Praise for *A Companion to Classical Recep*

"It is impossible in a short review to do justice to every single contribution of this multifaceted volume. One of the many attractive features of this collection is that it offers not only innovative essays about the reception and translation of the most read authors of antiquity . . . but also expands the horizon of the reception studies by introducing into the discussion untraditional themes and providing original approaches to the concepts frequently discussed in the context of reception."

The Classical Outlook

"This volume is an essential introduction to reception studies for both school and university students. Written in an accessible and engaging manner with useful sections for further reading."

Journal of Classics Teaching

". . . importantly, this volume exemplifies the recent boom in reception studies, and its potential to critique our subject and methodology."

Greece and Rome

"Hardwick and Stray's *Companion* pushes lingering worries about elitism and irrelevance right off the table. It offers bold reasons to treat classical studies as the cosmopolitan glue of the postmodern world. The book sparkles with the excitement that makes *A Companion to Classical Receptions* such an eye-opening delight."

Times Literary Supplement

"A spectacular volume from the massive series of *Blackwell Companions to the Ancient World*. The editors have pulled in a wider splay of trades and topics than any of their companions' companions or their own now mushrooming rivals can boast."

Bryn Mawr Classical Review

"There is sufficient careful scholarship, critical analysis, and contextualisation in this collection to warrant the claim that it provides a sophisticated and far-ranging overview of this burgeoning and dynamic field."

Scholia

BLACKWELL COMPANIONS TO THE ANCIENT WORLD

This series provides sophisticated and authoritative overviews of periods of ancient history, genres of classical literature, and the most important themes in ancient culture. Each volume comprises between twenty-five and forty concise essays written by individual scholars within their area of specialization. The essays are written in a clear, provocative, and lively manner, designed for an international audience of scholars, students, and general readers.

ANCIENT HISTORY

Published

A Companion to the Roman Army
Edited by Paul Erdkamp

A Companion to the Roman Republic
Edited by Nathan Rosenstein and Robert Morstein-Marx

A Companion to the Roman Empire
Edited by David S. Potter

A Companion to the Classical Greek World
Edited by Konrad H. Kinzl

A Companion to the Ancient Near East
Edited by Daniel C. Snell

A Companion to the Hellenistic World
Edited by Andrew Erskine

A Companion to Late Antiquity
Edited by Philip Rousseau

A Companion to Archaic Greece
Edited by Kurt A. Raaflaub and Hans van Wees

A Companion to Julius Caesar
Edited by Miriam Griffin

A Companion to Ancient History
Edited by Andrew Erskine

A Companion to Byzantium
Edited by Liz James

A Companion to Ancient Egypt
Edited by Alan B. Lloyd

A Companion to Ancient Macedonia
Edited by Joseph Roisman and Ian Worthington

In preparation

A Companion to the Punic Wars
Edited by Dexter Hoyos

A Companion to Sparta
Edited by Anton Powell

LITERATURE AND CULTURE

Published

A Companion to Classical Receptions
Edited by Lorna Hardwick and Christopher Stray

A Companion to Greek and Roman Historiography
Edited by John Marincola

A Companion to Catullus
Edited by Marilyn B. Skinner

A Companion to Roman Religion
Edited by Jörg Rüpke

A Companion to Greek Religion
Edited by Daniel Ogden

A Companion to the Classical Tradition
Edited by Craig W. Kallendorf

A Companion to Roman Rhetoric
Edited by William Dominik and Jon Hall

A Companion to Greek Rhetoric
Edited by Ian Worthington

A Companion to Ancient Epic
Edited by John Miles Foley

A Companion to Greek Tragedy
Edited by Justina Gregory

A Companion to Latin Literature
Edited by Stephen Harrison

A Companion to Ovid
Edited by Peter E. Knox

A Companion to Greek and Roman Political Thought
Edited by Ryan K. Balot

A Companion to the Ancient Greek Language
Edited by Egbert Bakker

A Companion to Hellenistic Literature
Edited by Martine Cuypers and James J. Clauss

A Companion to Vergil's *Aeneid* and its Tradition
Edited by Joseph Farrell and Michael C. J. Putnam

A Companion to Horace
Edited by Gregson Davis

In preparation

A Companion to the Latin Language
Edited by James Clackson

A Companion to Greek Mythology
Edited by Ken Dowden and Niall Livingstone

A Companion to Sophocles
Edited by Kirk Ormand

A Companion to Aeschylus
Edited by Peter Burian

A Companion to Greek Art
Edited by Tyler Jo Smith and Dimitris Plantzos

A Companion to Families in the Greek and Roman World
Edited by Beryl Rawson

A Companion to Tacitus
Edited by Victoria Pagán

A Companion to the Archaeology of the Ancient Near East
Edited by Daniel Potts

A COMPANION TO CLASSICAL RECEPTIONS

Edited by

Lorna Hardwick and Christopher Stray

A John Wiley & Sons, Ltd., Publication

This paperback edition first published 2011
© 2011 Blackwell Publishing Ltd

Edition history: Blackwell Publishing Ltd (hardback, 2008)

Blackwell Publishing was acquired by John Wiley & Sons in February 2007. Blackwell's
publishing program has been merged with Wiley's global Scientific, Technical, and Medical
business to form Wiley-Blackwell.

Registered Office
John Wiley & Sons Ltd, The Atrium, Southern Gate, Chichester, West Sussex, PO19 8SQ,
United Kingdom

Editorial Offices
350 Main Street, Malden, MA 02148-5020, USA
9600 Garsington Road, Oxford, OX4 2DQ, UK
The Atrium, Southern Gate, Chichester, West Sussex, PO19 8SQ, UK

For details of our global editorial offices, for customer services, and for information about
how to apply for permission to reuse the copyright material in this book please see our website
at www.wiley.com/wiley-blackwell.

The right of Lorna Hardwick and Christopher Stray to be identified as the author of
the editorial material in this work has been asserted in accordance with the UK Copyright,
Designs and Patents Act 1988.

Library of Congress Cataloging-in-Publication Data

A companion to classical receptions / edited by Lorna Hardwick and Christopher Stray.
    p. cm. — (Blackwell companions to the ancient world)
  Includes bibliographical references and index.
  ISBN 978-1-4051-5167-2 (hardback: alk. paper)
  ISBN 978-1-4443-3922-2 (paperback: alk. paper)   1. Classical literature—History and criticism.
I. Hardwick, Lorna.   II. Stray, Christopher.

PA3009.C66 2008
880.09—dc22

2007022246

A catalogue record for this book is available from the British Library.

Set in 10/12.5pt Galliard by Graphicraft Limited, Hong Kong
Printed in Singapore by Markono Print Media Pte Ltd

1   2011

Contents

Figures

Contributors

David W. Bebbington is Professor of History at the University of Stirling. He is the author of *The Mind of Gladstone: Religion, Homer and Politics*, 2005.

Sarah Annes Brown is Chair of the Department of English, Communication, Film and Media at Anglia Ruskin University, Cambridge, England. As well as numerous articles and chapters on various aspects of classical reception, she is the author of *The Metamorphosis of Ovid: From Chaucer to Ted Hughes* (1999) and of *Ovid: Myth and Metamorphosis* (2005), and is preparing a volume of essays, *Tragedy in Transition* (co-edited with Catherine Silverstone). Her current projects include an article on Pygmalion and Queer Theory and a monograph on transhistoricism.

Felix Budelmann is a Fellow of Magdalen College, Oxford. He is the author of *The Language of Sophocles: Communality, Communication and Involvement* (2000). His research interests include Greek drama and lyric, and their reception. He is currently working on a Greek lyric anthology.

Bryan E. Burns is Assistant Professor in the Department of Classics, Wellesley College. He is an archaeologist specializing in Aegean prehistory, with publications on interregional exchange in the Late Bronze Age and Archaic periods. His research interests also include the construction of the prehistoric and classical body in the modern arts and scholarship.

Gregson Davis is Andrew W. Mellon Distinguished Professor in the Humanities, Professor of Classics and Comparative Literature, and current Dean of Humanities at Duke University, Durham, NC. A native of Antigua in the anglophone Caribbean, he attended Harvard College (AB *magna cum laude* in Classics, 1960), and the University of California at Berkeley (PhD in Comparative Literature [Latin, Greek, French] in 1968). His publications on both Greco-Roman and Caribbean literary traditions include: *Polyhymnia: The Rhetoric of Horatian Lyric Discourse* (1991) and *Aimé Césaire* (1997).

Freddy Decreus is a philologist, specializing in the reception of classical Antiquity during the nineteenth and twentieth centuries. He works at the University of Ghent, where he is responsible for courses in Latin Literature, Literary Theory, Comparative Literature and Theatre History. His publications have addressed classical tragedy and the modern stage, mythology and modern painting, postmodernism and the rewriting of the classics, and feminism and the classics.

Catharine Edwards is Professor of Classics and Ancient History at Birkbeck College, University of London. Her book *Writing Rome: Textual Approaches to the City* (1996) focuses on ancient literary responses to Rome but also considers aspects of later responses. With Michael Liversidge, she edited *Imagining Rome: British Artists and Rome in the Nineteenth Century* (1996). She is also the editor of *Roman Presences: Receptions of Rome in European Culture 1789–1945* (1999).

Chris Emlyn-Jones is Emeritus Professor in Classical Studies at the Open University, Milton Keynes. Publications include editions and commentaries on a number of Platonic dialogues published by Bristol Classical Press: *Euthyphro* (1991, 2nd edn, 2002), *Laches* (1996), *Crito* (1999) and *Gorgias* (2004). Forthcoming (2007) is an edition, translation and commentary of Plato *Republic* Books 1–2 (Aris and Phillips). He has also published on Homer (*Homer: Readings and Images*, 1992, ed. with L. Hardwick and J. Purkis). He is currently working on a study of style, form and culture in Plato.

Ahmed Etman is Professor of Classics and Comparative Literature, Faculty of Arts, Cairo University; Chairman of the Egyptian Society of the Graeco-Roman Studies (ESGRS); Chairman of the Egyptian Society of Comparative Literature (ESCL). He has written a number of plays including: *Cleopatra Adores Peace* (1984, English tr. 2001, Italian 1992, Greek 1999, French 1999); *The Blind Guest Restores his Sight* (French tr. 2005); *Al-Hakim Does Not Join the Hypocritic Procession* (1988, Spanish tr. 2006); *The Goats of Oxyrhynchus* (2001 English and French tr. forthcoming); *The Wedding of Libraries Nymph* (2001, French and Italian tr. forthcoming); *A Beautiful Woman in the Prison of Socrates* (2004 French and English tr. forthcoming).

Michael Ewans is Professor of Drama and Research Facilitator in the School of Drama, Fine Art and Music at the University of Newcastle, Australia. He is the author of *Janáček's Tragic Operas* (1977), *Wagner and Aeschylus* (1982), *Georg Büchner's Woyzeck* (1989) and the Everyman Classics complete set of accurate and actable translations of Aeschylus and Sophocles in four volumes, with theatrical commentaries based on his own productions. His most recent book, *Opera from the Greek* (2007) contains eight case studies in the appropriation of material from Greek tragedy and epic by composers from Monteverdi to Mark-Anthony Turnage. An edition of Aristophanes' *Lysistrata, The Women's Festival and Frogs* will appear in 2011 from Oklahoma University Press, and will be followed shortly by *Achamians, Knights and Peace*.

Barbara Graziosi is Senior Lecturer in Classics at Durham University. She is the author of *Inventing Homer* (2002) and co-author, together with Johannes Haubold, of *Homer: The Resonance of Epic* (2005). Together with Emily Greenwood she has edited *Homer in the Twentieth Century: Between World Literature and the Western Canon* (2007). She is currently working, together with Johannes Haubold, on an edition and commentary of *Iliad 6* for the Cambridge Greek and Latin Classics.

Emily Greenwood is Associate Professor in Classics at Yale. She is the author of *Thucydides and the Shaping of History* (2006) and various articles on the reception of Classics in the Caribbean. She is co-editor, with Barbara Graziosi, of *Homer in the Twentieth Century: Between World Literature and Western Canon* (2007) and, with Elizabeth Irwin, of *Reading Herodotus: Studies in the Logoi of Book 5* (2007). Her latest book *Afro-Greeks: Dialogues between Caribbean Literature and Classics in the Twentieth Century* was published in 2010.

Edith Hall After holding posts at the universities of Cambridge, Reading, Oxford and Durham, Edith was appointed, in 2006, to a joint chair in Classics and Drama at Royal Holloway, University of London. She is also co-founder and co-director of the Archive of performances of Greek & Roman Drama at Oxford. Her books include *Inventing the Barbarian* (1989), *Greek Tragedy and the British Theatre* (2005, with Fiona Macintosh), *The Theatrical Cast of Athens* (2006) and *The Return of Ulysses* (2007).

Lorna Hardwick teaches at the Open University, Milton Keynes, where she is Professor of Classical Studies and Director of the Reception of Classical Texts Research Project. She is the author of many articles and books on Greek cultural history and its reception in modern theatre and literature, including *Translating Words, Translating Cultures* (2000) and *New Surveys in the Classics: Reception Studies* (2003). She is particularly interested in how Greek and Roman material has been used in postcolonial contexts and is currently working on a monograph on the relationship between classical receptions and cultural change.

Stephen Harrison is Fellow and Tutor in Classics at Corpus Christi College, Oxford, and Professor of Latin Literature in the University of Oxford. He is the author of a commentary on Vergil *Aeneid* 10 (1991) and of *Apuleius: A Latin Sophist* (2000) and editor of several volumes including *Texts, Ideas and the Classics* (2001), *A Companion to Latin Literature* (2005) and *Living Classics* (2009).

Thomas Harrison is Rathbone Professor of Ancient History and Classical Archaeology at the University of Liverpool. He is the author of *Divinity and History. The Religion of Herodotus* (2000) and *The Emptiness of Asia. Aeschylus'* Persians *and the History of the Fifth Century* (2000), and the editor of *Greeks and Barbarians* (2002) and (with Ed Bispham and Brian A. Sparkes) *The Edinburgh Companion to Ancient Greece and Rome* (2006). He is now working on a study of the modern historiography of ancient Persia.

Johannes Haubold is Leverhulme Senior Lecturer in Greek Literature at Durham University. He is the author of *Homer's People: Epic Poetry and Social Formation* (2000) and co-author, with Barbara Graziosi, of *Homer: The Resonance of Epic* (2005). He specialises on Greek epic and its relationship with Near Eastern literatures. Together with Barbara Graziosi, he is currently writing a commentary on *Iliad* 6.

David Hopkins is Professor of English Literature in the University of Bristol. Among his recent publications are (edited, with Paul Hammond) the Longman Annotated English Poets edition of John Dryden (5 vols, 1995–2005) and (edited, with Stuart Gillespie) vol. 3 (1660–1790) of *The Oxford History of Literary Translation in English* (2005). He has a special interest in English/classical literary relations in the seventeenth and eighteenth centuries.

Rosalind Hursthouse After twenty-five years in the Philosophy Department of the Open University, Rosalind Hursthouse returned to her home department at the University of Auckland, New Zealand, where she is now Professor. She wrote two course books on ethics for the Open University, *Beginning Lives* (1987) and *Ethics, Humans and Other Animals* (2000), as well as her definitive *On Virtue Ethics* (1999), and has published numerous journal articles on ethics and Aristotle.

Miriam Leonard is Lecturer in Greek Literature and its Reception at University College, London. Her research explores the intellectual history of classics in modern European thought from Hegel to Derrida. She is author of *Athens in Paris* (2005) and co-editor with Vanda Zajko of *Laughing with Medusa: Classical Myth and Feminist Thought* (2006). She is currently writing a short book on *How to Read Ancient Philosophy* (forthcoming 2008) and working on a project on Greeks, Jews and the Enlightenment. She is also editing a collection on *Derrida and Antiquity*.

Fiona Macintosh is Director of the Archive of Performances of Greek and Roman Drama and Fellow of St Hilda's College, University of Oxford. Her publications include *Dying Acts: Death in Ancient Greek and Modern Irish Tragic Drama* (1994) and with Edith Hall, *Greek Tragedy and the British Theatre 1660–1914* (2005). Her edited volumes include *Medea in Performance 1500–2000* (2000), *Dionysus Since 69: Greek Tragedy at the Dawn of the Third Millennium* (2004), and *Agamemnon in Performance, 458 BC to AD 2004* (2005).

Marianne McDonald is Professor of Theatre and Classics in the Department of Theatre at the University of California, San Diego, a member of the Royal Irish Academy, and a recipient of many national and international awards. Her published books include: *Euripides in Cinema: The Heart Made Visible* (1983); *Ancient Sun, Modern Light: Greek Drama on the Modern Stage* (1992); *Sing Sorrow: Classics, History and Heroines in Opera* (2001). Her performed translations include: Sophocles' *Antigone* (1999); Euripides' *Children of Heracles* (2003); Sophocles' *Oedipus Tyrannus* and *Oedipus at Colonus* (2003–4); Euripides' *Hecuba*, 2005; Sophocles' *Ajax*, 2006; and versions: *The Trojan Women* (2000); *Medea, Queen of Colchester* (2003), *The Ally Way* (2004), and also . . . *and then he met a woodcutter* (2005: after Noh), which was awarded the San Diego Critics Circle award for 'Best Play of 2005'.

Pantelis Michelakis is Senior Lecturer in Classics at the University of Bristol. His research interests are in early Greek literature and culture as well as in Greco-Roman drama and its ancient and modern reception. He is the author of *Achilles in Greek Tragedy* (2002) and *Euripides' 'Iphigenia' at Aulis* (2006). He has also co-edited two collections of essays, *Homer, Tragedy and Beyond: Essays in Honour of P. E. Easterling* (2001) and *Agamemnon in Performance, 458 BC to AD 2004* (2005).

Joanna Paul is Lecturer in Classical Studies at the University of Liverpool, having completed her doctoral thesis, 'Film and the classical epic tradition', at the University of Bristol in 2005. She is publishing articles on various aspects of cinematic receptions of antiquity, including adaptation and translation, and the films of Federico Fellini. Her current research project concerns modern receptions of Pompeii and its destruction.

James I. Porter is Professor of Classics at the University of California, Irvine. He is author of *Nietzsche and the Philology of the Future* and *The Invention of Dionysus: An Essay on the Birth of Tragedy* (both 2000) and editor, most recently, of *Classical Pasts: The Classical Traditions of Greece and Rome* (2006). He has just completed *The Origins of Aesthetic Inquiry in Antiquity: Matter, Experience, and the Sublime* (forthcoming), and is at work on a sequel volume, *Literary Aesthetics after Aristotle*, in addition to a study on the reception of Homer from antiquity to the present.

Cashman Kerr Prince is Associate Professor of Classics, Wellesley College. He is trained in Classics and in Comparative Literature, holding degrees from Wesleyan and Stanford Universities as well as the Université de Paris VIII. He works on early Greek poetry, including didactic, larger questions of Greek poetics, and the reception of classical texts primarily in the nineteenth and twentieth centuries.

James Robson is Senior Lecturer in Classical Studies at the Open University, Milton Keynes. His research interests include Aristophanes, humour theory, translation and Greek sexuality: he is co-editor of *Lost Dramas of Classical Athens: Greek Tragic Fragments* (2005) and author of *Humour, Obscenity and Aristophanes* (2006) and *Aristophanes: An Introduction* (2009). He is co-author of *Ctesias' History of Persia: Tales of the Orient* (2010) and is currently working on books on Greek Language and Classical Athenian sex and sexuality.

Hanna M. Roisman is the Francis F. Bartlett and K. Bartlett Professor of Classics at Colby College, Waterville, Maine. She specializes in Early Greek Epic, Greek and Roman tragedy, as well as in Classics and Film. In addition to numerous articles and book chapters in her various fields, she has written *Nothing Is As It Seems: The Tragedy of the Implicit in Euripides'* Hippolytus (1999), *Sophocles: Philoctetes* (2005). She is co-author with Fred Ahl of *The Odyssey Re-Formed* (1996), and with C.A.E. Luschnig, of *Euripides'* Alcestis: *A Commentary for Students* (2003). She has also co-edited with Joseph Roisman several issues of the *Colby Quarterly* on Greek and Latin literature. She is currently working on the translation with notes, introduction and interpretative essay to Sophocles' *Electra*.

Seth L. Schein is Professor of Comparative Literature at the University of California, Davis, and works mainly on Homeric epic, Attic tragedy, and institutional receptions of classical literature and culture. He has written *The Iambic Trimeter* *in Aeschylus and Sophocles: a study in metrical form* (1979), *The Mortal Hero: an introduction to Homer's Iliad* (1984), and *Sophokles' Philoktetes: Translation with Notes, Introduction and Interpretive Essay* (2003), and he edited *Reading the Odyssey: Selected Interpretive Essays* (1996). Currently he is working on an edition with commentary of *Philoktetes* and a translation of Aeschylus' *Oresteia*.

Christopher Stray has been Honorary Research Fellow in the Dept of Classics, University of Wales, Swansea, since 1989, and is Senior Research Fellow at the Institute of Classical Studies, School of Advanced Study, University of London. His publications include *Classics Transformed: Schools, Universities, and Society in England 1830–1960* (1998) and articles and books on the history of Classics, institutional slang, and examinations. He is currently working on an edition of the correspondence of Sir Richard Jebb and on a study of Classics in nineteenth-century Cambridge.

Gonda Van Steen is Cassas Chair in Greek Studies at the University of Florida. Her first book, *Venom in Verse: Aristophanes in Modern Greece* (2000) was awarded the John D. Criticos Prize by the London Hellenic Society. She has also published articles on ancient Greek and late antique literature, on the reception of Greek tragedy, on Greek coinage, and on post-war Greek feminism. Her most recent books are *Liberating Hellenism from the Ottoman Empire* (2010) and *Theatre of the Condemned: Classical Tragedy on Greek Prison Islands* (forthcoming 2010).

Betine van Zyl Smit taught at the University of the Western Cape, the Rand Afrikaans University and Stellenbosch University in South Africa for more than thirty years. One of her main research interests is the reception of Greek and Roman literature in South Africa. She was appointed as a senior lecturer in the Classics Department of the University of Nottingham in 2006.

Elizabeth Vandiver is Associate Professor of Classics at Whitman College, Walla Walla, and received her Ph.D. from the University of Texas at Austin. She has published two books, *Heroes in Herodotus: The Interaction of Myth and History* (1991), and the first English translation of Cochlaeus' biography of Luther in *Luther's Lives: Two Contemporary Accounts of Martin Luther* (2002). Her third book, *Stand in the Trench, Achilles: Classical Receptions in British Poetry of the Great War* (2010) is published in the series Classical Presences. She has published articles on a variety of topics, including Catullus; Livy; classical reception; and translation.

Angeliki Varakis is Lecturer in Drama in the department of Drama, Film and Visual Arts at the University of Kent, Canterbury. She has a number of publications including 'Research on the Ancient Mask', *Didaskalia* (2004) and 'The use of Mask in Koun's stage interpretations of *Birds*, *Frogs* and *Peace*' in Hall and Wrigley 2007 forthcoming *Aristophanes in Performance 421 BC–2005 AD: Peace, Birds, Frogs* and has written the commentary and notes for the Methuen Student Edition of *Antigone* (2006) and *Oedipus the King* (2007). She has actively participated in a series of practice-based research projects involving the mask.

J. Michael Walton is Emeritus Professor of Drama at the University of Hull and was founder/director of the Performance Translation Centre. He was General Editor of Methuen Classical Dramatists from 1988 to 2002, a series which included the whole of Greek Tragedy and Comedy in translation in thirteen volumes, with three further compilations including one of Roman Comedy. Twelve of his translations (several in collaboration with Marianne McDonald) from Greek and Latin are currently in print and have been performed widely in Britain and Ireland, America, Greece and Cyprus. The more recent of his seven books on Greek theatre include *Euripides our Contemporary* (2009), *Found in Translation: Greek Drama in English* (2006) and *The Cambridge Companion to Greek and Roman Theatre*, which he has edited with McDonald (2007).

Ruth Webb is Honorary Research Fellow at Birkbeck College, London, and Professeur Associé at the Université Paris X. She has published articles on post-classical Greek rhetoric and performance and is author of *Ekphrasis, Imagination and Persuasion in Ancient Rhetorical Theory and Practice* (forthcoming) and *Demons and Dancers: Performance in Late Antiquity* (forthcoming).

Nurit Yaari is Senior Lecturer and chair of the department of Theatre Studies at Tel Aviv University, Israel. She has published a book, *French Contemporary Theatre 1960–1992* (1994), and edited several books in English and Hebrew: *On Interpretation in the Arts* (in English, 2000), *The Man with the Myth in the Middle: The Theatre of Hanoch Levin* (with Shimon Levy, in Hebrew, 2004) and *On Kings, Gypsies and Performers: The Theatre of Nissim Aloni* (in Hebrew, 2006). Her articles are published in international journals focusing on Ancient Greek theatre and its reception and on Israeli theatre. Since 1997 she has served as Artistic Consultant and Dramaturg for the Khan Theatre of Jerusalem.

Vanda Zajko is Senior Lecturer in Classics at the University of Bristol. Her recent publications include a chapter on women and myth in *The Cambridge Companion to Greek Myth* (2007), an essay entitled 'Hector and Andromache: Identification and Appropriation' in C. Martindale and R. Thomas (eds), *Classics and The Uses of Reception* (2006), *Laughing with Medusa: Classical Myth and Feminist Thought* (ed. with Miriam Leonard, 2006) and *Translation and 'The Classic'* (ed. with Alexa Lianeri, 2008).

Acknowledgements

The editors would like to thank the contributors for their scholarship and flair. We also thank Al Bertrand of Blackwell for instigating the project along with Hannah Rolls and (especially) the energetic Graeme Leonard for their expertise in bringing the book to fruition. Special thanks to Carol Gillespie for her invaluable help at all stages of the work, and especially for keeping the contributors happy and the editors sane.

Figure 0.1 *The Sea God*. 1977. Collage with mixed media on board. Photograph courtesy of Romare Bearden Foundation. Art © Romare Bearden/Licensed by VAGA, New York, NY

Figure 0.2 *Odysseus Leaves Circe.* 1977. Collage on masonite. Photograph courtesy of Romare Bearden Foundation. Art © Romare Bearden/Licensed by VAGA, New York, NY

Introduction:
Making Connections

Lorna Hardwick and Christopher Stray

The chapters in this book show how receptions of Greek and Roman texts, ideas, myths and visual and physical culture are at the centre of myriad debates. These debates not only investigate the historical features and subsequent impact of the ancient world but also cover related areas throughout the intervening periods – in education, artistic practice and public and private senses of cultural identity. By 'receptions' we mean the ways in which Greek and Roman material has been transmitted, translated, excerpted, interpreted, rewritten, re-imaged and represented. These are complex activities in which each reception 'event' is also part of wider processes. Interactions with a succession of contexts, both classically and non-classically orientated, combine to produce a map that is sometimes unexpectedly bumpy with its highs and lows, emergences and suppressions and, sometimes, metamorphoses. So the title of this volume refers to 'receptions' in the plural.

We have used the word 'classical' in its specific sense of reference to Greek and Roman antiquity. Additional volumes would be needed to do justice to the classical cultures of (for example) India or to the cultures of the ancient near east and their receptions. Neither have we attempted to probe the conception of the 'classic' in general in its relationship to matrices of receptions (for an approach to the last, see Lianeri and Zajko 2008). We have included chapters that discuss how Greek and Roman culture represents and is represented by non-western perspectives, both in antiquity (T. Harrison) and more recently (Etman, Yaari, van Zyl Smit). Each of these could also be the basis of a further volume. The chapters that discuss the interaction between Greek and/or Roman material and various contexts in western culture should not be read as identifying the origins and subsequent genealogies and importance of Greek and Roman material primarily with Europe. Ancient Greece, after all, was at the interface of west and east, and recent research in ancient history has established the cultural diversity of the ancient Mediterranean context (Davies 2002; Morris 1992; West 1997). The Romans not only drew on and refashioned Greek material but also engaged in cultural exchange across their empire, with effects right up to the present day (see Maritz 2007 and Evans 2007 for African examples). The book also shows something of the sheer diversity of western receptions and distinguishes between the different traditions and contexts from which they have emerged. This extends to exploration of ways in which western and non-western literary and artistic strands converge and redefine each other (see Davis, this volume, ch. 30).

We hope our collection is not only cheerfully and creatively anarchic but also prescient in suggesting ways in which work in the field might develop in the future. There was no 'party line' in the invitations and guidance given to contributors. The aim has been to produce a volume that shows reception scholars actively at work. Contributors were asked to contextualize their discussions and to make their working methods transparent, but to avoid 'surveys' and to concentrate on texts, debates and trends which they judged to be of current and future importance.

In spite of the long-standing interest in the afterlife and influence of ancient texts in the field of classical learning, classical reception research as such is a fairly new area of prominence in anglophone scholarship, both within classics and in the relationship of the subject area with other disciplines (the influence of German scholarship both in Rezeptionsgeschichte and in theoretical approaches is of course extensive: see Martindale 2006). The relative newness of the specialism is reflected in the variety of backgrounds of the contributors. Some are distinguished scholars in classics or closely related fields who have developed their interest in reception as a result of questions prompted by their earlier research or in response to teaching new generations of students. Others are newer voices, some of whom have specialized in classical reception, including its theories and methods, in their doctoral and post-doctoral research. The work of early and mid-career researchers and teachers is already transforming the scope and practice of classical reception. We hope this mix of voices will enrich the debates inside and outside this volume and we only regret that the volume could not be even larger. (In a spirit of virtuous self-denial the editors sacrificed their own planned contributions.)

Contest and Debate in Classical Reception Research

The comparatively recent 'mainstreaming' of classical reception within classics has inevitably raised crucial questions about its theoretical bases, intellectual scope and relationship with existing specialisms such as the Classical Tradition, Intellectual History and Comparative Literature. In terms of working methods and theoretical frameworks, there has been intense debate about the relative merits of a variety of approaches (a study of the terms of abuse used might make an amusing and instructive article). Possible approaches include: starting from particular examples in order to draw out patterns and trends (condemned by some critics as 'list-making' or 'positivist'); concentrating on the historical contexts of ancient and subsequent receptions (which may prompt charges of cultural materialism, a.k.a. covert Marxism, or of ignoring the text); emphasizing the formal and aesthetic or 'transhistorical' relationships between the ante-text and its receptions (challenged for ignoring the social and political elements in the construction of judgements or for neo-Kantian idealism); charting the histories of particular texts, styles or ideas (attacked variously for privileging the influence of the ancient, for assuming that the meaning of the ancient is fixed or unproblematic or for replacing this with the 'progress' or 'presentism' of the modern); emphasizing the impact of receptions in shaping perceptions of the ancient texts and contexts (criticized for cultural relativism and denial of the autonomy and value of the ancient material).

Of course, all these summaries are over-simplifications of carefully argued positions. They also create false polarities in that much of the most interesting work operates against the grain of such perceived oppositions or in the spaces between them. Nevertheless, such shorthand does sometimes creep into reviews and conference debates, especially since doing classical reception has become more fashionable and the possibility of staking claims to desirable intellectual empires has increased. Of course, the arguments that take place are not always so reductionist (or so dismissive of the work of those with whom one does not agree) and the debates are becoming more sophisticated. There are indeed pressing issues to be addressed, not only in academia but also in the collaborative working relationships between researchers and arts practitioners (see further Harrison 2008).

There is also an embryonic debate that seems likely to gather momentum concerning the scope of the so-called 'democratic turn' in classical reception analysis. The 'democratic turn' covers a number of issues, both historical and philosophical. The first is that assumptions about the inherent superiority of ancient works were questioned and the independent status and value of new works accepted (see Hopkins, this volume, ch. 10, which situates reception issues firmly in literary debates from the late seventeenth century onwards). Second, research has tracked ways in which (partly through education) both the ancient and the newer works became better known among less privileged groups, with the newer sometimes acting as an introduction to the ancient. Third, the range of art forms and discourses that used or refigured classical material has been extended to include popular culture (with all the associated problems of conceptualization and association, see Steinmeyer 2007 and Hall, this volume, ch. 29). Furthermore, there has been extensive debate about the extent to which ancient texts and performance, especially in Greece, were products of democracy (Cartledge 1997; Goldhill 1990; Goldhill and Osborne 1999; Rhodes 2003) and about the resonances of ancient democratic processes and concepts to the modern world (Ober and Hendrick 1996). Conceptually, the notion of the 'democratic turn' is partly derived from the impetus given to reception studies from the theories of German scholars such as Jauss and Iser, particularly in the decisive role given to reader (and audience) response (for summaries see Hardwick 2003a ch. 1 and Martindale 2006). However, if readers and audiences do indeed have a role in the 'construction of meaning at the point of reception' (Martindale 2006) there are further questions to be asked about the relative importance of immediate response based on experience as against deferred and reflective response. It is also necessary to consider the relative status of the multiple meanings represented by the responses of unconnected individuals and the more consensual judgements arrived at among groups of different kinds (including the classically educated or 'reception-orientated' students or general readers or spectators; a 'reception-friendly' doctrine of the expert may yet see a revival).

This collection reflects the 'democratic turn' to the extent that it has been constructed on the basis that the activators of reception are many and varied and that we all gain from encountering examples from outside our own immediate areas of knowledge. This also entails a willingness to look at possible alignments of the history of scholarship with aesthetic and ideological trends outside academia and to view these alongside practice in art, literature, theatre and public discourse. So we hope that readers of this collection will want to create their own dialogues and debates, based not only on the chapters published here but also in comparison with other works of scholarship. For example, other volumes in the Companions series discuss a variety of contexts and insights for classical receptions. *A Companion to the Classical Tradition* (Kallendorf 2007) contains sections on the classical tradition in different historical and artistic periods from the middle ages to Modernism, as well as area studies of how classical material has been transmitted, interpreted and reworked in different places (including Africa, Central-Eastern Europe, Latin America and the United States). It also has a section on contemporary themes (including reception itself, postcolonialism, psychoanalysis and film), which in some respect serves to mutate classical tradition into reception. *A Companion to Greek Tragedy* (Gregory 2005) contains a substantial section on reception, ranging from issues of text and transmission within antiquity to modern translations.

It is significant that in many such books reception is kept in a separate section, usually at the end. This tends to artificially divide reception processes from analysis of the classical texts and contexts themselves and in particular to deny the dialogical relationships between reception and the analysis of the ancient contexts. A partial exception is the *Cambridge Companion to Virgil*, which puts chapters on reception at the beginning but, nevertheless, does divide them from the rest of the book (Martindale 1997). It remains to be see how Companions in preparation (for instance on themes such as Classical Mythology or on authors, such as Ovid, Catullus and Horace) will tackle the relationship between the ancient story or text and its transmission and dialogical reconstructions. It is sometimes said that reception sheds light on the receiving society but not the ancient text or context. Most people involved in reception would accept that on the contrary the relationship between ancient and modern is reciprocal (although they may disagree about how best to assess this) and some argue that classics itself is inevitably about reception (Martindale 1993 and Porter, this volume, part IX).

Thus there are significant revisions taking place in how the relationships between the classical tradition and classical reception are conceptualized and evaluated. The term 'the classical tradition' has in the past been used to focus on the transmission and dissemination of classical culture through the ages, usually with the emphasis on 'influence' or 'legacy' (Hardwick 2003a: ch. 1). This was sometimes combined with the assumption that classical works yielded a 'meaning' which could be grasped and passed on, as could the aesthetic and (sometimes) moral and political values of antiquity. As a result there was sometimes a misleading conflation between the values represented in the ancient context and those of the societies that appropriated them. One of the achievements of reception studies has been to examine this interface and to bring about a partial liberation from this confusion for both ancient and modern. Sensitivity to the possibility of a more dialogic relation between ancient and modern has also focused attention on the interface between tradition and reception. If it is accepted that tradition is not something merely inherited but is constantly made and remade (Hobsbawm and Ranger 1983), then reception and tradition may be seen as related parts of an extended process. For example, it has been suggested that tradition becomes reception when alternative modes of interpretation and transmission are not only recognized but are positively expected to contest and change how classical material is perceived and used (Stray 2006). Put another way, reception becomes decisive when traditions intersect or are in conflict. This may be important when classical material interacts with non-classical or partly-classical material (for example in literary traditions).

A revisionist approach to the relationship between tradition and reception is explored by Johannes Haubold and Felix Budelmann in the chapter that begins this volume. They suggest that a desire for a 'democratic turn' is a poor reason for shedding the term 'tradition' in favour of 'reception' and on the basis of specific examples from antiquity and beyond they argue that the reciprocal relationship between the two is fluid, both in practice and in theory. Other chapters also promote reflection on this fluidity. Sometimes the question raised is also about the balance to be struck in reception analysis between diachronic and synchronic approaches. Transmission and the construction of meanings through time is emphasized in chronologically structured histories but each reception is also located synchronically in a wider context of lateral relationships that may extend across space rather than time or may be a common feature in a number of receptions, irrespective of timeframe. Once value is decoupled from one-directional transmission through time, then the cultural authority of the ancient work and hence of concepts such as 'authenticity' and 'faithfulness' is bound to be changed in some degree, although the question of *how* the reception relates to its Greek and/or Roman springboard is still vital. The dynamics of creativity in the work of artists and writers, both ancient and modern, also have implications for the relationship between reception and tradition in that writers and artists position themselves in relation to their predecessors and contemporaries and are deeply conscious of being part of a tradition (Sluiter 2000). Yet they also wish to transcend that tradition. How scholars model and discuss that process is at the heart of reception debates. This 'meta-commentary' on cultural practices also involves its own re-assessments of tradition and innovation in scholarly practice and is one of the underlying strands running through the book.

Themes and Approaches in This Book

We have grouped the chapters in parts that highlight key topics and themes in classical receptions. We could, of course, have used other groupings (period, provenance, genre, theory). We hope readers will enjoy making their own rearrangements to reflect other cross-currents.

After the introductory discussion of Reception and Tradition by Budelmann and Haubold, the rest of part I concentrates on reception within antiquity and its subsequent implications. The topics covered all introduce material which also fed into later conceptions of what antiquity was like and the moral values it should exert. Barbara Graziosi discusses the ancient reception of Homer in a chapter that relates not only to strands in the discussion by Budelmann and Haubold but also to Gregson Davis' treatment of modern reframings of Homer. Chris Emlyn-Jones examines Plato's reception of drama and the tensions between its place in the presentation of his dialogues and in the development of his thought and its subsequent interpretation. Tom Harrison's analysis of Persia: Ancient and Modern juxtaposes the forms and contexts of ancient representations of Persia with modern responses, both in museum display and cultural politics. Ruth Webb picks up the theme of ancient attitudes to theatre and its popular manifestations and analyzes the impact of Christian and theological arguments.

Part II takes forward systematically some of the strands of transmission, acculturation and critique that emerged from the first part and considers these in the contexts of education and public policy. Seth Schein looks at conceptualizations of cultural debt as developed in college programmes in the USA, especially in respect of the association between cultural value and the construction of a common knowledge base for students of diverse origins. Emily Greenwood considers colonial education and the impact of classical figures and allusions on political discourse in the Caribbean. David Bebbington's chapter turns the focus from society to the outstanding individual and discusses the reciprocal relationship between W.E. Gladstone's work as a classicist and as a statesman while Stephen Harrison addresses the impact of Virgil's poetry in educational, literary and public frames of reference from the nineteenth century to the present.

The relationship between classical material and the public sphere that emerged from part II is explored in different ways in part III, in which the focus is on the practices and effects of translation. David Hopkins examines the tensions between conceptions of translation, attitudes to it and the creation of new work. Ahmed Etman discusses the symbiotic relationship between Arabic poetry and drama and translation from classical languages. He suggests that in the Egyptian literary tradition there is an occidentalism in approaches to Greek and Roman texts that can be compared with the orientalism of western approaches to eastern culture (cf. T. Harrison's discussion of constructions of Persia). Michael Walton also discusses drama translation, but from the point of view of audiences and staging and the gains and losses that arise from different approaches and criteria. James Robson's chapter focuses on comedy. Using the concepts and methods of translation studies research, he examines how Aristophanes' humour has been represented to different readers and audiences.

Part IV discusses the theory and practice of reception and provides an opportunity for readers to 'stock-take' on the extent to which theoretical perspectives affect the questions that are asked of classical receptions and thus the interpretative outcomes. Vanda Zajko reflects on the impact of feminist models of reception, relating these both to the successive 'waves' of feminism and to the female icons of the ancient world. Miriam Leonard examines the relationship between history and theory, arguing for theory to be firmly grounded in the historical contexts in which it originates and to be tested in those to which it is applied. In her case study she brings together psychoanalysis and the historiography of the repressed, adding Hebrew sources to the ancient world material discussed in this book. Pantelis Michelakis explains and evaluates methods in categorizing receptions, especially the dominant organizing ideas of period, canon and genre. His discussion gets to the heart of the tension between the need for organizing concepts and their effect on what is then considered, and how. Cashman Kerr Prince's chapter on André Gide's rewriting of myth engages with the impact of modernism on conceptions of the past. Gide foreshadows some current debates on the relationship between the use of myth in creative writing and the ensuing perceptions of antiquity and its figures that pass into public consciousness via reading.

In part V the focus shifts to the performing arts. Michael Ewans discusses Apolline and Dionysiac receptions of Greek tragedy in opera, with detailed attention to the relationship between poetry and musical form. Fiona Macintosh explores the potential of performance histories to illuminate decisive moments both in the reception of ancient plays and in the societies that are performing them and can profitably be read alongside that of Michelakis. Angie Verakis' chapter describes the relationship between body and mask in the staging of modern performances and considers the extent to which this can communicate an experience analogous to that of the ancient theatre. Freddy Decreus pushes to their limits post-modern approaches to ancient drama with a discussion of post-dramatic reworking of ancient tragedy in avant-garde performances that also bears on the discussion of physicality in Verakis' chapter. Finally, Nurit Yaari combines personal experience and academic analysis in her discussion of adaptation of Aristophanes into the very different traditions of Hebrew theatre and the highly charged political and cultural context of modern Israel. She demonstrates how classical drama can provide a field for practitioners and audiences to recognize and confront their own situations and dilemmas.

Part VI moves to film. The chapters by Joanna Paul and Hanna Roisman should stimulate debate because of their different starting points and the contrasts in their methods of identifying and evaluating the relationship between modern films and the ancient texts and contexts on which they draw (one primarily Roman and historical, one Greek and literary in emphasis). Roisman's analysis of Classics and Film emphasizes how classical narrative can emerge from a post-classical art form. Paul approaches from the perspective of the cinematic inscription of classical material. Marianne McDonald's chapter explores another possible starting point. She examines the potential of film as a teaching tool for engaging students' interest in the ancient world and also for helping them to be more critically aware of their own by identifying and exploring some of the correspondences that will promote debate.

The cultural politics that is never far from reception analysis has been an underlying strand in a number of chapters and part VII turns to some key examples and approaches. Catharine Edwards' chapter brings together material culture, imagination and politics in her discussion of the politics of ruins in Rome. Gonda van Steen considers the violent reception in Greece of the *Oresteia* of 1903, drawing out the traumatic relationship between the transformative power of performance and the cultural and political genealogies of drama in Greece itself. Betine van Zyl Smit's discussion of cross-cultural performances in South Africa draws on the most recent research on the astonishing impact of translations and adaptations of classical drama, not only in the struggle against apartheid but also in the subsequent move in the new South Africa for the construction of new performance traditions that bring together the histories and cultures of citizens of all races. Finally in this part, Edith Hall introduces a new topic in classical reception by arguing that it should be concerned with class as well as culture. Stressing the linked classical roots of both 'class' and 'classical', she provides a series of questions to be addressed to the contents and contexts of receptions.

Part VIII addresses the theme of changing contexts and unexpected juxtapositions that underlay part VII. Gregson Davis discusses the mutually illuminating images of Odysseus in the work of Derek Walcott and Romare Bearden, thus contributing also to the themes of Caribbean receptions and cross-genre transplantation. Sarah Annes Brown turns the lens to science fiction and breaks new ground in her exploration of how the genre both draws on myth and changes it. Bryan Burns also examines classical material in a post-classical art form, contextualizing photography in terms both of aesthetic judgements and social values and practices and contributing to the volume's discussion of physicality and the body. In a further foray across discipline boundaries, Rosalind Hursthouse then discusses the development of virtue ethics in contemporary moral philosophy, with special reference to the impact of the return to Aristotle's texts as a starting point for changing the questions asked in modern philosophy and the categories used to explore them. Elizabeth Vandiver's discussion of Homer in the poetry of World War One is also revisionist. She uses a wide range of examples to challenge previous judgements about the role of poetry in expressing and shaping rejection of the war (and by extension also contributes to current debates about how the war was regarded at the time, as opposed to subsequently). She argues that Homer receptions in the poetry of the war as a whole actually suggest that serving soldiers continued to support the ideals for which they thought they were fighting.

The volume ends with an impassioned polemic by James Porter in which he calls for teaching and research in classical reception to develop a fuller portfolio and to expand more positively into the sphere of public debate. In his chapter, which provides a provocative counterpart to that of Hursthouse, he calls for an increased role for the classically-orientated public intellectual in contributing to analysis and debate in areas of social, cultural and political identity and policy. Here we are back with the 'democratic turn' (Euben, Wallach and Ober 1994; Cartledge 2006).

Thus at a time of almost explosive expansion and variation in studies of classical receptions we hope that this collection not only offers a window on to a particular moment in time but that it will also provoke further debates in the wider world, as well as feeding into teaching and research. Work now in progress or planned is likely to add further dimensions to the issues raised here and to introduce new ones. In particular we expect to see more research on reception within antiquity, on the relationship between classical material and creativity (Harrison 2008; Rees 2008), on reception across genres, on alignments between scholarship and creative practice, on the role of the translator as mediator and activator (Lianeri and Zajko 2008) and on the cross-cultural genesis and impact of receptions. Work on classical metamorphoses in popular culture is posing questions about how perceptions of the ancient world are constructed in media and art forms that did not exist in antiquity and about the extent to which these resonate with the ancient forms. Another emerging field brings classical reception together with the history of education and of books – including textbooks (Stray 1994 and 2007).

The role of myth in reception practice and analysis is becoming more prominent, as is excerpting and the role of the iconic figure as means of transmission and reinvention, especially when whole texts are not directly known by most readers and audiences (or indeed by the modern writers and artists who are creating the new works). This means that there are questions to be asked about what will be the 'entry' points in the future for people encountering the world of the Greeks and Romans for the first time and how those entry points will change perceptions of what that world was like and how it relates to the modern. Addressing these new kinds of 'connections' may involve further disruptions to conventional models of investigation and reviews of temporal relationships and formal structures. It will surely also require an increased focus on the nature and role of mediating texts, translations, rhetoric and allusions. There are exciting times ahead.

Lorna Hardwick and Christopher Stray

PART I

Reception within Antiquity and Beyond

CHAPTER ONE

Reception and Tradition

Felix Budelmann and Johannes Haubold

Introduction

This chapter is concerned with the use of the term 'tradition' in studying the reception of classical antiquity. Tradition is a remarkably open and wide-ranging concept. Its core meaning of 'passing on' has relevance in numerous contexts, and as a result tradition has a role in a wide range of disciplines well beyond the arts.

Within Classics, tradition has had a particular history which centres on the concept of the 'classical tradition'. Long before 'reception' gained the prominence that it has now, the classical tradition was discussed and popularized by books like Gilbert Murray's *The Classical Tradition in Poetry* (Murray 1927) and Gilbert Highet's *The Classical Tradition* (Highet 1949). Such work needs to be seen on the one hand in relation to contemporary thinking about tradition outside Classics: outstanding here are T.S. Eliot's 1920 essay on 'Tradition and the individual talent' and Aby Warburg's 1932 *The Renewal of Pagan Antiquity* (see Kennedy 1997: 40–2, and the preface to Warburg 1999). On the other hand, work on the 'classical tradition' represents a more or less explicit engagement with debates over how and why Classics fits into the modern world. These debates go back to the nineteenth century – witness the altercations between Friedrich Nietzsche and Ulrich von Wilamowitz-Moellendorff in the 1870s, both classicists by training but with diametrically opposed viewpoints about the subject (Henrichs 1995) – and then gained fresh relevance after the crisis of World War One: Murray's work on the classical tradition is not an isolated phenomenon in the post-war years (on Murray as responding to the war see West 1984: 209–33). Already a few years earlier, two high-profile volumes had appeared devoted to the 'legacies' of Greece and Rome, edited by Murray's friend R.W. Livingstone (1921) and Cyril Bailey (1923) respectively, and a multi-volume series *Our Debt to Greece and Rome* was published in the US between 1922 and 1948 (cf. Schein, this volume, ch. 6).

Today, work on the classical tradition from the first half of the twentieth century leaves a mixed impression. Murray's book in particular reads with hindsight as a blend of sensitive analysis that still continues to be suggestive and a now rather dated eulogy of what he regards as 'classical' poetry. A similar point could be made about the notion of a classical tradition as a whole. It remains a useful and indeed evocative term referring to the engagement with classical antiquity in later periods: note for instance the *International Journal of the Classical Tradition* and the Blackwell *Companion to the Classical Tradition* (Kallendorf 2007). At the same time, some scholars, anxious because of the connotations of conservatism and elitism that the classical tradition cannot always shed, avoid it altogether at the expense of the term 'reception'. Especially in Britain, reception is sometimes thought to be the less problematic concept of the two.

In this chapter, we will not step into the debates over the classical tradition, nor will we focus on discussing 'tradition' in general. Rather, we want to pick up on areas of classical scholarship in which tradition has an established role – by which we mean areas where scholars have become accustomed to using the term 'tradition', partly for historically contingent reasons but partly also because it seemed appropriate and helpful to do so. Most famously, tradition is at the heart of Homeric studies, but books have been published in recent years also on, for example, the Epicurean tradition, ritual lament in the Greek tradition, the Augustinian tradition and the Anacreontic tradition. All these traditions are of course also cases of reception, usually of whole strings of reception. Tradition and reception tend to overlap, though the precise relationship between the two terms, and their implications in any given area of study, is not always easy to pin down. So what we will do in this chapter is take the two traditions of Homeric epic and Anacreontic lyric and discuss what they have to offer to the student of reception. The reason we devote the bulk of the chapter to case studies is that we want to reflect the way both the study of tradition and that of reception depends on its material. Like many critical terms, 'tradition' and 'reception' are most effective when they are tailored from case to case. This is not to say that there are no general points to be made, and we will indeed make some such points; but we believe that it is important to stress the variation in possible approaches to tradition and reception, both in practice and at a more abstract conceptual level.

Reception and the Anacreontic tradition

Our first case study in reception and tradition is taken from the early modern reception of the Greek lyric poet Anacreon (sixth/fifth century BCE). Anacreon's output is only preserved in fragments, with few complete poems. What is preserved fully, however, is the *Anacreontea*, a collection of mostly anonymous poems inspired by Anacreon, written between the first century BCE and the ninth century CE (text and translation of both Anacreon and the *Anacreontea* in Campbell 1988, discussion in Rosenmeyer 1992). When the *Anacreontea* were first printed, in 1554 by Henricus Stephanus (= Henri Estienne) in Paris, they were widely taken to be by Anacreon himself, and spawned a rich reception history in most European languages, especially in the seventeenth and eighteenth centuries. Our example will be a poem of unknown date by Abraham Cowley (1618–1667), published among his 1656 *Miscellanies* as one of eight 'Anacreontiques: or, Some Copies of Verses Translated Paraphrastically out of *Anacreon*'.

> *Drinking*
> The thirsty *Earth* soaks up the *Rain*,
> And drinks, and gapes for drink again.
> The *Plants* suck in the earth, and are
> With constant drinking fresh and faire.
> The *Sea* it self, which one would think
> Should have but little need of *Drink*,
> Drinks ten thousand *Rivers* up,
> So fill'd that they oreflow the *Cup*.
> The busie *Sun* (and one would guess
> By's drunken fiery face no less)
> Drinks up the *Sea*, and, when'has don,
> The *Moon* and *Stars* drink up the *Sun*.
> They drink and dance by their own light,
> They drink and revel all the night.
> Nothing in *Nature*'s *Sober* found,
> But an eternal *Health* goes round.
> Fill up the *Bowl*, then, fill it high,
> Fill all the *Glasses* there; for why
> Should every creature drink but *I*,
> Why, *Man of Morals*, tell me why?

In analyzing this poem as an act of reception the first thing to point out is its close connection with one of the *Anacreontea* (21 in today's standard numeration).

Ἡ γῆ μέλαινα πίνει,	The black earth drinks,
πίνει δένδρεα δ' αὐτήν.	the trees drink it.
πίνει θάλασσ' ἀναύρους,	The sea drinks the torrents,
ὁ δ' ἥλιος θάλασσαν,	the sun the sea,
τὸν δ' ἥλιον σηλήνη.	the moon the sun.
τί μοι μάχεσθ', ἑταῖροι,	Why fight with me, my friends,
καὐτῶι θέλοντι πίνειν;	if I too want to drink? (tr. Campbell)

Clearly, Cowley's poem uses the structure and conceits of the *Anacreontea* piece, expanding on it in length and level of rhetoric. Cowley imitates the basic sequence of the drinking earth, plants, sea, sun and moon, leading up to the question about the speaker's own drink, but elaborates throughout and so produces a poem that is three times as long.

   The next point to note is that Cowley's poem (unlike his Greek source) is clearly tied to a particular political situation. It is one of a rash of English Anacreontic pieces written in the early to mid-seventeenth century by poets including Robert Herrick, Richard Lovelace, Alexander Brome and the Aeschylus editor Thomas Stanley. As Oliver Cromwell's Parliamentarians were gaining more and more political control their austere cultural and religious outlook was becoming increasingly dominant. Royalists found themselves beleaguered and many of them, including Cowley, spent some time in exile. It is in this context of Puritan supremacy that Cowley's punchline about the 'man of morals' is to be understood. While the nameless Greek author just addresses his friends, Cowley makes a thinly veiled allusion to Puritans, perhaps even Oliver Cromwell himself, and their clampdown on drinking.

It is obvious that these socio-political connotations of the poem could be pursued in more detail (Revard 1991), but here we want to discuss three aspects of Cowley's poem as part of the Anacreontic tradition more broadly.

1 Tradition as a chain of influence

One thing the Anacreontic tradition does for the student of Cowley is to bring into view a vast number of earlier Anacreontic poems, more or less directly relevant to Cowley's own. Cowley's 'Drinking' is linked with Anacreon through a long chain of what we might call intermediate acts of reception. Without doubt the most influential is the late antique and Byzantine *Anacreontea* collection, which itself constitutes a reception of Anacreon. The Anacreon of Cowley and his contemporaries was not the Anacreon printed in today's editions but the *Anacreontea*. Most intermediate acts of reception are less momentous, of course, and do not reshape perceptions of an earlier text or author to the same degree. One such intermediate reception is a version of the same *Anacreontea* piece by the German poet Georg Rudolf Weckherlin, published in 1641 as 'Ode oder Drincklied. Anacreontisch' (Fischer 1884: 501–3). Like Cowley, and unlike most other poets writing versions of *Anacreontea* 21, Weckherlin expanded significantly on his model. The similarities in the detail of Cowley's and Weckherlin's expansion, together with the fact that Weckherlin spent time in England, have suggested to some scholars the dependency of one version on the other. Weckherlin may have drawn on Cowley, or Cowley on Weckherlin, alongside whatever other sources they used (Zeman 1972: 45–8; Revard 1991 traces other influences on Cowley).

Influence-spotting has sometimes acquired a bad name and can in fact be misleading. The complete set of literary influences (let alone cultural influences more broadly) that bear upon a poem is ultimately untraceable. In our example, even the role of Weckherlin is unclear. Moreover, we may ask which other Anacreontic poems Cowley was familiar with, and what drinking songs more broadly. What other poems may have shaped his habits? What anti-puritan jokes? We simply will never know what earlier material, consciously or unconsciously, went into Cowley's poem, let alone what in turn had shaped that earlier material. We are able to point, in certain cases, to obvious influences, but those influences will always only be a few among many. That said, it is undeniable that Cowley's creative act has behind it an enormous number of earlier creative acts. Even though we cannot delineate all or even most of them in an archaeology of influence, the influence of the past as such is undeniable. Anacreon is not transported onto Cowley's desk or to Cowley's period by a time machine (and the same is of course true for our reading of Anacreon or Cowley today). Renaissance or modern engagements with antiquity are shaped by many centuries of cumulative earlier engagements, starting in antiquity itself. Bearing in mind the wider Anacreontic tradition does not give us a key to tracing this build-up in exhaustive detail, but it shows us the importance of giving historical depth to any analysis of individual moments of reception, such as Cowley's 'Drinking', and indeed to our own reading of Anacreon, Cowley or anything else.

2 Tradition as an imaginary context

The amorphous and elusive nature that the Anacreontic tradition shares with many other traditions is not just a hindrance but can also be an advantage. It offers poets a place of belonging. Homeric rhapsodes called themselves 'sons of Homer', making themselves part of a wider family (Graziosi, this volume, ch. 2). The *Anacreontea* collection does something comparable with Anacreon, whose name opens the first poem. The poets of the *Anacreontea* often remained anonymous, and in various ways positioned themselves as continuing a project started by Anacreon rather than advertising their own originality. Cowley is less self-effacing. He publishes in his own name and leaves his mark. Not least because of his rhetorical expansions, Cowley has often been regarded as the most important English Anacreontic poet (Baumann 1974: 73–9; Mason 1990: 107–9). The jibe at the 'man of morals', too, distinguishes this poem not just from *Anacreontea* 21, but also from other, less polemical, versions of it. Even so, Cowley can still be looked at as part of a larger project. He calls his piece a paraphrastic translation, and uses the term 'Anacreontiques' almost as the marker of a genre. He thus places his poem among other poems carrying this label, like Weckherlin's 'Ode oder Drincklied. Anacreontisch' and like several of Herrick's *Hesperides* (published 1648, see Braden 1978: 216–17). The ways individual authors place themselves in or against a tradition vary enormously. In most cases, like here, there is some blend of innovation, indeed flaunted innovation, and seamless integration.

Just as the nature of this blend varies so do its effects. In Cowley's poem, one effect is a playful pretence of innocence. The piece poses as just an Anacreontic translation: there is nothing new. The fact that this mere translation is provocative in a context in which drink is a political issue would of course not have escaped Cowley's readers. So the traditionality of Cowley's stance sharpens rather than blunts the poem's political edge.

But that is not the only effect it has. It would probably be wrong to see the avowedly Anacreontic aspect of the poem merely as mock-camouflage used for political attack. Even though Cowley is rarely harmless, this is probably the punchiest of his *Anacreontiques*, which suggests that Anacreon held further attractions for him. Arguably, he and his royalist friends also drew some comfort from communing with Anacreon and Anacreontically minded people of the past. As they had to keep themselves to themselves, in a world that was hostile to their practices and beliefs, the Anacreontic tradition will have given them a more sympathetic imaginary home. They were not alone in enjoying drink and song.

3 *Tradition as continuity*

Much recent literary and cultural criticism focuses on what is particular about a given text or author. Why does Anacreon appeal to a royalist under the Protectorate? How does Cowley's piece relate to Weckherlin's? How does Cowley adapt *Anacreontea* 21? Not that these questions can be settled with certainty, but they can be discussed in interesting ways.

Thinking about the Anacreontic tradition gives a different vantage point. Of course, as we just pointed out, tradition too has room for particularity. Cowley created his own lastingly recognizable place within it. But tradition also puts a premium on continuity, sometimes even timelessness. Anacreontic poetry continued to be widely popular across a number of centuries. The appeal of each individual poem will have had something to do with its particular features and circumstances – such as Cowley's anti-puritan snipe for the consumption of other anti-puritans – but for a balanced understanding of Anacreontic poetry one needs to come to terms also with the many features that one finds again and again, in different periods and languages: brevity (Cowley's poem is at the long end of the spectrum); simplicity of metre (here: the iambic tetrameters); simplicity of language (Cowley is unusually rhetorical, but even Cowley's language is quite straightforward); wit (here: the punch line); a small number of usually apolitical and unspecific themes (especially drink, which here has a political application, and love); and, above all, a light-hearted tone.

Perhaps one of the most helpful observations to make about these repeated features is to point out that many of them are shared with the ever-popular genre of drinking song, and to note that Anacreontic poetry weaves together refined poetry and banal forms of conviviality (Achilleos 2004). The connection with drinking song is important because it helps explain both the remarkable degree of stability in the tradition and its popularity in many contexts in which popular forms of song and high-cachet poetry could be brought together (Roth 2000 is particularly suggestive).

This is a rewarding but challenging line of enquiry to pursue further. What, one is led to ask, is it that gives drinking song and the way Anacreontic poetry uses it such wide appeal? Homeric criticism has learned to discuss formulae and types scenes, and the power that is locked up in them (see our second case study). In addition to providing convenient building blocks for composition in performance, such repeated material contains pieces of cultural memory in condensed form. Comparable models for thinking about other poetry are rare, even though the Anacreontic tradition like many other literary traditions is repetitive in its own way: repeated metrical patterns, repeated themes, repeated jokes, etc. The recent rise in the use of cognitive science in literary studies is promising here, and may eventually help analyze the traditional aspects of Anacreontic poems like Cowley's. There is almost certainly something hardwired in the appeal of particular simple forms and particular themes like drink and desire. The risk in looking for cognitive patterns is of course that one goes too far and starts treating Anacreontic poems as exemplars of more or less universal patterns, ignoring their individuality, their links with certain contexts and the fluctuations of their popularity. The potential pitfalls are obvious, but so is the need to understand more fully why Cowley and others chose to write 'Anacreontics', rather than simply using the Anacreontic poems they read as a quarry, or a foil against which to present their own ideas.

Reception and the Homeric Tradition

From the reception of Anacreon in early modern Britain we move on to another area where the concept of tradition is of particular interest to students of reception. In the first half of the twentieth century, Milman Parry influentially defined Homeric poetry as the product of a traditional art form (Parry 1971). Linguistic formulae and other traditional patterns provide the performing bard with an economic means of responding to the constraints of oral improvisation. This idea was taken up and refined by Parry's student Albert Lord (Lord 2000). According to him, the traditional nature of Homeric poetry extends beyond language to type scenes such as arming, bathing or supplication (compare already Parry 1971: 404–7); and even to large-scale story patterns such as the return of a hero after an extended period of absence. More recent scholarship has further developed Parry's ideas, pointing out the expressive potential of traditional language and combining an aesthetic of traditionality with an emphasis on audience response (e.g. Nagy 1999; J.M. Foley 1999; Scodel 2002). What remains a largely unresolved problem is Homer's relationship with other, earlier literatures in the ancient Mediterranean (Burkert 1992; Morris 1997; West 1997). This is another area of obvious interest to anybody wishing to study the reception of ancient material; though it raises different questions from the ones we encountered when looking at Cowley's subversive drinking song.

Broadly speaking, the epic tradition from which Homeric poetry grows is both more pronounced and less open to change than the tradition of Anacreontic poetry within which Cowley was operating. Whereas Cowley was free to reshape *Anacreontea* 21 quite radically, albeit within the wider traditional framework of Anacreontic song, the language, themes and narrative patterns of early Greek epic tend to be more stable. The reasons for this are complex and are certainly not exhausted by labelling Homeric poetry an 'oral' art form (Foley 2002). Recent scholarship suggests that the traditional features of Homeric poetry have much to do with its claims to truth and authority (Graziosi/Haubold 2005). Whatever the reasons behind the phenomenon, such is the level of repetition and formulaic stylization in Homeric poetry that it is often difficult to pinpoint the contribution of individual composer-performers. This has an obvious impact on the terms of our inquiry: with Cowley we asked what thinking about tradition can add to our understanding of reception. With Homer and his predecessors in the ancient Mediterranean the most pressing question becomes how best to understand the act of reception itself, in the face of an obvious and thoroughgoing commitment to tradition.

To get a sense of the issues involved, let us start with an apparent echo of Babylonian literature in Homer. Homer, like Hesiod, sees the gods as descendants of Uranus (= 'Sky'). The only exception to this view is a passage from the *Iliad* where Oceanus and Tethys are described as the ancestors of the gods (Homer, *Iliad* 14.197–205):

> Τὴν δὲ δολοφρονέουσα προσυήδα πότνια Ἥρη.
> 'δὸς νῦν μοι φιλότητα καὶ ἵμερον, ὧι τε σὺ πάντας
> δαμνᾶι ἀθανάτους ἠδὲ θνητοὺς ἀνθρώπους.
> εἶμι γὰρ ὀψομένη πολυφόρβου πείρατα γαίης,
> Ὠκεανόν τε θεῶν γένεσιν, καὶ μητέρα Τηθύν,
> οἵ με σφοῖσι δόμοισιν ἐὺ τρέφον ἠδ' ἀτίταλλον,
> δεξάμενοι Ῥείας, ὅτε τε Κρόνον εὐρύοπα Ζεὺς
> γαίης νέρθε καθεῖσε καὶ ἀτρυγέτοιο θαλάσσης.
> τοὺς εἶμ' ὀψομένη, καί σφ' ἄκριτα νείκεα λύσω.'

> Then, with cunning intent the lady Hera answered her:
> 'Give me loveliness and desirability, graces
> with which you overwhelm mortal men, and all the immortals.
> Since I go now to the ends of the generous earth, on a visit
> to Okeanos, whence the gods have risen, and mother Tethys
> who brought me up kindly in their own house, and cared for me
> and took me from Rheia, at the time when Zeus of the wide brows
> drove Kronos underneath the earth and the barren water.
> I shall go to visit these, and resolve their division of discord.'
>
> 						(tr. Lattimore; modified)

The extract is taken from a longer speech: Hera asks Aphrodite for the *kestos*, a magic piece of clothing with which she hopes to distract Zeus from the battlefield and thus ensure an Achaean victory. She pretends that her plan is to reconcile Oceanus and Tethys (in reality she wants to seduce Zeus), and in this context depicts them as the ancestors of the gods (*Il.* 14.201). Walter Burkert and others (Burkert 1992: 91–6; cf. Morris 1997: 602; West 1997: 147–8) have pointed out that this apparently innocent detail is highly unusual in the context of early Greek epic; and that it recalls the Babylonian account of creation, the *Enūma eliš*, where two watery creatures, Apsu and Tiamat, give rise to the gods (*Enūma eliš* I.1–5, Talon):

> *o nu mu e-liš la na-bu-ú šá-ma-mu*
> *šap-liš am-ma-tum šu-ma la zak-rat*
> ZU.AB-*ma reš-tu-ú za-ru-šu-un*
> *mu-um-mu ti-amat mu-al-li-da-at gim-ri-šú-un*
> A.MEŠ-*šú-nu iš-te-niš i-hi-iq-qu-ma* ...

> When the sky above was not yet named
> and below the earth did not yet have a name,
> Apsu, the first one, their ancestor,
> and creative Tiamat who bore them all,
> were mixing their waters together . . .

There are some striking similarities between the two ancestral couples of Hera's speech and the Babylonian *Enūma eliš*. According to Burkert, even the name Tethys is derived from that of Tiamat, the corresponding mother figure in the Babylonian text. Homer, it would seem, has adopted and reworked a Babylonian classic 'down to a mythical name' (Burkert 1992: 93; for further discussion of the possibility that Tethys = Tiamat, see West 1997: 147–8 with n. 200).

Now, it is important to note that we do not actually know for certain whether *Enūma eliš* is the model behind Hera's speech. With Cowley, things were very much more straightforward: not all his sources can be traced, but he clearly had *Anacreontea* 21 in mind and assumed that at least some of his readers did too. By contrast, it cannot be proved that Homer ever came into contact with non-Greek poetry, including *Enūma eliš*. Sceptics have even suggested that parallels between Homeric epic and earlier Near Eastern texts are largely a reflection of standard human patterns of thought; though this position seems extreme and is becoming increasingly untenable. Assuming that Hera's speech in *Iliad* 14 does bear a meaningful resemblance with *Enūma eliš* beyond what is simply human, the question remains how to interpret it. Burkert emphasizes the fact that Oceanus and Tethys as a primordial couple are untraditional by the standards of Homeric (and Hesiodic) poetry. His claim is correct in so far as these deities do not normally occupy such a prominent role. But to conclude, as he does, that their depiction must be the result of external influence because it could not have been traditional raises a host of problems. At a very general level, Burkert's model of reception as 'influence' has severe limitations (Haubold 2002): as has become clear when we looked at Cowley and the Anacreontic tradition, acts of reception – however conceived – need not exclude continuity of tradition. We shall return to this point in a moment; but since the devil in reception studies is often in the detail, let us first revisit some of the details of Burkert's case.

To begin with, neither Oceanus nor Tethys can fairly be called untraditional characters in early Greek epic, no matter where their names originated. Oceanus makes appearances throughout Homer (*Il.* 1.423 etc.; *Od.* 4.568 etc.) and Tethys is well known to Hesiod (*Th.* 136 etc.). Turning to their role as described by Hera, we note that the goddess speaks δολοφρονέουσα 'with cunning intent'. Under such circumstances we expect a fair amount of rhetorical distortion, especially from a deity who has a habit of manipulating cosmogonic 'facts'. In the *Homeric Hymn to Apollo*, Hera gangs up with the Titans to engender Typhaon, the enemy *par excellence* of Zeus' rule (335–6). In this context, she describes the Titans as the progenitors of gods and men (337), a half-truth which is transparently intended as a challenge to Zeus as 'father of gods and men' (πατὴρ ἀνδρῶν τε θεῶν τε). Hera's speech in *Iliad* 14, from which our passage is taken, is likewise born of insubordination and contains similar half-truths: her description of Oceanus and Tethys in particular seems only a slight exaggeration when compared to the *Theogony*, where they give rise to no fewer than 6,000 divine children (Hes. *Th.* 337–70). Declaring Oceanus the 'origin of the gods' is not so much wrong as it is tendentious. A similar point can be made about Hera's claim to be his foster daughter, and about the alleged time of her adoption during the battle of the Titans. That battle was the defining

Felix Budelmann and Johannes Haubold

moment of Zeus' rule. Hera claims that she was with Oceanus (himself a Titan) when it happened, thus distancing herself from the current world order. In the process, she becomes an adoptive daughter of Oceanus, one of the powerful *Okeaninai* who are prominent throughout the epic tradition, often as a challenge to Zeus' rule (e.g. Hes. *Th.* 358, 886–90 for Zeus' wife Metis and her children).

It would thus appear that a simple dichotomy between 'traditional' and 'untraditional' material does not do justice to the complexities of Hera's speech. Nor will it help us understand the dynamics of reception in the context of early Greek epic. Later epic poets often engaged in a conscious game of adopting and transmuting earlier literary habits (e.g. Fantuzzi and Hunter 2005; Hinds 1998). That this was so was well understood by their contemporaries and was an important part of the enjoyment the texts had to offer. We look in vain for a similar awareness among the audiences of Homer. The Homeric scholia notoriously fail to comment on possible connections with earlier non-Greek texts: even such glaring parallels as *Iliad* 14 and *Enūma eliš* 1 are passed over in silence. One might argue that the relevant Near Eastern texts had simply fallen into oblivion; though later Greeks certainly knew some of them, and they could have known even more had they cared to find out. The point is that they did not care: as Glenn Most observes, there is no evidence to speak of that Greek audiences were ever interested in identifying Homer's sources (Most 2003: 85). Most's observation poses a problem for the student of reception: even if we accept as likely that Hera's speech in *Iliad* 14 depends ultimately on *Enūma eliš*, it is far from clear what exactly follows from this. The problem can be formulated in even more general terms: what, if anything, does our knowledge of older non-Greek texts contribute to our understanding of Homeric poetry?

In pursuing this question further, we must beware of judging Homeric epic by literary standards other than its own. In their search for a viable model, scholars of Homer have sometimes looked to the reception of Greek poetry on the part of Latin authors. But even the most superficial of glances suggests that the analogy is a false one: Latin poets partake in a poetics of allusion and imitation (*imitatio, aemulatio* etc.) of which the reception of Greek literary models is an integral part. These are important aspects of the early modern reception of classical literature too (including Anacreon), but with Homer the situation is very different: as Scodel 2002 in particular has shown, Homeric epic does not highlight borrowings of any kind because this would run counter to its 'rhetoric of traditionality'. In other words, the Homeric narrator wants his story to look familiar even when there are strong reasons to suspect that it is not.

This takes us back to the more fundamental question of whether Homer had 'sources' in any relevant sense of the word; or whether the undoubted similarities between, say, *Iliad* 14 and *Enūma eliš* call for an altogether different model of how texts relate to other texts. The question is best tackled by stepping back and looking at Homer's treatment of the gods more generally. By common consent, this is an area where Greek epic comes particularly close to neighbouring narrative traditions (Morris 1997: 616). The notion of a divine family with a history, a shared abode and a hierarchical structure with Zeus at its head all point eastwards. So far, scholars have tended to assume that the Homeric gods represent little more than literary embellishments, perhaps borrowed from eastern sources for orientalizing effect. But the relatively serious deities of Hesiod's *Theogony* are as 'oriental' as the laughing and feasting deities familiar from the *Iliad*. More generally, the gods are of central importance to epic as a genre, and even the details of their description mattered enormously to ancient audiences. Zeus, for example, was the 'gatherer of clouds' (cf. Ugaritic Ba'al as 'rider of the clouds'; Burkert 1992: 116) for very good reasons. Everyone knew that it was he who ruled the heavens and wielded the thunderbolt. It could not be otherwise: no less than the stability of the universe depended upon it. Zeus and his fellow gods, then, cannot be brushed aside as 'oriental imports', but they were not contained within the confines of Greek culture either (however understood). Like everyone else in the ancient Mediterranean, the Greeks conceived of their gods as universal forces. Zeus ruled the entire world, not just Greece. Poseidon caused earthquakes all over, not just in Greece. More generally, what Herodotus (2.53) calls the Greeks' 'theogony' had to account for the making of the entire world, not just Greece. It is here that we find some of the common ground between epic tradition and near eastern reception that so often proves elusive: Homer's gods may well have reached the Greeks from the East and they are certainly *meant* to look international; but at the same time they are also perfectly traditional.

This last point can now be generalized: in the context of strongly traditional art forms like early Greek epic, the study of reception acquires a specific meaning. As we have seen, one should not think of Homer as reworking individual source texts in the sense in which Cowley reworks *Anacreontea* 21; nor should one divorce individual passages from the wider context of the Greek epic tradition. Our point here is not to emphasize the uniqueness of Homer so much as to insist that there is no one single kind of relationship between tradition and reception; different texts require us to define this relationship in different ways, depending on the value they place on continuity, cultural authority and political relevance. Homeric poetry is only one among many examples one might use to illustrate the wider point that reception and tradition can be linked in complex and often unpredictable ways. There are of course differences in texture even within the overall framework of early Greek epic. Hera's deceptive speech in *Iliad* 14 is clearly meant to stand out as *relatively* idiosyncratic. But even here, the fabric of the tradition is stretched rather than simply torn. More generally, almost anything that we might wish to study under the heading of reception in Homer can also, with almost equal justification, be called 'tradition'.

Conclusions

Both case studies illustrate, we hope, that considerations about tradition have much to add to discussions of reception. In spite, or probably rather because, of their different vantage points, 'tradition' and 'reception' go together well and can mutually enhance one another. Cowley's Anacreontics and Homer's epics become richer texts when they are looked at in terms of both tradition and reception. One central contention of this chapter, therefore, is that we need to keep tradition in view when studying reception, and vice versa.

Beyond that, it is difficult to speak in general terms, and that is our second conclusion. The way 'tradition' and 'reception' relate to one another varies greatly. Our two case studies differ in many respects, and further examples, drawing on other texts or indeed on non-textual traditions, would produce further differences. The notions of tradition and reception owe much of their currency to their vague and suggestive quality, which makes both of them flexible umbrella terms for a wide range of critical pursuits. This volume demonstrates just how wide a term 'reception' is, and here we have tried to adumbrate the similarly broad range of 'tradition'. Such flexibility can be challenging in practice. It requires changes in approach when transferring the terms from one example to the next. Not just the poems, sculptures, pamphlets and ideologies that fall under the rubrics of tradition and reception are context-dependent, but so are the concepts themselves.

This need for sensitivity to context prompted us to concentrate on case studies rather than general discussion, and we hope this focus has justified itself. Before we end, though, we need to address an issue that is raised by our particular choice of examples. We picked two traditions that between them cover a certain breadth, trying to demonstrate that our topic embraces both ancient (Homer, Anacreon) and more recent (Cowley), and both conventionally classical and non-canonical (*Enūma eliš*) material. Yet in a different way our choice has been rather limited. Both case studies are taken from traditions that are firmly established within classical scholarship. Both are in a sense obvious choices.

One reason for this focus on the well established is the fact that the concept of 'tradition' is both epistemologically and politically problematic. Traditions, as Eric Hobsbawm and Terence Ranger influentially put it, are often invented, individually or collectively, consciously or unconsciously (Hobsbawm and Ranger 1983). There are few traditions whose existence cannot somehow be questioned, and there is no objective way of establishing whether something is a tradition, or what is and what is not part of a particular tradition. Marx neatly quipped 'I am not a Marxist'.

This awareness of the role of invention in forming traditions leads on to questions about the reasons for their invention. Here as elsewhere, the question *cui bono* can prompt interesting answers. Discussions of the classical tradition from the first half of the twentieth century, for instance, often have an element of self-justification: classicists give themselves a particular role by placing themselves in a continuous and value-laden tradition that reaches from antiquity to their own day. More sympathetically perhaps, some African thinkers have claimed certain kinds of continuity between their culture and the ancient Greeks as part of their struggle against dominant models that see everything that is valuable in African cultures as a colonial import (Howe 1998: index s.v. 'Greece/Greeks'). At the other end of the political scale, and with blatantly invidious intent, the Italian Fascists portrayed themselves as part of a tradition started by the Romans (Stone 1999). Clearly, talk of tradition is often self-interested, and the self-interest may be judged admirable or contemptible.

Our two case studies are less highly charged. Homer can be said to have been invented (Graziosi 2002); there is no reliable test for determining what is and what is not an Anacreontic poem; and as we have discussed Cowley's use of Anacreon is not innocent. But it is obvious that questions of *ad hoc* manipulation and politics are less immediately prominent in Cowley's 'Drinking' and Homeric uses of non-Greek motifs than in fascist or postcolonial uses of tradition. Clearly, therefore, our two cases studies can claim to be representative only to a very limited extent. We chose two unusually well-established traditions because we wanted to give ourselves room for illustrating ways in which tradition as a critical term can help studying acts of reception. With different examples, the chapter would have looked rather different.

But that is of course part of our point. The important thing to understand here is that one of the most interesting questions about traditions is what they allow people to do. Traditions are enabling. They enable people – scholars as much as poets, politicians and whole societies – to make certain connections. Traditions derive their power from people believing in them and using them in the way they choose. They do not exist as such, and they are not intrinsically good or bad. So for a last time we are reminded of the need to follow the lead of one's subject matter. In the study of reception as indeed elsewhere, 'tradition' should not be invoked, defended or attacked as a Platonic idea, but should be seen as a pliable tool for suggesting new perspectives, in different ways on different occasions. The concept is there for the taking.

FURTHER READING

Martindale 1993 contains important material on tradition in the study of reception (especially ch. 1.5), as does Lianeri 2006. Hardwick 2003a: ch. 1 charts a path 'from the classical tradition to reception studies'. The classical tradition is first expounded at length by Murray 1927; for recent work see Kallendorf 2007. Burke 2004: chs 1 and 2 has some concise comments on tradition from a cultural history perspective. The standard volume on invented traditions is Hobsbawm and Ranger (eds) 1983. The introduction to Machor and Goldstein (eds) 2001 traces the changes in the use of reception as a critical term. Stimulating perspectives on tradition outside the humanities may be gained from Boyer 1990 and Aunger (ed.) 2001.

Rosenmeyer 1992 discusses Anacreon and the *Anacreontea*; text and translation of both in Campbell 1988. Zeman 1999 is an overview of Anacreontics in post-Renaissance literature, with further literature on the various periods and countries. Brown 1999 and Roth 2000 treat Anacreontics as a genre, especially in English literature. For Homeric epic as a traditional genre see Parry 1971, J.M. Foley 1999, Lord 2000. Up-to-date discussions of tradition and reception in Homer can be found in Scodel 2002 and Graziosi this volume. Burkert 1992 and West 1997 collect and discuss much of the relevant material for the Homeric reception of Near Eastern poetry. Haubold 2002 suggests an alternative framework for comparative study.

CHAPTER TWO

The Ancient Reception of Homer

Barbara Graziosi

In terms of method, there is no easy starting point for studying the reception of Homer in antiquity, because all the terms involved in the enterprise constantly shift in relation to one another.

First, there is the issue of defining what 'Homer' might mean: the name itself is first attested in the sixth century BCE and, in the ancient sources, describes the author not just of the *Iliad* and the *Odyssey* but sometimes also of other poems: for example, the *Homeric Hymns*, the epics of the Theban and the Trojan cycle, *The Capture of Oechalia*. It seems that in the course of antiquity, definitions of what counted as the true work of Homer became gradually more stringent (Wilamowitz 1884: 353). In the sixth century, many epics were thought of as Homeric, whereas Xenophon, in the fourth, defined Homer's work as the *Iliad* and the *Odyssey* (*Symposium* 3.5). Those two poems had clearly dominated the cultural and literary landscape of Greece long before Xenophon, but we must bear in mind that the gradual redefinition of Homer's oeuvre in antiquity is itself part of reception history.

A second, and related, problem concerns what might count as an act of Homeric reception in ancient Greece and Rome. It is clear that many poems were composed after the *Iliad* and the *Odyssey*, but belonged to the same tradition of poetry: the *Homeric Hymn to Pan*, for example, is not likely to have been composed before the fifth century BCE (this is when Pan first made it as a Panhellenic god: Herodotus, *Histories* 6.105; cf. Parker 1996: 164), yet it adopts a Homeric point of view (e.g. ἔννεπε Μοῦσα, 'tell me Muse' in line 1). So we must ask: where exactly is the act of reception to be located in the case of this poem? It may be in the perception of ancient audiences, who heard the poem as Homeric; or in the work of the poet, who updated the Homeric tradition by introducing a new god. The issue is not limited to poems belonging, like the *Hymn to Pan*, to the Greek hexameter tradition. Throughout Greek literature (and, indeed, art and culture more generally) it is very difficult to distinguish between specific engagements with the Homeric poems and wider evocations of the epic past. The issue remains alive when approaching Roman receptions of Homer: the Trojan saga seems to have been known on the Italian peninsula since the eighth century (on 'Nestor's Cup', see e.g. Farrell 2004: 256). It reached the Romans through the Greeks of southern Italy and the Etruscans, as well as through a direct engagement with the *Iliad* and the *Odyssey*. As a result, scholars have wondered whether we should see Livius Andronicus' translation of the *Odyssey*, in the third century BCE, simply as an act of Homeric reception, or whether we should approach it as a particular manifestation of broader Roman engagement with the Trojan saga (the significance of Troy in early Rome has been the object of much debate: Gruen 1992 v. Erskine 2001).

Finally, there is the fairly intractable problem of distinguishing ancient from modern receptions of Homer. The definition of Homer's *oeuvre* and the place of Homer in Greek and Roman culture have been important issues in modern cultural history: classical philology was fundamentally shaped by the Homeric Question, that is, a sustained inquiry into the authorship of the Homeric poems (see further the 1985 edition of F.A. Wolf, *Prolegomena ad Homerum*, originally published in 1795). More generally, the discipline of classics is built on a particular understanding of the relationship between Greece and Rome – a relationship exemplified by Livius Andronicus' translation of the *Odyssey* (Leo 1913; Barchiesi 2002). At a basic level, we may ask two questions: in what ways the ancient reception of Homer shaped modern readings; and, conversely, how modern views about Homeric epic affect our understanding of its ancient reception. But these two questions are, in fact, inadequate. Many ancient and, indeed, modern acts of reception challenge linear notions of time, or of literary history, so that any neat division between the ancient and modern reception of Homer is called into question by the very acts which are usually studied under those two labels.

This short chapter investigates the ancient reception of Homer by focusing on the three issues outlined above. The first section, 'Defining the Subject', discusses how Homer's work was conceived in a range of ancient contexts. The next section, 'Modes of Reception', investigates a broad spectrum of possible engagements with Homeric epic in antiquity. Finally, 'Temporalities' investigates how readers make connections across time when engaging with Homeric epic; and questions the viability of separating ancient from modern receptions. The aim of the chapter is not to give a comprehensive overview of the reception of Homer in antiquity (that would be difficult even in a series of long monographs, or an encyclopaedia); rather, it aims to present some basic issues likely to confront students of ancient (and, indeed, modern) receptions of Homer.

Defining the Subject

How and by whom the Homeric poems were composed, when and for what reasons they were written down, how the Alexandrian editors arrived at their text of the *Iliad* and the *Odyssey* are questions that have exercised generations of scholars. Depending on the answers given, the name 'Homer' acquires different meanings. When studying the ancient reception of Homer, it is first of all imperative to be clear about the uses of his name. For some, Homer is the personification of a tradition of epic (e.g. J.M. Foley 1999); for others, he is the man who first wrote down the poem about the wrath of Achilles (e.g. Powell 1991; cf. West 1998, though he would resist calling the man 'Homer': West 1999). These different conceptions dramatically affect the project of studying his ancient reception since, depending on our conceptual framework, we may focus on the texts of the *Iliad* and the *Odyssey* as they have reached us, or consider the broader epic tradition out of which those two poems gradually emerged. I propose to start with a brief overview of ancient uses of the name Homer.

The *Iliad* and the *Odyssey*, as is well known, are resolutely silent about their author and so, it seems, are the other hexameter poems which were sometimes described as Homeric in antiquity. Of those, only the *Homeric Hymns* survive as complete poems; but it seems likely that the poems of the Theban and the Trojan Cycle did not contain explicit references to their authors (the ancients, who endlessly debated their authorship, did not apparently know of autobiographical passages within the poems which would help settle the question). Griffith (1983) offers an explanation as to why the Homeric poems remained silent about their author: according to him, poems that addressed themselves to a universal audience maintained anonymity and thus gave the impression of being equidistant from all possible listeners. (For this 'rhetoric of traditionality' in early hexameter epic, see also Scodel 2002.) There is one extant departure from this general rule: *The Homeric Hymn to Apollo*. Here the singer addresses himself to a chorus of girls and tells them that, should they be asked who the best singer is, they should answer: 'A blind man, he lives in rocky Chios, and his poems are the best for ever' (*Homeric Hymn to Apollo* 172ff). This, as Burkert (1987: 55) remarks, was 'meant to be Homer'; but not everybody in antiquity accepted as true the boast embedded within this poem: a scholion to Pindar, *Nemean* 2.1 (in Drachmann 1903–27) claims that a performer of Homeric poetry, called Kynaithios, actually composed the hymn and then tried to pass it off as the work of Homer. The report tallies with modern assumptions about the *Homeric Hymns*: there is little doubt that rhapsodes – that is, travelling performers – composed poems in the Homeric tradition down to the classical period and later still. Usually, their poems were received as Homeric; yet it seems that being too explicit about Homeric authorship could have the reverse effect to the one intended: in the case of the *Hymn to Apollo*, the implication that the author of the poem is a blind poet 'whose poems are the best for ever' provoked ancient critics to expose one Kynaithos as the actual author of the hymn (see further Burkert 1979, 1987). Anonymity, then, is a marker of the Homeric tradition, and is linked to the equidistance of the poems from all possible audiences: the poet does not name himself and does not single out any privileged listeners or readers.

The earliest extant authors who mention Homer by name are his critics; that is, people who explicitly want to distance themselves from the Homeric tradition. In the sixth century BCE, Xenophanes objected that Homer's gods are immoral (fr. 11 DK), while Heraclitus complained that Homer failed to understand the most obvious things (fr. 56 DK). From our earliest sources, Homer emerges as a poet of great authority, though the exact range of his subject matter and the definition of his work remain vague (Pindar, for example, ascribes to him stories that are not found in our *Iliad* or *Odyssey*: Fitch 1924, pace Nisetich 1989). The earliest extant author who explicitly discriminates between genuine works of Homer and epics wrongly attributed to him is the fifth-century historian Herodotus, at 2.117 – a passage to which I return below. It seems, however, that in some contexts Homer continued to be seen as the author of a vast number of poems long after Herodotus' time. *The Lives of Homer*, for example, are late compilations (cf. West 2003) but ascribe to Homer many poems: not just the *Iliad* and the *Odyssey*, but the *Margites*, the *Hymns*, the *Battle of Mice and Frogs*, many poems of the Theban and the Trojan cycle, the *Capture of Oechalia*. It seems, then, that contrasting definitions of Homer's *oeuvre* are not just a matter of historical development (wider range of poems in the archaic period, stricter definitions later on), but also depend on context.

Professional rhapsodes who earned their livelihood by travelling from city to city and reciting epic at local festivals would have found it expedient to insist that they were performing the works of Homer. In this way, they could rely on one name which had Panhellenic fame and status, in order to attract audiences to their performances. We know of a group of rhapsodes called the Homeridae, or 'descendants of Homer', who were thought of as being particularly authoritative (cf. Plato *Ion* 530d6–8): clearly, a close association with Homer, 'the blind poet whose works are best for ever' was advantageous to the rhapsodes (Burkert 1987). The context of their performances, and the particular pressures of their profession, help to explain some aspects of the ancient reception of Homer. First, because they invoked and even embodied Homer as the author of the poems they were performing (Nagy 2004), they naturally aroused the curiosity of their audiences about this poet, and then satisfied it by telling stories about his life: the surviving *Lives of Homer* have strong rhapsodic influences, and often attempt to establish special connections between Homer and particular places or audiences (Graziosi 2001, 2002). Thus, the anonymity of the epics, and their equidistance from all audiences, was counterbalanced by biographical narratives which could be adapted to suit individual circumstances and local preferences. We can also imagine that it might have been tempting for the rhapsodes to present whatever poems they were reciting as the work of famous poets like Homer or Hesiod. It is clear that the *oeuvre* of these two poets was rather fluid in antiquity: today, poems like the *Homeric Hymns* or the Hesiodic *Catalogue of Women* are thought to belong to the same traditions as the *Iliad* or the *Theogony*, but are usually denied full Homeric or Hesiodic authorship. The problem here has as much to do with modern concepts of authorship and the focus on the individual, as with ancient performances and performers. It seems that the *Iliad* and the *Homeric Hymns* were not composed by the same individual, or even in the same century (cf. Janko 1982), but that they were Homeric according to the exacting standards of ancient audiences. Those standards emerge not just from the report about the *Homeric Hymn to Apollo*, but from other evidence too.

Some fourth-century sources, for example, mention a decree passed by Peisistratus or his sons, according to which 'Homer and Homer only' was to be performed at the Great Panathenaea – the most prestigious festival in ancient Athens (for full discussion of the sources and the decree, see Kotsidu 1991). It has often been assumed that rhapsodic performances were checked against an official text (the so-called 'Peisistratean recension') so that individual reciters would not stray, embellish, cut or reshuffle. It seems very plausible that the technology of writing was used early on in the transmission of the *Iliad* and the *Odyssey*, as a means of preserving those two extraordinarily authoritative and bulky works. Yet it is important to note that classical sources focus all their attention on correct performances, not texts. Nietzsche already drew attention to this mismatch between ancient and modern priorities in *Wir Philologen*: 'How classicists torment themselves asking whether Homer wrote, without grasping the much more important principle that Greek art exhibits a long inward hostility to writing and did not want to be read!' (tr. Arrowsmith 1963: 15). The ancient sources on the Panathenaic decree tell us nothing about texts and are similarly useless when it comes to establishing what was meant by 'Homer' in the sixth century BCE: we are left to wonder, for example, whether rhapsodic performances may have started with a hymn to Athena (for the possibility that the *Homeric Hymns* were used to introduce longer epic recitations, cf. Bremer 1981). There is, however, one issue on which the reports about Homeric performances at the Panathenaea are informative: clearly audiences exerted some control over the rhapsodes and wanted to ensure stability of performance over time. Every four years, at the Great Panathenaea, Homer only would be recited.

Rhapsodes, then, were expected to keep the Homeric poems free of innovation. Playwrights, by contrast, were expected to create new versions of traditional stories every year, at the second most important Athenian festival: the Great Dionysia. This difference may account for the fact that contradictions abound in the work of the playwrights (for example: Euripides' portrayal of Helen changes drastically from play to play), whereas they were considered a problem in Homer. In an interesting passage, Herodotus observes: 'The *Cypria* is not by Homer, but by someone else; for in the *Cypria* we are told that, when Paris led Helen away, he arrived from Sparta to Troy in three days, enjoying a fair wind and a smooth sea, whereas in the *Iliad* Homer says that he wandered off course when he took her away' (2.117; cf. 4.32). It is a commonplace, among handbooks of mythology, to suggest that different versions of the same story circulated freely in the Greek world and could always be adapted to suit individual contexts. What Herodotus shows, however, is that there was also a need to establish one authoritative – that is to say – Homeric version of the myth, which was not constantly open to negotiation or alteration depending on context.

What begins to emerge here is the authority, and fixity, of the Homeric poems through space and time. Other snippets of information confirm the picture. We know, for example, that Solon or Pisistratus were suspected of having added one line to the *Catalogue of Ships*, in order to justify Athenian claims over Salamis against those made by Megara. The story is mentioned by Aristotle and duly recorded, next to the incriminated line, in the Homeric scholia, that is, the comments found in the margins of the medieval manuscripts (*Rhetoric* 1375b26–30; Scholia b *ad Il.* 2.558 in Erbse 1969–88). The anecdote confirms that the *Iliad* was thought to be common property among the Greeks: it was expected to be relevant to the Megarians, and to be free of Athenian additions.

Gradually, the ancient sources become more explicit about written texts of Homer. We know that Homeric epic dominated the school curriculum from early on and that schoolboys were expected, for example, to translate difficult Homeric words into ordinary language (cf. Aristophanes fr. 233 K–A). But it is in the library of Alexandria that the Homeric poems became the focus of the most detailed and comprehensive textual scholarship. It seems that before the third century, texts of Homer were noticeably more fluid than afterwards: the early papyri, as well as the Homeric quotations found in classical authors, vary significantly and sometimes report entire lines which have since disappeared (West 1988: 45, on the 'wild' papyri; and Labarbe 1949, on Plato). After the work of the Alexandrians in the third century – most notably Zenodotus, Aristophanes and Aristarchus – the texts of Homer became more uniform, although the Alexandrian scholars also appear to have introduced some conjectures and corrections of their own. Unlike the manuscripts of other ancient authors, the medieval manuscripts of Homer display few examples of straightforward mistakes or corruptions: variations are often the result of inherited views and preferences, and are based on rationales grounded in ancient Homeric criticism. In the case of Homer, more even than in that of other classical authors, textual criticism is inextricably bound with reception history (Battezzato 2003 is a rare and successful example of how textual criticism and reception studies can be combined). The modern editor of Homer often has to adjudicate between the views of different interpretations and versions of Homer, rather than simply having to restore a corrupted text. More fundamentally still, the editor must choose between different goals: s/he can try to reconstruct the text available to the Alexandrians (a task which van Thiel, 1991 and 1996, admirably succeeds in accomplishing) or attempt to produce a viable seventh-century text (this is the overall intent of West, though he makes considerable concessions to the transmitted text; cf. the introduction to his edition of the *Iliad*: West 1998). When studying the ancient reception of Homer, it is crucial to bear in mind that the transmitted text of Homer is probably very close to the Alexandrian editions (and to what Virgil read); but that it is much more difficult to know what versions of the *Iliad* Spartan school boys copied out in the fifth century, or even the exact wording and number of lines in Plato's copy of Homer (Nagy 2002).

For all that the Alexandrian scholars made a considerable contribution to shaping the text of Homer, it is also important to realize that they shared the concerns and interests of earlier generations. For example, we know that they went to the trouble of collecting and comparing versions of the Homeric poems which originated from different cities (the so-called 'city editions' αἱ κατὰ πόλεις ἐκδόσεις: Ludwich 1884: 3–8), and that they devoted more effort to establishing, preserving and explaining the text of Homer than to working on the poems of any other author. They were also keen to safeguard the impartiality and distance of the Homeric poems from all possible readers and interpretations: an important principle attributed to Aristarchus was that Homer should be explained only with reference to what was contained in Homer (Ὅμηρον ἐξ Ὁμήρου σαφηνίζειν): all comparisons with other works of literature, local customs, and material culture were thus subordinated to the internal coherence of the Homeric poems (cf. Herodotus 2.117, discussed above). The corollary is that, by then, the Homeric poems were clearly defined: they were the *Iliad* and the *Odyssey*, very much in the form in which they have reached us.

Modes of Reception

According to one definition, students of reception are essentially concerned with 'the artistic or intellectual processes involved in selecting, imitating or adapting ancient works' (this view of reception studies is discussed by Hardwick 2003a: 5). On this definition, the 'ancient works' in question seem to be a given. However, as the previous section indicates, the shaping of the Homeric poems, with the attendant shift of focus from performances to texts, and the ongoing redefinition of Homer's *oeuvre*, can itself be seen as a process of reception. The interconnection between the works and their reception emerges clearly when we try to identify any ancient selections, imitations or adaptations of Homer. For reasons of space, I discuss a small number of possible receptions, moving from small-scale selections to engagements with the *Iliad* and the *Odyssey* in their entirety.

Homeric epic is composed in a very distinctive language – an artificial mixture of dialects which was never spoken by a real community in their daily life, but which developed in the course of many centuries precisely as a means of expressing the great deeds of gods and men in the dactylic hexameter. Distinctive words, verbal forms and recurrent phrases characterize the Homeric language and, as soon as they are heard, evoke the epic deeds of gods and heroes (Graziosi and Haubold 2005). When they are used by later Greek authors, it is notoriously difficult to establish whether they represent a conscious allusion to the *Iliad*, the *Odyssey*, the *Homeric Hymns*, or even to specific passages within them, or whether they evoke the epic tradition more generally (cf. Hunter 2004: esp. 239). The word φύλοπις, for example, is an obscure term which apparently means 'battle' or a more specific aspect of war (its exact meaning was debated already in antiquity, see the scholia b to *Iliad* 6.1 in Erbse 1969–88). The Hellenistic poet Theocritus used it once, in order to describe the battles of the heroes and, more specifically, the language of the bards when they sang of them: φυλόπιδας προτέρων ὕμνησαν ἀοιδοί, 'the bards sang the battles of earlier generations' (*Idyll* 16.50). Moving backwards in time, Aristophanes, in the fifth century BCE, used it once, in a mock version of an oracle (*Peace* 1076). For Hesiod, earlier still, it was associated with the heroic age (*Works and Days* 161). In the *Iliad*, it was already treated as an obscure and heroic word: within the poem, it is often accompanied by more ordinary synonyms. Such internal explanations, or glosses, are common in the *Iliad* and suggest that ancient expressions were actively received and explained for the audiences of the poem. For the purpose of this article, we may ask when the use of the word φύλοπις can be described as an instance of Homeric reception.

Theocritus clearly knew the word primarily from the *Iliad*, though he talked about its use by 'the bards' in general, because he understood it to belong to a wider tradition of epic. Aristophanes used it in a mock oracle: we may be tempted to think that his use of the word has nothing to do with Homer; but in fact his usage reminds us that the language of epic and that of divination were close, and that Homer was often portrayed in the guise of a prophet in Aristophanes' time (Graziosi 2002: ch. 4). Finally, within the *Iliad* itself, there is a sense that the word was already treated as old and heroic: 'Homeric', we may say.

A sense that different forms of Homeric reception can be traced all the way back to the Homeric poems themselves emerges also when we consider other features of the poems, such as the celebrated simile of the leaves in *Iliad* 6.146–9. The basic comparison between the generations of mortals and the regeneration of leaves seems to have been widespread: it recurs, in a different form, at *Il.* 21.464–6, and the Greeks attributed it also to Musaeus, whom they considered an ancestor of Homer's (Musaeus, fr. 5 DK). So, for them, Homer was already working with an established poetic cliché (modern scholars agree: cf. Burgess 2001: 117–26). When Mimnermus compared mortal life to the ephemeral existence of leaves in fr. 2 W, there is little reason to suppose that he was engaging closely with *Iliad* 6; he too was working with a traditional image. Similarly, when Bacchylides compared to scattered leaves the souls of the dead whom Heracles encountered near the river Kokytos in the Underworld (5.63ff), we need not suppose an Iliadic model. When Simonides, however, quotes the exact wording of *Il.* 6.146 and calls it 'the single best thing the Chian bard said' (fr. 19 West) we know that he is thinking specifically of *Iliad* 6 and Homer. He too, however, proceeds to use the line as a piece of traditional wisdom, rather than engaging specifically with its meaning in *Iliad* 6. Later, Apollonius Rhodius and Virgil, imitators of Homer *par excellence*, do their own version of the simile of the leaves (at *Argonautica* 4.216ff and *Aeneid* 6.305ff respectively): here we can assume that *Iliad* 6 is a significant model, but other manifestations of the simile in Greek literature also seem relevant. Virgil, in particular, compares to leaves the souls which Aeneas encounters at the banks of the river Cocytus, when he descends into the Underworld. Many have supposed that Heracles' journey to the World of the Dead is at least as significant for the Virgilian passage as is Glaukos' speech, and have suggested that Bacchylides was probably not the only poet to have used a leaf simile in connection with Heracles' descent to the Dead (cf. Austin 1977: 309ff). It thus seems that although references to specific passages and episodes in the Homeric poems become more pointed in the course of time, the wider resonance of traditional images and expressions remains important.

Visual engagements with Greek epic confirm the picture outlined so far. It is only in the course of the sixth century BCE that vase paintings – both in Greece and in Italy – start to privilege Iliadic and Odyssean scenes over other stories about the epic past (Friis Johansen 1967: esp. 223–30; Kannicht 1982; Snodgrass 1998). But even when the Homeric models are clearly recognizable, images often speak of a wider and remote past which is not contained within a Homeric allusion: Lilian Balensiefen (2005) has recently shown how the Odyssean monsters which decorated Roman villas speak of a terrifying and distant past, which is reassuringly framed within an orderly architectural plan. Similar processes of framing and distancing, together with the attendant celebration of human progress, are at work in the *Odyssey* too;

so we may wonder whether, as we stroll through the villas and confront the monsters, we are looking at the *Odyssey*, or at what Odysseus saw.

If, instead of focusing on individual words, images or scenes, we look for engagements with the texts in their entirety, similar tensions between the *Iliad*, the *Odyssey*,
and the wider epic tradition emerge. When Aeschylus described his tragedies as 'slices
from the banquets of Homer' (according to Athenaeus, *The Sophists at Dinner*, 8.347e),
he was referring to the many poems that were loosely considered Homeric in his
time. The *Iliad* or the *Odyssey*, as Aristotle shrewdly remarked in the *Poetics*, 59b,
would provide the plot and material for just one play, whereas the poems of the
Cycle offered a basis for several. Generally, it seems that Athenian playwrights
avoided direct reworkings of the *Iliad* and the *Odyssey*, preferring instead to base
their plays on stories featured in the cyclic epics. These, as we have seen, were also
considered Homeric; though it seems that playwrights expected audiences to be particularly familiar with the *Iliad* and the *Odyssey*, and perhaps avoided covering the
same ground as those two poems precisely for that reason. Euripides' *Trojan
Women*, for example, is set after the fall of Troy but before the Achaeans have set
off on their return journey. The two other plays in the same trilogy (now lost) also
fall outside the scope of the *Iliad* and the *Odyssey*; yet Euripides assumes that his
audience can recognize detailed allusions not just to particular scenes of the *Iliad*
and the *Odyssey*, but to their entire structure. The portrayal of Andromache can serve
as an example to illustrate this point, though others could be adduced. In the *Iliad*,
she is depicted as the paradigmatic good wife who, however, always fails to be where
she might be expected. In book 6, Hector looks for her at home. When he fails to
find her, he imagines that she might be visiting one of her sisters in law, or have
gone to the temple; but, in fact, she is on the city wall, looking at the battlefield
and trying to identify Hector. Later, in book 22, everybody is watching Hector's
duel with Achilles from the wall, except for Andromache herself, who is preparing
a bath for him at home, even though by then he is already dead. Euripides'
Andromache is a self-righteous young woman: she knows that she is – unavoidably,
after her Iliadic portrayal – a good wife, and she congratulates herself on always knowing where a good wife should be (647–50): clearly a comment on her unpredictable
whereabouts in the *Iliad*. (For a different take on this Homeric passage and its reception, based on the psychoanalytic theory of identification, see Zajko 2006.)

In the Hellenistic period, the *Iliad* and the *Odyssey* were held in exceptionally high
esteem and were treated as paradigmatic examples of epic, far superior to the cyclic
poems and other epics that had once been attributed to Homer (cf. for example,
Callimachus, *Epigram* 32: 'I hate the cyclic poem . . .' and *Epigram* 55, which
suggests that Creophylus' poem *The Capture of Oechalia* was good enough to pass
as Homeric, though not in Callimachus' eyes). It was assumed that the scale and
structure of the *Iliad* and the *Odyssey*, as well as their language and themes, defined
the epic genre. Yet the monumentality of the Homeric poems was also considered
a problem. In an extremely influential passage of the *Aetia*, Callimachus complained
about critics who berated his miniature poems and expected him to write epics
in thousands of verses, featuring kings and heroes. It was once assumed that

Callimachus was alluding to a literary quarrel with Apollonius, the author of the most influential Hellenistic epic. But Apollonius' *Argonautica* itself tries to rework the *Iliad* and the *Odyssey* into a much shorter epic which displays many of the modernist traits we associate with Callimachus (cf. Nelis 2005).

In Rome, Hellenistic perceptions of Homeric epic were extremely influential. We do not know why Livius Andronicus decided to translate the *Odyssey* into Latin in the third century BCE: his plays were commissioned, but the occasion and motives for his translation of the *Odyssey* remain obscure. The fragmentary state of his work makes it especially difficult to gauge the exact relationship between the *Odyssey* and his Latin version (for an excellent brief appraisal of Livius as a Homeric translator, see Hinds 1998: 58–62). Beyond doubt, however, is the fact that the continuously high esteem in which the *Iliad* and the *Odyssey* were held in the Greek world deeply affected Roman perceptions of the poems. Similarly, the Greek pre-occupation with not repeating Homer is reflected in the earliest Roman engagements with his epics: although only fragments of Naevius' *Carmen Belli Poenici* and Ennius' *Annales* survive, those two works, together with Livius' *Odyssey*, testify to the variety and ambition of early Roman engagements with Homer (see further Boyle 1993). Later Roman poets approached Homer through Livius Andronicus, Naevius and, especially, Ennius, as well as through Hellenistic reworkings and their attendant value judgements. Virgil echoed Callimachus' hatred of the cyclic poem in *Georgics* 3.4, only to rework the epic cycle in his *Aeneid*, especially in books 2 and 3. His approach was meant as a challenge: he could fashion a poem equal to the *Iliad* and the *Odyssey* out of the cyclic material, which the Alexandrians considered infinitely worse than the genuine Homer. His attitude in turn became a model for later Roman poets, who defined their relationship with Homer (and Virgil) by reworking the most obscure, marginal and unappreciated Greek epics in their own work (see further Heslin 2005: 102ff).

The variety of Homeric receptions in Greece and Rome is bewildering, as is the esteem in which Homer was held throughout antiquity. Homer was thought of as the river Oceanus, from which everything else flows. Poets sought to justify whatever they were doing by claiming Homer as their predecessor: in his philosophical phase, Horace described Homer as the first and best moral philosopher (*Epistles* 1.2); while Ovid defended his own work by pointing out that, after all, the *Iliad* was just a fight over a slave girl, and the *Odyssey* a competition over a married woman (*Tristia* 2.1.381–6). The problem, for those approaching the ancient reception of Homer, is to try and identify what may not have been Homeric. For all that the ancients constantly debated the question, definitions of the truly Homeric constantly shifted, and thus ultimately reinforced the authority and influence of the poet.

Temporalities

The ancient reception of Homer can be made to fit into a rather cosy vision of literary history, and of the classical tradition, where artists and intellectuals steadily build on what previous generations have achieved. It is tempting, for example, to present Augustan epic as reworking Homer through the filter of Ennius, Alexandrian poetry and Athenian drama. Later receptions are then assumed to approach the Homeric poems through the poetry of Virgil. Yet such linear models of reception are problematic not just because Greek engagements with Homer continued long after the Hellenistic period (Hunter 2004), while the Romans may have been interested in the Trojan saga before Livius Andronicus (Farrell 2004), but most importantly because ancient approaches to Homer often defy linear concepts of time and, consequently, any neat division between antiquity and modernity. In order to see how they do so, it may be useful to take our cue (with committed anachronism) from recent receptions of Homer.

> Many contemporary artists and intellectuals have challenged conventional literary histories where, say, modern receptions of Homer tidily follow on from ancient antecedents. Derek Walcott, for example, has vigorously expressed his unhappiness with the colonising effect of a certain kind of literary history.
>
> I think it is this whole freshness of experience that made me feel that my references to Homer, and all the other writers I was indebted to in the book [i.e. *Omeros*], were perfectly valid. And I knew it would lead to a kind of academic acclaim that I'm not very happy about – 'Oh, so much is owed to so-and-so' – I hate that. It is a patronizing way of saying about, for instance, Romare's work: 'Look at those black cutouts. They are like Greek vases'. Yes, they may be like Greek vases, but they are *simultaneous* concepts, not *chronological* concepts. (Walcott 1997: 240, italic his own).

In Walcott's *Omeros*, the past is most strikingly evoked as a simultaneous experience when the fisherman-hero Achille makes a submarine journey to Africa, in the form of a hallucination or dream, caused by a sunstroke. His 'trip' is configured simultaneously as an ancient Greek *katabasis* (filtered through Dante and Virgil) and as a return of the slave's soul to West Africa – a motif prominent in neo-African eschatological belief-systems (see further Davis 2007; for other discussions of Walcott and temporality see also Haubold 2007 and Hardwick 2007a, 2007b). A visit to the Underworld and/or a return of the soul to Africa do not tidily belong to 'antiquity', because they defy death and, consequently, linear concepts of time.

Simultaneous experiences characterize what we may call the ancient reception of Homer too. At the beginning of Ennius' *Annales*, for example, the poet describes a dream in which he meets the soul of Homer. Literary historians have been keen to point out how the passage is indebted to Callimachus, who in turn alludes to Hesiod. But Ennius' dream does not fit tidily into a linear history of literature, because Homer swiftly reveals to Ennius that they share the same soul, and that, in an earlier incarnation, that soul belonged to a peacock. Ennius, then, does not simply receive, select or adapt an ancient work of literature: he turns out to be Homer incarnate. The business of the peacock was much ridiculed in antiquity (for sources and discussion, see Skutsch 1985: 147–53) but the reincarnation of Homer perfectly illustrates my main point. Studying the ancient reception of Homer demands of us that we think hard about what we mean by 'antiquity', 'reception' and – last but not least – 'Homer'.

FURTHER READING

The ancient reception of Homer is a central issue in many publications on classical literature and culture; I offer here some very brief suggestions for further reading. Two useful introductory articles are Hunter 2004 and Farrell 2004. J.M. Foley 2005 includes several articles which discuss the reception of Homer in later epic poetry. On Homer in early Greek lyric, Fowler 1987 and Nagy 1990; on drama, Goldhill 1986. For various aspects of Homer in early and classical Greece, see also Zanetto, Canavero, Capra and Sgobbi 2004. On Homer in Hellenistic poetry, Fantuzzi and Hunter 2005. For ancient Homeric scholarship, Pfeiffer 1968 and Montanari 1979–95; for Homer in Hellenistic and Roman education, see Morgan 1998. The Homeric scholia (that is, the marginal comments found in the medieval manuscripts and often summarizing ancient works of criticism) are edited by Erbse 1969–88 (*Iliad*) and Dindorf 1855 (*Odyssey*). For Homer in early Rome, Hinds 1998 offers a concise and stimulating discussion. On Livius Andronicus, see Mariotti 1986; on Naevius, M. Barchiesi 1962; on Ennius, Skutsch 1985. For Homer and Virgil, Knauer 1964a remains important (for an English summary, see Knauer 1964b); see also A. Barchiesi 1984. For Homer in the Greek world of the imperial period, see Zeitlin 2001; for allegorical interpretations, Buffière 1956 and Lamberton 1986. For Homer in Greek art, Kannicht 1982 and Snodgrass 1998; for Etruscan and Roman art, Brilliant 1984.

CHAPTER THREE

Poets on Socrates' Stage: Plato's Reception of Dramatic Art

Chris Emlyn-Jones

This chapter aims to consider the engagement of the philosopher Plato (*c.*429–347 BCE) with the contemporary dramatic art forms of the Athenian city-state (*polis*) in which he lived. Plato's attitude is developed extensively in books 2–3 and 10 of his central work, *Republic*, where the outline of an ideal state ruled by a philosophical elite involves the banning of virtually all existing poets from writing or performing as actors on a number of related grounds: they represent and portray undesirable qualities and emotions which pander to the lowest part of the human character rather than the intellect, for example heroes of epic and tragedy like Achilles and Agamemnon who exhibit arrogance, anger, despair and are generally out of control of their emotions. Since Plato, in common with many of his contemporaries, believed that you inevitably become the kind of person you are portraying, this led to the conclusion that drama has a bad moral and psychological effect on performers who, in their turn, pass this influence on to their audiences. Underpinning all this is the conviction that poetry (in fact all art, but poetry is Plato's chief target) is an imitation (*mimesis*) of reality, in which the artist has the apparent knowledge of what he portrays, but actually lacks the real thing because his product is an inferior copy of reality (*Republic* 10. 595–607; see also P. Murray 1996). Plato's view has had considerable influence on some anti-theatrical movements in later western culture (see Barish 1981).

Since all poetic activity in Greece up to Plato's time, whether Homeric epic, lyric poetry or Athenian tragedy and comedy, could be called to a greater or lesser extent 'theatre' or 'drama', in the sense that it was performed, formally or informally, before an audience, Plato's criticism could hardly be more wide-ranging in its application. The Homeric poems in particular, Plato's chief target in *Republic*, were regarded as a blueprint for Greek culture and despite the separation of three centuries from their composition, were contemporary with the fifth/fourth century BCE in the sense that they were recreated year after year in dramatic recitations by *rhapsodes* (professional reciters of poetry) at popular civic festivals in Athens and elsewhere. Plato's reception of drama would therefore seem the boldest of enterprises – to take on and largely reject the inherited cultural wisdom of the *polis*. In his final work, *Laws*, he brings together art and politics by identifying what he considers the excesses of the theatre as the key to the licence affecting popular democracy, a form of government he particularly dislikes and which, he claims, heralded the political decline of Athens. Instead of *aristocratia* (literally 'rule of the best') there is 'base *theatrocratia*' = 'rule of the *theatron*' (*Laws* 3.701a). The *theatron* was the curved viewing area in the theatre complex where the massed, and vocal audience (Plato calls them a 'mob' (*ochlos*)) sat on seats (wooden in the fifth and early fourth centuries BCE) to watch the performance (Wallace 1997).

A clear case, it would seem, of contested rather than assimilated cultural values (see Hardwick 2003a: 28). Most critical approaches to Plato's theory of art have either asserted the importance of some kind of autonomous aesthetic value, to which concept Plato, like most of his contemporaries, would have doubtless presented a 'mask of incomprehension' (Janaway 1995: 203), or have alternatively pointed out that Plato's hierarchical intellectual and moral universe simply failed to recognize and accommodate the plurality of voices involved in the conflicts and ethical dilemmas presented by epic, tragedy and comedy (Gould 1992: 24–5). Moreover, it is important to remember that our perspective on Plato is not that of most of his contemporaries. In the broader picture of fourth-century Athenian culture and politics, Plato's elite cultural values would have seemed something of a backwater (Brunt 1993: 300–1), and in their wider context much less influential than his younger contemporary Aristotle's more effective assimilation of the moral and emotional world of drama to rational principles in his *Poetics*.

What makes Plato's reception of drama not just interesting for aestheticians but of value for cultural historians is the form in which he casts his critique, which suggests not, as outlined above, a simple adversarial stance, but a more complex engagement with the popular culture of his day. He wrote not treatises but dramatic dialogues in which were developed a variety of scenarios featuring a wide range of individuals, prominent among them his teacher Socrates (469–399 BCE), who come together to converse in a variety of venues around Athens, and often in recognizable historical contexts. It has increasingly been recognized that Plato's dialogue form is not an ornamental facade, dressing up a philosophical message (as in, say, Cicero or Berkeley), but is part of the message itself – an expression of his inherent dramatic sense (Rutherford 1995). The dialogues (*c*.26 thought to be genuine, and about half a dozen of doubtful authenticity) vary considerably in length, form and content, but many of them have in common the characteristics of the dramatic genres Plato professes to criticize, including a genuine interaction of three-dimensional characters who feel strong emotion, joke and tease one another, as well as engaging in intellectual confrontation, discussion and debate. The total absence of the voice of Plato himself, either as author or character in his dialogues, strengthens, if anything, the generic link between the dialogues and conventional drama, and the dramatic element in his work extends well beyond structure and characterization, into copious quotation from poets and a pervasive use of theatrical imagery (Yamagata 2005; Tarrant 1955).

There is no evidence that any of the dialogues were actually performed by pupils or associates in Plato's school (the Academy) or elsewhere, and what form a performance might have taken is not easy to imagine (for a hypothetical reconstruction see Ryle 1966: 21–32); but this is less important than the fact that the individual scenarios are clearly composed to be 'performed', if only on a stage in the mind of the listener/reader, as 'meta-theatrical prose dramas', to adopt a recent coinage (Charalabopoulos 2001; Blondell 2002: 23–8). The idea of performance as something linking a variety of activities in the fifth/fourth century Athenian polis such as politics, theatre and law, has assumed increasing significance in Athenian cultural studies (Cartledge 1997; Goldhill and Osborne 1999); the inclusion of Plato in this development by examining the dialogue form as itself a performance (see e.g. the chapter by Goldhill and von Reden in Goldhill and Osborne, 257–289) has had the interesting effect of moving Plato in some respects closer to his contemporary culture. In the movement from oral to written communication in Greece Plato is no longer quite so obviously on the later side of a dividing-line which, it was argued a generation ago in the influential publications of E.A. Havelock, marks a watershed in the development of Athenian culture in the fourth and later centuries BCE (see in particular Havelock 1963). Plato's stance, rather than simply adversarial, is an attempt to engage with existing popular genres of discourse and turn them to his own purposes (see Nightingale 1995, developing and applying theories of intertextuality associated with Mikhail Bakhtin (Bakhtin 1981)). As such, Plato's interest in these genres extends well outside drama, to include, in particular, rhetoric, to which he tries, with only partial success, to assimilate tragedy (see *Gorgias* 502c–d, on Socrates' definition of poetry simply as oratory with the addition of music, rhythm and metre).

Drama in Plato's Dialogues

In considering Plato's 'meta-theatricality', *Republic*, written in the later 370s BCE and generally thought to be the authentic voice of Plato on dramatic art (see above), is itself far from typical of the dramatic scenarios of the dialogues written earlier. Following a lively introduction, the dialogue of *Republic* settles down into what is largely a monologue by Socrates, interspersed with the familiar 'Yes, Socrates, no Socrates'. In contrast, earlier dialogues such as *Protagoras* and *Euthydemus* (380s – we don't have any precise dates) are notable for their exploitation of the theatricality of semi-public encounters, featuring intellectual clashes between Socrates and sophists (renowned teachers of the day professing to impart wisdom). These intellectual 'bouts' are accompanied by semi-choreographed choruses, acolytes and bystanders who act as a claque, supporting one side or the other with theatrical *thorubos* (a 'din' – noisy appreciation or the reverse) (*Protagoras* 315b; *Euthydemus* 276b). Here Plato is not commenting on drama so much as re-enacting it, with philosophical argument about virtue (*aretē*) and knowledge representing dramatic debate.

It is notable that in both of the above dialogues, as in most of the dialogic scenarios, Socrates is presented as a visitor, an intruder into the sophists' arena, often an eccentric or comic figure, and sporting his customary ironic pose of the ignorant seeking knowledge (Vlastos 1991: 21–44); in *Protagoras* he is persuaded by an excited young friend to accompany him to the house of the wealthy patron Callias where the distinguished sophist Protagoras is lodging. They are initially rebuffed by the doorman in a stock comedy routine (' "Oh, sophists – he's busy!", and saying this, he slammed the door shut as hard as he could with both hands. We knocked again, and he answered us through the closed door, "Look, you fellows, didn't you hear me say he's busy?" ' (*Protagoras* 314d–e). In *Euthydemus* Socrates poses as an over-age student wanting instruction from the experts ('Aren't you afraid you're too old for that at your time of life?', says a solicitous friend, Crito (*Euthydemus* 272b). The same 'visitor role' is also true of *Republic* where the real purpose of the dialogue is introduced almost incidentally: Socrates makes a journey to the Piraeus where his ostensible object is to attend a religious festival, after which he is jokingly prevented by *force majeure* from going home and 'compelled' to visit the house of the *metics* (non-citizen residents) Cephalus and Polemarchus. However in each case Socrates' subsequent domination of the exchanges means that the setting swiftly transforms itself into his stage, as it were, onto which he receives his hapless opponents. The rules of the contest become his rules. Plato is dramatizing the reception and contest of cultural values as a physical reality.

In two dialogues Socrates' attention is focused on dramatic poet-performers. The first, *Ion*, is a short exchange between Socrates and Ion, a travelling rhapsode (performer of the Homeric poems, see above), otherwise unknown to us, whom we are told comes from Ephesus on the Asia Minor coast and has just celebrated a success in the competition of rhapsodes at the festival of the god Asclepius at Epidaurus (in the Argolid, south-west of Athens, famous for its theatre). Ion's skill, of which he is very proud, is to attract and manipulate the emotions of large audiences: 'At each performance I look down on them from up on the platform as they weep and look at me with dire emotion, astounded, in keeping with my story' (*sunthambountas* – 'their amazement matching [my words]' emphasizing the connection between his and their emotion). 'So I need to keep my mind very much on them, because if I make them cry I will laugh all the way to the bank, whereas if they laugh it's I who will do the crying for loss of my money' (535e). Like many actors through the ages Ion wishes to present his art as poised between the expression and communication of emotion and rational awareness of the need for effective presentation, and so his livelihood (see Janaway 1995: 23, quoting the actor Simon Callow: 'No matter how intense or painful the emotions of a part, the more you enter into them in a good performance, the less you are affected by them' (1985: 167)). Socrates, however, is keen to separate out the rational and the emotional: when Ion agrees that his job is to interpret the poet's 'thought' (*dianoia*) Socrates slips in (past the unsuspecting Ion) a 'strong' interpretation of this word: can Ion claim that he has more knowledge about divination than the expert in this skill? How can he claim to be an expert? Ion gratefully embraces Socrates' other suggestion – to take the initiative out of the performer's hands entirely and say that the rhapsode and, by implication, the poet he interprets succeed not by reason and skill but by 'possession': relieved of their reason, poets compose in a divine frenzy, possessed by the god, and pass on this possession to their audiences (533d–534e, and, on poetic 'possession', see Murray (1992)).

As with many of the Platonic dialogues we have no date of composition, but by its form *Ion* is, it would seem, an early dialogue, with only two speakers and an apparently early development of the 'anti-poetry' position. Socrates' argument is, in some respects, crude: the attempt to polarize the possible sources of poetic skill leaves open much middle ground: the traditional idea of poetic inspiration, for example the Homeric muse, invoked at the beginning of the *Iliad* or *Odyssey*, does not, and never did, imply entire passivity and absence of personal skill on the part of the poet, and we can assume that Socrates is not meant to be taken entirely seriously in putting it forward. However, the other extreme – the argument that poets and performers need to be expert in the subjects they treat – is fundamental to Plato's position and potentially more damaging to the poets: if Ion does not 'know about', for example, medicine or generalship (subjects which Homer speaks about), what are his grounds for claiming to 'know about' morality? Where does this leave the poet's traditional claim to be the teacher of his fellow citizens? In eagerly embracing one alternative – to be thought inspired – Ion shuns the other, the need for knowledge, at his peril.

The dramatic scenario is here the simplest: two characters meeting by chance somewhere in Athens. Socrates is initially cast as the host ('Welcome Ion; where have you come from?'). Egged on by Socrates, who pretends to envy the chance he has to dress up and look as fine a possible, Ion, vain, and flushed with recent success at Epidaurus, wants to be the one who takes the stage to give Socrates an exhibition (*epideixis*) of his skill as a poet, only to be ironically headed off by Socrates: 'and I will find time to listen to you one day' (530e). Behind a deferential pose, Socrates takes over the argument, initially contesting Ion's claim that it is only Homer's works which he can perform; this leads seamlessly into Socrates' claim that if Ion is right, it must be by possession that he can do this, since knowledge of a subject would surely imply the ability to judge success or otherwise of the treatment of this subject in any poet, and not just in Homer. This leads to the third section, which returns to the question of knowledge; in the case of Homer's assertions about military matters the person to judge whether these are correct must be the expert and not the rhapsode. The final conclusion, gratefully embraced by the perplexed Ion, that his status must derive from divine possession rather than any knowledge, is exploited with dramatic irony by Plato: is Ion unfair (in refusing to reveal his expertise) or divinely possessed? Ion replies: 'it's a much finer thing to be thought divine'. 'Well then', says Socrates, 'let's allow you this finer status in our eyes (*par' hēmin*)' (542b). Plato's ironic ending is emphasized by the little addition 'in our eyes' (Socrates does not believe for a second that the vain and stupid Ion is divinely inspired), but also depends on the unseen audience at whom, throughout the dialogue, Socrates has been winking over his shoulder. Ion, the representative of dramatic poetry, is not only intellectually unmasked, but through his personality and interactions made to look a fool on his own stage. The closure, the attribution of divinity, is transparently hollow. The audience is left tittering.

The other dialogue in which Socrates encounters a poet is the later and dramatically much more complex *Symposium* or 'wine-party', the setting of which mirrors an elite Athenian institution of some antiquity, with distinctive characteristics and procedures (Murray 1990). The host is Agathon, a tragedian writing at the end of the fifth century, whose work survives unfortunately only in fragments, but who is, unlike Ion, known to us from other sources, e.g. Aristotle in his *Poetics* (1451b21, 1456a29). Agathon is celebrating as host his recent victory in the competition of tragedies at the Lenaia (a winter festival) of 416 BCE (an unusually precise dramatic context). At the other extreme from *Ion*, the narrative structure is complex: the party is being presented by a minor character as narrator, describing an event at third hand some fifteen years after its presumed dramatic date ('he told me he said . . .' etc). Despite (because of?) the complexity of narrative structure the event is given an authentication as an important gathering which, despite its remoteness in time, many people are anxious to hear about (Rowe 1998: 5–6). Agathon was a tragedian of major importance, enough in the public eye to be the object of comic ridicule for his effeminacy by Aristophanes in his comedy *Thesmophoriazousai* (101–265).

Socrates is here the interloper; having (significantly?) avoided Agathon during his actual public celebratory feast ('for fear of the crowd' (*ochlos*)), he feels obliged to accept an invitation to the private celebration, an exclusive party on the following day. He arrives late, having dallied over a philosophical problem on the way. Meanwhile the other guests are already reclining on couches, and excuses for Socrates are given to Agathon by a companion of Socrates, Aristodemus (the primary narrator), embarrassed because he himself has not been formally invited but just asked to come along by Socrates. Socrates finally turns up and his eccentricity is smoothed over in social politesse ('this is just the habit he has' (175b)). The guests are all friends of social and intellectual consequence and include, besides Agathon, the comic playwright Aristophanes. They decide, on the proposal of one of them, Eryximachus, a somewhat humourless expert in medicine, to forgo the usual drinking bouts and instead make speeches in praise of Love. These all relate to Love as a mythical entity or as a social or natural force, Aristophanes producing a characteristically quirky and amusing 'myth' of Love as the force which compels originally separated human 'halves' to unite.

Agathon, as a climax to this part of the dialogue, makes a bravura and highly rhetorical speech, the sort of thing expected of a victor in a dramatic competition, relating the mythical qualities of Love (*Eros*) to traditional virtues, and this is greeted, for the first time in this party, with applause ('at the appropriateness of the lad's speech both for himself and for the god' (198a)). The ironic undertones of this assessment come to the surface, however, when, following extravagant praise, Socrates proceeds to use his dialectical method to refute Agathon's position, arguing that Love, far from being beautiful, implies a 'lack' of something, i.e. beauty. When Agathon is forced to say that 'It would appear, Socrates, that I knew nothing about what I said then' (i.e. when making his speech) (201b), this admission is revealing not only of the poet's character, but also, perhaps, how he regards his professional activity: at no stage in his encounter with Socrates does this appear to matter much to him: his willing concessions throughout the refutation (199–201) make him appear detached from the content. Its effectiveness is what is important; truth-value is neither here nor there. As with Ion, Agathon's intellectual shortcomings are dramatically exposed; but, unlike Ion, he is perceptive enough to admit intellectual weakness without, however, being able to see its implications for his profession.

The theatrical aspect of Socrates' relationship with Agathon comes to the surface in a short exchange which precedes Agathon's speech. Under the polite surface all the speeches have been highly competitive (conforming to a general symposium pattern), and Socrates takes advantage of this to bring the agonistic element to the surface. Only Agathon and Socrates are left to speak and Eryximachus, the unofficial master of ceremonies, hands over to Agathon. Eryximachus begins:

> 'If I didn't know that Socrates and Agathon are formidable on matters to do with love, I'd be awfully afraid that they'd be at a loss for words, because of the many and varied things that have already been said; but as it is I'm confident about them nevertheless.'
>
> Then Socrates said: 'Yes, well, you can say that, Eryximachus, because you've already competed successfully in the competition; but if you were in my position, or perhaps rather the one I will be in when Agathon too gives us a good speech, you'd be as terrified and desperate as I am now.'
>
> 'You mean to cast a spell on me, Socrates,' replied Agathon, 'so that I'll be thrown into confusion by the audience's high expectation of a good speech from me.' 'I'd be pretty forgetful, Agathon,' replied Socrates, 'if, when I'd seen your courage and self-confidence as you mounted the platform with your actors and looked straight out at such a large audience – not in the slightest way overcome by the prospect of displaying compositions of your own – I now thought you'd be overcome on account of the few of us.'
>
> Agathon said: 'What's that, Socrates? You surely don't think me so full of the theatre that I actually don't know that to an intelligent person a few sensible people are more frightening than a lot of stupid ones?'
>
> (*Symposium*, 193e–194b)

This exchange brings to the surface the hitherto implicit strongly competitive element in the speeches. Socrates' mock fear plays on Agathon's consciousness of his position in another world where status matters – that of the theatre – a performer facing an audience who might (but he doesn't really think they will) throw him into confusion by their expectations (he can pretend apprehension!). Agathon recognizes and attempts to deflect to his advantage the social pressure placed on him. Ostensibly he refers to this small exclusive audience, but the language gives him away; 'thrown into confusion' (*thorubēthō*) is cognate with *thorubos*, the roar of approval or disapproval of the theatrical crowd, and this word obviously colours what we are to understand by 'audience', when he uses the theatrical term *theatron* ('theatre' = the part of the whole complex where the audience sat, see above p. 39). Although pretending reluctance, Agathon is attempting covertly to bring his much-lauded recent public status to bear on the present company to secure victory in advance by blurring the boundary between the theatrical *ochlos* he has recently encountered and the apparently exclusive present theatron. He is trying to bring his 'street cred' with him, as it were, and cannot afford to fail his public. Socrates makes this explicit by extending the theatrical terminology: 'platform' (*okribas*) is the wooden structure where performances took place. Agathon is at the *proagon* (an event preceding the play in which the author mounts a stage with his players in order to introduce his work); he emphasizes words appropriate to performance in a big gathering:

'courage', 'self-confidence'. This is a trap, into which Agathon falls; in valuing his present audience ('a few intelligent people') over 'a lot of stupid ones', he reveals his real feelings about the environment in which he has to perform. It is a master-stroke to put the standard Platonic denigration of the mass audience into Agathon's own mouth. Socrates has momentarily converted the gathering into a stage on which Agathon will shortly perform, but it is a stage on which, as we have seen above (when discussing his speech on Love), he founders, and on which he suffers intellectual humiliation.

In *Symposium* Socrates exposes two aspects of Agathon's plight: on the one hand there is his intellectual defeat; Agathon is the only one of the symposiasts whom Socrates exposes in this way: his encomium of Love does not stand up to Socrates' polite probing. On the other hand there is Agathon's failed attempt to be part of both worlds – he wishes to bring the prestige of the public theatre to bear on the exclusive audience of the symposium, while at the same time being forced by Socrates into the position of revealing how little he really rates the theatrical crowd compared with his aristocratic friends. But how far are even these friends to be seen as discerning? They qualify by virtue of their class background and cultural status as an intellectual elite, but this does not prevent them from having greeted with *thorubos* Agathon's subsequently discredited speech.

Socrates' ability to play with the ironies here depends on the establishment of the public and private stage as clear polar opposites (as is indicated by his and Agathon's use of theatrical terminology). In contrasting the public mass audience of the theatre with the private or semi-private gatherings in which he presents his dialogues Plato is not attempting faithfully to reflect the historical reality of the divide; rather, he is engaged in constructing the contrasted identities which support and underline the emphasis he wishes to give to those who have knowledge and those who do not – 'the many', 'the foolish' or 'the ignorant', near-synonymous terms Plato regularly deploys to indicate the *ochlos*. Agathon is squarely caught between these identities.

Plato and the Athenian Polis: Centre and Periphery?

There is a sense in which Plato's public/private polarity, reflected, as we have seen, in some of the dialogues, also mirrors the geography of the *polis*. The focus of Plato's critique, the public institutions of democratic Athens, involving mass participation by a wide class-range of citizens, were closely centralized around the Acropolis, the religious centre: the Pnyx (Assembly area), the Agora (commercial, law-court and Council building) and, on the southern slopes of the Acropolis hill, the theatre of Dionysus where most theatrical performances took place, attended by up to 14,000 spectators. The contexts which Plato constructs for his dialogues tend, in contrast, to be the more exclusive venues frequented by the wealthy and socially privileged, such as gymnasia and the private houses of friends and patrons. These places and people are, in a sense, centrally placed in the social and intellectual life of the *polis*, but nevertheless exist in a tangential and complex relationship to the democratic core.

At some point in the 380s BCE Plato founded the Academy, a school on the site of a public gymnasium sacred to the hero Academus, more than a kilometre north-west of Athens. There is a serious shortage of information about the Academy – who attended, and what was studied (for the evidence, see Field 1930; Nails 1995: 213–31). The Academy was a legal entity with membership and a constitution, and Plato had a private house nearby. It is here, we must assume, that most of his dialogues were composed. Plato may well have been selective in choosing those who attended, and there are indications in the works of the orator Isocrates, for example, that there was some competition in the fourth century among schools for the attention of aspiring intellectuals and those likely to influence political and social affairs (Isocrates, *Against the Sophists*, 291.1).

While little is known about what went on in the early (fourth-century) Academy, there is evidence that the ambivalence of centre and periphery was very much in Plato's mind. In one of his later dialogues, *Theaetetus* (composed probably soon after *Republic*), a closely argued discussion of the perennial philosophical problem of knowledge and the role of sense data, Plato, in a digression, has Socrates play with the image of the philosopher as the person who has the *scholē* (leisure) to follow the argument whither it leads. This is not granted to the orator who has to talk against the clock (the *klepsydra*, the 'water-clock' used to time speeches in Athenian law-courts) as a 'slave disputing about a fellow slave, with a master sitting in judgement . . .'. In contrast, the philosophers, on the outside, 'from their youth up . . . have never known the way to the market place or law court or Council Chamber'. As a result, when they are forced to participate, they look ridiculous and are mocked. However 'our philosophical chorus . . . is not in a court under the judge's eye, nor in a theatre with an audience to criticize our philosophical evolutions' (*Theaetetus* 172e–173d). The appropriation of imagery is familiar and unmistakeable.

There is little doubt that for his own purposes Plato exaggerated the historical reality of the polarity; his picture of the Athenian dramatic audience as in progressive decline from a previous early fifth century BCE orderliness (see the reference to *Laws* at p. 39 above) does not entirely fit the evidence (Wallace 1997: 99–101); and, as has often been observed, his 'philosophical chorus' and Athenian democracy have much more in common than he was prepared to concede, for example in the emphasis on the importance of debate and reasoned argument (Monoson 2000). So his exaggeratedly polarized stance in the reception of Athenian popular culture itself needs explanation. By challenging the conventional theatre, and probably exaggerating its disorderliness, I would argue that Plato may have been attempting to reverse the polarity and make his stage, peripheral as it was in all senses of the word, the real cultural centre. Rather than denying the entire theatrical experience, he attempts to take it over, discredit its practitioners and substitute his own 'fringe theatre', outside the walls of Athens ('extra-murally' as it were).

In the 'theatre' of the dialogues poets are not at the centre (as many of them were in real life): Agathon is only equivocally so in *Symposium* (as the host of the party), whereas Ion is presented as the travelling poet who goes round the festivals and comes to Athens from outside and performs. This peripatetic nature of the dramatic artists as visitors and the (in an actual physical sense) temporary construction of their theatre, as well as Plato's conviction that his was the real theatre, is emphasized in *Laws* (Plato's last work, composed in the late 450s BCE; the speaker, as in several of the late dialogues, is not Socrates, but an 'Athenian Stranger'):

> As for our so-called serious tragic poets, imagine that some of them approach us and ask some such question as this: 'Strangers, may we pay your city a visit or not? And may we bring our poetry along with us, or what have you decided to do on this point?' In my judgement this should be the answer: 'Most excellent of visitors . . . we are also poets . . . rival artists and rival actors, and that, in the finest of all dramas, one which can be produced only by a code of true law . . . So don't imagine, then, that we shall light heartedly allow you to pitch your booths (= *skenai*, temporary stage-buildings) in our market square and give permission to those imported actors of yours, with their euphonious tones drowning out ours, to harangue women and children and the whole populace (*ochlon*) . . . Why, we would be stark mad to allow that.'
>
> (*Laws* 817a–c)

This picture of the poet in Plato's ideal society as a transient visitor with makeshift, movable props, as opposed to the 'true' theatre of the *polis*, is made clear earlier, in the *Republic*. All the usual institutions of state (occupying in reality the central geographical position) have been subsumed in the government by the Guardians (the philosophical élite); the poets, whose stamping ground is the theatre of Dionysus and other prominent places, are no longer at the centre. The question which Socrates continually repeats to his audience is whether or not dramatic poets should be 'admitted': (*paradechesthai* and cognates) from outside the *polis*; for example (378d5) on whether elements from mythology, e.g. warring gods from Homer, which fail to provide a morally suitable example, should be admitted into the city, along with their presenters:

> Take, then, a man whose wisdom enabled him to become multifarious and imitate every-thing; if he were to arrive in person in our city together with the poems he wished to exhibit, we would bow down before him as someone holy, amazing, and pleasing. But we would tell him that there is no man like him in our city, and that it is not in accord with law for there to be one. Then we would anoint his head with perfumes, crown him with a woollen wreath, and send him away to another city.
>
> (*Republic*, 397e–398a)

Along with the ironical Socratic praise and deference for the inspired 'holy divine poet', strongly reminiscent of *Ion*, we have a clear image of negative physical recep-tion of 'foreigners' from outside the city peddling subversion, followed by expul-sion. Poets can be welcomed back (cf. imagery of return from exile – in Greek the verb *katienai*) only in the unlikely event that they can show that they have a place in a 'well-governed city' (607c5). By the time of *Republic* Socrates no longer wishes to capture the poets' stage, but actually to deny them any place which is not closely allied with his state aims. In his state, the poets, even the 'harmless' ones, no longer have their traditional place at the centre. Indeed, those who come from outside with their following, drawing large crowds with their loud voices, like the peripatetic sophists, are even politically dangerous (568c). In a series of discussions from *Gorgias* through to *Republic* Plato emphasizes the close association of poets and rhetoricians with undesirable political associations such as tyranny; the link is the 'enslavement' to appetites at the expense of the exercise of reason which both the tyrant and his willing henchman, the poet, bring about in the mass of the populace (Lear 1992: 214).

Republic takes place dramatically in a 'fringe' area, the Piraeus (port of Athens), at the house of 'fringe' people, the *metics* (resident non-citizens) Cephalus and Polemarchus, during a religious festival involving foreigners, Thracians, from north-eastern Greece. Socrates, the visitor, notorious for his unwillingness to stir outside the walls of Athens, makes a journey, in reality of some nine kilometres, from the centre of Athens to Piraeus (still staying, it may be noted, within the fortifications between Athens and Piraeus constructed for defence during the fifth century); this provides a setting which enables Plato to explore a Utopia (Kallipolis) removed from the traditional polis centre both ideologically and geographically. The symbolism of 'going down' to Piraeus (327a) is significant: later in *Republic* in the famous image of the cave, the unenlightened masses sit bound underground in a cave watching shadows flickering on the walls, cast by objects passing behind them. The philosopher who has reached enlightenment 'above' is given the task of 'going down' to the everyday world and learning to live amongst the shadows, although initially ridiculously bad at operating in this world (*Rep.* 514ff; Burnyeat 1997). Just as the polarity of centre and fringe has been reversed horizontally in the *Theaetetus* example of philosophers in pursuit of real knowledge not 'knowing their way' to the political and social centre of the city (above p. 46), so here, in Plato's most radical departure from existing politics, the masses, and, by implication the institutions which support them, have been consigned, in a vertical polarity, to the unenlightened depths.

Plato's ability to lay claim simultaneously to both territories – centre and periphery – owes a great deal, as we have seen, to his dramatic manipulation of the image of Socrates. The long-disputed issue of the historicity of Plato's image of Socrates in the dialogues (see, for contrasted positions, Vlastos 1991: 45–80; Stokes 1992) has recently largely resolved itself into the more interesting question of the ways in which Plato uses his teacher: in particular the dual focus of Socrates presented as the fifth-century 'man in the agora', questioning so-called intellectuals, artists and other 'experts' about their claims to knowledge (and, incidentally, generating considerable resentment (*Apology* 21–2)), and, in contrast, the more typically fourth-century representative of Plato's alternative culture, seen notably in *Republic* and taken further in the more abstract speculations of the later dialogues.

We can, however, already see in the 'early' Socrates a critical attitude to conventional 'performance' in the widest sense: for example, in his explicit refusal, during his trial for impiety which resulted in his condemnation and death, to resort to conventional jury-pleasing rhetoric and, in particular, in his contempt for those who stage 'pathetic dramas' (*eleina dramata*), dragging weeping family members into the dock, displaying inappropriate emotions in order to elicit the sympathy of the jury and secure acquittal (*Apology* 35b, and, on the influence of drama on forensic activity generally, see Hall 1995a). In the sequel to Socrates' trial, *Crito*, the Laws of Athens, personified by a Socrates under sentence of death answering his friend Crito's plea that he should save himself by fleeing Athens, point out the necessity of Socrates' staying and facing death under their aegis rather than dragging out his life out in exile, 'living it up in Thessaly' (*Crito* 53e).

Plato's presentation of Socrates was of a lifelong loyal Athenian who did his military service with distinction during the long war Athens waged with the Peloponnesians in the latter part of the fifth century BCE (*Apology* 28e). In a striking Homeric comparison Socrates compares himself to Achilles in the *Iliad*, who chose death rather than an ignoble life (*Apology* 28c). However, for Socrates, 'staying at his post' involved not only fighting for his city but also wandering around the agora (the social and commercial centre of Athens) and turning up at other venues, directing at so-called experts awkward questions about values and conduct. This, which could be described as a critique of the Athenian performance culture, was, as we have seen, itself a drama, in which Socrates' 'performance of philosophy' (Goldhill and von Reden 1999) gave conviction to Plato's critique of the institutions of his *polis* and force to his 'alternative dramatic stage'.

FURTHER READING

Plato's writings on poetry are accessible in good recent English translations and commentaries, mainly in the Penguin Classics Series: *Ion* in Saunders 2005: 39–65 and *Laws*, Saunders 2004; *Symposium*, Gill 1999; *Republic*, Lee 1987. The definitive commentary on the Greek text of *Ion* and the relevant parts of *Republic* is Murray 1996. For the dramatist Agathon outside Plato, see Sommerstein 1994, and for the references in Aristotle, *Poetics*, see Heath 1996.

The recent secondary literature on this topic is enormous, and a strictly limited selection is included here. A short, reliable account of Plato's attitude to poets can be found in Ferrari 1989. The fullest and most helpful (and perhaps sometimes over-sympathetic) guide to Plato from the viewpoint of modern aesthetics is Janaway 1995. The last thirty years has, however, seen a radical reassessment of the interaction of Plato and the contemporary Greek theatre, which has come about partly as a result of a realization that Plato's philosophical content cannot be studied in isolation from the literary and dramatic aspects of the dialogues (compare Barish 1981, with e.g. the more nuanced Halliwell 1992). The study of intertextuality in Plato, developed from the seminal studies of Bakhtin 1981, has been advanced by Nightingale 1995, who analyzes the subtleties of Plato's incorporation of elements of contemporary Athenian literary genres, including tragedy and comedy, into his dialogues. The dramatic qualities of the dialogues themselves, including the significance of characterization, have been recently analyzed in some detail by Blondell 2002, who also provides the fullest survey and analysis to date of the speculative external evidence for Plato's methods of composition (compare also Nails 1995 on the relationship of Socrates to Plato's Academy). On Plato's debt to previous theories of inspiration and mimesis in Greek literature, see Murray 1992. For a short but trenchant critique of Plato, unusually (in current scholarship) from the perspective of ancient drama rather than Plato, see Gould 1992.

CHAPTER FOUR

'Respectable in Its Ruins': Achaemenid Persia, Ancient and Modern

Thomas Harrison

There are two ways of approaching the reception of ancient Persia, both through antiquity and into the modern world. The first would be to look at the representation of Persia (that is, in this context, the history of the Achaemenid Persian empire) in a sequential fashion – to show how it relies on a small number of stock images, of decadence and cruel power, replicated and then projected onto subsequent eastern enemies; one could then trace similar images continuing into the modern world, coloured by a variety of modern experiences. One could also, however, see this topic as a case study of what one might term 'historical reception', and to show how reception work is integral to sensitive historical interpretation. This chapter will attempt, within a limited compass (focusing in particular on the original formation of a western tradition of Persia and on the popular and scholarly reception of that tradition in the nineteenth and twentieth centuries), to do both.

The Formation of 'Persia'

Achaemenid Persia is in a number of ways an exceptional and a sensitive case, however. Running from its mid-sixth-century foundation under Cyrus the Great to its demise at the hands of Alexander, the history of the Persian empire (and of its reception) is a history in which the Greeks are always present both as arbiters and as foils. This is a fact with a number of consequences. First, leaving aside for now the modern Iranian reception of ancient Persia, in the west – as a result in particular of Edward Said's hugely influential *Orientalism* (Said 1979) – the Greeks' representation of the Persians has been seen as the first moment in the history of western ideological dominance over the East; Aeschylus' *Persians* has been described as the 'first unmistakable file in the archive of Orientalism, the discourse by which the European imagination has dominated Asia' (Hall 1989: 99). How should we respond to this continuity (or imagined continuity)? Secondly, unlike the study of Greek history (usually envisaged as a process of filling in of gaps, or of building on earlier foundations etc. – with only occasional currents of revisionism), the recent study of Achaemenid Persia is founded on an imagined break with past scholarship and past understanding and on a rejection of the framework of the Greek sources on which historians have been forced (and indeed still are forced in substantial measure) to rely. In the words of Heleen Sancisi-Weerdenburg (the first convenor of the Achaemenid History Workshops, which did so much to revitalize the study of Achaemenid History), historians have needed 'to break away from the dominant Hellenocentric view' (Sancisi-Weerdenburg 1987a: xiii) 'to dehellenise and decolonialise Persian history' (Sancisi-Weerdenburg 1987b: 131). In place of the stereotypes of Achaemenid kings and queens as oriental despots, or the view of the Persian empire as prone and decadent from the Persian wars to the conquests of Alexander, the new Achaemenid historiography – relying crucially on Persian administrative records, not solely on the accounts of Greek historians – has emphasized the resilience of the Achaemenid empire and the tolerance and pragmatism of its rulers.

The reception of Achaemenid Persia is also problematic in ways that the reception of a text cannot be. When can Persia's 'reception history' be deemed to begin? Our starting point here is not a (more or less fixed) literary text, or even a set of such texts, but a historical society and empire. This society and empire can only be reconstructed from, and in a sense may only be constituted by, a whole range of different perspectives: the administrative perspective of the Persepolis fortification and treasury texts (written in cuneiform on clay tablets, and baked for posterity as an accidental result of Alexander's destruction of Persepolis); the grandiose perspective of the (early) Persian kings, setting the world to order in their inscriptions; and in large part, especially when it comes to creating any kind of narrative of the Persian empire, the accounts of Greek outsiders.

None of these sources provides unmediated access to the reality of Achaemenid Persia. The Persian kings in their iconography, as in their inscribed pronouncements (the two relate closely to one another in terms of imagery), themselves borrow motifs from previous near-eastern kingdoms; Persian kingship and Persian power are presented as the summation of previous empires (Nylander 1970; Root 1979). Darius' own account of his accession as inscribed at Bisitun – the only narrative account of Persian history in Old Persian that survives – is markedly problematic (Wiesehöfer 1978). The relationship of Greek writers with the reality of Achaemenid Persia is more complex still; inevitably it also varies widely from author to author. Though the Persians undoubtedly made a vivid impression on the memories of the Greeks of the Persian war period, and though a small number of individual Greeks (such as the fourth-century BCE doctor Ctesias of Cnidus) may have had experience of the Persian court, direct experience of Persians or Persia was undoubtedly scarce. We are often forced into surmising what the possible route for information may have been – guessing for example that the Herodotean version of Cambyses as a mad tyrant derives from hostile Egyptian sources, or that the embassy of Kallias may have been the means by which inspiration for the festival metaphor of the Acropolis came from the Persian royal capital of Persepolis (Miller 1997: 3–133; cf. Root 1985). Despite this distance between the Achaemenid and Greek worlds, however, clear traces of Persian administrative records or of Persian royal ideology do survive in Greek sources. Herodotus' catalogues of the Persian empire and of the Persian army or his account of Darius' accession clearly derive in part from Persian records (the latter from Bisitun: e.g. Lewis 1985) – notwithstanding the deformation that they underwent en route. The King's self-styling as a kind of global policeman sorting out the petty squabbles of his subject peoples (Kent 1953: DSe 30–4; cf. DNa 32, DNb 16–21) also finds reflection in Greek accounts, in Greek descriptions of the senseless Greek way of war (by which even 'the victors come off with great harm' and the defeated are destroyed, Hdt 7.9.b1–2) or of the pathetic prizes for which they fight, 'strips of land of no great worth' (Hdt 5.49).

The distortion that Persian society or Persian ideology undergoes can be for a number of reasons. First and foremost, distortion is the result of a variety of Greek ideological agendas, the need for Persia to provide an exemplum of moral decadence (or of benign monarchy), or to create a tidy narrative of decline from the austere heyday of the elder Cyrus (Briant 1989). In parallel to these factors, Persian material is subject to exactly the same 'deformation' that affects other oral sources, for example for the history of the archaic Greek world (for deformation, see Murray 1987). Where it differs, however, is in the relative lack of controls on that deformation: where an oral account of contemporary Athenian or Theban society would have been circumscribed by (some knowledge of) the historical reality it is easy to imagine that accounts of Persia might have been limited only by their relationship to an easily recognizable stereotype (cf. Bovon 1963 on artistic representations). As Edward Said wrote on Aeschylus' *Persians*, the play 'obscures the fact that the audience is watching a highly artificial enactment of what a non-Oriental has made into a symbol for the whole Orient' (Said 1978: 21). Even where an author has witnessed Persian society at close hand, such autopsy is not the panacea for inherited prejudice that one might have hoped. Though Xenophon, on the back of his encounter with the fringes of the Persian empire in the course of the revolt of Cyrus the Younger, preserves many details of Persian etiquette, for example, in his *Anabasis* (Tuplin 1990), his idealization of Cyrus the Elder (and denunciation of the subsequent decline in Persian society) in the *Cyropaedia* suggests that experience is still being subordinated to preexisting conceptions (Gera 1993). Ctesias is usually deemed to have reaped little advantage from his spell in the court of Artaxerxes (Sancisi-Weerdenburg 1987c; Bigwood 1978; Tuplin 2004).

Rediscovery and reappropriation

It is this melange of sources, this mirage (partly an ideal version of Greek society, partly its antithesis), that is the exclusive starting point for the reception of Achaemenid Persia – or was, until the 'discovery' of the royal capital of Persepolis by western travellers (especially from the seventeenth century onwards). For the most part, the early reception history of Persia (if we define that as starting from after the fall of the Persian empire at the hands of Alexander) merely elaborates on these first traditions. In the context of Roman expansion, Greek resistance to the Persians can be aligned, by Polybius, with their later resistance to the Gauls as inspirational models of the Greek struggle for liberty (Pol. 2.35.7–8). Conversely, Xerxes can become the type of the oriental pleasure-seeker (Cicero *de finibus* 2.111–12), or an example of the excesses of human vanity or the transience of human fortune (Juvenal *Satires* 10. 172–87, Lucretius *de rerum natura* 3.1029–33). Just as for Ammianus allusions to the Persian war reverberated in the context of Rome's struggles against the Sassanian Persian empire (Fornara 1992), and just as classical reperformances of Aeschylus' *Persians* may have stimulated Athenian patriotism in the face of other enemies, so the first Renaissance performance of the play (1571) significantly celebrated the victory of a western naval alliance over the Ottomans at Lepanto (Hall 2007a). A performance of the play in Constantinople on the eve of the Greek uprising of 1821 again implicitly equated Persians and Turks (van Steen 2007); and one of the first reconstructions of the palaces of Persepolis by a western traveller, that of Cornelis de Bruijn, also cast them in a distinctly baroque Ottoman light.

Though armchair historians (notably the eighteenth-century Mitford) were capable of a questioning attitude to the Hellenocentric bias of their classical sources (Brosius 1991), the crucial turning point in the representation of ancient Persia seems to coincide with the growth of contact between western Europe and Iran in the nineteenth century – and it is in this period, and in particular on British travellers and writers to Iran, that this chapter will dwell. We are dealing now with a much greater number and variety of travellers – missionaries, doctors, scholars, but predominantly diplomats and soldiers (see e.g. Wright 2001; for three key individuals, Bosworth 1993, 1995; Lambton 1995) – for all of whom Persepolis and other Achaemenid sites are an essential detour, and for a minority of whom (notably Henry Rawlinson, the decipherer of cuneiform) they become an obsession. Moreover, though the earlier nineteenth-century travellers, not least Sir John Malcolm (Malcolm 1815; cf. Ouseley 1819–23) show a refreshing reliance on (post-Achaemenid) Persian sources such as the Shahnameh or the 'Book of Kings' (Firdausi's historical epic, written around the turn of the first millennium), this is also the period in which the primacy of Greek and Roman sources begins to erode in favour of an attention to Persian monuments and inscriptions. The background to British and other western contact with Iran in this period is, of course, political – the so-called Great Game, the concern on the part of the British to protect India from (first, French and then Russian) encroachment from the west and north. In the words of St John Simpson, it is 'a story strongly shaped by the professional duties of civil servants, diplomats and soldiers . . . for whom antiquarian pursuits were a minority hobby in an overwhelming environment of heat, disease, boredom and excessive drinking' (Simpson 2003: 192). Despite this political context, and despite the often passing nature of their interest in ancient Persia, British and other writers of this period, far from adhering unquestioningly to a romantic model of the Greco-Roman world, evince a much more complex and (in many instances) a more positive approach to the Achaemenid past than is commonly presented – and they also preempt many of the conclusions of more recent scholarship.

Stereotypes of Persian decadence do make appearances. George Rawlinson relies heavily on Ctesias and other fragmentary fourth-century authors, dwelling on the moral weakness of Xerxes (with 'scarcely a trait whereon the mind can dwell with any satisfaction', Rawlinson 1885: 502). The Persian wars are seen as a turning point, at least in hindsight (Grundy 1901: 1–2; Rawlinson 1885: 298; Jackson 1906: 26, 322). However, the picture of the empire waiting enervated for Alexander's knock-out blow is scarcely ever developed in any detail. At the same time, moreover, one popular historian can be found insisting that Persia 'played the leading part in the history of the known world' for the 150 years after Salamis (Sykes 1922: 18–19); or making the argument, familiar from recent scholarship, that to assume the Persian empire decadent robs Alexander of credit for his military achievement (Sykes 1922: 20ff; cf. Kuhrt 1995: 675).

There is a similar spread of responses to imperial Persian art and architecture. Again, of course, there are negative judgements. George Rawlinson churlishly finds nothing in either sculpture or architecture 'indicative of any remarkable artistic genius' (Rawlinson 1885: 317, cf. 380; see also Kinneir 1813: 76, cf. 51). Others complain of precisely the features of the sculpture of Persepolis that are now rightly interpreted as reflecting an imperial ideology of stability (Root 1979): most memorably, one later American writer moans of the monotony and formalism of the sculptures, and of the 'bored composure' with which the Great King plunges 'a dagger into rampant unicorns and lions and griffins' (Amory 1929: 68, 61). These negative judgements are, however, quite clearly the exceptions to a tone of breathless excitement. 'Standing in the gathering twilight in front of the vast platform', the colonial official Bradley-Birt wrote (to give just one example), 'the modern Western mind half fails to grasp the thought of so much splendour and antiquity' (Bradley-Birt 1909: 180; cf. Ouseley 1819–23 ii. 288–9). Moreover, far from sharing the damning judgement of Bernard Berenson on Achaemenid art, that it displayed the 'originality of incompetence' (Berenson 1954: 186, cited by Nylander 1970: 148), a number of writers foreshadow more recent work in emphasizing the extent to which Achaemenid art combined and added a twist to its various models, Greek, Babylonian or Egyptian (e.g. Arnold 1877: 331–2; Curzon 1892: i. 194; Millspaugh 1925: 4–5; Ross 1931: 103; Morton 1940: 175; cf. Root 1979, 1991, Nylander 1970; for a more recent judgement, Philip Hensher, *Mail on Sunday* 11 September 2005, 64). Others also understand that the apparent sameness of Persepolitan sculpture is intentional, that it reflects in the words of an English doctor 'a oneness in composition which is exceedingly remarkable' (Collins 1896: 78–9); see links between the processions of the Apadana at Persepolis and of the Panathenaia (Curzon 1892: 161, cf. Root 1985) or develop the thesis of Persian influence on Greek art and music (Arnold 1877: 331–2; Benjamin 1887: 336–7; Rawlinson 1885: 412).

For the most part, Persia and the Persians are viewed as frozen in an undeveloped state from ancient to modern times (e.g. Malcolm 1815: 621; Benjamin 1887: 169; Anderson 1880: vii). Writers focus, for example, on Persian deceit, 'the love of finesse and intrigue [which] is congenital to Orientals (Rawlinson 1885: 319), their slavish submission to despotism (Malcolm 1815: 637–8), or their lack of emotional control (Rawlinson 1885: 319), finding 'Aeschylus' tragedy of the *Persae* . . . in this respect, true to nature' (cf. Bell 1928: 55). At other moments, however, this imagined continuity breaks down in favour of an identification with the ancient Persians by explicit contrast to the Iran of the contemporary dynasty of the Qajars (the shahs of the nineteenth and early twentieth centuries). This identification in many cases trumps any with the classical Greek and Roman past.

There are three main (overlapping) focuses to this identification. The first is the Persians' Zoroastrian religion – 'of a more elevated character than is usual with races not enlightened by special revelation . . .', according to the Anglican canon George Rawlinson, a 'pure spiritual monotheism' (Rawlinson 1885: 316, 444). This admiration for Persian monotheism is clearly in part the result of Cyrus' biblical image (p. 425; cf. Rice 1916: 11), but Zoroastrianism is also seen not only as a *symptom* of moral discrimination (Ross 1931: 31), but also as a powerful *cause* of Persian supremacy. This position merges with a (rarely explicit) racial distinction. '[When] their religion with its lofty and sane ideals is taken into consideration', according to Percy Sykes, 'it is little wonder that these enlightened Aryans founded an empire and held in subjection the lower Semitic and Turanian races whose civilization they had absorbed' (Sykes 1915: ch. 2; cf. Rawlinson 1885: 315; Benjamin 1887: 88; Sykes 1902: 198; Ross 1931: 35).

Secondly, clearly the identification with ancient Persia rests also on an admiration for the built remains of the Achaemenids. It is in this area more than any other that continuity between ancient and modern Persia is represented as having broken down: the ruins of Pasargadae and Persepolis convey both ancient grandeur and modern desolation (Bradley-Birt 1909: 183, 200–1; Sykes 1902: 325; Amory 1929: 49). Western identification with the Persian past is sharpened also by what is perceived as a (modern Persian) neglect and ignorance of their history. 'The love of travel, visiting the remains of former grandeur, and of tracing the history of ancient nations, which is so common in Europe, causes wonder in the Asiatics, amongst whom there is little or no spirit of curiosity or speculation', according to Sir John Malcolm (Malcolm 1827: ii. 236; cf. Baker 1876: 127, Williams 1907: 188, 215, 231, Bradley-Birt 1909: 181, 223, 228, Moore 1915: 352; for contrast with Greeks, Ross 1931: 34).

Thirdly, a number of writers reveal an admiration for the Achaemenids' administrative achievement – again by contrast with the perceived corruption and inefficiencies of Qajar Persia. The 'desolation' of Persepolis and Pasargadae is only representative of Persia's more general decline from ancient greatness. 'The Persia of Herodotus and Xenophon was immeasurably superior to mediaeval Persia in its attributes and is even now more respectable in its ruins', according to George Curzon (Curzon 1892: 10; cf. already Fowler 1841: ii.44–5; see also Baker 1876: 336). 'A paternal despotism is undoubtedly all that Persia is fit for today' (Bradley-Birt 1909: 323–4). Paternal despotism had, of course, been the Achaemenids' speciality – and their administrative achievements take on a distinctly British flavour. 'Bent on settling and consolidating his Empire', according to Rawlinson, '[Darius] set up everywhere the satrapial form of government, organized and established his posts, issued his coinage, watched over the administration, and in various ways, exhibited a love of order and method, and a genius for systematic arrangement' (Rawlinson 1885: 474).

The identification is perhaps even stronger in the case of the soldier Percy Sykes (whose history is dedicated 'to British administrators in India and at Whitehall'). Sykes focuses on the Kings' construction of a network of roads, the building up of trade links, and above all the empire's vast extent: 'We thus see an empire which included the whole of the known world and a good deal of territory then unknown, which stretched from the burning sands of Africa to the icebound borders of China, vast but obedient' (Sykes 1915: 180; for Sykes's career, see Wynn 2003).

As one moves into the twentieth century, a significant trend in representations of ancient/modern Persia is towards a greater appreciation (if no less condescending) of the prospects for modern Iran. This coincides crucially with the birth of the Iranian Constitutional Movement and the complex history of the western-backed and western-looking Pahlavi Shahs. Rather than noting modern Persian neglect of the Achaemenid past then, writers tend instead to note a deep (but emotional and somehow inchoate) identification. 'The Persians come to Persepolis to gain courage to forge ahead with the modernization of their country' (Merritt-Hawkes 1935: 87–8; cf. Williams 1907: 231). The link between Persians and Persepolis is 'a close, deep feeling, due to their racial identification with all that Persepolis signifies, and their belief that in their time, or in that of their children, Iran will again be great' (Morton 1940: 173). Needless to say, this representation of the novelty and unformed nature of the Persian relationship with the Persian past elides a whole history of Iranian (pre-decipherment) views of Persepolis from the Sassanians onwards (see Vasunia 2007b).

The Pahlavis' own identification with the Achaemenids was notoriously taken to its extreme by the last Shah in his 1971 celebration of the foundation of the Persian empire – an event which in turn discredited the Achaemenids, especially in the early years of the revolutionary government. Though the post-revolutionary attitude to the Achaemenid past may have been predominantly one of 'disdain' (*Economist*, 17 September 2005: 63), the picture is increasingly mixed. Just as ancient Iranian names are still in fashion (and not exclusively among middle classes or emigrés), tourist copies of the Persepolitan reliefs (if these are a measure of popular identification) are ubiquitous. A documentary film on the statue of Darius I was a popular success, winning a prize at the Tehran film festival (*Financial Times Magazine*, 3–4 September 2005: 34). Even at a high political level, identification with the Achaemenid past is clearly possible. At the opening of the British Museum exhibition, *Forgotten Empire*, the newly elected Iranian Vice-President made the claim that the values of Achaemenid Persia (notably, integrity) had only been fully realized through the Islamic Revolution. (No less opaquely, a British journalist has described the Persian empire as '[living] on in the consciousness of modern Iran, providing a language of justice, protest and difference at home and shaping the country's relationships abroad', Martin Woollacott, *Guardian*, 13 October 2005, B32.) The tented city that the last Shah built at the side of Persepolis to house the visiting foreign dignitaries is now itself due to be recreated (*Guardian*, 22 September 2005, 24). On the other hand, claims persist of the current government's disregard for pre-Islamic sites – over the siting, for example, of a gypsum factory or of a railway line close to the royal tombs of Naqsh-i-Rustam.

If we turn to the current western representation of ancient Iran, it is undeniable that this is coloured by the current political context. This was artfully exploited by the British Museum in the context of their exhibition. 'At this difficult time', the Director Neil McGregor was quoted as saying, 'when East–West relations and understanding are at a low ebb, it is instructive to see what a remarkable contribution the ancient Near East has made to the cultural heritage of the world'. (In another context, he talked of the Athenians' need to maintain the negative image of the Persian empire to keep together their 'coalition of the willing', *Guardian*, 12 October 2005, G2, 22–3.) While Iranians might look to ancient empires as a high water mark of Iranian greatness, and of the territorial extent of Iran, Western responses have tended to express or imply a more negative analogy – even as they have sought to reverse it. This has again emerged most clearly in the context of the British Museum exhibition. The exhibition in many ways presented an accessible version of the more positive view of Achaemenid Persia that has become the consensus over the last twenty years. Critics faithfully followed this line, stressing the tolerance of the Persian empire (noting that the 'Cyrus Cylinder', the Babylonian account of Cyrus' conquest of that city, has been called a declaration of human rights, even if not approving that view; cf. Kuhrt 1983), its cosmopolitanism or multiculturalism (e.g. *Sunday Times Magazine*, 14 August 2005, 20–6; *Mail on Sunday*, 11 September 2005, 64), and the role of Greek propaganda or 'spin' in perpetuating the Persian empire's negative image. The Persians may have used violence, one journalist found, but unlike the Assyrians, it was violence as a means to an end (*Spectator*, 24 September 2005, 73–4). At the same time, however, the exhibition elicited a significant backlash against this more positive view of the Persian empire, leading to the claims, for example, that the Persian empire 'turns out to be as grandiose, luxurious and remotely despotic as Herodotus says it was' (*Guardian*, 8 September 2005, 10), or that the exhibition had gone 'too far in emphasising the softer sides of Achaemenid achievements' (*Apollo*, November 2005: 80–1). More specifically, earlier negative views of Achaemenid art have been reprised: the lack of 'humanity' or movement in Achaemenid sculpture (*Sunday Telegraph* 18 September 2005, 6), or according to one blogger ('Heraclitean fire') its lack of 'visual pizazz', the fact that 'the stuff in the exhibition was all relentlessly about power and wealth'. In the lack of any Persian development of the ideas of citizenship or of the freedom of the individual, Greek prejudice was found (by Peter Jones) to be justified (*Spectator*, 8 October 2005, 24). Very little mention was made of Islam (except in the context of the Iranian government), but the monotheism that had seemed to some nineteenth century writers to make ancient Persia the nearest thing to Christian Europe, is perhaps implicitly seen as a shadow of an aggressive Islam.

The Modern study of the Achaemenids

Academic currents do not map neatly on to contemporary events. While the Islamic revolution within Iran disrupted Iranian identification with the pre-Islamic past, at roughly the same time a western-led movement (as we have seen) set out to reclaim the Achaemenids from an orientalizing, Hellenocentric viewpoint. It should be clear from the account given above of nineteenth- and of popular twentieth-century responses to the Achaemenid past that (in the current author's view) the rupture in the understanding of Persian history that has taken place in the last twenty years can be exaggerated. The negative view of the Persian empire that is regularly invoked by recent scholars can, as we have seen, certainly be found in the work of previous generations, notably in the histories of A.T. Olmstead or of George Rawlinson (emblematic for Sancisi-Weerdenburg of the pejorative view of Persia: Sancisi-Weerdenburg 1987b: 128–31). So, for example, Olmstead reprises Herodotus' account of the personal dimension of that defeat (9.108–114): 'failure of the European adventure opened the way to harem intrigues, with all their deadly consequences' (Olmstead 1948: 266–7). But this founding tenet of the new Achaemenid historiography has arguably had the effect of eliding more positive views of the Persian past, and more constructive attempts to understand Persian empire, kingship and society in their own terms. At the same time as focusing on Persian harems, Olmstead for example minimizes the significance of the Persians' defeat in the Greek-Persian wars, forcing them into a chapter on 'Problems of the Greek frontier'. Even as early as 1864, a young British diplomat mocked Greek accounts of the Persian wars: 'The real fact is', Edward Eastwick wrote, 'young Europe is whipped and schooled into admiration of Greece, till no one dares give a candid opinion. Otherwise, how can men in their senses affect to believe all that stuff about the invasion of Xerxes?' (Eastwick 1864: 26–7). It is worth noting also that ancient Greek writers convey a much more textured picture of the Achaemenid empire than might be supposed from catch-all ascriptions of Hellenocentrism: if the picture of a Persia neutered for 150 years by the experience of the Persian wars has been redressed, it is in no small part due to classical sources, not least, to Thucydides' description of the crucial Persian intervention in the Peloponnesian war (see Lewis 1977).

The new Achaemenid historiography raises other interesting questions about our response to the Achaemenids. First, it is worth noting that – by sharp contrast to the study of Athenian or Roman imperialism, say – there is an almost universal assumption that imperial expansion is a good thing. So, most markedly, Cambyses can be rehabilitated from the image perpetrated by the Greek sources by the recognition that he, like Darius, was a builder of the empire (in Briant's chapter heading: Briant 2002). Secondly, although (or because?) it begins from the need to reverse the pattern of Greek stereotypes, the examination of such stereotypes usually forms only a brief detour (contrast Briant 1989). As evidenced, perhaps, by the absence of the two most significant landmarks in the understanding of Greek representations of barbarians from the bibliography of Briant's monumental history (Hall 1989, Hartog 1988), there seems to be a reluctance to examine this material, a desire to emphasize the reality of friendly contact and to minimize the significance of Greek pejorative ideas of foreign peoples by describing them as, for example, official Athenian propaganda. Thirdly, and related to this, there appears to be a certain selectiveness in the use of Greek sources evident in the new historiography. A key task of the Achaemenid historian, according to Briant, is to 'distinguish the Greek interpretative coating from the Achaemenid nugget of information' (Briant 2002: 256; contrast Briant's formula, ibid.: 8). Such an operation can only be valid, however, on the assumption that Greek pejorative bias (itself not a wholesale phenomenon) is relatively superficial – that it affects the selection of one nugget of information rather than another, for example, rather than dictating the very heart of the anecdote – and that the nugget can indeed be distinguishable from its coating. (There is a parallel here with archaic Greek history, and in particular with the argument of Christiane Sourvinou-Inwood that some later accounts are 'articulated in a mythological idiom', and that they cannot therefore be filleted to reconstruct a narrative of events: see Sourvinou-Inwood 1991.) A good example of this problem is the modern discussion of the role of Persian women (esp. Brosius 1996; Wiesehöfer 1996: 79–88). Stories from Greek sources of Persian queens intervening in political affairs (and performing violent acts of vengeance) are distilled into an outline of the constitutional limits of their intervention. Justification is offered for their violence (they are acting to defend their family interest), and an implicit contrast is offered with the Greeks (the Persians have enterprising resolute women, so the Greeks have wilfully misunderstood the prominence of Persian women). Leaving aside the scarcely veiled competitiveness between Greek and Persian cultures evident here, this arguably elides the Greek context for stories of Persian cruelty (as well as underestimating evidence for the possibility that such cruel punishments were indeed inflicted): in particular, to use the personal motive as an excuse for political intervention ignores the clear moral of such stories in their Greek context, that such cruel acts are the inevitable result when you allow the political to become personal (cf. Nitocris, Hdt. 2.100; wife of Sesostris, Hdt. 2.107).

How then should one proceed from here? One desirable development in the study of Achaemenid history might be a turn to a more cultural focus, one in which Greek representations are seen as the matter of Persian history rather than just the chaff. One benefit of such a change of focus might be an appreciation of the fluidity of Greek representations and their complexity, their being contingent on a number of different factors. This discussion has proceeded as though the image of ancient Persia received in different ways in different modern contexts was uncontested. It is worth, in conclusion, emphasizing that this is not the case. First, ancient sources reflect markedly different positions. If a modern critic (Waldemar Janauszcak) asks of the burning of Persepolis 'Who was the barbarian in that exchange?' (*Sunday Times*, Culture, 11 September 2005: 8) he is going no further than Euripides in the context of the Trojan War (Hall 1989: ch. 5; Said 2002). Secondly, it is important to emphasize that secondary literature on the Greek representation of Persians and others has moved on to a significant degree from any ascription to the Greeks of a simple Greek-barbarian polarity; if the new Achaemenid historiography has sprung up in equal step with the focus on the Greek invention of the barbarian, a further irony is that the clearcut image of the Persian 'other' has been significantly undermined. Recent literature has seen, for example, the attempt to diminish the currency of the barbarian ideology and to claim that it was purely a manifestation of the Athenian empire, or the view that luxury borrowings from Persia to Greece 'disprove' the old stereotypes of the barbarian (Miller 1997: 1). Such revisionist positions are, of course, open to question. Though Athenian imperialism may have been a focus for many of the contrasts between Greek and non-Greek, there is reason to suppose (unless you deem Herodotus to have been operating in an exclusively Athenian context) that such ideas had a broader currency. As for Greek cultural borrowings from Persia, if items of dress (such as parasols) reserved for the Persian King are adopted in the Greek world by well-to-do Athenian wives, it is evident that such borrowings *need* not contradict the ideology of Persian effeminacy. More generally, it is hard to suppress the suspicion that beneath this backlash against the Greek–barbarian polarity (reminiscent of some of the anti-anti-imperialist backlash against Said and Orientalism) there lies an unwillingness to 'taint' classical authors by ascribing to them chauvinist attitudes.

There is perhaps a bigger problem, however, which is in common both to the proponents of the Greek-barbarian polarity and to its critics – and that is the assumption of continuity from the ancient world to the present day. How much do 'western' relations with ancient and with modern Persia really have in common? First, without necessarily subscribing to the patriotic myth of the Greeks as heroic underdogs, it is beyond doubt that, up to the conquests of Alexander, the relationship of Greeks and Persians was one in which the military-political boot was on the Persian foot (e.g. Lewis 1977, Miller 1997: ch. 1). In some ways there is a defensive or reactive quality to Greek chauvinism, evident for example in their mocking naming of pyramids after their own cheesecakes and crocodiles after lizards and so on, or in the pathetic claims of fringe courtiers in Herodotus' *Histories* to be close to the Persian court (e.g. Hdt. 5.30). This quality in Greek chauvinism is perhaps masked by what happens next: that is, Alexander's conquest of Egypt and the Near East and the 'hellenization' that it triggered.

Secondly, the Greeks were by no means unique in their claim to a superior civilization (if we can use such an anachronistic gloss for the Greek–barbarian polarity). What Herodotus claims of the Persians, that they considered themselves the most virtuous, their neighbours the next most virtuous and so on, seems to be borne out by Persian sources for royal ideology (Hdt. 1.134). Similarly (as Herodotus was again well aware), the Egyptians shared the linguistic ethnocentrism of the Greeks, calling any who did not speak the same language 'barbarian' (Hdt. 2.158; cf. Donadoni 1986). Though Alexander's conquest may in part have been fed (and in a sense have fulfilled) earlier Greek representations of eastern barbarians (Flower 2000; Vasunia 2001), there was nothing inevitable about it – and nothing inevitable likewise about the long genealogy that has since been generated for 'orientalism'. (To say – doubtless as a shorthand – that a tragedy 'experiments with Orientalism': Hall 1989: 73, as if it were a pre-existing body of thought, underestimates the complexity of such ideologies in the modern as well as the ancient world.) Only perhaps if we challenge such genealogies can we begin to transcend the Us-and-Them contrasts and the disciplinary boundaries that are a block to an understanding of both Persians and Greeks.

FURTHER READING

For an introductory account of ancient Persia, see especially Wiesehöfer 1996. For Greek representations of (or reception of) Persia, see Hall 1989 and Harrison 2000; for Persia and the Persian wars in the western tradition, see Sancisi-Weerdenburg and Drijvers 1991, and (from a very different perspective) Bridges, Hall and Rhodes 2007. For British travellers to Persia, the fullest account is Wright 2001. The website *Achamenet* is a rich source of material on ancient Persia and increasingly on reception.

CHAPTER FIVE

Basil of Caesarea and Greek Tragedy

Ruth Webb

A new papyrus fragment with some lines of Greek script comes to light in the case of a mummy dating from the second century CE. Miraculously, the scrap contains the first few lines of a work, complete with its title and the name of the author. Papyrologists puzzle over it: the Greek is recognizably the language of the Gospels and the Septuagint but it's a different dialect. The heading gives a name known only from one or two references in the sacred texts – Sophocles – and the words *Oidipous Tyrannos*, the swollen-footed king. Mystified, the papyrologists shrug and file away the fragment for future examination as they move on to the serious task of deciphering other fragments, a new Gospel written in Coptic, a collection of sayings of the Desert Fathers.

It is hard to imagine a scenario like this, in which Sophocles, his language and culture are entirely unknown and where the only form of ancient Greek civilization is that of the early Christians. Without Sophocles and the other tragedians there would be no opera and modern drama, if it existed at all, would be vastly different. There might be no cinema, except perhaps for documentaries, no literary fiction (compare the comments of Zuntz 1965: xix on a world without Iphigeneia). Freud would certainly not have been able to read *Oedipus* in Greek at school or to see the play on stage in Vienna or Paris (on the performance history of *Oedipus* see Macintosh 2005).What would he have called his complex? Would he have identified the attachment of son to mother in the same way and with the same clarity as his knowledge of the play allowed him to do?

A world very like this hypothetical world without Greek tragedy is evoked in Jorge Luis Borges' short story, *Averroes' Search* (1949), in which the central character tries and fails to imagine, in a culture without formal drama, what Aristotle could possibly have meant by 'comedy' and 'tragedy' in his *Poetics*. It could, even should, have been our world. How have the scripts of plays performed in religious festivals in a small town in Attica nearly 2,500 years ago survived through the centuries, despite the effort required to understand them in their original language? How did they escape nearly two millennia dominated by Christianity with its radically different view of the world, divinity and the nature of humanity? This chapter will look at the treatment of tragedy (or rather its lack of treatment) in one text from a key moment in that process, 'To the young men on how to benefit from Hellenic texts' by Basil of Caesarea (*c.* 330–79CE).

The survival of Greek drama depended on a set of interrelated phenomena in the ancient world. First, the scripts of Athenian plays had to be preserved and valued – an important step was the institution of a contest in old tragedy at the City Dionysia of 386 BCE. Then they had to be read on their own merits as texts and judged worth preserving from one generation to the next (Easterling 1997b: 211–27). The prestige that the language and culture of fifth- and fourth-century Athens enjoyed throughout the Hellenistic and Roman periods was a key factor: tragedy was read in schools at least partly to train young men in the ancient Attic dialect. Particularly after the successful revival of Attic as *the* language of culture that took place from the first century BCE, culminating in the linguistic purism of the Second Sophistic, a knowledge of classical literature and its idiom was essential for a public career (Swain 1996: 17–64). Were it not for the prestige of the classical Attic dialect and the requirement that all educated men in civil life and in the administration be able to express themselves in it, knowledge of the language of Sophocles, Thucydides and Plato would surely have died out in antiquity. Modern students of the ancient world would study Coptic, Syriac and New Testament Greek. As it is, we owe our knowledge of classical Greek to the unbroken tradition of learning that stretches from the Hellenistic period, through late antiquity and into Byzantium, a thread whose fragility at certain times and places is frightening to contemplate.

Even so, our knowledge of Greek tragedy has been severely limited by the actions of antiquity. The corpus available to us is largely the selection made for teaching in Greek schools, probably in the second century CE. Gradually, other tragedies were lost from view. We have two words of Aeschylus' play about Oedipus' father, Laius. Of the same author's *Oedipus*, precisely nothing survives because these plays were not included in the school selections (Radt 1985: 231–2, 287–8). Nothing illustrates more dramatically the fate that awaited the plays, however moving or enlightening we might have found them, and however victorious they were in their day, that were not taught in the schools of later antiquity.

Even when classical Greek – that is to say, mainly Athenian – literature had found its place in the curriculum its survival was far from assured. Logically, the rapid spread and triumph of Christianity should have been the end of the old literature. Christians should have had no use for texts full of the exploits of the old gods they were combating. The language of the Greek Old and New Testaments, closer to the spoken language of the period, should have become the norm. Religious and theological works, written in accessible language, that instructed individuals in the truly serious business of saving their souls should have dominated, replacing the tortuous phrases of over-educated intellectuals. If all this had happened, the manuscripts of classical authors, if they had survived this long, would no longer have been copied. We would have no medieval manuscript tradition and our knowledge of tragedy and much of classical literature would be confined to the fragments contained in a handful of ancient papyri. Even then, like our puzzled papyrologists, we would not have the linguistic or the cultural background to make sense of the little that did survive.

Christians and the Classics

The acceptance of classical literature by the Christian community of the first centuries CE was a crucial factor in the survival of ancient poetry and non-technical prose. As Henri-Irenée Marrou outlined in his *History of Education in Antiquity*, Christians adopted the school curriculum of the surrounding pagan culture with surprisingly little resistance (Marrou 1956: 318–32; Harl 1993). This curriculum involved the reading of the poets (notably Homer and the tragedians) followed by a study of prose authors and an intensive training in the techniques and practices of rhetoric (accompanied by the continuing study of poetry) (Cribiore 2001, 2007). This acceptance of the traditional education was inspired by practical considerations: the prestige of the traditional classical education and its practical utility (Heath 2004). The primary purpose of reading poetry in the schools of antiquity was not appreciation of its aesthetic qualities, although such appreciation is shown by adults in their mature reading, like Dio Chrysostom in his report on the three versions of Philoctetes that were available to him (*Or.* 52). The ancient commentaries do show some interest in questions of staging and the actor's interpretation of the role, but they focus on details of language and on the appreciation of the rhetorical qualities of the plays.

Poetry served as an introduction to the study of rhetoric and logic, the ability to express oneself clearly, in conformity with expected norms. Christians needed these skills as much as their pagan neighbours did, they too needed to celebrate marriages and deaths, to preach, to argue. Indeed, the refutation of opponents is often presented as a reason for acquiring these skills (Harl 1993: 421). To this end, Christians studied alongside non-Christians in the traditional schools, John Chrysostom and other Christians studying with Libanius, a committed pagan. The greatest obstacle to the adoption of the traditional curriculum by Christians came in the form of the edict by the Emperor Julian, a convert from Christianity to a paganism of his own design, who pointed out the contradictions inherent in Christians teaching a literature whose content they rejected (even then, he only banned Christians from *teaching*, not from attending schools and was thus in line with the least forgiving currents of Christianity itself) (Marrou 1956: 323–4).

But the relevance of post-classical rhetorical skills for Christian preachers was immediate, as was the utility of a training in logic and argumentation for demonstrating Christian thought both to the converted and the unconverted. The success with which the Christian elite of the fourth century absorbed the skills of the rhetorical schools and went on to use them in their own writing and preaching is remarkable and has led to the Church Fathers of the fourth and early fifth centuries being defined as a 'Third Sophistic' (Amato 2006). The works of Basil of Caesarea, John Chrysostom, Gregory of Nyssa and Gregory Nazianzen are all examples of this marriage of

Christianity and classical learning whose influence was instrumental in preserving the Greek classical tradition throughout the Byzantine middle ages.

The acceptance of the traditional education by members of the educated Christian elite was not, however, a simple and straightforward matter of pressing a neutral set of techniques into the service of the new religion. Even if educated Christians like Gregory Nazianzen argued passionately against Julian's attempt to identify classical literature with the pagan religion, their attachment to their cultural heritage was often ambivalent. Even attending the rhetorical schools presented a certain risk. In his funeral oration for his friend Basil of Caesarea, Gregory himself describes the care the two young men had to take in Athens to avoid being corrupted by contact with the still flourishing paganism and with the distractions of the late antique city: festivals, theatrical performances and parties. 'In brief', he says, 'for others, Athens is danger-ous to the soul because she is richer than the rest of Greece in the harmful type of wealth, idols, and it is difficult not to be seduced by those who praise them and speak on their behalf. But we did not suffer any harm because our minds were solid and well-guarded' (*Or.* 43, 21).

Recent studies of Gregory's writings have underlined the ways in which he pre-sents a carefully edited image of himself and his life. We may wonder how immune the young Cappadocians were from the temptations of the city, temptations that worried non-Christian teachers like Libanios just as much as their Christian coun-terparts. It is clear that the marriage of Christianity and the traditional training in rhetoric was not a simple matter. The complexities involved are evident in the work that Basil himself wrote for his nephews in defence of the reading of classical texts, 'To the young men on how to benefit from Hellenic texts'. Far from being a whole-hearted paean to the values of the classical tradition, the work makes its young readers acutely aware of the dangers presented by classical texts and the need for a guide like Basil who can show them which authors are safe and approachable and which, like Sirens, lure readers to a spiritual death (Saïd 2004: 227).

For the modern classicist, it is something of a disappointment. There are no unknown quotations from lost works, no insightful readings of literature. Indeed, although the first author cited by Basil is Hesiod, there is little discussion of poetry. Most of Basil's examples are drawn from prose, mostly from philosophical or moralizing works, and he has a marked preference for improving anecdotes. Classical literature is use-ful, above all, as an introduction to Christian sacred texts. Such texts can only be approached by readers who are sufficiently mature and intellectually prepared to pen-etrate to their depths. For Basil, the Christian must prepare him or herself (though in the context of the letter the Christian is resolutely male) for 'another life', which he declines to describe in the present context, but which far surpasses their present 'human life' (*anthropinos bios*) (2). The way to this life is through the scripture, which teaches by way of mysteries (*aporrheta*). Nothing else is of true value, but Basil finds a role for traditional education as a propaedeutic. Until the reader is of an age to understand the meaning (*dianoia*) of the scripture, he can practise with classical texts. Basil provides us with a dazzling sequence of similes to convey the relationship between classical and Christian literature. Classical works are like shadows and mirrors, read-ing them is like play fighting and dancing in preparation for real war, or like the first stages of the dyeing process in which the fabric is prepared to receive its final indelible colour, or again like looking at the reflection of the sun on water in preparation for the true light (2). To these images of active preparation, Basil adds another drawn from nature: if truth (*aletheia*) is the fruit on the tree, external wisdom is represented by the leaves that surround the fruit (3, cf. Plutarch, *How to Study Poetry* 28D–E).

However, the key image for Basil's enterprise is that of bees (4) carefully selecting the flowers they visit and taking only what is useful to them. Each classical text must be vetted to see whether it is in conformity with Christian morality. Basil's approval is reserved for works that depict good moral behaviour. He recommends Prodikos' parable of the choice of Herakles as recorded by Xenophon, *Memorabilia*, 2.1.21 (but adjusts the details to give a more Christian flavour) (5) and admires anecdotes about the self restraint of Perikles, Sokrates and Alexander (7). The examples illustrate the type of text the young men should be gathering to make their moral honey, but there are no clear guidelines as to who is to do the vetting and exactly which criteria should be used. There are many such puzzles in Basil's approach, including his failure to make explicit mention of his principal source in the opening chapters of the treatise (4–5): Plato's discussion of education in Books 2 and 3 of the *Republic*.

Basil shares with the figure of Sokrates in the *Republic* a conviction that what one reads can affect the soul, particularly when that soul is young (5, cf. *Rep.* 378e). Reading about virtuous acts can make the soul virtuous, but the reverse is also true (4). Basil therefore advises rejecting all representations (*mimeseis*) of wicked characters, which should be avoided 'Just as those people say Odysseus avoided the songs of the Sirens. For being acquainted with bad words is a path that leads to acts.' Literature is seductive because of the pleasure it offers, like honey disguising poison. A list of actions described in poetry follows, all of which have parallels in Plato's discussion of poetry (*Rep.* 377e–378e; 389e–390c):

> We will not praise the poets when they utter insults, or joke or represent (*mimeisthai*) people in love or drunk, nor when they equate happiness (*eudaimonia*) with a groaning table and licentious songs. We shall pay least attention of all when they talk about the gods, particularly when they speak about several gods who don't even agree with each other. For they show brother at odds with brother, father with children, and the children in turn waging war against their parents.

Oratory, too, is suspect because of the lies involved. In stressing the moral content of classical literature over its form, Basil is close to Plato in the *Republic*, who is ready to admit the poetic representation of worthy and disciplined behaviour, such as the obedience of Diomedes in *Iliad*, 4.412 (*Rep.* 389). Though Basil also appears to have known Plutarch's treatise *On Reading Poetry*, he does not adopt the new strategy offered there of recognizing the art (*techne*) of the author as a quality of literary texts that could excuse the representation of things that are untrue or inappropriate (Bréchet 1999). In some respects, however, Basil is closer to Plutarch, as in his emphasis on the good examples that can be found in Homeric epic. Indeed, Basil is even willing to make some interpretative leaps that come close to allegory in his reading of Homer.

The most striking example is his treatment of the episode in *Odyssey* 6 in which the Phaeacian princess, Nausikaa, encounters Odysseus, naked and shipwrecked, and takes him home to meet her parents. Basil begins by attributing to an anonymous authority the view that 'All of Homer's poetry is an encomium of virtue (*arete*)' before giving the following illustration:

> Not least the lines in which he makes the Cephallenian leader, who has been saved naked from the shipwreck, first inspire respect in the princess [Nausikaa] by his appearance alone, far from feeling shame at being seen naked, since he represented him cloaked in virtue instead of a robe. Then he shows the rest of the Phaeacians conceiving such admiration for him that they abandoned the life of luxury in which they used to live and all looked to him and emulated him so that not a single one of the Phaeacians would have wished for anything more than to be Odysseus, even though he had just escaped from a shipwreck.

This is far from a modern understanding of Homer. But ancient interpreters did use Homeric characters as embodiments of moral ideals and much-enduring Odysseus in particular was used as a model for the philosopher (Richardson 1975). Basil's reading of the encounter with Nausikaa is ingenious, as long as one does not press the details too much. The claims about the Phaeacians, however, appear to be entirely imagined by Basil and one modern reader has gone so far as to suggest that Basil's reading is intentionally absurd, intended to spur the inquiring and informed reader to contemplate the irremediable distance between Homeric poetry and Christian morality (Fortin 1981). But, as Suzanne Saïd has pointed out (Saïd 2004), ancient readers constantly adapted ancient texts to their own needs. The sense that a text had an original meaning belonging to the historical context in which it was composed that dominates our approach to classical literature was absent.

The lengths to which Basil was prepared to go to save Homer for the Christian reader are particularly striking when we consider the place of tragedy in his selection of classical literature. Tragedy appears only twice, in the form of two lines quoted out of their context. One is the infamous line from Euripides' *Hippolytos*, 612, which was already notorious in classical antiquity: 'My tongue swore, but my mind remains unsworn'. Basil uses this to sum up a life in which one's words are in conflict with one's life. The other is from Euripides' *Rhesus*, 84 expressing a heroic sentiment that was entirely out of sympathy with a Christian understanding of human relations: 'Quite simply, anger arms the hand against one's enemies'.

This unexplained absence demands further inquiry. One very obvious reason for the exclusion (implicit or otherwise) of tragedy from a young man's reading list is the scandalous nature of much of tragic action. This indeed is the reason given by Basil's brother, Gregory of Nyssa, for their mother's refusal to allow their sister, Makrina, to read tragedy. Makrina's mother considered it shameful and unsuitable (*aischron kai aprepes*) to induct a tender young soul through the sufferings depicted in tragedy, or the inappropriate behaviour of comedy or the misfortunes of Troy (*Life of Makrina*, 3). So Makrina's education was limited to the sacred texts and she did not encounter the traditional, 'external' (*exothen*) learning dispensed by the schools that her brothers attended. A glimpse of the type of education she might have received is given in John Chrysostom's treatise *On Vainglory and the Education of Children* where he advises parents on how and when to read Old Testament stories with their children, showing far more concern for the learner than did most representatives of the traditional, classical education.

Makrina's education, as recorded by Gregory, goes some way towards explaining Basil's unspoken aversion to tragedy. But it raises even more questions. Makrina read no classical poetry at all. Although the harshest words are reserved for tragedy, comedy and epic are also excluded while Basil, as we have seen, finds ways to make Homer palatable. If Odysseus' encounter with Nausikaa could be made acceptable to a Christian audience, surely there were ways to include tragedy. It is true that the text of a play, consisting of speeches by characters, lends itself less easily to allegorical treatment than a narrative. But Basil was certainly not averse to quoting out of context and there were sentiments and figures in tragedy that he could have cited as examples of laudable behaviour: Antigone's devotion to her father, Alcestis' devotion to her husband, to name but two. Plutarch, by contrast, finds quotations from two plays of Euripides (both now lost) that can be used by the moralist (*On the Education of Children*, 10B and 11F; *How to Study Poetry*, 36C).

The Theatre in Basil's Treatise

A further indication of the real nature of the problem posed by drama is to be found in the few references to the theatre in Basil's work. These are uniformly pejorative. Basil crowns his list of subjects to be avoided by the young reader (sex, drink, songs, polytheism) by saying 'adultery between gods, love affairs and making love in the open air . . . things that one would be ashamed to mention even speaking of animals, all this we shall leave to the people of the stage' (4). Further on, in a passage criticizing people whose words do not accord with their behaviour, he cites the example of the actor who pretends to be what he is not: 'they appear as kings and lords when they are neither kings nor lords and perhaps not even free men at all' (6). Accusations of immorality and remarks about the low social status of the actors who paraded on stage are familiar refrains in the anti-theatrical polemic of late antiquity and point to the fact that, for Basil, the theatre was still a living tradition. That these are the only references to the theatre in the work suggests, too, that he did not see a strict distinction between classical drama and the performance traditions of his own day. This association may go a long way towards explaining the absence of tragedy from his list of approved readings.

Theatrical performance was an active and important part of civic life in Basil's lifetime and, in the Greek East, for a long time afterwards and one of the temptations that Gregory Nazianzen claims that they avoided as students in Athens. Tragedy was no longer performed in its original form, but excerpts were sung by expert singers, *tragodoi* (Theocharidis 1940; Hall 2002). The *tragodoi* prompt some criticisms from Church fathers, but above all their ire is reserved for the most popular forms of theatrical entertainment, mime and pantomime. In the pantomime, the myths of the gods and the tragic plots were still represented in danced forms by hugely popular dancers while the mime represented the latest development of comedy, showing scenarios from everyday life performed by a mixed group of men and women (Jory 1996; Webb 2006). Tales of adultery, though by no means the only subject matter of the mime, were prominent and popular. The Church fathers, like pagan moralists before them, found much to object to in these performances, from the 'harlots' on stage to the unnerving 'men-women' of the pantomime, male dancers performing female roles. Added to the perceived immorality of the performances them-selves was a centuries-old stigma surrounding stage performance that led actors and actresses to be treated as socially unacceptable outcasts (Leppin 1992). The old Roman treatment of performers as infamous persons deprived of the rights of the normal citizen was adopted by the early Church which refused to accept practising performers (though retired performers were able to convert) (Lim 2003). Basil's com-ment about leaving adultery and sexual promiscuity to the people of the stage reveals a common stereotype of actors and actresses as immoral, and an association of the theatre with sexual licence which continues earlier Roman prejudice against the stage professions (Edwards 1997). It is striking that in counting 'love-making in the open air' among the depraved acts to be left to the people of the stage, Basil transfers one of Plato's examples of inappropriate behaviour in Homeric epic (*Rep.* 390c; cf. *Iliad* 14, 294–351) to the theatre, exploiting the poor image of the performer to relieve epic of at least one charge.

Although the theatre of Basil's day was very different from the theatre of classical Athens in both artistic and social terms, it was still a vigorous institution that attracted many Christians, despite the best attempts of preachers to describe the dangers it presented to the soul. It is very likely that the existence of this living theatrical tradition coloured Basil's attitude to classical tragedy. Unlike Homeric epic, tragedy was not simply text but still potentially a performance. It had not entirely been neutralized and transformed into literature that could be an object of inter-pretation. Tragedy, from Basil's perspective, could thus be seen as closely bound up with the life of the city and with celebrations that still held associations with idolatry, even if they were no longer overtly pagan.

The Theatre, Mimesis and Morality

However, just as the silences in Basil's treatise leave open many questions, one can-not help but feel that the Christian complaints about the theatre leave aside many of the most important issues. Christian writers represent the theatre of their day as immoral, as the heir to pagan traditions and as frankly anti-Christian. The charges of immorality are especially frequent in the sermons of John Chrysostom, Basil's younger contemporary (Brown 1989: 305–22; Mayer and Allen 2000: 118–25). Paganism is less of an issue by this time, but Chrysostom frequently plays on the contrast between Church and theatre to persuade his listeners that the psychological impact of the latter makes them unclean and unable to participate in Christian rites. In addition to this depiction of the theatre as unchristian we find the depiction of the theatre as a fundamentally anti-Christian institution disseminated through the tales of pagan actors who dared to mock Christian rites, like baptism, on stage but were miraculously converted as they did so and immediately martyred (Panayotakis 1997; Lim 2003).

If we follow Basil's own practice of searching for a deeper meaning, we can perhaps detect some urgent unspoken concerns behind these complaints about the theatre. One, noted by Peter Brown, is the intuition that the theatre presented a rival institution to the Church, an alternative form of sociability (Brown 1989: 314). Another fear that runs throughout the anti-theatrical discourse of pagans and Christians alike is the fear of the power of mimesis itself. As the tales of the actor-martyrs so vividly show, theatrical mimesis could be transformative. Acting like some-one could actually change the person engaging in the mimesis. It was precisely this fear that led Plato to ban the poets from his ideal city: he feared the impact on the young of reading aloud the words of an insubordinate Achilles or a gluttonous Odysseus (*Rep.* 395b–d; Halliwell 2002: 51–2). In the late antique discourse on the theatre the fear that the audience will themselves be transformed into what they see is evident in many passages from many different authors (Webb 2005).

The boundary between literary mimesis – the imitation by an author of language, of style or of a particular work – and theatrical mimesis – acting the role of another person – was fluid. It is interesting to consider some other absences from Basil's treatise in this light. One is his failure to name Plato at the point when he practic-ally reproduces the philosopher's arguments against poetry. In so doing, Basil elides the fact that he himself is engaging in precisely the type of mimetic activity whose risks he warns against. Another is his omission of the most obvious and practical reason for reading classical literature: the linguistic skills that it imparted. The major justification for the traditional education is encoded in Basil's own language, in the carefully classicizing Greek that can only have resulted from years of mimetic activity, absorbing the language of classical authors including, of course, the trage-dians. Indeed, mimesis is essential to Basil's conception of reading. His preference for anecdotes portraying worthy behaviour falls within a long tradition of *exempla*, designed to inspire emulation in the reader. Emulation also plays an important part in the interpretation Basil offers of Odysseus and the Phaeacians, with the islanders vying to be like their visitor. The multiple levels of mimesis in Basil's account of reading show that classical literature was not conceived of as a form of inert matter but as a representation that could affect those that encountered it. Reading, more-over, was still an active practice (like the play-fighting used by Basil as an image of reading as preparation for theology) that could transform the reader.

It would therefore seem that tragedy was bound up with too many taboos to be acceptable to Basil. Above all, it underlined the negative associations of the mim-esis that was an essential, if potentially dangerous, part of the reception of classical texts. Basil's avoidance of tragedy shows the multiple factors that affected the Christian reception of a classical literature that had yet to be entirely separated out from a civic life that contained so many grey areas and dangers for the committed Christian, as Gregory Nazianzen makes clear in his account of Athens. If Basil had been our only gatekeeper to the classical past, it is likely that our knowledge of ancient literature would be closer to the imaginary scenario evoked at the beginning of this chapter than to the current state of affairs. But, just as the majority of Christians continued to attend the theatres, the Christian elite did not in the end choose to avoid reading tragedy. Instead, strategies of reading were found which allowed the content of tragedy to be made acceptable matter for teaching in schools. But there was always a certain contradiction involved, and infinite shades of grey and degrees of accommodation to be found between unconditional acceptance of Greek literature and outright rejection. In his defence of the mime, the sixth-century rhetor, Chorikios of Gaza, gleefully pointed out the discrepancy. Defending the morality of the adultery mime which depicts, he claims, the punishment of the guilty parties at the end, he points out the equally shocking content of the traditional curriculum that he himself dispensed which demanded that young men know and tell the stories of Helen, Klytaimnestra, Pasiphae, Prokne and Philomela and Oidipous. 'We train young men to tell these stories', he goes on, 'and we take it so seriously that we chastise any boy who doesn't do it properly with blows' (*Or.* 8, 36–40). The blatant inconsistency is possible because these are the subjects of writings (*suggrammata*) and, Chorikios points out, we know they are a form of game (*paignion*) (*Or.* 8, 41).

Chorikios' analysis, playful as it is in itself, identifies the factors that, in the end, enabled tragedy to be read: the creation of a category of canonical literature whose content is not judged by the same standards as a 'low' form of art, like the mime, or of real life. Basil's deeply moralizing interpretation of Homer and his deletion of tragedy from his reading list show how long and uneven this process was and how much the perception of what we now know as 'classical literature' was affected by the simultaneous presence of living phenomena, like the late antique theatre.

FURTHER READING

The classic account of Christian receptions of classical literature is that of Marrou 1956: 314–29 and this survey is still invaluable. However, Marrou's approach has long needed revision. His belief in the supreme value of classical literature and in its 'humanistic' ideals left little space for the more practical concerns of late antique readers or for consideration of the social phenomena that motivated the transmission of classical literature. Three articles bring these questions up to date: Inglebert 2004: 333–41, Saïd 2004: 227–39, and Rappe 2001: 405–32. In addition there is the excellent and nuanced study by Harl 1993: 417–31. On the study of Latin literature in Late Antiquity the definitive work is Kaster 1988.

On the wider social and culture background see Brown 1971 esp. Part One, 'The Late Roman Revolution' and 1992, esp. ch. 2. Cameron 1991 analyzes the development of specifically Christian forms of communication while Chuvin 1990 traces the story of the rise of Christianity from the pagan perspective (the English translation contains only the first part of the French publication: *Chronique des derniers païens*, Paris, Les Belles Lettres/Fayard, 1990).

PART II

Transmission, Acculturation and Critique

CHAPTER SIX

'Our Debt to Greece and Rome': Canon, Class and Ideology

Seth L. Schein

Civilization is on the whole a simple and easily understood phenomenon.

Showerman (1922: xiii)

The power of the 'classical' does not spring, as is usually thought, from its relation to a real or imagined past, but from its relation to current social, political, and moral values that it helps to legitimate (Settis 2004: 104). In other words, the 'classical' is ideological. An ideology may be defined as 'a self-serving set of deeply held, often unconscious beliefs [and values]' (Rose 2006: 103) and a way of expressing these beliefs and values in a 'legitimating discourse' that 'takes for granted a particular, established social order', but 'fails to include an analysis of the institutional mechanisms that maintain this order, and is liable to be no more than a contribution to the efficacy of the ideology itself' (Bourdieu 1977: 188). Since antiquity, the discourse of the 'classical' has functioned in just this way to legitimate a social order and a set of institutions, beliefs, and values that are commonly associated with western civilization and 'our' western cultural heritage.

'Our Debt to Greece and Rome' is a series of forty-four books, published between 1922 and 1948 and dedicated, in the words of the founding editors, to the influence of 'virtually all the great forces . . . of the Greek and Roman civilizations upon subsequent life and thought and the extent to which these are interwoven into the fabric of our life to-day' (Hadzsits and Robinson 1922: ix). The series assumes a historical continuity between 'the Greek and Roman civilizations' and our own, the distinctive excellence of those civilizations, and the transparency of their influence upon us. By constant reference to a classical past to which 'we' are so indebted, the books in the series legitimate the ideals and practices of 'our life to-day', which turn out to be those of an educated, elite stratum of Anglo-American society in the early twentieth century. The process of legitimation recalls Hannah Arendt's characterization of ideology as 'the logic of an idea' applied to history, with the 'movement' of history explained as 'a consequence of the "idea" itself . . . The movement of history and the logical process of this notion are supposed to correspond to each other, so that whatever happens, happens according to the logic of one "idea"' (Arendt 1973: 469). In the case of the influence of classical civilization on our own, the idea is the typical, late nineteenth-century notion of the progressive development of civilization, culminating in the Greek and Roman civilizations. The 'movement of history' is the continual manifestation of the 'living and vital force' of these civilizations (Hadzsits and Robinson 1922: x), their 'universal and eternal verities' (Showerman 1922: xiv) over time, up to and including 'our' own era.

In the present chapter I try to elucidate the 'classical' as an ideological construct by discussing briefly the multiple, changing meanings of the word and the conceptions of canon, class, and ideology with which it has historically been associated. I then focus on the history and ideology of the 'classical' and 'canonical' in the United States, especially in institutions of higher education in the twentieth century. Finally, I reflect on our actual debt to Greece and Rome and suggest the educational and liberatory potential of the 'classical' in the world we live in.

The documented use of the word 'classical' goes back to a famous passage (19.8.15) in the *Noctes Atticae* (*Attic Nights*) of Aulus Gellius (second century CE), where Gellius attributes to M. Cornelius Fronto, a noted orator and friend of the emperor Marcus Aurelius, a figurative use of the adjective *classicus*, which properly describes someone in the wealthiest of the five property-owning classes (*classes*) of Roman citizens established by Rome's sixth king, Servius Tullius (cf. Livy 1.43.5, Gell. 6.13.1.3) (see Hall's chapter in this volume). Gellius says that he heard Fronto tell 'some learned and eminent poet', in a discussion about correct linguistic usage, to 'investigate whether any orator or poet, provided he belongs to that older group – that is, some first-class, first-rate [lit. 'landowning'] writer, not one of the lowest class – has ever said "four-horse chariot" in the singular and "sand" in the plural'; (*quaerite an quadrigam et harenas dixerit e cohorte illa dumtaxat antiquiore vel oratorum aliquis vel poetarum, id est classicus adsiduusque aliquis scriptor, non proletarius*). Gellius's final words may also mean 'some writer suitable to be read by members of the first class and by landowning people, not by members of the lowest class', but with either translation he makes Fronto transfer the language of economic and social stratification to the realm of literature by this contrast between a 'landowning' (*adsiduus*) author 'of the highest class' (*classicus*) and a member 'of the lowest of the five classes' (*proletarius*). To be sure, Gellius'/Fronto's metaphor is not entirely new: earlier Roman authors had also used the language of social stratification to indicate cultural standing. Thus Cicero, in speaking of the Stoic philosophers Cleanthes and Chrysippus, says, 'In my view they belong to the fifth [i.e. the 'lowest'] class in comparison with [Democritus]' (*qui mihi cum illo* [*sc. Democrito*] *collati quintae classis videntur, Acad. 1.2.73*). Similarly, Quintilian figuratively uses the word *ordo* ('social rank', 'social status') to refer to a canonical list of select authors in a particular genre: for example, 'Apollonius [of Rhodes] does not come into the canon given by the literary scholars' (*Apollonius in ordinem a grammaticis datum non venit, Inst. Orat.* 10.1.54; '[the old literary scholars] have included some authors in the canon but excluded others entirely from the number' [*veteres grammatici*] *alios in ordinem redegerint, alios omnino exemerint numero'*, *Inst. Orat.* 1.43). It has been argued that in his nearly unique figurative use of *classicus* to mean 'first class' (paralleled only by Arnobius *Adv. Nat.*, 2.29, where *testis classicus* seems to mean a 'reliable witness'), Gellius is coining a metaphor not to describe a writer who is 'outstanding' and has been included in a canonical list, but to refer, in a more limited way, to one of a 'group of older writers' (*cohorte . . . antiquiore*) who exemplify correct usage (Citroni 2006: 206–9). The earliest known Renaissance humanist to imitate Gellius' metaphorical use of *classicus*, Filippo Beroaldo, does so precisely in reference to linguistic usage (1496, 1500). Other humanists, however, including Melanchthon and several authors associated with Erasmus, use *classicus* more generally of the 'best' authors (Rizzo 1986: 389–90; Pfeiffer 1976: 84; Citroni 2006: 209–11) and *proletarius* of the 'worst'. Thus in 1548 the mythographer Gyraldus (Lilio Gregorio Giraldi) criticizes his fourteenth-century predecessor Albricus (Pierre Bersuire), *qui auctor mihi proletarius est, nec fidus satis* ('who is in my view an author of the lowest class, and not sufficiently reliable' (*De diis gentium . . .* (Giraldi 1696: col. 153, quoted by Panofsky 1955: 47 n.19).

Like ecclesiastical, legal and educational elites in antiquity and the middle ages, the Renaissance humanists skilfully deployed the knowledge, techniques and status of the classical to achieve and maintain power. The pursuit of the *studia humanitatis* or *studia humaniora*, especially the ability to read and write classical Latin and, to a lesser extent, Greek, was a path toward upward social mobility, enabling students of the 'humanities' in the fourteenth and fifteenth centuries to gain employment as secretaries and legates of city-states and teachers in noble families. The best known teacher of the *studia humanitatis* was Guarino Guarini of Verona (1374–1460), who had studied Greek in Constantinople and whose pedagogical values and practice, especially at Ferrara in the service of the ruling Este family from 1429 on, made him the most sought after and influential of humanist teachers (Grafton and Jardine 1986: 1–28). Guarino offered an education modelled on that of ancient Rome. It was heavily reliant on rote memorization, repetition and arduous oral and written drilling, and it aimed at the same mastery of classical works and authors that was achieved in ancient Rome elite education. Guarino's students then proceeded to advanced rhetorical training based mainly on the pseudo-Ciceronian *Rhetorica ad Herennium*. As they progressed they wrote formal essays, mastered epistolary forms, and had to speak and write extemporaneously in Ciceronian Latin (Grafton and Jardine 1986: 9–20).

Whatever the intellectual virtues of Guarino's educational values and practices, their main aim was pragmatic: to produce potential employees of aristocratic families and city-states. He complemented his technical training with worldly advice, as when he wrote to his son in 1443: 'whatever the ruler may decree must be accepted with a calm mind and the appearance of pleasure. For men who can do this are dear to rulers, make themselves and their relatives prosperous, and win high promotion' (Grafton and Jardine 1986: 24). Guarino's pragmatism helped make his course of training more a valuable socio-economic commodity than an intellectual enterprise. Insofar as his school, which 'became the arts faculty of the new university of Ferrara', served as a model for other humanistic educational institutions, he was 'the modern equal of Theophrastus and Isocrates' (Grafton and Jardine 1986: 1). For example, Guarino's pedagogical ability to make classical Latinists and humanists out of students who were not to the manner born recalls Isocrates' boast of the civilizing power of education: that 'the students of [Athens] have become teachers of others, and that the name of "Hellenes" has come to be not [the name] of a race but of an intelligence, and those sharing our education are better called Greeks than those sharing our physical nature', *Panegyricus* 50.

Renaissance humanism, like the 'classical', was to some extent a figurative construct, masking a fundamentally socio-economic enterprise beneath idealistic claims for the value of literary studies. The noun *humanitas*, from the adjective *humanus*, may originally have meant 'human nature or character', but by the second century BCE it had come to signify too the cultural refinements that distinguish civilized human beings from beasts or from barbarians like Caesar's *Belgae*, 'bravest . . . because they are farthest away from the cultural refinement of the province' (*fortissimi . . . propterea quod a cultu atque humanitate provinciae longissime absunt, BG* 1.3). The *studia humanitatis* aimed not only at mastery of a particular style of Latin, but at a superiority claimed by the ancient Romans over foreigners (*barbari*), and, in the Renaissance, by the educated over the uneducated – a superiority that was at once economic, social, and cultural.

Through the fourteenth and fifteenth centuries, the word 'classical' continued to be used of Greek and Latin authors who were considered first-class, authoritative models of literary excellence and were read and imitated in schools. In the sixteenth century, especially in France, 'classical' also began to describe writers in modern languages whose works were considered to have exemplary value (Wellek 1968: 451; Settis 2004: 68). The earliest known occurrence is in Thomas Sebillet's *L'Art poétique* (1548), where 'les bons et classiques poètes français' ('the good and classic French poets') are Jean de Meun (thirteenth century) and Alain Chartier (fifteenth century). The practice of calling writers in modern languages 'classical' became more widespread in France and England after the foundation of the French Academy in 1635, the Royal Society in 1662, and the Society of Dilettanti in 1732. 'Classical' could thenceforth be used of any writer in an ancient or modern language acknowledged to be a normative model of excellence.

The same use, however, is not found in connection with ancient or modern visual artists in the early modern period, despite the intense engagement by leading painters and sculptors with the fragments of ancient sculpture found in Italy in the fifteenth and sixteenth centuries. Instead, 'ancients' and 'moderns' were the key evaluative terms for painters and sculptors, and the desire to reassemble the fragments of ancient statues and imitate ancient sculpture was part of an antiquarian enthusiasm for all things ancient. Only in the eighteenth century did students of ancient art, notably J.J. Winckelmann, develop a new, periodizing model of art history in which the word 'classical' was used for the first time to describe the period of highest achievement in a given culture and the art most worthy of imitation (Winckelmann [1764] 2006, 1755; Settis 2004: 74–82). Winckelmann's periodization was based on two different organic models of the rise and decline of a life form: that of the development, flowering and decay of a seed and that of human birth, childhood, youth, maturity, ageing, old age and death. He found the latter model of rise and decline in Pliny the Elder's chapters on art and artists in Books 34 and 35 of his *Natural History* (first century CE), and Pliny in turn derived it from such earlier writers on art as Xenocrates of Athens and Antigonos of Karystos (third century BCE) and perhaps too from cultural histories such as the *Life of Greece* by Dikaiarchos (fourth century BCE) and the *Life of the Roman People* by M. Terentius Varro (first century BCE). Although earlier artist-writers, including Lorenzo Ghiberti (fifteenth century) and Giorgo Vasari (sixteenth century), and scholars such as Joseph Scaliger (seventeenth century) also built on Pliny's model, it was Winckelmann who definitively revived ancient retrospective views of ancient artistic style; he used terms like archaic, classical, and baroque to describe the art of fifth- and fourth-century Athens, Hellenistic Greece, and republican and Augustan Rome, which gave rise to the use of these terms and others like classicism and neoclassicism in connection with modern imitations of ancient style (Settis 2004: 74–5). 'Classical' and 'classicism' in the sense developed by Winckelmann and his followers came to be distinguished, sometimes polemically, from 'romantic' and 'romanticism' in the late eighteenth and early nineteenth centuries. 'Classical' and 'classicism' referred to the harmony, formal balance, rational consistency and emotional restraint that Winckelmann and his followers attributed to the 'first-class' art and literature of fifth-century Athens and Augustan Rome, and 'romantic' and 'romanticism' to art and literature characterized by individualism, innovation, rejection of canonical models and lack of emotional restraint. The contrast was first made by German and French critics such as the brothers Schlegel and Germaine de Staël, then by authors throughout Europe and America (Wellek 1968: 451, 454; Wellek 1973: 188–90; Lokke 2004: 18; *OED*, *s.v.* 'classical' 6.a).

Winckelmann's model of the classical as the fullest flowering of a natural organism, along with his conception of the classical as the highest style, inviting imitation, come together in a remarkable definition of a classical work of art by the German scholar Gerhart Rodenwaldt: 'Klassisch ist ein Kunstwerk das vollkomen stilisiert ist, ohne von der Natur abzuweichen, so dass dem Bedürfniss nach Stilisierung und Nachahmung in gleiche Weise Genüge getan ist' ('A work of art is classical that is completely stylized without deviating from nature, so that the requirements of both stylization and imitation are equally well met', Rodenwaldt 1916: 125, quoted by Wellek 1968: 455–6). If the work of art in question is 'first-class' and either from Greco-Roman antiquity or from a peak period in another artistic or cultural tradition, the four main uses of the word 'classical' would all be present: (1) to denote worth, rank, or perfection and recognition of exemplary status; (2) to denote a chronological period considered best; (3) to denote a specific historical style; (4) to denote an aesthetic category (Tatarkiewicz 1958; cf. Porter 2006b: 14–15). In all four senses, 'classical' involves an implicit or explicit contrast with an opposing quality, period, style, value, or aesthetic category.

Toward the end of the eighteenth and the beginning of the nineteenth centuries, at the same time as the conflict between classicism and romanticism, antiquarian and aesthetic interests in ancient art, which previously had gone hand in hand, diverged radically. Aesthetic responses became the domain of artists and critics, while antiquarianism combined with art history in the new academic discipline of *klassische Altertumswissenschaft* ('the science of classical antiquity'). This new discipline soon became of fundamental importance in schools and universities, owing both to the popularity and influence of F.A. Wolf's *Darstellung der Alterthums-Wissenschaft nach Begriff, Umfang, Zweck und Wert* (*Description of the Science of Classical Antiquity in Conception, Range, Goal, and Value*, 1807) and to the central role of classical studies in the University of Berlin, founded in 1809–10 under the leadership of Wilhelm von Humboldt and soon the model for new and revamped universities in Germany and throughout continental Europe (Lenz 1910: 73–5, 81–92, 107–8, 157–62, 352–6, 359; Fuhrmann 1959: 196–7, 206; Sweet 1978–80: II. 55–6, 58–9). Paradoxically, this new specialization, dedicated to 'highest-class' ('classical') culture, had its home in schools and universities whose aim was to educate the children of bourgeois families to take their places in a new governing class. At roughly the same time, public museums meant mainly for the middle class (e.g. the British Museum in London, the Altes Museum in Berlin) not only displayed classical antiquities as one of their most popular features, but distributed plaster casts of Greek and Roman sculptures to schools, universities, and museums throughout Europe and the Americas, where they similarly helped spread 'classical' culture to the bourgeoisie (Settis 2004: 69–71).

    In other ways, however, the new science of antiquity continued the work of traditionally elite classical studies in promoting and preserving economic and social inequality. If one could not afford to attend a school that offered a humanistic education, or if one were barred on racial or religious grounds, upward social mobility was virtually impossible. Unequal access to education was also an important means of maintaining the subordination of women. For centuries, only a few girls and women of the upper class had the opportunity to learn Latin and even fewer, Greek. In Germany, where the word *Humanismus* was coined by F.I. Niethammer to denote the emphasis in the *gymnasium* (secondary school) on the Greek and Latin classics (Niethammer 1808), girls were legally barred from public humanistic gymnasia, and rarely achieved any secondary schooling until late in the nineteenth century (Albisetti 1988: 15, 18–19; Marchand 1996: 31). Girls in England and France received a secondary education in greater numbers, but in those countries too this education hardly ever included the study of Greek and Latin, knowledge of which was a prerequisite both for a university education and for the kinds of employment that could lead to higher social status and political influence (Mayeur 1979: 116, 149, 156, 170–1; Ringer 1979: 208–10, 232; Margadant 1990: 18). The educational barriers to a classical, humanistic education both expressed and reinforced the lower status of girls and women and their inability to share in the prestige and power to which knowledge of the classics might lead.

    The importance of the school as the site of transmission of the classical languages and cultures cannot be overestimated. By the second half of the nineteenth century, especially in France, the most important meaning of the word 'classical' no longer was 'belonging to or used of the highest rank or class of writers', but 'having educational or institutional authority'. M.P.E. Littré, in his *Dictionnaire de la langue française* (1862–73), *s.v. classique*, gives as the *primary* definition of the word, 'used in or belonging to the classes of colleges and schools', and the OED, *s.v.* 'classic', suggests that Littré's definition probably led to the word being used of 'the ancient authors generally as studied in school or college, together with the associated languages, literature, geography, art, etc.'. The OED adds, 'It is probable, also, that the transference of the epithet to these languages themselves has been partly owing to the notion that the latter are intrinsically excellent or of the first order, in comparison with the modern tongues'. Thus the OED entry brings together (1) what was historically the earliest figurative meaning of 'classical': a writer 'intrinsically excellent or of the first order' (with its implied corollary sense of 'serving as a model of correct usage'); (2) the developed, educational-institutional meaning of the word: 'used of or belonging to the classes of schools or colleges', where 'class', from Latin *classis* ('economic or social rank or division'), denotes 'a division of the scholars or students of an institution, receiving the same instruction or ranked together as of the same standing' (OED *s.v.* 'class' 3a; cf. Williams 1983: 60). As the OED points out, *s.v.* 'classic', 'The extension [of the meaning of 'classical'] has probably been in the main unthinking or unanalyzed: the Greek and Roman authors read in school were actually the classical writers [*sc.* in Gellius' sense] in these languages, and thus "classic" became practically synonymous with "ancient Greek or Roman" '. In other words the 'classical' is, by this definition, in large part an ideological construct benefiting the students who attended the schools in which Greek and Latin were offered, the teachers who taught in them, and the parents who paid the fees for the education that would reproduce, in their children, their own elite status or enable those children to attain it for the first time.

The reading of the classical Greek and Roman authors in schools is one aspect of the key role of the school in the formation of what we now call the literary canon. (Guillory 1993: 3–82). Historically, the conception and authority of the 'classical' has been inextricably linked to school, college and university use of certain texts and authors as models of language and style and the basis of educational and moral formation. This process began in ancient Greece, with the educational use of Homer, Hesiod, and the lyric poets to which Plato objected so strongly in Book 1 of the *Republic* and elsewhere. The education (*paideia*) of which Isocrates boasts in the passage from his *Panegyricus* quoted above included the study of these poets and, perhaps, of the major dramatists, historians and orators of fifth-century Athens. In Hellenistic Alexandria, the authors whose works were studied and made the subject of scholarly commentaries were known as the *prattomenoi*, and those 'selected' and 'included' on lists of the best writers in each genre were called the *engkrithentes*. As Gellius implies, these writers were known by Roman scholars as the *classici*, the canonical authors, along with such Latin writers as Cicero, Vergil, and Horace, whose works became school texts in or shortly after their own lifetimes, as Horace ruefully anticipated (*Ep.* I.20.17–18), and they have served in that capacity ever since.

It is probably no accident that lists of, and technical terms for, these writers of the first rank came into fashion during the Hellenistic and Roman imperial eras, when the Greco-Roman world was ruled by monarchs, whose courts were marked by elaborate hierarchies. A new sense of decorum prevailed in both politics and art and is reflected in critical writings like Horace's *Ars Poetica*, which begins by rejecting the grotesque and eccentric and calling for unity and consistency in the best visual and verbal art. Similarly, Horace's *Letter to Augustus* (*Epist.* II.1) praises Alexander the Great's 'accurate taste' (*iudicium subtile*) in visual art, which led him to make Apelles his favorite painter and Lysippus his favorite sculptor (239–41), and endorses Augustus' favourable judgement of the poets Vergil and Varius, in whose works 'the character and mind of famous men are visible' (245–50). These judgements, which associate the *classici* both with a ruler and with the harmony, balance, and rational order of the art appropriate to that ruler, are perhaps the first stage in the simultaneous association of the 'classical' with simplicity, symmetry and authority in both art and politics.

It is worth noting that in antiquity *kanon* (Latin *canon*) meant 'rule', 'model', or 'standard' and thus could serve as the title of the sculptor Polyclitus' book on what we now would call the artistic 'canon of proportions' and of his famous statue illustrating that canon (Easterling 1996: 286). *Kanon*, however, never denoted the lists of artists or writers in various literary genres who were considered 'first class', though in the fourth century CE it came to be used of the books of the Bible that were recognized by the Church as genuine and divinely inspired. This led the Dutch scholar, David Ruhnken, in 1768 to extend its meaning cautiously to the lists of chosen authors, for which Quintilian had used *ordo* and *numerus*: 'out of a great abundance of orators, [Aristarchus and Aristophanes of Byzantium] assigned just ten to what one might call the canon' (*ex magna oratorum copia tamquam in canonem decem dumtaxat rettulerunt* [*Aristarchus et Aristophanes Byzantius*], Ruhnken 1825: 386, quoted by Pfeiffer 1968: 207). 'Then', as Pfeiffer observes, 'Ruhnken dropped the cautious *tamquam* ['what one might call'] and went on referring to the selective lists as *canones* [canons]' (Pfeiffer 1968: 207). This is the source of the modern use of the word 'canon' to mean a generally acknowledged list of preeminent literary works, though as P.E. Easterling observes, 'Out of the ancient works that were known or rediscovered during the Renaissance, markedly different "canonical" selections have been made in different periods, and the changing process of reception continues, with new theoretical and political implications as western culture itself is held up to scrutiny' (Easterling 1996: 286).

One good example of this 'changing process of reception' is the varying manner in which, in the United States during the past two centuries, the content and authority of the canonical and the classical has been linked to the use in schools, colleges, and universities of a relatively few texts and authors as models of style and the basis of academic and moral education. Through the first decades of the twentieth century, knowledge of Greek, Latin and sometimes Hebrew was an entrance requirement at the older, elite private colleges; insofar as they were read at all, the 'classics' were read in the original languages. The influential Yale University report of 1828 argued that '[f]amiliarity with the Greek and Roman writers is especially adapted to form the taste and to discipline the mind, both in thought and diction, to the relish of what is elevated, chaste, and simple . . . Every faculty of the mind is employed, not only the memory, judgement, and reasoning power, but the taste and fancy are occupied and improved' (Day and Kingsley 1829: 328–30). By the late nineteenth century this kind of argument fed into a new conception of the humanities. No longer were they the traditional *studia humaniora* that could help students get ahead in life economically and socially. Instead, at least in the context of college curricula, they came to mean 'the elevating, holistic study of literature, music, and art' (Winterer 2002: 118–19), and they were distinguished from studies in the natural and social sciences by the claim that they had nothing to do with economic and social utility. Rather, they emphasized knowledge for the sake of knowledge, and the books in the classical canon were read as paths to inward reflection and self-cultivation.

The conception and exploitation of the classical and canonical changed again in the first few decades of the twentieth century, as new kinds of students entered American colleges and universities in unprecedented numbers. Many were the children of Catholic and Jewish immigrants from southern and eastern Europe, who, owing to their poverty and low social status, had for the most part been excluded from humanistic education in the countries from which they had emigrated. These students could not be expected to know the classical languages or be familiar with the cultural values that the canonical works written in these languages had historically transmitted. In response to this new wave of students, and under the influence of 'war aims' courses developed on various campuses during World War One to teach the reasons for American participation in the war (Schein 2007), beginning in the 1920s many colleges and universities instituted so-called 'great books' courses in 'western civilization' and 'humanities', with syllabuses consisting of canonical texts from antiquity through the nineteenth century, as many as 50% of which were by Greek and Roman authors. (The publication of the first volumes in 'Our Debt to Greece and Rome' in 1922 and of the Oxford University Press 'Legacy' books the following year is a related phenomenon: Bailey 1923; Livingstone 1923.)

The 'great books' courses not only aimed to introduce the new kinds of students to texts and traditions with which they were unfamiliar, but to 'acculturate' them and prepare them to take their places in the middle class, to which their college education would entitle them. As a result the 'classical' again came to be seen as a commodity, the consumption and conspicuous display of which could help students fulfil their desires for upward social mobility. It was as if classical works had an 'aura', to use Walter Benjamin's term, and would allow students to realize their most ardent wishes (Benjamin 1969: 221–3, 245 n.5; Schein 2007). At the same time, these 'classics' served the interests of the colleges and universities in 'acculturating' their students and maintaining their own privileged positions as gatekeepers to the middle and upper classes.

In the past few decades, as women, African–Americans, and the children of non-European immigrant families have begun to attend college in greater numbers, the selective version of the western canon traditionally offered in great books courses has increasingly seemed insufficient and at times disrespectful of these new groups of students and their diverse cultural background. In most cases students have objected not to the quality and content of the individual works read in great books courses, but to the assumptions that only western texts can be 'classical' and 'great', and that their own identity and their economic and social prospects as college graduates should depend on acculturation through exposure to the 'heritage' of western civilization.

As a result of the cultural critique of great books courses, many colleges and universities have modified the content of these courses to include non-western texts or introduced new courses focused on the 'great books', the classics, of various non-western cultures. Predictably, these changes have angered some students, faculty, and alumni, who feel that *their* identity and worth have been diminished by what seems to them the disestablishment of western culture and its traditional texts, institutions, and values (Guillory 1993: 28–35, 38–47; Levine 1996: 68–73).

It is often said that canonical great books are 'timeless' (or 'timeless classics'), but in fact each work was written in particular historical circumstances, and the varying institutional versions of the canonical list are themselves historical constructions. In its own time, virtually every work now read in a great books course called into question specific institutions and values of the culture in which it was created, whether to challenge and change them or, in the end, to reinforce and reaffirm them. If, as often happens in these courses, such works are read mainly in relation to one another, with insufficient attention to their original historical, social, and institutional contexts, they are mystified as timeless classics, lose their critical edge, and become mere affirmations of a supposed cultural heritage. This in turn masks their ideological power and allows them to be manipulated by opportunistic teachers and political leaders to promote themselves and their political purposes in the name of the 'eternal-classical'. At best, this has resulted in students misreading the canonical works or reading them one-dimensionally; at worst it led to the perversion of classical studies in German universities between 1933 and 1945, when, in Arnaldo Momigliano's telling phrase, the 'fascination of barbarism' led numerous scholars and Classics departments to put their scholarship and teaching at the service of racist Nazi ideology, Hitler as a political leader, and the legitimation of the exile or murder of their Jewish colleagues (Momigliano 1945: 131 = Momigliano 1966, II: 748; cf. Hartshorne 1938; Losemann 1977; Irmscher 1980; Näf 1986, 2001; Lohse 1991; Wegeler 1996).

I hope that my brief historical sketch of the meanings and uses of the words classical and canonical will have demystified the ideology underlying 'Our Debt to Greece and Rome' and similar attitudes to classical civilization and classical studies. We classical scholars and teachers have a particular opportunity and responsibility to understand and resist the institutional construction of a self-serving literary canon and classical tradition, and to help students grasp the historical process by which texts are de-historicized, appropriated, and transformed, so that they lose their power to criticize and call into question. Our work becomes easier when we free ourselves from the assumption of elitism that has historically been associated with the classical. In this way we can think more clearly, and help our students think more clearly, about the ways in which 'classicism' and 'humanism' are implicit and complicit in the institutions and ideology that support class exploitation, gender hierarchy, and political and economic domination. Similar institutions and ideology were features of the societies and cultures in which our canonical classics were created and handed down. By recognizing this historical reality, we can rediscover the liberatory power of these classics as critical works that are good to think about and good to think with.

NOTE

I would like to thank Carolyn Dewald for encouragement and criticism that improved this essay in content and organization, and Liz Irwin and Chris Stray for further criticism, corrections, and suggestions.

FURTHER READING

On the meaning of ideology, see Gramsci 1988: 196–200, 330, 380–1; Bourdieu 1977: Index *s.v.* 'ideology', 'norm', 'rule'; Williams 1983: 145–7; Guillory 1993: 61–6, 77–8, 134–41, 238–40, 262–5. On 'class', 'culture', 'elite', and 'education', see Williams 1983: 60–9, 87–93, 111–5. On canonicity and educational institutions, see Guillory 1993: 3–82; Easterling 2002.

On Renaissance humanism and education, see Jensen 1996: 63–81 and Mack 1996: 82–99.

On Classics in education, see Stray 1998; Beard and Henderson 1995: 109–12; Goldhill 2002: 191–231; Schein 2007.

On Classics and classicism, past and future, see Wellek: 1968: 449–56; Porter 2000: 167–288, 356–423, and 2006b; Settis 2004.

CHAPTER SEVEN

Gladstone and the Classics

David W. Bebbington

William Ewart Gladstone's writings about antiquity deserve more attention than they have received. Among his contemporaries the four-times Prime Minister of the United Kingdom achieved some celebrity for his scholarship. One of his Homeric works, and a minor one at that, was acclaimed in grandiloquent style by Heinrich Schliemann, the excavator of Troy. 'This work', he told its author, 'the masterpiece of the greatest scholar of all ages, will for ever remain classic and will for ever be considered as the pearl of all that has been written or may still be written about Homer' (Schliemann to Gladstone, 8 May 1876, Gladstone Papers, British Library, Add. MS [hereafter GP] 44450, f. 25). Schliemann's praise, a symptom both of his extravagant personality and of his hopes of continued support from the statesman, was wide of the mark. Even in his own day some of Gladstone's theories created incomprehension or astonishment among classicists in the mainstream of scholarship. Thus Jane Harrison of Newnham College, Cambridge, remarked soon after the statesman's death that, though two of his works were extraordinarily good, he had 'gone dotty' in some of his ideas about Homer (Stewart 1959: 66). Gladstone was in the older tradition of the gentleman amateur who spun theories of his own devising and lamented the regular distractions from scholarship forced on him by his profession. But the effect of the disdain of the experts has been to encourage writers about Gladstone to treat his classical endeavours with wry amusement. Lord Jenkins, for example, writes of his main campaign of work on Homer as 'one of the most bizarre of all his intellectual exercises' (Jenkins 1995: 181). Likewise Sir Philip Magnus compares his efforts on the Greek poet to the attempts to decipher the hidden message of the Great Pyramid (Magnus 1964: 124). It is true that Sir Hugh Lloyd-Jones has offered a sympathetic appreciation of the statesman's Homeric scholarship, but he treats the enterprise solely in the context of the history of classical learning (Lloyd-Jones 1975: 15–17). The possibility that Gladstone's classical studies helped mould his politics, both in theory and in practice, is often tacitly ignored.

Certain historians would probably go so far as to claim that Gladstone's politics could not have been affected by his work on Greece and Rome. The so-called 'high politics' school of interpretation would argue that the classics, along with religion, formed a dimension of the ideology that he was careful to keep apart from his public career (Cooke and Vincent 1974: 53). That understanding of Gladstone, however questionable on broader grounds, is dealt a mortal wound by Frank M. Turner's admirable examination of the statesman's contributions to Homeric study, the predominant aspect of his work on antiquity. Turner shows that Gladstone is a prime example of the common tendency of the Victorians to use the ancient world as a cockpit for the struggles of their own day. Gladstone allowed his reading of Homer to be shaped by the preoccupations of a mid-nineteenth-century politician (Turner 1981: 234–44). That interpretation of Gladstone's scholarship will be followed here. Yet Turner misses a dimension of Gladstone's examination of Homer that carries considerable significance for his political life. Of the commentators on Gladstone's intellectual concerns, in fact, only Agatha Ramm has noticed that the statesman's views on Homer changed over time (Ramm 1989–90: 14–17). Far from remaining constant, his estimate of the poet underwent substantial transformation. The analysis that follows attempts to bring out the implications of the development in Gladstone's understanding of the Homeric poems. At the same time it tries to do greater justice than has hitherto been done to other aspects of the statesman's debt to the classics. It will become apparent that the direction of influence that Turner has identified, of Gladstone's politics on his classical researches, does not stand alone. The classics also impinged on his politics.

The Classics and Gladstone

Although Homer was the focus of Gladstone's mature *oeuvre*, other ancient authors occupied him at various stages in his career. At Eton he received a thorough grounding in classical literature and at Oxford he spent the bulk of his working hours with ancient texts. During the 1830s, while establishing himself as a young Member of Parliament, he dedicated a great deal of time, especially in each recess, to systematic reading, much of it in classical authors. As late as 1852 he studied in turn Propertius, Tibullus, Longinus, Plautus and Suetonius, taking careful notes on each (GP 44740, ff. 70–92, 97–110, 133–55, 156–63, 280–312). He found certain writers compulsive. Once he had taken up Thucydides, as he remarked to Lord Acton late in life, he could not bring himself to stop (Gladstone to Acton, 1 April 1888, GP 44094, f. 15v). There were, however, limits to the catholicity of his taste. He held the Greek tragedians to be lacking in 'life-likeness'. He assigned Aeschylus the highest place among them, but in the daily diary record of his reading there is no mention after Oxford of looking at Sophocles in the original even though the statesman considered him superior to Euripides (Gladstone 1857: 10). In general he preferred Greek to Latin authors, and he despised Virgil as an inferior epic poet who had distorted subsequent generations' appreciation of Homer (Gladstone 1858: 3. 512–13). Yet Gladstone included passages from Horace in a collection of translations that he issued in 1861 with his brother-in-law and on his final retirement in 1894 he completed *The Odes of Horace*, a set of translations of his own (Lyttelton and Gladstone 1861; Gladstone 1894). Like Stanley Baldwin after him, Gladstone clearly found Horace the most appealing of Latin authors (Dilks 1977: 275).

From the late 1840s, however, it was Homer who held pride of place in his gallery of ancient writers. In 1858 Oxford University Press published on Gladstone's behalf his weightiest classical work, *Studies on Homer and the Homeric Age*. It was a massive treatise, each of the three volumes containing over five hundred pages. Subsequently Homer was the subject of four other books, three public lectures and over two dozen articles. He was working on a further book based on the poet, to be called 'The Olympian Religion', within five months of his death in 1898 (GP 44713, ff. 80–2). A fair proportion of this output deals directly with what can be gleaned from the poet on themes relating to public life. The political arrangements of the *Iliad* and the *Odyssey* form the subject of roughly a quarter of the third volume of *Studies on Homer*, of one of the fifteen chapters in *Juventus Mundi* (1869), of one of thirteen in Gladstone's primer called simply *Homer* (1878) and of one of the seven in *Landmarks in Homeric Study* (1890). In each case the undergirding conviction is that, as Gladstone puts it in his earliest work on Homer, 'the first real foundations of political science were laid in the heroic age' (Gladstone 1858: 3. 8).

Gladstone's discussion of 'The Polities of the Homeric Age' in *Studies on Homer* was conceived as a liberal Conservative defence of constitutional monarchy. George Grote, the radical republican historian, had depicted the kings in Homer's pages as absolute despots from whose yoke the peoples of Greece subsequently rejoiced to free themselves. Gladstone directly challenges this interpretation. In the Homeric poems, he claims, the king receives personal reverence because monarchy was 'always and essentially limited', possessing only 'moderate powers' (Gladstone 1858: 3. 27). The *boule*, the council of chiefs, had been described by Grote as 'a purely consultative body' without power to resist the king (Grote 1846–56: 2. 91). Gladstone insists, however, that the members of the council could differ from Agamemnon, the supreme ruler on the Greek side, and even overrule him. The *boule*, Gladstone alleges, was 'a kind of executive committee', operating very like the British cabinet (Gladstone 1858: 3. 98). Grote had been even more disparaging about the *agore*, or public assembly. It gathered merely to hear the royal instructions and so had 'a nullity of positive function' (Grote 1846–56: 2. 92). Gladstone contends that, on the contrary, the account of the military assembly in book 2 of the *Iliad* assumes that 'the army was accustomed to hear the chiefs argue against, and even overthrow, the proposals of Agamemnon'. The authority of the ruler was therefore circumscribed by the power of a body very similar to parliament. 'The position of Agamemnon', Gladstone concludes, '. . . bears a near resemblance to that of a political leader under free European, and, perhaps, it may be said, especially under British institutions' (Gladstone 1858: 3. 138). Homer depicted constitutional arrangements close to those in which Gladstone participated.

As the statesman subsequently evolved from a liberal Conservative into a fully fledged Liberal, there was no substantial alteration in his understanding of the Homeric polity.

In his later books on the poet there is a similar exposition of the way in which the king ruled responsibly in consultation with the council and under potential criticism from the assembly. Despite the continuities in the statesman's treatment of political themes, however, there are certain alterations in *Juventus Mundi*. As Turner has noted, the previous criticism of voting by majorities is suppressed by the Liberal Prime Minister; and there is an intriguing acceptance, as there had not been thirteen years before, that most of the people in early Greece were probably peasant proprietors – which reflects the author's preoccupation in 1869 with the Irish land question, on which he was to legislate in the following year (Turner 1981: 242). By 1890, when the 'Grand Old Man' was pressing Home Rule as the panacea for Ireland, there is rather more change in his discussion of politics in *Landmarks of Homeric Study*, though still in terms more of emphasis than of substance. Now the first place in the analysis is given to the idea of freedom. The poet is said to set 'a high value on the personal freedom of the human being as such', a point vindicated by his 'emphatic condemnation of slavery'. There is also a whole chapter on 'Homer as Nation-Maker', in which he is praised for blending the diverse ethnic elements of the Greek world into a single nation (Gladstone 1890: 97–8, ch. 2). Freedom and nationality were leading components of the case Gladstone was then arguing on behalf of Ireland, and it clearly affected his treatment of Homer. There was an outcropping of Gladstone's Liberalism in his later scholarship.

There is therefore abundant evidence that Gladstone's stance in public affairs shaped his attitude to Homer. His initial liberal Conservatism set out the contours of discussion in his first book on the poet and then his subsequent political evolution left its mark on his later writings. So much is generally agreed. But how far did the reverse process operate? To what extent were Gladstone's political ideas moulded by his classical interests?

The Classics and Gladstonian Conservatism

In the earliest phase of his thinking, at Oxford and during the following decade, Gladstone immersed himself in classical philosophy. Already by the time he was examined in the Oxford Schools in 1831 he was able to compose, in the five hours between 10 a.m. and 3 p.m., a powerful answer to a question contrasting Aristotle's teaching with the Stoic principle of *apatheia* (GP 44812, ff. 63v–64v). In the autumn of 1836, in parallel with the study of Augustine's *City of God*, he undertook a campaign of reading Cicero. Beginning with the *De Oratore*, he passed on in turn to the *Academica*, the *De Finibus Bonorum et Malorum*, the *Tusculanae Quaestiones*, the *De Natura Deorum* and the *De Officiis*, taking careful notes on each (GP 44726, ff. 95–108, 132–3, 149–50, 245–8, 249–54, 269–73, 292–4). He records finding the exposition of Stoic doctrine put in the mouth of Cato in the *De Finibus* 'more elaborate than clear' (GP 44726, f. 231). Gladstone disagreed with the supposition of the Stoics that affections and passions could be rooted out of the personality, but he valued them for their defence of what would now be called a non-natural theory of morality. Evil, they taught, was irreducibly evil, something malignant and not, as utilitarians of Gladstone's day such as Grote held, merely a label for pain (GP 44726, f. 230). The Epicureans, by contrast, seemed guilty of upholding the utilitarian teaching that the rightness of an action depends on its consequences; and in the eyes of Gladstone, who cast himself as a champion of traditional Christian morality, that was sufficient condemnation (GP 44812, f. 64v). Plato was rather more of a shaping influence. Gladstone studied the *Phaedo* at Oxford, the *Timaeus* and the *Critias* in 1837 and in the same year began the *Laws*, but, like many other readers, he found the work unpalatable and did not complete it (GP 44720, ff. 14–16, 209–13; 44727, ff. 111–16, 133, 134–5). Between August 1832 and October 1833, at the outset of his parliamentary career, he scrutinized the text of the *Republic* with immense care. Book 8, he noted, was 'very pungent' on democracy, vividly portraying the character of a demagogue. The communitarian temper of the philosopher appealed to Gladstone as the natural correlate of the Christian teaching about mutual responsibilities. 'We seek', Gladstone noted, 'the good of the whole not a part' (GP 44722, f. 50v). The same holistic axiom, however, was to be found in virtually every ancient school of philosophy, and it would be a mistake to follow Colin Matthew in attributing as much weight to Plato as to Aristotle in the statesman's formation (Matthew 1997: 33–6). Gladstone's considered estimate of the two appears in a paper apparently composed in 1835. Aristotle had enunciated 'many noble truths', while Plato merely contained 'thoughts exquisitely beautiful' (GP 44725, f. 23). Plato made a real but only a subordinate contribution to Gladstone's early thinking.

It was Aristotle who exerted the most specific sway over the young politician. Gladstone used to refer to the philosopher, along with Augustine, Dante and Bishop Butler, as one of his four doctors (Morley 1903: 1. 207n.). There was an Aristotelian tone to his earliest and longest piece of writing on political theory, an unpublished paper 'On the Principle of Government' written at Oxford during the Reform crisis of 1831. The *Nicomachean Ethics*, which Gladstone was then studying almost daily, is quoted four times. The writer falls naturally into Aristotelian jargon. Thus in order to downgrade the value of freedom in the abstract he argues that it is only 'a *dynamis* of contingent quality and application, determined to good or evil according to its *telos*'. Gladstone follows the philosopher in holding that authority must be restricted to those with the proper qualification of a disposition towards justice. There is no question of equal rights for all – or indeed of equality in any respect. Subordination is the 'natural law of humanity'. The whole essay, like Aristotle's writings, claims to be about what is natural for human beings. The result is a highly conservative statement of principle which identifies the limitations of human nature with the will of the Almighty. Like the long tradition of Christianized Aristotelianism that preceded him, Gladstone does not distinguish sharply between the divine and the human constraints on possible political arrangements. But the starting point is not the Bible, for Gladstone insists that he is taking as his subject 'the original circumstances of human nature' rather than the human condition as modified by the fall (GP 44721, ff. 6, 4, 15). Aristotle provided the foundations on which Gladstone erected the structure of his earliest political thought.

The debt to Aristotle persisted. Four years later, when writing a private memorandum 'Of the law of Social obligation', Gladstone appeals to him, 'the same great authority', for the basic premise that 'society is a body naturally formed and not optionally' (GP 44725, f. 172). Richard Helmstadter has shown that the greatest intellectual influence on Gladstone's first book, *The State in its Relations with the Church* (1838), was Aristotle; and Agatha Ramm has pointed out that his aversion to Roman Catholicism was partly the result of his Aristotelian cast of mind (Helmstadter 1985: 15–17; Ramm 1985: 329–32). In *Studies on Homer* the combination of discipline with freedom in the constitutional arrangements of the heroic age is said to have achieved a 'mean of wisdom' that the philosopher would have approved; and in *Juventus Mundi* the same Aristotelian 'spirit of moderation' is (rather surprisingly) claimed as the mark of the good or great man in Homer (Gladstone 1858: 2. 527n.; Gladstone 1869: 393). When *Studies on Homer* had been issued, the next publishing venture that Gladstone contemplated was actually an edition of Aristotle's *Politics*. In the autumn of 1860, while Chancellor of the Exchequer, he spent nearly a month beginning an annotated translation, promising those of his future readers who gave 'unsparing effort' to the text not only 'augmented knowledge' but also 'increased capacity'. He did not manage to complete more than the first three of the eight chapters, together with fragments of the last two, before he was distracted by other tasks and so the edition never appeared. In his draft Gladstone is willing to criticize Aristotle, on the grounds, for example, that he depresses the status of women, but the prevailing tone of the comments is favourable. Gladstone approves the concept of 'absolute justice' (*to kyrios dikaion*) for approximating to 'what we term natural justice'; and he offers no qualification of Aristotle's fundamental contention that 'the state is both natural and prior to the individual' (GP 44750, ff. 9v, 58, 108, 57; Arist. Pol. 3.9.1, 1.2.14). These premises still undergirded his own attitude to public affairs as he sat for the first time in a Liberal cabinet.

If Aristotle contributed an enduring conservative element to Gladstone's social philosophy – a stress on duty, community and subordination – the statesman owed another rather different debt to the philosopher. From an early date Aristotle's principled pragmatism gave Gladstone a reasoned justification for political flexibility. He undertook his first thorough reading of the *Politics* during 1834–5. Because he was simultaneously studying Sir William Blackstone's *Commentaries on the Laws of England*, the classic eighteenth-century exposition of the principles of the constitution, and Alexis de Tocqueville's newly published *Democracy in America*, it seems clear that he was putting himself through a stiff course in political theory. A detached memorandum shows that he found a passage in book 4 chapter 12 of the *Politics* particularly instructive. 'But at all times', Gladstone read, 'a legislator ought always to attach the middle section of the population firmly to the constitution'. The task that Aristotle laid down was precisely the mission of Peelite Conservatism. 'It is a mistake made by many', the philosopher went on, 'even by those seeking to make an aristocratic constitution, not only to give too great preponderance to the rich, but to cheat the people' (Arist. Pol. 4.12.4). Here was a lesson that Gladstone took to heart, ever seeking to stabilize the aristocratic order by carefully judged concessions to public demands. Nine days after completing the examination of the book, he composed a paper entitled 'Of concession', exploring how and when government

should give ground to calls for change. The lodestar, he decided, was this: 'To concede when right is good: and to concede liberally when we concede at all' (GP 44725,
f. 189v). It was a formula that was to epitomize Gladstone's reforming technique
over, for example, Irish disestablishment or Home Rule. It was not left, as has
usually been supposed, to Peel's administration of 1841 for Gladstone to imbibe
these maxims from his leader. A combination of influences had brought him to this
eminently practical stance in the previous decade. Experience of serving under Peel
in 1834–35 no doubt contributed to the ideas of the paper; Tocqueville and general historical knowledge certainly did. Yet Aristotle's ancient wisdom also played its
part in making Gladstone, already by the mid-1830s, not Macaulay's 'stern and unbend-
ing' Tory but a mild and malleable one (Macaulay 1877: 468).

The Classics and Gladstonian Liberalism

Homer became an intellectual enthusiasm too late to be a formative factor in
Gladstone's Conservatism, but it is worth investigating the relationship between
the poet and Gladstonian Liberalism. The significance of Homer for Gladstone's
later politics, however, can be appreciated only by examining other aspects of the
statesman's engagement with the poet. Far more space in *Studies on Homer* –
two of the three volumes – is allocated to questions of race and religion than
to political topics. Gladstone's approach to the two themes was shaped by many
of the assumptions of contemporary social anthropology. The dominant school
until the 1850s, calling itself 'ethnology', was still heavily indebted to the pioneering work of the Asiatic scholar Sir William Jones, who, in 1784, had argued for an
affinity between Indian culture and the classical civilization of the Mediterranean.
Jones appealed to linguistic and mythological similarities to demonstrate the links
between the branches of the Indo-European family of nations (Cannon 1990:
296–7). The leading exponent of ethnology in the earlier nineteenth century
was J.C. Prichard, a Bristol physician who followed Jones in fitting his researches
into a biblical framework based on the dispersion of the descendants of Noah
after the flood. Culture, on this view, had advanced by its diffusion from a common
centre to the various quarters of the globe. Comparative philology enabled the scholar
to trace the patterns of migration. Gladstone consulted one of Prichard's works
while *Studies on Homer* was in the press in order to check the acceptability of the
view he was setting out (Prichard 1831; Foot and Matthew 1968–94: 5. 275). The
first volume of Gladstone's book, headed 'Ethnology of the Greek Races', was an
exemplary instance of Prichard's technique. Gladstone carefully sifts Homer's vocabulary in order to establish the characteristics of the two main constituents of
the Greek nation, the earlier Pelasgians and the later Hellenes. The statesman was
able to draw on the conclusion of the great German historian B.G. Niebuhr that
the Pelasgians were a peaceful agricultural people (Gladstone 1858: 1. 297). The
Hellenes, by contrast, were poorer and less civilized but more energetic. The broad
outline of Gladstone's anthropological analysis was in the mainstream of contemporary scholarship.

The statesman's understanding of ancient religion was framed by his ethnology. The migrating peoples had carried with them the faith that they had originally shared with each other at the common centre. Their earliest religion, Gladstone supposed, was what had been disclosed by the Almighty to Adam and Eve in the Garden of Eden. This primitive revelation contained not only the basic features of monotheism but also such distinctively Christian features as acknowledgement of the Holy Trinity and expectation of a Messiah. As the dispersal of the nations progressed, however, memories of these sublime doctrines faded and erroneous conceptions of the supernatural mingled with the inherited truths. Among the Greeks, therefore, there were valid ideas about divine things received by tradition as well as debased notions, the fruit of more recent invention. Gladstone divided Homer's gods and goddesses into two corresponding categories, the 'traditive' and the 'inventive'. In the traditive group, which had Apollo and Athene as its leading figures, the traces of the original revelation were detectable by the perceptive eye. Apollo, for example, was never at odds with the will of his father Zeus, and so reflected prophecies of the coming of Christ, who would always conform to the will of his heavenly Father (Gladstone 1858: 2. 71–2). The whole burden of the second volume of *Studies on Homer* was that truth could be discerned on Olympus.

Gladstone, a High Churchman who had been deeply affected by Tractarianism, was attempting to protect the twin theological beliefs in revelation and tradition. The Almighty had made known his purposes to humanity; and possessors of revealed truth were able, by resisting threats to the deposit of faith, to transmit it down the ages. The underlying message of *Studies on Homer* is that they should not succumb, as had the Greeks, to innovations in matters of religion. Amongst them the inventive element in the Homeric creed had debased the divine image. In the poet's pages the attribution of human traits to the Greek divinities, a phenomenon Gladstone labels 'anthropophuism', injects corruption into the Olympian community. Thus to the character of Zeus it adds 'earthly, sensual, and appetitive elements', rendering him 'human and carnal'. Although Gladstone acknowledges a 'capacity for good' in human beings, his stress is on their being 'the prey of vicious passions' because they suffer from an 'inward disease'. An Augustinian sense of the prevalence of sin dominates the statesman's treatment of Homer's divinities. The account of Olympus, he concludes, 'wherever it reproduces the human, reproduces it in degraded form' (Gladstone 1858: 2. 174, 186, 18–19, 333). This estimate was later to be transformed, but in *Studies on Homer* Gladstone was confident that the defining characteristic of humanity is its sin.

Scholarly opinion, however, was veering decisively at the time in favour of the view that early religion was not the result of divine revelation. There was a growing consensus that, on the contrary, awe in the presence of stupendous natural forces had given rise to the spirit of worship (Müller 1830: 1. 16; Thirlwall 1835: 1. 183–90). In *Studies on Homer* Gladstone had rejected this supposition, but, faced with a barrage of critical reviews of the book, over the next few years he was forced to accept that Homer's divinities could be explained as an outgrowth of the veneration of nature. Yet Gladstone still wished to defend the idea of a primitive revelation, which remained for him a bastion of orthodox Christianity. Having conceded that nature worship existed in archaic Greece, he faced the problem of explaining how Olympian religion could nevertheless bear witness to the earliest revealed truth. The answer lay in the power of anthropomorphism, 'that principle which . . . casts the divine life into human forms' (Gladstone 1869: 232). This feature of Homer's poems was an echo of the idea of the incarnation, the union of the divine with the human, that had been revealed at the dawn of history. Unlike the word that Gladstone had previously used, anthropophuism, the new term has almost entirely favourable connotations. Anthropomorphism is the force that prevents the admiration of nature from ruining the religion of Homer. The depiction of the gods and goddesses as human beings dominated the poet's pages, relegating the older nature worship to the margins of the supernatural cosmology. In place of his previous antithesis between the inventive and the traditive, Gladstone postulates in *Juventus Mundi* an antithesis between the natural and the anthropomorphic. The same contrast recurs in all his subsequent writings on Homer, right down to the unfinished treatise on 'Olympian Religion'. Sometimes, as in *Landmarks of Homeric Study*, he prefers to use the term 'theanthropism' to describe the attribution of human qualities to the divine (Gladstone 1890: 65–6). Whatever the terminology, the effect of the need to minimize the element of nature worship in Olympian religion was to elevate the role of the human element in the pantheon.

The new stress on the dignity of the human was prominent in a lecture delivered by Gladstone in 1865 on the 'Place of Ancient Greece in the Providential Order'. The ideal of humanity is presented as the central classical legacy to Western civilization, balancing the Christian inheritance. The Greek mind, Gladstone declared, was 'the secular counterpart of the Gospel'. If Christianity was the salt of civilization, the Greek contribution was the thing salted. The '*idée mère* of the Greek religion, the annexation of manhood to deity' entailed, especially in the golden age of Homer, the upgrading of whatever could be called human. It dictated the banishment of the inhuman: the sacrifice of human beings, incest, polygamy, cannibalism, infant exposure and (in Homer's time) homosexuality. Even caricature, to which the Chancellor of the Exchequer seems to have been particularly sensitive at the time, was unknown to the Greeks. In their place were admiration of human beauty and a respect for the status of women higher than that displayed in the Old Testament. Divorce, for example, was less acceptable to the Greeks of the heroic age than under the law of Moses. Art and philosophy could blossom because the human element was so prominent in the Hellenic mind. Hence Socrates propounded 'as the prime subject for the study of man, the nature, constitution, and destiny of man himself' (Gladstone 1865: 77, 59, 73). The dignity attached to human beings could be demonstrated from the story in Pausanias of the person who, after the death of his enemy, was killed by the fall of the man's statue. The sons of the victim successfully prosecuted the statue for the crime and it was duly thrown into the sea. So sacred, concluded Gladstone, was human life. The principle was the glory of Greek culture.

A profound feeling for the importance of the human therefore pervades Gladstone's later thought. No longer were human beings considered primarily as sinners needing restraint. A measure of discipline was indeed required, but an excess of it could stunt and maim. 'The principles of repression', he wrote, 'which were indispensable as the medicine of man, were unfit for his food' (Gladstone 1865: 85). The Greeks taught, on the contrary, that the whole of human life was richly to be enjoyed. The account of the shield of Achilles in book 18 of the *Iliad*, with its scenes of marriage, a lawcourt, war, agriculture and dancing, is taken as an illustration of the range of common life calling for celebration (Gladstone 1874). In an article written for an American periodical in 1887 summing up the message he would wish to leave to posterity, Gladstone declares that the most fruitful area for study lies 'in man and the world considered with respect to man'. Human beings, though defaced by the fall, have enormous potential for great moral achievements. The stress is now on the capacities, not the deficiencies, of the human race: 'humanity itself', he goes so far as to say, 'touches the bounds of the superhuman' (Gladstone 1887: 590). The echo of his treatment of the Olympian divinities illustrates the way in which Homeric researches had left their mark on his broader thinking. He had turned from a pessimistic to an optimistic estimate of the human condition.

Gladstone's assumptions about Homer coloured his way of conceptualizing the human race, marking him out from the prevailing contemporary trend. During the later nineteenth century the inherited cosmopolitan emphasis, inherited from the Enlightenment, on the qualities that human beings possess in common was steadily undermined by doctrines asserting the distinctiveness of particular races. In particular it was often contended, for instance by the Oxford philologist Friedrich Max Müller, that there was a great gulf fixed between the Aryan and Semitic peoples. Appealing to etymology and myth, Max Müller dwelt on the fundamental unity of the Indo-European peoples and their difference from the Semites. Gladstone, however, was committed to resisting such speculation. It is true that he sometimes used the terminology of Aryan and Semite, even on one occasion quoting an authority positing 'a remarkable contrast' between the two (Gladstone 1869: 140–1). But he was careful not to endorse this judgement, and explicitly took issue with Max Müller on this question. The professor, in repudiating any Semitic influence on Greek mythology, once suggested to Gladstone that it was a product of nothing but Aryan myths and the Greek national mind. The statesman replied that there was another constituent element, what he labelled 'x', the legacy of primeval truth (Gladstone to Max Müller, 19 October 1864; GP 44251 (2), f. 279). Gladstone always insisted on the common intellectual stock of the 'Aryan' Greeks and the 'Semitic' Jews. His whole aim in his last unfinished treatise was to establish the substantial identity of the traces of primitive revelation in Homer and the Old Testament. As he insisted against a disciple of Max Müller, each ethnic group shared the inheritance of 'one gift, associated with the worship of the one God, given at one centre'. The notion of a single original revelation bound together 'all the tribes, races and nations' of the world (Gladstone 1879: 257). Evidence drawn from Homer seemed to vindicate the unity of the human race. Gladstone was not swept along by the drift of European thought towards racist and specifically anti-Semitic conclusions.

The results of the attitudes towards human beings generated by his work on Homer were evident in Gladstonian Liberalism. The statesman's speeches as party leader are pervaded by references to the demands of human need and the duties of humane response. There is a profound sense of the solidarity of the whole race. Perhaps the most famous passage from Gladstone's Midlothian addresses of 1879 calls attention to the sufferings caused by the Conservative 'forward policy' in Afghanistan, urging that his hearers are united with the victims 'as human beings in the same flesh and blood' (Gladstone 1971: 94). The speeches on the Bulgarian horrors in 1876 and on Irish coercion in the later 1880s equally appeal to the values associated with humanity. Gladstone's last public speech, at Liverpool in 1896 recommending British intervention to defend the Armenians against the Turks, disavowed any motive of denouncing Muslim rulers in the interest of Christian subjects. 'The ground on which we stand here', he declared, '. . . is human. Nothing narrower than humanity could pretend for a moment justly to represent it' (*The Times*, 25 September 1896, p. 5). The cluster of ideas surrounding the assertion of the dignity of the human being was near the kernel of the political message that Gladstone delivered. That is certainly not to propose that freedom or nationality was less important in the Gladstonian scheme of things, but it is to suggest that humanity was a third member of the statesman's triad of supreme values. No doubt it owed its place partly to Gladstone's acute sensitivity to human suffering and his equal awareness of what the Liberal press would applaud; and it definitely had some of its roots in his theological development. But it was also indebted for its content to his changing appreciation of Homer.

The legacy of Gladstonian humanitarianism has been immense. The same values that animated his version of Liberalism were transmitted, though with less stress on the implications of liberty for restricting the role of the state, to the next generation of Liberal theorists and to the Labour party. It is easy to see how humane concern for the welfare of one's fellow beings could ease the transition to greater collectivism. Furthermore, Gladstone's vision of a concert of powers enforcing standards of humanity against oppressors did not expire at his death. On the contrary one of the Americans at whom his article of 1887 was directed, Woodrow Wilson, who as a young man looked to Gladstone as his hero (Baker 1928–39: 1. 87), was to make this internationalism the foundation of his idea for the League of Nations. The global police actions of its successor body, the United Nations, in the early twenty-first century owed a little of their ultimate inspiration to the ideals that Gladstone expounded in the later Victorian years. Those, in turn, were conditioned in part by the statesman's idiosyncratic celebration of the human element in the Olympian pantheon. Gladstone may have read his politics into the exploration of Homeric constitutional arrangements, but there was also a reverse flow of influence from the study of the ancient world to modern public affairs. Gladstone's political thinking was not immune to reflection on classical themes. His early Conservatism, together with his enduring technique of concession, was formulated in Aristotelian terms. Perhaps more surprisingly, his mature Liberalism was affected by his classical scholarship. The humanitarianism of late Victorian Liberal policies owed something to the values of Homer's Greece. Gladstone's politics were inevitably coloured by antiquity because they were shaped in the matrix of a mind steeped in classical learning.

FURTHER READING

The place of Gladstone in classical scholarship is evaluated by Lloyd-Jones 1975. Turner 1981 discusses the impact on Gladstone's Homeric scholarship of his changing political stance. For an overall discussion of Gladstone's scholarly endeavours see Ramm 1989–90: 1–29, and for a consideration of the impact of Aristotle on his thought see Ramm 1985: 327–40. Bebbington 2005 contains a developed version of the argument of the present chapter. The debate between Grote and Gladstone on Homeric Greece is analyzed in Bebbington 1998. Clarke 1945, Ogilvie 1964 and Jenkyns 1980 provide the wider context.

CHAPTER EIGHT

Between Colonialism and Independence: Eric Williams and the Uses of Classics in Trinidad in the 1950s and 1960s

Emily Greenwood

Reading will give you some of the confidence that is so badly needed in the society dominated by this powerful sense of inferiority. You are small and impotent and the countries you come from and go to are not particularly influential in world affairs, but there is nothing in the world to stop you from cultivating and developing independent minds.

> Extract from an address by Eric Williams to the
> graduating class at the University of the West Indies,
> Mona, Jamaica, 16 February 1963 (Williams 1981: 255)

The career of the politician-historian Eric Williams offers a dynamic example of the shifting uses to which Classics could be put in colonial and postcolonial Trinidad. This chapter presents a study of Williams's strategic use of Classics during his rise to political prominence in the 1950s. I begin by putting Williams's classical education in context by describing the civilizational authority that Classics commanded in the education system in the British colonies in the Caribbean. I then examine an episode called the 'Aristotle debate', which took place in the Port of Spain public library in November 1954 and pitted Williams's interpretation of Aristotle against that of Dom Basil Matthews. Williams claimed an affiliation between his popular education movement and the climate of political debate in classical Athens. Accordingly, in my analysis of the 'Aristotle debate' I suggest analogies between Williams's demagogic rhetoric and the strategies employed by politicians under Athenian democracy. Athenian politicians sought to strike a balance between the elite learning that qualified them to offer expertise in instructing the citizen body, and popular, democratic personae. In Williams's case his varying use of Classics is symptomatic of a broader tension in his career between the erudition that first brought him to prominence on the political stage and the folk credentials that he tried to cultivate in order to ensure his popular appeal. The politics of the emerging nation were such that the conspicuous use of Classics, which played an important part in launching Williams's political career, fell away sharply in the decades after independence.

Eric Williams was an academic by training – an acclaimed historian of the trans-Atlantic slave trade – who co-founded the PNM (the People's National Movement) in 1956, and subsequently became the first Prime Minister of the independent nation of Trinidad (an office he held from 1962 to 1981). What is more, as one who campaigned for independence from colonial rule, and who wrote about the experiences of domination and independence, Williams's writings provide a salutary commentary on postcolonialism that is unburdened by the regime of postcolonial theory. Trinidad and Tobago did not gain full independence until 31 August 1962, but prior to this Eric Williams used his public speeches to argue that the culture and society of colonialism was defunct and that it was time to move beyond colonialism – most famously in the speech 'Massa Day Done', which was delivered as a public lecture in Woodford Square, Port of Spain, on 22 March 1961. As an economic historian, Williams was acutely aware that colonialism could persist under different guises, and was familiar with the theory of neo-colonial economic imperialism whereby former colonies risked becoming dependent upon the economies of Europe and North America, swapping the culture of exploitation that had existed in the Caribbean under the plantation economies for a new form of economic servitude (Nkrumah 1965). Indeed, Williams had already reached his own conclusions about capitalism as a mode of imperial domination in his 1944 work *Capitalism and Slavery*. However, he distinguished between the threat of neo-colonialism and global capitalism, on the one hand, and an independent mentality on the other – what we might call a postcolonial ideology. It is no accident that, in his address to the graduating class of the University of the West Indies in 1963 quoted at the beginning of this essay, Williams tells his audience that 'there is nothing in the world to stop you from cultivating and developing independent minds'. While he struggled with the politics of economic development and agricultural cultivation in the Caribbean, he promoted the feasibility of independence and development in the intellectual sphere.

However, as Williams's shifting use of Classics on the political stage illustrates, the supposedly autonomous sphere of education was itself subject to colonial and postcolonial politics. In the period leading up to independence Williams used his mastery of the classics to challenge the mastery of British colonial rule, and held up Periclean Athens as a model for democratic self-government in Trinidad (Williams does not address the problematic issue of Athens' own empire). During this phase of Williams's thought there was a very strong equation between the cultivation of a liberal education, grounded in a knowledge of 'world civilization' reaching back to the ancient Greeks, and the attainment of political independence. However, the political agenda driving this educational programme imposed its own constraints. This was a demagogic style of education with a particular end in mind. In the period after independence Williams fluctuated between continuing to advocate a liberal education and independent thinking, and, conversely, evoking the 'national needs' of Trinidad and Tobago to argue against a predominantly literary education in a predominantly agricultural society. Whereas prior to independence Williams had recourse to analogies with ancient Greece, classical allusions are largely jettisoned after independence. This shift in Williams's use of Classics is part of a larger shift in his thought. In his study of the development of Williams's political historiography, Anthony Maingot identifies several conflicting Williamses corresponding to the different roles that he fulfilled, which ranged from scholar, academic, international civil servant (under the auspices of the Caribbean Commission), and politician to Prime Minister (Maingot 1992: 165–9, 'Williams Versus Williams').

Classics as the Height of Foolishness

In order to appreciate the cultural and political significance of Williams's use of Classics, it is necessary to understand the status of Classics in the educational curriculum in the British Caribbean colonies in the decades prior to independence. In British Caribbean colonies in the 1950s, there was a tight equation between education and social mobility. Both fictional and historical works relating to this period reveal the paradox that, although education could change one's situation in life, it was so closely associated with social status that for many people it was considered foolish to aspire to an education at odds with one's position in society. This attitude had its origins in the society of the plantocracy where the education of slaves and, subsequently, indentured labourers was held to be counterproductive. In his historical and political works, Eric Williams describes the legacy of the plantation economy – and indeed the slave economy – in terms of a society that does not have the leisure for the arts or intellectual pursuits for their own sake (Williams 1964: 212–14, 247).

In the memoirs of his school days in Barbados at the intermediate school Combemere in the 1940s, the Bajan (Barbadian creole) author, journalist and some-time politician Austin Clarke describes the awe and alienation that greeted young black boys who broke established patterns by excelling in their studies. For the lower socio-economic classes Latin was generally considered off limits, and amongst the other classes it was regarded instrumentally, as the key to professions such as medicine, or law. Competence in abstruse academic subjects is referred to, paradoxically, in terms of 'folly'. Clarke frequently uses the expressions 'Latin fool', 'French fool', and 'Mathematics fool' (Clarke 2003 [1980]: 66). The popular prejudice that education for its own sake is perverse recurs throughout the literature of the Anglophone Caribbean (fictional and historical), either published in or relating to this period.

The phrase 'sociology of knowledge' needs to be applied literally in this context; one cannot understand the significance of a classical education in Trinidad in the decade leading up to independence, without understanding the role of education in social mobility in islands such as Barbados, Trinidad, Jamaica, and St Lucia. This social hierarchy was reflected in a hierarchy of subjects with the most 'useless' subjects being the most elitist. Needless to say, in the period leading up to independence,

Classics was at the top of this educational hierarchy. In most schools Classics meant Latin, but in a few schools – most notably Harrison College in Barbados (see below) and Queen's Royal College in Trinidad – Greek was also on the curriculum.

Austin Clarke recalls a conversation with one of his classmates about the lethal academic environment of Harrison College, the foremost secondary school in Barbados, if not the entire Anglophone Caribbean:

> I hear that there's a lotta fellows going to Harrison College who does go mad, because of the amount of work they have to study. I hear that for one night of homework they set a hundred lines o' Latin, a hundred lines o' Greek, five chapters o' Ancient History, five chapters o' Greek history, a distinction Latin prose, a distinction Greek prose, a pass Latin prose, and a pass Greek prose, plus Unseens, plus Shakespeare, Milton, Chaucer, Ben Johnson.
>
> (Clarke 2003 [1980]: 178)

The intellectual stature of the school is quantified by the amount of Latin and Greek that the students have to study, with Chaucer, Milton and the Elizabethan dramatists tacked on for good measure. This passage epitomizes the familiar image of the collegiate schools in the English colonies in the Caribbean, founded with the express purpose of providing a 'classical education' to colonials. In Barbados this school was Harrison College, while in Trinidad it was the Queen's Royal College, inaugurated in 1859 (on the colonial philosophy behind the founding of this school, see Williams 1964: 202–3). Clarke himself was to enter the sixth form of Harrison College in 1950. The quantification of the sheer amount of Latin and Greek that pupils had to study at Harrison College illustrates the stamina that pupils in the colonies had for learning Latin and Greek, in competition with the students at the famed public schools in the mother colony (James 1994: 24–8; Williams 1969: 23; and Walcott in Rowell 1996: 125–6). Whereas English literature could always be claimed by the colonizing powers, Greek and Latin were as much the property of pupils in the Caribbean as they were of pupils in Britain and represented a greater degree of cultural exclusivity. It is in this context that we should make sense of C.L.R. James's recollection that the first Bajan Prime Minister, Grantley Adams, claimed that his Greek was as good as his English by the time he left Harrison College (James 1996: 164). For these authors who were schooled in the classics, the traditions of ancient Greece, Rome and Egypt represented parallel cultures with claims to antiquity and civilization that surpassed those of the colonial metropolis.

Another dimension of the focus on Latin in Austin Clarke's memoirs of his school days is what may be termed the creolization of Classics, whereby the ancient Romans are translated into the Caribbean and given Caribbean identities. The play of affiliation involved is complicated and not always consistent. For example, in the following passage the Romans – as Italians – become co-opted into Caribbean male culture through their love of wine and drink.

> We didn't know at first that Mussolini was an Italian, a Roman. All the Italians we knew were in books, dead; speaking a dead language; and wearing togas, and eating while lying on their sides: grapes from a bunch and wine from an urn.

> We in Barbados loved rum. We loved the Italians (and hated Mussolini) because they were like us, like the men in our village who loved rum and women more than work. And the Romans, like our own men, talked and sang hymns ancient and modern all drunklong.
>
> (Clarke 2003 [1980]: 46)

And yet, the reader is also informed that Clarke and his peers championed Hannibal – Rome's Carthaginian enemy – as a 'black' hero:

> Hannibal, whom we loved (and no one told us he was black like us!) climbed mountains and was smart. Alas, he lost one eye: *in occulo altero* [sic]. But he had crossed the Alps, one of the highest mountain ranges in the whole whirl! We loved Hannibal.
>
> (p. 46)

It is surely significant that the European cultural affiliation being claimed via the Italians bypasses the British colonial power under which this schooling took place. Clarke's nostalgic account glosses over the latent contradictions in these associations. We may wonder, for example, how the affiliation for the 'black' Hannibal sits alongside love of the Romans, or quite how the blurring of modern-day Italians with ancient Romans is supposed to work. The first we might attribute to the Eurafrican double consciousness that is a legacy of colonialism in the Caribbean, and the second as a subversive reflection of the ahistorical appropriations practised by European colonial regimes in claiming continuity between the civilizations of ancient Greece and Rome and their own civilizational authority (see Stam and Shohat 2005: 297). The main point is the way in which Clarke and his Bajan contemporaries reinterpreted the cultural presuppositions that were latent in their colonial education.

Clarke's emphasis on his classical education belongs to a tradition among the Caribbean intelligentsia of this period of rooting one's intellectual credentials in the Classics. Eric Williams also wrote about his classical education in his autobiography (for comment see Greenwood 2005: 65–7). Not only does Williams politicize the Classics in his account, but he also represents his achievements as a classicist as a political qualification. This notion of a classical education as a political qualification is exemplified by the so-called 'Aristotle debate' – an episode that commentators widely regard as the making of Williams's political career (Cudjoe 1993: 49; Oxaal 1968: 104; Rohlehr 1997: 851).

The Aristotle Debate

For two weeks in November 1954, a debate about the interpretation of Aristotle's political and ethical philosophy gripped Port of Spain, the capital of Trinidad and Tobago. That year, Eric Williams had embarked upon a demagogic campaign to educate the Trinidadian masses in politics and Caribbean nationalism, with a view to political independence. To this end he set up an adult education programme in September 1954, under the auspices of the People's Education Movement (PEM). This educational programme consisted of a series of lectures centred on the Trinidad

Public Library in Port of Spain, but also touring other venues in Trinidad. On 8 September 1954, for example, Williams had lectured on 'The Educational Problems of the Caribbean in Historical Perspective', and on 10 September, he addressed the question 'Is there a Caribbean Literature?' (for a summary of the adult education programme, see Williams 1969: 113–15). On 4 November, Williams selected the theme of 'Some world famous Educational Theories and Developments relevant to West Indian Conditions.' During the course of this lecture, he quoted from Aristotle's *Politics* to support his thesis that state control of education was desirable.

At question time, the Rev. Dom Basil Matthews, a black Trinidadian Benedictine monk with a Ph.D. in theology from Fordham, rose to challenge Williams's citation of Aristotle in support of his argument for secular education. Matthews followed this up by giving his own lecture in the public library on Tuesday 9 November on 'Aristotle, Education and State Control' in an attempt to refute Williams's interpretation of Aristotle. This was followed, in turn, by a lecture from Williams on 17 November on 'Some Misconceptions of Aristotle's Philosophy of Education'. This debate, con- ducted through public lectures, was covered in the *Trinidad Guardian*, which, in addition to providing editorial commentary on the debate, also quoted at length from both Williams's and Matthews's lectures. To my knowledge, complete texts of the lectures that Williams and Matthews gave do not exist; consequently I have relied on the excerpts published in the *Trinidad Guardian*. An important proviso is that the excerpts, divorced from the full texts of the lectures, not to mention the ori- ginal contexts for performance, may misrepresent the arguments of the speakers. However, this reliance on journalistic coverage is not entirely distorting, since the newspaper itself played a role in the debate. For instance, in his lecture of 17 November, Williams supplemented his recollection of Matthews' speech of 9 November with excerpts from the speech as published in the *Trinidad Guardian*.

As Gordon Rohlehr has remarked, 'the Williams/Matthews debate was a piece of intellectual stick fighting that was totally irrelevant to the concrete issues of Trinidad and Tobago' (Rohlehr 1997: 851). However, he concedes that the debate was cent- ral in establishing Williams's intellectual charisma – a commodity that was extremely important in Trinidadian politics. The way in which Williams and Matthews wielded Aristotle in this debate gives a good insight into the politics of using Classics dur- ing this transitional period between colonialism and independence.

On Thursday 11 November 1954 the *Trinidad Guardian* carried an article on 'Religion the Essence of Civilized Living', in which the editor summarized Matthews' argument that Aristotle's stress on the ethical aims of education is fully compatible with religion in education (p. 12). Judging from the published excerpts, Matthews' interpretation of Aristotle's views on the role of ethics in education involved a close reading of passages from the *Politics*, with the proviso that he placed a strong Christianizing spin on Aristotle's text, claiming that Aristotle's arguments for ethics in education 'support' Christianity's claim for religion in education (*Trinidad Guardian*, Thursday 11 November 1954: 12).

On 18 November, the *Trinidad Guardian* covered Williams's rejoinder to Matthews in his lecture on the previous day, under the headline ' "Dom Basil Concealed Slavery in Aristotle's Ideal State": Dr William replies to Monk's Eulogy.'

> Dom Basil's enthusiasm for Aristotle's ideal state was said by Dr. Eric Williams last night to conceal 'slavery, the exclusion of workers from citizenship, the subordination of women and imperialism'. But, Dr. Williams added later, 'he can't smack his lips at the thought of his ideal omelette and then say he doesn't want, however, the ideal eggs of which it is made'.
>
> (*Trinidad Guardian*, Thursday 18 November 1954: 10)

Williams's tactic was to turn this debate about education into a debate about slavery. Aristotle's theory of natural slavery in Book one of the *Politics* is undeniably relevant to a history of the arguments for and against the slave trade in modern history and, correspondingly, would have been an emotive, indeed explosive, issue in Trinidadian society in 1954 – where slavery was, and is to this day, a 'live' issue. But it was disingenuous of Williams to turn a debate about secular versus religious education into a debate about slavery. Furthermore, it was sophistic of Williams to argue that, in citing Aristotle as an authority, Matthews was endorsing slavery implicitly. When tackled on his omission of Aristotle's ideas about slavery, Matthews seems to have played into Williams's hands:

> 'Dom Basil in his lecture,' said Dr. Williams, 'said not so much as a whisper of the slave basis of Aristotle's state. I had to drag it out of him with a question. What was his reply? Listen to it as given in the *Trinidad Guardian*: "slavery was sometimes necessary to the common good but that you could enslave men's bodies but not their minds." So slavery was sometimes necessary to the common good!'
>
> 'Necessary for whom?' Dr Williams asked. 'And what was the definition of the common good? The moral and religious excellence of the life of the Greek citizen which Dom Basil so extols is nothing more than the life of the slaveowner. If Dom Basil is so enthusiastic about Aristotle's ideal state which is based on slavery, then I must ask Dom Basil whether he opposes the abolition of slavery.'
>
> (*Trinidad Guardian*, Thursday 18 November 1954: 10)

Dom Basil Matthews' (alleged) argument at this point, that 'slavery was sometimes necessary for the common good' perhaps needs to be seen in the context of the quietist Christian theological tradition which played down the appalling institution of physical slavery by applying the metaphor of enslavement to sinful human existence to argue that all men are slaves (see the texts and discussion in Garnsey 1996: 157–235). Williams's rhetorical opportunism in the above passage is evident if we read Williams against himself. In his famous 'Massa Day Done' speech, delivered in 1961, he places a different gloss on the same material. In the present speech he dismisses 'the moral and religious excellence of the life of the Greek citizen' as 'nothing more than the life of the slaveowner'. Conversely, in the later speech Williams claims that 'Ancient Greek society, precisely because of slavery, has been able to achieve intellectual heights that so far have had no parallel in human history' (Williams 1997: 728). Granted, in the latter speech Williams plays up the cultural achievements of the slave society of ancient Greece in order to ridicule the cultural impoverishment of the Caribbean plantation societies. Nonetheless, this inconsistency is a good example of Williams's versatility and sophistry in spinning the same material in different ways to meet the needs of the rhetorical occasion.

Williams's rhetorical strategy is reminiscent of the demagogic style of oratory in Athens in the fifth and fourth century BC. Think, for example, of Demosthenes in speech 19 (*On the False Embassy*) attempting to turn the jury against Aeschines by pointing out that Aeschines quoted from tragedies in which he had never acted and was thus showing off about his extensive knowledge of literature. Williams's tactic of calling attention to Matthews' failure to mention Aristotle's theory of slavery parallels Demosthenes' tactic of pointing out that Aeschines overlooked the 'ship of state' passage in Sophocles' *Antigone* (lines 179–210) – a play in which Aeschines had acted – failing to grasp its democratic message (Demosthenes *On the False Embassy* 245–50). Williams was to replay this strategy in later speeches, expressing contempt for opposition politicians in the Democratic Labour Party whom he accused of taking quotations from books in order to appear intelligent, but taking their quotations out of context and thereby exposing their ignorance (see Cudjoe 1997: 759–60).

Throughout the Aristotle debate Williams plays the role of the populist demagogue who alerts the Trinidadian *demos* to the elitist, pro-racist, and pro-imperialist strain in Dom Basil Matthews' arguments. At the same time, Williams styles Matthews as an academic who tries to obfuscate the truth with scholarly quotations from professors:

> 'Dom Basil in one of his numerous quotations from professor this, professor that, and professor the other, says that Aristotle would have but scant sympathy with any scheme of education that laid the emphasis on technical and utilitarian training . . .
>
> 'I am not going to allow Dom Basil any longer to hide his light under the bushel of odd quotations from stray professors . . .' Then he addressed the question to the parents in the audience. 'Would you be willing to pay the price of slavery, subordination of women, contempt for work in order that your sons should become what Aristotle calls a great-minded man, and *what we would today call a dilettante and a snob?*'
> (my italics)

Williams, like Matthews, commanded authority by virtue of his doctorate: in the *Trinidad Guardian* he is invariably referred to as 'Dr. Williams' (Williams had gained his D.Phil. from Oxford for the doctoral dissertation 'The Economic Aspect of the Abolition of the West Indian Slave Trade and Slavery', later revised for publication as *Capitalism and Slavery*, 1944). And yet here Williams uses Matthews' elite education as a weapon against him – to throw doubt on his democratic and patriotic credentials. Williams deliberately eschews an academic approach to Aristotle, plays down his own elite education to side with the audience ('what *we* would today call . . .'), and encourages the audience to think of themselves as competent judges of these questions.

> Ladies and gentlemen, it has been my privilege this evening to teach you more Aristotle than is known by many learned people with university degrees. You are in a position now to judge for yourselves how profound is the gulf separating Dom Basil and myself on this question, and how very closely related to your own problems of today is the Aristotelian philosophy handed down to us 2,300 years ago . . .

> Have not Dom Basil and I moreover been the humble instrument for bringing out
> the very best in the Trinidad community and positive evidence of the emergence of an
> active and enlightened democracy in Trinidad? Neither Dom Basil or I will win this
> battle. The victors are you, the people of Trinidad and Tobago.
>
> (*Trinidad Guardian*, Saturday 20 November 1954: 10)

The strategy of instructing the audience and then praising their knowledge, which
they have as a result of the speaker's instruction, is also a classic Demosthenic
tactic (see Demosthenes 18.88). The idea that rhetorical instruction was a crucial
propaideutic for political debate was fundamental to Athenian political oratory (see,
for example, the statement of this idea in Pericles' funeral oration – Thucydides *History*
2.40.2). Williams turned this didactic motif in democratic oratory into a reality by
instituting a public education programme to educate the masses in politics.

Democracy and Elitist Knowledge

The Athenian democracy of the fifth and fourth centuries was committed to the
sovereignty of the citizen body en masse (*dêmos*). As various scholars have noted,
the nature of this political system meant that, in practice, political rhetoric was acutely
audience centred (see, in particular, Ober 1989, passim and Yunis 1998, especially
239–34). Williams's references to Athenian democracy are subject to similar constraints insofar as he was presenting his arguments to mass audiences. Examination
of his political rhetoric reveals similar techniques to those used by Athenian politicians in order to co-opt their audiences into the privileged knowledge that qualified them to speak in the first place. At the same time, the context for speaking
demanded an air of studied amateurism – of not knowing anything that the audience could not know in principle. The irony in Williams's case is that his use of
Classics would eventually become a victim of the need to use accessible, popularist
rhetoric in order to succeed as a politician.

Writing in his autobiography, Williams makes the intellectual calibre of his public
lectures a point of pride:

> Particularly in my lectures at the University of Woodford Square, I made it a point not
> to talk down to the people. It was straight university stuff, in content and in form as
> well as in manner, designed to place the problems of Trinidad and Tobago in interna-
> tional perspective.
>
> (Williams 1969: 149)

However, this was not exactly 'straight university stuff'; in the Aristotle debate Williams
omitted dissent between scholars, and pursued an argument that was politically expedient, whereas Matthews' lectures included copious references to scholarly discussions. Williams deliberately cultivated this anti-academic style in order to ingratiate
his historical works with popular audiences and readership. This trend increased as
Williams made the shift from historian trying his hand at politics to the politician
putting his hand to history. Anthony Maingot notes that Williams's 1970 study *From*

Columbus to Castro: The History of the Caribbean 1492–1969 does not contain any footnotes or source citations for the data that he cites (Maingot 1992: 155; see p. 151 of the same work where Maingot cites Williams's admission that he set about popularizing his history of the Caribbean – Williams 1969: 109). In an article entitled 'Trinidad and the Revolution in Intelligence', originally published in the *PNM Weekly* on 30 August 30, the Bajan novelist George Lamming identified Eric Williams's flair for public lecturing as the ability to turn history into news, and to give it the character of street-corner gossip (Lamming 1993: 322). In the same vein, writing about Williams's 'Massa Day Done' speech, Selwyn Cudjoe comments that Williams had finally 'liberated himself from the psychological constraints of his formal academic training' (Cudjoe 1997: 760).

On the back of the lectures in the Public Library Williams established an independent political voice. When he left the Caribbean Commission (an Anglo-American institution that was set up to conduct research on the Caribbean) in June 1955, he announced his plan to form a political party by giving a lecture in Woodford Square – an open square in the Port of Spain – to an estimated audience of 10,000 people. This square became the venue for frequent lectures/political speeches, and Williams referred to this square as the 'University of Woodford Square', drawing parallels between this open-air auditorium and ancient Athenian institutions in which the *dêmos* was schooled in the ways of politics:

> The University of Woodford Square has for the past 12 years been a centre of free university education for the masses, of political analysis and of training in self-government for parallels of which we must go back to the city state of ancient Athens. The lectures have been university dishes served with political sauce.
>
> (Williams 1969: 133)

Williams's account of the University of Woodford Square is self-aggrandizing and the analogies with ancient Athens are loose. However, in this Williams was closer to the politician-historians of ancient Athens than he may have intended. Surviving Athenian political oratory is also self-aggrandizing. For all that the intelligence and power of the demos as audience is extolled, the leading role goes to the oratory of Demosthenes, Aeschines, Lycurgus, or Pericles (the last in Thucydides' account). The looseness with historical detail is also a feature of Athenian political oratory, where differing spin can be put on identical data and historical *exempla* depending on the needs of the occasion.

These traits are illustrated in the passage in *The History of the People of Trinidad and Tobago* in which Williams highlights the role of the University of Woodford Square in educating the masses for government:

> The political education dispensed to the population in these centres of political learning was of a high order and concentrated from the outset on placing Trinidad and Tobago within the current of the great international movements for democracy and self-government. The electorate of the country was able to see and understand its problems in the context of the ancient Athenian democracy or the federal systems of the United States and Switzerland, in the context of the great anti-colonial movements of Nehru

and Nkrumah, and in the context of the long and depressing history of colonialism in Trinidad and Tobago and the West Indies.

(Williams 1964: 243)

This education in self-government seems to have specialized in movable, changeable analogies, which had the effect of collapsing the historical, cultural and social differences between different democratic forms of government, and blurring democratic ideology with anti-imperialism and anti-colonialism. This can be attributed to the populist tenor of the lectures and the target audience, and yet Williams has another 'audience' in mind when he writes up the reputation of the University of Woodford Square. Namely, he has in mind the outside reader who will be impressed at the 'formal' arrangements for the Higher Education of the Trinidad people. The 'constituent colleges' that Williams refers to earlier in the same passage were actually district libraries, or public spaces at which intellectuals from the PNM might address local audiences when they did their peripatetic lecture tours.

Speaking on 'Party Politics' in Woodford Square on 13 September 1955, Williams ended his lecture with a quotation from Pericles' funeral oration (Thucydides *History* 2.35–46), promising that the People's Education Movement would hold up to the electorate 'the ideal of the ancient democracy of Athens'. After recounting the occasion of this lecture in his autobiography, Williams recalls that when Harold Macmillan visited Trinidad and heard about the institution of the 'University of Woodford Square', he described Trinidad and Tobago as 'the Athens of the Caribbean' (Williams 1969: 135–6). However, there are deep tensions underlying Williams's use of the analogy with Athenian democracy. Like the Athenian politicians referred to above, Williams's political rhetoric is largely audience-centred, and shifts depending on the audience being addressed. The mass Trinidadian audiences attending his public lectures at the University of Woodford Square were encouraged to think of themselves as qualified judges of any argument, and to participate in the egalitarian society that was being held out to them.

In the context of the 'Aristotle debate', Williams flattered his audience – and himself, in so far as he claimed to have taught them – with the claim that having listened to the debate, they knew more than 'many learned people with university degrees'. However, once this 'revolution in intelligence' – to use George Lamming's phrase – had served its purpose, and Trinidad had achieved independence, Williams offered a more pessimistic analysis of the reality of democracy in Trinidad and Tobago. Addressing the Library Association of Trinidad and Tobago on 5 March 1966, Williams took issue with a society in which professional expertise and specialization were undermined by the prevailing ideology 'that one person is as good as another to do a particular job that requires a particular competence' (Williams 1981: 257–8). And yet, by his own account, Williams himself had instilled in his audiences the belief – enshrined in Athenian democratic ideology – that the ordinary citizen, by virtue of his (and her, in Trinidad) political education, was qualified to play any role in society. Williams's political rhetoric was heavily propagandistic, offering his audience opinions on subjects of concern to their society under the guise of 'education', but without giving them the critical perspective to evaluate his speeches independently, or to think for themselves. This mode of oratory is not so far away from the sketch of Pericles at 2.65.8 of Thucydides' *History*, where Thucydides comments that Pericles 'held the mass in check in independent fashion' (*kateiche to plêthos eleutherôs*). Thucydides' Greek is ambiguous: the statement can be given both a pro-democratic spin and an anti-democratic spin. I interpret this statement anti-democratically, to mean that Pericles showed independence (independent thinking) in his dealings with the Athenian people while their democratic 'freedom' was subtly constrained by his rhetorical hold over them. This interpretation fits Eric Williams's brand of populist oratory well: the outcome may have been political independence for Williams's Trinidadian audiences, but his speeches did not allow them much independent thought.

However, the intellectual condescension in Williams's speeches was counterbalanced by the popular flavour of his rhetoric, which was shaped in part by the audiences that Williams addressed. As with Athenian political rhetoric in the era of democracy, there was an implicit contract between speaker and audience, which established the broad terms of cultural reference and socio-political ideology for the speaker. Eric Williams spoke as one of the most educated men in Trinidad to audiences that included men and women with only the rudiments of education. Consequently, he had to develop an appropriate rhetoric and to attune his educated prose to the language of his audience. It would be interesting to examine the alternation of pronouns in Williams's speeches, along the lines of the analysis that has been done for Demosthenes' speeches, studying his subtle modulations between the pronouns 'I', 'we' and 'you' as he speaks *to* the people, *with* the people and *about* the people (Sinclair 1988: 123). Conversely, reading back from Williams to Demosthenes and other Athenian orators of the fourth century BCE can offer a fresh perspective on the long-standing debate about how democratic political oratory in ancient Athens really was.

When Williams does philosophy with the masses in the context of the 'Aristotle debate', one is reminded of the boast in Pericles' funeral oration that the Athenians 'love knowledge' without it making them soft (Thucydides *History* 2.40.1): 'We love what is beautiful without giving way to extravagance; and we love knowledge without it making us soft.' This qualification is a nod to the popular prejudice – familiar from Aristophanes' comedies and Plato's dialogues – that philosophers were soft and weak creatures who spent their time indoors abstaining from outdoor work and exercise. When Pericles tells his audience that 'we love knowledge', he pre-empts this prejudice and co-opts his mixed audience into a single, shared identity that is at some remove from the reality of the different groups and cultures within the Athenian citizen body (see the excellent discussion in Wohl 2002: 43–7). As Nicole Loraux has convincingly demonstrated, the genre of the funeral oration is an ideological hybrid that sustains parallel elite and democratic discourses, addressing a divided audience as though it was one, yet containing traces of the different interests and affiliations of the audience members (Loraux 1986: 184 and ch. 4 more generally).

Although Williams evokes the spirit of Athenian democracy, the loose way in which he does so suggests an opportunistic use of democratic *topoi* (commonplaces), that were already *topoi* when used by orators such as Cleon and Nicias in the late fifth century BCE (as reported in Thucydides' *History*), or by Demosthenes, Aeschines and

Lycurgus in the 340s and 330s BCE. Concentrating on the rhetorical commonplace 'as you all know', Jon Hesk has explained the importance of these *topoi* in democratic rhetoric as 'the means by which mass and elite colluded in dramatic fictions' (2000: 227, see further 227–31). Williams deploys similar *topoi*, but the additional irony is that in citing ancient Greek orators and philosophers he is playing the elite card. To offset this elitism he interprets these authors in a popularist, post-slavery, and anti-colonial light. Furthermore, he makes a show of elite education, but purports to share this education with the audience at the same time. Williams's performance in this debate, and his adoption of the slogan of the 'Athens of the Caribbean' provides an excellent example of how audiences (ancient and modern) shape 'democratic' political rhetoric. Although Williams's position was undeniably elitist, the rhetoric is populist – a tension which haunts political rhetoric in democratic societies.

This popular character is further evident when we consider the social and cultural idioms that inform Williams's speeches. In the case of Williams the linguistic exuberance of his rhetoric certainly owed much to local Trinidadian culture. Selwyn Cudjoe and Gordon Rohlehr have both written excellent studies of the performance context for Williams's speeches in terms of Trinidadian oral culture and the audience expectations reflected in and manipulated by Calypso (Cudjoe 1993: 36–100; Cudjoe 1997; Rohlehr 1997). Rohlehr has analyzed Williams's rhetorical prowess in terms of the role of the folk hero-intellectual who blends erudition with popular culture (Rohlehr 1997, especially 852–3). Williams's political rhetoric was influenced by its local cultural context: most notably the 'lime' (a social mode of persuasive argumentation that places emphasis on body language), the give and take of 'picong' (a mode of playful criticism, which ranges from friendly teasing to sharper invective), and the cultures of Calypso and carnival (Cudjoe 1993: 41, 46, 75, 100; on Calypso furnishing the performance context for Williams's political rhetoric, see Rohlehr 1997: passim).

Although the debate on Aristotle may have gone over the heads of many of the members of the audience in the Trinidad Public Library, the learned idiom would not have been foreign to the audience. Trinidad in the 1950s was a society that prized educated language and rhetorical finesse (see Cudjoe 1997: 755–7 on the premium placed on 'speaking properly'). To construct another analogy with Athenian democracy, Williams's popular audiences liked their politicians to tell them something they didn't know whilst flattering them with the assumption that they were intelligent enough to take it all in and to evaluate what they heard. Josiah Ober has suggested that Athenian audiences willingly suspended incomprehension in listening to speeches that went over their heads in order to 'smooth over ideological dissonance' and latent inequalities of birth, wealth, and education between speaker and audience (Ober 1989: 190). We can compare the image of Athenian audiences offered by the Athenian politician Cleon in the Mytilene debate (as narrated in Thucydides' *History*, 3.38.6–7): according to Cleon, Athenians were highly self-conscious about their own intelligence and rhetorical powers and were obsessed with being seen to keep up with speeches. The analogies between Williams's political rhetoric and Athenian democratic rhetoric work both ways; reading Williams reveals the need for further research into the different types of rhetorical give-and-take (including flyting and signifying) in surviving examples of Athenian oratory, in order to get a better measure of how the speeches relate to the broader speech culture in which they were delivered.

Conclusion

Eric Williams modelled aspects of his political rhetoric on his understanding of Athenian democracy, but he also drew inspiration from Trinidadian culture and local institutions. In the period after independence, Williams largely abandoned his citation of ancient Greek authors and analogies with ancient Athenian democracy, presumably in response to the prevailing politics in the post-colony. However, some of his post-independence speeches contain wistful references to 'what happened to the ancient Greeks and how that relates to modern Trinidad and Tobago', and how such dry-as-dust subjects are integral to a 'liberal education' (Williams 1981: 262). It is one of the ironies of Eric Williams's career that his elitist colonial education at Queen's Royal College, and subsequently at Oxford, led him to distinctly postcolonial conclusions. However, Williams's postcolonial ideology played a decisive role in bringing into existence a postcolonial society in which the kind of 'liberal' education that he had received under the colonial era was constrained by both the economic needs and the political climate of the post-colony.

Studying Classics in postcolonial worlds should involve more than studying how Classics has 'influenced' intellectual traditions in post-colonies and how, in turn, these intellectual traditions have appropriated Classics (see Goff's introduction: 2005: especially 5–12). There is also a need to pay attention to the phenomenon of 'the empire writing back' and giving its interpretation of world history. Many of the paradigms for understanding Athenian democracy have been developed with reference to European and North American models of democracy. Hence Athenian democracy is compared and contrasted with a restricted model of what democracy looks like in the modern world. Eric Williams's experiments with direct democracy in Trinidad in the 1950s (ironically under the mantle of colonial rule) provide fruitful comparative material for re-examining the give-and-take between politicians and their audiences in ancient Athenian political rhetoric.

FURTHER READING

For an introduction to Williams's life and works, the reader should start with Williams's autobiography (Williams 1969). Early critical comment can be found in the appraisals by C.L.R. James (1993) and George Lamming (1993). For more recent criticism and analysis of Williams's political oratory in the context of Trinidadian culture and society, see the excellent studies by Selwyn Cudjoe (1993: 36–110, and 1997) and Gordon Rohlehr (1997). A general critique of Trinidadian society in this period, as a society in transition between colonialism and independence, can be found in the jaundiced travel account by the Indo-Trinidadian author V.S. Naipaul (2001: 33–82; originally 1962). Naipaul's account was prompted and sponsored by Eric Williams.

Michael Dash has explored the trope of turning to the ancient Mediterranean in Caribbean fiction in the chapter 'A New World Mediterranean: The Novel and Knowledge' (Dash 1998: 82–106). Greenwood 2005 offers a broad introduction to different uses of classics in Caribbean literature in the twentieth century; while Greenwood 2004 offers a case study involving the politics of the use of classics in pre-independence St Lucia, which offers fruitful comparative material for the current chapter.

CHAPTER NINE

Virgilian Contexts

Stephen Harrison

This chapter presents some case-studies in the reception of Virgil in literature in English in the nineteenth, twentieth and twenty-first centuries. It aims to show how different aspects of Virgilian texts appeal to and can be mapped on to different cultural and literary contexts, and to present a few detailed interpretations of English poetic texts in the light of their intercultural and intertextual modifications of Virgilian models.

Virgil and the Victorians

The reception of Virgil in England in the Victorian period was somewhat mixed (see Turner 1993: 284–321; Vance 1997: 133–53). The Romantics could view Virgil as a pallid and artificial stylist compared to the vigorous and 'primitive' Homer: 'if you take from Virgil his diction and his metre, what do you leave him?' (Coleridge, *Table Talk*, May 1824; for other similarly negative opinions see Sellar 1897: 68–77). This view continued into the mid-nineteenth century: Macaulay in the introduction to his *Lays of Ancient Rome* (1842; cited from Macaulay 1860: 10) claims that 'the best Latin epic poetry [i.e. the *Aeneid*] is the feeble echo of the Iliad and Odyssey', and Gladstone's influential work on Homer similarly contrasts Homer and Virgil in detail to the latter's disadvantage (Gladstone 1858: III.500–35). Though Virgil later found defenders amongst scholars and historians (see Rogerson 2007), and struck more of a cultural chord during the rise of British imperialism in the last third of the nineteenth century, he is generally viewed as inferior to Homer in the Victorian period.

Matthew Arnold's essay 'On the Modern Element in Literature' (1857, cited from Keating 1970) had a considerable influence on Victorian (and later) views of Virgil: 'over the whole of the great poem of Virgil, over the whole *Aeneid*, there rests an ineffable melancholy; not a rigid, a moody gloom, like the melancholy of Lucretius;

no, a sweet, a touching sadness, but still a sadness, a melancholy which is at once a source of charm in the poem, and a testimony to its incompleteness' (p. 74). This view found notable expression in Tennyson's 1882 poem 'To Virgil':

> Roman Virgil, thou that singest Ilion's lofty temples robed in fire,
> Ilion falling, Rome arising, wars, and filial faith, and Dido's pyre;
>
> Landscape-lover, lord of language, more than he that sang the Works and Days,
> All the chosen coin of fancy flashing out from many a golden phrase;
>
> Thou that singest wheat and woodland, tilth and vineyard, hive and horse and herd;
> All the charm of all the Muses often flowering in a lonely word;
>
> Poet of the happy Tityrus piping underneath his beechen bowers;
> Poet of the poet-satyr whom the laughing shepherd bound with flowers;
>
> Chanter of the Pollio, glorying in the blissful years again to be,
> Summers of the snakeless meadow, unlaborious earth and oarless sea;
>
> Thou that seest Universal Nature moved by Universal Mind;
> Thou majestic in thy sadness at the doubtful doom of human kind;
>
> Light among the vanished ages; star that gildest yet this phantom shore;
> Golden branch amid the shadows, kings and realms that pass to rise no more;
>
> Now thy Forum roars no longer, fallen every purple Caesar's dome –
> Tho' thine ocean-roll of rhythm sound for ever of Imperial Rome –
>
> Now the Rome of slaves hath perished, and the Rome of freemen holds her place,
> I, from out the Northern Island, sundered once from all the human race,
>
> I salute thee, Mantovano, I that loved thee since my day began,
> Wielder of the stateliest measure ever moulded by the lips of man.

Tennyson interestingly treats Virgil's works in reverse chronological order and inverse generic hierarchy, and there are signs here that the Victorian poet is focusing on points of contact with his own poetry as well as with his own more general cultural context. The *Aeneid* is presented immediately in the first stanza, with a predictable emphasis on the ever-popular *Aeneid* 2 (fall of Troy) and 4 (Dido), but then follow two balancing pairs of stanzas (2–5) largely on the *Georgics* and *Eclogues*, looking perhaps to the interest in nature shared with Tennyson himself. The point about Virgil's 'lonely words' in line 6 is taken up about Tennyson himself by a contemporary critic (Collins 1891, 14–18), and the famous expression of Virgil's pessimism in stanza 6 not only echoes Arnold's view but also the general outlook of the Tennyson who wrote such magnificently melancholic lines as 'Break, break, break / On thy cold gray stones, o sea' (the opening line of the eponymous poem, published in 1842) or 'O Death in life, the days that are no more' (*The Princess* [1847]: IV.40) and was most famous for *In Memoriam A.H.H.* [1850], a vast poem lamenting the premature death of a youthful friend. A melancholic Virgil melded well with the Victorian cult of death, mourning and sentiment of which Tennyson could be viewed as the arch-spokesman (see e.g. Joseph and Tucker 1999).

Just as stanza 1 looks to *Aeneid* 2 and 4, stanzas 6 and 7 look to *Aeneid* 6, another consistently popular part of the poem, especially for a Victorian society much taken with religion and the afterlife. Stanza 6 echoes Virgilian phrasing; the 'Universal Mind' underlying 'Universal Nature' recalls Anchises' account of the Stoic *pneuma* infused through nature at *Aeneid* 6.726–7 *totamque infusa per artus / mens agitat molem*, 'mind spread through every limb [of the universe] moves the whole mass'. Stanza 7 again echoes *Aeneid* 6 (with 'Golden branch amid the shadows' compare the *umbrae*, shadows, (6.139), which protect the grove of the Golden Branch, *aureus . . . ramus*, 6.137), but strikingly presents Virgil 'as himself the golden bough that gives mysterious access to the Underworld, *Aeneid* vi 208' (Ricks 1989: 630). This suggests that as in his *Ulysses* (Ricks 1989: 138–40; Redpath 1981: 121–4; Markley 2004: 121–6) Tennyson is reading classical texts through the prism of Dante, who famously introduces Virgil as Dante's guide through the underworld at the beginning of the *Inferno* (1.62–93). Dante was highly popular in the Victorian period and also used by Tennyson in *In Memoriam* (cf. Millbank 1998: 1 on 'the Victorian cult of Dante' and 185–93 on *In Memoriam*), and his presence in this poem is surely confirmed by the address 'Mantovano' in stanza 10, a direct citation from Dante *Purgatorio* 6.74, where the Mantuan Sordello addresses his fellow-citizen Virgil; the address also speaks to the Accademia Vergiliana of Mantova, the commissioning body for Tennyson's poem (Ricks 1989: 628).

Tennyson's poem is firmly placed in the nineteenth century by stanzas 8 and 9. The contrast of Virgil's everlasting glory with the fall of ancient Rome looks to the ideology of Gibbon's *Decline and Fall* and the Romantic interest in Rome's ruins (Vance 1997: 29–30), and the allusion to recently found Italian freedom nods to reunification and the Risorgimento. Though Tennyson presents himself as belonging to a northern and non-classical culture (stanza 9 'sundered once from all the human race)', that separation is itself expressed in a Virgilian phrase (*Eclogues* 1.67 *penitus toto divisos orbe Britannos*, 'the Britons sundered far away from the whole world'). The last line brings the two poets together again: 'Wielder of the stateliest measure ever moulded by the lips of man', referring to the Virgilian hexameter, surely looks to Tennyson's own interest in noble sound and dignified expression, and reminds us that Tennyson himself experimented with hexameters among other Greco-Roman metres (Markley 2004: 87–120). It is important to know that Tennyson's autograph sets this poem out in two-line stanzas, reproduced above and echoing in a long ten-stress line the impressive length of the Latin hexameter which the poem itself praises; modern editions ought to do the same (Markley 2004: 103–4).

The contemporary idea that Tennyson was the English Virgil, encouraged by this poem, has a certain amount of plausibility (see Collins 1891: 1–23; Mustard 1904: 91–105 and especially 105 'the most Virgilian of modern poets'; Markley 2004: 1–8; Harrison 2007). Indeed, Tennyson's *Idylls of the King*, his set of narrative poems which narrates the career of King Arthur and romantic tales of the Knights of the Round Table, presents a kind of medievalizing *Aeneid* for the Victorian age (Markley 2004: 7–8), with some echoes of Homer and Virgil and a mythical heroic plot of the national past which has ideological consequences for the present, but here as elsewhere Tennyson avoids complete confrontation with ancient epic and its ambitions. The *Idylls* are indeed twelve in number like the books of the *Aeneid* and are collectively not far short of the *Aeneid* in length, but they are much more episodic and considerably more loosely linked than the books of Virgil's epic, being written separately over several decades and only put together for complete publication in 1872. This reticence about direct confrontation with the full majesty of ancient epic is a feature Tennyson shares with several other Victorian poets (see Jenkyns 2006).

Arnold's judgement that Virgil was sweetly melancholic but ultimately not adequate for the greatness of Roman culture (Arnold 1857; see above) did not prevent him from using Virgilian allusion in his poetry. Arnold's pastoral *Thyrsis* contains echoes of the *Eclogues*, his *Sohrab and Rustum* (1853) and *Balder Dead* (1855) make use of the *Aeneid* (see Allott and Allott 1979: 319–55, 376–421), and (perhaps most interestingly) his 1850 *Memorial Verses* for Wordsworth set up a fascinating parallel between Wordsworth and Lucretius on the one hand and Arnold himself and Virgil on the other. Arnold's commemorative lines

> And he was happy, if to know
> Causes of things, and far below
> His feet to see the lurid flow
> Of terror, and insane distress
> And headlong fate, be happiness.

clearly pick up Virgil's famous laudation of Lucretius at *Georgics* 2.490–2 (cf. Allott and Allott 1979: 241):

> Felix qui potuit rerum cognoscere causas,
> Atque metus omnes et inexorabile fatum
> Subiecit pedibus strepitumque Acherontis avari.

[Happy was he who succeeded in knowing the causes of things, and in putting into subjection under his feet all kinds of fears and inexorable fate and the din of the greedy Underworld.]

Wordsworth, the great philosophic poet of nature, is constructed as a latter-day Lucretius, which leaves Arnold as the latter-day Virgil, plausible enough given that Arnold himself shows a good deal of the melancholy he has attributed to the *Aeneid*.

Arthur Hugh Clough is another poet who makes interesting use of Virgil. His *The Bothie of Tober-na-Vuolich, A Long-Vacation Pastoral* (1848) is a remarkable narrative poem of a Highland reading-party and eventual marriage of its undergraduate hero in 9 brief books, all 200 lines or less, resembling the 10 *Eclogues* both in length and (almost) in number, and written in accentual hexameters, an English version of the *Eclogues'* metre. Though it is principally a mock-epic with many comic imitations of Homeric style, Clough's poem is prefaced as a whole with two epigraphs from the *Eclogues* (as are four of its nine books); these epigraphs sometimes suggest reworkings of original Virgilian contexts. All these fit the plot quite well – e.g. Book II, where the poetic contest of Thyrsis and Corydon from *Eclogue* 7 activated by the epigraph is turned into an undergraduate intellectual discussion, or Book III, where the poetic catalogue of Silenus (*Ecl.*6) becomes the Piper's narrative (for more see Hayward, 1983). Interestingly, this use of Virgilian pastoral is downplayed when the poem explicitly reflects on its own genre in its last book: there it refers (IX.139) to 'Muse of great Epos, and Idyll the playful and tender', using the title of Theocritus' Greek pastoral poems ('Idylls') which were the chief model for the *Eclogues*, rather than referring to the work of Virgil. Though the use of Virgil is much more significant in the *Bothie* than the use of Theocritus, the naming of the Greek form rather than the Roman suggests that Theocritus is the 'real' pastoral poet and Virgil the pale imitator, thoroughly consistent with the general Victorian view sketched above. A further key way in which the *Bothie* appropriates Virgilian models for its own cultural context is its obvious affinity with the Oxford novel, in which a student moves through undergraduate frivolity to respectable married life (cf. e.g. Bradley 1853 and Hughes 1861); like other texts such as E.B. Browning's *Aurora Leigh* (1857), the *Bothie* seeks to accommodate the leading ancient poetic tradition to the leading literary genre of Victorian England (see further Harrison 2007).

Thus Victorian authors appropriate Virgil for effective literary reasons, but also to show their gentlemanly education and to appeal to the similar education of their model readers, thus incorporating the Roman poet into a model of contemporary class and cultural solidarity.

Twentieth and Twenty-first Centuries: Virgil's *Eclogues*, Culture and Politics

The diverse cultural backgrounds for the use of Virgil in earlier twentieth-century literature have been brilliantly illuminated by Theodore Ziolkowski (Ziolkowski 1993), to whom the reader is referred for orientation as well as much telling analysis. In this section I will look at a few examples of the use of Virgil's *Eclogues* in twentieth-century poetry in English, showing how the political and ideological force of these poems can be activated in quite different directions and cultural settings.

Robert Frost: from Roosevelt to Kennedy

I begin with Robert Frost, whose use of classical texts has often been remarked (see e.g. Bacon 2001). Frost appropriated Virgil's *Eclogues* in two poems written nearly thirty years apart, 'Build Soil: A Political Pastoral' (1932), and 'For John F. Kennedy: His Inauguration' (1960–1). These two poems show quite different political engagements with Virgilian pastoral, reflecting the original mixture of optimism and pessimism in Virgil's *Eclogue* book. In 'Build Soil', suggestively subtitled 'A political pastoral', Frost presents a conservative manifesto against Roosevelt's declared farm policy for the 1931 election, which Frost saw as too socialist and collectivist (cf. Tuten and Zubizarreta 2001: 43–5). The poem overtly recalls the first of Virgil's *Eclogues*, in which Tityrus, whose farm has been saved from the land-confiscations after Philippi, converses with Meliboeus, whose land has been taken and who faces the prospect

Stephen Harrison

of emigration (here I build on Ziolkowski 1993: 160–3). Frost's poem is rather longer than Virgil's (292 against 83 lines) and departs from it considerably, but evokes it closely at the beginning in order to highlight its still relevant themes of land-confiscation and the problem of governmental interference in rural life. The Virgilian characters retain their names, and their roles are subtly altered. As in the Virgilian poem, Meliboeus begins by addressing Tityrus (1–12):

> Why, Tityrus! But you've forgotten me.
> I'm Meliboeus the potato man,
> The one you had the talk with, you remember,
> Here on this very campus years ago.
> Hard times have struck me and I'm on the move.
> I've had to give my interval farm up
> For interest, and I've bought a mountain farm
> For nothing down, all-out-doors of a place,
> All woods and pasture only fit for sheep.
> But sheep is what I'm going into next.
> I'm done forever with potato crops
> At thirty cents a bushel. Give me sheep.

They meet on a university campus (Frost's poem was read at Columbia on 31 May 1932), thus like Virgil's shepherds presenting a mildly surreal combination of peasant and intellectual (cf. e.g. *Eclogue* 3.40–2, where Menalcas seems to be an expert on astronomers; for a rustic astronomer in Frost see 'The Literate Farmer and the Planet Venus' [1942]), but also perhaps reflecting the *locus amoenus* or conventional peaceful paradise where Tityrus is located in *Eclogue* 1 (1.1–2). Meliboeus has not lost his land as in Virgil's poem, but has been forced to move to an inferior mountain farm ('interval' is English 'intervale', located on a plain in a river valley); however, that newly-purchased poor farm is described in three lines which clearly echo the three lines spoken in Virgil's poem by Meliboeus on the poor farm *retained* by Tityrus in the confiscations (*Build Soil* 7–9, followed by *Eclogue* 1.46–8):

> I've bought a mountain farm
> For nothing down, all-out-doors of a place,
> All woods and pasture only fit for sheep.
>
> Fortunate senex, ergo tua rura manebunt
> et tibi magna satis, quamvis lapis omnia nudus
> limosoque palus obducat pascua iunco.

[Fortunate old man, then your country place will remain, big enough indeed for your needs, though it's all bare stone and though a marsh covers its pastures with muddy rushes.]

Here we see some skilful variation of the original Virgilian scenario. As in Virgil, the character Tityrus, sometimes identified with the Roman poet and clearly to be identified with Frost here, is presented as a poet as well as a farmer, and

Meliboeus suggests that he uses his literary talent to do something for Depression-hit farmers (22–5):

> Why don't you use your talents as a writer
> To advertise our farms to city buyers,
> Or else write something to improve food prices?
> Get in a poem toward the next election.

This is a somewhat self-reflexive moment, as 'Build Soil' is in a sense 'a poem towards the next election' of 1932, though it was not in fact published until 1936. But it also recalls *Eclogue* 9, the other poem in Virgil's pastoral collection which centres on the issue of land-confiscation, where the capacity of poetry to effect change in the countryside through persuading the powerful is raised but presented as ultimately ineffectual (9.7–13).

Tityrus picks up this point in his first contribution to Frost's dialogue (26–30):

> Oh, Meliboeus, I have half a mind
> To take a writing hand in politics.
> Before now poetry has taken notice
> Of wars, and what are wars but politics
> Transformed from chronic to acute and bloody?

This political role of poetry is then pursued in the rest of the poem, where Tityrus preaches his doctrine to Meliboeus, who interrupts only with brief questions and comments, more like a token Platonic interlocutor than the Meliboeus of *Eclogue* 1, who in fact speaks more lines than Tityrus (46 against 33), and whose distress receives much more attention in Virgil than in Frost. Like Virgil's poem, Frost's emerges at a time of political disturbance, land-confiscation and disruption in Virgil's Italy providing a match for the Depression and the 1932 election: Meliboeus' comment at 31–2, 'I may be wrong, but, Tityrus, to me / The times seem revolutionary bad', picks up the view of his Virgilian namesake at *Eclogue* 1.11–12: *undique totis / usque adeo turbatur agris*, 'everywhere there is such disturbance over the whole of the countryside', where Virgil's symbol of agricultural for political trouble (indelibly linked through the land-confiscations, consequence of civil war) is literalized by Frost.

Tityrus' message is summarized in the slogan which gives the poem its title (234–6):

> Build soil. Turn the farm in upon itself
> Until it can contain itself no more,
> But sweating-full, drips wine and oil a little.

Here we find an 'invisible hand' solution diametrically opposed to Roosevelt's socialistic statism: let the self-reliant farmer produce a surplus and thus stimulate the economy. Though 'wine and oil', the standard agricultural products of ancient Israel rather than modern New England, provides a Biblical rather than a classical reference (cf. e.g. Joel 2.24), the symbolism of agriculture for the more general political and economic situation clearly reflects Virgil's discourse in the *Eclogues* and indeed the *Georgics*. Though the middle section of the poem presents a political view of a much more detailed and focused kind than anything found in Virgil's quasi-allegorical pastoral world, some of its elements recall Virgil, in particular Tityrus' opposition to urban outsiders coming in and taking possession of the country, a clear parallel to the soldiers who form the new owners of Meliboeus' confiscated land (*Eclogue* 1.70–1 *impius haec tam culta novalia miles habebit, / barbarus has segetes*, 'so a wicked soldier will possess these well-tilled fallow fields, a barbarian these crops') – cf. 185–91:

> Needless to say to you my argument
> Is not to lure the city to the country.
> Let those possess the land, and only those,
> Who love it with a love so strong and stupid
> That they may be abused and taken advantage of
> And made fun of by business, law, and art;
> They still hang on.

Frost's closing sequence again recalls the Virgilian model. Meliboeus, moved by Tityrus' advocacy of sturdy agrarian self-reliance, takes his leave to think about what he has heard (286–92):

> I can tell better after I get home,
> Better a month from now when cutting posts
> Or mending fence it all comes back to me
> What I was thinking when you interrupted
> My life-train logic. I agree with you
> We're too unseparate. And going home
> From company means coming to our senses.

The return of Meliboeus to his poor mountain farm is a symbolic return to self-contained smallholding: he will ponder the issues when engaged in lonely rustic tasks. This is a strong contrast with the end of *Eclogue* 1, where the two do not part but Tityrus offers the dispossessed Meliboeus hospitality for the night (1.79–83). Frost's Meliboeus concurs with his Tityrus that 'we're too unseparate', and mirrors this in his return to solitary agriculture from this political discourse, while Virgil's shepherds present some solidarity and mutual sympathy in the face of political *force majeure*. Frost presents a bottom-up view of the world where a determined and self-reliant individual, farmer or poet, can make a difference, modifying for his own ideological reasons the pastoral landscape of Virgil and its constant vulnerability to larger top-down political change.

Similarly political, but very differently framed, is Frost's other engagement with Virgil's *Eclogues*. The octogenarian Frost was commissioned well in advance to write a poem for the Presidential inauguration of John F. Kennedy on 20 January 1961 (cf. Tuten and Zubizarreta 2001: 118–19). Famously, he was unable to read his new poem in the glare from the snow and instead recited from memory a nationalistic sonnet of some twenty years before, 'The Gift Outright'. In later publication this conflation was marked by the printing of the inauguration poem and the reprinting of the sonnet under the collective title 'For John F. Kennedy His Inauguration' with the subtitle 'Gift outright of "The Gift Outright" (With some preliminary history in rhyme).'

The inauguration poem begins by celebrating the poet's public role in taking part in the ceremony and praising the current age of decolonization and the origin of freedom in the United States (1–18). It is in the next section that engagement with Virgilian pastoral becomes clear (19–23):

> Now came on a new order of the ages
> That in the Latin of our founding sages
> (Is it not written on the dollar bill
> We carry in our purse and pocket still?)
> God nodded his approval of as good.

The common-touch reference to the dollar bill conceals a sophisticated set of Virgilian references. The reverse of the dollar bill presents a pyramid surmounted by an eye, inscribed with the date 1776 in Roman numerals and accompanied by two Latin mottoes, one above (*annuit coeptis*) and one below (*novus ordo seclorum*). The designer was clear about the symbolism (Thomson 1782): 'The pyramid signifies Strength and Duration: The Eye over it & the Motto allude to the many signal interpositions of providence in favour of the American cause. The date underneath is that of the Declaration of Independence and the words under it signify the beginning of the new American Æra, which commences from that date.' Both Latin mottoes are Virgilian: *annuit coeptis*, '[God] approved our enterprise', seems to derive from a prayer to Jupiter in the *Aeneid* (9.625 *adnue coeptis*, 'approve our enterprise'; Frost's 'nodded' points to the etymology of *adnuo*, literally 'nod in agreement'), and *novus ordo seclorum*, 'a new order of the ages" varies *Eclogue* 4.5 *magnus ab integro saeclorum nascitur ordo*, 'a great order of ages is born afresh'.

That Frost alludes to Virgil as well as to the greenback in his 'new order of the ages' seems likely from his poem's close, in which he expresses the general optimism of the period (70–7):

> It makes the prophet in us all presage
> The glory of a next Augustan age
> Of a power leading from its strength and pride,
> Of young ambition eager to be tried,
> Firm in our free beliefs without dismay,
> In any game the nations want to play.
> A golden age of poetry and power
> Of which this noonday's the beginning hour.

This closure evokes Virgil's *Eclogue* 4 in a number of ways. That poem greets the coming of a new age with a prophecy of the birth of a marvellous boy, perhaps the potential son of Augustus or Mark Antony (8–45). Frost looks back to this Virgilian prophetic stance: 'The glory of a next Augustan age' picks up *Eclogue* 4.11 *decus hoc aevi*, 'this ornament of the age', referring to the marvellous boy and thus perhaps evoking the *Wunderkind* status of JFK himself, the youngest man to be elected President (cf. 'young ambition'). The idea of a new golden age associated with Augustus is Virgilian but not from the *Eclogue*: here Frost picks up *Aeneid* 6.792–3, where it is foretold that Augustus *aurea condet / saecula*, 'will found ages of gold', linking the fresh young JFK and the fresh young Augustus, a ready analogy (cf. Lubin 2003: 97; Kleiner 2005: 207–8). The 'golden age of poetry and power' marks the poet's collaboration in this new and exciting national enterprise; as in Build Soil's 'poem toward the next election' (25), here we find Frost appropriating the framework of a Virgilian *Eclogue* to engage with a Democratic President and his programme, but from a completely different perspective. Where 'Build Soil' mounts a fierce critique of Roosevelt, the inauguration poem participates fully in the myth of America renewed under the youthful Kennedy (for this ideology see e.g. Rorabaugh 2002).

Seamus Heaney: millennial echoes

Seamus Heaney's engagement with classical texts has been a fascinating feature of his recent output. Whether or not this is an attempt to 'insinuate himself into an Eliotean-European line of poetry' (Burrow 1997: 36), one of the most striking aspects of this engagement has been that with Virgilian pastoral (see Twiddy: 2006), and there are clear links with Frost's use of the same genre (see Buxton 2004: 53–6). In a lecture on the 'staying power' of pastoral, Heaney himself has argued that the form of the eclogue has successfully survived in literary history owing to its capacity to adapt to a wide range of historical and cultural circumstances, and to its paradoxical ability as a very 'literary' form to confront even the most terrible aspects of life with truth and realism (Heaney 2003). In his collection *Electric Light* (Heaney 2001), we find Heaney approaching the Virgilian eclogue form in three different ways: a translation of *Eclogue* 9 ('Virgil: Eclogue IX'), a transposition of *Eclogue* 4 to the political situation of the north of Ireland ('Bann Valley Eclogue'), and a poem which juxtaposes the world of the *Eclogues* with that of Yeats ('Glanmore Valley Eclogue'). Here I offer a treatment of 'Bann Valley Eclogue' (see also Bloomer 2005a).

This poem uses the first line of *Eclogue* 4 as its epigraph (*Sicelides Musae, paulo maiora canamus*, 'Muses of Sicily, let us sing of something a little greater'), which directs us not only to Virgil's poem but also to its thematic elevation within the *Eclogue* collection. Virgil's millenarian poem alludes to myths of religious cycles of renewal in connection with the end of civil war (see Nisbet 1995: 47–75); Heaney's poem indeed deals with similar themes as a self-consciously millennial work: it was read live on the Irish television channel RTE 1 on 31 December 2000, amid hopes for peace in the north of Ireland in the twenty-first century after a generation of civil war in the twentieth. The Virgilian monologue of *Eclogue* 4 is recast as a dialogue between 'Poet' (Heaney) and Virgil, but its status as model is easily recognizable in the Poet's opening speech (1–6):

> Bann Valley Muses, give us a song worth singing,
> Something that rises like the curtain in

> Those words *And it came to pass* or *In the beginning*.
> Help me to please my hedge-schoolmaster Virgil
> And the child that's due. Maybe, heavens, sing
> Better times for her and her generation.

Virgil's Sicilian Muses (an allusion to his Greek model Theocritus) are here transplanted to the Bann Valley in County Derry, core Heaney territory, and a symbolic borderland between Protestant-dominated east Ulster and the Catholic-dominated west. The 'song worth singing' suggests like the Virgilian 'sing of something a little greater' a theme of higher significance. The expected male child of Virgil's poem becomes a girl here, suggesting perhaps 'feminine' peace rather than the renewed 'male' martial prowess to which the boy will grow up in the Latin original; there is also a reference to Yeats' famous poem 'A Prayer for My Daughter', which Heaney's poem echoes several times (cf. Twiddy 2006). This is the key theme of the poem: 'better times for her and her generation' looks to a millenarian feeling that the 'troubles' will be a thing of the past for the next generation as they have dominated the past. This political application of Virgil's new age of peace after civil war is highly appropriate. This is further stressed in Virgil's reply to the poet (7–19):

> Here are my words you'll have to find a place for:
>
> *Carmen, ordo, nascitur, saeculum, gens.*
> Their gist in your tongue and province should be clear
> Even at this stage. Poetry, order, the times,
> The nation, wrong and renewal, then an infant birth
> And a flooding away of all the old miasma.

'Your tongue and province' puns neatly on the Province of Northern Ireland and the Latin *provincia*, Roman imperial province: Virgil's poem has specific political meaning here and now. The word-games of pseudo-translation here provide English words not in the Latin ('wrong and renewal') and an aural play (*nascitur*/nation): the metaphor of 'flooding away', not in the original, is appropriate to the Bann river valley, and the idea of blood-pollution in the Greek word 'miasma' (see Parker 1983) again clearly points to the washing away of the guilt of civil war. 'Infant birth', like the biblical phrases evoked in the Poet's opening words (*And it came to pass, In the beginning*), points to a Christian element here, and suggests the old interpretation of *Eclogue* 4 as a prophecy of the coming birth of Christ. In a poem set in 1999 there is also a reference to the current bimillennium of that event: the idea of redemption through new birth and the removal of previous blood-guilt clearly applies in the Poet's 'tongue and province'.

The idea of blood-guilt itself provides a fertile parallel with the Augustan poets' own analysis of the problems of their times, as Heaney's next stanza shows:

> Whatever stains you, you rubbed it into yourselves,
> Earth mark, birth mark, mould like the bloodied mould
> On Romulus's ditch-back. But when the waters break
> Bann's stream will overflow, the old markings

Will avail no more to keep east bank from west.
The valley will be washed like the new baby.

The allusion to Romulus plainly recalls Horace's use in *Epode* 7 (16–20) of the
Romulus/Remus fratricide as a symbolic parallel and origin for Rome's current civil
war: like the Romans of the first century BC, the people of Ireland have been their
own destruction. The healing overflowing of the Bann, symbolically bridging the
sectarian divide ('old markings', both stain and boundary) of Co. Derry/Co. Antrim
marked by the river's banks, may be a neat reversal of the ominous inundation of
the Tiber in Horace *Odes* 1.2, clearly a symbol of Rome's internecine guilt. This
idea and that of the saviour child are brilliantly combined in the image of 'The valley will be washed like the new baby.'

The Poet replies, picking up Virgil's earlier citation of his own Latin:

Pacatum orbem: your words are too much nearly.
Even 'orb' by itself. What on earth could match it?
And then, last month, at noon-eclipse, wind dropped.
A millennial chill, birdless and dark, prepared.
A firstness steadied, a lastness, a born awareness
As name dawned into knowledge: I saw the orb.

Paradoxically this stanza, which begins by literal citation of Virgil's Latin (cf. *Eclogue*
4.17 *pacatumque reget patriis virtutibus orbem*, [of the marvellous boy] 'he will rule
over a *world pacified* by his father's virtues'), moves swiftly away from the classical
model into a typical Heaney experience of the natural landscape and strong contemporary allusion: 'noon-eclipse' surely refers to the total solar eclipse of 11 August
1999, visible in the UK about noon, and 'millennial' chill reminds us of the millenarian aspect of this poem already noted.

Virgil's response looks to the rosy future for the coming child, who will experience the peaceful cycles of nature:

Eclipses won't be for this child. The cool she'll know
Will be the pram hood over her vestal head.
Big dog daisies will get fanked up in the spokes.
She'll lie on summer evenings listening to
A chug and slug going on in the milking parlour.
Let her never hear close gunfire or explosions.

This clearly reworks *Eclogue* 4.15–23:

ille deum vitam accipiet divisque videbit
permixtos heroas et ipse videbitur illis
pacatumque reget patriis virtutibus orbem.
At tibi prima, puer, nullo munuscula cultu
errantis hederas passim cum baccare tellus
mixtaque ridenti colocasia fundet acantho.

ipsae lacte domum referent distenta capellae
ubera nec magnos metuent armenta leones;
ipsa tibi blandos fundent cunabula flores.

[He will enjoy the life of the gods and will see the heroes mingling with the gods, and will himself be seen by them, and will rule over a world pacified by his father's virtues.
But, child, the earth will pour forth small gifts for you without cultivation, wandering ivy everywhere with cyclamen, and lotus mixed with smiling acanthus; your cradle too will itself pour forth charming flowers. The she-goats will bring home of their own accord their udders filled with milk, and the flocks will have no fear of great lions; the snake will be no more, no more too the deceptive poison plant.]

The religious status of Heaney's girl as a 'vestal' picks up with a suitable Roman allusion the Virgilian idea that the boy will be divine and mix with the gods, and the marvellous fecundity of the Virgilian landscape is repeated in Heaney's dog daisies, nicely anchored in modern Ulster with the dialect term 'fanked up' (caught up, enclosed). The Virgilian miracle of the she-goats returning home for milking of their own accord is matched by the miracle of peace in Heaney ('Let her never hear close gunfire or explosions') as the cows submit to the regular and tranquil cycle of modern milking – the miracle of normality restored rather than millennial and enchanted abnormality.

The poem's last two stanzas are narrated by the Poet, some return perhaps to the monologue structure of Virgil's original. In the penultimate stanza Heaney diverges from *Eclogue* 4 with lines about being sent by his mother to look for shamrocks on St Patrick's Day, but in the last stanza there is some return to Virgil:

Child on the way, it won't be long until
You land among us. Your mother's showing signs,
Out for a walk on her own among the bales.
Planet earth like a teething ring suspended
Hangs by its world-chain. Your pram waits in the corner.
Cows are let out. They're sluicing the milk-house floor.

A variant version of the poem, entitled 'Child that's Due' and sold for the Save the Bogs Campaign (still available from the Irish Peatlands Conservation Council, see http://www.ipcc.ie/artgalleryform.html; accessed 8/8/07) contains an additional final stanza in some ways closer to the Virgilian original, with an allusion to smiling (cf. *Eclogue* 4.60 and 62), and a ring-compositional ending (not in Virgil) which picks up the opening line:

We know, little one, you have to start with a cry
But smile soon too, a big one for your mother.
Unsmiling life has had it in for people
For far too long. But now you have it in you
Not to be wrong-footed but to first-foot us
And, muse of the valley, give us a song worth singing.

The removal of this stanza in *Electric Light* provides an ending which is still effect-ively Virgilian: the address 'child on the way' and the allusion to pregnancy pick up Virgil's similar address to the coming child as *parve puer*, 'small boy' (4.60, 62) and his reference to the mother's long gestation (4.61). Furthermore, the stress on regular animal behaviour and the farming cycle in this *Electric Light* ending recalls poem-endings elsewhere in the *Eclogues*: *Eclogue* 6.85–6 (time for flocks to return home) and *Eclogue* 10.77 (calling the she-goats home). The millennial miracle of normality, restored under conditions of peace and optimism, is rightly stressed at the poem's closure. Thus Heaney, like Frost in his inaugural poem, uses Virgil's eclogue of prophecy and renewal to look to a new age in his own culture and times.

Conclusion

These case studies suggest how Virgilian texts can be received and appropriated in different ways in different cultural contexts in poetry in English. Both the melan-cholic tendency in Virgil and the political aspect of the *Eclogues* are key critical features picked out for comment and exploration in later poetic texts, suggesting that poetic successors are often poets' best and most perspicacious readers.

FURTHER READING

On the reception of Virgil in the Victorian period, Vance 1997: 133–53 and Turner 1993: 284–321 provide excellent modern orientation. For Tennyson's use of classical texts and affinities with Virgil, Collins 1891 and Mustard 1904 are still of interest as contemporary receptions; most recently, Markley 2004 gives a decent general guide, especially on the evidence of Tennyson's personal library. On Arnold's use of classical epic there is some material in Jenkyns 2006 and the detailed notes in Allott and Allott 1979 are very useful, but a full modern treat-ment is needed; the classical sources for Clough's *Bothie* are partly explored by Tillotson and Tillotson 1965 as well as Hayward 1983, but again a fuller discussion would be useful. On the reception of Virgil in the earlier twentieth century, Ziolkowski 1993 is outstanding: his treatment of Frost's 'Build Soil' (160–3) can be set against the wider survey of Frost's use of classical literature in Bacon 2001. Heaney's own lecture on pastoral (Heaney 2003) is very informative for his methods in 'Bann Valley Eclogue', also treated in Bloomer 2005a, and Twiddy 2006 is a recent and helpful treatment of Heaney as pastoral poet, focusing especially on *Electric Light*.

PART III

Translation

CHAPTER TEN

Colonization, Closure or Creative Dialogue?: The Case of Pope's *Iliad*

David Hopkins

The second half of the twentieth century witnessed a significant revival of academic interest in the tradition of English verse translation from classical poetry. An important agent in this process was the journal *Arion*, founded at the University of Texas in 1962 and edited by a group of American and expatriate-British classicists, including W. Arrowsmith, D.S. Carne-Ross, C.J. Herington, and J.P. Sullivan. *Arion* was the first classical journal with an avowedly literary-critical, as opposed to historical and philological, agenda. It would, its editors hoped, perform within Classics a similar role to that of *Scrutiny* or *Essays in Criticism* in English studies, and would apply to the study of classical literature the critical methods and assumptions familiar at that date in university English departments.

The founders of *Arion* were all university teachers – though D.S. Carne-Ross was a relative newcomer to the academic world, having previously worked as a producer for the BBC Third Programme – but a crucial influence on the journal's conception and early activity came from a stridently non- (even anti-) academic source, in the form of the writings and example of the poet, Ezra Pound. Several of the *Arion* team were passionate Poundians, and had been particularly influenced by Pound's oft-stated conviction that one of the most effective forms of literary criticism is translation, in which texts from other cultures and periods are reinterpreted and 'made new' for the modern world. Consequently, an important part of *Arion*'s activity was the publication of new translations from the classics – versions which, the editors hoped, would cast as much light on their originals as the discursive analyses which occupied the rest of the journal.

One of the most distinguished and widely discussed contributions to the early numbers of *Arion* was the essay, 'Is Juvenal a Classic?' by the British scholar, H.A. Mason (H.A. Mason 1963), in which central use was made of English translations and imitations of Juvenal by Ben Jonson (1605), John Oldham (1683), John Dryden

(1692), and Samuel Johnson (1749) to suggest a major reinterpretation of the Roman poet's satirical stance and tone. Like the *Arion* editors, Mason had long been, in his own words, a 'cranky devotee of all Pound's efforts as a translator' (H.A. Mason 1969: 245), but his study of Pound had led him not to the promotion of new translation, much of which struck him of inferior quality and insight, but to a deep immersion in the translation theory and practice of the English poets of the sixteenth, seventeenth and eighteenth centuries.

Mason's study of the English translator-poets, pursued in a series of books and articles appearing between the late 1950s and his death in 1993 (see particularly H.A. Mason 1959, 1963, 1969, 1972, 1976–7, 1981), led him to a number of convictions about the activity of poetic translation which he never voiced collectively in one place, but which find piecemeal expression throughout his *oeuvre*. They might be broadly summarized as follows. Once translations of poetry move beyond the humble 'crib' – a plain prose version that makes no pretension to preserve any of the artistic quality of its original, but is merely designed to assist students in their attempts to construe the ancient text – they become answerable to a number of inexorable laws. A translation of classical poetry which itself claims poetic status – one which seeks, in George Chapman's phrase, 'with Poesie to open Poesie' (G. Chapman 1967: 1:10) – can only be written by a genuine poet, not a Professor of Latin or Greek *pretending* to be a poet. Since such translated verse must display, no less than any other poetry, the 'genius' famously described by Samuel Johnson as 'that power which constitutes a poet . . . that energy which collects, combines, amplifies, and animates' (Johnson 1905: 3. 222), it is fully deserving of epithet 'creative'. It will necessarily take freedoms with the literal sense of the original, since it is impossible to render with word-for-word fidelity the full range of verbal nuance, expressive effect and verse-music in a foreign poetic text, while simultaneously preserving an 'answerable style' in the host language. An English translator, if he wishes to be readable, can no more preserve the metrical procedures and form of his original than he can retain its syntax and word-order, for verbal and artistic forms that seem natural to one language and literature will seem merely bizarre if transported mechanically into another. Such principles, Mason thought, had been given memorable expression by two of the English translator-poets, Sir John Denham and William Cowper. 'Whosoever offers at Verbal [i.e. word-for-word] Translation', Denham had written in his Preface to *The Destruction of Troy* (1656), 'shall have the misfortune of that young Traveller, who lost his own language abroad, and brought home no other instead of it: for the grace of the Latine will be lost by being turned into English words, and the grace of the English, by being turned into the Latine Phrase' (Denham 1969: 159–60). In a similar vein, Cowper had argued, in a letter of 1794, written shortly after the completion of his own translation of Homer, that 'there are minutiae in every language, which transfused into another will spoil the version. Such extreme fidelity is in fact unfaithful; such close resemblance takes away all likeness. . . . A translation of Homer so made . . . will be written in no language under heaven; – it will be English, and it will be Greek; and therefore it will be neither' (quoted in H.A. Mason 1972: 185–6). For these reasons, it is quite inappropriate to judge verse translations by their apparent lack of fidelity at the phrase-by-phrase and line-by-line level. What should concern one is the intelligence with which the translator has engaged with the larger tone, manner and spirit of his original. To such ends, a translator might legitimately add to, or abridge the sentiments found at any particular place in his original. He might import into his rendering of a particular poem or passage sentiments found not in that passage, but elsewhere in his author – or even in another poet who had been fruitfully inspired by that author. To produce a genuinely poetic rendering, moreover, a translator must engage with his source as intensely as he would engage with the raw material of his 'original' work. In this respect, Mason fully endorsed T.S. Eliot's belief that good translation 'is not merely translation', since, in good translation, the translator is 'giving the original through himself and finding himself through the original' (Eliot 1948: 13). 'There must,' Mason wrote,

> be a degree of concern amounting to passion both on the part of the translator and of the reader before an alien body can be assimilated. The foreign book must be deeply required. Both translator and reader must come to self-expression, self-completion, self-transcendence through the act of assimilating.
>
> (H.A. Mason 1972: 180)

Translation is, on such a view, simultaneously an act of submission and surrender and of self-discovery and self-realization. It depends for its success as much on the resources and potentialities of the host language and the host poet as on the linguistic qualities and characteristics of the original. Good translation, moreover, challenges its readers by discovering 'the real needs of its age', incorporating sentiments and insights from 'foreign' cultures and periods as a challenge, complement, even rebuke, to the commonplace or superficial assumptions of the translator's own contemporaries. The translator must write in an idiom accessible and acceptable to his own age, but not in one that merely reflects the cliché wisdom or cliché expression of the present moment. Thus, when Dryden declares that he has tried to make an original speak as he would 'if he were living, and an *Englishman*' (Dryden 1956–2000: 3. 4), the claim is not merely that the original has been cut down to familiarly modish size. Dryden is, rather, affirming his conviction that a translator must find what Mason calls 'mediate terms' to negotiate between an 'alien' past and an apparently familiar modernity. 'It is . . . a claim', wrote Mason,

> that can be made for a creative translation of a Classic text that it destroys [any] false sense of approximation and reveals the classic work as at one and the same time forever alien and yet, mysteriously, *abordable* [accessible, approachable]. It is in fact only possible to do creative translation when these two opposed orientations are simultaneously strongly felt. The translator must stand like Virgil's dead stretching out his arms *ripae ulterioris amore* ['in yearning for the farther shore': *Aeneid*, 6. 316], but there must be genuine voices coming back from the further shore.
>
> (H.A. Mason 1969: 247)

Mason's 'creative translation' overlaps to a large extent with Dryden's 'Paraphrase, or Translation with Latitude, where the Authour is kept in view by the Translator, so as never to be lost, but his words are not so strictly follow'd as his sense; and that too is admitted to be amplyfied, but not alter'd' (Dryden 1956–2000: 1. 114). But Mason's ideal also encompasses Dryden's growing conviction (for which, see D. Hopkins 2005), that successful translation is achieved not merely by applying a particular stylistic or compositional method, but as the result of a complex, dialogic meeting of minds across the ages.

A number of developments in academic life and publishing practice over the last half-century might seem to testify to the success of Mason and the *Arion* school, and of other distinguished late twentieth-century critics – most notably George Steiner – in establishing the claims of poetic translation on the attention of students in both English and Classics. *Arion* is itself still in business, after two phoenix-rises from the ashes. 'Translation studies' is now an established 'field' within the literary academy. And the last few decades have seen the republication of many of the most famous English translations of classical poetry, both as individual texts, in such series as the Penguin Classics and Wordsworth Classics of World Literature, and in anthologies such as *The Oxford Book of Classical Verse in Translation* (eds Jeremy Maule and Adrian Poole) and the volumes devoted to classical poets in Christopher Ricks's Penguin Poets in Translation series. Poetic translation from the classics, moreover, as the work of Tony Harrison, Seamus Heaney, Ted Hughes and Christopher Logue eloquently testifies, continues to be prominently practised by some of the most celebrated writers of our own day.

But there are signs that English verse translation of kind admired by H.A. Mason have not taken as secure and permanent a root in academics', students' and general readers' minds as its advocates might have hoped. Commercial pressures have, significantly, already forced some of the new editions of the older poetic translations out of print. Teachers of Classics in Translation, anxious about the disconcerting freedoms of 'creative translations' with the literal meaning of their originals, have tended to favour modern academic renderings of the classical poets over more para-phrastic versions (see Carne-Ross 1968). And teachers of English Literature, worried about translated verse's lack of 'originality' – in a way that, despite all the recent talk about the textually mediated nature of reality, betrays their lingering enthralment to a post- or sub-romantic aesthetic of self-expression – regularly exclude it from their consideration of the major poets, even when, as in the cases of Dryden and Pope, it is absolutely central to those poets' achievement. The great translations consequently receive little or no coverage in the textbooks, such as *The Norton Anthology of English Literature*, most regularly consulted by undergraduates on English Literature courses.

Recently, moreover, there have been a number of academic attacks specifically tar-geted on the paraphrastic mode of verse translation. In his widely discussed book *The Translator's Invisibility* (Venuti 1995), Lawrence Venuti has promoted the cause of 'foreignizing' translation – translation which seeks to preserve the 'otherness' of its original by the deployment of a deliberately un-English vocabulary, syntax, and form – against the 'domesticating' and 'assimilative' methods advocated and adopted by such poets as Denham, Dryden, Pope and Cowper. The practice of the 'domesticating' translator, Venuti claims, rests on an 'ethnocentric violence'. Such translation 'elid[es] the linguistic and cultural difference of the foreign text', thus constituting a species of colonization, in which the 'ethnodeviant' is occluded or denied, and the foreign text is appropriated to the dominant values of the host culture, deceitfully masquerading as transcendental truths (Venuti 1995: 41, 76, 79, 148; see also Venuti 2000).

A similar resistance to 'domesticating' translation is displayed in Jan Parker's *Dialogic Education and the Problematics of Translation in Homer and Greek Tragedy* (2001), a book which combines literary criticism with educational theory, and draws on its author's experiences as a teacher of classical literature to Latin- and Greek-less students in university and adult education classes. Classical literature, Parker argues, should be taught not *in* but *through* translation. The essential tool for such a project is the 'glossed text', a translation that leaves key terms and concepts in the original language, thus allowing the reader access to semantic, cultural, and philosophical implications that would be obscured by a more thoroughgoing substitution of English 'equivalents'. Such glossed texts have the additional advantage of highlighting the ways in which, in the work of Homer and the Greek tragedians, key ethical and religious values and concepts are constantly debated and contested, rather than merely assumed. To isolate, for example, the essential terms of the Homeric heroic 'code' – *kleos, timê, geras, kudos* – is to stress the degree to which, in the unfolding narrative of the *Iliad*, such terms are unstable and fragile entities, as likely to be questioned and subverted as assented to by Homer's warriors, and by the poem's readers. Moreover, Parker argues, such a recognition of the radically ambiguous and polyvocal nature of ancient epic and drama encourages, at the pedagogical level, a democratic, open-ended exchange between teacher and student, in which both parties engage in a genuinely collaborative exploration of issues which were always a site of contest, and which can never be finally settled. Such a model contrasts sharply with the habits of mind encouraged by the 'assimilative' translations of such poets as Pope, which, by offering a thoroughgoing recreation of their original, effectively impose an authoritarian interpretative 'closure' on the ancient text.

Such closure has been thought to be conspicuously in evidence in Pope's treatment of the celebrated speech of Sarpedon to Glaucus in Book 12 of the *Iliad*. The speech occurs at a crucial moment in the siege of Troy. Sarpedon, a Prince of the Lycians, clients of the Trojans, turns to his companion Glaucus, exhorting him to join him in leading an attack on the Greeks, who have retreated behind their fortifications. Why, Sarpedon asks, are he and Glaucus afforded honour (*timê*) above the other Lycian chieftains, with the finest seats, food and wine at banquets, and a great domain (*temenos*) of rich farmland, if they do not fight in the forefront of the battle, thereby inspiring the admiration of their fellow Lycians? If they could live for ever, Sarpedon would neither himself enter the battle where men win *kudos*, the god-given charm that secures victory, nor would he exhort Glaucus to do likewise. But since the demons of death are standing all around them in their thousands, they should both go forward into battle, whether this results in their granting some other warrior his victory-wish (*eukhos*) or his granting them theirs.

Sarpedon's speech has often been taken to define with particular force and clarity the values of the Homeric hero, and modern classical scholars have stressed different details in Sarpedon's terminology and logic, in an attempt to convey the precise structure of relationships and ethical convictions which they imply. In his celebrated study of Indo-European language and society, Émile Benveniste argued that the honour (*timê*) that is owing to the chieftains, and paid as a tribute (*geras*) by their people is their right, part of the life-lot afforded them by fate (*moira*) or the gods (see Benveniste 1973: 341–2). And Christopher Gill, drawing on the findings of W. Donlan, has recently suggested that Sarpedon's words should be seen as the expression of a 'generalized reciprocity', according to which the warlord is willing to take a potentially self-destructive course of action not out of a modern sense of 'altruism', or (*pace* Hainsworth 1993: 352) to honour an immediate contractual obligation, but in deference to a longer-term social ideal of reciprocal benefits. At the moment of delivery, Gill argues, Sarpedon's resolve to lead the assault is offered as a 'favour' (*kharis*), rather than as 'a determinate . . . quid pro quo for determinate privileges and status' (Gill 1998: 310–11).

Here is Pope's rendering of Sarpedon's speech (first published separately, 1709; incorporated in Pope's complete rendering of the *Iliad*, 1717):

Why boast we, *Glaucus!* our extended Reign,
Where *Xanthus'* Streams enrich the *Lycian* Plain,
Our num'rous Herds that range the fruitful Field,
And Hills where Vines their purple Harvest yield,
Our foaming Bowls with purer Nectar crown'd,
Our Feasts enhanc'd with Music's sprightly Sound?
Why on those Shores are we with Joy survey'd,
Admir'd as Heroes, and as Gods obey'd?
Unless great Acts superior Merit prove,
And vindicate the bount'ous Pow'rs above.
'Tis ours, the Dignity they give, to grace;
The first in Valour, as the first in Place.
That when with wond'ring Eyes our martial Bands
Behold our Deeds transcending our Commands,
Such, they may cry, deserve the sov'reign State,
Whom those that envy, dare not imitate!
Could all our Care elude the gloomy Grave,
Which claims no less the fearful than the brave,
For Lust of Fame I should not vainly dare
In fighting Fields, nor urge thy Soul to War.
But since, alas! ignoble Age must come,
Disease, and Death's inexorable Doom;
The Life which others pay, let us bestow,
And give to Fame what we to Nature owe;
Brave tho' we fall, and honour'd if we live,
Or let us Glory gain, or Glory give!
                    (*The Iliad of Homer*, 12. 371–96;
                    Pope 1939–69: 8. 95–6)

Since the later eighteenth century, Pope's *Iliad* has been criticized for imposing on Homer a Virgilian grandeur, rhetorical orderliness, and self-conscious philosophical abstraction and sententiousness, which are alien to the more concrete and plain-spoken original. In his lectures *On Translating Homer* (1861) Matthew Arnold famously used the example of Sarpedon's speech to support his contention that in Pope's translation 'Homer's thought has passed through a literary and rhetorical crucible, and come out highly intellectualised' (M. Arnold 1972: 206). And Lawrence Venuti has recently added a political dimension to such criticisms in claiming that Pope's translation of Homer 'was a strategic choice, an appropriation of the 'wild' Greek text to display the refinement of his literary talents and build a readership of equally refined tastes' (Venuti 2000: 57).

In her discussion of Sarpedon's speech, Jan Parker argues that Pope has depicted Sarpedon's heroic resolve in straightforwardly stirring terms, glossing over Sarpedon's fundamental reluctance to fight, affirming his conviction that his bravery will certainly be rewarded by 'Glory', and thereby imposing a false univocality on Homer's more equivocal presentation (J. Parker 2001: 117–20). But are such criticisms quite fair? It certainly cannot be denied that Pope's rendering heightens the measured shapeliness of Sarpedon's words. But what is not so often stressed is the English poet's searching and cogent reaching out towards the distinctive ethical structure and assumptions which he intuited to be present in the Homeric speech. In his stress on their privileges as gifts of 'the bounteous powers above' which they owe to 'nature', Pope can be seen (*pace* Brower 1959: 111) not to be confusing divinely bestowed honour with human tributes, but to be observing the Homeric distinction between *timê* (honour) and *geras* (tribute), as described by Émile Benveniste. And in his portrayal of the heroes' decision to fight as an act of aristocratic magnanimity ('The life which others pay, let us bestow'), Pope can be seen (again *pace* Brower 1959: 110) not to be merely imposing upon Homer with an 'upper-class insolence' or 'Restoration swagger', but to be anticipating Christopher Gill's description of Sarpedon's speech as an expression of 'generalized reciprocity' rather than narrowly contractual obligation. Sarpedon's speech, in Pope's rendering, steers a middle course between the noble gesture of 'royalist' self-immolation with which Sir John Denham (1668) had imagined the two heroes offering themselves as 'A common sacrifice to Honour', and the hard-headed Whiggish contractualism with which Peter Motteux's Sarpedon (1707) had urged that they should 'justifie their Title by their Worth' (on these translations, see further D. Hopkins 2000: 81–2). Pope's Sarpedon, moreover, articulates a system of values far removed from the providential Christianity of the English poet's own culture.

The suggestion that Pope's version offers stirring heroic sentiments to which the poet is simple-mindedly committed seems questionable, since Sarpedon's fundamental unwillingness to fight is signalled as clearly – perhaps more so – by Pope as in Homer's original. Sarpedon's significant 'alas' of heartfelt regret ('But since, alas! ignoble Age must come') is Pope's addition, and the English poet has also subtly enhanced the loving relish with which Sarpedon remembers the 'purple' harvests, 'numerous' herds, 'foaming' bowls, and 'purer' nectar, which he and Glaucus enjoyed in peacetime, and the 'sprightly' music which 'enhanc'd' their former feasts (all Pope's additions).

And Pope's replacement of Homer's *kêres thanatoio muriai* ('countless spirits of death'), 'which no mortal may escape or avoid', with 'ignoble Age', 'Disease' and 'Death', can be seen not merely as the sonorous expression of a melancholy of the kind later associated with Tennyson or Housman, but as a measured reminder of the inexorable conditions of life which, as in Homer's original, form the backdrop to the warriors' heroic decision. It is also questionable whether Pope's warriors feel that they are certain to be rescued by 'Glory'. For Pope's final antithesis ('Or let us Glory gain, or Glory give!') can be seen not as a confident swagger but as a sober acknowledgement that though they *may* gain 'Glory', the 'Glory' of the occasion may go not to them, but to those at whose hands they will meet their death. Pope thus seems fully alive to the fragile and questionable values that Homer associates with the heroic code. And when he comes to render Homer's depiction of the death of Sarpedon in Book 16, he offers an unflinching acknowledgement of the horror and degradation of the battle which Sarpedon enters, and in which he is killed, and does not balk the 'buzzing Flies' that 'Incessant swarm' around the 'heav'nly Form' of Sarpedon's corpse 'defac'd with Dust and Gore' on the plain (Pope 1939–69: 8. 273; for an interesting recent discussion see Sowerby 2004: 55–6).

Pope's capacity for imaginative negotiation with the alien world of Homeric values is even more strikingly apparent in another celebrated passage from his *Iliad*: the episode in Book 21 when Achilles, having returned to the fight in fury after the death of Patroclus, encounters Priam's son, Lycaon. Lycaon begs to be spared as a *xenos* (guest-friend) and suppliant, but Achilles denies his plea, and kills him brutally. Jan Parker describes how her classroom discussions of this passage centred on the tone of two words used by Achilles to Lycaon, 'poor fool' (*nêpios*) and 'friend' (*philos*), which are 'arguably either sarcastic or denoting a commonality between them despite their seemingly distinct status' (J. Parker 2001: 84). Students debated the mood of Achilles here – '(sadistic? cold? insanely angry? philosophical? sardonic? gently sad?)' – and also discussed questions of narrative focalization. Is the episode being told from Achilles' point of view? Where do the values come from by which to judge Achilles' behaviour? Various possibilities were floated and discussed, but no firm conclusions were reached, the debate suggesting, rather, the 'multi-voicedness' of Homer's text. One of the advantages of the 'glossed text' method, indeed, is that 'the reader is free to run a plurality of possibilities and hold off decisions' in a way that would not be possible when 'experiencing an interpretation in the theatre or an authoritative recreating translation' (J. Parker 2001: 85–6, 90). Here is Pope's rendering of Achilles' speech (1720):

> Talk not of Life, or Ransom, (he replies)
> *Patroclus* dead, whoever meets me, dies:
> In vain a single *Trojan* sues for Grace;
> But least, the Sons of *Priam*'s hateful Race.
> Die then, my Friend! What boots it to deplore?
> The great, the good *Patroclus* is no more!
> He, far thy Better, was fore-doomed to die,
> 'And thou, dost thou bewail mortality?'
> See'st thou not me, whom Nature's Gifts adorn,
> Sprung from a Hero, from a Goddess born;

> The Day shall come (which nothing can avert)
> When by the Spear, the Arrow, or the Dart,
> By Night, or Day, by Force or by Design,
> Impending Death and certain Fate are mine.
> Die then!
>
> (*The Iliad of Homer*, 21. 111–25;
> Pope 1939–69: 8. 426)

Jan Parker notes Pope's failure to translate Homer's *nêpie* ('you poor fool'), and argues that he renders Homer's *philos* (friend) 'univocal' by turning Achilles into someone who 'has faced squarely the human condition and can condemn Lykaon for not doing so': 'It may be noble and brave to have looked one's own death in the face and come to terms with it, but I dare to say it is not Homeric' (J. Parker 2001: 91). But such a view of the quintessentially Homeric is not shared by all recent commentators. In the first chapter of *Epic Romance: Homer to Milton* (1993), Colin Burrow offers a powerful description of the distinctive and disturbing nature of Homeric 'sympathy' and 'pity', forms of those emotions quite different from those with which we are accustomed. In most post-Christian literature, Burrow argues, 'the inescapable similarity between mortal experiences' is associated with 'the desire to save, cherish, and regenerate'. But Homeric pity and sympathy, in sharp contrast, are usually associated with death:

> You can kill someone through Homeric pity, not because you want to put him out of his misery, but because you accept the fact of your mortality in his death. When warriors in the *Iliad* pity a dead comrade, they rarely pause in fighting to tend their wounds. They go straight on and kill. This is usually more than revenge, or is at least an unusually complex form of revenge: it is more like an activation of mortality, a recognition that things must die, which leads to an urge to universalize that recognition. . . . Sympathy of this kind, the kind that recognizes death, turns back into something which it is tempting to call ruthlessness.
>
> (Burrow 1993: 22–3)

On his return to the battle, Burrow comments, Achilles 'becomes Homeric sympathy militant', wishing to affirm his shared sense of mortality 'by bringing death'. Commenting specifically on the Lycaon episode, Burrow remarks:

> Where sympathy ceases to be the conscious relation of particular sorrows to particular sorrows, and becomes a sense of general and universal fragility, then the mortality of another person becomes identifiable with one's own, with one's friend's, with that of any sufferer. This attitude is simultaneously a kind of universal sympathy and a form of despair, which blurs suicidal and homicidal desire into a deadly composite. . . . The horror of [Achilles'] ruthless *aristeia* is not that it is inhumane; in a way it is so superhumane that it presses the poem's own recurrent sense of shared fragility into horror: why, if death is universal, should it not be *made* to be universal?
>
> (Burrow 1993: 24–5)

Pope's rendering of the Lycaon episode shows him, I think, to be recreating the emotional and conceptual temper of Homer's episode in ways which strikingly anticipate Burrow's commentary, and which simultaneously cast doubt on Lawrence Venuti's assertion that Pope characteristically transforms Homer's brutal heroes into dignified 'English gentlemen' (Venuti 2000: 57). In a note on the passage, Pope expressed his distress at Achilles' implacable rejection of Lycaon's supplication:

> I must confess I could have wished *Achilles* had spared him: There are so many Circumstances that speak in his Favour.
>
> > (*The Iliad of Homer*, 21. 84n.; Pope 1939–69: 8. 425)

But such qualms in no way inhibited him from rendering Achilles' final terrifying words to his victim with absolute conviction, and in a plain, unadorned diction which conveys the hero's sentiments with a measured but formidable directness. And in the same note from which I have just quoted, Pope expressed his admiration – in the old sense of the word, if not the new – of Achilles' behaviour:

> There is an Air of Greatness in the Conclusion of the Speech of *Achilles*, which strikes me very much: He speaks very unconcernedly of his own death, and upbraids his Enemy for asking Life so earnestly, a life that was of so much less Importance than his own.
>
> > (*The Iliad of Homer*, 21. 84n.; Pope 1939–69: 8. 425)

Pope's translation tellingly reinforces his sense of the 'greatness' of Achilles' sentiments by imbuing his words – and marking the fact in his text by inverted commas – with an echo of Dryden's translation (1685) of the moment in Lucretius' *De Rerum Natura* (3. 1025–6) where Lucretius had himself echoed the sentiments of the Homeric Achilles to support his own haughty rejection of the fear of death:

> > Mean time, when thoughts of death disturb thy head;
> > Consider, *Ancus* great and good is dead;
> > *Ancus* thy better far, was born to die,
> > And thou, dost thou bewail mortality?
> > > ('Lucretius: Against the Fear of Death',
> > > 236–9; Dryden 1956–2000: 3. 54)

Though on one level Pope's allusion might be thought to introduce into the speech a distinctly un-Homeric intertextual sophistication, his echo of the Drydenian Lucretius' scornful repetition ('And thou, dost thou'), simultaneously offers an effective equivalent for the Homeric Achilles' *nêpie* (you fool) which, as we have seen, he had left untranslated at the opening of the speech.

In the foregoing discussion, two brief examples from Pope's *Iliad* have had to stand proxy for the whole wealth of paraphrastic translation from classical poetry in English. And nothing has been said about the alternative 'foreignizing' tradition championed by Lawrence Venuti. I offer, by way of a coda, two brief comments on that subject. First, it is true that the 'foreignizing' mode has achieved a number of notable successes in English. The most celebrated – though it is, for several obvious reasons, a very 'special case' – is the tradition of Biblical translation from Tyndale to the Authorized Version. A more recent instance might be the Confucian Odes of Ezra

Pound (see Carne-Ross 1989; Haynes 2003: 87–8). But the dangers of the mode surely remain those signalled by Denham and Cowper: that the 'alien' stylistic elements preserved from the original will only be recognizable as such by those who know the source in its original language; to others they will seem merely bizarre. As Kenneth Haynes has observed, 'it is, obviously, harder to write well enough to change the norms of one's own language than it is to write competently within them, and most successful translations with greater ambitions than that of the crib have been assimilative' (Haynes 2003: 87). Second, there is, in practice, by no means the hard-and-fast polar opposition between 'foreignizing' and 'domesticating' translation that Venuti implies. Few 'foreignizing' translations are, in fact, without their local 'domesticating' elements, and vice versa. The translations of Dryden, for example, though broadly 'assimilative' in their method, contain, as Dryden himself acknowledged (see Dryden 1956–2000: 5. 319–36), numerous local importations of Latin idiom, style, and diction (for discussion of one particularly interesting instance – Dryden's 'pause of life' (rendering the Latin *vitai pausa*) in his translation of Lucretius – see Jones 1985: 56–7).

Pope's translation of Homer, moreover, though its general methods may place it in Venuti's 'assimilative' and 'domesticating' category, involves, as I hope my examples have shown, a much more searching and subtle imaginative dialogue with the 'otherness' of the Homeric world than such a categorizing would suggest. Pope's relationship with Homer is, I believe, far more aptly characterized by H.A. Mason's model of a translatorly stance which acknowledges ancient texts as 'forever alien, and yet, mysteriously, *abordable*', than by the alternative model of a 'familiarizing' translator confidently 'appropriating' and 'colonizing' his original. And Pope's sensitivity to the developing drama of the *Iliad*, with all its turns, reversals, and ambiguities, also casts doubt, I believe, on the suggestion that Pope has imposed on Homer a consistently monovocal interpretative 'closure'.

Pope's endeavour was to make sense of every element and every moment in Homer's narrative in ways which genuinely respond to the alien world of the Greek poem, while simultaneously effecting those 'structural substitutions' of custom and belief (for the term, see B. Williams 1993: 18–19) necessary to relate that world to modern readers' concerns. Pope, moreover, sought to make every element and moment of Homer's text intelligible *in relation to every other element and moment* (see Sowerby 2004 *passim*). 'Glossed texts', however useful they may be as a stimulus to classroom discussion, can ultimately only offer *disiecta membra*: discontinuous speculations *about* a Greek text and suggestions of possibilities *within* that text, rather than a sense of the unified effect *of* the text as a whole. They can do little, that is, to provide the absorbing imaginative experience, continuously unfolding in time and cumulative in its effect, that the reading or performance of epic and dramatic texts entails. There are undoubtedly good educational reasons (tellingly expounded by Jan Parker) for encouraging students to keep open a variety of possibilities when exploring Homer's use of his key conceptual, ethical, and religious terms. But such a luxury is simply not available to the reader of or listener to – as opposed to the participator in seminars on – classical epic and drama. In the Preface to his *Iliad* (1715), Pope offered a vivid evocation of the experience of reading Homer:

It is to the Strength of [his] amazing Invention we are to attribute that unequal'd Fire and Rapture, which is so forcible in *Homer*, that no Man of a true Poetical Spirit is Master of himself while he reads him. What he writes is of the most animated Nature imaginable; every thing moves, every thing lives, and is put in Action. If a Council be call'd, or a Battle fought, you are not coldly inform'd of what was said or done as from a third Person; the Reader is hurry'd out of himself by the Force of the Poet's Imagination, and turns in one place to a Hearer, in another to a Spectator.

(Pope 1939–69: 7. 4)

Only a translation of Homer that constantly displays a 'Fire', 'Rapture' and 'Imagination' commensurate with those of its original can produce a readerly involvement of the kind that Pope describes. And if a translation does not produce such an effect, it is, surely, untrue to its original in as fundamental a way as can be imagined? In many obvious, important, and well-documented senses, Pope's *Iliad* is 'unfaithful' to the letter of Homer's text. Indeed, Pope himself constantly signals in the notes to his translation his conviction that it is impossible to render Homer's text with transparent and unmediated directness in the very different cultural and linguistic circumstances of a later culture (see G.F. Parker 2005). But in other, equally important, ways – or so it might be argued – Pope's version is by far the most radically 'faithful' rendering of Homer that we possess. If we are taking the etymological root of the term 'translation' seriously, to indicate a genuine 'bringing across' of something of the total effect of an ancient text (not merely of its construable content or discussable elements), might it not be argued that it is *only* versions which offer the fullness of imaginative and experiential participation allowed by Pope's *Iliad* that properly deserve the title 'translation' at all?

FURTHER READING

H.A. Mason's principal studies of translation are to be found in H.A. Mason 1959, 1963, 1969, 1972, 1976–7, 1981. Steiner 1998 has become a standard reference-point for subsequent discussion of literary translation. Tomlinson 2003 offers a poet's view of the verse translator's art. Shankman 1996 provides a complete text of Pope's *Iliad* in one volume. This is the only popular edition ever to have included all of Pope's own notes, with quotations from classical sources conveniently translated. For studies of Pope's *Iliad*, see Knight 1951, Mason 1972, Rosslyn 2002, Shankman 1983. Sowerby 2004 argues convincingly that the decorum of Pope's translation results from the poet's desire to preserve narrative and dramatic coherence rather than from any mechanical concern to observe neoclassical 'correctness'. G.F. Parker 2005 illuminates Pope's intelligent awareness of problems of rendering Homeric 'simplicity' in English.

CHAPTER ELEVEN

Translation at the Intersection of Traditions: The Arab Reception of the Classics

Ahmed Etman

The main aim of this contribution is to clarify the cultural results of introducing classics in the modern Arab world. It is therefore necessary to explain the historical background dealing with the roots of the interrelation between Egypt and the ancient east on one side, and Classics on the other. (All translations are the author's unless stated otherwise.) The Arab world, particularly Egypt, contributed in making and preserving the mediterranean heritage, which includes what we mean by Classics. In the golden age of Islam in Baghdad (second and third centuries H., equivalent to the eighth and ninth centuries CE), the main classics were translated into Arabic. Consequently this very ancient connection with the classics was bequeathed to modern Arabs. It is noteworthy, however, that some fields of the classics such as mythology, drama and epic were neglected or ignored in the Baghdad of the Abbasids. Nowadays Arabs do not hesitate to deal with these fields freely. They have adopted Greek myths in their creative writings in prose and poetry. Classical scholarship in Egyptian universities played a great role in this cultural change. This rising Occidentalism in the east is, in a way, a very positive response to a long history of western Orientalism.

The Oriental Origins

The origins of Greek civilization are Oriental rather than European. Geography, history, archeology and anthropology confirm this fact. Greek authors from Homer to Lucian acknowledge the debt to Egypt, Phoenicia and the Orient in general. Bernal (1987) has been published in Arabic, having been revised, edited and introduced by Etman (1997). The Arabic introduction deals with the endless discussions in the Arab world, Greece and in the western world as a whole (see, for example, Lefkowitz and Rogers 1996; Berlinerblau 1999; Moore 2001). This debt, however, has to be duly repaid now by the peoples of the east and in particular the Arabs. They know that they cannot understand their own national heritage without Greek and Latin sources. For example the writings of Herodotus, Strabo and Plutarch are the main introduction for any Egyptologist. The hieroglyphics of the Rosetta Stone were deciphered by the help of a Greek version on the same stone. On the other hand, a great part of the classical heritage was discovered in the sands of Egypt, that is, on papyri. Therefore, there is no exaggeration if it is said that Egypt is, in a way, a partner in making and preserving the classical heritage, which in any case became one of the universal and human possessions.

Arabic Versions of the Classics

From Alexander's expeditions to the Arab conquest, that is, about a thousand years, the area known now as the Arab world lived under the impact of Greco-Roman influence, or rather cultural exchange. This was strengthened by the fact that in the golden Age of Islam, the Abbasid period of the eighth and ninth centuries CE, Dar El Hikmah (Wisdom House) was founded in Baghdad for translation, especially from Greek. There the main books of Greek heritage were translated particularly in the fields of applied sciences for example, medicine, mathematics, astronomy and philosophy (Rosenthal 1992: passim).

   These translations from Greek helped to promote cultural and academic activities in Baghdad, which actually witnessed a golden age of multilingualism and multi-culturalism. At the same time these translations offered an invaluable help to modern and contemporary Classics in the following respects:

1   They throw a light on some extant texts and their meanings.
2   They correct some fragmented texts, filling up the lacunae.
3   They preserve some texts in Arabic, the Greek origins being lost.
4   They fill many gaps not only in some texts, but also in the literary history of different genres and sciences.

Consequently these Arabic versions cannot be neglected in modern classical studies generally, and in textual criticism particularly (Walzer 1962: 29, 59; Etman 1997–8: 29–38). However, the great works of Greek literature remained unknown to the Arabs. The little that was known of Homer, Hesiod, Pindar, the tragedians, Aristophanes, etc., was known indirectly, for instance, through the works of Aristotle and Galen and gnomic literature. However, some forms of Greek literature persisted and re-emerged in Arabic guise (Rosenthal 1992: 255ff.). The descendants of the Ancient Muslim translators of Baghdad, that is, contemporary Arabs, reasonably feel now that they should revive and continue the same approach to the Classics, but with wider perspectives suitable for the contemporary knowledge society.

Classics in the Arab Renaissance

The Egyptian Renaissance began immediately after the French expedition led by Napoleon Bonaparte (1798). Under the rule of Mohamed Aly, an Albanian born in Cavala-Greece, many student missions were sent to Italy and France. Rifa'a Rafie El Tahtawy (1801–1872) went to Paris as an Azhar preacher on one of those missions. On returning to Cairo he became the leader of cultural Egyptian Renaissance based on three main projects: revival, modernization and translation.

He founded the school of Alsun (languages) which is still active at the present time, having graduated tens of generations of translators from (and into) different languages. El Tahtawy himself translated the work of François de Salignac de la Mothe Fénelon (1651–1715), *Les aventures de Télémaque* (1699). This work, written by a Christian priest, was intended to have an educational function. This aspect attracted the Azhar Muslim preacher and convinced him to translate it with great hopes of an agreeable reception from the Muslim audience. In any case it is the first translated work based on classical mythology in modern times.

Three features of this translation should be noted. First, it is a translation achieved by an amateur, that is, one who is not a classicist. Second, the work itself is not directly from the classics, but it is inspired by the *Odyssey* of Homer. Third, a modern European language is used to connect the Arab reader with classical culture. This mediation was necessary because there were no classicists in Egypt and the Arab world at that time. A similar mediation took place in some countries of western Europe during the Renaissance. For example, William Shakespeare read an English translation (1597) of Plutarch's *Parallel Lives* by Thomas North (1535–1603). This was a translation of a French translation (1559) by Jacque Amyot (1513–1593). These three features of translation were to be dominant in the classical culture of Egypt and the Arab world until the 1950s and 1960s.

Egyptian Classical Scholarship

The establishment of the Classical Studies Department in Cairo University (1925) marks a turning point. Writing a book with the title *The Future of Culture in Egypt* (1938), Taha Hussein (1889–1973), the founder of classical scholarship in Egypt, asserted that the historical connections between Egypt and Greece, or the Mediterranean culture as a whole, are unique, and they are perhaps stronger than any connections between Egypt and the other countries of the Middle East. He even believed that there would be no cultural renaissance in Egypt if the Egyptians neglected the classical heritage (Etman 1998: 687–770). These opinions of Taha Hussein were strongly resisted by some nationalists and some Muslim conservative scholars of the university of El Azhar. The philhellenism of Taha Hussein calls to mind the Dutch Desiderius Erasmus and his role in the revival of Classics in the European Renaissance. Taha Hussein was the first to translate Sophocles' plays into Arabic (Committee of Writing, Translation and Publishing 1939). This translation played a great role in developing Arab theatre, although the translator depended on a French translation rather than the Greek original itself. The success of this translation is partly due to the charming style of the translator, who was undoubtedly one of the best modern Arab prose writers. Lewis Awad (1916–1990), Shoukry Aiad (1921–1999), Tharwat Okasha (1921–) and others followed the model of Taha Hussein and published many translations and studies on classics depending mainly on their wide reading in English and French.

At the present time, however, many Egyptian Universities, among which is El Azhar the most ancient Islamic University, include a Classical Department. So there are new generations of classicists who completed their studies in England, France, Germany, Italy, USA and Greece. They diffuse philhellenism not only in Egypt but also all over the Arab world. They publish new translations of the Greek and Latin authors, especially the dramatists, directly from the original texts. These efforts are promising, they pave the way for composing a Greek–Arabic and a Latin–Arabic dictionary and a classical encyclopedia. Egyptian cultural life is badly in need of these tools.

The Egyptian Society of Greek and Roman Studies (ESGRS), founded in 1985, has its own Annual (AESGRS) and its own electronic website (www.esgrs-escl.com) and it is a member of FIEC. It organizes international congresses, and it publishes specialized monographs and some translations:

> The Egyptian output in Greek and Classical Studies developed naturally in all decades [of the twentieth century], but it reached its peak in the eighth decade (1982–1994) because of the establishment of ESGRS in 1985. This Society enriched writing and translation in the field as a result of its annual publication AESGRS, the first specialized periodical in the Middle East.
>
> (El Kafoury 2004: passim; cf. AESGRS 2004–5: 211–14)

I believe that the revival of the Ancient Bibliotheca Alexandrina and the opening of the new Alexandria Library (October 2002) embodies the greatest concrete achievement of Egyptian classical scholarship. I have discussed this in some published papers and in my play *The Wedding of the Libraries' nymph* (Khedr 2002: 309–29).

The major result of all these efforts is that Egyptian classical scholarship has passed the stage of 'mediation' and established a direct relation between Classics and Arab culture. The influence of classical scholarship on creative writings in the Arab world from the second half of the twentieth century onwards is very obvious (Etman 2001b: 3–10). People now are not satisfied with the amateur translations, they seek translations by the Egyptian classicists. This is exemplified by Homer's *Iliad* which has been translated previously five times by amateurs and through 'mediation'. But when the classicists' translation appeared in 2004, the intellectuals felt that this chronic challenge had been finally overcome and they now asked: 'where is the *Odyssey*?' They meant that, since the challenge of the *Iliad* had been overcome after a whole century of attempts, let us turn to the *Odyssey*. The recent translation of the *Iliad* (Etman 2004b) and the reaction of cultural life in Egypt and the Arab world is discussed in *The Translation of the 'Iliad' and Classics into Arabic* (Etman forthcoming). For the papers from a symposium held on this occasion, see Etman 2006.

Arab Poetic reception of Greek Mythology

Ancient Arab Muslims did not translate Greek poetry because Arabs of those times felt no need to translate foreign poems. They already had a well-established poetic tradition even from the pre-Islamic period. Also, Arab Muslim translators and critics believed that poems are untranslatable. There is a quotation from *Siwän al-hikmah* of Abu Sulaimän al-Mantiqï as-Sijistänï (according to Istanbul MS Murad Molla 1408, fol. 35a), which states the following: 'Stephan son of Basileus [seventh century CE] has translated part of the Homeric poems from Greek into Arabic. It is known that poems lose most of their special splendour in translation and that the ideas expressed in them become largely corrupted when the artistic form of the poetry is altered.'

In Al-Jähiz, *Kitäb al-Hayawän* (Cairo, 1323–5, I: 37; Cairo, 1938–45, I: 74f.) the same perspective is repeated:

> Only the Arabs and people who speak Arabic have a correct understanding of poetry. Poems do not lend themselves to translation and ought not to be translated. When they are translated, their poetic structure is rent; the metre is no longer correct; poetic beauty disappears and nothing worthy of admiration remains in the poems. It is different with prose. Accordingly, original prose is more beautiful and appropriate than prose renderings of metric poetry.
>
> (quoted in Rosenthal 1992: 18–19)

Actually there are numerous Arabic references, quotations and the like concerning Homer and his two Epics. Yet the Homeric verses quoted in Arab tradition are in fact a translation of the *Monostichoi* attributed to Menander (Kraemer 1956: 259–316; Stromaier 1980: 196–200). There is a tradition that Hunain bin Ishaq (194–260 H = 809–873; CE), the best Arab translator from Greek, translated the *Iliad*, yet we have nothing at all to confirm this. But it is said in Arab traditional anecdotes that Hunain bin Ishaq was heard loudly reciting Greek verses from the *Iliad* during his walks in the streets of Baghdad.

There are still some questions without any convincing answer. Did Arabs actually translate the *Iliad*? If not, why not?

I believe that the main obstacle in the way of Muslim Arabs translating Homeric epics was mythology. Arab pre-Islamic poetry – as it has reached our hands – deals with myths only rarely and vaguely. This phenomenon, together with the circumstances of oral tradition, convinced Taha Hussein to declare his doubts concerning the genuiness of pre-Islamic poems. Taha Hussein's book *Pre-Islamic Poetry* developed these opinions and raised great troubles for the author in the 1920s. The book itself was banned. Later the author published a modified edition with the title *Pre-Islamic Literature*.

Here the main difference between the Arab oral poetic tradition and its parallel in Greece is marked – that is, the function of myth in the concept of poetic creation itself. On the Arab side, as far as it is known, there is no essential function of myth. On the Greek side it is almost impossible to separate myth from poetry. They are two faces of the same coin, or rather, myth is the *sine qua non* of *poiesis*. This is obviously exemplified in the *Iliad* and *Odyssey*. The main protagonists of these two epics are divine or semi-divine. This hero or that is the son of a god or goddess. The human and divine actions are inter-woven and reciprocal in the daily events of the Trojan wars and the adventures of Odysseus. In the *Iliad* there is a divine struggle on Olympus among gods and goddesses who divide into two parties; one supports and the other resists the Greeks (or the Trojans). It is a divine and heavenly battle parallel to the earthly. Human beings in the two epics behave as if they are divine beings (apotheosis), while gods and goddesses behave like human beings (anthropomorphism): they quarrel with each other, they suffer and cry with tears, they fall in love and they are victims of cruel passions. This essential concept is the key to understanding Homeric epics and Greek tragedies (Etman 2004b: 281–99).

However, this concept cannot be transferred precisely to Arab Muslim mentality. Even in pre-Islamic times, as far as it is known, they have nothing similar. It is exclusively a Greek concept which cannot be transplanted in Arab cultural soil. After Islam it was considered impossible to translate Greek epics (and tragedies), in which this mythological concept is a *sine qua non* of composing and receiving poems.

Arabs translated many Greek prose works, some of which contain complicated philosophic ideas concerning life and death, man and gods and the like. One can probably read Herodotus, Thucydides, Demosthenes or Plato putting aside the mythological hints. In contrast, the concept of poetry itself includes the mythological way of thinking. Muslim Arabs could not adapt this concept of poetry to their own poetic tradition, nor to their mentality. For this reason they did not translate Homer's epics.

From ancient times, then, Greek pagan myths represent the main impediment for Arab Muslims to absorb Greek poetry. In particular they avoided the Greek poems based on polytheism and myths of love stories between gods/goddesses and human beings for example, the epics and tragedies. In modern times this problem was overcome step by step. Rifa'ah El Tahtawy', as has been noted, translated Fénelon's *Les aventures de Télémaque* which was written by a pious Christian priest and with an educational function. Such justification was also the pretext of Soliman El Bostany translating the Homeric *Iliad*. He did not mention the word *myth* in his lengthy title:

> *The Iliad of Homeros translated into poetic Arabic with historical and literary explanation and with an Introduction on Homeros and his poetic work and on Greek Literature and Arab Literature.* Entailed with a General Glossary and Index by Soliman El Bostany, Published in El Hilal Press, Egypt 1904.

The title includes Greek Literature, History and Homeric poetic art, but it avoids any allusion to the myth of Trojan Wars. This means that, until the publication date in 1904, men of letters in the Arab World did not have the courage to deal with mythology so openly. The *Iliad* in this translation, the introduction and the comments contain basically and naturally mythological materials, but the translator was extremely careful to omit this essential element from the title.

The importance of El Bostany's poetic translation is due to the three following factors:

1   It represents a turning point in the cultural and academic life in Egypt and the Arab world. It was published 21 years before the foundation of the Department of Ancient European Culture (= Classics) in Cairo University (1925) by Taha Hussein, as has been mentioned above. Therefore, it can be reasonably said that this translation partially contributed to the establishment of Greek and Latin Studies in Egypt. Soliman El Bostany had tried to teach himself Greek. However his translation of the *Iliad* depends on French, Italian and English translations rather than on the Greek original.

2   The introduction to El Bostany's translation is extremely interesting. It is a serious comparative study of Greek and Arabic poetry. It also deals with the problems of translating poems into poetic translations. This introduction, appearing so early, can be considered as a leading study in classics and comparative criticism.

3   It is the first complete translation of the *Iliad* into Arabic.

El Bostany's translation was received with great enthusiasm. A well known Islamic thinker, Gamal El Din El Afghany addressed the translator saying:

> It much pleases us to do to-day what Arabs should have done more than thousand years ago: Would that the men of letters gathered by El Maamoun [in Baghdad] began by translating the *Iliad*, even if this should have obliged them to sacrifice Greek philosophy as a whole.

On the same occasion Munif Pasha, Otthoman minister of Education said:

> 'If the Arab poet who said: I am as Omeros [= Homer] for the Religion of Muhamed . . .' if he actually did for the East what Homeros did for the West, West could have not been able to anticipate us with such a great distance.

The translation of the *Iliad* into Arabic took Soliman El Bostany almost twenty years of hard work. It has about eleven thousand Arabic verses, parallel to about sixteen thousand Greek original verses. The problems which El Bostany faced are numerous. Such translation requires wide reading in the mythology, history, archeology, geography, economy and politics of Ancient Greece. How did he get such knowledge? How did he solve the problems? Such questions cannot be answered without a detailed comparative textual study of the Arabic translation and the original. Gihad Kazem an Iraqi living in Paris, prepared a PhD thesis on El Bostany's *Iliad* (see *Revue d'Etudes Palestiniennes*, 56, 4 n.s. 1995: 79–100; cf. Etman 1995: 511–13).

In the 1960s Dreeny Khashabah published an *Iliad* and an *Odyssey*. A Lebanese, Anber Salam by name, published simplified texts of the two epics. Amin Salama also published the two epics in Arabic. The last serious effort was that of the great Syrian poet Mamdouh Udwan who published in Abu Dhabie (2002) a complete prose translation of the *Iliad*, made from an English translation.

The different translations of the Classics as well as the classical scholarship in Arabic were warmly received by the creative Arab writers. This is reflected in the influence of Greek mythology upon modern Arabic lyric poetry, which is too extensive to be examined here in detail (see further Hamdy 1966; Daif 2003). This phenomenon is partly due to the stamp of T.S. Eliot on Modern Arabic Poetry in general. And from the thirties of the twentieth century a group of poets in Cairo, led by Abu Shady, Aly Mahmud Taha and Abu El-Qasem El-Shabby (from Tunisia), tried to revive the Greek myths in their poems. They even called themselves and their periodical after the name of the Greek god of music, poetry and oracles, *Apollo*. This trend in Arabic poetry is still strong in the works of the contemporary poets such as the Iraqi poets El-Sayab, El-Bayati and Nazik al Malaika as well as Adonis of Syria and Salah Abd El-Sabour and Mohamed Afifi Mattar of Egypt (Ghazoul 1994, 2002; Etman 1982, 1983a, 1983b).

It is not a matter of mere Greek mythological references here and there in modern Arabic poetry. The influence extends to include the poetic techniques themselves. For instance, the imagery of the contemporary Arabic poetry is highly affected by the symbols of Greek myths. It is enough to deal here briefly with one example, namely the image of fire. I think that the Tunisian, Abu El-Qasem El-Shabby, is the first Arab poet to connect the idea of fire with Prometheus in a poem under the title *The Hymn of the Titan, or thus Prometheus Sang*. It was published on 15 December 1933. The poems of Aly Mahmud Taha also are full of images of fire with the mythological background borrowed from the Greeks. Nazik al Malaika admires and imitates him. In one of her poetic collections, *The Sea Changes Its Colour*, she published a poem under the title *Sanabil el Nar* [*The (Wheat) Ears of Fire*]. In this poem, dated 9.2.1974, the image of fire embraces the essence of the meaning as well as the external form itself. The poem deals with the theme of love passing through three stages: physical love, patriotism and divine love. Love here is represented as a holy fire which purifies and deifies its sufferer lifting him to be united with the highest level of existence. This image of fire is obviously close to the apotheosis by fire in Greek mythology and philosophy, for example, the stoic concept of Divine Fire (Etman 1974: 50–63).

But no Arab poet exploits the myth of Prometheus better than the Iraqi poet El Bayati (1926–1999). In the introduction to his collection *The New Nisabour* [*Muhakama fi Nisabur*] (1963) he says: 'In fact the crisis of Arabic Modern poetry does not lie in the form, but rather in the very existence of the poet himself.' And he adds that 'the traditional poetic form does not enable the non-talented poets to be inspired by the flame of Prometheus'. And once more in another collection, *The Death of the Myth*, El Bayati introduces the myth by saying 'the poetic fires which have been inflamed during the forties and the beginnings of the fifties [that is, of the twentieth century] are still alive and blazing and they finally turned to be a forest of flames'. And speaking about his poetic experience he says 'In the foregoing part of my poetic career I stood at the gates of Thebes as an exile and as a witness. This was not but an indication of my return into the fiery circle'.

It is remarkable that El Bayati and some other Arab poets, use such words as: revolution, innovation, and the fire (of Prometheus) as synonyms in the context of their poetic diction. Thus El Bayati considers himself as the 'fire-stealer', that is, Prometheus Pyrophoros. In his collection *The Book of the Sea* there is a poem with the title *The Worshipped* in which he says:

> Imprisoned in fire and chains,
> I return to my exile with birds and caravans.
> Waiting for the resurrection of the poet,
> The magician and the fighter.
> I worship these fires in your eyes.

All the pieces of El Bayati's collection *An Autobiography of the Fire Stealer* use the myth of Prometheus as a symbol of the Arab revolution, both cultural and political (Etman 1982).

On the other hand, some critics consider the mythological trend in modern Arabic poetry as a revolution in Arab letters. They underline the revival of pagan myths and the open-mindedness of the Arab poets. These critics note also that the use of myths helps the Arab poets to go beyond lyricism which has been a traditional characteristic symptom of Arabic poetry from the antiquity. Yet Arab poets exaggerate using the myths so much that they sometimes resort to footnotes and annotations. This fact alone denotes very obviously that the myths are misused, or in other words they are not required by any artistic necessity. Indeed so extensive is the use of mythology in the poems of El Sayab, for example, that critics have differed on his success/failure in putting it to artistic use. In one short poem only – 'The Blind Prostitute', in his collection *The Song of the Rain* – he mixes together Oriental and western myths, referring to the following Greek names: Medusa, Oedipus-Jocaste, Thebes-Sphinx, Apollo, Daphne and Aphrodite.

Sometimes, however, a Greek myth is successfully interwoven in the poetic essence itself. Moreover, this is achieved sometimes without any explicit reference to the Greek myth. One example only is to be mentioned here quoted from the Syrian poet Nazar Qabany. On the first anniversary of Taha Hussein's death, in a ceremony held under the auspices of the Arab League in Cairo, October 1974, Nazar addressed the late great philhellene saying: 'O you scholar of Al Azhar/Stealer of the fire.'

'Stealer of the fire' is an expression which originally means nothing in Arabic traditional poetic language. But now, with the Greek mythological background of Modern Arabic Poetry, it means a lot. Taha Hussein, having graduated from Al Azhar, went to Europe and from there he (although being blind) stole the fire of enlightenment, and, exactly as Prometheus, he was severely punished.

Classical Drama in Arab Theatre

It is curious, that although the Arabs of the golden Islamic Age translated many Greek texts into their own language (among these was Aristotle's *Poetics*) and although some of these translations were the basis of very important classical studies in Europe in the beginnings of the Renaissance, yet they did not translate any Greek play into Arabic. They even did not even understand the meaning of such words as 'drama', 'tragedy' and 'comedy', identifying each of them with this or that genre of their native lyric poetry. At the same time in some of their poems they use a certain kind of dialogue based on dividing every verse between two speakers (El Mumatanah). This, on the one hand, reminds us of the *antilabe* in Greek tragedy and, on the other hand, it denotes that Arabic poetry could have been adapted to dramatic dialogue, if they had known about dramatic performances.

During the nineteenth century missions of students to Europe continued. Khedewi Ismail wanted Egypt as a piece of Europe. To mark the opening of the Suez Canal (1869) he built the Opera House in Cairo with the plan to perform the opera *Aida* (1871), composed by Giuseppe Verdi (1813–1901). Many French, Italian and British theatre groups performed their works in Cairo and Alexandria. Many of these works were from neo-Classics whether French, British or Italian. In other words, the theatre of Shakespeare, Corneille, Racine, Molière and Goldoni were performed in Egypt from the second half of the nineteenth century, but only to the foreign communities and local aristocracy.

Local theatre groups began to imitate or adapt these foreign performances. They translated or remodelled the neo-Classics. For example, Soliman El Naqash came from Lebanon, stayed in Alexandria and wrote a play (1868) with the title *Maie* (Etman 2000). It is an adaptation of Corneille's piece, *Horace*, which is based on a myth taken from Titus Livius on the legendary foundation of Rome. Jacob Ssannoue adapted many comedies in the same way. At the beginning of the twentieth century Osman Galal successfully adapted Molière to the extent that some critics called him the 'Egyptian Molière'. George Abyad, a Syrian by origin, was the first to be sent by the Egyptian government to France to study theatre in 1904. On his return he organized an Egyptian company in 1912. The first plays performed by his company were translated into Arabic, from French, by Farah Antun. Thus the first pure Egyptian theatre company began with a Greek play, namely *Oedipus*, Abyad himself was known as the 'Oedipus of Arab Theatre', being the first to act this role (Etman 2002: 223–6). Munira El Mahdiah and Mohamed Abd El Wahab, famous singers, performed Cleopatra, as a reaction to the performance of Shakespeare's *Antony and Cleopatra* (Etman 2001a: 56–71). This tendency towards the Cleopatra theme in the early twentieth century culminated in the poetic work of the prince of Arab poets Ahmed Shawqy's *The Death of Cleopatra* (1927) (Etman 2003: 107–16; Mazhar 2003: 97–133).

Yet introducing dramatic art into Arabic poetry requires, beside Shawqy's poetic genius, a systematic study of the origins of drama, a thing which Shawqy lacked. Dramatic education must begin with the Greeks, that is, with Aeschylus, Sophocles, Euripides and Aristophanes. This rule was to be established later in the Arabic dramatic literature through the rich experience of Tewfik El Hakim. But as for Shawqy, on reading all his poems, *El Shawqiat*, and on following the circumstances of his education and its sources, we do not find any indication that he knew the Greek dramatic masterpieces. Of course we do not mean simple knowledge, which as a matter of fact Shawqy had obtained even before his stay in France. I believe that the dramatic education of Shawqy as a whole is neither high, nor systematically complete. No doubt he knew the neo-classical writers of France and the heads of the Romantic revolution there, such as Victor Hugo. He also knew many other dramatists, yet he did not digest their works. Even the performances which he attended in Egypt and in France, were not so fruitful for him. The genius of the prince of Arabic poetry had been previously directed otherwise, to fields different from the dramatic art.

Arab critics assert that composing any play of classical origins, such as *The Death of Cleopatra* and *Cambyses* of Shawqy, needs two basic requirements. First the author has to keep a direct and systematic contact with the classical sources. Second, he must possess a long experience in dramatic art and technique. Fortunately the new generation of Arab verse dramatists tries to achieve these two requirements. This trend is exemplified by the plays of Naguib Sorour and Salah Abd El Sabour.

Arabic prose drama profited from classical culture more fruitfully than did the poetic. Tewfik El Hakim went to France to study law but devoted himself to drama. From his wide readings in French literature he was convinced that if he wants to achieve any success as a playwright he must begin from the natural beginning, that is, to go back to the Greek authors, 'the eternal masters of drama'. He read them, but in French translations.

The result was that Tewfik El Hakim wrote three plays with Greek themes, namely *Pygmalion, King Oedipus, and Praxa*. The last one is an imitation of Aristophanes *Ecclesiazousai* or *Women in the Assembly*, the Arabic title *Praxa* being an abbreviated form of Praxagora, the protagonist. Yet the Greek influence upon Tewfik El Hakim is not confined to these three plays but it extends to all his works and even to his very way of thinking. In his play *Food for Every Mouth* he adapts the myth of Orestes to a contemporary theme. And in his semi-autobiographical story *A Bird from the Orient* he fell in love with a beautiful French girl during his stay in Paris; and he revealed his feelings to her for the first time through a French translation of a poem by Anacreon (fr. 11) entitled 'To Love' (*eis Erōta*) although he translated it into Arabic as meaning 'the combat'.

The influence of Tewfik El Hakim was tremendous. It is enough to mention here that there are no less than six Arabic adaptations of Oedipus. Each play reflects a certain period and is closely connected with this political event or that from the debacle of Palestine in 1948 to the defeat of Arabs in 1967. This means two things. First that Oedipus has been absorbed into Arabic modern life at least on the stage. Second, many other plays on the Oedipus theme are to be expected in the coming years. El Hakim was taken as the Model by many other writers in Egypt and the Arab World. They tried to adapt Greek plays into Arabic versions. All of them do not read Greek. All of them depend on their European culture and their knowledge of this European modern language or that. Some of them can read only Arabic (Etman 1979: passim; Carlson 2004b: 368–375, 2005: passim).

Thus from the beginnings of modern Egyptian theatre in the middle of nineteenth century Greek drama was known indirectly through the neo-classics. In the early twentieth century some Greek plays were translated. From that time onwards many Greek plays were published in translations from English or French, not only in Egypt but also in Kuwait, Iraq, Lebanon and Syria. Some of these plays were performed. An extraordinary example is to be mentioned here, the director of National Theatre of Greece by name Mouzinides was invited to direct the *Libation Bearers* of Aeschylus on the stage of the National Theatre in Cairo. The translation was in blank verse by Lewis Awad, who knows little Latin and less Greek, being a professor of English in Cairo University and a translator of the *Ars poetica* of Horace (1947). The performance took place in the early 1960s and achieved a great success and warm reception from the Egyptian audience.

The translations of the classicists, for example, Mohamed Saqr Khafaga (1919–1964), Selim Salem (1904–1993) and their students, began to appear from the 1960s. Generally speaking Greek Theatre won the greater part of Arab attention. Every piece was translated more than once (Carlson 2005). It is possible to say that there is no Greek or Roman play still without an Arabic version. Yet the translations from the original, Greek and Latin, are still incomplete, although they are increasing year after year. Some of these translations were performed on the stage for example, *Oedipus, Antigone, Electra* of Sophocles, *Medea* of Euripides, the *Clouds* and *Frogs* of Aristophanes.

Many Greek and Roman plays were acted and broadcasted on Cairo Radio, that is, the Second (now Cultural) programme. This programme had three hours of broadcasting every evening and I was astonished when my translation of Seneca's tragedy *Hercules Oetaeus* was broadcast. The play is so difficult, being full of myths and philosophic references (note that there is no evidence, to support or to reject that Seneca's tragedies were performed on Ancient Roman Stage). The Arabic *Hercules Oetaeus* was also too long and it was broadcast in two successive evenings (more than five hours). The protagonist was one of the superstars in the cinema, theatre and television, the late Abdallah Ghaith. This took place in 1989/90. I also translated *The Women of Trachis* of Sophocles as well as the *Clouds* of Aristophanes and both were broadcast in the same way and on the same programme.

However, another mode of reception, namely adaptation, has been more successful. Here it is almost impossible to count all the adaptations from Greco-Roman myths and plays in Arabic performances. Many Greek myths have been performed one way or another on the Arab stage (see Loulidi 2004: 399–405, 1998: passim, which discussed the works of Aly Oqla Arasan, Walid Ikhlassi, Riad Essmat, Hassan Hamada, Ahmed Etman and Mohamed El Kughatt as Greek mythological themes dramatized in Arab theatre). The study of the classical sources of modern Arabic theatre (Etman 1985: 126–9) is recommended as a promising approach for a well-balanced understanding of philhellenism in the Arab world.

To conclude, it is noteworthy that contemporary Egyptians and Arabs are interested in ancient Greece and its heritage and generally they know more about it than about modern Greece and modern Greek literature (except for a few names like Kavafy and Kazantzakis). The branches of ancient Greek culture which have warmer reception are: mythology, criticism, theatre, epic, philosophy, history and archeology. Lyric poetry is almost unknown except Sappho and Pindar from Greek and Ovid from Latin.

FURTHER READING

Etman 1990, 1993, 1995; Gutas 1998.

CHAPTER TWELVE

'Enough Give in It': Translating the Classical Play

J. Michael Walton

Introduction

Special and specialist areas of translation cover so much ground that their practitioners inevitably have clashing priorities. The poetry translator operates within a different constituency from the UN interpreter, the scientific journalist or the sur-titler
for opera. The biblical scholar, the cultural historian, the gender critic, all have their
agendas, agendas different because of their individual priorities and constituencies.
Manchester University's Centre for Translation and Intercultural Studies has a programme which incorporates lectures on, amongst other topics, translation and
conflict, video games, the language of young children, philosophy, journalism in Iraq,
Italian fascism and computer technology. TRIO (Translation Research in Oxford)
once devoted a full day to translating nonsense. All such translators enthusiastically
rehearse and debate the issues of their discipline, sometimes fruitfully, sometimes in
so arcane a fashion as to defy penetration. All have in common, though it does not
always seem so, that their discourse revolves around a source and a target language
and the transference from the former to the latter.

Translating drama is different. The source may be there but the target is not:
at least not as a finished article but only as an intermediate stage. Where most
translation involves a bond between source as mother and target as child, theatre
translation serves as midwife between the playwright's pregnancy and a living,
breathing performance baby. If this seems no more of a distinction than is the polysys-
temic approach to literary or poetical translation and the open-ended possibilities
of a target which allows for a variety of 'true' (in the sense of 'equally suitable')
translations, it is not so. A stage play on the page – any play of any shape or form
from the long-dead Sophocles to the contemporary Botho Strauss – is still in
transit, a potential only, its breath of life to be determined by directors, designers
and players in as many different ways as there may be productions.

My aim here will be threefold: in the first instance, to provide some sort of introduction to the individual nature of translating of drama, and especially ancient Greek

tragedy, as opposed to other forms of literary translation; second, to identify the parameters that may be set between a respect for the original text and the imperatives of a modern production, together with the function of the translator within the process; third, to consider specific examples from each of the Greek tragedians which highlight the transition in ancient Athens from the formal tragedy of Aeschylus to the more human and humane plays of Sophocles and Euripides. Overall, the intention is more to provoke discussion than to provide solutions to the problems: for the nature of translation and the nature of the theatre both show there are no absolute rules and no easy answers.

Translating the Stage Play

The responsibilities of the translator of a piece first intended for performance are complex. The task is a different one depending on whether a translation is commissioned for a specific production by a specific director, or for publication, where it may lie comatose on the shelf waiting, like Princess Aurora, for her prince to fight his way through the forest and wake her with a kiss. The classical canon offers the worst of all worlds, that of trying to marry, at one terminus, a playwright whose every mindset was dictated by a socio-political aesthetic two and a half thousand years old, to, at the other, a contemporary audience who will expect to be touched, affected or amused within their own set of cultural references and expectations.

Until the beginning of the twentieth century, the translator of a Greek tragedy or comedy was not faced with as much agonizing because few if any of the translators had any expectation that their plays would ever be exposed to an audience. Greek drama, as opposed to drama inspired by Greek mythology, was simply not performed on the professional stage. Many of these translators into English, and they numbered well over three hundred before 1900 alone, were clerics or schoolmasters with both time and occasion to publish. Some were playwrights, in Dryden's case a playwright and poet laureate with a sophisticated interest in translation, for whom the writing of an *Oedipus* with Nathaniel Lee (performed 1678, published 1679), paid no more than the occasional lip-service either to Sophocles or to Seneca. Up to, arguably Lewis Theobald (1688–1744), but in reality Gilbert Murray (1866–1957), translation of Greek playtexts showed the barest understanding of the theatrical nature of the originals, or the stage conditions for which they were first created. The last hundred years have borne witness to appropriation of classical drama by various interests which were united in a desire to bridge the gap between the ancient Greek text as source and a contemporary audience as target. Some have been more successful than others. Most have tended to become dated fairly quickly. The sources, on the other hand, have never seemed more alive as metaphors for the issues of today as modern directors have returned for their inspiration to the theatre's own earliest history.

Classical scholarship has always tended to view the world of the fifth century BC through the preoccupations of its own time. This is inevitable. Perspectives shift and so they should. But if one thing about the Athenian drama may be regarded as certain it is that, had not *The Oresteia* been well received by its audience at the first production in the spring of 458 BC, we would not now have it. The corollary to this is that, had it not similarly appealed purely as text to generations of scholars and to translators from Robert Potter (1721–1804) onwards, we would not have seen, amongst a host of others, two full productions of the whole trilogy in English at the National Theatre (Harrison's translation, 1981 and Hughes', 1999); and outstanding European productions such as Ariane Mnouchkine's under the title of *Les Atrides*, (1990–2) and Peter Stein's (1980, 1994). (See Macintosh et al. 2005 for full details of these productions.) There is something within *The Oresteia* and all the other extant plays of Aeschylus, Sophocles, Euripides, Aristophanes and Menander that accounts for their appeal to their original audience. It is up to the translator, not only to locate this factor, but to reveal it in such a way that modern practitioners can find ways of renewing the plays on stage.

Translation of a Greek play, then, is far more than a simple act of transmission from one language into another. It involves the transference of a context and finding a balance of reference which will both keep faith with the original and allow for the creative act of performance. Reduced to a simple argument, it is not about translating 'chariot' as 'motor-car' or 'bow' as 'rifle', but rather finding a language that will allow a director to create a stage world where either chariots and bows, or cars and guns, may seem appropriate. This is not the place for a more detailed consideration of the production of Greek plays on the contemporary stage. It may be a place to offer a challenge to the current thinking that the translator has little need to know the original language or context.

One of four English-language productions of Euripides' *Hecuba* in 2004/2005 was 'translated' by Frank McGuinness, who does not work directly from ancient Greek. The three others were translated respectively by John Harrison, by Tony Harrison and by Marianne McDonald, all of whom do work from the Greek. Is the text of John Harrison (Cambridge University Press, 2004), Marianne McDonald (Nick Hern Books, 2005) or Tony Harrison (Faber and Faber, 2005) 'better', by definition, than that of McGuinness, simply because the other three do know the original language? McGuinness is a prolific and highly accomplished playwright (also published by Faber and Faber) who claims of his *Hecuba* only that it is 'a new version'. W.B. Yeats had no Greek, neither did Robert Lowell nor Ted Hughes; nor do Seamus Heaney and Brendan Kennelly. Does that make them worse 'translators' of Aeschylus, Sophocles and Euripides *as playwrights* than those literal translators of the nineteenth-century Bohn editions, or the Kelly's Keys to the Classics, or, in the twentieth and twenty-first centuries, the Loeb editions, with Greek on one page, the English opposite?

The Spirit of the Original

Robert Lowell's *Oresteia* (published 1978) was picked out for intense criticism by Sir Kenneth Dover in an essay originally published in 1980 and reprinted in a slightly revised version as 'The Speakable and the Unspeakable' (Dover 1987: 176–81). Suggesting that Lowell's plays in English bear 'an intermittent resemblance to three plays which Aeschylus wrote in Greek', Dover identified substantial cuts, imported material and a sense beyond either that Lowell 'does violence to the Greek sense of occasion'. The words of criticism are carefully chosen and represent separate concerns which he believes the translator should bear in mind.

The first is cutting the text. *The Oresteia* is certainly long, three plays which together tend to play for upwards of five hours – seven in the case of Peter Stein's production – and are often spread over two nights. Even the first 'full' production in English, that of Frank Benson at Stratford in 1904, promised in the publicity to come in under three hours, with intervals of only eight minutes and ten, and incurred the wrath of several critics with deadlines by lasting for a full three hours and a half. Aeschylus, intense and condensed in his language, is fiendishly difficult to cut.

More to the point, one suspects, and with a few honourable exceptions, a poet's loyalty is to his own work and it is here that Dover's second concern, importation, most often shows its face. Though the question of whether verse should only be translated into verse, rather than into prose, has been debated at length, there can be little dispute that the later Greek playwrights, Euripides, Aristophanes and Menander, are easier to render in prose than are the plays of Aeschylus. Translating any classical play demands an ordering of priorities. Dover gives licence to the poet's claim to 'fidelity to the spirit of the original', but concludes that 'What goes wrong in this genre of pseudo-translation is not just ignorance of the literature and culture to which the original work belongs, but narrowness of vision and indifference to character, plot and the intelligence and imagination of the original author' (Dover 1987: 177).

In a brief introduction to the published text Lowell justified his personal approach as 'to satisfy my own mind and at first hearing the simple ears of a theatre audience'. There is no denying that the better known the translators, either as poet or playwright or both, the harder they seem to find it to resist the temptation to leave their own signature on the original. This is where, it seems to Dover, translators are at fault who get carried away by an emotional reaction to a single moment or incident and over-translate it at the expense of a play's rhythm.

Linking these concerns, and underlying them, is Dover's conviction that translating 'the spirit of the original' depends not on 'intuition' but in finding out what the spirit of the original was. This is, perhaps, a parallel layer to the need to locate a dramatic throughline which will open up the original to the imagination of the practitioner, though for Dover this is optional: 'The compulsory task is say what the author said; the option to be taken if he wants the play to be performed, is to say it in a way which actors will relish speaking and an audience relish hearing' (Dover: 179).

If the questions raised by the Lowell translation are cut and dried, the answers are less so. The prolific Victorian playwright, James Robinson Planché, whose one hundred and eighty stage works included numerous adaptations from the French and also what was arguably the first translation of Aristophanes' *Birds* to be performed on the English stage (Theatre Royal, Haymarket, 13 April 1846), subsequently justified his own cavalier attitude to originals in his memoirs by stating that 'There is much more art required to make a play actable than a book readable' (Planché 1872: 246). And that was the extent of his heart-searching.

Dover's scholarly sense of dismay at liberties taken with the work of the first great playwright makes him a proper apologist for the source text: Planché, the pragmatic actor-manager, conscious of his paying audience and his own security, speaks for the true target, a satisfied audience. So where do classical translators stand: are they the in-betweens or go-betweens?

Three responses may help to provide a platform from which to find a significant example. Hilaire Belloc in his Taylorian lecture delivered in Oxford in 1931 homed in on the phrase 'the atmosphere of the word'. He began that lecture with the defensive suggestion that 'The art of translation is a subsidiary art, and derivative'. He did not deal specifically with the classics, nor, except in passing, with the dramatic text, but offered a number of ground rules which can be applied to either field, leading him to the statement that '[W]hat is . . . important when one is attempting the rendering of any great matter – great through its literary form or its message – is the atmosphere of the word' (Belloc 1931: 17).

Thirty-six years later, Theodore Savory, in a comprehensive study of translation from its early history, through translating poetry, the Bible and eventually science, included a chapter specifically on 'Translating the Classics'. One of his key statements came in the first paragraph of this chapter where he suggested that 'the translation of Greek must be more than linguistic practice, because Greek is one of the supreme languages of the world' (Savory 1957: 60). He proceeded to initiate the debate on 'Hellenizers and Modernizers' before concluding that 'If ever there were a phase of translation in which the principle of the modernizer was uncontestably to be preferred, it is in the rendering of the Greek play.' This fighting stance, however, may be influenced by Savory's unequivocal response to Greek drama that it 'never reached the supreme perfection of Homer' (Savory: 67–8; see also Walton 2006a: ch. 4).

Tom Stoppard was interviewed in *The Daily Telegraph* in October 2005, having just completed 'translating' a play for the first time, *Le Vent des Peupliers*, by a young French dramatist, Gérald Sibleyras (Sierz 2005: 25). Stoppard is known, apart from his own original work, for his updatings of plays by a variety of European authors, among them, Molnár (*Rough Crossing*); Schnitzler (*On the Razzle*); and Pirandello (*Henry IV*). In tackling the Sibleyras play his first problem was with the title. *Wind in the Poplars* would have had too much of an association with *Wind in the Willows* for an English audience. In the end the English title came out as *Heroes*. Stoppard's own confessed approach to what was his first real translation was interesting: 'The starting point is to be utterly faithful to the original. But if you abide by that completely you are doing the author a disservice. An absolutely strict translation would not have *enough give in it*' (my italics and hence my title).

A salutary example of what this entails comes from what may actually have been a piece of 'lazy translation', to use one of George Steiner's terms (Steiner 1975). In Act Two of Pinter's *The Birthday Party* Stanley Webber is being browbeaten by Goldberg and McCann. They aim a whole string of accusations at him and the dialogue reads as follows:

GOLD: No society would touch you. Not even a building society.
MCCANN: You're a traitor to the cloth.

GOLD: What do you use for pyjamas?
STAN: Nothing.
GOLD: You verminate the sheet of your birth.
MCC: What about the Albigensenist heresy?
GOLD: Who watered the wicket in Melbourne?
MCC: What about the Blessed Oliver Plunkett?
GOLD: Speak up, Webber. Why did the chicken cross the road?

(Pinter *The Birthday Party* 1960: 51)

The first German translator, reputedly, came to the line 'Who watered the wicket in Melbourne?' and looked up the words in his dictionary – 'wicket' means 'gate', 'watered' means 'urinated'. So he came up with a translation in German which translates back into English as 'Who urinated over the gates of Melbourne?'

The analogy is, however, a cricketing one. Melbourne is a cricket ground. Watering the wicket is *not cricket*. It is cheating by sprinkling water on the playing pitch to advantage the home team. This would be understood in Australia or Britain or anywhere else where cricket is a national sport; it would be appreciated by a major percentage of the white population and an increasing percentage of the black population of South Africa; its innuendo would reverberate in Sri Lanka, Pakistan, India, the Windward Islands or Jamaica. It meant something to Pinter, a wartime evacuee from his London home, whose cricket bat was his comforter; and for whom ever after cricket has been a comfort. It would have to be explained to all but the rarest American, and then only partly, by a cultural equivalent, through baseball perhaps. Christina Babou-Pagoureli, the translator into modern Greek of Stoppard, Beckett and Pinter (cricketers all), as well as Shakespeare and Webster, translates cricket references into tennis ones. It would, and did, mean nothing to a German.

Nor, if that translator had appreciated the implications, would it *have had* any meaning for a German audience to whom 'watering the wicket at Melbourne' might as well be 'urinating over the gates of Melbourne'. In other words, this translator's cultural oversight may have been nothing of the sort. What he recognized, perhaps, to give him the benefit of the doubt, was that the context implied threat; it suggested bullying and brainwashing. Linguistic equivalent was irrelevant in a stage situation which was rooted in emotional tensions beyond language.

Here is surely the nub for classical drama, perhaps for any dramatic text, the amount of 'give' being dictated by the most careful of tightrope walking between the original (frequently disputed anyway by scholars of ancient Greek) and the kind of flexibility or fluidity required by actors and directors; what Fiona Shaw once described in conversation as 'neutrality'. Writers with strong beliefs, it might be argued, make the worst translators. Poets want to write their own poetry; playwrights to write their own plays; critics to build in their own interpretation; philosophers to share their own recipe for living. The infliction of Christian virtues on Antigone, Alcestis or even Hippolytus may be feasible in production. But in the translator, a lack of attitude is probably more use than any strongly held conviction.

What is necessary is the ability to 'read' a play properly. Anyone who can read can read a play on the page but alarmingly few, translators as well as directors, pick up on the dramatic rhythm that underpins any theatrical performance and is as present in Aeschylus as it is in Shakespeare. Greek tragedy is intense, but it is not so intense that it should be played relentlessly with all the stops out. So the following examples, comparing early and contemporary translations for their sensitivity to dramatic pattern, will not be from the most intense moments, the passionate speeches, the *anagnorisieis* (recognitions) and *peripeteiai* (reversals) that are the dramatic highlights of Greek tragedy, but the quieter moments where the everyday, the gently comic, the human touch is allowed to impinge on matters of moment.

Aeschylus and *The Oresteia*

Starting with Aeschylus is logical, especially as only *The Oresteia* as a connected trilogy offers the opportunity to consider the full dramatic shape. *Agamemnon* opens, as does *Hamlet*, at a human level with a minor character and a night scene on the ramparts. Aeschylus' Watchman is disgruntled and bored. The first translator of Aeschylus into English, Robert Potter, goes straight to the point with the opening lines:

> Ye fav'ring gods, relieve me from this toil:
> Fixed, as a dog, on Agamemnon's roof,
> I watch the livelong year.
> (Potter 1777: ll. 1–3)

Aeschylus refers to 'the Atreidae' here, not to 'Agamemnon', but Potter's licence is understandable in the cause of clarity.

Anna Swanwick, some ninety years later, however, offers:

> I pray the gods deliverance from these toils,
> Release from year-long watch, which, couch'd aloft
> On these Atreidan roofs, doglike, I keep.
> (Swanwick 1865)

Not only does she settle for the obscure 'Atreidan', but her opening is in the form of a prayer – the first word in Aeschylus is *theous*, accusative plural of *theos*, a god, whereas Potter, though a cleric and schoolmaster, seems to opt for the monotony of the man's task, rather than his piety.

Gilbert Murray (1920) takes a monotheistic stance but is otherwise arcane to the point of requiring an additional translation:

> This waste of year-long vigil I have prayed
> God for some respite, watching elbow-stayed,
> As sleuthhounds watch, above the Atreidae's hall.

Richmond Lattimore (1953) has a similar struggle with elbows:

> I ask the gods some respite from the weariness
> of this watchtime measured by years I lie awake
> elbowed upon the Atreidae's roof dogwise.

Lowell (1978) opts for:

> I've lain here a year,
> crouching like a dog on one elbow
> and begged the god to end my watch.

A dog on one elbow?
  Tony Harrison (1981), similarly, though with his signature poetic dimension:

> no end to it all, though all year I've muttered
> my pleas to the gods for a long groped for end.
> Wish it were over, this waiting, this watching,
> twelve weary months, night in and night out,
> crouching peering, head down like a bloodhound.

Ted Hughes (1999), in what is described in the printed edition as a 'version' rather
than a translation – Hughes had no grounding in ancient Greek – opens with:

> You gods in heaven –
> You have watched me here on this tower
> All night, every night for twelve months,
> Thirteen moons,
> Tethered on the roof of this palace
> Like a dog.

A few lines further on (11–12) the Watchman reviews the orders he has been given
to wait for the beacon which will signal the fall of Troy:

> . . . these high hopes
> My royal mistress thinking on her lord
> Feeds in her heart (Potter).

> . . . for so proudly hopes
> A woman's heart, with manly counsel fraught (Swanwick).

> So surely to her aim
> Cleaveth a woman's heart, man-passionèd (Murray).

> . . . to such a high end a lady's
> male strength of heart in its high confidence ordains (Lattimore).

> Clytemnestra
> stationed me here to waken her when the beacon
> shall flame in the east proclaiming Troy has fallen. (Lowell)

> The woman says watch, so here I am watching.
> That woman's not one who's all wan and woeful. (Harrison)

Hughes's opening speech has forty-two graphic lines before the Watchman spots the
beacon, compared to Aeschylus' twenty-one and so deviates from the original, though
not necessarily its 'atmosphere', as to make direct comparison with 'accurate' translators pointless.

If we want to make some judgement between these approaches, and there are more than another fifty English *Agamemnons* at least where a similar comparison could be exercised, any individual preference will come down to the balance to be struck between the original text, its associations, structure, language, metre, perceived emphases and mood. It is in Harrison that Stoppard's 'give' may most clearly be found, with the opportunity for character, situation and even humour – 'The woman says watch, so here I am watching' – which a director might be looking for in the opening scene of such a lengthy piece of theatre. The sense of dramatic pacing or rhythm needs to allow in its 'give' for a relaxing of concentration, for an equivalent breathing-time within the individual scene to what the Greek playwright creates throughout a play by alternating scenes of action with choral ode.

One brief further example shows the extent to which this already exists in Aeschylus, as we will see it does in Sophocles and Euripides. *Libation-Bearers*, the second play of the trilogy is the most dense and concentrated of the three plays, revolving around the return of Orestes, his reuniting with Electra and the murder of Aegisthus and Clytemnestra. Breathing-time in this play comes in the interlude after Orestes' first scene (incognito) with his mother after which she invites him into the palace. The choral ode lasts only for eleven lines before being interrupted by the unexpected entry of Orestes' former Nurse who has heard of the death of Orestes but does not have the privileged knowledge of the Chorus that the news is pretence. She has a speech of over thirty lines in which she recalls him as a baby, his help-lessness, his crying, even cleaning up after him. Potter is appropriately tender but, from the same deference to the solemnity of tragedy that allowed him to translate the whole of Aeschylus, Sophocles and Euripides but omit *Cyclops*, has the Nurse say of her duties 'nor with a squeamish niceness / Thought scorn of any office' (Potter 1777: 759–60).

Anna Swanwick (1865), under the influence more of St Luke than Homer, has her Nurse speak of herself as 'cleanser of his swaddling bands' (though what might seem an old-fashioned coinage, 'swaddling bands', is a phrase to which Shapiro and Burian choose to return in their dignified 2003 translation). George Warr (1900) has her claim 'The babish belly waits no help. / How oft I prophesied amiss, how oft / To make amends I washed his clouts again'. Murray opts for ''twas clothes to wash and dry, and fuller's work as much as nurse's'. Lattimore: 'and had to wash the baby's clothes. The Nurse and laundrywoman had a combined duty'. Lowell concurs, 'both nurse and laundress'. Hughes has her speak of the baby Orestes with touching affec-tion: 'Like a blind kitten . . . A baby is helpless at both ends', but draws the line at dirty nappies. Harrison's nurse is more straight-thinking, musing on babies: 'You have to read minds, keep one jump ahead / or else you get caught with their crap to clean out.'

Sophocles and the Common Man

Sophocles offers a similar wealth of examples, notably in a series of down-to-earth messengers in *Oedipus Tyrannus* and *Antigone*, with others in *Electra, Women of Trachis* and *Philoctetes* who the audience know or suspect to be lying through their teeth. All of this sets up an intriguing series of questions for the translators (never mind actors and directors) about how much to signal to an audience. In terms of a play's structure such equivocation serves as a kind of distraction factor, but also as a means of elaborating or delaying the plot.

In *Antigone* the Guard makes two entrances, the first reluctantly to confess to Creon that the body of Polyneices has been buried; the second time, one choral ode after his first exit, to bring in Antigone whom he has discovered re-burying the body. His second entrance is briefer than the first, principally due to his initially dragging his feet. The first English *Antigone* was in prose by George Adams in 1729 who has his Messenger enter with the lines:

> O King, I will not say that swift and hardly breathing I came with nimble Pace; for I had many Resistances of Cares, turning myself round in the way for to return. My thinking Soul spoke many Things to me. Miserable Man! Whither goest thou? Whither wilt thou go and suffer Punishment. Thou Wretch, wilt thou still tarry?
>
> (Adams 223–9)

The speech continues in the same vein. Initially Creon responds calmly, until provoked:

MESSENGER: Do you permit me to speak anything? Or shall I return and go as
             I came?
CREON: Do you know how troublesome your Talk is?
MESSENGER: Are you bit in the Ear or Mind?
CREON: Why did you search out my Grief, and where it lies?
MESSENGER: He who did it torments your Mind but I your Ears.
CREON: Wo is me. How thou art all mere talk . . . Palliate your crime with
             florid speech; but if you will not shew me who did this Thing. You
             shall say that Gains unjustly got are dangerous.

(315–26)

The Messenger retreats with an aside:

> ['Apart'] But whether he be ta'en or not (for Fortune will determine that) you shall not see me returning hither again.
>
> (327–9)

It may well seem that Adams is uncomfortable with, or at least resistant to, the idea of a comic messenger amidst the gravity of a tragedy. Subsequent translators seem less concerned. Potter (1788) offers the line from Creon 'What a quaint prater this!' (Greek *lalêma* (babbler) is the common reading but *alêma* (cunning man) affords an alternative).

The prominent translators of Sophocles from the end of the nineteenth century, Plumptre, Whitelaw, Coleridge and Campbell, seem unwilling to commit themselves, but Jebb introduces something of Launcelot Gobbo from *The Merchant of Venice* ('Use your legs, take the start, run away', Act II, sc. 2) for his Guard: 'Fool, why are you going to your certain doom? Wretch, tarrying again?' There is an interesting note in T.A. Buckley's first Bohn edition (1849) at the end of this scene:

Mitchell [probably Thomas Mitchell, translator of Aristophanes] observes, 'The Phylax [Guard] retires, it is to be presumed, amid much laughter from the audience.' If so, their risible powers must have been below the standard of the New Cut [possibly a reference to the Royal Victoria Theatre, commonly called The Old Vic]. An audience so excited to risibility would be invaluable to a modern farce-writer.

(Buckley 1849: 173)

Hugh Lloyd-Jones's second Loeb edition (1994) certainly allows for comic playing ('Ah, you are a chatterer by nature, it is clear!'), without dictating it. Don Taylor (1986), another non-Greek reading playwright, seems to demand it:

SOLDIER: Am I allowed to speak, sir?
CREON: No.
          Why should you speak! Every word you say
          Is painful to me.
SOLDIER: Well, it can't be earache,
          Can it sir, not what I said!
          It must stick in your gullet. Or further down
          Maybe, a sort of pain in the conscience.
CREON: Do you dare to answer me back, and make jokes
          About my conscience?
SOLDIER: Me, sir? No, sir!
          I might give you earache. I can see that.
          I talk too much. Always have done.

(p. 144)

Comic potential too for Mueller and Krajewska-Wieczorek (2000):

First let me get myself off the hook, king
I didn't do it and swear I don't know who did.
So, please sir, don't take it out on me!

(p. 116)

and the beguiling Heaney in *the Burial at Thebes* (2004) who seems to insist on the accent too:

I was over a barrel. One part of me was saying, 'Only a loony would walk himself into this' and another part was saying 'You'd be a bigger loony not to get to Creon first.' It was, 'You take the high road, I'll take the low road.' . . . So here I am, the old dog for the hard road. What will be, says I, will be.

(p. 12)

Marianne McDonald (2000b) manages to be faithful to Sophocles, while hinting, without dictating, at the approach the actor might take:

If Creon hears about what happened from somebody else, how do you think you're going to get out of trouble then?' Turning this over and over, looking at it again and again, I dragged my feet, and made a short road long. Finally I screwed up my courage and decided to come. And here I am!

(229–34)

Euripides and the New Realism

Two brief examples will have to do for Euripides, though suitable candidates are queuing up in every one of his surviving plays. The first is purely linguistic, in fact the translation of a single word at the end of *Alcestis* (1128) when the bemused Admetus asks if the woman he sees before him is really the wife he saw die or some phantom. Heracles who has wrestled with Death to bring her back says, jokingly, that he is no *psuchagôgos*, the word meaning 'leader of souls', used elsewhere as an epithet of Hermes; in verb form to describe Socrates in Aristophanes' *Birds* (1555); as a metaphor of persuasion and illusion; and of the attraction of *opsis*, the visual element in tragedy, by Aristotle in the *Poetics* (1450ª33). *Psuchagôgoi* is even the title of a lost play of Aeschylus. Heracles is making a joke, but this is a word of rippling meaning, especially in the only Greek play to feature a resurrection. Charlotte Lennox (1759), herself translating the partial *Alceste* of Father Pierre Brumoy, ducks Heracles' *psuchagôgos*, substituting: 'She lives. Speak to her'. Potter (1781) translates the word as 'one that evokes the shades'; Way (1894) 'ghost-upraiser'; Aldington (1930) 'sorcerer'; Roche (1974) 'spirit-raiser'; Vellacott (1953), Lattimore (1955) and Hadas and McLean (1936), 'necromancer'; Kovacs (1994) 'raiser of spirits'; Davie (1996) 'Conjurer of spirits' (1996); Blondell (1999) 'conjurer'; Walton ([1997] 2002) 'witch-doctor'. The range reflects the range of nuances possible in this remarkable scene.

Ion is only one of several Euripides' plays which look forward to New Comedy, with its plot of a foundling, intrigues and deceptions, unexpected revelations and a crib full of miraculously new-looking trinkets. Any potential tragedy is prevented or circumvented, and everyone ends up happy, though in some cases as the result of only a partial view of what has really happened. The sub-tragic tone is established, after an expositional prologue from Hermes, in the opening scene proper in lyric metre (hence musical), where Ion, a temple-servant at Delphi, is tidying the stage while trying to prevent the local birds from leaving their calling cards on the shrine of Apollo. The Chorus accompanying Creusa, queen of Athens, and full of admiration for the stage décor, are followed by Xuthus, king of Athens who has come to consult the oracle about his and Creusa's childlessness. Told by the oracle that the first man he meets on leaving the temple shall be his son, Xuthus accosts Ion.

Not all early translators were comfortable with Euripides in skittish mood. The first English *Ion* was that of Potter in 1781, closely followed by that of Michael Wodhull a year later. Potter certainly saw something of the humour (517–23):

XUTHUS: Health to my son! This first address is proper.
ION: I have my health: be in thy senses thou,
                  And both are well.
XUTHUS: Oh let me kiss thy hand,
                  And throw mine arms around thee.
ION: Art thou, stranger,
                  Well in thy wits; or hath the god's displeasure
                  Bereft thee of thy reason?

XUTHUS: Reason bids,
         That which is dearest being found, to wish
         A fond embrace.
ION: Off, touch me not, thy hands
         Will mar the garlands of the god.

Arthur Way (1894), more than a hundred years later, has little time for such frivolity, or indeed, intelligible sentence structure:

XUTHUS: Let me kiss thine hand, and let me fold thy form in mine embrace!
ION: Stranger, hast thy wits? – or is thy mind distraught by stroke of heaven?
XUTHUS: Right my wit is, if I long to kiss my best-beloved regiven.
ION: Hold – hands off ! – the temple-garlands of Apollo rend not thou!

This is hardly an improvement on the strange 1889 translation of H.B.L. [Lennard], one line of which reads: 'Has't thy wits, sir-stranger, maddens thee some god despite?'
    Ronald F. Willetts (1958) is much more jaunty:

XUTHUS: Son, my blessing – it is right to greet you in this way.
ION: Sir, my thanks. We are both well – if you are not mad.
XUTHUS: Let me kiss your hand, embrace you.
ION: Are you sane? Or can the god have made you mad somehow?
XUTHUS: Mad, when I have found my own and want to welcome him?
ION: Stop. – or, if you touch it, you may break Apollo's crown.
XUTHUS: I will touch you. And I am no robber. You are mine.
ION: Must I shoot this arrow first, or will you loose me now?

                                                              (517–25)

This, as might be expected, is a much more fluent piece of dramatic dialogue, which the playing would enhance, but it seems to depend on Ion's doubting Xuthus' sanity. A different comic potential can be seen in Philip Vellacott's translation (1954), from four years earlier than the Willetts:

XUTHUS: My son! All happiness to you, my son! Before anything else I must wish
          you joy.
ION: Thank you, I am quite happy. If you will behave sensibly it will be bet-
          ter for us both.
XUTHUS: Let me kiss you and embrace you.
ION: Sir, are you in your right mind or has some god sent you mad?
XUTHUS: I have found what I longed for. Is it mad to show my love?
ION: Stop! Take your hands away. You'll break my wreath.

The implication that Ion believes he is being propositioned by Xuthus, no doubt something of an occupational hazard for young temple attendants, certainly makes the scene funny. Davis Lan's 'version' (1994) spells it out:

XUTHUS:	My child! My boy! My happiness! Oh!
	I wish you all that I feel!
ION:	Thank you.
	I'm glad it went well and the answer was pleasing.
	Now, if you're finished –
XUTHUS:	Let me embrace you!
ION:	You feel weak? Incense can affect people oddly.
	Sit here, Let go!
XUTHUS:	I'll never let go.
ION:	Don't paw me!
	If that's what you want, there's a place. I'll direct you . . .
	You're creasing my clothes.

Kenneth McLeish (1997) used elliptical and fragmented dialogue but it is recognizably Euripides:

XOUTHOS [different transliteration]:	Son! Son!
	How are you, son?
ION:	Er. Thank you.
	If you're well, we're both well.
XOUTHOS:	Give me your hand.
	Kiss me. Hug me.
ION:	Pardon. What's happened?
	Have the gods – ? Are you all right?
XOUTHOS:	All right? I've found it.
	Got it. Found it.
ION:	Please let go.
	You'll tear my garland.

Conclusion

The real issue in translating, as well as in directing, plays from ancient Greek, is of restraint and licence, or, if you prefer, faithfulness to or freedom from the original; of finding a cultural context into which these ancient dramas will fit both theatrically and as a historical translocation. Many of the seminal directors of the twentieth century were wary of the Greek repertoire, unless, like Brecht (1948), they ransacked *Antigone* for her name and a message, or, like Oklopkhov (1961), they managed to persuade an audience to find a confluence between Medea and Stalin, both Georgians, both murderers of their children (Worrall 1989: 192–5). Definitions of what may or may not qualify as a 'translation' ebb and flow like the tide and leave as much flotsam. Beachcombing is not the purpose here. It is still worth reopening the debate about translation and translators, their qualifications and their responsibilities, less in the hope of finding any definitive solutions than in suggesting that our theatre does deserve, alongside the plethora of currently fashionable plays based on classical mythology from Sarah Kane to Chuck Mee, the odd reminder of what superb craftsmen the Greek tragedians and comedians really were.

TRANSLATIONS USED

Aeschylus

Agamemnon: Potter, R., 1777, Norwich; Harrison, T., 1981, London; Hughes, T., 1999, London; Lattimore, R., 1953, Chicago; Lowell, R., 1978, New York; Murray, G., 1920, London; Raphael, F. and K. McLeish, 1979, Cambridge; Shapiro, A. and P. Burian, Oxford, 2003; Swanwick, A., 1865, London; Warr, G., 1900, London.

Libation-Bearers: Warr, G., 1900, London.

Sophocles

Antigone: Anonymous (The Oxford Translation), 1823, Oxford; Adams, G., 1729, London; Buckley, T., 1849, London; Heaney, S., 2004, (*The Burial at Thebes*), London; Lloyd-Jones, H., 1994, Cambridge, Mass.; McDonald, M., 2000, London; Mueller, C. and A. Krajewska-Wieczorek, 2000, Hanover, N.H.; Potter, R., 1788, London; Taylor, D., 1986, London.

Euripides

Alcestis: Aldington, R., 1930, London; Blondell, R., 1999, New York; Davie, J., 1996, London; Hadas, M. and J. Harvey McLean, 1936, New York; Kovacs, D., 1994, Cambridge, Mass.; Lattimore, R., 1955, Chicago; Lennox, C., 1759, from the French of Pierre Brumoy, in *Le Théâtre des Grecs*, London; Potter, R., 1781, London; Roche, P., 1974, New York; Vellacott, P., 1953, Harmondsworth; Way, A., 1894, London; Walton, J.M., [1997] 2002, London.

Hecuba: Harrison, J., 2004, Cambridge; Harrison, T., 2005, London; McDonald, M., 2005, London; McGuinness, F., 2004 (in a new version), London.

Ion: Potter, R., 1781, London; McLeish, K., 1997, London; Lan, D., 1994, London; Lennard, H.B., 1889, London; Vellacott, P., 1954, Harmondsworth; Willetts, R.F., 1958, Chicago.

FURTHER READING

Arrowsmith and Shattuck 1961. Barsby 2002; Bassnett 1991; Burian 1997; Johnston 1996; Scolnicov and Holland 1989; Walton 2006a.

CHAPTER THIRTEEN

Lost in Translation? The Problem of (Aristophanic) Humour

James Robson

Après avoir parcouru, toute l'après-dînée, à peu près la millième partie de la ville, on les ramena chez le roi. Candide se mit à table entre Sa Majesté, son valet Cacambo et plusieurs dames. Jamais on ne fit meilleure chère, et jamais on n'eut plus d'esprit à souper qu'en eut Sa Majesté. Cacambo expliquait les bons mots du roi à Candide, et quoique traduits, ils paraissaient toujours des bons mots. De tout ce qui étonnait Candide, ce n'était pas ce qui l'étonna le moins.

The afternoon had passed, and they had seen little more than a thousandth part of the city, but it was time to go back to the royal palace for supper. Candide sat down to table with His Majesty, and Cacambo and several Court ladies were of the company. Never was entertainment so lavish as that supper party, and never was anyone so witty as His Majesty. Cacambo interpreted the King's witticisms to Candide, who found them still witty in translation, a point which surprised him as much as anything he heard or saw.

> Voltaire, *Candide*, ch. XVIII, 'What they saw in El Dorado'
> (*Ce qu'ils virent dans le pays d'Eldorado*), tr. John Butt (Voltaire 1947: 82)

That a character like Candide finds it quite so remarkable that wit survives translation is, on the face of it, extraordinary. After all, this is a man who has had much to be surprised about. He seems regularly to see his nearest and dearest die horrible deaths only later to find them alive and well in bizarre circumstances and has recently stumbled upon the lost kingdom of El Dorado complete with its huge red sheep and abundance of gold and jewels. To be sure, the English translation may well be more emphatic than the French original – 'a point which surprised him as much as anything he heard or saw' is no doubt a little more forceful than 'ce n'était pas ce qui l'étonna le moins' – but the point still stands: Candide was greatly surprised.

But why should it be so surprising for humour successfully to transfer from one language to another? After all, when I (and, I suspect, most anglophone readers) read *Candide* I am reading a novel in translation which I unhesitatingly recognize and would categorize as humorous and which actually makes me laugh out loud at times. Is this not proof enough that humour can happily survive the rigours of translation at the hands of an able translator?

What I shall be addressing in this chapter is the extent to which certain types of humorous passages do, or do not, translate straightforwardly from one language to another. In particular, my discussion will address the apparent paradox thrown up by this passage, namely that humour can on the one hand be very fragile (so fragile that Candide can be justifiably surprised at its preservation) and on the other extremely durable (so durable that a reader would be entitled to be surprised if a translation of *Candide* were *not* humorous). The chapter examines the problems that humour creates for the translator through the lens of both translation and humour theory and draws its examples from English translations of Aristophanes. The focus on translations of Aristophanic plays throws up a range of pertinent issues concerning not just linguistic but also cultural transfer and provides a corpus of texts from which it is possible to discern the practical ways in which translators tackle the problem of humour.

Translating Verbal Humour

To return to the topic of Candide's surprise, it is relevant to point out that the successful transfer which raises Candide's eyebrows is a specific type of humour: 'witticisms', or 'bons mots' in the French. Puns, witticisms, poetic ambiguities, rhyme: these all rely on the specific form that words have in a language – and since (as linguists from Saussure onwards have maintained) these forms comprise an arbitrary system of signs, we cannot expect one language's set of signs to map easily onto that of another. To be sure, the more closely related two languages are the more likely that (i) there will be cognate words the two will share and (ii) these will have the same or a similar range of multiple meanings, but even here the situation is complex. Certainly the differences between Classical Greek and Modern English are such that a translator must count him or herself lucky to find lines like *Acharnians* 1210–11 whose translation into English causes few practical difficulties.

Λα: τάλας ἐγὼ ξυμβολῆς βαρείας.
Δι: τοῖς Χουσὶ γάρ τις ξυμβολὰς ἐπράττετο;

In the Penguin version of the play, Sommerstein translates (Sommerstein 1973a: 103):

LAMACHUS: O dreadful, fatal charge –
DICAEOPOLIS: What, you've been *charged* for your entertainment on Pitcher Day?

The humour of the Greek passage relies on the fact that *xymbolē* has multiple meanings: in line 1210, the listener/reader is led to understand *xymbolē* with reference to one meaning of the word, *xymbolē* (1) = 'encounter, engagement', whereas in

1211 another meaning, *xymbolē* (2) = 'contribution, subscription', is appealed to. Humour theorists call the polyvalent word on which the pun is based – in this case *xymbolē* – the 'connector' (or 'locus'). Each instance of humour also has its 'disjunctor', namely a word or phrase which causes the listener/reader to look for the connector's secondary meaning. In this example, the disjunctor in the Greek is *epratteto*, 'was collecting': the phrasing prior to *xymbolē* may well serve to indicate that a pun is on its way, but it is only at *epratteto* – 'someone *was collecting* subscriptions' – that the listener/reader becomes aware just what that pun will be. It is not always easy to be precise about such matters, but in the English translation the phrase 'for your entertainment' is most likely the point at which a listener/reader would become aware of the precise nature of the pun (though the word 'charged' itself might even act as the disjunctor for a sharper-witted listener/reader – and it is not uncommon for the same word to act as both connector and disjunctor). The stroke of luck enjoyed by the translator of these lines is that the two relevant, distinct meanings of a single polyvalent Greek word, *xymbolē* – the word on which the pun relies – also happen to be two distinct meanings of a single polyvalent English word, 'charge'. On this vital point, the two language systems coincide rendering the pun translatable.

Of course, an anglophone translator of Aristophanes can hardly rely on such luck every time there is a pun in the Greek. Even when there is no coincidence between the connector in the Source Language (SL) and a word in the Target Language (TL), however, an inventive translator can often find a substitute pun. A good example is *Clouds* 545, which translators have successfully tackled in a variety of ways. The line reads:

κἀγὼ μὲν τοιοῦτος ἀνὴρ ὢν ποιητὴς οὐ κομῶ
And I, being just such a man do not, as a poet, *komaō*

where *komaō* means (1) 'give myself airs' and (2) 'wear my hair long'. Sommerstein in his Aris and Phillips translation follows the ingenious proposal of Borthwick (1979), who suggests rendering *komaō* 'give myself *h*airs' (Sommerstein 1982: 61):

And I myself, being a poet of the same stamp, do not give myself *h*airs

(here, as in the Greek, the connector and disjunctor coincide: *komaō*, 'give myself *h*airs'). In another vein, Meineck attempts a pun on 'bald' and 'bold', playing on the fact that, as we know from references in his plays (e.g. *Knights* 550; *Peace* 767–73), Aristophanes was himself folically challenged (Meineck and Storey 2000: 38):

and I, the playwright, am cast from the same mold. I have always been bold (bold, not bald – I know I'm bald!)

However, felicitous translations are not always possible. Various translators' attempts at a passage such as Demos' description of Paphlagon at *Knights* 75–9, for example, neatly demonstrate that inventiveness has its limits.

ἔχει γὰρ τὸ σκέλος
τὸ μὲν ἐν Πύλῳ, τὸ δ' ἕτερον ἐν τῇκκλησίᾳ.
τοσόνδε δ' αὐτοῦ βῆμα διαβεβηκότος
ὁ πρωκτός ἐστιν αὐτόχρημ' ἐν Χάοσιν,
τὼ χεῖρ' ἐν Αἰτωλοῖς, ὁ νοῦς δ' ἐν Κλωπιδῶν.

In his Aris and Phillips edition, Sommerstein renders these lines (Sommerstein 1981: 17):

> He stands with one leg in Pylos and the other in the Assembly, with his feet this far apart; so that his arse is right in Chasmos, his hands in Extortia, and his mind in Larcenadae.

The humour in the Greek is conveyed by puns on *en Chaosin*, 'amongst the Chaonians' and *chaos*, 'open void' (a particularly suitable term to describe Paphlagon's arsehole since politicians are regularly mocked in Old Comedy for being pathics or prostitutes); on *en Aitōlois*, 'among the Aetolians', with a pun on *aiteō*, 'demand', and on *en Klōpidōn*, 'in Clopidae', with a pun on *klōps*, 'thief' (the places seem to have been chosen purely for their potential as puns). The lack of double meaning for these words in English, however, forces Sommerstein merely to signal the humour with weak, invented quasi-humour: 'Chasmos . . . Extortia . . . Larcenadae'. In his 1970 translation of the play for Oxford Paperbacks, Patric Dickinson weakens the puns even further: he anglicizes (and thus 'domesticizes': see below) two of the placenames ('Beggarland', 'Borough of Theft') and glosses the pun on the third ('open-mouth Chaonia') (Dickinson 1970: 54):

> he straddles
> One foot in Pylos, the other in
> The Assembly, and his arse is right
> Bang above open-mouth Chaonia
> His fist in Beggarland, and his wits
> In the Borough of Theft.

'Verbal' and 'Referential' Humour

To take the discussion forward, it will be useful to draw on a distinction which goes back at least as far as Cicero (but which is probably Aristotelian in origin), one between humour which is on the one hand *in verbis* (and hence generally called 'verbal humour') and on the other hand *in re* (generally called 'referential humour': for other translations of these terms, see Attardo 1994: 27). In his *De Oratore* Cicero discusses the rephrasing of humour in the same language – i.e. paraphrase or what is sometimes called 'intralingual translation' – and arrives at the following formula.

> *nam quod quibuscumque verbis dixeris facetum tamen est, re continetur; quod mutatis verbis salem amittit, in verbis habet leporem omnem.*

> For the joke that, said in whatever words, is nevertheless funny, is contained in the thing (*res*); the joke that loses its saltiness if the words are changed has all the funniness in the words (*verba*).
>
> (Cicero, *De Oratore*, 2.62 (252))

> *quare ea quoque quoniam mutatis verbis non possunt retinere eandem venustatem, non in re sed verbis posita ducantur.*
>
> Therefore also such jokes which, after the words are changed, cannot retain the same funniness, should be considered to lie not in the thing (*res*) but in the words (*verba*).
>
> (Cicero, *De Oratore*, 2.64 (258))

Cicero's distinction between verbal and referential humour provides the beginnings of an explanation for the paradox noted earlier – that sometimes humour displays fragility when it comes to translation, sometimes durability. The examples we have been looking at so far have all been instances of *verbal* humour and – to formulate things in a slightly different way from Cicero – what characterizes this kind of humour is the presence of a bivalent or polyvalent connector (i.e. a word with double or multiple meanings which forms the basis of a pun) or, alternatively, two words with a strong formal similarity (e.g. 'airs' and 'hairs'). Whereas *referential* humour tends to be durable (more on this below), the successful transfer of *verbal* humour from Source Language to Target Language is problematic for the reason that it relies on a word-for-word translation of the polyvalent word or phrase (be it in the form of an equivalent lexical item in the Target Language, e.g. 'charge' for *xymbolē*, or a substitute item, 'give oneself *h*airs' for *komaō*). If no word or phrase in the Target Language can be found to convey the same range of meanings as the connector in the Source Text, then the humour is essentially untranslatable: hence verbal humour's fragility. This is the case in the *Knights* example above, for instance, where the place names chosen by Aristophanes for his puns resist effective translation into English (we shall look at tactics used by translators when they reach this impasse later).

To return one last time to the case of Candide, if we can assume that the King of El Dorado's witticisms were examples of verbal humour (a fact which would explain Candide's surprise at their successful translation), it must be the case that they relied on a series of connectors which either just so happened to have equivalents in Candide's native German and/or for which his valet Cacambo nimbly found a series of substitute puns. In the latter case, all credit would be due to Cacambo who, far from being *bad* (*kakos*) at *both* (*ambo*) languages, must have been particularly adept at finding the *mots justes* to translate the King's *bons mots*.

Translating Referential Humour

So much for verbal humour, then; now let us consider referential humour. As the Ciceronian distinction implies, verbal and referential humour form a contrastive pair: in other words, any instance of humour that is not verbal may be categorized as referential and *vice versa*. Cicero's test for referential humour is that it can survive *intra*lingual translation or paraphrase, but the terminology introduced earlier allows a slightly subtler formulation, namely that the defining characteristic of referential humour is that it relies *neither* on a polyvalent connector (a punning word) *nor* on any other formal similarity between words (such as required by a Spoonerism, 'the queer old dean', or by near-puns such as Sommerstein's 'airs'/'hairs'). The importance of the distinction between verbal and referential humour to the present discussion is that referential humour can survive not only *intra*lingual translation but, all things being equal, *inter*lingual translation, i.e. translation into another language: with no punning connector to convey from the Source Language to Target Language a major obstacle to the successful rendering of humour is removed.

To remove any possibility for confusion it ought to be stated that referential humour still relies on words. Indeed, the term 'verbal humour' is somewhat unfortunate since it might be thought to imply that referential humour is somehow *non*-verbal (and contrariwise, verbal humour – like referential humour – can concern 'things', like 'airs' and 'hairs'). So to restate, referential humour as a category covers all humour which is non-punning and as such naturally covers a wide range of phenomena. It can, for example, be sustained for long sequences, but can equally be conveyed in – and successfully translated by – one-liners, such as the fear expressed by the Second Woman as to one possible way in which the plans of the Assembly women could fail (*Ecclesiazusae* 264–5).

τὰς χεῖρας αἴρειν μνημονεύσομεν τότε.
εἰσθισμένοι γάρ ἐσμεν αἴρειν τὼ σκέλει.

The somewhat wordy translation by Dillard in the Penn Greek Drama series reads (Slavitt and Bovie 1999: 299):

> But we've yet to figure just how we're going to remember to raise our hands to vote when most often we find ourselves in positions where we raise our legs!

Here the humour revolves around the activity of 'raising' (*airein*) – which, when it concerns arms, is a non-sexual act connected with voting (as Dillard's added gloss 'to vote' reminds us) but when it concerns legs, takes on a sexual dimension.

Ecclesiazusae 264–5 is an instructive passage to consider from the point of view of the divide between verbal and referential humour. At first glance, one might be tempted to categorize these lines as an example of verbal humour relying on the connector *aireō*, 'to lift'. However, key to its categorization as referential is the fact that *aireō* is *not* polyvalent here – in the phrases *tas cheiras airein*, 'raise our hands' and *airein tō skelei*, 'raise our legs', only one meaning of *aireō* is appealed to. In fact, this extract provides a neat demonstration of the robustness of the categories: *Ecclesiazusae* 264–5 *does* survive paraphrase, does *not* rely on a polyvalent connector (or any other formal feature of language) and is *therefore* an example of referential (and *not* verbal) humour.

As countless examples could illustrate, the translation of referential humour is often relatively unproblematic. However, there are times when it can be far from straightforward. Take the following one-liner from *Lysistrata*, for instance. When Cinesias is being tormented by his wife, Myrrhine, with promises of sex which she keeps failing to fulfil, he says (928):

ἀλλ' ἢ τὸ πέος τόδ' 'Ηρακλῆς ξενίζεται;
Well, is this Heracles' cock you're entertaining?

The joke only makes sense when we know that Heracles regularly features in Old Comedy as a character who was promised a meal, but either received it too late or not at all. Henderson's device of including necessary information in the text of his translation – the so-called 'intruded gloss' – is a common one. In his Loeb edition, he translates (Henderson 2000: 395):

KINESIAS: Is this cock of mine supposed to be Herakles waiting for his dinner?

What the problems of translating this line highlight is a further reality of translation: namely that it comprises cultural as well as linguistic transfer. Indeed, the successful translation of much referential humour relies on the existence of certain shared cultural assumptions between the Source Text (ST) and Target Text (TT) audiences: even the *Ecclesiazusae* humour would fail if the Target Text culture failed to recognize 'arm-raising' as a constituent part of voting or 'leg-raising' as a constituent part of sex (and on this point it is interesting, as noted above, that Dillard makes a small 'intruded gloss' of his own: 'to vote'). A further complicating factor in the cultural transfer of humour is taboo: when faced with translating the *Ecclesiazusae* lines, translators in given cultures and historical periods might not be able to rely on their audiences to categorize brazen female sexuality as humorous. Even in the context of the modern anglophone world it is not unknown for North American translations to underplay ethnic and sexual stereotyping to accommodate cultural sensitivities (see Scharffenberger 2002: 435 and esp. 456–60 on the controversy surrounding Arrowsmith's portrayal of the *Thesmophoriazusae*'s Scythian archer as African-American, for example).

Translation Studies and the 'Cultural Turn'

Not every translations studies scholar would be as bullish as Bassnett and Lefevere in the introduction to their 1990 book *Translation, History and Culture* when they talk of how the so-called 'cultural turn' is, and should be, sweeping translation studies (Lefevere and Bassnett 1990). However, this book marks an important staging post in the metamorphosis of translation studies from a discipline interested chiefly in texts at the level of words and sentences to one concerned more with broader cultural issues. Certainly 'culture', whether narrowly or broadly defined, is of vital importance to the present discussion since the translation of humour is deeply affected both by changing sensibilities in the target culture and changing perceptions of the source culture. In addition, the cultural differences between the everyday worlds of the two cultures is also determinative of the translation produced (especially since it is at the level of the everyday that humour often operates). Whilst a situation is imaginable where the cultural knowledge of the putative audiences of the Source Text (ST) and Target Text (TT) are practically indistinguishable, the gap between modern anglophone and Classical Greek culture is certainly wide. Thus there are numerous artefacts and institutions which feature in Aristophanes' Greek which have little or no equivalent in modern anglophone culture (e.g. 'Pitcher day' at *Knights* 1211) or whose associations are starkly different (e.g. Heracles at *Lysistrata* 928) and there appear people, places and works of literature which a modern audience may never have heard of.

When dealing with these cultural differences, translators must be clear about who their target audience is and what effect they hope to achieve. In theoretical terms this means, for instance, a translator having to decide the extent to which he or she will aim to make a translation what has been called 'adequate' (that is, preserving the norms and values of the source culture) or 'acceptable' (i.e. adapted to those of the target culture: Toury 1995; reformulated as 'TT-orientated' and 'ST-orientated' by Hermans 1999). A slightly different distinction is made by Venuti who uses the terms 'domestication' or 'foreignization' (Venuti 1995 et al. very much argues for 'foreignization' as a translation strategy, i.e. that translators should lose what he calls their 'invisibility' and make readers aware that they are reading a translation rather than a Source Language text by highlighting differences in the cultural and stylistic norms of the two cultures, texts and textual traditions). Perhaps more relevant still for the translator of Aristophanes is Katarina Reiss's triadic model of 'Informative', 'Expressive' and 'Operative' translations (articulated in Reiss 1989, for example). To what extent is the translation to be 'informative' and convey factual information about, e.g. its source culture? To what extent are the aesthetic ('expressive') dimensions of the text to be highlighted? And to what extent is the text to be 'operative' and induce certain behaviour in the audience, be that behaviour feeling sympathy with a certain point of view conveyed by the Aristophanic text, or even perlocutionary effects such as laughing or smiling in response to instances of humour? I suspect few translators would wholly ignore any of these vectors, but the relative importance attached to each will inevitably differ depending on the extent to which the translation is intended as, say, a teaching text, a crib, a performable or performance text, and so on. Needless to say, even when the aims of two translators largely coincide, widely different products can nevertheless result.

It is worth at this stage stating the vital point that not all humour will induce laughter in a listener/reader. Laughter can be caused not just by humour but by a range of stimuli (e.g. tickling, relief, shock) and texts we recognize as humorous do not always cause us to laugh – a joke which we have heard before, which we find offensive or which we do not 'get', for instance, may fail to induce laughter but may nevertheless usefully be categorized as 'humorous'. Thus the translator's position as to the extent to which he or she will aim to make the target audience laugh will have an important impact on the translation. In terms of Reiss's triadic model, it will depend on the value placed by a translator on the 'informative' dimension compared to the 'operative' dimension of the Aristophanic text (with 'expressive' considerations playing a role, too): the more 'informative' a translation, the more it will aim to convey the sense of the original Aristophanic joke; the more 'operative' a translation, the more the translator will be at pains to amuse the listener/reader (and therefore the more likely to eschew a 'literal' translation of the Source Text). In practice, it is stage rather than page translations that traditionally employ more substitute jokes – topical humour replacing humour concerning ancient personalities and social phenomena – but practice varies.

One question which arises here is whether a substitute joke can still be called a 'translation' in any meaningful sense and this, in turn, raises important issues of *trust* between translator and audience (a surprisingly under-explored concept in translation studies). How many topical jokes or non-classical references will a reader bear before he or she decides that what he or she is experiencing is less a play by Aristophanes, and more a version or adaptation by the translator? A listener/reader expecting or requiring an 'adequate' (ST-orientated) or 'informative' translation, for instance, might rapidly lose faith in a translation which is avowedly 'acceptable' (TT-orientated) or 'expressive', whilst for another listener/reader it may be that topical illusions and the visibility of the translator/adaptor's hand add to a given version's appeal.

Humour Theory

A further fruitful way to address the problem of translating humour is from the point of view of humour theory. The most influential theory of humour in recent years has no doubt been that of Victor Raskin and Salvatore Attardo, whose General Theory of Verbal Humour (GTVH) emerged out of work that both scholars published in the mid-1980s to 1990s. The GTVH is in origin a theory of jokes but has been applied with more or less success outside this immediate sphere. The theory is based on what Raskin and Attardo call 'script opposition' and is in essence a theoretically sophisticated incongruity model. As such it shares similarities with a long line of theories which see humour as being predicated on some sort of surprise which is painless to the listener ('painlessness' being a quality of humour suggested by Aristotle: ἄνευ ὀδύνης, *Poetics* 1449a). The 'scripts' which are opposed are abstract entities made up of the conventional experiences and utterances connected with a given activity or situation – in a more casual moment, Attardo calls them 'an organized complex of information about something' (Attardo 2002: 181) – and so, for instance, the 'script' connected with 'going shopping' would include, say, all the sentences and assumptions behind a phrase book entry on that subject. Two or more scripts must overlap in a joke and then be shown to be 'opposed' – the normal model being that there is one 'obvious' reading of the humorous text or situation presented but that another less obvious reading is shown also to be possible at a key moment, i.e. the punch line, which tends to appear at or towards the end of the text. So, to take an example:

A pair of suburban couples who had known each other for quite some time talked it over and decided to do a little conjugal swapping. The trade was made the following evening, and the newly arranged couples retired to their respective houses. After about an hour of bedroom bliss, one of the wives propped herself up on her elbow, looked at her new partner and said, 'Well, I wonder how the boys are getting along.'

Here the punch line leads the listener to re-evaluate his/her initial expectations. What was set up as an instance of heterosexual intercourse is shown to be an instance of homosexual intercourse: thus two scripts are 'opposed'. Jokes can be referential or verbal in nature, just like other forms of humour. The 'partner swapping' joke is referential, the following joke, complete with its connector, 'tank', is verbal.

Two fish in a tank. One says to the other, 'Where's the gun?'

The GTVH gets more complex still: it posits that any given joke can be broken down into six components, known as Knowledge Resources (KRs). These are:

LA (Language: i.e. the precise wording of the text)
NS (Narrative Strategy: e.g. simple narrative, riddle, conversation, etc.)
TA (Target, or 'butt' of the joke: not all jokes have a target)
SI (Situation: what the joke is 'about')
LM (Logical Mechanism: the way that the incongruity is built in to the joke and thus resolved)
SO (Script Opposition: the way in which the key frames of reference present in a joke – the 'scripts' – are 'opposed' to one another).

Relevant to the translation of humour is that, according to Attardo, these six Knowledge Resources form a hierarchy: and so each Knowledge Resource in the list above is more deeply integral to the joke than the last. Experiments using paraphrased jokes suggest that listeners are most likely to rate two jokes as being 'the same joke' when the Knowledge Resource changed is most superficial: Language is thus the least important, Script Opposition the most essential (although a significant number of listeners rate Situation as more key than Logical Mechanism: see Ruch et al. 1993). We might see fit to scratch our heads at this point since puns might reasonably be said to rely on Language, which is the Knowledge Resource that Attardo reckons to be the least important. However, in his 2002 article, 'Translation and Humour: An Approach. Based on the General Theory of Verbal Humor (GTVH)', Attardo defends the hierarchy by arguing that punning is actually reliant on a kind of Logical Mechanism: one called 'cratylism' (Attardo 2002: 188) which relies on the notion that if two words sound the same or similar they must therefore have the same or similar meanings. Thus, according to Attardo, punning lies at the deepest level of the joke bar one (only Script Opposition is deeper) and it is simply that 'the Logical Mechanism "cratylism" preselects some features of Language (i.e. it limits the options of the Language Knowledge Resource to any of the options which fulfil the requirements of the Logical Mechanism)' (Attardo 2002: 189).

Whether or not we accept Attardo's reasoning on this point, the conclusions which he arrives at bear a strong resemblance to those we reached earlier with the help of the Ciceronian distinction. To oversimplify: verbal jokes do *not* translate (unless we are lucky) and referential ones *do* (unless we are *un*lucky). Attardo concludes that, with the notable exception of puns, the mere fact of translating a joke into a foreign language ought not to cause any particular difficulty – as long as the Narrative Strategy, Target, Situation, Logical Mechanism and Script Opposition are 'available' in the target culture. And it is here that we are faced with the realities of cultural exchange outlined earlier. With an Aristophanic text the Target may or may not be available in modern anglophone culture (politicians yes, 'the Paphlagon' no); likewise the Situation (voting with hands yes, feeding Herakles no), and so on. The logic of Attardo's argument is that a translator should make a substitution at the most superficial level possible for the translated joke to be most like the original – the problem of puns notwithstanding.

Aristophanes' Translators

Naturally, the difficulty of translating humour is a topic which exercises Aristophanes' translators themselves, and as we should perhaps expect it is verbal humour, and puns in particular, which appear to cause them the most anxiety. Sometimes translators proudly single out instances of puns they feel they have successfully transferred from Greek to English while preserving most of the letter and flavour of the original. They are seldom as candid about their less admirable efforts, however, as Robin Bond, a New Zealand academic who has translated plays of Plautus and Aristophanes. Reflecting on his translation work, he says (Beacham et al. 2002: 178):

> in comedy one has to adapt and change to a certain extent. As a matter of technique the hardest thing, of course, is puns. Occasionally translations of puns fly into your head but sometimes they don't. Sometimes therefore you ignore the pun in the Greek or the Latin and sometimes you import one which is not there, because whatever you've lost you can compensate for by invention.

Sommerstein says something similar in the introduction to his Penguin edition of *Lysistrata*, *Acharnians* and *Clouds* (Sommerstein 1973a: 36):

> To give an idea of the verbal humour . . . I have found it necessary to adapt his jokes, or, where even this is impossible, to compensate for their loss by adding something elsewhere. I have generally at such points given an idea in the notes of what the author wrote.

Douglass Parker, recalling his work with (and sometimes against) William Arrowsmith, expresses this strategy of 'compensation' more starkly still, calling the technique 'the surrogate joke' (Parker 1992/3: 253):

> The *fact* of the joke is more important than the particulars of that joke . . . But verbal jokes are normally lost. So, we were to *compensate*. Put in other jokes.

A good example of an adaptation made by Sommerstein when faced with a challenging piece of verbal humour comes in his translation of *Clouds* 688–92. The Aristophanic humour is based on the formal similarity between the vocative singular of first declension masculine and feminine nouns, the joke being that – according to the comic Socrates' hair-splitting logic – some men's names are not really 'masculine' at all. Naturally this word play is impossible to replicate in English and Sommerstein's solution is to employ, in place of the Aristophanic Amynias (vocative: *Amynia*), an English man's name whose abbreviated form can similarly be construed as belonging to a woman (Sommerstein 1973a: 141; commented on at Sommerstein 1973b: 152; revised in Sommerstein 2002: 100):

Σω: . . . ἐπεὶ
        πῶς ἂν καλέσειας ἐντυχὼν Ἀμυνίᾳ;
Στ: ὅπως ἄν; ὡδί. "δεῦρο δεῦρ', Ἀμυνία."
Σω: ὁρᾷς; γυναῖκα τὴν Ἀμυνίαν καλεῖς.
Στ: οὔκουν δικαίως, ἥτις οὐ στρατεύεται.

SOCRATES: . . . If you met Alexander, what would be the first thing you'd say
                   to him?
STREPSIADES: I'd say – I'd say 'Hullo, Sandie!'
SOCRATES: There you are; you've called him a woman.
STREPSIADES: And rightly too – the way *she* manages to dodge the call up . . .

In terms of Attardo's model the Target has been changed (the real-life Amynias has become a non-specific Alexander) and the Logical Mechanism has undergone a shift (humour relying on the similarity of Greek vocatives has become humour relying on the similarity between a male and female name) but in other respects (Narrative Strategy, Situation, Script Opposition – i.e. male versus female) the joke remains largely unchanged.

The contrast between Sommerstein's concept of 'compensation' and Parker's 'surrogate joke' is clearly discernible from an extract such as Parker's version of *Acharnians* 719–26. Like his erstwhile mentor Arrrowsmith, Parker writes in a distinctive and lively idiom introducing humour not present in the Aristophanic original (though evidently inspired, in part, by Aristophanes' pun on *Phasianos*, which can indicate 'from Phasis', 'pheasant' and 'informer'). Dicaeopolis is speaking directly after the play's parabasis.

ὅροι μὲν ἀγορᾶς εἰσιν οἵδε τῆς ἐμῆς.
ἐνταῦθ' ἀγοράζειν πᾶσι Πελοποννησίοις
ἔξεστι καὶ Μεγαρεῦσι καὶ Βοιωτίοις,
ἐφ' ᾧτε πωλεῖν πρὸς ἐμέ, Λαμάχῳ δὲ μή.
ἀγορανόμους δὲ τῆς ἀγορᾶς καθίσταμαι
τρεῖς τοὺς λαχόντας τούσδ' ἱμάντας ἐκ Λεπρῶν.
ἐνταῦθα μήτε συκοφάντης εἰσίτω
μήτ' ἄλλος ὅστις Φασιανός ἐστ' ἀνήρ.

A more-rather-than-less literal version of these lines might begin:

> These are the boundaries of my market place. All the Peloponnesians, Megarians and Boeotians can trade here – as long as they sell to me and not to Lamachus. I place these three leather straps . . .

Whereas Parker's version reads (Parker 1961: 70–1):

> I herewith fix the boundaries of my place of business
> and send abroad a blanket invitation to the citizens
> of Megaria, Boiotia, and the Peloponnese.
>
> HURRY
>
> ON DOWN
> TO DIKAIOPOLIS' FREE BAZAAR!
> Contract Acceptance
> Contingent on Absolute Avoidance of Business with Lamachos.
>
> (*He produces a huge paddle.*)
> I now present my Board of Trade – the pick of a
> large panel – well-seasoned, rigid and unbending
> in its application of the solitary Rule of Commerce, *viz.*:
>
> THIS IS NOT A BIRD SANCTUARY! ALL STOOL
>   PIGEONS, PEEPERS,
> MEDDLING NARKS, AND FINKS ARE HEREBY
>   INFORMED:
> OFF LIMITS! STAY OUT! THIS MEANS YOU!

This extract raises a number of interesting issues – impressionistically we might say that it does not 'feel' like a translation in the way that, say, bilingual facing-page translations generally do, such as those found in Loeb or Aris and Phillips editions. In this regard, it is relevant to recall some of the concepts discussed earlier – 'expressiveness' and 'adequacy' in particular – with a view to examining the ways in which Parker's vision of translation is distinct. Further, though, Parker's idiosyncratic approach to Aristophanes highlights an issue which has been ducked up to now – namely, how the text *as a whole* affects a listener's or reader's perception of, and reception of, its humour. And, it must be said, humour theory in general has tended to avoid this issue until recently, with scholars such as Raskin and Attardo choosing to focus on free-standing jokes – i.e. like the 'partner-swapping' and 'fish-tank' examples, sometimes called 'canned jokes' – rather than whole texts. Indeed, one danger of adopting an 'informative', 'adequate' (ST-orientated) or 'foreignizing' approach to translation may well be that the resulting work runs the risk of treating instances of Aristophanic humour on too ad hoc a basis with insufficient regard for how, for example, 'the verbal details of the text . . . cumulatively create the flavour of Aristophanic humour' (Halliwell 1997: lii). What is more, the rhythms and moods set up by a humorous work and the collective force of the *foregoing* humour are often important factors in an audience member's appreciation of each *successive* instance of humour. Or to put it another way, successful translation of an instance of humour within the context of a novel or play will often rely on a successful build-up to the lines concerned – and not just on the careful handling of the passage itself.

Conclusion

This seems a good a point at which to draw a line under this discussion and to look ahead to what work remains to be done in this area. Certainly, examining the translation of Aristophanes' (and other writers') humour in terms of the whole text is one issue which will merit further investigation but what other issues will benefit from investigation? Doubtless other fruitful areas for research will include the translation of typical Aristophanic joke-types – especially those which rely on devices which are relatively foreign to modern humour, such as the surprise final item, the discontinuous list, or the irreverent change in register. How do these work in terms of cultural transfer? In a similar vein, how do different translators deal with jokes for which we simply lack enough information fully to understand or which are all too often found lame by modern tastes? And what of 'found' humour: do puns emerge or non-humorous sequences *become* humorous in translation? Also crucially in the case of Aristophanes, any investigation is further complicated by the difficulty of deciding just where to draw the line in the Source Text between 'humour' on the one hand and his 'playfulness' and 'exuberance' on the other (Robson 2006: 184–6).

Lastly, there is no doubt mileage in exploring the precise nature of the divide between verbal and referential humour and its usefulness for scrutinizing the process of humour translation. Table 13.1 summarizes the key suggestions made in this chapter about

Table 13.1 Summary of strategies used for the translation of humour

← Coincidence		Non-coincidence →
		Substitute pun
		Compensation
	Verbal humour	
Translation possible		
	Referential humour	
		Intruded gloss
← Cultural similarities		Cultural differences →

the translation of humour, but doubtless there is more to say on this rich and complex area. I look forward to future discussion.

FURTHER READING

An essential first step for those interested in the issues raised in this essay is to read English translations of Aristophanes: the editions mentioned in these pages should serve as a useful cross-section. Aside from occasional pearls of wisdom to be gleaned from the introductions to translations of Aristophanes, more sustained testimonials by translators include Sommerstein 1973b, whose comments concern his Penguin translations, Arrowsmith 1961 and Parker 1992/3 on their Mentor editions and the 'Translators' forum' in Beacham et al. 2002. Halliwell 2000 provides a concise overview of the history of Aristophanic translation in English which is usefully supplemented by the work of Walton 2006a and 2006b, chs. 8 and 9, who draws out a number of key themes. In the course of her analysis of Arrowsmith's unpublished version of the *Thesmophoriazusae*, Scharffenberger also provides a thoughtful account of the issues surrounding the translation of Old Comedy. On Aristophanic humour, see Kloss 2001 and Robson 2006.

'Translating Humour' is the theme of a 2002 edition of the translation studies journal *The Translator*, in which are to be found a number of useful contributions, including Attardo 2002. Also pertinent and highly readable is Venuti 2002. Rojo López's 2002 analysis of humour translation in terms of frame semantics and Larkin Galiñanes' 2005 study of the narrative characteristics of humorous novels are also of interest.

A key starting point for those wanting to engage in humour theory itself is the work of Raskin and Attardo (e.g. Raskin 1985; Attardo and Raskin 1991; Attardo 1994, 2001). There are few aspects of modern humour research not touched on in the pages of the journal *Humor*, which is both essential and addictive reading.

Translation studies is, of course, a broader field. Here, Bassnett 2002 still serves as a useful starting point, with Munday 2001 and Venuti 2004 easing the reader into more complex areas. Underwood 1998 and Hardwick 2000a are essential reading in the area of classical studies.

PART IV

Theory and Practice

CHAPTER FOURTEEN

'Making It New': André Gide's Rewriting of Myth

Cashman Kerr Prince

For the ancient Greeks, the Delphic injunction γνῶθι σέαυτον [know thyself] defined an ethics of introspection and self-awareness. Fittingly, Delphi as the centre of the ancient Greek world enjoined ancient Greeks to know their own centre. Both knowledge and the self are privileged, and knowledge of the self represents *the* privileged site of classical Greek culture (even as we, from the distance of historical perspective, can pinpoint the shortcomings and blind spots of ancient self-knowledge). Such a cultural climate creates an ethics of reflection (such as Aristotle's notion of *theoria*, 'contemplation', encapsulated in *Nicomachean Ethics* 1178^{b}21–2), and, in the context of ancient Athenian democracy, creates a society of voluble individuals (many of whom may well have privileged the ideal of introspection over true self-knowledge). The afterlife of the Delphic injunction is long and varied, but this aphorism affords us an entry into the work of André Gide (1869–1951), and a means to examine his use of the classical past. In this chapter, I will focus on two early works of André Gide: *Le Traité du Narcisse* (*The Treatise of Narcissus*, published in 1891, the first work Gide signed as author) and *Le Prométhée Mal Enchaîné* (*Prometheus Poorly Chained*, 1899). In both works, we shall see Gide, in the spirit of literary modernism, making the classical past anew. Gide invents new versions of the classical past; these serve as scrims upon which he can project his own themes and concerns, and allow him to articulate his ideas of self-knowledge and introspection within a larger, and more culturally privileged, context. At the same time, these invocations of the classical past become occasions to comment symbolically upon our relationship to that past.

For Gide – as for other modernist luminaries such as Pound, Eliot, Stein, Cocteau or Yourcenar – the question of a work's form was a source of anxiety and concern. The two works we shall consider are pieces of literary prose, but neither is what Gide ever considered a novel. Indeed, Gide thought the only novel he ever wrote was *Les Faux-monnayeurs* (*The Counterfeiters*). *Le Traité du Narcisse* is, in name, a treatise, and as such belongs to Gide's earlier literary works when he wrote several such *traités*, the same could be said for *Le Prométhée Mal Enchaîné* even though the title does not bear the name of *traité*. Both works are published in the Pléiade edition of Gide's works entitled *Romans, Récits, Soties, Œuvres Lyriques* (1958), expanding on Gide's own title for a collection of his works in 1948 (*Romans, Récits, Soties*); I will cite texts in the original French from the more recent Pléiade edition, together with my own translations. The title of these volumes reflect Gide's own anxieties about the genre of his works, as do the classifications and statements he made during his lifetime (*Prométhée*, for instance, was first announced in 1899 as a *roman*, then without generic marker, then a *sotie* – a farce offering satiric commentary on people and society). I do not propose to dwell on the question of genre for its own sake, but rather view it as an index of Gide's literary concerns, and so see the generic uncertainties he voiced about his literary prose in counterpoint with the tensions those works set up between a scholarly view of the classical past and Gide's more modernist view of antiquity. At the same time, this counterpoint mirrors the ethical dilemmas of self-knowledge which Gide explores in his versions of the classical past.

Le Traité du Narcisse, subtitled *Théorie du Symbole*, revisits a myth made famous in Ovid's *Metamorphoses* (3.339–404, Echo, and 3.405–508, Narcissus), even as it reflects this myth in a wholly new light. First, Echo is wholly absent from Gide's version of this myth, so without the spurned love of the nymph and the machinations of Nemesis granting her prayer (*sic amet ipse licet sic non potiatur amato!*, So let him love, but not be loved in return!; 3.403) Gide must create another motivation for Narcissus' contemplation of the fountain. This change of motivation prefigures Gide's radically divergent reading of this myth, even as this change only becomes apparent once we have read Gide's work in its entirety; I begin in this way in order to underscore the rewritings of the classical past which Gide undertakes from the opening sentence of this work. Gide's Narcissus opens, 'Books are not, perhaps a thing truly necessary; at first, some myths suffice; they provide the basis for an entire religion' (3). In this written, literary work, we read a *recusatio*, or disavowal, of all literature; Gide begins his published literary career with a statement of dissimulation, renouncing precisely the books which he spends his lifetime writing. From these myths spring a religion, wherein the people unknowingly adore the images while priests slowly penetrate the intimate sense of the hieroglyphs which the myths present. Myths are linked to mysticism, and the literality of the opening *recusatio* takes on a mystical cast.

Recusatio gives way to *praeteritio* (rhetorically omitting details of this tale) as Gide sketches the received myth of Narcissus in a few lines of sentence fragments. Like a recitation of a tale already well known, Gide sets up the received version of the tale of Narcissus precisely in order to *unwrite* what we think we know, and to offer in his rewriting a new version, a true version. This recitation begins, 'Narcissus was perfectly beautiful, – and that's why he was celibate' (3). Here beauty is a deceptive sign, an invitation to desire and attraction which is simultaneously renounced, foreclosed; here is a Narcissus unlike Freud's, or indeed the *triste beauté* of Narcissus in Valéry's poem, 'Narcisse Parle'. Yet this sketch of the tale of Narcissus is promptly set aside; the *praeteritio* reminds us of it in order to turn away from it, challenging and rewriting it. The sketched history ends, 'You know the story. Still, we shall recite it again. All things are said already, but since none listen one must always begin again' (3). Here the lack of reception necessitates repetition; the combination of repetition with the mysticism announced in the second sentence of the *Traité* (quoted above) places us as readers in the presence of knowledge which is hermetic (inspired, mystical, revelatory).

Gide returns to the fountain of beautiful knowledge which the myths represent, to tell a story (one already displaced by being a written or literary work, in Ovid's hands as in Gide's hands) which we as readers are already led to suspect none will hear or read. Within this literary dynamic, a choice of classical myth seems an apposite choice: we all always already know the story, so we can always already dismiss it as known. None will listen. Yet Gide writes the myth anew. This rewriting becomes a challenge; Gide works to actualize the modernist credo, 'Make it new.' Gide actualizes what he writes in his 'Considérations sur la mythologie grecque (Fragments du *Traité des Dioscures*)') ('Considerations on Greek Mythology [Fragments of the Treatise of the Dioscuri]'). Here he works reverently to excavate the rationale of ancient myth, while fully admitting this rationale will not be the same as such predecessors as Keats, Goethe or Racine. From the shards of mythology left us by mythographers, Gide recreates the myth in its full profundity rather than repeating the oft-told nursery tale. The classical past is remade, no longer so classicizing or classical, but something new in the guise of something old, and this new version bears the weight of authority granted by the foundations of the classical past.

Gide's version of Narcissus is a figure of the Poet and, like Poet or Wise Man (*Savant*), a seeker after knowledge. Narcissus does not observe his reflection in a still pool but sits beside the river of time (3) outside (or, beside) time; Narcissus observes, enraptured, the present, the future as it approaches, and the past as it flows by and away. All these are imperfect historical events, always beginning again, always in a quest for their lost first, or Ideal, form (4). In this state of utter presence, observing the passage of time wholly and fully and commingling soul with history to the point where he cannot tell them apart here Narcissus dreams of Paradise (4). We turn from Narcissus to the Paradise which he dreams.

Section I of this Traité opens with an ecphrastic description of Paradise. This Paradise is a place of perfection where all is crystalline, in full and perfect bloom (5). All is unchanging in this 'Chaste Eden! Garden of Ideas!' (5). Like Narcissus, this Paradise is an image of celibate beauty. In the midst of this paradisal Eden stands *Ygdrasil, l'arbre logarithmique* (5); (Ygdrasil, the mathematical tree), at whose base rests, open, 'the book of Mystery – where can be read the truth which must be known, its pages leafed all day long by the wind' (5). The classical *locus amoenus* (or, idealized, idyllic place) where sits Ovid's Narcissus merges with elements drawn from other traditions. As with the opening mysticism, we have here again hieroglyphs: Egyptian elements find themselves in the Christian Garden of Eden. At the same time, the Garden contains Ygdrasil, the world-tree drawn from Norse mythology. Gide syncretically combines Rangnarok and Eden. The idea of an arithmetical tree and the Book of Mystery recall elements of kabbalah. This syncretic and celibate garden of ideas is the paradise dreamed by Gide's Narcissus. Here lives Adam, an expected inhabitant of Eden, who is still unsexed and this man is *Hypostase de l'Élohim* (5; incarnation of Elohim). This combination of Christian (Eden) and Jewish (Elohim) elements makes sense, given the overlapping texts between these two traditions; combining these with elements drawn from Norse and classical mythological tradi- tions is both more shocking (in their surprising juxtapositions) and more typical of the late nineteenth century. An encyclopedic and empirical quest for knowledge coupled with fascination and early critical study of world religions in the nineteenth century created the conditions of possibility for innovative (or, shocking) theories of religious syncretism. Gide's juxtaposition of mythic elements drawn from disparate traditions shares these same conditions of possibility.

For Gide, however, this mythic portrait is not the creation of a new religious creed. Adam observes this paradisal world, in a sense creating it as the sole being existent who can observe it (6). At the same time, Adam does not rest in perfect harmony with this crystalline, celibate, perfect world. Breaking off a branch of Ygdrasil, he wrenches apart this Eden. For his act he finds himself sexed, accompanied by a woman (here unnamed) who tries blindly to recreate the now-lost perfect state of being (6). This new being, the creation of these humans, is incomplete, imperfect, and no sub- stitute for the lost perfection. Among this fallen race dispersed across the earth (7) are the poets who piously gather together the pages ripped from the immemorial Book where one could read the truth which must be known (7). With the etiology of the poets, section I closes.

Section II of this *Traité* returns us from the paradise dreamt to its dreamer, Narcissus. The narrator speaks, pondering what Narcissus might see were he to turn his gaze from the river of time. This invites the consideration of when the river will stop its flowing, time will stop its flight. Gide returns to the received myth of Narcissus, pondering when the water, 'stagnant mirror, in the purity equal to an image – equal, finally, to the point of confusing itself with the images – will say the lines of these fatal forms – to the point of finally becoming them' (7). This is not mirror-still water in which Narcissus views his reflection to the point of confusing image and reality, but the flowing waters of time in which Narcissus observes events pass. These reflections on what Narcissus might see, on when the waters might cease, when time might cease, lead to one of Gide's major points in this *Traité*, namely a theory of the sym- bol (announced in the work's subtitle). We read, 'Paradise must always be remade; it is not in some faraway Thulé. It rests beneath appearances. Every object possesses, virtual, the intimate harmony of its being, like each grain of salt possesses in itself the archetype of its crystal' (7). For Gide, Paradise is this deeper, or hidden, reality – not the world of appearances: Paradise is lost over and over by those who look to themselves, to the world of appearances. In this account, Narcissus is not a young boy who fell in love with his own appearance (a figure of the tragic loss of Paradise), but the improperly understood story of a young man whose observations of the deeper truth, hidden reality, of the symbol was little understood by others.

In the final section (III) of this *Traité*, Gide returns to the figure of the Poet. Like Narcissus, the Poet is an observer who sees Paradise. Paradise, we learn, is every- where despite imperfect appearances. It is the job of the Poet to understand these imperfect appearances then restate these truths (9). In this vision of the world, all is not what it appears. The Poet, like a Learned Man, searches for archetypes and universals; while the Learned Man searches slowly and fearfully through countless examples following a process of induction (9), the Poet plumbs the profound depths of things. The Poet, 'knows that the appearance is but a pretext, a garment which cloaks the symbol and where the profane eye stops. But the appearance shows us the symbol is there' (9). For Gide, unlike for Freud, Narcissus is not a tragic figure of egotistical self-involvement and self-love; this Narcissus contemplates not his own reflection but rather Paradise in the depths of the river of time. The mystical truths the Poet observes, restates, in some senses reveals, are crystalline works of art (10). These works crystallize in the silence in which the Poet seeks refuge, like Narcissus contemplating the river of time. This process requires the Poet: 'in him, slowly, the Idea rests then, lucid, opens in bloom outside of time'. Within this remove of calm and silence, Narcissus contemplates. For Gide, this is the real meaning of the myth of Narcissus; the *Traité* ends with a *recusatio* recalling the opening, 'This treatise is perhaps not something truly necessary. First some myths suffice' (12). The Traité opens with a *recusatio* of all literature; it concludes with an echoing *recusatio* in the same language but this time specific to this particular piece of literature. Despite this dissimulation, the suffering solitude of the Poet is here rendered public in the hope that others will admire that which the Poet admires. The public is now re-admitted to this world, but at a distance of the written page, which particular written page seems a stand-in for pages torn from the book of the Mystery propped open against the trunk of Ygdrasil, the mathematical Tree of Life in the Garden of Eden. What Narcissus and Poet contemplate are ideal visions of the world, calling us to less pro-fane, more ideal, lives and worlds. According to Gide, contemplation is a necessary dynamo in this world, and a rewritten version of the myth of Narcissus explains this necessity for us readers. Teiresias in Ovid's Metamorphoses tells Liriope that Narcissus will live so long as he does not know himself (*si se non noverit*, 3.346); for Gide's Narcissus, not knowing oneself is not a life, so this comment does not concern the span of a life but sum total of what constitutes a life. Gide's use of a classical myth adds cultural weight and import to this vision of contemplation; at the same time, the repeated *recusatio* calls into question the naturalized connection with the classical past (a connection which is not something truly necessary), while also opening up this valorized classical past to influences (some myths) from other traditions.

We see a similar questioning of the connections between classical past and the time of Gide's writing (this time made explicit in the text through the Gidean *mise-en-abîme*) in *Le Prométhée Mal Enchaîné*. The tale begins, 'In the month of May 189., two o'clock in the afternoon . . . On the boulevard which runs from Madeleine to the Opera House' (303). In this bourgeois, Parisian milieu at a pre-cise moment in historical (indeed, at the time of publication, contemporary) time, appears an uncommonly large man of middle age. While walking down the sidewalk he drops a handkerchief; a skinny man retrieves and returns it to the first, who thanks him wordlessly then walks on. But the first man quickly turns around, asks the other man something, then takes out pen and ink, and has the other man write an address on an envelope. As our observing narrator, a spectator among the crowd when all this transpires, notes, this is where the story becomes odd (303): the second man returns pen and envelope but before he can even smile good-bye, the first man 'by way of thanks, abruptly slapped the other man on the cheek, then jumped into a cab and disappeared' (303). Now the clincher: our narrator tells us 'I learned later that it was Zeus, the banker' (303). Thus the tale which sets up this entire work translates Zeus from physically and temporally remote Olympus to contemporary Paris; no longer father of gods and mortals, Zeus is now a different sort of all-controlling figure: a banker. Further, the introduction of Zeus into a history of odd behaviour on the streets of Paris in May 189. grants a mythic dimension to an otherwise precise and detailed history. From this opening tale, we embark on a section of *Prométhée* entitled 'Chronique de la moralité privée [Chronicle of private morality]' in which we read straightaway, 'I shall not speak of public morality, because there is no such thing' (304); as with the two Aphrodites in Plato's *Symposium* ($180^d5-{}^e2$), here we see a division or separation of morality, even as Gide refuses to discuss the public half of this binarism.

The scene suddenly changes with the beginning of the next paragraph: we then learn that Prometheus, chained to the peak of the Caucausus, contorts himself to turn around then, 'between four and five o'clock in the autumn, walked down the boulevard which runs from Madeleine to the Opera House' (304). Seeing the various Parisian celebrities hurry by Prometheus asks himself where they are going, and takes a table at a café, striking the quintessential Parisian pose of the *flâneur* (observer, spectator, stroller – although the word is not used in Gide's work, the concept is clearly present). Prometheus discusses these passers-by with the waiter, who says these people hurry by in search of their personality which here (Paris, but also within the culture of the café) is called idiosyncrasy (*personnalité; ce que nous appelons ici, idiosyncrasie*, 304). The waiter then explains how he observes (or, we might prefer, collects) personalities in this restaurant with tables only for parties of three. Prometheus consents to dine, and is seated with two other gentlemen whom he has not yet met: Cocles and Damocles. Over the course of dinner, Prometheus learns that Damocles is the recipient of the envelope mailed by Zeus and addressed by the same Cocles with whom he now shares a table, the Cocles who had returned the handkerchief of Zeus on the sidewalk and received a mighty slap for his efforts. Inside the envelope Damocles received, with no note or explanation, was a 500 franc note. This unexpected windfall is the work of Zeus the banker, but for Damocles it is not a benefice; as he explains to his dinner companions, 'Before, I was unremarkable, but free. At present, I belong to him. This adventure marks me; I was nobody, I am somebody' (310). The receipt of the money is for Damocles an act of interpolation, calling him into being as an individual, unique being. For Cocles, this history weighs differently; as he reminds Damocles, 'So know and do not forget that your gain comes at the price of my misery' (312). For Cocles this is a history of a zero-sum game in which he is the loser: Damocles is only able to acquire wealth at the expense of Cocles, as Cocles reiterates later in this *récit*. As we have seen, Damocles does not experience his windfall as wealth but as responsibility, obligation. The fundamental difference in their points of view remains an animating tension in Gide's literary work.

Returning to the diners, they turn to Prometheus and demand his story. Prometheus has no story to tell, no past to recount; all he has is an eagle (314). When the others desire to see his eagle, Prometheus calls it, it flies in through the front glass, accidentally knocks out one of Cocles's eyes, and with tender yet haughty cries perches on Prometheus's right side, whereupon Prometheus opens his vest and feeds the eagle some of his liver (314). This commotion, surprisingly, provokes less reaction from the other people in the café than does Prometheus displaying his eagle in Paris and publicly feeding it his liver; as one person tells him, it's great if you want to feed your liver to the eagle, but for those who see this, it is terrible and you should hide yourself when you engage in this act (315). Here Gide demonstrates the absolute lack of a public morality (so-called), and the *récit* promptly returns to a consideration of private morality. These expressions of public disapproval provide a distraction and give Damocles the occasion to use his 500 francs to pay the bill for dinner, a new front glass, and a glass eye for Cocles, all while the other two are unaware. By this act of private morality, Damocles seeks to be free of the money and the obligations it has imposed upon him; we learn that this gesture provides only temporary relief. When the waiter sees him the following day his anxiety was worse (316) because of the state of health of Cocles.

Gide uses the different reactions of Damocles and Cocles, and the actions of Zeus the banker (the *miglionnaire* as Gide names him in the text), to explore the possibility and consequences of an unmotivated act; it is the character Prometheus who reflects on this story and offers a parable of self-knowledge derived, as he says, from this history. After the eventful dinner, Prometheus is jailed as an unlicensed fabricator of matches (314); while jailed Prometheus continues seeing his eagle, feeding it his liver so that the eagle becomes more and more beautiful even as Prometheus wastes away. Once the eagle is strong enough, Prometheus light enough, the eagle carries him out of his jail. Cut to Damocles and Cocles, meeting again in person, if not in spirit; their dispute is interrupted by a notice of a lecture at eight o'clock that evening by Prométhée Délivré speaking about his eagle, followed at eight-thirty by the eagle making a flight around the hall, and at nine o'clock a collection on behalf of Cocles (320). As Prometheus announces in the opening of his speech, in keeping with his classical spirit he has three points: one must have an eagle, we all have an eagle, and a third point which will flow naturally from the preceding during the course of his speech (321). Self-referentially, Prometheus's classicism highlights the liberties Gide takes with the classical past, altering to his own ends what he finds in the received figures and texts.

Gide's Prometheus is not the altruistic philanthropist of ancient Greek mythology, nor the crafty trickster described by Hesiod. In his speech, Gide's Prometheus announces that his philanthropy towards mortals was the suggestion of his wife, Asia (323). This Prometheus has already announced that, 'I do not love man; I love what devours him' (322). Reluctant though Prometheus may be as a philanthropist, he takes pity on mortals and invents some fires for them; this act marks the commencement of Prometheus's self-knowledge and the existence of his eagle (323). These fires provide mortals with self-consciousness, and in turn Prometheus provides mortals with a goal, *raison d'être*, which is, 'the devouring belief in progress' (324). This belief is, for mortals, their eagle (324). It is this eagle, this reason for living, which Prometheus loves, both among mortals and also in his own life. The goal of Prometheus's speech is to share his love for his now-beautiful eagle with the humans present at his performance, and to instil love of eagles in all men. As he explains, conscience is an ugly, wretched lot, but whatever it be it will devour us; once we embrace and love this obligation which calls us into existence as individuals, as some-bodies, then it becomes our destiny and is beautiful (326–7). This speech, in the centre of Gide's *Prométhée Mal Enchaîné*, is the heart of this *récit*: Prometheus offers instruction to Damocles and Cocles, as well as all other mortals present, to embrace their lot and make the best of it. This is the altruism of the latter-day Prometheus.

In the last part of the *récit* we see how neither man follows the advice of Prometheus. As Damocles lies dying, he expresses to Cocles and Prometheus the horrors of an obligation, a debt to be repaid; these horrors are amplified because Damocles does not know to whom he owes the debt (332). These obligations called into being in face of another human being are worse still, posing moral and ethical dilemmas which are not easily resolved. In Damocles' case, these dilemmas, the anguish of being indebted to someone unknown, lead to his death, as his dying words attest, 'I hope at least that my dying has not deprived him, the one who gave me some-thing' (333). At the funeral, Prometheus speaks, recounting an amusing history of Tityrus which serves to amuse and distract those present; when Cocles later asks the relevance of the tale, Prometheus says if it had been more relevant, Cocles and the others present would not have laughed. In fact, it is only since the death of Damocles that Prometheus found the secret of laughing (339–40). Prometheus's knowledge of laughter no doubt owes less to the death of Damocles than his own decision after that death to kill his eagle; the *récit* concludes with Prometheus, Cocles, and the waiter dining on the eagle in the café in which the narrative began. The author tells us the tale is written with one of the eagle's feathers, being the part Prometheus kept of the bird's beauty. The final epilogue adds another mythic element to the mix: Pasiphaë expresses her regret that she did not sleep with Zeus as did Leda, so she did not give birth to one of the Dioscuri, but thanks to the animal with which she so famously coupled she brought into the world a calf (341), better known to us as the Minotaur.

The elegiac tone of regret with which the *récit* ends begs the question of this Prometheus's regret. Unlike the classical antecedent, Gide's character moves beyond philanthropy and punishment. The moral of Prometheus's lecture, embracing one's lot and converting obliged duty into consciously chosen activity, seems lost by the end; the eagle, symbol of this conscience, is no longer the beloved devourer of Prometheus but devoured by Prometheus. Roles are reversed. Prometheus is no longer the wily but punished trickster of Hesiodic poetry nor the tragic and revolutionary figure of Aeschylean drama who prefigures the ultimate downfall of Zeus's reign. Gide continues the story where the ancient sources leave off, bringing Prometheus back from his mountain-side punishment. In properly Greek fashion, Gide looks to the end of Prometheus's life; so let us examine Gide's work teleologically. In Gide's *récit*, Prometheus becomes a *bon vivant* enjoying life. This transformation is accomplished through the agency of Zeus and the history of Damocles and Cocles.

The death of Damocles marks the final judgement of a tragic worldview imbued with an overly heightened sense of responsibility. The perseverance of Cocles in the face of tragedy (Zeus's slap, the loss of an eye) and the alteration of Prometheus's character point up the benefits of a life more idyllic (as in Virgil's Tityrus) and more concerned with the present moment and with happiness. Zeus presides over mortal lives from a distance, insulated but also deeply alienated by his extreme wealth; Cocles, seemingly instinctively, and Prometheus, reflectively (as articulated in his public speech) partake in human society and mortal life, enjoying the pleasures it has to offer.

In both *Le Traité du Narcisse* and in *Le Prométhée Mal Enchaîné*, Gide invokes the classical past to argue for a theory of Narcissistic egotism. In each work, Gide has taken such liberties that connections between the classical past and Gidean modernism are difficult to discern. But there is a stronger connection here than just the use of classical names as appended details. Using classical characters to argue for a theory of Narcissism or egotism, Gide adds historical and cultural depth to this theory of self-centredness. At the same time, we can read the characters of Damocles and Cocles symbolically, commenting on the uses of the classical past. Their different approaches to the classical past represent what the Waiter would call the personality of each character; these values, or traits, of individual personality take on larger meaning in Gide's symbolic language, with each character representing a different critical demeanour – and Prometheus, the titular hero, representing Gide's chosen path. Damocles represents the exhausting burdens of inescapable indebtedness to the classical past; dwelling always already on the classical past, as Damocles does on his personal past and the debt he can never discharge, leads to misery and separation from the contemporary world in which we live. Cocles represents a less burdensome relationship to the classical past: what he sees from his one remaining eye allows him to continue living in the modern world. The partial vision of Cocles represents a respectful relationship to the past while also transcending Damocles's rigid fixity on what's past. Cocles is closest to the demeanour embodied by Gide's Prometheus: Prometheus escapes the bounds of classical mythology and its storied bondage as punishment for his philanthropy, to go in search of his own personality on the streets of Paris. Prometheus merges the classical ideal with modern urban life. At the same time, Prometheus' discourse on his eagle calls attention precisely to our relationship with the past (mythic, historic, and personal); the past, like the eagle, becomes that which sustains and nourishes us in the present. It serves us; we do not (like poor Damocles) serve it. This lesson, learned by Prometheus during the course of the *récit*, is the latest philanthropic act of Prometheus, marked symbolically by the feasting on the eagle after the funeral of Damocles. The past may be beautiful, as was the eagle, and that beauty may live on, as it does in the eagle's feathers, but those feathers now serve the author as a quill to convey precisely this lesson to the audience. In more compact form, Gide's Narcissus represents the same lesson. Narcissus is an observer, combining the elements of multiple traditions. Like poets, Narcissus contemplates the crystalline beauties of art; but such contemplation exists outside of the river of time. Narcissus represents the need to transcend time, history, arguably cultural specificity and reliance on only one tradition.

Gide's ego-centrism represents, then, an ethics of relating to the classical past. Like Aristotelian *theoria*, we are left to contemplate the classical past and its beauty. But this contemplation must be modified by the self-knowledge inspired by the Delphic injunction: we must know ourselves in order to know others (especially those at a temporal remove from us). We are instructed not to lose sight of our selves in this transhistorical contemplation. Gide's ethics of the classical past, rather than easily dismissed as quirky Narcissism, thus gains cultural authority by presenting itself as the realization of two classical ideals. The mediation of self-knowledge with concern for others prevents Gide's theory from being merely self-centredness. Rather Gide, like Prometheus, likes what devours men; in these two works we see Gide examining our devouring fascination with the classical past. Like Prometheus, Gide may be a reluctant philanthropist, but he does offer lessons in how to negotiate this fascination. While the classical past calls into being our ideal selves, Gide also acknowledges that we do not live in a classical nor ideal world. We must temper our ideal selves or risk dying miserably like Damocles; only by pursuing the transhistorical syncretism and the conditions of possibility which that presents (as in *Le Traité du Narcisse*) can we productively combine classical past and present reality. Otherwise, we die devouringly. In these early works, Gide announces themes which will run throughout his literary career, including his final work, *Thésée* (Theseus, written in 1943–1944, published in 1946). Like Prometheus, Gide himself philanthropically models for readers the ethics of combining the classical past with his modernist present.

FURTHER READING

The French texts of Gide cited in this chapter can be found in Gide 1958, except for 'Considérations' which can be read in Gide 1924 or Gide 1935. Although Gide re-wrote the classical past throughout his literary career, the study of reference for Gide's use of classical myth remains Watson-Williams 1967; on *Narcisse* see now Genova 1994. The fundamental study of Gide's theory of narcissism is Delorme 1970; Goulet 1985 finds in Gidean Narcissism a personal myth of the super-ego, and this work could be expanded in light of recent explorations of Nietzsche's influence on Gide. On the importance of Zeus being a *miglionnaire* in *Prométhée*, see Lacan's fifth seminar, dating from 1957, 1998: 51–57. For more on twentieth-century receptions of the classical past in France, see now Leonard 2005.

CHAPTER FIFTEEN

'What Difference Was Made?': Feminist Models of Reception

Vanda Zajko

When Penelope, the narrator of Margaret Atwood's 2005 *Penelopiad*, decides that, finally, it is her turn to do a little story-making she complains vociferously about the cultural authority of her husband's version of the events that shaped both their lives. In particular, she expresses her loathing of the way in which her example has been used to coerce other women into toeing the wifely line:

> He was always so plausible. Many people have believed that his version of events was the true one, give or take a few murders, a few beautiful seductions, a few one-eyed monsters. Even I believed him, from time to time. I knew he was tricky and a liar, I just didn't think he would play his tricks and try out his lies on me. Hadn't I been faithful? Hadn't I waited, and waited, and waited, despite the temptation – almost the compulsion – to do otherwise? And what did I amount to, once the official version gained ground? An edifying legend. A stick used to beat other women with. Why couldn't they be as considerate, as trustworthy, as all-suffering as I had been? That was the line they took, the singers, the yarn-spinners.
>
> (Atwood 2005: 2)

Unable to control her reputation and forced to witness the jeering, jokes and speculation that surround her, this Penelope comes to the conclusion that patience has been the most effective weapon in her armoury: now that all the others 'have run out of air' and the stakes have been lowered since the main protagonists are dead, at last she has a chance to tell her side of the story and to 'address the various items of slanderous gossip that have been going the rounds for the past two or three thousand years' (Atwood 2005: 143). The long view her endurance allows her guarantees that she can give an account which incorporates whatever details of the earlier versions she chooses and similarly can reject any particulars which do not flatter her or suit her purposes. Thus Atwood's heroine, in her self-conscious belatedness and awareness of the dynamics of appropriation and selection, functions as an allegory of reception theory with its insistence on the way that 'the very history of effects and the interpretation of an event or work of the past enables us to understand it as a plurality of meanings that was not yet perceivable to its contemporaries' (Jauss 2001: 7). Is she, however, a feminist heroine? And what might it mean to make such a claim?

Surveying the figure of Penelope from another, more overtly scholarly perspective, Barbara Clayton describes how in her original and more familiar context of the *Odyssey* she has been the centre of controversy as to whether the Homeric poem can be described as either feminine or feminist. Famously it was the nineteenth-century novelist and essayist Samuel Butler who launched the modern debate when he claimed that the poem must have been written by a woman since the point of view from which the story is told is a feminine one. Pointing to the numerous ways that Butler's idea of the feminine inevitably draws heavily upon the values of his nineteenth-century friends and acquaintances, Clayton comments wryly that 'Butler finds that the *Odyssey*, when conceived of as written by a man, is an inferior poem, but a masterwork when conceived of as written by a woman' (Clayton 2004: 2). She shows how the terms of validation used by Butler (words such as 'charming') reoccur in the scholarship to the extent that they have contributed towards a tradition of reading the differences between the *Odyssey* and *Iliad* as gendered: the *Odyssey* slight, superficial and feminine; the *Iliad*, since antiquity considered the earlier and more serious of the Homeric poems, profound, forceful and masculine (Clayton 2004: 1–19).

Butler's critique of the *Odyssey* was contemporaneous with the later part of what has come to be known as the 'first wave' of feminism, namely the struggle to achieve universal suffrage that occurred throughout the nineteenth and early twentieth centuries. The reclamation of Butler as a 'proto-feminist' critic by scholars in the second half of the twentieth century can be seen as analogous to the rediscovery of this first wave by the 'second wave' of feminists in the 1960s and 1970s, many of whom had been unaware that anything like a women's movement had hitherto existed. More recently, in the 1990s, 'third-wave' feminists positioned themselves more self-consciously in relation to the earlier movements. Astrid Henry describes the relationships between these successive 'waves' as follows:

> Second-wave feminists describe the first wave as their 'heritage,' a history that had been intentionally hidden but that once discovered could embolden them. In this regard, the second wave's relationship to the first is noticeably different from the third wave's relationship to the second. In constructing a relationship to the past, second-wave feminists had to first unearth first-wave feminism; their recovery of the past and, ultimately, their identification with it did not involve a direct confrontation with feminists of the nineteenth and early twentieth centuries. The encounter with feminism looks decidedly different to third-wave feminists who grew up with feminism 'in the water' and with second-wave feminists as teachers, mentors, family and friends.
>
> (Henry 2004: 60)

We shall return to the significance of the metaphor of the waves later in the chapter, and to the differences between different models of feminism, but for now let us consider how the debate about the *Odyssey* developed. In the last few decades of the twentieth century feminist-inspired studies were concerned to investigate the subject matter and value systems of the poem with more precision and to consider how gender might play a role in its interpretation. For some critics it was the preponderance of vital female characters that led them to consider the *Odyssey* the more 'feminine' a text; for others it was the emphasis on qualities of mind such as cunning and intelligence rather than physical prowess that determined its gendered identity. One result of the growth in popularity of reader-centred modes of analysis was a switch of attention from the content of the poems to the dynamics of the reading process itself: some critics reconstructed possible responses of the ancient audiences to the poems to provide clues as to the gender ideology they were likely to promote (see, for example, Doherty 1995); others considered the attitude and perception of the contemporary reader to hold the key to whether the *Odyssey* should be judged as either a feminist or a failed feminist text (see, for example, Felson Rubin 1994).

Certain topics began to dominate the debates. For example, the question of whether the 'like-mindedness' of Odysseus and Penelope celebrates the idea of equality within marriage, or merely gestures towards a promise of female power that is never truly fulfilled preoccupied commentators such as Sheila Murnaghan, who concluded that 'the Odyssey's unusually sympathetic portrait of the exemplary wife is placed in a wider context of suspicion towards women from which even she cannot altogether escape' so that 'Penelope becomes an exception to the general rule' and 'the poem self-consciously depicts the formation and authorization of a tradition of misogyny even as it places the counter-example at the centre of its story' (Murnaghan 1987: 107). Linked to this point is the broader inquiry as to whether the androcentric values of the poem are ultimately reinforced or destabilized by the temporary authority of certain female figures. Froma Zeitlin articulates a popular position when she suggests that 'every female figure in the poem – including Calypso, Circe, Arete, and even Nausikaa – contributes some element to the complex and composite portrait of Penelope' (Zeitlin 1996: 45). Indeed, however various the details, feminist critics of this period tend to share the strategy of making Penelope the focus of their readings of the *Odyssey*. It is as if, for their interpretations to have authority, they must locate a voice or figure *within* an ancient text which will validate them. This model of reception is one which typifies a second-wave feminist response to ancient texts more generally.

The focus on Penelope continues into the twenty-first century, although in a different critical climate we find a shift in the emphasis of the work she is required to do. Clayton gives the following explanation for the Penelope-centred title of her book (*A Penelopean Poetics: Reweaving the Feminine in Homer's Odyssey*), concentrating on the metaphor of a weaving that she suggests, in Penelope's case, is predicated on the notion of unweaving in order to reweave:

> Reweaving, as we shall see in subsequent chapters, is at the heart of an Odyssean poetics that is essentially Penelopean in nature . . . A Penelopean poetics of unweaving brings together notions of gender, language, and poetic production in a way that challenges androcentric ideology, i.e. the very phallocentric principles which have sanctioned the equation of the *Odyssey*'s femininity with the poem's alleged weaknesses. It allows

us to identify difference at the level of narrative production and to understand how
pervasively the poet has woven a feminine alterity into the fabric of the *Odyssey*. Thus,
a Penelopean poetics manages to be both feminist and feminine at the same time.

(Clayton 2004: 19)

Here, then, in a bold having-your-cake-and-eating-it move, Penelope's activity is figured
as mediating not only between different ways of conceptualizing poetic activity,
but also between the different, not to say oppositional, positions regarding gender
difference signified by the terms 'feminist' and 'feminine': the idea of a 'feminist
heroine' is likely to be associated with the kind of 'images of women' criticism that
depends on measuring textual representations of women against the real women
outside of those texts; 'feminine', on the other hand, is more commonly used in
the contexts of psychoanalytically informed criticism where the feminine is seen as
a position taken up by the subject within language and the social order that is not
dependent on bodily difference. Penelope may be 'a difficult, if not unsatisfactory,
feminist heroine' (Clayton 2004: 18) but under her more recent description she
manages to achieve a synthesis of intellectual positions that are usually held apart,
at times with a considerable degree of rancour.

Clayton's Penelope notwithstanding, more often than not it is the 'inter-generational'
quarrelling of feminists that receives attention, particularly within progressivist narratives that equate the most recent mode of analysis with the most sophisticated.
Such narratives incline towards urging a commitment to models of reading that stress
plurality above all in terms of engagement with both writers and readers, perhaps in
order to avoid the charge of naiveté that has tended to be laid against feminism.
The following extract from the introductory essay to Sally Minogue's edited collection *Problems for Feminist Criticism* typifies this trope: attempting an overview of
feminist theory and praxis, Minogue attacks a certain variety of feminist criticism for
its judgemental tendencies and its predilection for censoring the choices of readers:

> In telling us which authors we should and should not read, and what area of those
> authors we should and should not approve, and what aspects of behaviour of female
> characters we should and should not take as models of identity, it narrows our area of
> interest in literature in a distorting manner. It assumes the link between the depiction
> of certain sorts of male and female behaviour in fiction and authorial misogyny . . . And
> in doing this it puts the claims about gender above any other consideration in our approach
> to literature.

(Minogue 1990: 11)

The object of denunciation in this chapter is that variety of feminist poetics which
concerns itself with exposing misogyny in its various manifestations in the works of
male writers and 'correcting' its distortions. The supposition of this kind of poetics
is that misogynistic representations in literature are damaging to men and women,
both those who are exposed to them and those who are exposed to others whose
attitudes have been shaped by them. Several generations of scholars have by
now attacked this early version of feminist criticism, preferring, with Minogue, an
emphasis on the aforementioned plurality and the open-endedness of the reading

process. Indeed it has become characteristic of feminist collections to undertake a scrutiny of methodological positions at the outset and to emphasize that feminism should not be considered a monolithic frame of reference. For example, in another such introductory essay, Margaret Higonnet argues that feminism, like comparative literature, is not a singular theory or entity but rather 'it juxtaposes different voices, to stress not homogeneity but conflicts and discontinuities' (Higonnet 1994: 5). She suggests that far from being narrow or limiting, feminist theories have the capacity to renovate literary studies in a thoroughgoing way and to generate innumerable new readings of both canonical and non-canonical texts. But is there a tension between these sorts of radical claims made for the potential of feminist interpretation and the disavowal of the idea that it should put gender above any other consideration in its approach to literature? If the representations of gender are not made central, is it possible to distinguish readings described as feminist from a whole variety of others that are self-consciously working against, or re-writing, aspects of a tradition?

In terms of the tradition constituted by feminist criticism itself, the contentious area of debate, as demonstrated both by the extracts above and, more implicitly, by Clayton's synthesizing methodological statement, is which models of gender difference should underpin its readings. This is connected to the question of the relation of feminism to the other disciplines or sub-disciplines which it both seeks to influence and which inform its procedures. Feminist research has tended to identify as strongly interdisciplinary for both pragmatic and ideological reasons and Hilde Hein and Carolyn Korsmeyer suggest that this has given it a distinctive eclectic feel:

> This is deliberate, for many feminist scholars discovered early in their work that their own disciplines not only ignored gender but also lacked adequate disciplinary tools to revise their fields suitably to cope with issues of women's experience and gender differences. Few feminists give high priority to disciplinary purity, and eclectic studies have replaced narrower research methods. Just as feminist philosophy has benefited by the use of strategies of textual, representational and psychological analyses, so too feminist scholars of literature and art have profited by employing philosophical views to illuminate their own studies.
>
> (Hein and Korsmeyer 1993: ix)

Feminist work in Classics is no exception. As feminist ideas started to make an impact in the kinds of ways that have been discussed, an expansion of the geographical, historical and conceptual boundaries of the discipline became hard to ignore and new critical vocabularies borrowed from cognate areas of study began to require translation and dissemination. Doing 'feminist Classics' involved the rethinking of the possibilities for the field of study in terms both of subject matter and methodology and the pressing need to participate in debates across the humanities was apparent to those who acknowledged that Classics, a discipline 'that confers status by evoking tradition with all its weight', was falling behind in the race for modish intellectual credibility (Rabinowitz and Richlin 1993: 3). Nancy Rabinowitz and Amy Richlin have described how feminists working in Classics who attempted a dialogue with emergent feminist theory initially felt themselves doubly marginalized as their work was for the most part unrecognized by those positioned in the mainstream of their subject and their affiliation as classicists rendered them virtually invisible to 'feminists in the theoretical avant-garde' (Rabinowitz and Richlin 1993: 2). The attempt to 'play catch-up', far from resulting in a mutually beneficial symbiosis, could on occasion lead to a feeling of voiceless exclusion and invisibility so that instead of being a cross-disciplinary mode of textual analysis, academic feminism within the fairly small world of Classics sometimes seemed a barely acknowledged sub-grouping of the discipline.

The struggle for recognition and authority during these years could in part explain the keenness of more recent scholars to disassociate from it: it is as though the taint of intellectual disreputability potentially still clings to any endeavour that explicitly identifies as feminist. Given that subsequent to the period depicted by Rabinowitz et al. above, there was a time when gender-related research can be said to have dominated Classics or, at least, the self-consciously progressive faction of the discipline, such a claim might be regarded as suspect, particularly by those who will have felt that their lack of interest in such topics actively counted against them. But the constant recourse to history lessons in prefatory remarks and the avoidance of commitment to explicitly feminist positions continues to suggest a degree of defensiveness. The transmutation of Women's Studies into Gender Studies into Lesbian and Gay Studies into Queer Theory into Post-feminism can be regarded as a natural and healthy evolution of thought in response to changing social circumstances and where we are now might indeed be measured against where we once were with a certain amount of complacency. However, such an account does rather beg the question of whether 'feminist' these days continues to have valency as either a descriptive or an exhortative term. Or has it, rather, become part of a historicizing vocabulary? Has the moment of feminist reception quite simply been and gone?

The question of how a feminist reception of, say, a literary text, differs from other kinds of receptions is crucial here. There can be no doubt paying particular attention to issues of gender has, in the past, given rise to the kind of fresh and invigorating readings that Higonnet claims for feminism: we have only to think of the Penelope who in a widely read and highly regarded book of 1990 could be described as 'the real centre of the Odyssey's plot' (Winkler 1990: 133) to realize how richly feminism at one time irrigated even the most dryly canonical of classical landscapes. But what about involvement with current debates and ideas? Is the process of engagement with contemporary theories of gender continuing to have an impact on the ways we read ancient texts? It is clear that it does not work to try and turn back time and return to a more innocent age when wrongs to be righted in relation to men and women seemed, at least in some quarters, to be more obvious and urgent. But neither is it necessarily viable, in terms of retaining the intelligibility of the need for feminist interpretation, to position it as simply one of many ways of understanding textual relations. A commitment to feminist modes of analysis depends upon a belief that systems of representation structured around the binary of sexual difference continue to propagate imparity. If no such belief is held, there is no comprehensible reason for retaining them at all. It can easily be demonstrated that feminism never has been univocal, any more than any other critical position that is conveniently caricatured – there have always been fierce debates about aims, strategies, and sites of identification. But the question presses whether a discourse that prioritizes and theorizes gender difference over and above any other persists in having the capacity to generate debate and provide intellectual sustenance for those inhabiting a world where, for some at least, the possibilities for identification are multiple and multiplying.

One of the questionable issues here is whether feminism can operate as meta-narrative, as somehow 'outside' or in the vanguard of other discourses, commenting critically upon them. The postmodern turn in reading has highlighted the problems in claiming such status for any interpretive position and distrust for the claims of grand narratives characterizes the work of contemporary scholars in the majority of disciplines. There have also been changes in the composition of departments and other academic groupings that have altered the way that feminist topics and approaches are positioned in relation to others taught and researched under a particular heading. Marjorie Garber describes the resulting shifts in intellectual focus as follows:

> In the wake of 'studies' that were anti- or cross- or interdisciplinary by design, the traditional disciplines have in some cases begun renaming themselves as 'studies': English studies, literary studies, Romance studies. And these new 'studies' include issues like culture, history, language, cartography, gender, and sexuality in the range of courses they offer. The cluster model more and more obtains, with or without the 'studies' designation. To make a long story short, the once outside has become the new inside. Or, to take a longer historical view, that which was once considered collectively (in the grand old days of unified knowledge: the trivium and quadrivium) and was later individualized, categorized, classified, and assorted into 'departments' is now again being viewed as a collectivity. With a difference. Whether we call this poaching, cultural imperialism, hegemony, interdisciplinarity, or the end of the intellectual world as we know it will depend upon where we're coming from, where we think we're going, and in what company.
>
> (Garber 2001: 78)

Given the ongoing metamorphosis of the academic landscape, where do feminist readings of classical texts belong? Within Classics? Or within some other (sub)disciplinary grouping? Should they be subsumed within the increasingly dominant field of 'reception studies' or do they have the potential to offer a distinctive gendered critique of just such intellectual expansionism? Some would argue that it is by positioning itself continuously on the borders or margins of other areas of activity and isolating itself from 'company' that feminism remains aloof enough to protect the integrity of its procedures and retain its facility for appraisal. However, others would maintain that there are times when this kind of distance leads to complacency that may result in a feeling of immunity from rigorous ideological critique. As can happen with any radical movement or mode of thinking, the successful dissemination and incorporation of its ideas into mainstream institutions has thrown up new challenges for feminism in terms of how to proceed responsibly and fix upon new directions. Now that some aims of the original movements have been fulfilled to a greater or lesser extent, quite what the *telos* of feminism should be is still an open question both within and without the academy. In self-aware mode, feminism has played a major part in opening up debates about the processes that both construct and destabilize the identity categories which ground its assumptions. In the words of Judith Butler who strongly urges the need for their continued interrogation: 'How is it that the very category, the subject, the 'we', that is supposed to be presumed for the purposes of solidarity, produces the very factionalization it is supposed to quell?' (Butler 1995: 49). The emergence of 'third-wave' or 'post-feminism' as an antidote to, or extension of, the earlier 'second wave' varieties can be seen as demonstrating precisely this kind of factionalization, as can the arguments between and about the advocates of each of these two 'movements'.

It is fair to say that as yet, with a few notable exceptions (see, for example, Liveley 2006), the impact of these new brands of feminism has yet to be felt in Classics (or classical *studies*), even though, in line with Garber's depiction above, the boundaries of the discipline have continued to shift and evolve. Nowadays many more programmes are offered that entail reading ancient authors in translation as well as in the original languages, studying texts in different media, and considering a wide range of critical theoretical positions from a variety of sources within the humanities, and yet it is still the case that for the latest feminist theory we have to look elsewhere. This may have a lot to do with the subject matter that is distinctively the concern of classicists and historians of the ancient world: both third-wave and post-feminist insights have tended to come from those working within one of the latest academic groupings, 'cultural studies', and often from the scrutiny of texts in a variety of media from the domain of popular culture. As such, the kinds of issue they are able to address move far beyond the parameters of those that arise from the consideration of (for the most part) male-authored literary, historical and philosophical texts of one kind or another. The participatory contexts made possible by the new technologies and the opportunities to survey and interrogate contemporary readers and audiences have resulted in an explosion of reception-orientated research that cannot but cause those working with more traditional material to salivate at the spectrum of freshly revealed opportunities. And yet it is probably from this direction that some of the challenges to readings of classical literature and culture will come, challenges both in terms of innovative interpretations and in terms of expanding the concept of what constitutes a 'classical text'. Anita Harris has shown how important it is when narrating a history of feminism to look 'in places often disregarded as sites for feminist work' (see reference to website below). She argues that the resources of contemporary societies enable and encourage new ways of conducting political organization, protest, and agitation:

> This is certainly the case for much young feminist debate, for example, as evidenced in the creation of grrrzines, girls' webpages, and chat rooms. 'Zines', short for fanzines, are independently produced informal news letters, which usually include reviews, information sharing, editorials and creative writing around issues relevant to young women. They are distributed through wide networks for the purposes of sharing information and building a community of young feminists.
>
> (www.chloe.uwa.edu.au/outskirts/archive/VOL8/
> article4.html, last accessed October 2006)

We might argue that for both feminism and Classics, there is a need to listen to unfamiliar voices, and to look in unfamiliar places in order to open up debates about new modes of thinking that will result in changes to conceptualizations of their subject. Within all varieties of academic discourse, there is a tendency for certain ideas and methodologies to be posited as outdated in order to justify and glamorize the adoption of the new. Within feminism, this tendency has become fossilized by the use of generational metaphors to represent the changes in dominant modes of understanding. Second-wave feminism is figured as a mother figure to the third wave and the metaphor or 'matrophor' (Dakin Quinn 1997: 179) can result in the older generation's representation as stuffy, prissy, and embarrassingly outdated when compared with the sexy vitality of the younger. Astrid Henry points out how although the term third wave is frequently employed 'as a kind of shorthand for a generational difference among feminists, one based on chronological age' (Henry 2004: 3), it over-simplifies the differences between and within each 'generation' of women:

> Though plural, the term 'generations' is almost always dyadic, referring to just two generations. We seem unable to think of generations – or even of waves for that matter – in threes or fours . . . In other words, rather than recognizing the variety of 'relations between women,' the metaphor reduces these potential *relationships* to a single *relationship*: that of mother and daughter. Describing second-wave feminists – and second-wave feminism – as 'mothers' to the third wave may have been inevitable, given that the age difference between each wave's representatives is roughly the equivalent of one familial generation. Yet . . . within the second wave's imagined relationship to feminism's first wave – a generational relationship that cannot so easily be represented as familial – the language of the family was already being deployed.
>
> (Henry 2004: 3)

The dominance of the mother–daughter trope may explain some of the disgruntlement and rancour that can characterize feminist deliberations. The categories 'third-wave feminism' and 'post-feminism' are heatedly debated by those who identify with them and those who oppose them. In yet another, recent, introductory essay, Joanne Hollows and Rachel Moseley discuss the problem as follows: 'The very idea of successive "waves" of feminism has been seen to produce – or reproduce – antagonistic relationships between generations of women structured along the lines of the bad mother–daughter relationship that prevents a constructive dialogue and stops an inheritance being shared' (Hollows and Moseley 2006: 14). Genevieve Liveley, however, is more conciliatory and stresses the continuities between third wave feminism and what went before. She approves the image of the wave 'precisely because of the relationship with previous movements and moments in the history of feminism that it suggests' (Liveley 2006: 3). The idea here, presumably, is that when one stares at the ocean it is impossible to tell where one wave stops and another one begins. The self-representation of post-feminism is sometimes considered to be somewhat more confrontational in that it is associated with the discourses of individualism and choice and with the rejection of the kinds of collective narratives that Butler earlier described as 'supposed to be presumed for the purposes of solidarity'. But there is a more conciliatory perspective available here too and the 'post' in 'post-feminism' can be read not only as marking a point of rupture but also as reconnecting vital contemporary debates to earlier ones, thus signifying a process of ongoing transmutation and change:

> Postfeminism, as an expression of a stage in the constant evolutionary movement of feminism, has gained greater currency in recent years. Once seen, somewhat crudely, as 'anti-feminist', the term is now understood as a useful conceptual frame of reference encompassing the intersection of feminism with a number of other anti-foundationalist movements, including postmodernism, post-structuralism and post-colonialism. Postfeminism represents . . . feminism's 'coming of age', its maturity into a confident body of theory and politics, representing pluralism and difference and reflecting on its position in relation to other philosophical and political movements similarly demanding change.
>
> (Brooks 1997: 1)

Hollows and Moseley point out how post-feminism, like the idea of third-wave feminism, is 'a fraught term used in multiple and uneven ways across geographical contexts'. They describe how at an ESRC funded conference on 'New Femininities' in Cardiff in 2005 what became apparent were 'not only geographical differences, but also disciplinary ones: post feminism had a currency in making sense of texts within film, media and cultural studies, but was outside the frame of reference of many scholars working in sociology and education' (Hollows and Moseley 2006: 12–13). And, one might add, so far, of those working in Classics. Despite the uncertainties of scope and definition, these new varieties of feminism have emerged as a result of dissatisfaction with the existing plant life. Kathleen Rowe Karlyn describes the unpopularity of existing feminism thus:

> while girl power may be hot, feminism is not. Rarely has feminism been viewed in the culture with such ambivalence, indifference or downright disdain. Many women, especially young women, simply do not want to associate themselves with feminism, despite the belief of most self-identified feminists that women of all ages have benefited, and continue to benefit, from feminism as a political movement and a mode of cultural and political analysis . . . mainstream or 'hegemonic' feminism – still largely associated with the second wave – has lost its appeal because of (1) its failures regarding class and race; (2) its censoriousness regarding sexuality, especially heterosexuality; (3) its resistance to the pleasures of the popular; and (4) its growing institutionalization and refusal to examine its own stakes in the power structure. The second wave, of course, was hardly monolithic, despite efforts to make it appear so and to reduce it to caricature. However, the new feminisms have distinguished themselves from the second wave by staking out different positions and priorities on these matters.
>
> (Rowe Karlyn 2006: 57, 59–60)

But the process of transmutation and change looks set to continue: Henry reports that there is now talk of a 'fourth wave' of feminism among women in their late teens and early twenties (2004: 181).

If feminism is to survive as 'a mode of cultural analysis' let alone as 'a political movement' it looks as though it will be the energy of the debates surrounding its hybrid new forms that will help to 'keep it real'. From the point of view of those who share a commitment to reading, teaching and disseminating the texts of antiquity, an effort must be made to become involved with these debates in order that the present and future creative presence of classical culture continues to have a role in invigorating them. For if there has as yet been little communication between academic Classics and the 'new feminisms', within the realm of popular culture there are numerous examples of textual productions inspired by the myth and literature of the ancient world and this is the material from which post- and third-wave feminism largely draw their inspiration since 'popular cultural forms can be seen as 'sites of opposition' and 'sites of resistance' for a range of groups who wish to open up the possibilities for the creation of new sites of meaning and knowledge' (Brooks 1997: 189). This constant reference to classical texts forms a continuity between the new forms of feminism and the old because classical myth, in particular, has always been central to the development of feminist thought. Zajko and Leonard (2006: 1–17) is devoted to exploring this centrality and shows how the tensions involved in the commitment to classical myth exposes many of the conflicts within feminism itself. By what is sometimes a circuitous route, then, the influence of Classics persists and offers something distinctive to emergent feminist debates.

At the end of her wide-ranging survey of Classics and reception studies Lorna Hardwick concludes the chapter entitled '(Why) Do Reception Studies Matter?' with a discussion of the likely vocabularies of the receptions of the future. Arguing that 'above all, reception studies have shown that classical texts, images and ideas are culturally active presences', she suggests that 'the key evaluative question both for the relationship with the past and for the present, may well be "what difference was made?"' (Hardwick 2003a: 112). A key issue also for any kind of feminist praxis, it is sometimes impossible to answer such a question without a measure of temporal and analytical space and detachment:

> Some of these judgements about the making of differences and their impact require time and critical distance before they can be made. In this respect the study of very recent appropriations and refigurations has special requirements for the finding, preservation and analysis of the data which will inform judgements that can only be made in the future. The growth of reception studies in recent years contains an explicit claim that classical culture will continue to be a significant strand in cultural history. It also implies a requirement to develop transparent rationales and practices in cultural philology that will make critical inquiry a reality in the present and form a coherent basis for investigation by the cultural historians of the future.
>
> (Hardwick 2003a: 113)

Genevieve Liveley, working with an idea first mooted by Amy Richlin in 1993, suggests that this length of perspective is precisely the distinctive bequest of Classics to feminism. It is this, she advises, that provides the necessary distance and displacement to facilitate reflection on the historicality of positions and ensure the continuing efficacy of feminism as hermeneutic (Liveley 2006: 18). For Liveley, the long view of Classics draws attention to the contingency of all interpretations and it leads her to conclude that feminist literary criticism does not differ from any other mode of reading in as much as, whilst it may have distinctive priorities, it cannot determine or control its reception any more than, say, the allegoresis that produced the Ovid Moralisé. We are reminded here of Atwood's Penelope who struggles to regulate the stories people tell about her and eventually, due to the long span of time that she spends in Hades, is able to retaliate by telling one of her own. Throughout *The Penelopiad*, Atwood's own revisionist tale, Penelope's jealousy of Helen is one of the dynamics that drives forward the narrative. A glamorous and destructive figure on the fringes of her life ever since she was a child, Helen has tormented Penelope with her insouciance and effortless desirability and Penelope has been waiting for a considerable time for the opportunity to undermine her confidence and begin to take her revenge. Atwood rejects what might be characterized as a second-wave feminist move in her refusal to countenance any empathy between the two women, a rejection of any declaration of sisterhood in the face of male oppression. Her Penelope is perhaps a third-wave feminist, intent on differentiating herself from a feminine identity that does not meet her needs. She is also, as mentioned earlier, a reception theorist, and her model of reception, like Liveley's above, depends on drawing upon a sense of historical distance in order to reject the gender ideology of her 'original text'. In her last exchange with Helen she makes the point very clearly that, in the words of Hans Robert Jauss, 'literary communication opens up a dialogue, in which the only criterion for truth or falsity depends on whether significance is capable of further developing the inexhaustible meaning of the work of art' (Jauss 2001: 27).

Helen has had more than a few excursions. That's what she calls them – 'my little excursions'. 'I've been having such fun,' she'll begin. Then she'll detail her latest conquests and fill me in on the changes in fashion. It was through her that I learned about patches, and sunshades, and bustles, and high-heeled shoes, and girdles, and bikinis, and aerobic exercises, and body piercing, and liposuction. Then she'll make a speech about how naughty she's been and how much uproar she's been causing and how many men she's ruined. Empires have fallen because of her, she's fond of saying.

'I understand the interpretation of the whole Trojan War episode has changed I tell her, to take some of the wind out of her sails. Now they think you were just a myth. It was all about trade routes. That's what the scholars are saying.'

(Atwood 2005: 187)

FURTHER READING

Those interested in thinking about the engagement of classicists with feminist theory from a historical perspective should look at: Sorkin Rabinowitz, N. and Richlin, A. (eds) 1993; Skinner (ed.) 1987, and Pomeroy (ed.) 1991. Other notable works include Zeitlin 1996; Wyke (ed.) 1999; and Doherty 2001. Zajko and Leonard (eds) 2006 explores the centrality of classical myth to the development of feminist thought.

CHAPTER SIXTEEN

History and Theory:
Moses and Monotheism and the
Historiography of the Repressed

Miriam Leonard

'Historians', Peter Gay argues, 'like to reject psychoanalysis as an auxiliary discipline with one sweeping, summary denial: you cannot psychoanalyze the dead. To make the attempt would be to introduce inappropriate techniques into historical inquiry, allow baseless speculation to subvert the explanatory process that has served historians so well for so long, and reduce the beautiful, variegated bouquet of thought and action to drab, depressing psychopathology. Historical individuals, groups, classes, nations, are not patients on the couch', Gay ventriloquizes, 'not even an imaginary couch' (Gay 1985: 3). The postulate of a universal human nature, so often attributed to psychoanalysis, has been particularly displeasing to many scholars of the ancient world whose resolutely historicist training has warned them against such colonizing presumptions. Indeed, those historians who have been open to modern interdisciplinary perspectives would be much more inclined to follow the lead of a figure such as Michel Foucault (1926–1984) whose writings on antiquity are explicitly premised on understanding its social and sexual discourses as the manifestations of a society which has not known psychoanalysis.

And yet, as Gay points out, 'the professional historian has always been a psychologist – an amateur psychologist' (Gay 1985: 6). Gay argues that despite his or her professions to the contrary, the historian always functions with some notion of human nature. Such a conception has to be the precondition of exploring historical causation and of attributing motives to the actors of the past. Only a rigorously structuralist or systemic analysis which denies agency to the individual and insists on the decisive role of external, supra-human structures can avoid the retrojective postulation of a common understanding of mind. Gay argues that even the historical materialism of Marxism which insists so heavily on the determinism of external economic and social pressures relies for its analyses on a certain theory of the mind (Gay 1985: 6).

In this chapter I want to argue that beyond this inescapability of a certain psychological vocabulary, Freudian psychoanalysis, in particular, has something to contribute to our understanding of the past. In studying the relationship between 'history' and 'theory' I shall be exploring how psychoanalysis can offer reception studies a different way of understanding the temporality of meaning, a different way of conceptualizing how the pastness of the past impacts on its meaning in the present. Reception studies have often been figured within the field of Classics as antithetical to history. This vision is articulated most clearly by Charles Martindale (1993, 2006) but has been opposed by a number of other practitioners of classical reception, most notably by Simon Goldhill (2002) who has argued for the idea of reception as a form of cultural history. In this sense, the debates within Classics parallel the changing understanding of reception theory within other disciplines. Machor and Goldstein's collection *Reception Study: From Literary Theory to Cultural Studies* (2001), clearly marks the trajectory for reception set out by Goldhill. But it is worth remembering that the impetus for Hans-Robert Jauss's (1921–1997) formulation of a *Rezeptionsästhetik* was a desire to move beyond overly historical models of reading where the meaning of a text was exclusively located in its 'original' moment of production. Indeed, Jauss presents reception theory as an explicit attack on positivism and its desire to reconstruct the 'past as it really was' divorced from its meaning in the present (Jauss 1982). It would be difficult to deny that by studying the evolving meanings of the artefacts of antiquity across time, the scholar of reception removes the classical text from its original context and threatens to erase the essential historical dimension of the object of her/his inquiry. Reception theory and historicism have thus often been seen as competing and even irreconcilable discourses.

The charge of ahistoricism which has been laid against reception theory could perhaps be seen as the most explicit example of a more generalized desire to oppose the study of the past 'as such' to theoretically informed models which highlight the essential role the process of recovery of the past plays in our understanding of historical cultures. Reception theory, then, is just one of a number of 'theories' which has been seen as standing in the way of exploring antiquity in its own terms. But reception perhaps more than any other field has explicitly set itself the task of probing this supposed opposition between 'history' and 'theory'. In this chapter I want to explore how thinking of Freudian psychoanalysis as a form of reception can help one develop a better model for explaining these tensions which have lain behind many of the debates between classicists in recent decades. More specifically, by investigating Freud's (1856–1939) own writings about history, I shall argue, that the scholar of reception can begin to articulate a more subtle understanding of the trace of the past which is able to resist the most aggressive of modern appropriations. Reading Freud can expose not just the necessary historicism of reception studies but it can also show how reception theory has a significant role to play in redefining the project of history for scholars of the ancient world.

'Nothing That Ever Took Shape Has Passed Away'

Contrary to the consensus about the ahistoricism of psychoanalysis which has become an orthodoxy within classical scholarship (see Vernant 1988; Leonard 2003), Freud's theory and practice of analysis is through and through historical. His understanding of the human mind arose from the insights he gleaned from the case histories of his patients. Freud thus makes 'history' play the decisive explanatory role in his exploration of pathology. At the very core of psychoanalysis is a recognition of the historicity of human experience and of the pre-eminent role the past plays in our understanding of the present. As Freud's well-known use of the metaphor of archaeology affirms, the past is absolutely central to the construction of the Freudian process (see Spence 1987; Gamwell and Wells 1989; Mertens and Haubl 1996; Armstrong 1999, 2005a). So Freud claims that the role of the analyst, 'is to make out what has been forgotten from the traces it has left behind' and writes:

> In the face of the incompleteness of my analytical results, I had no choice but to follow the example of those discoverers whose good fortune it is to bring to the light of day after their long burial the priceless though mutilated relics of antiquity. I have restored what is missing, taking the best model known to me from other analyses; but like the conscientious archaeologist, I have not omitted to mention in each case where the authentic parts end and my construction begins.
>
> (Freud 1953–74: 7, 12)

The description of Freud's method wavers between extreme positivism and self-conscious constructivism. While Freud seems to be placing emphasis on the incompleteness of the historical record, he nonetheless, 'like the conscientious archaeologist' wants to draw a clear distinction between where the 'authentic parts end' and the 'construction begins'. For Freud there is no problematization of the 'authenticity of the past'. Freud's comments here are all the more striking given his recognition elsewhere that the narrative that the analyst and analysand construct together is never simply an account of events that happened. But the latent positivism of his archaeological analogy suffuses Freud's own study of the Classics. Thus, in his famous description of Rome as a 'psychical entity' in *Civilisation and its Discontents,* it is the recoverability of the past which is foregrounded:

> Now, let us make the fantastic assumption that Rome is not a place where people live, but a psychical entity with a similarly long, rich past, in which nothing that ever took shape has passed away, and in which all previous phases of development exist beside the most recent. For Rome this would mean that on the Palatine hill the imperial palaces and the Septizonium of Septimus Severus still rose to their original height.
>
> (Freud 1953–74: 21. 70)

There is no doubt that Freud's reconstruction of the past here exists in a chaotic and destablizing juxtaposition. History becomes a synchrony of discordant historical moments. But what the Freudian account loses in terms of diachrony, what it lacks in reliable historical narrative, it gains in the assumption that nothing which happens in the past is ever truly lost to the historical record. If the tools of the historian or the analyst are sufficiently finely tuned they will be able to recover the concrete historical moments that have left material remains on the physical landscape. Nothing, in this account 'passes away'. There is, therefore, no bar to the onward march of science.

Freud repeatedly worries in this section about the status of his analogy, even going so far as to say: 'Our attempt seems to be an idle game' (71). In fact, in the face of the imagined objection that it is possible for buildings of a city, and 'even' elements in the mind, to be destroyed, he nuances his position: 'We can only hold fast to the fact that it is rather the rule than the exception for the past to be preserved in mental life' (72). And yet, despite these modifications, Freud leaves undiscussed one of the most puzzling aspects of his depiction of Rome as a human mind – the extent to which the traces of the past are so manifest to the viewer. In Freud's account, the tourist needs no archaeologist to discern the historical movements of Rome's development. By analogy one is led to believe that the analyst is able to read his patient's psychical history, as it were, as an open book. Freud's neglect of the process of recovery in the Rome analogy effectively leaves both the archaeologist and the analyst out of a job.

But in his earlier reading of Wilhelm Jensen's (1837–1911) *Gradiva* (a novel which traces the young archaeologist Norbert Hanold's 'Pompeian phantasy' as he tries to discover the origins of relief of a young girl he sees in a Roman museum) a different emphasis emerges. In Freud's comparison between Pompeii and the human mind, it is not so much what can be recovered as what has been 'repressed' which is at the forefront of the analogy:

> There is, in fact, no better analogy for repression, by which something in the mind is at once made inaccessible and preserved, than burial of the sort to which Pompeii fell victim and from which it could emerge once more through the work of spades. Thus it was that the young archaeologist was obliged in his phantasy to transport to Pompeii the original of the relief which reminded him of the object of his youthful love. The author was well justified, indeed, in lingering over the valuable similarity which his delicate sense had perceived between a particular mental process in the individual and an isolated historical event in the history of mankind.
>
> (Freud 1953–74: 9. 40)

The dialectic between what 'has been preserved' and what is 'inaccessible' which had been so strangely occluded in Freud's vision of the Eternal City is brought out in all its complexity when Freud turns to Pompeii. Here it is the difficulty of 'the work of spades' which is insisted upon. In the Pompeian analogy it is not just the fragility of the past which is foregrounded but also the fallibility of the process of its recovery. In this version, repression, phantasy and transference all take their place in the Freudian depiction of the work of the archaeologist. And yet, the optimism of Freud's enlightenment seems to operate at both levels of the analogy. Just as the buried city of Pompeii 'emerges' through the labour of archaeology, the archaeologist's own processes of repression, phantasy and transference can be exposed through the process of analysis. It is not just the object of science but science itself which becomes self-critical and ultimately self-transparent.

Freud's use of the archaeological metaphor has been extensively critiqued in recent years, not least by Donald Spence who has subjected the analogy to his postmodern suspicion (Spence 1987). But as Richard Armstrong has shown, Freud's profound investment in Roman culture owes as much to the precepts of 'critical history' as it does to the emerging discipline of archaeology. As Armstrong convincingly demonstrates 'psychoanalysis was born in dialogue with the larger considerations of historical consciousness from the nineteenth century' (Armstrong 2005a: 160). In particular, Armstrong has ingeniously teased out the relationship between Freud's analytic model and Barthold Niebuhr's investigation of Livy's early history of Rome:

> A great hallmark of nineteenth-century German historiography was the critical analysis of the Livian narratives of early Rome by Barthold Georg Niebhur (1776–1831) in his *Römische Geschichte* (1811–32), in which he proclaimed these hallowed accounts to be poetical fictions responding to national *psychological* needs, not historical truth. This type of source criticism became the model for critical history that was to dominate German thought well into the twentieth century. So it is not surprising that *both* the spell of the Livian narrative, and its dispelling could stand behind an account of childhood memory in Freud.
>
> (Armstrong 2005a: 162)

Armstrong is able to track down a direct reference to Niebuhr's methodology in Freud's own *Autobiographical Study*:

> It will be seen, then, that my mistake was of the same kind as would be made by someone who believed that the legendary story of the early kings of Rome (as told by Livy) was historical truth instead of what in fact it is – a reaction against the memory of times and circumstances that were insignificant and occasionally, perhaps, inglorious.
> (Freud 1953–74: 20. 35, quoted in Armstrong 2005a: 163)

By exploring the influence of Niebuhr on Freud's critical attitude to the myths and legends of Livy's *Ab urbe condita*, Armstrong shows how Freud's historical method was profoundly involved in the nineteenth-century debates about the power and limits of positivism.

Repression and Reception

Freud's engagement with the historiography of the ancient world is perhaps even more explicit in the work which he described to his son as his 'first appearance as a historian'. Published from his exile in London, *Moses and Monotheism* was to be Freud's last major work. It is here that he develops the now notorious theory that Moses was not a Hebrew but an Egyptian priest, who far from being chosen by the Jewish people as their leader, himself chose the Jewish people to be his followers. The origins of monotheism are then to be discovered in the transposition of the Egyptian religion of Aten via Moses to the Jews. In addition to the suggestion of the Egyptian origin of monotheism, at the centre of Freud's provocative rewriting is the claim that the Jews, in their impatience with the harsh strictures of his monotheistic religion, murdered Moses. The history of ancient Judaism is the site of an oedipal murder whose consequences for the Jewish people continued to be felt well into Freud's lifetime. Written on the eve of World War Two and only published after

Freud had fled Vienna in the aftermath of the *Anschluss* (annexation of Austria by Nazi Germany), the contemporary political implications of this text were not lost on either Freud himself or on the text's many subsequent readers. This work functions not just as investigation of the origins of monotheism but also as an exploration of the pathology of anti-Semitism. Freud's characteristically slippery opening has found itself at the centre of an impassioned debate about his Jewish identity: 'To deprive a people of the man whom they take pride in as the greatest of their sons is not a thing to be gladly or carelessly undertaken, least of all by someone who is himself one of them' (Freud 1953–74: 23. 7). Is *Moses and Monotheism* a brave return to his paternal religion at a time of extreme persecution or is it, in one critic's words, 'an excavation into the Jewish past' which, in the name of a 'selfish desire to display the impersonal vigour and superiority of *Wissenschaft*' (science) is 'quite to the detriment of his own people on the eve of their greatest catastrophe'? (Armstrong 2005b: 253)

The structure of Freud's last work is notoriously complex and self-consciously displays the difficult circumstances of its own composition. As Samuel Weber argues: 'It is as if the nonlinear, discontinuous, repetitive temporality that marks the historical process as Freud construes it had contaminated the structure of the text' (Weber 2005: 65). Its generic complexity can be uncovered in an excavation of its proposed titles. Freud had originally intended to publish the work under the title *The Man Moses and Monotheistic Religion: A Historical Novel*. Yosef Yerushalmi has written extensively about the implications of Freud's generic qualification in this repressed subtitle (Yerushalmi 1989, 1991). In particular, he focuses on the overtly historical character of the first two essays which parade their affiliation to historical writing and historically inspired biblical scholarship. Freud not only draws on a large range of historical sources, but he also repeatedly anticipates the objections to his historical method in a manner which again recalls the precepts of 'critical history' explored by Richard Armstrong.

But what is perhaps more interesting than Freud's always contentious and now largely discredited historical narrative is what this remarkable text has to say about the transmission of the historical record. Freud signals the departure from the historical material of the first two essays towards the analytic focus of the third: 'All this, however, is still history, an attempt to fill up the gaps in historical knowledge . . . Our interest follows the fortunes of Moses and his doctrines, to which the rising of the Jews had only apparently put an end' (Freud 1953–74: 23. 62). In other words, the murder of Moses rather than being the conclusion of his historical story is only its beginning. Far from being the *telos* of the Freudian analysis, Oedipus is only its starting point. 'It might very well have signified the final end of the Moses episode in the history of the Jewish people. The remarkable thing, however, is that that was not the case – that the most powerful effects of the people's experience were to come to light only later and were to force their way into reality in the course of many centuries' (Freud 1953–1974: 23. 62). Freud's interest in historical reconstruction here departs from the positivist premise of the previous chapters. He has no desire to return to the originary moment of monotheism's conception, nor, unlike in his previous work *Totem and Taboo*, does he want to prove the historicity of the Oedipal complex by designating the murder of the father as a concrete and specific moment in the history of humanity. Freud's primary interest in *Moses and Monotheism* is rather with the complex reception of this event in the long history of the west from antiquity to the present.

For 'how' Freud asks 'are we to explain a delayed effect of this kind and where do we meet with a similar phenomenon?' (Freud 1953–74: 23. 66). It is at this moment that Freud's much anticipated analogy makes its appearance: 'There is no difficulty in finding an analogy in the mental life of an individual corresponding to this process' (Freud 1953–74: 23. 67). Moses' stubborn persistence in the historical consciousness of the Jewish people resembles the mind in which nothing 'ever passes away'. The death of father, even and especially when he has been murdered, can never be erased from the memory of the son. But unlike the analogy with Rome where the historical record lies manifest in disturbing synchrony, Freud's Moses story can only be understood from a diachronic perspective. Like Pompeii, the period of burial is as important as its ultimate 'emergence'. So drawing on the comparison between delayed recollection and the phenomenon of repressed memories, Freud writes, 'On reflection, it must strike us that, in spite of the fundamental difference between the two cases – the problem of traumatic neurosis and that of Jewish monotheism – there is nevertheless one point of agreement: namely, in the characteristic that might be described as latency' (Freud 1953–74: 23. 68).

What is more, Freud sees this period of 'latency' as crucial to the very development of history as such. For history, the process of recording the past is, Freud argues, the necessary byproduct of the latency period. History is, as it were the symptom of 'latency'. But Freud again challenges the positivist notion of history which he seemingly embraced in the earlier sections of his work. For here the phenomenon of repression is absolutely crucial to the emergence of the historical record. As he writes 'the people who had come from Egypt brought writing and the desire to write history along with them; but it was to be a long time before historical writing realized that it was pledged to unswerving truthfulness' (Freud 1953–74: 23. 68). Distortion, fantasy and repression are all integral to the 'desire to write history'. Freud's distrust of the official historical record seems fully in tune with his hermeneutics of suspicion: 'All the tremendous efforts of later times failed to disguise this shameful fact. But the Mosaic religion had not vanished without leaving a trace; some sort of memory of it had kept it alive – a possibly obscured or distorted tradition. And it was this tradition of a great past which continued to operate (from the background, as it were), which gradually acquired more and more power over people's minds' (Freud 1953–74: 23. 70). It is significant that Freud turns to the history of Greece to explain this 'unfamiliar idea':

> With our present psychological insight we could, long before Schliemann and Evans, have raised the question of where it was that the Greeks obtained all the legendary material which was worked over by Homer and the great Attic dramatists in their master-pieces. The answer would have had to be that this people had probably experienced in their prehistory a period of external brilliance and cultural efflorescence which had perished in a historical catastrophe and of which an obscure tradition survived in these legends.
>
> (Freud 1953–74: 23. 70)

Archaeology here, is for Freud, no longer functioning as an analogy for psychoanalysis. Freud and Schliemann are rather in competition and in Freud's fantasy chronology the spades of psychoanalysis discovered the remains of Troy long before Schliemann set sail. Homer's *Iliad* is, for Freud, the neurotic symptom of a repressed trauma. 'Early trauma- defence-latency-outbreak of neurotic illness – partial return of the repressed. Such is the formula which we have laid down for the development of a neurosis. The reader is now invited to take the step of supposing that something occurred in the life of the human species similar to what occurs in the life of individuals'. (Freud 1953–74: 23. 80).

In Freud's theory of the return of the repressed, I would argue, we can find a compelling theory of historiography and of reception. And yet, what is interesting about *Moses and Monotheism* is that its very content could be seen as the delayed manifestation of an obscured historiographic tradition. Freud's theory of the Egyptian origins of Moses places him at the heart of the debate about the primacy of different ancient cultures (Greek, Roman, Egyptian, Phoenician and others) that dominated the intellectual landscape of the nineteenth century. What is more, as Jan Assman has shown, in his privileging of Egyptian culture Freud comes at the end of a long line of Enlightenment thinkers who had invested in Egypt as a 'counter-religion' to the dual forces of Christian monotheism and secular European philhellenism. As Moses comes to occupy the role of Oedipus in Freud's account of the collective psyche, Freud's historical narrative shifts its focus from Hellenism to Hebraism. Freud's investment in the biblical Moses as he approached his death has been interpreted by Yerushalmi, amongst others, as a return of the Hellenized Freud to the repressed Hebraic religion of his father (see also Robert 1977; Rice 1990). Yerushalmi's emphasis on the role of Freud's father in the son's struggle between Hellenism and Hebraism finds an echo in Freud's own account of his visit to the Acropolis:

> The very theme of Athens and the Acropolis in itself contained evidence of the son's superiority. Our father had been in business, he had had no secondary education, and Athens could not have meant much to him. Thus what interfered with our enjoyment of the journey to Athens was a feeling of *filial piety*.
>
> (Freud 1953–74: 22. 247–8)

But as we have seen, far from a resurrection of the father, *Moses and Monotheism* is launched by a parricide: 'To deprive a people of the man whom they take pride in as the greatest of their sons is not a thing to be gladly or carelessly undertaken, least of all by someone who is himself one of them' (Freud 1953–74: 23. 7). By making Moses an Egyptian, Freud affirms the Semitic character of the European monotheistic tradition while denying its specifically Jewish origin. Like his earlier and well-documented identification with the Carthaginian general Hannibal ('To my youthful mind Hannibal and Rome symbolized the conflict between the tenacity of Jewry and the organization of the Catholic church' (Freud SE 4, 196; see also Armstrong 2005a), Freud's Jewish identity is transposed on to a Semitic tradition which, while existing in opposition to the Greco-Roman civilization, cannot be easily assimilated into the religion of his father. Freud seems to be rejecting the exclusionary rhetoric of the Eurocentric and Judaic accounts alike. Written at a time when the polemics of the Aryan/Semite debate had reached its most frenzied literalization in the politics of Nazism, *Moses and Monotheism* stands as a provocative example of a universal history – a history, that is, that covered the development of humanity in general without distinctions of race or culture. Freud thus champions a model of historiography which for both scholarly and ideological reasons had been exiled from the academy. It is fascinating from this perspective that the ancient historian that Freud cites most extensively in this work is Eduard Meyer (1855–1930) whose own brand of universal history Arnaldo Momigliano (1908–1987) identified as an anachronism even though Meyer was writing more than half a century before the publication of Freud's *Moses*:

> In the situation that existed around 1880 Meyer's notion of the history of antiquity was therefore in one respect the continuation of an old idea of universal history now in decline, but was in another respect an affirmation of concrete political and cultural relations extending from Mesopotamia to the Iberian peninsula, which were not generally recognized by contemporaries.
>
> (Momigliano 1994: 213)

Meyer was an increasingly rare late nineteenth-century phenomenon, a scholar who was as familiar with the Semitic cultures of the Near East as he was with Greece and Rome. Meyer thus positioned himself both against the increasing specialization of the academy and the climate of racial intolerance which made the juxtaposition of Semitic and European cultures so distasteful to his contemporaries. But Eduard Meyer's untimely scholarly radicalism went hand in hand with his fierce political conservatism and personal anti-Semitism (see Calder/Demandt 1990: 446–504; Momigliano 1994: 207–22). That Freud should have chosen to base his historical account of Moses' Egyptian origins on the writings of an anti-Semite who held on to the belief in the possibility of a universal history long after the political circumstances made this impossible is perhaps one final irony of this text that we will have to leave unexplored.

Murderous Distortion and Solicitous Piety: History and Theory

What, then, can Freud tell us about the role of 'history' and 'theory' in reception studies? In the Freudian project, the analyst cannot but see himself as a historian. An analyst who does not show an interest in the historical experience of his analysand has fundamentally misunderstood his vocation. Reception, like psychoanalysis, concerns itself with exploring cultural memory. Moreover, the receptionist and analyst alike understand literature and culture as crucially historically embedded. Just as Freud has no hope of understanding his patients without recourse to the case history, so the scholar of reception who does not interest herself or himself in history of a text, that is to the say the historical circumstances of its composition as well as its long history of reading, cannot hope to understand its meaning in the present. Such an understanding of history can guard one against the presentism of certain strands of reception studies which focus on late twentieth century engagements with the Classics with little awareness of their place in a longer dialogue between antiquity and modernity which extends over several centuries (the analysis of such present-day cultural artefacts as the film *Gladiator* might fall into this category, as might some of the less reflective studies of the modern performance of ancient drama; on this phenomenon see Beard 2004). But a respect and sensitivity to the role of 'history' in the recovery of 'meaning' does not condemn one to an unthinking positivism. By laying his emphasis on the process of recovery, Freud exposes the dialectic between construction and reconstruction which is involved in any encounter with the past. The question that many sceptical readers might ask when confronted with a reading of a modern text informed by reception theory might be: 'Did Freud actually ever read Strabo?' or 'How can we know if Derrida read Plato in the original'? Freudian theory makes one more aware of delays, displacements and repressions involved in the so called 'chain of reception'. The complex dynamic between memory and forgetting, revelation and distortion, which is at the heart of any encounter with the past is perhaps most interestingly illustrated in Freud's famous comparison of the act of textual distortion to a murder:

> The text, however, as we possess it to-day, will tell us enough about its own vicissitudes. Two mutually opposed treatments have left their traces on it. On the one hand it has been subjected to revisions which have falsified it in the sense of their secret aims, have mutilated and amplified it and have even changed it to its reverse; on the other hand a solicitous piety has presided over it and has sought to preserve everything as it was, no matter whether it was consistent or contradicted itself.
> (Freud 1953–74: 23. 43)

In his description of the biblical text, Freud seems to be creating perfect character sketches of the receptionist and the positivist, the 'theorist' and the 'historian'. The receptionist 'mutilates' the text with her/his 'own secret aims', while the positivist in his/her 'solicitous piety' attempts to preserve 'everything as it was'. However, despite the conscientious historian's desire to 'let the text speak for itself' the past cannot help but implicate its receiver in its reception:

> Thus almost everywhere noticeable gaps, disturbing repetitions and obvious contradictions have come about – indications which reveal things to us which it is not intended to communicate.

In Freud's version it is the positivist who ends up having to confront disturbing contradictions and it is for her/him that authorial intention and original meaning become most difficult to control. When one tries to 'preserve things as they are' in Freud's account, the text appears to have an even more transformative power on its reader than when one actively tries to appropriate it. The most transformative readings in Freud's version are the ones which seek to stay closest to the original:

> In its implications the distortion of a text resembles a murder: the difficulty is not in perpetrating the deed, but in getting rid of the traces. We might well lend the word '*Entstellung* [distortion]' the double meaning to which it has a claim but of which to-day it makes no use. It should mean not only 'to change the appearance of something' but also 'to put something in another place, to displace'. Accordingly, in many instances of textual distortion, we may nevertheless count upon finding what has been suppressed and disavowed hidden away somewhere else, though changed and torn from its context. Only it will not always be easy to recognize it.
>
> (Freud 1953–74: 23. 43)

The scholar of the ancient world must always work with texts which are torn from their context, displaced and in disguise. But the ineradicable traces of history always return to haunt the receiver. What is more, the past has a transformative effect on the present no historian can hope to control. Just as the positivist historian can never hope to stand outside her/his object of study, the receptionist can never fully appropriate the text s/he receives. Cathy Caruth has argued:

> For many readers, the significance of Freud's questioning of history has been a tacit denial of history. By replacing factual history with the curious dynamics of trauma, Freud would seem to have doubly denied the possibility of historical reference: first, by himself actually replacing historical fact with his own speculations; and second, by suggesting that historical memory, or Jewish historical memory at least, is always a matter of distortion, a filtering of the original event through the fictions of traumatic repression, which makes the event available at best indirectly.
>
> (Caruth 1991: 185)

But by reconfiguring history as traumatic history, Caruth argues, Freud has a more interesting point to make about the relationship between the original historical moment and its reception: 'the experience of trauma, the fact of latency, would . . . seem to consist, not in the forgetting of a reality that can never hence be fully known; but in an inherent latency within the experience itself'. 'For history to be a history of trauma' Caruth concludes 'means that it is referential precisely to the extent that it is not fully perceived as it occurs; or to put somewhat differently, that a history can be grasped only in the very inaccessibility of its occurrence' (Caruth 1991: 187). In the same way that Freud's understanding of history as history of trauma undermines the opposition between a positivist and more constructivist view of history, so reception studies ought to make more problematic any perceived incompatibility between 'original meaning' and the meaning of the receiver. In Freud's version the process of reception is fully constitutive of the 'original meaning' of an event. It is only through reception that one can have access to the past. This does not mean the denial of history but rather, as Caruth puts it, the recognition of the 'inherent latency' within history itself. For the receptionist recognizes that like the murdered Moses, the ancient world has 'not vanished without leaving a trace; some sort of memory of it [keeps] it alive – a possibly obscured or distorted tradition. And it [is] this tradition of a great past which continue[s] to operate (from the background, as it were), which gradually acquire[s] more and more power over people's minds' (Freud 1953–74: 23. 70).

FURTHER READING

For the debate about the role of history in reception studies see Jauss (1982), Machor and Goldstein (2001), Martindale (1993) and (2006), Goldhill (2002) and Whitmarsh (2006). For Freud and history see Gay (1985), Horden (1985) and Stannard (1980). Freud's archaeological metaphor is discussed by Gamwell and Wells (1989) and Spence (1987). Armstrong (2005a) is a masterful account of Freud' relationship to antiquity. On *Moses and Monotheism* see Robert (1977), Rice (1990), Yerushalmi (1991), Bernstein (1998), Derrida (1995) and Said (2003). Assmann (1997) provides the background to Freud's Egyptian Moses. For another account of the relationship between reception and psychoanalysis see Zajko (2006).

CHAPTER SEVENTEEN

Performance Reception: Canonization and Periodization

Pantelis Michelakis

In recent decades, the performance reception of Greco-Roman drama has emerged as a subfield of classical reception at the intersection between classics and theatre studies. Despite its complex relationship of affiliation and influence with literary and dramatic criticism and its openness to semiotics, translation studies, post-colonialism, and hermeneutics, performance reception has established itself as a field indebted above all to history in all its different forms and guises. The nature of the theatrical event may be transient and contingent and the traces it leaves behind fragmentary, but the appeal to performance reception of the empirical methodology of sources and of the 'impartiality' of the research practices of historiography remains strong. This is not least because of the vast amount of new knowledge and information into which the performance reception of Greco-Roman drama has tapped. New knowledge has contributed to a reconceptualization of the afterlife of Greco-Roman drama but at the same time it has also resulted in an easing off of the pressure from adjacent critical fields. However, the most interesting work in perform-ance reception is taking place not at the level of the discovery and accumulation of empirically accurate knowledge, but at the level of identification, evaluation, syn-thesis, and analysis of this knowledge and of the purposes of its investigation. Factual statements have undeniable usefulness, but it is the methodologies involved in their making and uses and the narratives of their interpretations which make performance reception a field of critical inquiry.

The purpose of this chapter is to revisit two of the most commonly used practices in theatre history and historiography, and to explore the methodological basis on which they have been or might be constituted. Periodization and canonization are both central to the ways in which knowledge of the theatrical past is organized, classified, categorized, and made available in performance criticism. Periodization shapes perceptions of change, providing ways of compartmentalizing and controlling the passage of time, whereas canonization provides selection criteria and value judge-ments for dramatic texts and their authors as well as for stage performances and their directors or stars that remain, or should remain, unaffected by the passing of time. Both canons and periods are commonly used as empirical tools because they facilitate performance analysis and interpretation. But, far from descriptive and unproblematic, they are inevitably implicated in the questions of historicism raised above. One of the disciplinary contexts in which the two practices have come under a lot of critical scrutiny is that of literary studies, and theatre research could certainly benefit from a more productive engagement with it. The aim of this chapter is to rethink some of the assumptions we make in the process of canonization and periodization of stage performances of Greco-Roman drama, and to examine the implications of such practices both for what we are looking for and for what we find in our encounter with the theatrical past. Canonization and periodization condition not only the way we look at the past, but also the kind of past we look at.

Canonization

It may at first seem strange that canonization, often associated with literary and dramatic criticism, has a central role to play in performance research. If anything, performance reception has sought to challenge the rigidity and elitism of dramatic canons which privilege printed play-scripts and condemn their stage enactments as derivative. Instead, it has drawn attention to the cultural diversity and enabling power of previously overlooked and transitory aspects of the reception of Greco-Roman drama on the ancient and modern stage. But this is not to say that the reception and criticism of theatre performances are alien to processes of value formation and determination. For instance, the canon of the three great tragedians was formed long before any of the cultural, educational or scholarly processes of textual transmission and selection gave shape to the canonical body of dramatic texts that survived into the Renaissance and the invention of the printing press. Just a few months after the death of the last of the three tragedians, Sophocles, in the winter of 405 BC, Aristophanes devoted the second half of his *Frogs* to an assessment of the gap created – both in the world of theatre and in the world of Athenian politics and culture near the end of the Peloponnesian War – by the absence of Aeschylus and Euripides. The *Frogs* has often been seen as a piece of literary or dramatic criticism associated with textual models of analysis. However, its preoccupation with issues of performance criticism and with the enabling impact of the stage on play-scripts is by no means insignificant. The characters of the play introduce concepts such as the archaic style and pompousness of Aeschylus' theatre and the novelties and realism of Euripides' theatre, which play a decisive role in debates about the canonization of their work and the meaning of timelessness and originality on both the ancient and the modern stage. Since Wagner's time, the archaic elements of Aeschylus' work have been associated with the originality, authenticity and monumentality of the theatrical genius, but in earlier centuries they were associated with naivety, antiquatedness and primitive roughness, and were deemed wholly inappropriate and a violation of the norms of neo-classical theatre (Michelakis 2005). Similarly, the novelties of Euripides' theatre have been associated with tragedy's flexibility and adaptability but also with its popularization, conventionalization and vulgarization (Michelini 1987: 3–51). Contrasting attitudes towards the canonical status of the three tragedians and their theatre clash not only between periods but also within periods, and even within the same play or text, as in the case of Aristophanes' *Frogs*. Had the superiority of Aeschylus' theatre over Euripides' been self-evident to Aristophanes' ancient – and modern – spectators and readers, the competition between the two dramatists would not be hanging in the balance for a third of the play, nor would it go on to inspire and symbolize opposing performance strategies and methods in antiquity and in the modern world.

Like the formation of the canon of the three tragedians, the process of canonization of their plays through and as performance begins in fifth-century Athens itself. Euripides' *Bacchae* and *Iphigenia at Aulis* and Sophocles' *Oedipus at Colonus* were first performed when the two playwrights were already dead. The direction, choreography, music, set design and training of the actors and the Chorus were based on decisions which could not be taken by, or in consultation with, the playwrights and which must have been the product of an engagement with their previous work. The revival of Aeschylus' plays must have begun before the last decade of the fifth century. The interest by Sophocles, Euripides and Aristophanes in works such as Aeschylus' *Libation Bearers* shows familiarity not only with Aeschylus' dramatic script but also with its stage enactment (Bain 1977; Easterling 2005). The transformation of the Athenian tragedy of the fifth century, the product of a specific temporal moment and of a particular political and cultural context, into a symbol of a wider linguistic, artistic and cultural heritage, what we call today *classical* and *Greek* tragedy, is another sign of the early canonization of the genre through performance. The plays of the three tragedians started being re-performed from 386 BC with the introduction of a theatrical competition for the 'classical' plays of the fifth century (Pickard-Cambridge [1968] 1988: 124–5). The presence of tragedy in the Middle and New Comedy of the fourth century is striking (e.g. Porter 1999/2000). Also striking is the popularity of tragedy outside the Greek mainland, in the fourth-century iconography of south Italy, where tragedies must have been exported as specimens of Greek, rather than exclusively Athenian, culture and language (Taplin 1997, 2007). The first traces of this process can be dated to the time of Euripides, who wrote plays for King Archelaus of Macedon, if not even earlier, to the time of Aeschylus, who composed and produced plays in Sicily. If the play that Aeschylus was commissioned to compose for the celebration of the foundation of Sicilian Aetnae was performed in 476 BC, the process of canonization of tragedy outside Athens was under way before the oldest surviving play, the *Persians*, was even composed (Taplin 1999; Easterling 1994; Revermann 1999/2000; Allan 2001).

The reasons for which Greek tragedy has been so popular on the ancient and modern stage and the meanings and values attributed to canonical plays in different moments in their performance history are neither fixed nor self-evident. The Oedipus of the Renaissance or the Enlightenment has little to do with that of psychoanalysis (Macintosh 2007). If the contemporaries of Sophocles fully agreed with Aristotle that *Oedipus the King* is an exemplary play, they would probably not have given to the tetralogy with which it participated in the dramatic competition only the second prize (Dain and Mazon 1958: 69). Twentieth-century theatre would show greater admiration for Euripides' *Iphigenia among the Taurians* if modern views of the play coincided with those of Aristotle and Goethe (Gliksohn 1985). *Prometheus Bound* may today be better known for the debate around its authorship (Griffith 1977: 1–7) but throughout the nineteenth century and the beginning of the twentieth it played a central role in the revival of Greek drama on the modern stage and in the establishment of Aeschylus as the father of tragedy and of western theatre as a whole (Harrison 1998, vii–xxix; Dougherty 2005). *Iphigenia at Aulis* is a play which in the last two centuries has become infamous for its alleged interpolations; yet from the time of Racine and Louis XIV to the eve of the French Revolution it was one of the most popular Greek plays on the stage of neo-classical theatre and opera (Michelakis 2006a, 2006b). On the other hand one would search in vain for the concept of the trilogic *Oresteia* as a monumental work of art or for the performance history of the *Bacchae* before Nietzsche and Wagner in the second half of the nineteenth century (Bierl 1996; Macintosh et al. 2005; Zeitlin 2004; Garland 2004: 221).

The canonization processes of the reception of Greek tragedy on stage interact with those in poetry, philosophy or education in complex ways. Until the beginning of the twentieth century Oedipus and Electra had no complexes. Freud's most famous complex might have been known today under a different name if not for the popularization of Sophocles' character at the turn of the twentieth century by stars of naturalistic theatre such as the French Jean Mounet-Sully (Armstrong 2005a; Macintosh this volume: ch. 9). Conversely it is difficult to imagine how contemporary spectators, actors or directors can engage with Oedipus without also engaging, even through rejection, with the conceptual vocabulary of psychoanalysis. The political character of the dialectic confrontation between Antigone and Creon can be set within the context of the Athenian democracy of the age of Sophocles but its modern dynamic is to no smaller degree due to its position within a philosophical genealogy which originates in Hegel. The *Antigone* of modern theatre would have been different without Hegel, but the philosophical explorations of the Hegelian tradition might have also acquired a different orientation without *Antigone* (Steiner, 1984: index s.v. Hegel; Leonard 2005: 96–156). The social and psychological dimensions of Medea's infanticide, which explain the continuous presence of the play on the modern stage, did not have the significance they have today before the issues of gender and interculturalism acquire their modern dynamic (Hall et al. 2000). Similarly, the emergence of the disciplines of anthropology and history played an instrumental role in the establishment of the *Oresteia* as a landmark in the history of western theatre and civilization. In their turn, modern productions of the trilogy show how a dramatization of violence and of a critique of progress can comment on, or even participate in, moments of tumultuous historical change, for instance the Russian Revolution and the fall of the Iron Curtain (Bierl 1996; Macintosh et al. 2005).

Canons operate not only on the principle of exclusion of what is non-canonical but also on the principle of uniformity of what is included (Guillory 1995: 244). They can safeguard the qualities of great plays, but they can also threaten them with homogenizing standards which limit responses to them and obscure their uniqueness and singularity. What determines the significance of canonical plays is not necessarily an engagement with the plays themselves but canonizing processes related to, say, the reputation of their playwright or the prestige of Greek tragedy as an art form or as cultural heritage. In fact the value of canonical plays can be threatened by their canonicity even when the defence of the canon rests on this value (Guillory 1995: 236). What lessons in gender or intergenerational relationships did productions of Sophocles' *Electra* or Euripides' *Medea* provide to girls in women's colleges across Europe and North America to justify their great popularity in the educational canon throughout the first half of the twentieth century (Pluggé 1938)? What lessons in patriotism did the lead character of Sophocles' *Ajax* offer on the eve of World War Two, dividing as he did his army both when alive and after his death, to justify the selection of the play for the festival of fascist Syracuse in 1939? What kind of education did Aeschylus' *Prometheus* or Sophocles' *Antigone*, plays with a dialectic and anti-authoritative tone, provide to political detainees in prisons and correctional institutions in cold-war Greece (Van Steen 2005) or in South Africa during the apartheid regime (Hardwick 2003a: 99–101; Rehm 2007)? How can plays such as Aeschylus' *Agamemnon*, which focuses as it does on issues of historical discontinuity and political deadlock, be used to celebrate the beginning of theatrical institutions, such as the festival at Syracuse in 1914 or the National Theatre of Greece in 1932?

The preoccupations of canonical plays can be different from, or in fact contrary to, those of the social and cultural processes that contribute to their canonization. At the same time, canons, like individual plays, can have different and even contradictory values attached to them. Progressive and regressive can be the effects of the properties not only of plays but also of processes of value formation and determination (Guillory 1995: 243). Prevalent trends in contemporary performances of Greek and Roman drama in the USA reflect a preoccupation with inter-cultural, multi-cultural and trans-cultural understanding (H. Foley 1999) which can be construed as serving a socially progressive agenda but also as being essentially hegemonic and neo-colonialist. In the same way, the *Oresteia* of the Olympic Games in Nazi Berlin in 1936 (Bierl 1996: 28–9; Flashar 1991: 164–7), the many performances of Greek drama produced by the Italian 'National Institute on Ancient Drama' in Syracuse with the financial and ideological backing of Mussolini's Ministry of Propaganda from 1925 to 1939 (Corsi 1939; Amoroso 1997), or the support for the revival of ancient drama by the 1967–74 dictatorship of the Colonels in Greece (Van Steen 2001) can be studied as marginal phenomena of the abuse of cultural heritage by regimes with totalitarian and populist tendencies. Alternatively, they can be situated within a more general framework for the management of cultural heritage by political and cultural institutions, playing an instrumental role in a diachronic or comparative study of individual plays, artists, and theatrical institutions, or larger cultural and intellectual phenomena.

The imagination of different eras is captured not by Greek tragedy as a whole but by individual plays, playwrights or performance styles, whose features and qualities only metonymically, and not without the exclusion of many others, stand for a larger whole. Likewise, it is not the imagination of a whole era that canonical plays capture but that of specific communities, artistic, philosophical, national, ethnic or otherwise. The significance that a play acquires for a particular historical community may serve its values and beliefs, but it may also help articulate its fears and anxieties, or expose its internal tensions, inconsistencies or contradictions. In many of the peripheries of the modern and the ancient world, often defined through their relation to a metropolitan centre, the reception of Greek tragedy has been closely linked with issues of cultural or national identity. Since the 1960s, for instance, plays of western theatrical canons such as *Oedipus the King*, *Antigone* and the *Oresteia* have repeatedly been appropriated by African playwrights and directors to dramatize the complex nexus of confrontations (ranging from resistance to rejection or submission) and exchanges (from influence to assimilation or cross-fertilization) which often characterize the complex relations between peripheries and centres (Hardwick and Gillespie 2007; Budelmann 2004; Hardwick 2004a; Wetmore 2003). To take one example, Wole Soyinka's *The Bacchae of Euripides: A Communion Rite* is an exploration of aesthetic, political and cultural boundaries in the post-colonial Nigeria of the early 1970s, but the commission and production of the play was undertaken by the National Royal Theatre in metropolitan London. The conditions which enabled the production and reception of the play and which account for its canonical status among postcolonial adaptations of Greek tragedy do not cancel its criticism of colonialism but exemplify some of the complexities of the dynamic relation between centres and peripheries (Macintosh 2007a; Wetmore 2003: 81–97; Hardwick 2004a: 236–8).

Periodization

In the twenty-five centuries that have passed since the death of the three tragic playwrights, their performance reception has been marked by thematic, temporal and spatial continuities but also by periods of silence, false or tentative starts, violent or incomprehensible ruptures, and multiple deaths. The plays of the Greek tragedians may have been performed not even once in the fifteen centuries that separate the Renaissance from the Roman philosopher and playwright Seneca. In more recent centuries, their revival has often been incidental and precarious. The year 1585 is often considered to be a landmark date for the revival of Greco-Roman drama on the modern stage, with an impressive Italian production of Sophocles' *Oedipus the King* inaugurating the neo-classical theatre Olimpico of the Venetian Vicenza (Wiles 2000: 178–83). Yet, for all the interest that the production generated in its own time and still generates among theatre historians and classicists, it was a one-off event. Moreover, it was not the first performance of Greek tragedy in Europe, as several plays such as Euripides' *Hecuba* and *Medea* and Sophocles' *Electra* had been performed in colleges from the beginning of the sixteenth century (Boas [1914] 1966; Tanner 1934). The revival of Greco-Roman drama on the modern stage began not in 1585 but a full century earlier, and not with a Greek tragedy but with the Roman comedies of Plautus and Terence and the tragedies of Seneca which both linguistically and aesthetically appeared more familiar and attractive (Reinhardstoettner 1886; Sanesi 1911; Duckworth 1952). When exactly one decides that the performance history of Greco-Roman drama begins is inextricably linked with one's investment in different aspects of the subject. The preoccupation of much of recent scholarship (the present chapter is no exception) with Greek drama rather than Roman and with tragedy rather than comedy helps explain why 1585 is often used as a decisive date for the beginning of a process which may have actually started much earlier and which did not quite establish itself as a continuous theatrical tradition until the middle of the nineteenth century.

Scholarly debates around theatrical origins and beginnings can find themselves immersed in wider cultural and political conflicts. Should the origins of Greek tragedy on the modern Greek stage be sought at the beginning of the twentieth century, when the first systematic attempts were made to create theatrical traditions for the revival of Greek tragedy in ancient Greek or in close translation (Georgousopoulos 1993)? Should they be sought in the 1810s, at the eve of the Greek War of Independence, when free adaptations of tragedies were performed by the Greek diaspora, for instance the *Philoctetes* of Sophocles and of the French neo-classical playwright La Harpe, which was performed by Nikolaos Pikkolos in Odessa (Spathis 1986)? Or back in 1571, some fifteen years before the landmark production of *Oedipus the King* in Vicenza, when Aeschylus' *Persians* was staged in an Italian adaptation on the Venetian-occupied Greek island of Zante (Mavromoustakos 1999a)? The relative significance of continuities and ruptures, of free adaptations and close translations, and of amateur and professional productions raises issues of periodization which take us beyond a series of historical moments and show how historiographical problems can be grounded in larger debates around the politics of language, cultural heritage and national identity.

Scholarship on the performance reception of Greco-Roman theatre deploys a wide range of classificatory and typological systems for the division of the field into periods, movements, ages and styles. Period labels come from chronological dates (Hall et al. 2004), general concepts of periods (e.g. Renaissance), historical events ('Post-war Presences' Flashar 1991: 181), rulers ('Medea and Mid-Victorian Marriage Legislation' Hall and Macintosh 2005: 391), cultural influences ('Electra after Freud': Scott 2005), artistic movements (e.g. modernist sets), artists or intellectuals ('Gilbert Murray and the popularisation of Euripides': Garland 2004: 161), and genres (e.g. nineteenth-century burlesque). Periodization encourages a closer look at the plurality of micro-narratives of which larger historical sequences are constituted. As such it is an 'enabling instrument of history', 'marking decisive moments of difference, the 'rise' or 'emergence' or 'crisis' or 'waning' of the forms of social life' (Fulbrook 2002: 5). Yet, despite the fact that period labels are functionally necessary, and can be positively deployed, divisions into historical or cultural periods, movements and styles have repeatedly come under attack, and not without good reason (Besserman 1996: 4). They favour the assumption that change occurs between periods, in the margin of history, rather than in its midst. They obscure not only continuities or affiliations between periods but also changes within periods. Even annalistic labels such as 'the 1960s' or the 'millennial' can convey a false sense of singularity, homogeneity and coherence (e.g. 'the 1960s' standing for cultural counter-revolution, the 'millennial' for excitement or anxiety), thus failing to do

justice to the variety of complex and disparate historical processes and structures each
of them encompasses.

A period which foregrounds the problems of the period as a fixed, singular or
homogeneous entity is that of the 'present' or the 'contemporary' (e.g. Kruger 2003).
In the last few decades there have been more stage productions of Greek tragedy
than in any other similar period of time since the invention of the genre in the late
sixth century BC. Recent research (e.g. Hall et al. 2004) show how theatre and
cultural historians have sought to collect, classify and interpret a vast body of
empirical data amounting to hundreds of productions and thousands of sources
from around the world by demarcating the whole phenomenon as 'contemporary'.
'Contemporary' productions of Greek tragedy raise an issue of periodization whose
methodological and theoretical implications call for closer consideration. The 'contemporary' is not an empirically discrete period but a way of thinking about and
organizing time and history at large. It may be constructive to assume that the
'present' of the performance reception of tragedy in avant-garde theatre begins with
productions such as Richard Schechner's *Dionysus in 69*, but does the same hold
true for the reception of Greek tragedy on the commercial stage or in schools and
universities? How about countries with important theatrical traditions such as Spain
and Greece, which were in the middle of a dictatorship well into the 1970s, or East
Germany on the other side of the iron curtain? Or other geographical and conceptual peripheries existing away from the limelight of western metropoles? Can the
revolutionary or counter-cultural 'present' of the performance reception of Greek
tragedy during four decades of avant-garde theatre be the same as the fin-de-siècle
or post-millennial 'present' of valorization or institutionalization of this reception in
scholarship, in the classroom, or on stage? To focus on the artistically and socially
progressive tendencies of experimental theatre is to set Greek tragedy at the forefront of artistic innovation and creativity. However, this is also to obscure other,
competing aspects of this 'present' such as the marginalization and fragmentation of
theatrical experimentation, anxieties about the death of tragedy and the contested
role of Greco-Roman antiquity in the modern world, the (real or perceived) crisis
in humanities scholarship, and the regressive or highly regulated nature of many of
the socio-political contexts within which Greek tragedy is 'currently' being performed
and debated. Periodization does not account for the different positions available within
each period, nor for the different endpoints from which one looks at the past.

Periodization does not overcome the problems of totalization usually associated
with diachronic historical narratives. Even when we move away from larger historical sequences and concentrate instead on 'more specific, historically grounded,
propositions about the interrelation among particular elements in any given historical constellation' (Fulbrook 2002: 62), we cannot easily separate the defining
features of micro-narratives from the singularity and totality of grander narratives.
Like larger narratives, periods are not so much chronologically distinct stages in a
continuous historical time, but discursive tropes or modes of experience, providing
different structures for organizing historical meaning and significance. Concepts such
as avant-garde, modern and postmodern, or civil war, democracy and dictatorship
are shorthands, labels or categories for 'imposing order on disparate and complex

historical events, patterns of development, political structures.' (Fulbrook 2002: 86–7). Consider, for instance, the case of Aristophanes' *Frogs*, with which I began my discussion of canonization processes above. The play dramatizes not only contrasting value judgements on the theatre of Aeschylus and Euripides but also competing views of the history of tragedy itself, bringing historical and cultural change into the centre of interpretation. The *Frogs* does not contrast different 'moments' in the history of tragedy but different modes of understanding the development of tragedy. On the one hand it dramatizes evolutionary and teleological narratives of progress introduced by the character of Euripides. On the other hand it features narratives of decline and fall and schemes of birth-maturation-death supported by the character of Aeschylus. Aristophanes' *Frogs* rehearses some of the more powerful strategies of emplotment of historical processes available to scholars for the history of performance of Greek tragedy. On the one hand, there is the narrative of progress and triumph the popularity of which increases as scholars focus their attention on the twentieth century. Through such a narrative one can explain why in the last few decades Greek tragedy has been more widely performed than at any other similar period after the fifth century BC. On the other hand the performance reception of Greek tragedy can also be interpreted as a story of decadence or of nostalgia for what has been lost for ever: a story that begins with the death of the great dramatists and continues with the gradual loss of much of their work and the neglect, misunderstanding, or abuse of their surviving work by fourth-century actors, Roman tragedians, Byzantine scribes, modern intellectuals, postmodern directors and so on. The performance history of Greek tragedy on the ancient stage has often been cast in such terms, with the help of its ancient admirers such as Aristophanes and Aristotle (see, further, Easterling 1993). Inevitably, any attempt to tell the performance history of fifth-century tragedy is based on a certain vision of history, be it evolutionary, pessimist, cyclical or whatever. This holds true not only for narratives of continuity and revival but also for those focusing on rupture and fragmentation.

Conclusion

Performance research provides a revised and corrective genealogy of the reception of Greco-Roman drama in antiquity and in the modern world, allowing an expansion of knowledge and understanding beyond the spatio-temporal and conceptual boundaries of other fields such as poetry or education. On the one hand the numerous and diverse stage enactments of dramatic texts provide a large new empirical field that awaits exploration. On the other hand the nature of these enactments, best understood as events leaving only scattered traces behind rather than facts, poses a challenge to the dichotomy between contingency and timelessness which discussions of periodization and the canon often rely on. To be sure, periodization and canonization are necessary to discussion and central to the ways in which theatre histories are constructed and transmitted. But this is not to say that they are neutral, objective or simple. Their empirical use can be based on arbitrary or unexamined assumptions which obscure the same reception processes they set out to illuminate. To do without such concepts means to give up tools which not only make the construction of historical narratives possible but also differentiate them from the random collection and exposition of factual knowledge. But to use them as anything other than discursive strategies is to reduce their effectiveness and to miss some of the intricacies and complexities of the interaction between practice and theory that make reception performance a suitable ground for old paradigms to be put to new tests.

NOTE

I am very grateful to Lorna Hardwick, Miriam Leonard, Fiona Macintosh and Vanda Zajko for their generous and insightful comments on earlier versions of this chapter.

FURTHER READING

On the need to interrogate the research practices of theatre studies and more specifically the processes and effects of theatre history and historiography, see the essays in Zarrilli, McConachie, Williams and Sorgenfrei 2006, Worthen and Holland 2003, Reinelt and Roach 1992, and Postlewait and McConachie 1989. On the concepts of the canon and canon formation and the debates in literary criticism between enabling and authoritarian – or aesthetic and cultural – readings of the canon, see Gorak 2001, Guillory 1995, and the essays in Alter 2004 and Gorak 1991. For an overview of ancient and modern paradigms of periodization and their critique from Friedrich Nietzsche to Michel Foucault, Jacques Derrida, and Fredric Jameson, see the collection of essays in Besserman 1996, especially the introduction. On the concept of the 'classic', see the influential studies by Kermode 1983 and 1988, and the collection of essays in Porter 2006a, especially the introduction.

PART V

Performing Arts

CHAPTER EIGHTEEN

Iphigénie en Tauride and *Elektra*: 'Apolline' and 'Dionysiac' Receptions of Greek Tragedy into Opera

Michael Ewans

After reading the *Oresteia* in 1847, Wagner abandoned the composition of music for nearly five years and rethought his entire artistic ethos, in the light of the Greek achievement, in three substantial prose works: *Art and Revolution, The Art-Work of the Future,* and *Opera and Drama* (1849–50; in Wagner 1892–9: vols 1 and 2). Wagner's interpretation of the significance of Greek tragedy was designed to clarify in his own mind his feeling of disgust with the bourgeois drama of his day – and indeed also with the entire tradition of art in Christian Europe since the Renaissance (Wagner 1892–9: 1.58, 2.175–6, 1.39). Wagner symbolized his view of Greek tragedy as a synthesis between two modes of apprehension – rational and emotional (which, in Wagner's diagnosis, have been separated to their disadvantage in the art of modern Europe). In the first pages of *Art and Revolution* he states that two gods lie at the heart of the Greek tragic experience: Apollo, the lawgiver 'holding up, to those involved in passionate action, the peaceful, undisturbed mirror of their inmost, unchangeable Greek nature'; and Dionysos, god of the irrational forces which give inspiration to the tragic poet (Wagner 1892–9: 1.32–3). Wagner's image of the two opposed gods in creative tension is a useful frame of reference for examining two contrasted case studies in the appropriation of Greek tragedy into opera. Wagner revered Gluck, and Strauss shared Wagner's aesthetic to such an extent that he was popularly referred to as 'Richard the second'; so the application of Wagner's terminology to these two composers is very far from arbitrary.

This chapter will analyze the aesthetic stance of the librettists and composers; the relationship between the libretti and the source texts; and some of the ways in which the musical setting interpreted the Greek story for the contemporary audience. (Strauss's opera is cited by the rehearsal figures and bar numbers of the study score published by Boosey and Hawkes. Note that Strauss began a new set of rehearsal figures with 1a at the centre point of the opera, when Chrystothemis runs in with the news that 'Orest ist tot!')

Iphigénie en Tauride

In Vienna after 1760, Christoph von Gluck embarked on an ambitious quest 'to revivify the serious musico-dramatic arts, to free them from the convention-bound complacency in which they seemed to be mired' (Loppert 1992: 456). Gluck composed three Italian operas to libretti on Greek themes by Calzabigi – *Orfeo ed Euridice, Alceste* and *Paride ed Elena* (1762, 1767, 1770). Gluck subsequently reworked the first two of these operas in French for Paris, where he also composed two further operas embodying the new musico-dramatic style – *Iphigénie en Aulide* (1774) and *Iphigénie en Tauride* (1779).

Gluck's new aesthetic was, effectively, a call to return opera to the purity, economy and dramatic power imagined in the Camerata's original vision of opera as a modern revival of the spirit of Greek tragedy (for which cf. Strunk 1998: 363–415). He sought to abandon spectacle and display (especially vocal display) for their own sake, and eliminate all diversions from the main story. Using Greek myths – and, in *Alceste* and the two *Iphigénie* operas, adapting texts based on dramas by Euripides – Gluck was able to focus on re-creating in opera the original dramatic virtues of Greek tragedy, which he saw as simplicity, clarity, directness and intensity; in Wagner's terms, these are 'Apolline' characteristics. Calzabigi spoke for them both when he wrote of *Orfeo*, '[the plot is] simple, not romanticized; a few verses are enough to inform the spectators of the progress of the action which is never complicated . . . but reduced to the dimensions of Greek tragedy, and therefore has the unique advantage of exciting terror and compassion in the same way as spoken tragedy' (cited in Howard 1981: 23). Note that Calzabigi here claims for the new opera an affinity with Greek tragedy not only in simplicity of plot and economy of form, but also in emotional effect, evoking as he does the Aristotelian virtues of 'exciting terror and compassion' (*Poetics* 49b27).

However, Gluck continued to write works during his Paris years that do not conform to these ideals. Only much later did Gluck gain the independence and self-confidence to reassert in Paris, in *Iphigénie en Tauride*, the values that he had developed in Vienna. When he composed the second *Iphigénie*, Gluck was able to create a new operatic drama in which musical effects are employed solely for dramatic purposes, and the interaction between text and music is extremely close.

Gluck needed both confidence in his own Greek-derived aims and a text, which could inspire the Parisian audience for *tragédie lyrique* to suppress their taste for ornate arias and *divertissements*, and appreciate his transformation of the Greek ideal into a new kind of opera on its own terms. When he asked the young poet Nicolas-François Guillard (1752–1814) to adapt the play *Iphigénie en Tauride*, written in 1757 by Claude Guymond de la Touche (1729–1760), for an opera libretto, their collaboration succeeded so well that well that Baron Grimm felt 'when I hear *Iphigénie*, I forget that I am at the opera; I believe that I am listening to a Greek tragedy' (Glicksohn 1984: 70). Indeed, one contemporary critic even denied that the libretto was based on De la Touche's play, so convinced was he that Guillard had directly followed Euripides (Glicksohn 1984: 80).

De la Touche's Play and Guillard's Libretto

De la Touche's *Iphigénie en Tauride* conforms strictly to the conventions of French neo-classical tragedy. It is in the standard five Acts, and in rhyming Alexandrines; and in the interests of the neo-classical requirement of *vraisemblance* De la Touche expands on many details. There is of course no Chorus; in their place, Iphigénie is equipped, like Racine's Phèdre, with two attendants (the priestesses Isménie and Eumène), who act as her confidantes and as messengers.

De la Touche also clearly felt that Euripides' compact drama, with only four principal human characters (Iphigeneia, Orestes, Pylades and Thoas), needed a subplot. He therefore furnished one, involving Isménie's father and his friends, political enemies of Thoas who are in hiding (3.3ff). Guillard cut this subplot from his libretto. He also eliminated De la Touche's confidantes, reducing the named principal human characters back to Euripides' original four. He then introduced a Chorus of Priestesses, whose function is very close to that of the Chorus in Euripides' drama (see below). He also vastly improved on De la Touche's recognition sequence, creatively using both elements from Euripides and a suggestion that he found in Aristotle's *Poetics* to create a very powerful climax (see below). Finally, he restored two Euripidean scenes, Oreste's vision of the avenging Furies and the concluding *dea ex machina*, which had been suppressed because they lacked *vraisemblance* in all earlier eighteenth-century Iphigeneia plays and most Iphigeneia operas (Heitner 1964: 304–5).

Guillard's adaptation moves the French text back much nearer to Euripides. Indeed, his *Iphigénie en Tauride* is closer to its Greek source than either of Gluck's other two main Euripidean libretti. However, his libretto is far from being a close or literal arrangement of Euripides for the contemporary stage. Most strikingly, both De la Touche and Guillard effectively eliminate the whole last third of Euripides' drama. Iphigeneia's escape plan, and her successful deception of Thoas so she can take Orestes and Pylades to the seashore, simply disappear. Thoas does discover the escape of Pylade; but there is nothing in the new text to correspond with the messenger-speech in Euripides (1327ff), which describes the Taurians' subsequent discovery that all three Greeks are trying to escape, the hand-to-hand combat at the ship, and the wave, which forced it back towards the land.

These were crucial parts of Euripides' original design. Athena rescues Iphigeneia and Orestes when after fluctuations in their fortune their escape seems hopeless, and so affirms that the gods do care about human beings. By contrast Guillard and Gluck, for all their anxiety to re-create the form of ancient Greek tragedy, evidently did not feel – or did not wish to make their audiences feel – the anxiety about providence, which was a principal theme of Euripides' drama. In this libretto it is simply assumed, from Iphigénie's first words onwards, that the gods are ultimately benign; they hate barbarity, and will protect the good. Accordingly, Euripides' demonstration that despite initial appearances the gods do, in the end, help those who help themselves was now superfluous.

Iphigénie and Oreste

In her fear of the storm, which begins the opera, Iphigénie prays:

> Great Gods! Help us.
> Avert your avenging thunderbolts;
> Let them strike guilty heads.
> Innocence lives in our hearts.
> (1.1.176ff)

Guillard presents Iphigénie as innocent simply because her inner soul revolts against barbarism; in his libretto Iphigénie's pure moral character protects her from being tainted by the past deeds of her ancestors or by the customs of the Taurians. Iphigénie is also deprived of the complex, ambivalent feelings about human sacrifice, which afflict her Euripidean original (343ff). Euripides' Iphigeneia believes that her heart has been hardened against strangers (350) by her own traumatic experience at the hands of the Greek army at Aulis, and the supposed 'death of Orestes'. However, she feels pity for Orestes and Pylades as soon as she actually confronts her new victims (471ff). In the opera, Iphigénie simply regards her duty in the temple as 'sacred, but cruel'. In 4.1 she protests that she must 'stifle the pitiable voice of humanity'; nonetheless, she allows herself to be prepared to sacrifice one of the Greek captives.

Euripides' Orestes is calmly and stoically heroic. By contrast, before Guillard's Oreste has even arrived on stage a Scythian has reported that he was heard uttering the words 'crime' and 'remorse'. Oreste is racked by guilt, for having apparently caused the imminent death of his friend (2.1), as well as for the murder of his mother (3.4). Guilt and remorse are Christian, internalized feelings about a crime; they are absent from Euripides' Orestes simply because these concepts are alien to ancient Greek thought. In Euripides' drama the only ways in which his deed of kindred-murder continued to attach itself to Orestes were external; a near-indelible miasma or psychic pollution (946ff), and the presence of the Furies (a cowherd reports that he has seen Orestes suffering from an assault by the Furies, who are visible to Orestes but not to others; 281ff).

In his *Eumenides* (95ff, 244ff) Aischylos had made the Furies appear in person, urged on by Klytaimnestra, and pursue Orestes. This scene made a legendary impact in the Athenian theatre; late sources allege that children fainted, and women gave birth (Anonymous *Life of Aischylos*, 9). When Gluck discovered that Guillard's text, unlike Coltellini's *Ifigenia* libretto for Traetta (2.3), had no visible Furies, he did not hesitate to demand from his librettist a comparable scene for his new opera. 'The ending is bad because the Furies only appear to Oreste in a dream and in his imagination; this destroys the idea that he believes he is seeing his mother, when he sees Iphigénie. He must still be preoccupied with his dream, when he says these words: "My Mother!" "Heavens!" – otherwise they will have no effect' (cited in Noiray 1979: 81; further discussion at Cumming 1995: 229). So after he has been separated from Pylade and plunges into despair, Oreste first achieves a feeling of calm and deliverance (or thinks he does; Gluck memorably subverted this feeling of calm by his orchestral commentary, with its menacing viola *ostinato*: 2.3.23ff); but then the calm is shattered; the avenging and pitiless Furies (stirred up by the ghost of Clytemnestre herself, just as in Aischylos and in Traetta) suddenly appear (2.4).

The inclusion of this spectacular scene leads to inconsistency (or just plain overkill). Guillard and Gluck present an Oreste, stricken with internal guilt, who expects and pleads to be punished *aux enfers* – in a Christian Hell (2.1). Diane explicitly sends him home in 4.6 to reign in Mycènes because 'your remorse has wiped out your crime'. Like a good Christian, he has expiated his deed by repentance and self-knowledge. In spite of this, the (external) Greek Furies appear as well as the (internal) Christian guilt. Gluck contrives to have the best of two different worlds. Elsewhere he presents Oreste's sufferings with the psychological realism, and within the Christianized ethical framework, which *vraisemblance* demanded. However, he gladly included a Furies' scene drawn from the opposing tradition of baroque opera, because it adds an element of *le merveilleux* to a work that is otherwise extremely austere in theatrical effects, by the standards of its time.

Chorus

Guillard and Gluck integrated the *Iphigénie* Chorus into the action, in the manner of the best Greek tragedies (Aristotle, *Poetics* 56a25ff). The principal, female Chorus represents a group of Greek women who have been exiled to Tauria like Iphigénie, just as in Euripides; this important change from De la Touche, in whose play the priestess of Diane were Scythians, enabled the Chorus to be much more closely involved in the action than in *Alceste* and *Iphigénie en Aulide*. The Chorus of women is, so to speak, Iphigénie's collective confidante; and at times soloists emerge from the group to hold dialogues with her, exactly as in Greek tragedy.

Like Euripides' Chorus, they intrude vividly with comments on the action. Two good examples from Act 1 are the short Chorus 'Oh dreadful dream!' (1.1.298ff), and a powerful commentary on their own fate, 'When shall we see our tears run dry?' (1.1.398ff). There is also a remarkable sequence in Act 2, where Gluck's avoidance of full-blown arias in the baroque tradition can be seen by the way in which the women interact with Iphigénie. After she has heard the miserable fate of her royal house and the 'death of Oreste', Iphigénie launches into an *air* (aria), 'O unhappy Iphigénie'. This is not a monologue addressed to the audience, but a lament in which she asks the Chorus to 'join your plaintive cries to my laments' (2.6.25ff). The priestesses first punctuate and later conclude this section with their own passionate emotional response.

Act 2 then proceeds to a powerful musico-dramatic conclusion. In their despair, Iphigénie asks the priestesses to make funerary offerings for Oreste. A quirky, sombre sinfonia leads into a powerful Chorus, 'Behold these sad offerings' (2.6.148ff). Iphigénie's brief solo prayer (216ff) is marked *air* in some libretti; but it is subordinate to the choral prayer that surrounds it. Gluck reverses the traditional baroque priority of soloist over Chorus; in its place he re-creates for his modern audience the experience of a Greek *kommos*, an interactive lyric ritual lament shared between soloist and Chorus.

Recognition

Guillard and Gluck adopted a suggestion mentioned in Aristotle's *Poetics* (*Poetics* 55a7–8, 55b10ff); Orestes comments on the fact that he is about to be a victim of human sacrifice, just like his sister at Aulis, and this creates the climax of the opera. Oreste sings 'Iphigénie, dear sister; this is how you died at Aulis' (4.2.257ff) at the moment when Iphigénie herself is just about to execute him. In Euripides' drama Orestes (as yet unrecognized) expressed surprise at Iphigeneia's unpleasant tasks as the servant of the Taurian goddess – 'Will you, a woman, sacrifice men by the sword?' She replies that she will simply prepare him for death, and 'there are men within this house, who have that duty' (617ff). Less plausibly but more melodramatically, Guillard imagines a temple with no male executioners; Iphigénie's attendant Priestesses prepare Oreste for death, and she herself must strike him dead with the sacrificial knife. At this terrible moment, Iphigénie has to repress her humanity, and commit murder. The catastrophe, which Iphigénie's dream predicted, is prevented at the last minute; but the climax of the opera is the moment when an essentially innocent and horrified Iphigénie is almost forced to re-enact her mother's all too willing crime of kindred murder. This is far less plausible than Euripides' scenario; but it provides much more opportunity for emotional effect at the moment of recognition. Given the chance to stage a scene in which a sister holds the knife and is about to kill her brother, no eighteenth-century opera composer was going to worry about *vraisemblance*.

Euripides began the recognition process with Iphigénie's pity for the plight of the captive Greeks (479). However, he did not take this theme any further. By contrast, the principal appeal of the Iphigeneia myth for Gluck and Guillard lay in their ability to graft onto it the emotions that fascinated eighteenth-century society. Guillard injects right at the start the idea of a family affinity – first between Oreste's mother and his elder sister (Oreste comments aside on the 'astonishing likeness'; 2.5.19ff), and later between the brother and sister themselves. The contrast between Gluck and Euripides becomes overt in 3.1, where Iphigénie tells her priestesses how much she pities the stranger, and sings that he is Oreste's age. Iphigénie's pity for Oreste remains a theme throughout the subsequent scenes; in 3.5 Oreste insists that it misleads her into choosing that he, rather than Pylade, should be saved; but Iphigénie sings that she could not kill him:

> An unknown power, mighty, irresistible,
> Would stay my arm right at the altar of the gods!
> (3.5.29ff)

At the climax in Act 4, Iphigénie has not yet recognized the stranger; nonetheless, she trembles when the Priestesses urge her to take the knife, and feels unable to perform the sacrifice. Gluck conveys by an expressive upper string melody how Iphigénie's reluctance, when a priestess presents the knife to her, springs from her feeling of a deep affinity with Oreste. And then he shows that this feeling is reciprocated, when an even more eloquent melody flowers in the violins to illuminate the depth of feeling behind Oreste's 'last words', in which he thinks about Iphigénie's death at Aulis. Iphigénie and Oreste now recognize each other without hesitation, and Iphigénie voices the feeling that has been underlying the whole sequence; 'without yet recognizing you, I had you in my heart' (4.2, 128ff).

This recognition sequence constantly stresses the feelings of affinity between sister and brother. These are entirely absent from Euripides' drama, in which ironically neither Orestes nor Iphigeneia ever comes close to guessing that they are face to face with their sibling until it is proved to them. Gluck's musical dramatization of this affinity created a new and very powerful recognition scene. Iphigénie's deep natural feelings for Oreste represent the developed sensibilities of civilized humanity; she confronts barbarity and cruelty courageously, armed with the passionate feelings of an enlightened eighteenth-century woman. The conflict between love and duty had been a staple theme of Metastasian opera, since it dramatized the central social predicament of the upper classes, which formed the audience for opera in pre-revolutionary France (cf. Robinson 1982: 137ff). At the climax of this opera, Guillard and Gluck reworked Euripides' story of the recognition of Orestes by his sister so that it presents that conflict in an extraordinary new focus – far removed from the by then thoroughly conventional arias in which a hero debates whether to abandon his lover or his station in society. The conflict in the heart and soul of Iphigénie is between a barbarian duty and a fraternal love; and her narrow escape from unknowing fratricide is presented in a musico-dramatic sequence where the music speaks with compelling power, and truly evokes the Aristotelian emotions of pity and fear. This was, and remains, the fundamental reason for the success of *Iphigénie en Tauride*. And that success is due to Gluck's conscious decision to compose a work which re-creates, as far as was possible in an eighteenth-century opera, both the spirit and the form of classical Greek tragedy, and Guillard's ability to provide him with a text which made that possible.

Hofmannsthal's *Elektra*

(*Hofmannsthal's play is cited from the Gesamtausgabe; see Hofmannsthal 1997.*)

The Berlin public was both surprised and enthralled in 1903 when Hugo von Hofmannsthal, hitherto the author of delicate, allusive poetry and lyrical plays unleashed intense emotional forces in his verse 'tragedy after Sophokles', *Elektra*.

Hofmannsthal had been brooding on the theme of Elektra for some time, when he met Max Reinhardt and Gertrud Eysoldt in May 1903, following her success as Nastya in Reinhardt's expressionist production of Gorky's *Lower Depths*. They both urged him to complete his *Elektra* – doubtless sensing that Hofmannsthal's conception of the character would make his new drama a perfect vehicle for Reinhardt to direct Eysoldt again in the title role, after the great impact of their 1902 performances of Wilde's *Salome*. And the text that he created for them showed that Hofmannsthal had not only appreciated the almost animal power, which Eysoldt had brought to the roles of Salome, Nastya, and Wedekind's Lulu. He had also absorbed Reinhardt's symbolic, expressionist use of set, costume and particularly lighting in his recent productions (McMullen 1985: 642–4, 648).

Dionysiac Poetics

The spirit of eighteenth-century German neo-classicism is most finely embodied in Goethe's *Iphigenie auf Tauris* (1779) – a deeply felt drama of gentle irony, which presents a rational and noble vision of antiquity, as 'Apolline' as Gluck's contemporary opera on the same subject. It unfolds as a series of dialogues, bringing all its five characters on stage together only for a brief part of the final scene, and using almost no properties or stage effects. In Goethe's *Iphigeneia*, the Furies of the house of Atreus are finally tamed through the deep simplicity of the heroine, who refuses to be dishonest or untrue to herself. In the final scene, her female nobility finally inspires the men around her to rise to enlightened male chivalry and to abjure violence.

In later life Goethe himself wrote to Schiller that 'this Hellenizing work of art seems to me on a fresh reading to be devilishly humane' (cited at Hofmannsthal 1959: 131); and Hofmannsthal had Goethe's play and this comment very much in his mind when he conceived *Elektra*. 'My point of departure was the character of Elektra; I remember it very well. I was reading the Sophokles play in the garden and the forest, in the autumn of 1901. I remembered the line from *Iphigeneia*, where it says "Elektra with her tongue of fire" [Goethe, *Iphigenie auf Tauris* 1030], and as I walked I fantasized about the figure of Elektra, not without a certain pleasure in the contrast with the "devilishly humane" atmosphere of *Iphigeneia*' (1997: 383–4; cf. Mueller 1980: 93ff).

Hofmannsthal's *Elektra* was deeply influenced by the new, Dionysiac vision of Greece inspired by Wagner and enshrined in the work of Nietzsche (*The Birth of Tragedy from the Spirit of Music*, 1872) and Rohde (*Psyche*, 1893). (For Hofmannsthal's reading of Rohde cf. Worbs 1983: 272, 274.)

> The image of [Sophokles'] Elektra immediately transformed itself into a new one. The ending was there immediately as well; that she can go on with her life no longer, that, when the blow has fallen, her life and her inner nature must cause her ruin. I noted the relationship with, and the contradiction with, Hamlet. As for the style, there was present in my mind the idea of making something opposed to *Iphigeneia*, something which Goethe's words to Schiller ['devilishly humane'] would not fit.
> (Hofmannsthal 1959: 131; cf. Newiger 1969: 150)

Hofmannsthal and Sophokles

There are many surface features that make Strauss's opera seem, at first sight, to inhabit a quite different world from Sophokles' original drama. However, these are all due to its Wagnerian/Nietzschean emphasis on the Dionysiac forces, which make men and women act beyond the control of their rational faculties. Hofmannsthal subtitled his *Elektra* 'Tragödie in einem Aufzug/frei nach Sophokles' ('Tragedy in one act; freely adapted from Sophokles'); and he regarded it as a *Bearbeitung* ('arrangement') of Sophokles rather than as a new independent play, because every major theme of the new play and of Strauss's opera is already either explicit or implicit in Sophokles' original tragedy.

Both dramas are, first and foremost, detailed, psychological studies of the sufferings and vengeance of the heroine; and both are arranged so that after her early appearance Elektra remains on stage until the end, guarding the door of a palace which is hostile to her and confronting a succession of other, subordinate characters (Cf. Newiger 1969: 149). Hofmannsthal cuts the prologue, and adds Elektra's dance of death; he omits the Tutor's narrative of the 'death of Orestes'; but apart from these alterations, Hofmannsthal's action corresponds exactly to Sophokles' original plot.

It is almost as if Hofmannsthal was determined that every major element in the modern drama should be capable of being traced back to a source in Sophokles' *Elektra*: the fearfulness and psychological disintegration which Klytämnestra has suffered under the pressure of her own self-knowledge and her daughter's accusing presence (Soph. 780ff, Strauss 132ff); Elektra's determination not to believe in the report of Orest's death (Soph. 804ff; Strauss 4aff); her immediate decision, when once she has accepted it, that the sisters should avenge Agamemnon themselves (Soph. 947ff; Strauss 34aff); her attempt to persuade Chrysothemis by harping on her sister's desire for marriage (Soph. 961ff; Strauss 82aff); her ever-increasing madness, and her appalling blood-lust (Her response in the opera to Klytämnestra's death-shriek, 'Triff noch einmal' ['Strike yet again'], 191a, is straight Sophokles [= 1415]); her ingenious luring of Ägisth, and her ironic pretence to have finally accepted 'agreement with the stronger' (Soph. 1465 = Strauss 207a). Even the most obvious innovation of Hofmannsthal's play, Elektra's self-destruction, is foreshadowed in the original Sophokles (140ff).

There is one striking aspect of the Sophoklean version, which Hofmannsthal did not overtly pick up; Strauss seized upon it. Sophokles has Klytaimnestra's dream portend the return of Agamemnon to rule once again in Mykenai (417ff). Hofmannsthal discarded this, in order to create a Klytämnestra who is oppressed by indescribable – and so even more terrifying – dreams. However, Strauss brought out in his opera the implication of Sophokles' dream – that Orestes is, as it were, Agamemnon returned. Hofmannsthal prescribes that Orest, when he enters, should be 'silhouetted in black relief against the last rays of the sun' – like a warrior from a Greek black-figure vase; and this image almost suggests of itself that he is like a shade or a ghost. To reinforce this impression, Strauss introduced Orest with solemn, reticent chords on trombones and Wagner tubas (123a), which makes him seem almost the shadow of a person rather than the substance. He also cast Orest as a baritone, against the convention that young men should be tenors; at first Orest sings very solemnly and slowly, as if the son is echoing the deeper voice of an older man. Then Strauss set Elektra's rapturous celebration, when she has recognized him, as an extended development of the lustrous melody for *divisi* strings to which, in her opening monologue, she begged her father's ghost to appear (example 18.4; 45, developed at 147aff).

Immediately after this, in a revelatory passage, Hofmannsthal's Elektra refuses to allow her brother to embrace her, and explains her appearance. This passage explains Elektra's behaviour in the opera; in Freud's terms, Elektra's hysteria was caused by the trauma in adolescence of her father's murder. Strauss realized that this passage was the heart of Hofmannsthal's text, and he set it to music of extreme beauty and pathos (158aff):

> I know you shudder
> At my sight, and I was once a king's daughter!
> I think that I was beautiful; when I put out
> The lamp before my mirror, then I felt it
> With a virgin's rapture. I felt
> How the slender rays of the moon
> Bathed themselves in my body's white nakedness
> As in a pond, and my hair
> Was such hair, the hair at which men tremble –
> This hair, dishevelled, full of dirt, humiliated.
> Do you understand, brother?
> I have had to surrender all that I was.
> I offered up my shame,
> The shame that is sweeter than anything,
> The shame which, like the silver mist,
> The milky mist of the moon, surrounds
> Every woman and wards horror off from her
> And from her soul. Do you understand, brother?
> I had to offer all these thrills of sweetness to my father.
> Do you think,
> When I rejoiced in my body,
> That his sighs and groans did not press themselves
> Right to my bed;
> (*sombrely*) Jealous are the dead;
> And he sent Hate to me, hollow-eyed Hate
> as bridegroom. (155aff)

Hofmannsthal then brings back at the end of his play the diagnosis of Elektra as obsessed, like her mother, with the need for revenge; he foreshadows a new kind of tragedy, one very much of the twentieth century, in which Elektra can no longer exist after her deepest desire has been fulfilled in deed (cf. Corrigan 1958–60: 17–28).

Strauss's *Elektra*: Strategy and Style

A playwright alone could not create this modern tragedy. Hofmannsthal's *Elektra* cries out for musical setting, because at crucial moments throughout the drama words – as Hofmannsthal well knew – become an inadequate medium for conveying the psychological torment of the characters. Hofmannsthal felt that the moment of Elektra's self-fulfilment, when she is destroyed by the very passion which had given her life, could only be expressed through dance, in which humankind passes beyond the sphere of words into that of pure gesture and timeless movement (cf. Newiger 1969: 150ff; Hamburger 1954: xxv–xxxi). Hofmannsthal wanted Strauss to set *Elektra* to music because Strauss had achieved great success with *Salome*, which includes both an extended dance sequence and a closing soprano scena of the utmost pathos and intensity. The playwright undoubtedly hoped that Strauss would realize in musical terms not only the psychological dimensions underlying the earlier portions of his play, but also the Dionysiac power needed for the final dance, where Elektra is explicitly described in the stage directions as throwing her head back like a maenad.

Strauss did far more than this. He perceived that Hofmannsthal's play lacks a coherent theatrical structure, and he determined to furnish one. In Hofmannsthal, the murdered king is a dominant, background presence, so ominous that his name is spoken only once. Hofmannsthal failed to see that this device, which might have been effective in a written poem, would be coy and unsatisfying in the theatre. Strauss therefore introduced Agamemnon's name into the text at several different points, unified by its common musical setting. It is established as a dominant feature of the opera by its presence as a ritual refrain in Elektra's first monologue. Then, while developing the musical setting, Strauss abandoned his first idea, which was to end with mysterious, muted sounds, unrelated to any previous musical material (Gilliam 1991: 231–3). He decided to end the opera as he began it, with a violent, *fortissimo* declamation of the musical motif that has become totally associated with Agamemnon's name, by its use as a principal *leitmotif* throughout the opera (example 18.1).

Example 18.1

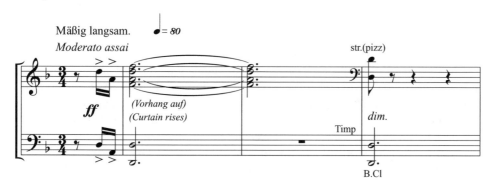

The resultant circularity is central to Strauss's final vision of the story. Sophokles' *Elektra* suffers a sequence of events, which gradually affect her sanity and drive her to savage bloodlust; Strauss' Elektra has her end implicit in her beginning.

Hofmannsthal's directions for the staging of *Elektra* make clear that for him the palace at Mykenai is a Byzantine, middle Eastern building, filled with corridors, nooks and crannies, strange colours and sinister chambers. He explicitly describes the back of the palace as having 'a mysterious and sinister appearance, like that of the great houses in the orient'. Its few, irregular windows are to have 'something of the lurking, veiled quality of the orient' and its low right-hand section is over-hung by a giant, twisted fig tree 'whose mass, sinisterly formed in the evening light, is spread out on the flat roof like a crouching animal' (Hofmannsthal 1947–59: 81–2).

The *mise-en-scène*, which Hofmannsthal imagined for his *Elektra*, is the 'orient' in which French and German writers and artists since the 1820s located their treatments of crimes and passions, sexuality and murder; the orient had become the preferred location for 'sensuality, promise, terror, sublimity, idyllic pleasure, intense energy' (Saïd 1979: 118). The geographical location of this 'orient' was flexible; the actual near east was preferred (e.g. Delacroix, *The Sack of Constantinople* and *The Death of Sardanapalus*; Gauthier, *A Night of Cleopatra*; Flaubert, *Herodias*; and Wilde, *Salomé*), but other locations could be 'orientalized' – most notably Carthage in Zola's *Salammbô*. Flouting the letter but not the spirit of Delacroix's prohibition, Hofmannsthal orientalized Mykenai in his *Elektra* to make it an appropriate venue for the monstrous crime of matricide. In Hofmannsthal's view Greece, as the nineteenth century had inherited it from the Apolline vision of eighteenth-century neo-classicism, was too classically pure to be the location for its own mythology.

Strauss and Reinhardt deliberately returned the musical and visual dimensions of Hofmannsthal's drama to Greek originals – but not those of eighteenth-century neo-classicism. Schliemann began to excavate at Mykenai and Tiryns in 1874, and for the first time modern Europeans could see pictures of the architecture of the fortified palaces, which stood in Agamemnon's kingdom at the actual period (*c.*1200–1100 BCE) in which the legends about the Trojan War took place. This was totally different from the gleaming white marble temples and statues (their original coloured paint long removed from the surfaces by the passage of time) which Winckelmann and other cultured eighteenth-century Germans had hailed as the quintessence of classical Greece.

Strauss first visited Greece in 1892; he was impressed by the 'gigantic forces and recklessness of expression' in the friezes from the temple of Zeus at Olympia (Adams 1989: 159). Like Nietzsche, he wanted to contrast 'this possessed, exalted Greece of the sixth century with Winckelmann's Roman copies and Goethe's humanism' (Strauss 1953: 155). Reinhardt also felt that this drama should evoke prehistoric Greece; the set which Strauss saw, when he attended the first production of Hofmannsthal's *Elektra*, replaced Hofmannsthal's oriental concept with 'the cyclopean walls of a Mykenean palace's inner court' (Niessen, quoted at McMullen 1985: 645). Many set designs for Strauss' opera have reflected this monumental aspect of the score, evoking the massive stone blocks out of which the walls of Mykenai and Tiryns were built (cf. Hartmann 1981: 54, 56, 58). Similarly, Strauss composed his *Elektra* in a different musical style, from which the Orientalism, sinuous melodies and exotic tone-colours of *Salome* have been banished.

Strauss was influenced, in the claustrophobic, monumental musical idiom that he created for this opera, by the ruins of Mykenai and Tiryns – the massive blocks of raw stone from which the fortresses are constructed, and the oppressive portals of the entrances. Although there are many passages of chamber-music delicacy for sub-sections of the vast orchestra, the biggest moments in the score seem as if hewn from granite – right from the opening gesture (example 18.1).

Strauss framed his opera, and gave it an overall shape, by returning in the final minutes to the motifs, which were introduced during Elektra's first monologue. Here Elektra invokes Agamemnon, as she has done each day since his death at this, the hour of his death. We are watching a ritual, in which a witch conjures up her famil-iar, and he retakes possession of her soul (example 18.2).

Example 18.2

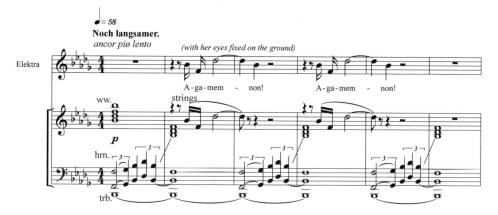

The horn/trombone motif is Elektra's solemn invocation, summoning Aga-memnon's spirit to rise. As she sings her father's name to the earth the audience realizes in retrospect that the gigantic gesture, which opened the opera in ominous, tragic D minor, represents the presence of Agamemnon.

Elektra summons Agamemnon's spirit by painting a vivid picture of the moments of his death. Then she imagines him returning, and octave brass fanfares start to rise in the orchestra; they are played *ff*, spanning six octaves, as she completes her word-picture (example 18.3). Like Götz Friedrich, who superimposed an image of Agamemnon at this point in his film of the opera, I believe that these rising fanfares portray the success of her invocation; Agamemnon's spirit rises from below the earth.

Example 18.3

Elektra is not aware of his presence, so she tenderly invokes her father, pleading to him with a rapturous A flat string theme which depicts the depth of her love (example 18.4). Later, it will return and be developed when she recognizes Orest. This melody expresses all the longing for Agamemnon, which she will then project onto her brother.

Example 18.4

After a vivid evocation of the carnage which will take place when Agamemnon's day of vengeance comes, Elektra concludes the monologue with the image of herself, Orest and Chrysothemis dancing round the funeral pyre of the usurpers, their supporters, dogs and horses (53ff).

In this passage a new 64 dance melody is heard (example 18.5), gradually swelling throughout the full orchestra to convey the power and intensity of Elektra's vision of the dance. It plays on after her last cry of 'Agamemnon', becoming almost perilously prolonged, until the brass fanfares rise again, just before the entry of Chrysothemis (63). This final sequence of the monologue is highly ominous, since the return of the fanfares shows that when Elektra dances herself into a state of ecstasy, the spirit of Agamemnon wells up inside her. That is precisely how Elektra will be destroyed at the end of the opera.

Example 18.5

In Hofmannsthal's original vision, Elektra destroys herself during the maenadic final dance. 'In *Elektra* the individual is dissolved in an empirical way, in which even the content of her life is burst asunder from inside, like water which has turned to ice in an earthen jug. Elektra is no longer Elektra precisely because she has consecrated herself to being wholly and completely Elektra' (1959: 201).

Strauss replaced this rather mystical and untheatrical concept with a different vision, in which Agamemnon's dominance over her psyche destroys Elektra's life. In the finale, the Agamemnon-related motifs from Elektra's monologue return to illuminate what has happened to her, as a result of the action of the opera. Strauss' massive orchestra depicts the driving force of the dance (example 18.5) welling up out of Elektra's psyche, with redoubled intensity and on a more expansive scale, from the moment when Chrysothemis rushes in terror from the scene, and Elektra plunges physically into her dance of death. The dance music develops as a gigantic waltz, with a combination of tragic exultation and banality that perfectly expresses the condition, at once both super- and sub-human, of those in a state of *enthousiasmos* or Dionysiac ecstasy (247aff).

The final bars of the orchestral score communicate the exact nature of the catastrophe. The dance reaches a climax of uncontrolled, reckless and unprecedented intensity (259a–260a); then, suddenly, the triple rhythms are halted, and Agamemnon's octave fanfares (example 18.3) rise up again in the brass (260a 4), now accompanied by an appalling sound effect, which is intensified to an unbearable intensity just before Elektra falls – the tam-tam scraped with a triangle stick (260a 4–12). The meaning is clear; Agamemnon's spirit rises up again, now inside his daughter's psyche – and destroys her. After Elektra lies still (261a 1), Strauss's response to the final moments is on the largest scale. To end the opera, the motif of Agamemnon's name (example 18.1) is declaimed by the full orchestra, at first alternating with a sombre lament in the form of sustained *piano* chords for the low brass, in the remote and sinister key of E flat minor. But first these chords, and then Chrysothemis' plaintive cries of 'Orest!', are swept away by monumental C major repetitions of the Agamemnon motif. However, the opera does not conclude in an unalloyed triumph of Agamemnon's desire for vengeance. Strauss (like Sophokles) felt that the triumphant revenge of the matricides should leave a nasty taste in the mouths of the audience. The horrible lurch of the *fff* brass- and string-dominated tutti away from a glowing, triumphant C major back for a moment to distant E flat minor, in the penultimate semiquaver, achieves just that.

This ending creates a real feeling of finality. Agamemnon's cataclysmic motif returns, its full symphonic implications now revealed, to conclude the opera as it began it, enforcing through music the central idea of Hofmannsthal's play, that her father's memory has first turned Elektra into a hideous, outcast prophetess of doom, and has now destroyed her utterly. *Elektra* is a tragedy of modern emotions, possible only in the age of Freud; and a tragedy, which completely reflects the Nietzschean, Dionysiac vision of Greece.

It has been argued that that vision is necessarily flawed, as well as limited, as the basis for a drama. Not only do Hofmannsthal's characters have few redeeming features; they are almost entirely the prisoners of their emotions – 'destinies' rather than 'characters' (Corrigan 1958–60). Klytämnestra, bound inside her own self

by her consuming guilt, is explicitly imaged as a prisoner; but this is equally true
of the other two principals – Chrysothemis reduced to desperation by her prolonged virginity, Elektra destroyed as a person by her obsessive love for her dead
father. For at least one critic, 'Sophocles' passion within rationality has greater
dramatic range than Hofmannsthal's pure feeling' (Forsyth 1989: 27). This is true
of Hofmannsthal's drama by itself; but Strauss' music, while it illuminates every nuance
of the characters' psychology, also enfolds and contains the Dionysiac power of the
play within an intellectually coherent music-dramatic structure (Cf. Whittall 1989:
72–3; Carpenter 1989: 76–7). The opera re-creates, in a distinctive modernist style,
the tension between 'Dionysiac' destructive passion and 'Apolline' formal structure,
which lay at the heart of ancient Greek tragedy.

FURTHER READING

The best CD recordings of these two operas are:

Gluck's *Iphigénie en Tauride* conducted by John Eliot Gardiner (Philips 416 148–2,
1986).

Strauss' *Elektra* conducted by Georg Solti (Decca 417 345, 1986).

Gardiner's *Iphigénie*, with Diana Montague in the title role, remains unsurpassed. There is
as yet no good DVD recording of this opera.

Solti's classic recording, with Birgit Nilsson in the title role, remains the best and one of
the few complete recordings of *Elektra*. Götz Friedrich's stunning film of *Elektra*, with Leonie
Rysanek in the title role, is now available on DVD. Its only drawback is that it observes the
standard theatre cuts.

There is no good modern introduction to *Iphigénie* in English, though Loppert 1992 provides an invaluable starting point. Glicksohn 1984 is the best and most extensive essay in a
good issue of *L'Avant-Scène Opéra* (no. 62) entirely devoted to the opera. And Howard 1963
remains basically sound, despite having been published so long ago.

Elektra is the subject of an uneven Cambridge Opera Handbook edited by David Puffett
1989. Carpenter 1989 and Whittall 1989 are the best of the essays. Gilliam 1991 is largely
devoted to the compositional process; Goldhill 2002 is a discursive and fascinating essay on
the opera's reception in England; but there is no discussion of the music.

Some of the primary sources are well worth finding. Wagner's sometimes obscure prose
style should not deter readers from grappling with his thoughts on opera, drama and the Greeks
(1982–9: vols 1 and 2). However, I offer a summary and analysis in Ewans 1982: ch. 2. The
Hofmannsthal/Strauss correspondence is also fascinating, since Hofmannsthal found Strauss
rather overbearing in person, and preferred to deal with all matters concerning the music-text
interaction by letter. More extensive analyses of Iphigénie and Elektra appear in Ewans 2007.

CHAPTER NINETEEN

Performance Histories

Fiona Macintosh

Performance histories of ancient plays are still relatively new. Surprising as it might seem now, writing about the theatrical afterlife of the ancient plays beyond the fifth century BCE was of little or no concern to classical scholars and/or modern literary specialists before the late 1970s (see Hall and Wrigley 2001 for comment). However, with Taplin's pioneering focus on the performative dimension of ancient tragedy (Taplin 1977, 1978) – followed shortly after by three milestone productions of the *Oresteia* between 1980 and 1982 from Greece (directed by Karolos Koun), the UK (directed by Peter Hall) and Germany (directed by Peter Stein) – came a new awareness that performance, like scholarship, has a history that shapes and determines critical responses to a text.

Like most things new, the performance histories that grew out of this performative turn have not escaped controversy. First, and by no means least, it has taken some time to convince the wider academic community – especially classicists and modern literary specialists – that this is an area worthy of study. My first realization that this might be a real struggle occurred in the early 1990s, shortly after I was asked to write a chapter on tragedy in performance in the nineteenth and twentieth centuries for the *Cambridge Companion to Greek Tragedy* (Easterling 1997a: 284–323). When I found myself explaining to George Steiner what I was currently researching, I was rewarded with a raised eyebrow and very faintly disapproving: 'You're a theatre historian, then!' Although I would not resist the label nowadays – indeed with so few theatre historians currently working in Departments of Drama and Theatre, it might even be flattering to be described as such – at the time, and as a young post-doctoral student overly conscious of my interdisciplinary background, to be dismissed as mere 'theatre historian' by the doyen of Comparative Literature was somewhat smarting.

My project was, of course, no *Antigones* in the Steiner-esque mould (Steiner 1984); but it was the first step on a path that has turned out to be much more intellectually challenging and rewarding than many at the time might have imagined. Not only did it entail exciting forays into the Lord Chamberlain's Play Collection at the British Library in order to consult play-scripts, which very often still retained the dust that had been gathering since they were first deposited; it also involved genuinely interdisciplinary research that was breathtakingly refreshing after much of the study I had previously undertaken. I myself had mistakenly feared that writing performance histories would involve rather too much time mechanically cataloguing, itemizing and processing somewhat dull production details, against which my training in English Literature and Comparative Literature bridled. And when I applied for a job in a Modern Literature department a few years later, I remember being advised against submitting the said chapter as an example of a recent publication: the appointments' panel members just would not understand what it was all about, I was warned, no doubt advisedly.

I only begin with these self-indulgent anecdotes to show how much things have moved on since the early 1990s. The rest of this chapter seeks to demonstrate the importance of performance histories to reception studies as a whole by looking at decisive moments in the reception of Sophocles' *Oedipus Tyrannos*, where particular productions have had wide-ranging consequences for our understanding and interpretation of the text. But before considering these key moments, it is important to outline precisely what is involved in this relatively new branch of classical reception studies.

Practising Performance Histories

Now with the combined work of the Archive of Performances of Greek and Roman Drama in Oxford, the Open University's Reception of the Texts and Images of Ancient Greece in late twentieth-century Drama and Poetry in English and the European Network of Performance of Ancient Drama based at the University of Athens, performance histories are not just respectable; their importance has also become widely appreciated in certain circles. Yet however respectable in some circles, in others performance histories of ancient plays are still ignored. For example, Martindale and Taylor's recent and very useful edited volume on *Shakespeare and the Classics* (Cambridge 2004) bizarrely makes only one reference to performance in its account of a period as deeply steeped in stage performance as was fifth-century Athens. It comes in Michael Silk's chapter when he makes the key observation that opera was developed in the 1590s in Italy just as Shakespeare began his career as a playwright (Silk 2004: 245). But there is no mention here, nor indeed elsewhere in this volume, that Greek tragedy had already enjoyed a considerable performance history: in the vernacular in Italy (1585 at Vicenza) in Latin at Cambridge (*Hecuba* 1559/60 at Trinity and *Antigone*, early 1580s at St John's) and in loose vernacular adaptation in London (Gascoigne and Kinwelmershe's *Jocasta*, Gray's Inn 1566 and Pickeryng's *Horestes* before 1567). This omission in an otherwise invaluable collection would suggest that performance histories of ancient plays still have important contributions to make to discussions of Shakespeare's classicism in the future.

It is, of course, true that much of the data gathered by those engaged in performance history has been hard to access or simply unavailable until relatively recently.
The online database of the Archive of Performances of Greek and Roman Drama
(www.apgrd.ox.ac.uk/database.htm, ed. and maintained by Amanda Wrigley), available since 2005, has been a boon to scholars working in the area of performance
history. The research lying behind the database has perforce been conducted in
areas where subject specialists (for a whole host of reasons, which are worth investigating) have rarely ventured before, or at least rarely in conjunction with one
another – in, say, popular culture and in the popular theatre in particular; in social
and legal histories; in opera, ballet and the cinema. For this reason, there has been
some work that has no doubt been overly empirical and raw – literally finding what
was performed where and when. But even this preliminary collation of data has
yielded important results, which have often called into question long-held assumptions about the reception of classical authors at particular times. For example, even
a cursory glance at Allardyce Nicholl's record of plays performed in the eighteenth
century, throws doubt upon Clarke's claim in *Greek Studies in England 1700–1830*
(1945) that Aeschylus was unknown at the time: Thomson's *Agamemnon* (1738),
which was a roaring success in the theatre and was very widely printed, demands
knowledge of Aeschylus no less than Seneca in its treatment of the Argive dynastic
struggle (Hall and Macintosh 2005: 99–127). Similarly, the orthodox assessment of
the reception of the Greek tragedians in nineteenth-century Britain, which labels
Aeschylus, the Romantic, Sophocles the mid-Victorian and Euripides the Modernist
needs some reconsideration in the wake of recent work on performance history.
Whilst this schema may still broadly be true in the case of Sophocles, whose
Antigone dominated the mid-nineteenth-century stages of Europe, it is deeply misleading for the other two tragedians. Euripides' tragedies were, in fact, widely performed from the 1840s onwards in England and Aeschylus in formal terms turns
out to be no less a Modernist than Euripides (Macintosh 2005b: 139–62).

In a review of a recent volume based on a conference on 'Agamemnon in
Performance' held at the APGRD in Oxford (Macintosh et al. 2005), Simon Goldhill reminds the reader how far performance reception has travelled in a relatively
short space of time; but also how far it still has to go:

> The central problem that has not yet been adequately faced by the field in its current
> state can be simply expressed: what sort of history is performance history going to be?
> How much politics, how much cultural study, how much intellectual history is neces-
> sary to understand a performance as a historical event? This volume shows how per-
> formance history has advanced far beyond the counting of new styles of stage sets, or
> lists of productions. But if we want to understand why some performances have a major
> cultural impact, then we must set the historical questions in a far wider frame.
> *Agamemnon in Performance 458 BC to AD 2004* provides a necessary basis for such
> advanced historical work to proceed.
>
> (Goldhill 2006)

Whilst Goldhill is right to point out the the narrowness of certain work carried
out in performance histories in the past ('counting . . . lists'), he is equally right to

emphasize that this is not typical of much recent work in the area, whose hallmark is its genuinely interdisciplinary and international nature. At its best performance history works extensively and intensively at the intersection between theatre history, histories of classical scholarship and the history of ideas. The question 'How much?' of each seems almost irrelevant because entirely contingent upon the particular object of the inquiry; for the performance historian, the need to be aware of the importance of all these perspectives is imperative. For example, the agonistic (and often parasitical) relationship between the London and (mostly) Parisian stages in key phases in British theatre history means that any British re-working of an ancient play is highly likely to be linked to another continental (and very often operatic) version of that play. In this sense, interdisciplinary work must occur across generic and (unusually for modern literary departments) geographical boundaries in performance histories of ancient plays. And just as the early, and well-documented, performance history of opera is inextricably linked to Greek tragedy, there is a parallel and largely untold story of the ways in which modern appropriations of the chorus are linked to developments in dance in the modern world. Non-verbal reception in music and movement has not had any refined and thorough-going treatment; and we need to be aware that ancient information about the theatre (not just the dramatic texts themselves) – for example in anecdotes preserved in Plutarch or Philostratus, and treatises on dance by Lucian and Choricius – has exerted a continual influence on the western founding fathers and practitioners of new genres of musical theatre.

Classical performance reception – as performance history is often described in order to situate the field within the broader category of classical reception studies – has begun recently to receive serious theoretical attention (Hall 2004; Michelakis 2006b). And Jauss's model of the interplay between the circumstances of a work's production (its context) and its (often multiple) reception(s) as the key to meaning is especially helpful in relation to performance (Jauss 1982). Since there are clearly inherent problems with the tools and the sources of performance reception – especially with reviews (Hardwick 1999, 2003a; Burke 2003; Burke and Innes 2004) – Goldhill's reminder that there is a need for a wide range of contextual evidence is paramount. Whilst diachronic studies might be seen by some to be the product of naïve historical positivism, they have often been in the early stages the only way to proceed. How do we know what happened to, say, the *Agamemnon* in Britain if no one has sat down and gone through the play lists to find out if and when it was performed; or, equally importantly, if no one has searched the catalogues for vernacular translations and adaptations of Aeschylus' tragedy and/or its trilogy?

Moreover, since the term 'Renaissance' has increasingly come under scrutiny from wide quarters – ignoring as it does the uninterrupted tradition of 'classical learning' that was sustained in Byzantium and the Arabic and Syriac scholarly traditions, especially Baghdad – the scope of these studies has widened with the growing awareness of the rich performance tradition of the plays in antiquity from almost immediately following their premières until beyond St Augustine, not only in the tragic theatre but in comedy, mime, dance and sung recital. The collection of essays, *Greek and Roman Actors: Aspects of an Ancient Profession* (Easterling and Hall 2002), is pioneering in the field. Tracing the performance history of ancient plays throughout antiquity involves the work of a few specialists who are able to piece together that complex early history from disparate Christian and pagan sources, including visual records, literary testimonia, papyri, graffiti and other inscriptions.

Diachronic studies, seen from this perspective, have yielded a substantial amount of fruit and continue to do so: they have not only provided the building blocks for further study; they have also widened the canon (so Michelakis, this volume, ch. 17). Furthermore, if diachronic studies of particular plays seem partial and distorting, this is simply because we are now in a position to know more about the impact of the plays on a synchronic level: so whilst the reception of the Mendelssohn *Antigone* some years ago might have focused on aspects of the performance and the set alone; now it would have to broaden its focus to include discussion of the actress, Helen Faucit, as cultural icon of the period, and especially the impact of her performance in the title role upon Thackeray, George Eliot and De Quincey (Macintosh 1997; cf. Macintosh 2005b).

Whilst Goldhill chooses to focus on what he sees as the narrowness of historical focus in performance histories, I would single out instead the absence of serious formalist analysis of the primary texts (the vernacular translations, adapations and performance texts) as a major weakness in the area. Jauss et al. were indebted to Russian Formalism in their formulation of reception theory; the context-driven work of many diachronic studies, by contrast, results in very little close textual work. Performance histories need to combine diachronic awareness with synchronic depth, together with formalist analysis of the texts in question. Form, as Jauss knew all too well, is always more or less political.

Mapping the *Oedipus* with Mounet-Sully

Kierkegaard's emphasis on 'the Moment' of apprehension of a live-performance and its indelible power on the imagination seems especially pertinent to performance histories (Kierkegaard 1987: 42, 68, 117–18, 239, 486–7). General reception studies of Sophocles' paradigmatic tragedy ignore these 'moments' – either because the texts upon which they were based are not themselves deemed worthy of study or because they are not 'written' texts at all. Charting the afterlife of Sophocles' *Oedipus Tyrannos* without the help of performance histories would be confined to some or all of the following: its reception in the Renaissance and its consequent dominance in neo-classical theoretical discourse; discussion of its French neoclassical adaptations by Corneille and Voltaire and, perhaps, the English version of Dryden and Lee; possibly some consideration of its German Romantic parodic treatment in Kleist's *Der Zerbrochene Krug* (1811); and then a leap to Freud and his fascination with the myth of Oedipus and its subsqent impact on twentieth-century thought and theatre (through the French versions of Cocteau and Gide, Stravinksy, perhaps later the film version by Pasolini). It would conclude today with reference, no doubt, to the post-colonial versions of Ola Rotimi and Rita Dove (Mueller 1980; Scherer 1987; Segal 2001; Goff and Simpson 2007; and for the early period, see Lurje 2004).

A performance history of Sophocles' *Oedipus Tyrannos*, however, might look somewhat different. It would begin with the reception of Sophocles' play in antiquity; and whilst the emphasis would be on the Senecan reception, it would also include discussion of other lesser known anecdotes from late antiquity, which suggest that Sophocles' play itself continued to enjoy a theatrical life beyond the fifth century. The discussion of the early modern period would open with the inaugurating production of *Edipo Re* at the Teatro Olimpico, Vicenza, in 1585. It would draw on histories of scholarship (so neo-Aristotelian readings would be central and as important as, say, discussion about versions by Corneille, Dryden and Lee and Voltaire) and histories of the book (so early texts and translations and versions of Oedipus would matter). But it would not result in a jump from Voltaire (1714) – or even the early nineteenth-century Kleistian parody – to the *fin de siècle* reception in early psychoanalytical theory. First it would need to include discussion of the French revolutionary staged versions of the play and their impact (albeit in closet performance) in Britain (Biet 1994; Hall and Macintosh 2005). But the most important focus for the discussion of the nineteenth century and early twentieth century would be upon the 1858 *OEdipe Roi* of Jules Lacroix.

Even though Lacroix' little known text is omitted by the eminent theatre historian Jacques Scherer from his major study *Dramaturgies d'Oedipe* (1987), this was the version that eclipsed Voltaire's from the repertoire of the Comédie Française, and then went on in 1861 to receive the prestigious prize from the Académie Française normally reserved for original works. Moreover, the fact that Lacroix's translation survived on the stage for over fifty years – surely an unprecedented and unparalleled achievement – is reason enough to grant it serious consideration; and especially so in a culture such as our own when the shelf-life of a translation is generally considered to be about, and definitely no more than, ten years. For it is Lacroix's translation – mediated especially through the supreme performative powers of Mounet-Sully from 1881 onwards – that can be considered to have played an instrumental role in shaping early twentieth-century critical readings of Sophocles' tragedy. Indeed it is hard to imagine Paris's preoccupation with Oedipus in the interwar period – which saw the multiple versions by Cocteau, Gide and others – without the Mounet-Sully renderings of Lacroix's version before the Great War.

Freud's biographer, Ernest Jones, records the deep impression that a performance of *Oedipe Roi* seen in Paris in the 1880s made on his subject; and even if there is some doubt nowadays as to whether Freud actually saw Mounet-Sully in the title role, there is no doubt that the reputation of the production had a considerable impact on him and on early psychoanalytic theory (Jones 1953: 194; cf. Armstrong 2006). In Lacroix's text, the chorus and Thebes itself both disappear into the background leaving an unerring focus upon a suffering hero. With Lacroix's version the French stage was able to witness the blinded Oedipus for the first time and to watch Oedipus' suffering being played out in all its poignancy within a harrowing family drama. Both Corneille and Voltaire had omitted the final scene for reasons of decorum; and it is significant that it is this part of Lacroix's version that seems to have captured the minds of the reviewers. For it is here in this scene, that Oedipus emerges as Everyman.

The part of Oedipus was taken in 1858 and in the revival of 1861 by the tragic actor, Geffroy, who had succeeded the famous French revolutionary actor, Talma at the Comédie Française. Geffroy's performance received unanimous acclaim especially for this final, hitherto unseen, act. By 1861 Geffroy had become so closely identified with the role of Oedipus that there was some doubt a successor would be found to take over the role. Indeed the ancient Oedipus now had to wait until the 1880s, when the star-system could produce Jean Mounet-Sully, the exemplary tragedien of the next generation, who was deemed worthy of donning Oedipus' heroic mantle.

If Freud theorized the concept of Oedipus as Modernist Everyman, it was Mounet-Sully who pioneered and popularized this view. With his powers of imper-sonation, he made audiences across Europe believe that the Greek tragic hero was really like them. Mounet-Sully's involvement with the twentieth-century's most popular and truly pioneering art-form, cinema extended and perpetuated this per-ception of Sophocles' tragic figure. It may be surprising that the actor, who was renowned for his extraordinary powerful voice (he was from all accounts an accom-plished baritone) was to have turned to silent film in the last phase of his life. But his dependence upon 'gestes' would have made that transition a particularly appropriate one.

As Pantelis Michelakis has shown (and to whom I am indebted both for supply-ing me with a clip of the film of the stage/film performance and for the discussion that follows), Mounet-Sully's silent film of *Oedipe Roi* of 1912, in which he per-formed and which he directed, was released not just in France but in America (January 1913) and in Austria (March 1913). It was unusually long (it lasted just over one hour and is therefore longer than any other extant silent film of an ancient play of the period). Its structure (which can be inferred from the publicity surrounding it and from stills in the French Bibliothèque du Film – the film itself has not survived) is most striking: the first act involves Oedipus' encounter with the Sphinx, in which Oedipus (we infer from the German Censor) unlike his Greek counterpart, kills the Sphinx and then decapitates her and brings the head to Thebes. Only the last two acts involve the Sophoclean play. Hofmannstahl's *Ödipus und die Sphinx* directed by Max Reinhardt (1906) had already treated this part of the legend in the theatre – the prequel to his version of *Oedipus Rex* at the Zirkus Schumann in 1910 in Berlin, also directed by Reinhardt. However, as Michelakis points out, what is important about the Mounet-Sully film is that it is clearly not a record of a stage performance, but an attempt to retell the Oedipus story 'in a manner appropriate to the generic parameters of the new art form' (Michelakis 2004b: unpublished paper).

This extraordinary development in the reception of Sophocles' tragedy had, I sug-gest, an important legacy. It encouraged the viewer of the film to 'read' the myth differently. *Oedipus Tyrannos*, the neo-Aristotelian paradigm, admired in France since at the very least Dacier's commentary on the *Poetics* of 1672 as the pinnacle of tragic form, had for obvious reasons never previously been so radically recast. This was in marked contrast to, say, the *Oresteia*, which for a whole host of reasons had been radically rewritten on numerous occasions since the Renaissance (Ewbank 2005). But now with the very different demands of the new genre, Sophocles' retro-active plot could be refigured as *Bildungsroman*. Furthermore, with the developments in anthropology, in which myths were now being read both across time and across cultures, the Oedipus myth was liberated from the Sophoclean formal strait-jacket in a way that it had not been since the Renaissance (cf. Alexander Neville's 1563 version of the Oedipus' story recast as medieval morality tale).

What is striking about the next version of Sophocles' tragedy, the *Oedipe Roi* of Saint-Georges de Bouhélier, directed by Firmin Gémier at the Cirque d'Hiver in 1919, is that it is indeed another recasting of Oedipus as *Bildungsroman*, and more particulary strongly reminiscent of a Medieval Mystery Play, with its octosyllabic verse form, familiar style and paratactic structure. For Bouhélier the theatre was to provide a sacred and inclusive space; and the choice of venue in 1919, above all, made that aspiration a serious one. As with Mounet-Sully's film version, the audience watching the play at the Cirque d'Hiver was very far from the *haut bourgeois* one at the Comédie Française: Gémier planned a genuine 'people's theatre' (he went on to become the first director of the Théâtre National Populaire). Taking his cue in many ways from Max Reinhardt in his choice of venue (a circus), his choice of play and his use of huge crowds (not to mention the set), he went even further that Max Reinhardt in trying to recreate the performance conditions of the ancient theatre (for Reinhardt's production, see Macintosh forthcoming). In addition to the play, with its cast of two hundred, including javelin and discus throwers and high jumpers, he attempted to recreate an Olympic Games (shortly to be staged in Paris) and make theatre truly 'popular'. Audiences loved it; critics less so – this was a *Gesamtkunstwerk* that was too ambitiously inclusive.

Now Oedipus as Everyman went on to be perpetuated by other adaptations and versions in the 1920s and 1930s. The Everyman was literally Everywhere. To think of Oedipus in the twentieth century is really to focus on that enormously concentrated period of productivity and achievement on the Paris stage in the late 1920s and early 1930s, which witnessed Stravinsky's Opera-Oratorio *Oedipus Rex* with the Latin libretto of Jean Cocteau in 1927, Gide's *Oedipe* in 1932 and Cocteau's full-length drama of 1934 *La Machine Infernale*. Stravinsky's opera is the exception that proves the rule with its hieratic and deliberately anti-Freudian Oedipus. The other versions here all rewrite Oedipus's life as *Bildungsroman*: Mounet-Sully's pioneering film freed Oedipus both from his formal mould and his kingly realm.

Mapping Oedipus with Martha Graham

If Mounet-Sully's role in the theatre and in the cinema was central to the formation of early twentieth-century views of Oedipus, the next pivotal performative moment I want to discuss here occurred in 1947 with Martha Graham's pioneering ballet, *Night Journey*. Most accounts of Oedipus in the twentieth century move from Paris of the 1920s and 1930s to the general reception of the 1960s and beyond, with Pasolini's film (*Edipo Re* 1967), and (maybe) Rotimi's version (*The Gods Are Not to Blame* 1968), before including recent versions like those by Berkoff (*Greek* 1980) and Rita Dove (*Darker Face of the Earth* 1994). But Graham's earlier ballet is a very important point in the reception history of Sophocles' play and serves as a salutory reminder to classical reception scholars of the necessity of including dance within their sphere of study (a 1961 recording of *Night Journey*, produced by Nathan Kroll, is available on DVD, *Martha Graham in Performance*, Kultur, USA, with Martha Graham as Jocasta, Paul Taylor as Tiresias, Bertram Ross as Oedipus). Graham's Greek-inspired ballets in general are predicated upon the complex relationship between myth, literature and psychoanalytical theory, and are thus central to any serious discussion of mid-twentieth-century reception of the plays. Furthermore, Graham's 'mythic' cues come directly from the giants of literary Modernism, Joyce and Eliot; and like them, her intuitions are often strikingly prescient.

The dance drama opens with Jocasta entering the stage, rope in hand ready to hang herself. As Tiresias slowly arrives, he strides rhythmically across the stage, beating his staff as if tolling the bell of doom. The blind priest goes to remove the rope from Jocasta's hands; but it is not to prevent her suicide, it is merely to postpone it. For here, in Martha Graham's dance drama, *Night Journey*, based on Sophocles' *Oedipus Tyrannos*, Jocasta has become protagonist; and she is forced (Noh-like) to relive the horrors of her life as she stands on the threshold of death.

Graham's work owes as much to Yeats's *Plays for Dancers* as it does to psychoanalytic theory; and like Yeats's Noh-inspired plays, it hovers between the realms of life and death; reality and other layers of consciousness. The 'night' of this particular journey refers as much to the dream world as it does to familial descent into lugubrious chaos. As Graham's Jocasta falls upon the schematic bed by the renowned Japanese designer, Isamu Noguchi, more rack-like than canopy, her dream world begins to unfold before our eyes.

A victorious Oedipus, ceremoniously welcomed by an all-female chorus carrying stylized laurel branches, treads upon the raised stepping stones that lead him to the royal bed and to his prize. Lifting the queen upon his shoulders, covering her head with his cloak before placing an imperious foot upon her thigh, he is alternatively tender child and dominant warrior in courtship. Slowly the victory dance gives way to an erotic and highly charged physical union that brings with it painful forebodings for Jocasta. She nurses Oedipus, then mounts his lap in a beautiful sequence of carress and enfurlment as they both become entwined in the (now umbilical) rope and the bed beneath. But when the chorus return, to the staccato strings of the orchestra and the dissonant piano accompaniment in William Schuman's score, the lovers' passion is reduced to (rather than consummated with) a series of restricted jerks.

Tiresias re-enters, his familiar pounding staff now evoking Oedipus' legendary lameness; and when the tip of the staff touches the 'umbilical' cord, husband/son and wife/mother collapse to the ground. The truth has been signalled: Oedipus discards the rope, reeling from the bed and recoiling upon the chorus in horror. Only once more, momentarily, does passion return before moral rectitude prevails to curb the errant son. Now that the skein of Jocasta's memory has broken in this familial drama of intergenerational chaos, future precedes the present as the husband/son appears to blind himself prematurely before taking flight from the incestuous bed. Alone now, Jocasta rises from the bed, removes her royal cloak, grabs the rope of kinship and of memory, wraps it round her neck and falls. Tiresias returns, his staff tapping in Noh-like invocation of the spirits of the dead; and as he walks, he walks on past the corpse which remains centre stage, presaging as he does, the exile of Oedipus to come.

Martha Graham has radically refigured the Sophoclean text in order to allow the mother-figure, Jocasta, to come centre stage. Graham's un-Sophoclean insistence upon the erotic nature of the incestuous encounter between mother and son, and the dance-drama's concern with the act of incest to the exclusion of the parricide is significant. Similarly both the inclusion of a female chorus and the centrality of the traditionally bisexual Tiresias to its structure bring a decidedly feminist reading to the ancient text. Indeed, these departures from Sophocles' tragedy are especially significant in hindsight because we can now see them as emblematic of a general shift in attitudes that becomes commonplace in many late twentieth-century reworkings of the Sophoclean tragedy.

Oedipus Tyrannos as Outsider

We have noted the large number of productions and adaptations of Sophocles' tragedy in the first half of the twentieth century. But what about Oedipus today in the theatre? It is now very hard to see a major production of Sophocles' *Oedipus Tyrannos* that is more than just a tired reconstruction. And when Oedipus does appear on the stage, he is very far from being Everyman in the Mounet-Sully mould. He is often so radically refigured as the Other that he provides an alternative rather than representative voice for humanity. I am thinking here of Berkoff's Oedipus, who hails from London's East End, of those post-colonial Oedipuses where Sophocles' tragic character is refashioned as a minority rather than a majority voice (witness especially the Deep South African-American version by Rita Dove). In Pasolini's film *Edipo Re* (1967), Oedipus is more sentient than cerebral man. In all of these versions, Oedipus is Outsider, not Everyman. As Outsider in these new versions, Oedipus is now more *tyrannos* in the ancient sense – the ruler who comes from without rather than the one who inherits the throne – than the Everyman of Mounet-Sully/Freud's interpretation. All these post-1960s versions are anticipated twenty years earlier in *Night Journey*.

Post-war scholarship on the *Oedipus Tyrannos*, in a move strikingly evocative if not directly inspired by the eighteenth-century Jesuitical readings of Sophocles' text, sought perhaps unsurprisingly to reinject the political dimension of Sophocles' play back into the Freudian familial romantic drama. In Knox's pathbreaking study *Oedipus at Thebes* of 1957, the lonely Modernist hero as Everyman was radically reformulated as the ruler from without, who is really a vision of imperial, tyrannical Athens. The readings of Vernant and Vidal-Naquet continue to emphasize the *tyrannos* of the title. In Vidal-Naquet's reading, Oedipus the tyrant becomes overtly politically problematic. He writes in 'Oedipus in Athens': 'As the chorus says in *Oedipus Rex*, "Hubris breeds the tyrant" (873), or, as Aristotle was later to put it, whoever cannot live within the community "forms no part of the city and so becomes either a beast or a god". Such certainly is the fate of the character created by Sophocles' (Vidal-Naquet 1988: 326–7).

These critiques were coincident with the counter-moves in psychoanalytical theory and clinical practice, where the Kleinian psychoanalytical model, in which the mother replaces the father as the focus for exploration, began to eclipse Freudian orthodoxy. If the eighteenth-century Oedipuses were insouciant tyrants, by the end of the play they were very frequently at odds with the tyrannical side of their own nature (Hall and Macintosh 2005: 215–42). Now in postmodern Paris, Oedipus has become inseparable from what is seen as the repressive aspects of psychoanalysis. In Foucault's terms in particular, Oedipus is a tyrant through and through: his search for truth is but one stage in the repressive pan-optic society that western liberal democracies have become. Mounet-Sully's Everyman, who battles nobly but vainly against an unjust world has himself now become the prime cause of social injustice. Foucault's critique gains even greater force and prominence in *L'Anti-Oedipe* of Deleuze and Guattari (1983 – Foucault wrote the introduction to the English translation), where Oedipus is a symbol of restraint and repression, racist, capitalist, patriarchal and imperialist.

The recent focus on Oedipus the *tyrannos* to the exclusion of what I have termed here Oedipus the Everyman, is not unrelated to this wider anti-Oedipal discourse in post-war France (see Leonard 2005 for a fascinating account of the centrality of post-war French classical scholarship to political and cultural thought at this time). Although Vernant's important essay 'Oedipus without the Complex' sought to dissociate Sophocles' Oedipus from Freud, paradoxically the valiant attempts to historicize Sophocles' tragedy with reference to the *tyrannos* of antiquity resulted in a coincidence of interest with those who in found Oedipus the modern tyrant (Vernant 1988). The relative absence of Sophocles' Oedipus from the modern international theatrical repertoire since the late 1960s is also, I suggest, an important aspect of this development. Whilst it is hard to see Oedipus in Sophocles' play as anything other than an embryonic Foucauldian tyrant – in say, the scene with Tiresias, the scene with Creon and most clearly perhaps in the scene of physical torture with the shepherd towards the end of the play – marginalization within the modern repertoire is clearly not unrelated to the Foucauldian view of him. Oedipus' new guises – no longer Everyman, but very often Otherman (as ethnic other – the outsider of the *tyrannos*) – all resist the traits that make him open to criticism; and very often Oedipus is totally marginalized in a world which is seen through the eyes' of Jocasta alone, as with Martha Graham's prescient ballet *Night Journey* (1947).

This very brief discussion of the performance history of Sophocles' tragedy demonstrates the important ways in which classical hermeneutics, the history of ideas and theatre history are interrelated; and it reminds us that performance often articulates important shifts in orientation first. Mounet-Sully's performances guaranteed that Oedipus became Modernist Everyman. When we consider the late twentieth-century, in particular, we can see that Martha Graham's ballet anticipated in many ways the radical re-siting of Oedipus in the post-Freudian world of the late twentieth century. Histories of classical scholarship must widen their brief to include not just the wider political, social and cultural contexts; but also ally themselves with that second cousin of classical reception, performance history.

FURTHER READING

In addition to the searching the databases of the APGRD, Oxford (www.apgrd.ox.ac.uk/), The Open University Reception of Classical Texts Research project, Milton Keynes (www2.open.ac.uk/ClassicalStudies/GreekPlays/index.html) and the European Network of Performance of Ancient Drama, Athens (www.cc.uoa.gr/drama/network/index.html), the following standard reference works are essential tools for the researcher involved in performance histories:

Avery, Hogan, Scouten, Stone and Van Lennep 1965–8; *DNB* 1908–9; *Enciclopedia dello spettacolo* 1954–62; Stanley 2001; Allardyce Nicholl 1925 and 1952–9.

ODNB 2004; Reid 1993; Wearing 1991.

CHAPTER TWENTY

'Body and Mask' in Performances of Classical Drama on the Modern Stage

Angeliki Varakis

A common object in classical and Hellenistic artistic representations that reflect theatrical performances is the mask, carried by actors before or after the performance, or used as decoration. A characteristic example is the late classical Gnathia fragment in Würzburg, which depicts a tragic actor holding his mask (Würzburg H 4600 (L832)). As Richard Green observes, 'It is one of the finer examples of Greek vase painting . . . in its depiction of the engaging contrast between the mean, rather shabby person of the actor and the heroic quality of the figure he has just portrayed' (Green 2002: 99). The mask appears similar to a disembodied entity of Hellenic beauty. Its features and hair are not in any way exaggerated, and the face is characterized by 'a calm and untroubled expression'.

The Greek masks of tragedy were not simple decorative objects or concealment devices, which aimed to hide the identity of the wearer (even though they did so) but embodiments of mythical characters of a heroic quality. Similarly, one could argue that the bodies of the tragic protagonists as depicted on the 'Oedipus' vase (London 1843.11–3.24 (E 169)), were also characterized by trimness and balanced proportions reflecting the heroic ideal of beauty as seen in most fifth- and fourth-century BCE art. More specifically, the tall and respectable figure depicted in the centre of the tragic scene, generally taken as representing King Oedipus, stands evenly balanced with his legs straight dressed in an elaborately decorated garment. His elaborate costume, balanced bodily posture and physical height seem to signal his heroic status, especially if compared to the figure of the messenger which is standing on his left. The messenger is considerably shorter and wears different clothing, short dress and boots. Finally, it is quite natural that the wearing of long robes must have imposed bodily discipline and restricted gesture, maximizing the actor's potential for speech (Wiles 2000: 159).

Recent scholarship has rightly shown an increasing interest in interpreting ancient drama in terms of its effect in performance practice. One could argue that the most credible source of information that benefits a theatrical interpretation of ancient drama is the limited but extremely valuable material evidence that has survived from antiquity for the physical appearance of actors and their masks. The earliest explicit depictions appear on a series of vases that date to the last decade of the fifth century BCE and the beginning of the fourth. The most important and best preserved example is the Pronomos vase which shows performers of a satyr play celebrating a victory in the dramatic competitions (Naples 81673 (H 3240)). In this vase we have good evidence for masks and costumes from Athens in about 400 BCE.

In the world of academia a great deal of research on the Greek mask has been built around the careful study of ancient iconography. An important example is the work undertaken by T.B.L. Webster and J.R. Green as part of 'the ancient theatre project' centred on the Institute of Classical Studies in London. This work involved building up a data-base of masks. Webster's catalogues of masks ($MOMC^3$, MNC^3, MTS^2) are historically valuable as they give an indication of the ancient theatrical masks' appearance and popularity by period and area. A more performance-based approach of the ancient mask that also uses ancient iconography as a precious source of information has began to develop since the 1980s with the work of academics from the field of theatre studies and classics such as David Wiles, Oliver Taplin, Michael Walton, Nurit Yaari, Martha Johnson, C.W. Marshall and Claude Calame. Their work aims to show how masks can develop and shape our understanding of Greek theatre performance and society. A great deal of work, however, remains to be done on such issues as body language and its impact on the perception of masks.

The Heroic Mask and Body of Tragedy

A number of distinguished modern practitioners have chosen to follow the classical performance tradition by representing the heroic figures of tragedy using full-headed masks. Their choices have been based mainly on the premise that Greek masks are not merely concealment devices but also embodiments of mythical figures. Likewise, the bodies are covered by archaic robes, which visually complement the full-headed mask, effecting a full visual transformation of the performer into a tragic hero or heroine. The rare occurrence of modern masked performances of Ancient Greek drama and the absence or limited extent of masked acting in the training programmes of most major drama schools meant that these productions had to revive a style of performing which was unfamiliar to the actors, presenting a strong physical and vocal challenge.

In the monumental Greek production of *Prometheus Bound*, performed in the ancient theatre at Delphi in 1927, full-headed masks were employed to signal the individuation of the heroic figures distancing the collective body of the unmasked chorus from the characters. The production was performed as part of a cultural festival which included sport, folk dancing and other demonstrations of popular arts and crafts as well as a lecture by archaeologist Wilhelm Dörpfeld. The performance itself was directed and choreographed by Eva Palmer-Sikelianos (tr. I. Gryparis, music K. Psachos, sets and masks by Foskolos, mask designs by H. Sandro). The use of masks was in line with the entire philosophy of the production, which was highly influenced by Nietzsche's views as manifested in his famous work *The Birth of Tragedy*. For Nietzsche the hero's individuation was marked through the use of the Apollonian mask, which underneath its ideal and wonderfully balanced guise contained and confined the true Dionysian ecstatic hero, the true embodiment of nature. This also explained the aesthetic principal of heroic beauty in the design of the non-exaggerated head-pieces, resembling the classical masks of tragedy in their lack of a readable cast of expression. The best source of the productions mask images are to be found in the photographic album, *Endymatologia sto Archaio Theatro (Costume-design in Greek Theatre)* edited by stage-designer Dionysis Fotopoulos.

The purpose of using masks was also connected to their metaphysical power, which allowed them to function as channels of communication between the human soul and the great world of myth. Once again, this points to Nietzsche's ritual theories and the notion of the Dionysiac mask, with its sacred powers of possession. As Angelos Sikelianos characteristically remarked, 'At least at an aesthetic level, the mask can today achieve a sacred communion between the great myth and the modern souls that our age is not accustomed to' (Fotopoulos 1986: 34).

It is questionable whether the masked performers were able to deliver or experience the neo-romantic visions of the director. The production was not well received, and it is interesting to reflect on why it failed to engage some of the Greek critics. Although everyone praised the noble cause and high aspirations of the entire project there was a substantial amount of negative criticism as far as the performance and masks were concerned. The Greek reviewers were most critical of the heroes' realistic acting and trivial bodily gestures, which in their view were inappropriate for communicating the mythical dimension of the play and for fulfilling the visual demands set by an outdoor environment. It is quite difficult to imagine how a realistic approach to acting could be reconciled with the use of masks but one thing that is certain from reading the extracts from the critical reviews was that there was an overall lack of consistency as far as acting styles were concerned, not only between chorus and characters but between the characters as well (Sideris 1976: 358). This lack of style homogeneity was also apparent in other aspects of the performance, with the chorus on one side trying to re-create the Greek experience through extensive archaizing, and the set, which on the other hand utilized special effects for the realistic representation of the rocky cliff on which Prometheus was chained. As Fiona Macintosh observes with regard to the setting, 'There was no attempt to re-create the fifth century skene, with the vast rock upon which Prometheus was pinioned owing more to the monumental sets of early Hollywood epics than to any Greek precedent' (Macintosh 1997: 306).

The negative reviews disclosed a common attitude of the time, which was in favour of a statuesque and rhetorical style of acting, primarily concerned with serving the text. Most critics did not hesitate to question the effectiveness of full masks, which in their opinion made the 'recitation of the lines very difficult' (Sideris 1976: 359). The design of the masks was also heavily criticized for being far too realistic, representing highly individual features inappropriate for the representation of a mythical figure, generating an aesthetic clash with the archaic robes that covered the performers' bodies (Sideris 1976: 361). It was a time when scholars were still under the false impression that the ancient production was performed in high masks and raised cothurni.

One can only wonder whether the same people would have been more favourable towards the archaic-in-feel production of Tyrone Guthrie's *Oedipus Rex*, performed in the Greek-style auditorium at Stratford, Ontario, in 1955 using Roman-style masks and platform shoes. Guthrie's *Oedipus* likened a stylized mode of delivery, which concentrated on serving W.B. Yeats's text whilst highlighting the symbolic dimension of the play.

Guthrie's fascination with Greek theatre, just like that of Eva-Palmer and Angelos Sikelianos, derived from its ritual context, religious content and symbolic quality. In his analysis of the Oedipus story he used Apollo's attributes for the explanation of the hero's quality and actions, suggesting a strong influence on his views from Nietzsche.

'The God principally concerned with Oedipus is not Dionysus, the wine god, but Apollo; and the drama is far from being a simple statement of devotion. It is the product of an extremely sceptical mind' (Guthrie 1965: 32).

The director's belief in the universality of the Oedipus myth lead him to make analogies between ancient and modern rituals comparing the performance of Oedipus to the Christian ritual of Holy Communion, a religious experience he desired to recreate on stage through his 1955 ceremonial production. The Oedipus tragedy, just like the story of Christ in the ritual of Holly Communion, was presented as a symbolic re-enactment of self-sacrifice in honour of God (Guthrie 1965: 32–3). The performance was therefore designed, with its slow, deliberate gestures and movement, and frequent carefully posed tableaux, to assist the audience to grasp that they were watching a solemn ritual.

The symbolism of the production was straightforward and strongly expressed through the use and design of the masks and colour-coded costumes. The heroic status of the protagonists' huge masks was further reinforced when seen on stage alongside the life-size masks that were given to the ordinary mortals in the chorus. The Oedipus mask in particular, designed by Tanya Moisewitsch, stage and costume designer of the production, was characteristic for its Apollonian references through its gold colour and 'rays rising from its crown' (see figure 20.1). After Oedipus blinded himself, the character changed into a red robe and mask with a black veil over his face. The colour choices heightened the symbolic aspect of the production, while many may argue they increased the audience's emotional involvement. Unlike Sikelianos's production, the Apollonian mask was not used as a means to evoke the god's connection to individuation but as a means of reinforcing the universal status of the god-like hero. This explains its large size, symbolic colour and non-realistic design.

The film version of the production suggests that the masks in connection to the platform shoes and traditional costumes added a grand and monumental dimension to the actors' rather static bodies. An interesting reading by Martin Winkler, who compares the effectiveness of masks to the cinematic technique of close-ups on expressionless faces, throws light on another dimension by which Guthrie's masks

Figure 20.1   The masked figures of Oedipus and the chorus in the production of *Oedipus Rex*, directed by Tyrone Guthrie in 1955

could exert suspense and intensity of emotion on the spectators. It also partly reflects what many scholars and practitioners have recognized as a characteristic and powerful element in the image of the tragic mask; the blankness in its facial expression. The lack of a readable cast of expression allows the spectators to project their imagination on the immobile and expressionless features of the mask, depending on how they perceive the meaning of the text and actions of the characters. According to Winkler, in Guthrie's film version of *Oedipus* the masks seemed to come alive at key dramatic moments by way of a slow but powerful movement of the character's head. As he suggests, 'It is the viewer's psychological involvement, not the actors and not the director, that makes the masks come alive at these moments' (Winkler 2002: 55). The psychological involvement, according to Winkler, is produced from the audience's foreknowledge of the hero's fate, which in conjunction with the mask's immobile and expressionless features, allow them to project their own perception of the character's emotions onto the face. Winkler's analysis of the power of the Greek masks is most appropriate when discussing key dramatic moments but the crucial question remains unanswered: How can an immobile full mask retain its life, truthfulness and intimacy throughout the entire course of a lengthy live performance and more precisely when the character is moving, speaking and interacting with other characters on stage? In most masked productions of Greek tragedy, the actors fail to make the full mask an integral part of their body, which entails the danger of losing the audience's attention, with the mask being perceived as a dead object. John Emigh in his insightful book on masked performance makes a very accurate observation with regard to the Balinese mask and its vitality on stage:

> If he [Balinese actor] finds that place of congruence between his physical and spiritual resources and the potential life of the mask, then a living amalgam is created: a character, a persona. This amalgam is at best unstable . . . but it moves, it speaks, it breaths, it is perceived . . . as having an organic integrity. If the performer fails to find such a meeting place within this field of paradox, ambiguity and illusion, then the mask will retain its separateness . . . whatever its worth as an object . . . it will at best function as a decoration, a costume element.
>
> (Emigh 1996: 275)

Peter Hall's formalistic production of the *Oresteia* that was presented at the Olivier theatre in 1981 (tr. T. Harrison, dir. P. Hall, music Harrison Birtwistle, sets and costumes Jocelyn Herbert) has often been criticized for lacking organic unity and plasticity in movement, mainly due to the performers' failure to make the full-headed masks an integral part of their bodies. A formal presentation might be aesthetically pleasing, presenting a series of effective and pleasantly balanced visual tableaux at key dramatic moments, but is this adequate to make the masked figure effective throughout the entire performance?

Peter Hall's formal approach to Greek tragedy lies in his belief that the effective communication of large-scale characters and emotions could be achieved by way of exterior formality. Whether through the poetic quality of the language or the masked presentation of the figures, the formal quality of Greek theatre was there to assist the actor to perform and the spectator to grasp the larger-than-life situations and characters. In his opinion formality in staging would offer a contained, but simultaneously liberating, experience for the audience and performers (Hall 2000: 25). Oliver Taplin explains Hall's insistence on masks as a desire to create and maintain a discipline, a chain in which the play can dance, implying that through confinement and formality a new strength of expression could be unleashed (Taplin 2001).

The notions of artistic discipline, control and balance were fundamental in classical art and theatre as they reflected aspects of the heroic ideal. In Peter Hall's *Oresteia*, these artistic principals were evident not only through the highly controlled physical movement and speech of the performers, but also through the shape and appearance of the full masks. The latter's designs drew on Greek iconography as well as the principle of neutrality. The heroic figures were distinguished from one another through colour and hair-styles, but their faces shared the same lack of expression, a deliberate choice which in Hall's opinion would permit the audience to project their imaginations onto the mask, effected through the meaning of the spoken lines. In other words, it was the text rather than the mask that dictated meaning. Similarly, the long robes covering the performers' bodies imposed a bodily discipline involving stillness, balance and restricted gesture, while it could be argued that the insistence on frontal delivery did not allow for the exploitation of the corporeal possibilities of the play or the effective communication between the characters.

There has been much discussion amongst scholars regarding the effectiveness of Hall's formalistic approach to Greek tragedy. The objections partly derive from what many indicate to be his misunderstanding of the nature of masked acting and the mask's value as a means of activating the body. As Wiles concludes,

> in Hall's productions the text drives and the masked body has to follow where it is taken. There is no Platonic equipoise of mind and body, poetry and gymnastics here: the function of the mask is rather to obliterate body so the mind and the word can triumph.
>
> (Wiles 2004a: 257)

Last, but not least, was the problem of audibility. The production was heavily criticized for preventing the audience from identifying the speaking character due to the full masks, which impeded the actors' voices. It was clear that Peter Hall also observed that effect and in his later productions incorporated a microphone within each mask. Many might argue that the use of a microphone is another type of masking, creating a separate voice to that generated by the body of the performer and sustaining a distance between body, mask and sound. It is still questionable whether this was just an easy solution to a much more complex issue of acoustics.

The issue of acoustics is vital when it comes to performing a vocally demanding authored text in full masks. Many modern practitioners have considered this issue, with Greek mask-maker Thanos Vovolis leading the way via his systematic practice-based experimentation and continuous development of a method. His process allows for the fusion of body, mask and sound through the discovery of key postures, necessary for the production of lament cries. In his view, these postures could maximize the production and direction of the voice with the body and skull turning into a resonance chamber for these sounds (Vovolis 2003: 74). Unlike Hall, in Vovolis's work the mask becomes an integral part of the body.

The Chorus Mask and Collective Body

Eva Palmer-Sikelianos did not use masks for the presentation of her highly stylized chorus. Her choice was based on the premise that a mask is primarily a means of identification and impersonation and therefore unnecessary for a group that is designed to remain anonymous. Masks, however, adopt different meanings on different occasions, depending on their shape, size and design, as well as the performance context. Even though their power to identify a new persona is considered a very significant function in classical performance, their ability to connect a group of people by homogenizing their appearance is equally important, especially with regard to the chorus, assisting the members to behave as an organic entity. The qualities of a chorus mask could also expand to the characters, especially if one approaches the tragic heroes as being born out of the collective spirit of the community. In this case the character's mask may be presented in a stylistically similar manner to the masks used to cover the members of the chorus as it is the actions rather than the heroic appearance that set the characters apart from the group.

The realization of the choral component of tragedy in modern re-enactment has most often been problematic. One of the reasons for this is that the religious context in ancient Greece informed much of the choral performance. The following productions were successful in that respect, by adopting a live language grounded in collective ritual activities rather than archaeological formality.

After witnessing a series of voodoo ceremonies in Rio (the ceremonies of the *mancumbe* and of the *candomblés*), Barrault appreciated the *Oresteia* under a new light. His vivid memory of the ritual ceremonies played a valuable role in his preparation of his performance of the trilogy produced by the Compagnie Madeleine Renaud-Jean-Louis Barrault for the Marigny theatre in Paris in 1955 (adaptation by André Obey, music Pierre Boulez, sets and costumes Marie-Hélène Dasté). The live body of ritual activities made him realize that Greek theatre was not something sterile or lifeless but 'a total theatre composed by singing, diction, breathing . . . the art of gesture, the dance, trances, mask, rhythm, etc.' (Barrault 1961: 79). The rediscovery of Greek theatre through the physicality of the ritualistically energized body highly influenced the way in which he used the mask in his *Oresteia*, an integral object of collective experiences, related to exotic ritual practices. The mask was approached as a means of rediscovering instinctual behaviour, by activating all the senses of the body while its religious quality was associated to its magic ability to connect people with the supernatural world. His appreciation of the mask is reflected through its design and shape, which tried to emulate African tribes 'preparing for religious festivals rather than conventional Greek masks' (Barrault 1961: 77). The masks designed by the commedia mask-maker Amleto Sartori (well known for designing masks following the tradition of the popular Italian theatre *Commedia dell' Arte*, where half close-fitted leather masks are used to identify the comic types) were close-fitting three-quarter leather masks, allowing greater freedom for the mouth, permitting the voice to come through and the intake of air necessary for the physical requirements of the performance. Primitive and tribal dances could in Barrault's opinion assist in the discovery of the inspiration for the dances painted on Greek vases (Barrault 1961: 79). It was the physical energy of the Greek theatrical experience he wanted to revitalize, rather than the archaic empty forms of classical Greece. This approach was in line with Barrault's overall perception of theatre as a total act in the Artaudian sense (Antonin Artaud's ideal of 'total theatre' was based on the concept that mind and body, words and actions cannot be separated on stage) and his working within the physical tradition of famous French director Jacques Copeau (the first theatre practitioner to have developed a teaching method through which the mask could be put into service, in training and performance) and classical mime.

The performance, however, was not as well received as Guthrie's, which was staged during the same year. Wiles identifies two key reasons for the production's lack of success. The first was related to the proscenium stage and its unsuitability to host the highly physical performance and the second to the inability of the audience to appreciate the intercultural reading of the play. It also remains unclear whether the performers were adequately trained to play in masks (Wiles 2004a: 253). In any case, Barrault's masked production was innovative in its attempt to distance itself from the static and highly formal approach to the Greek plays. Its physicality inspired by exotic collective rituals made the mask work, not only as a reminder of its ritual power but also as a tool, which assisted the body to regain its 'whole theatrical function'. According to Barrault, 'Under the mask, you no longer look with your eyes, but with your neck . . . it is the mask which enables us to regain the human being's totality of expression' (Hainaux 1957: 277).

Following a similar path to that of Barrault, the Greek director Karolos Koun tried to find a live ritual language to communicate the meanings of his performance of the *Oresteia*, presented at the ancient theatre of Epidaurus in 1982 (tr. T. Valtinos, dir. K. Koun, music M. Christodoulidis, sets and costumes Dionisis Fotopoulos, masks Stavros Bonatsos). He searched within the religious tradition of the Greek Orthodox church, producing an interesting interplay between past and present. For example, the images of mourning women in traditional Greek funeral rites and other eastern European images associated to death were influential for the presentation of the choruses, with the mask adding a ceremonial and religious feel to the entire experience (see figure 20.2). The ceremonial sense was not, however, associated with strict formality. In Koun's view 'military' formality was an alien concept for the Greeks because even within a traditional pattern of collective movement and vocal expression there was still room for spontaneity and individual creativity. When discussing this issue he brings forth as an example modern Greece's lament practices and the way in which they allow space for spontaneous movement and cries within the framework of the ceremonial (Koun 1997: 66). In his production of the *Oresteia* this element of spontaneity was responsible for producing a sense of plasticity and choral organic unity. The masks could also communicate this sense of creativity through

Figure 20.2 Drawing inspired by Karolos Koun's masked *Oresteia* in 1982

small and discrete variations in their design. Their most important function, however, was their power to conceal the excessive detail and trivial sensitivities of the human face, which in tragic actions and highly emotional situations, like that of mourning, were irrelevant. The mask of the Furies for example was nothing more than a gauze covering the female face, generating a powerful image associated with death. The student of Koun, Mimis Kougioumtzis explains that the main reasons for using masks on the chorus were connected to their function as a concealment device and neutralizing tool, giving primacy to the dramatic narrative (Kougioumtzis 1989: 141–2). This is not irrelevant to the director's belief that the one of the most important elements of the performance was the text and more specifically the poetic lines uttered by the chorus.

The idea of the mask as a concealment device that helps the actors maintain their impersonal nature also justifies Koun's and the Art Theatre's persistence in using the half mask. Instead of employing full headpieces, which were devices to reveal characters, Koun preferred using half masks, which were essentially a negative, by defining a break between the visible part of the face and the hidden. In this respect the use of the mask appears closer to Brechtian (Brecht's theatre aimed to draw attention to the overt artificiality of the play and performance signalling a distinction between role and actor) than to ancient theatre. Koun repeatedly admitted the impact of Brechtian theatre on his work, especially in regards to the mask (Koun 1997: 92). His influence from Brecht also explains his desire to destroy any illusion during his production of the *Oresteia* by having the actors who participate in the chorus getting rid of their chorus mask and wear the mask of their part on stage. As he characteristically describes in an interview for the newspaper *Ta Nea*,

> everything is constructed on stage in front of the audience. The actors who participate in the chorus, take off the chorus mask and wear the mask of their role and a piece of skin or cloak. By doing this I have no intention to create a scenic effect but to underline the magic of theatre.
>
> (Koun 1982)

This scenic invention also revealed the way in which he understood the tragic heroes of the play, as roles essentially being born out of the community.

Mask-maker Thanos Vovolis also appreciates the actors playing the roles as emerging from the collective body of the chorus and dissolving back into it. The convention of the chorus relates to his understanding of the concept of the acoustical mask. As he and his collaborator Giorgos Zamboulakis explain,

> According to this concept an initial and basic relation is developed between the mask and the voice of the actor, allowing him to become a fractal of the common body of the chorus, to emerge as the stage figure of the role and then dissolve back to the body of the chorus.
>
> (Vovolis and Zamboulakis 2004: 108)

Their view partly reflects Koun's belief that all people are essentially the same but vary in the way they physically and vocally react to a set situation and the unifying elements of mask and costume. However, Vovolis's masks are very dissimilar in shape, style and meaning and for this reason energize the body and mind in a different manner. In Vovolis's work the unresolved tension, which is experienced in Koun's productions between the 'alienating and political conception of the mask and the ceremonial conception', ceases to exist because his masks cover the entire face of the performer, disallowing the persons of the actors to remain visible. His work concentrates on the spiritual qualities of the mask and its ability to make the body function as a whole. The Greek mask is perceived as a body/mind state of being, a state of *kenosis* (total emptiness). He compares this state of being to the state that humans experience when delivering a type of vocalization observed in tragedy and tragic lament. During this active process of vocalization, the face radiates the maximum measure of life, through its intensity, but at the same time an emptiness, due to its lack of a recognizable expression. In Vovolis's method the text and especially particular sections of lamentation are paramount in our understanding of the tragic mask's nature and in the discovery of its acoustic qualities.

His systematic practice-based research on the mask is valuable not only because it develops a method of working with the mask but also because it presents a new approach to the mask as an integral part of the performance, which fuses body, text and sound into an organic whole.

The Comic Mask and Grotesque Body

In masked productions of tragedy the fusion of body, text and sound into an integrated unit is a requirement, so that the audience can experience a character who is alive and whose thoughts, feelings and actions are clearly visible. In classical comedy, this organic fusion is even more difficult to attain because the play demands a stronger physicality, with rapid and even violent movement. It is hard to imagine how a modern actor could physically cope with interpreting the highly active parts of Aristophanic comedy whilst wearing what in classical times would have been a full-headed mask, padding on the belly and backside and, in the case of male characters, a large leather phallus at the front.

This in part explains why in most modern revivals, the comic and gross quality of the ancient role is visually transmitted through the stage appearance and particular acting style of a famous leading actor rather than the artificial body of classical costume. On some occasions the padding and phallus may still be present but the face of the performer remains the key attraction of the performance. The Greek director Alexis Solomos in his book the *The Living Aristophanes* was the first practitioner to express such views comparing the spirit of the comic characters to famous comedians of the cinema (for a more detailed description of Solomos's work and a discussion on whether the use of a famous comedian is in fact another type of mask (see Varakis 2003: 176–205. Also on Solomos and his Aristophanic revivals see: Van Steen 2000: 197–8, 199–204, 226–7).

I shall discuss in detail some exceptions to the rule, the first being the Greek National Theatre formalistic production of *Clouds* in 1951, inspired by ancient iconography, and Karolos Koun's influential Greek productions of *Acharnians* (1976) and *Peace* (1977), in which masks and grotesque bodies were used as part of his folk interpretation of Greek comedy. The production *Clouds* was presented at the Agiou Konstantinou national theatre venue in Athens (dir. S. Karantinos, tr. K. Varnalis, music G. Kasasoglou, choreography R. Manou, sets and costumes N. Hajikyriakos-Ghikas, masks A. Spiteri in designs by Ghikas.) The productions *Acharnians* (tr. L. Zenakos) and *Peace* (tr. K. Varnalis) were presented at the ancient theatre Herodes Atticus in Athens. In both productions the music was composed by Chr. Leontis and the sets were designed by D. Fotopoulos.

Inspired by the work of Eva and Angelos Sikelianos, Karantinos tried to re-introduce Aristophanes to the modern Greek stage by focusing on the deeply formalistic nature of ancient theatre. He sought for inspiration from the ancient vases and statuettes as far as the images and movement were concerned because he believed in the diachronic power of the comedy's theatrical form (see figure 20.3). According to him, the theatrical form of comedy derived from ritual festivities in which the public was free to express its deeper instincts while being in full disguise (Karantinos 1951: 4).

The director's desire to cover individuality and free the performer from inborn constraints was closely related to the fact that the production used an unbowdler-ized translation that tried to remain faithful to the ancient text. The body mask made the performer and spectator feel free of shame and the actor irrepressible in the expression of risqué language, as happens in modern times in carnivals and other

Figure 20.3   The masked figures of Socrates and Strepsiades in the production of *Clouds*, directed by Socrates Karantinos in 1951

occasions where people are in disguise (Karantinos 1951: 4) Thirty-three years later
Peter Hall expressed the same view as part of the reason for using the mask in his
1994 production of *Lysistrata*: 'This is a play about erections . . . without masks it
would be too obscene, you could not do it' (Taylor 1993). However, Karantinos's
masks were not similar to modern carnival masks or masks used in live festivities and
it may be that this was exactly where the key problem of the production lay and
the main reason for its overall lack of success. He was using a dead performance
language to communicate a play that was already difficult to grasp due to its highly
ephemeral character.

The unsuccessful production of *Clouds* did not, however, precipitate the abandonment of masks and use of grotesque figures on the Greek stage. Koun's
innovatory work with regards to Aristophanic comedy was about to flourish and
in the next few decades his productions would become an international landmark for the interpretation of Greek comedy. Unlike Karantinos, Koun was given
the opportunity to stage his comedies in their natural outdoor environment, which
some may argue played a great role in the way he decided to stage the Aristophanic
plays. The open-air theatre demanded the creation of an atmosphere suitable for
large spaces, with the festive spirit of great festivals and celebrations. The creation
of a live celebration on stage became a priority, especially with regards to the comedies *Acharnians* and *Peace*, which not only include celebratory events but are
also sealed with celebrations. The presence of masks, puppets and grotesque bodies
more than in any other of his productions encouraged the creation of a festive
atmosphere inviting the spectator to imagine that the performer had vanished into
a real festival.

Driven by a strong ideological view, which Koun named 'Greek folk expressionism'
(Greek folk expressionism was an aesthetic theory, which aimed to display on stage
the Greek popular element in its purest form as it appears in the unchanged rural
life, folk traditions and older Byzantine religious paintings and ancient pottery.
See also Van Steen 2000: 161–78), the director, as with tragedy, tried to establish
a link between ancient and modern Greek traditions. Therefore in order to capture
the ritualistic feel of the ancient experience, Koun and his stage designer Dionysis
Fotopoulos searched within the folk traditions of modern Greece and other eastern
European festivals for grotesque images that would correspond to a live language,
allowing for the effective communication of the festive spirit to a modern Greek
audience. He chose to use them on secondary characters with a symbolic meaning
and members of the chorus, who in his view were responsible for determining
the overall atmosphere of the comedy through their dynamic presence as a group.
The leading characters were to wear only a false nose, which in conjunction with
their stylized movement and speech delivery (especially in the *Acharnians*) pointed
once again to a live popular form of entertainment, the Greek shadow theatre
Karaghiozes (Varakis 2003: 251–4). Finally, on a dramatic level, the expression of
vulgarities and excessive behaviour seemed much more natural and less profane when
presented within a carnival atmosphere.

There is an evident stylistic distinction in the productions I have discussed,
between the formal- and archaic-in-feel performances and the more physical ones.

It seems that the key reason for their difference stems from the directors' diverse appreciation of Greek theatre and the mask in particular. Sikelianos's, Guthrie's, Hall's and Karantinos' assumptions about the universality of Greek drama led them to approach the mask as an ancient device with a universal significance and thus easily transferable on the modern stage. For Barrault and Koun, on the other hand, the Greek mask was tied with the specific culture in which it first appeared. In order for it to be effective on the modern stage it had to be part of a live language grounded in contemporary theatrical reality or ritual activities. There is no doubt that performances that use a live language are far more successful in achieving a more fulfilling and emotionally engaging experience for a present-day audience.

Practice-based Research

In modern theatre practice the Greek mask and body matter for the creative possibilities they open for the present. Practice-based research is therefore essential as it could explore such potential through extensive experimentation. The following project is a representative example of how practical research can deepen our understanding of masked acting, producing an interesting interplay between past and present.

Richard William's 'New Comedy Masks Project', based at the University of Glasgow in collaboration with 'The Scottish Mask and Puppet Centre' and a group of professional commedia actors (performers who have been specifically trained to interpret the comic types of the *Commedia dell' Arte*) under the direction of Adriano Iurissevich, has used the information provided by the archaeological evidence as a valuable source for the reconstruction of New Comedy masks, which are then used in live performance. The key objective of the project is the recovery of a lost tradition of mask performance and its rehabilitation by internet dissemination, studio research and live performance. The research project deals exclusively with three-dimensional objects, such as miniature Hellenistic masks (most model masks that have been used in this project come from the island of Lipari and are held in the Art Gallery and Museum, Kelvingrove, Glasgow, 1903.70.dt.1–16), which through 3D scanning are enlarged to life size (for more analysis on the technical side of the project and to view images of the model masks see Richard Williams 'The Digital Matrix in 3D' *Digicult Info* 9, 2004: 3–9). By asking actors to work with costumes and masks based on a close analysis of the artefacts, one can appreciate the potential of the ancient masks in performance practice and further an understanding of how performers moved and acted in antiquity. It is well-accepted by mask specialists that the structure and overall design of the mask could be a very valuable source of information when exploring the corporality of the performer, because its form could guide the actor's movement depending on how willing the performer is to adjust his physicality to the requirements of the mask. The most exciting part of the entire project came when the group decided to perform a complete play, Menander's *Epitrepontes*, before a live audience in the Roman theatre of Lecce in 2003, using the mask reconstructions to cover the performers' heads, turning virtual reality into a real life performance.

The use of a vast range of research methods from the more traditional physical and vocal exercises (Vovolis) to the more revolutionary utilization of 3D technology (Williams) is the only way to achieve a vivid idea of the techniques of ancient theatre, for theatre is practice. It not only heightens a historical understanding of issues such as acting and audience perception but most importantly provides a basis for bringing the texts to life through generating creative possibilities in the present. The Greek mask that could act simultaneously as an aesthetic object of beauty, a ritual device, a dramatic persona, a unifying tool, an implement for activating the body and instrument for serving the text provides room, more than any other performance object, for the exploration and realization of such possibilities.

NOTE

Special thanks to my mother Athena Varakis for providing the drawings included in this chapter.

FURTHER READING

The mask and body on the ancient stage

For a fundamental discussion on masks on the ancient stage see: Bieber 1930: cols. 2070–120. Pickard-Cambridge 1968: 189–196.

On the aesthetics and function of the Greek mask in antiquity see: Calame 1986: 125–42; Halliwell 1993: 195–211.

On the use of masks in ancient performance see: Walton 1980: 163–186 and 1996: 41–57; Wiles 1991 and 2000: 147–153 with mention of modern performances; Rehm, 1992: 39–42; Marshall 1999: 188–202; Yaari 1993: 51–62; Johnson 1992: 20–34.

For a discussion on the body, costume and performance styles in ancient performance see: Foley 2000: 275–311; Valakas 2002, 69–91; Green 2002: 93–126.

The mask and body on the modern stage

For a historical account of the Greek mask on the modern stage see: Wiles 2004a: 245–263; On practice-based research: Wiles 1999 offers an insightful seminar discussion by leading scholars in the field of classics and theatre on key issues regarding the mask in performance practice; Vervain and Wiles 2001: 254–272 and Wiles 2004b: 206–214; Coldiron 2002: 393–4; Williams 2004: 415–426; Williams: 2004: 3–9; Vovolis & Zamboulakis 2004: 107–131; Vervain 2005: 245–264; Varakis 2004.

On Hall's masked productions see: P. Hall (2000); Harrison 1991: 7–29; On Guthrie's masked production *Oedipus Rex* see: Winkler 2002: 43–70 which offers an insightful view on the function of the Greek mask in modern performance from the perspective of filmic close-ups of the human face.

For a comprehensive study of the mask in modern and ancient performance see Wiles 2007.

CHAPTER TWENTY-ONE

The Nomadic Theatre of the *Socìetas Raffaello Sanzio*: A Case of Postdramatic Reworking of (the Classical) Tragedy

Freddy Decreus

You love them or you hate them. Radically, and absolutely, in either of the two directions. But what cannot been denied, is this company's radiating presence, all over Europe. They are much appreciated guests at all important theatre festivals and considered one of the worlds leading theatre companies, one of the most radical-thinking and inventive theatre groups of contemporary theatre. The tableaux they present are exceptionally provocative and alienating, 'shockingly beautiful and seductively repellent' in their own words, but always extremely demanding. Their images have been labelled 'iconoclastic' and 'super-iconic' (Castellucci 1992), seen as relicts of old ritual violence and sacredness, or elaborations of Artaud's idea of theatre as a plague. Mostly, however, they defy every attempt at description and easy interpretation and lead audiences into atmospheres and trance-like states that cannot be properly analyzed, but that take possession of all of their physical senses. The beauty they produce is extremely fragile, always on the edge of frightening and overwhelming people, 'a sensory shot straight to the veins, flooding the mind', as they use to qualify themselves.

Since they have been staging a lot of classical myths, tragedies and foundational stories and continuously are claiming that one of their most important artistic aims is to (re)interpret contemporary tragedy, the 'classical' heritage is often within their scope: classicists are invited to be first-class witnesses of the large cultural differences between this 'nuovo teatro' and more common (neo)classical styles, and therefore of the shift from the world as text to the world as performance. An interest was taken in Mesopotamian myths with *La discesa di Inanna (The descent of Inanna)* (1989) and *Gilgamesh* (1990), in Egyptian beliefs with *Iside e Osiride (Isis and Osiris)* (1990), in Persians ones with *Ahura Mazda* (1991) and in Christian salvation stories with *Lucifero (Lucifer)* (1993). More traditional topics were handed over from Shakespeare in *Amleto (Hamlet)* (1992), *Guilio Cesare (Julius Caesar)* (1997), *Ophelia* (1997) and *Orestea (una commedia organica?)* (*Orestea. An organic comedy?*) from Aischylos (1995). Top of the bill, of course, are the eleven tragedies, staged in ten different European cities, called *Tragedia Endogonidia*, started and concluded in Cesena (from 2002 to 2004), a series of performances mainly set up to analyze and investigate the functioning of tragedy today.

'Postdramatic' is a notion developed by Hans-Thies Lehmann, in his *Postdramatic Theatre* (2006), the English translation of his *Postdramatisches Theater* (1999). Lehmann introduced this approach, in order to cope with a diversity of productions that defy 'traditional', 'text-based' western European theatre. In her *Introduction* to this work, Karen Jürs-Munby notices: 'To call theatre "postdramatic" involves subjecting the traditional relationship of theatre to drama to deconstruction and takes account of the numerous ways in which this relationship has been refigured in contemporary practice since the 1970s.' Important, however, is the decision not to erase or forget the dramatic tradition as such. Therefore, Karen Jürs-Munby specifies that 'it will hopefully become clear that "post" here is to be understood neither as an epochal category, nor simply as a chronological "after" drama, a "forgetting" of the dramatic "past", but rather as a rupture and a beyond that continue to entertain relationships with drama and are in many ways an analysis and "anamnesis" of drama'. (2006: 2).

A Radically New Artistic Climate

As a theatre company, the *Socìetas Raffaello Sanzio* was founded in Cesena in 1981 by a group of young artists who were trained in various disciplines of arts and sciences and who showed an interest into the interaction of theatre, video and film, and more specifically, into the way that plastic, visual and acoustic materials resulted in a new 'Gesamtkunstwerk', ('a complete and unified work of art') as an aesthetic statement strong and persuading enough to shake the foundations of traditional western representation and philosophy. Referring to their Renaissance hero Raphael (sc. Raffaello Sanzio), who was admired 'because in the perfection of his compositions, the body bathes in metaphysics' (Bleeker et al. 2002: 217), Romeo Castellucci (artistic leader and stage designer), his sister Claudia Castellucci (choreography), Chiara Guidi (musical dramaturgy) and Paolo Guidi (light design) created a new theatre which could gather and integrate all other arts and disciplines and which resulted in performances disturbing all sensitive and acoustic perceptions.

For a number of reasons, we would like to call their work 'nomadic'. The first and most general reason is the amazing and continuous use they make of metamorphoses, transformations and uneasy transitions. In the initial production they realized in Cesena (C. #01) of the *Tragedia Endogonidia*, the first entrance is made by 'The Polymorphic Figure' who went through three successive transformations (indicated even by an armband pointing at the number corresponding to each change of state: 1, 2, 3). The Berlin version, the third stage in their *magnum opus* (B.#03), is a story about a woman without name, going through a number of rituals and hardly explainable actions, loosing and cherishing a dead child that reappears at the end and dances on her coffin. In the Brussels' version (BR. #04), within one and the same scene, an old man puts on several layers of clothes, first turning into a Jewish prophet, later on into a Belgian policeman, just in time to be beaten to death by another policeman, who pours fake blood onto the ground and marks the scene of the crime by some letters. Only then, one starts to remember that in the very first scene a floor cleaner has been washing the floor until it really was spotless. Subversion of the Aristotelean 'law' of temporal succession and of logic probability, resulting in an awareness of timeless and unnameable places, which can be situated anywhere. Theatre is no longer seen in terms of a number of clearly marked scenes, entrances and exits, on the contrary, it is continuously in a flux; sometimes the stage set is completely sealed off (a golden room in Avignon, A.#02, and Bergen, BN.#05, a marble chamber in Brussels, BR.#04) allowing no escape at all, some-times it is radically dismantled and open to every possible disturbing effect, charac-ters being obliged to force their way into the stage (a clown smashing through a window in Avignon, a tank breaking through the glass wall in Strasbourg, S.#08). Time is literally 'out of joint', the past glides over the present, the future comes and goes, slow motion disrupts 'normal' perception. In order to restore the compre-hensibility of what has been seen, we might try to normalize these alienating factors and reduce their strangeness by situating them within the realms of 'mythical' times. And indeed, on many occasions, Castellucci returned to the origins of things, to foundational moments in myth, society and religion. His art is surely nomadic in a mythical sense, since it deals with beginnings and with the fear of getting lost in the depths of the labyrinth, these mysterious areas that are not supposed to guide human nomads in their search for meaning. Since neither philosophical nor religious meta-systems still govern the west, theatre has to return to the very beginning of things, to the moment that Lucifer questioned Jahweh or that traditional Greek gods died in the fifth century and tragedy started as a kind of answer to this loss of presence and evidence. However, a performance like *Genesi* (1999) scares and fascinates him more than the Apocalypse itself, because it confronts the artist with the terror of sheer possibility. This very moment of returning to that point beyond language, beyond that first system that differentiated meanings, aims at recovering the preliminary conditions of our human nature, a moment where the humans still had commerce with talking animals, horses, rabbits, monkeys, or a billy-goat, a moment also where words were not needed yet. The uncertainty that lies between creation and destruc-tion, between Genesis and the murder of Cain, between the discovery of radium by Marie Curie and the destruction of the world by nuclear energy (topics in his production *Genesi*), is the same shocking and seductive experience that can be felt by the physicist, the artist, the politician, all human beings concerned with the pro-cess of creating, Castellucci suggests. They carry death and destruction in their very being, as an obscure part of themselves that they cannot deal with, a kind of vague mortal fear that is closely connected to sleep, hence *Genesi*'s subtitle, *From the Museum of Sleep*. This museum preserves all traces of the plague, vainly pushed aside and temporarily forgotten, but nevertheless recalling that black hole where every creation

returns to and gets its energy from, a sleep as black as the black sun. Every spectator of this and all other productions has the idea only to recognize small narrative
fragments or 'chunks' of information out of mythic stories: the larger picture always
fails and escapes, abandoning you along the tracks of a mysterious dream. A lot of
beds on the stage (the hospital bed in *Il Combattimento*, 2000; Orestes's bed in
Eumenides, 1995), a lot of dreams to cope with, but never a Doctor Freud to reduce
the chunk-like atmosphere. But whereas myths are stories which are meant to
suggest an escape from the labyrinth, these dreams densely loaded with mythic
fragments complicate our understanding, since they only suggest brief moments
of recognition before definitely drawing back. A return to one kind of invented
'reality', be it mythic or ideological, might be not sufficient to conceive and fill up
the life we live. In his production *Santa Sofia. Teatro Khmer* (1986), Castellucci stages
the super-iconoclast Pol Pot, the Cambodian dictator who emptied whole cities in
order to set up a new agrarian communist state and sanctified his bloody assumption of power by the introduction of a new beginning of times. Setting up *Raffaello
Sanzio* as a new theatre was the occasion for Castellucci to radically disrupt and
abolish 'reality' as we know it, staging what he considers to be empty bodies and
carnal forms, without shedding real blood. For him, this is an exercise in creating
parallel and multiple worlds, not surrealistic ones that mainly copy and presuppose
existing ones and sometimes heavily rely upon coincidence and the unconscious, but
rather 'ir-realistic' ones, always on the move (Castellucci 2001; Crombez 2005).

Therefore, in his opinion, direct communication and pure enactment of a literary
text on the stage are the worst possible enemies of theatre, since they became part
of the ideology of the so-called humanist western world.

> Our first preoccupation was to destroy that which exists, not out of a need for an empty
> space, but with the need for a rupture in the representation of the world as it was pro-
> posed to us. We need to recommence something from nothing. In effect, even if ico-
> noclasm tackles the reduction of images, the word is not negative at all, it is positive.
> Iconoclasm does not signify the 'anti-icon', nor 'without icon', but 'I break the icon',
> his sister affirms.
>
> (Castelluci 2001: 22–9; Tackels 2005: 70–2)

What the stage especially illustrates is the unlimited possibility of mingling 'realistic'
moments with unknown or uncertain ones, in a continuous struggle for domination, as an inexhaustible exercise in detecting and revealing new modes of per-
ceiving 'matter' and physicality. Statements like these make clear that his kind of
theatre challenges every reassuring (humanist) interpretation of literature and text
and undermines its essentialism and gender-typical definitions. In this way, Rosi Braidotti
called her book *Nomadic Subjects*, 'a move beyond the dualistic conceptual constraints
and the perversely monological mental habits of phallocentrism' (Braidotti 1994: 2).
This radical change of focus makes it clear that the theatre made by Raffaello Sanzio
asks for more than Aristotelean poetics, based as it is upon an easily recognizable organization of plot, action and character, since it requires a totally different
philosophic scope. In the worlds they create, difference rules over transcendental

hierarchy, intensity over logic, the pre-rational over the rational. Mixing human and animal 'actors' (cf. the 300 species of animals in *Le Favole di Esopo* (*The Fables of Aesop*), 1992), high technology and common objects, anorexic and bulimic bodies with fragments of texts, Castellucci is constantly creating border-zones, in-between-reality moments, mimetic-teases, in which we have the impression of seeing and hearing, but constantly have to admit that we only witness a highly sophisticated mechanic reproduction of reality. In this kaleidoscopic theatrical 'machine', every action is displaced, doubled and suspended, and neither a realistic nor mythic inter-pretation helps to interpret what we see.

In fact, much of this corresponds to the world of the 'energetic theatre' that Lyotard already discussed in 1977, to the 'rhizomatic' organization of the world put forward by Deleuze and Guattari, to the 'postdramatic' landscape defined by Hans-Thies Lehmann, to the 'open dramaturgy' practised by Jan Ritsema, or to the 'postmodern' dance project of Pina Bausch or André Lepecki. And, beyond all doubt, one of the major heroes in their iconoclastic universe is Antonin Artaud, whose name and her-itage figure in a lot of productions. Castellucci, more than once, refers to Artaud's idea of a 'Body Without Organs', a body which avoids as long as possible colonization by the usual forms of mental inclusion and representation. This 'organ-less body' attempts to stay out of traditional western philosophic attempts at conceptualizing experience and at obeying societal conditioning; it, rather, is a continuous transfor-mation of energy and sensation which is supposed to liberate the body. What Castellucci fancies, is the establishment of a dynamic and non-settled relationship between logos and non-logos, between rationalizing efforts and pre-linguistic experience, between essentialism and the process of becoming. Instead of choosing for the generalized western predilection for a well delineated plot and a clearly structured hermeneutical path he favours a climate of intensity, ambiguity and physicality.

The perfect aestheticism of his 'tableaux', the 'unjointed time', the sophisticated light engineering as well as the alienating sound design (mostly by Scott Gibbons) that often enough fundamentally modifies the human voice are set up in order to create a loosely structured neurological climate, as it is processing deeply within the spectator, one that does not lead to definite perceptions or interpretations and that generally is not set up as an invitation to know and judge, but rather to feel and experience. 'The theatre that tries to produce resolution is unacceptable', he says. 'It gives one the impression of being at school again. It is even worse, because this type of theatre wants to give us the truth that it calls the truth. Even Brecht has fallen in this crossing and this dogmatic pretension. It is more correct for the the-atre to leave a disturbance. This is preferred because one demands thus that people help to continue the story, to produce the part that lacks.' (Tackels 2005: 56). That is why he loves to stage a real *in-fans* in his *Tragedia Endogonidia*, BR.#04, where a baby sitting all alone on the ground, in the middle of the stage, suddenly dis-covers the public watching it. 'The infant's gaze provoked dizziness, a questioning, a physical and staggering awareness of our being-there. With this look, the child questions the performance, the theatre, the situation of being on stage, a physical questioning that has no words, nor performance leading to self-reflection', Céline Astrié comments (2003: 14). For the same reason, Castellucci likes to have his own six little children on the stage, innocent and playful creatures who, sometimes, are still able to free their brains from the world of representation and the inhibitions created by the super-ego. What a shocking experience when in the second act of *Genesis*, these white-clad children, in a complete white-washed environment, embedded in an unbearable sweet musical atmosphere, are driving in a very relaxed way a tiny toy train, heading towards their own extermination in the gas chambers of Auschwitz, and, later on, visceral organs fall out of the sky and are driven away in the same tiny train. What a clash between Artaud's artistic vision of the preconscious 'Body Without Organs' and the literal and ideological execution of it!

In the next section, we ask ourselves how the classical 'heritage' has been dealt with when confronted with these aesthetical and philosophic principles. We focus on three productions: *Orestea* (1995), *Giulio Cesare* (1997) and the *Tragedia Endogonidia* (2002–4).

Contemporary Tragedy

Never believe classics to be safe, Castellucci advocates, and never tackle them as a superstitious person who is afraid to put them to the test of fire (Valentini and Marranca 2004: 16–25). However, from the very start of his company till the present day, tragedy has been one of the favourite topics he has dealt with, though in a very personal and determinate way: 'I find all attempts to revive the fossilized shell vain and intolerable. To make a tragic text 'contemporary' is a lie, and especially pathetic when it is poets' doing. It betrays a missionary spirit in its perpetrators, an attempt to 'reconstruct the true spirit of the tragedy' in its contemporaneity, as if tragedy were a ball to be kicked around in the lofty realms of poetry', he mentions.

Orestea (una commedia organica?) *(1995)*

The *Orestea* clearly deals with Castellucci's fascination for mythic origins and the creation of totalizing imaginations, as a kind of meaning generating machines which create definite ways of organizing thought, and, as happened in the west, mostly in terms of binary oppositions and the privileging of one category over the other. Since he refuses to reconstruct tragedy in 'a missionary spirit', he chooses a recreation 'through the looking-glass', as one of the articles discussing this production is entitled (1997b: 190–9), in fact through the distorting glass of a whole hall of mirrors, one could say. Indeed, this production is so unique, astonishing and different from all others stagings of *Oresteia* that it is must remain a mystery, even after careful analysis. Both its title *Orestea (una commedia organica?)*, deliberately kept ambiguous (what is an 'organic' comedy?), and the extreme reduction of *Eumenides*, traditionally seen as the key episode of the trilogy (only twenty minutes survive), complicate any easy understanding. In fact, this production which stages the three tragedies, thrives on a double perspective of reversing and revisiting the trilogy: first, there is the importance Castellucci places on a series of remarks made by Walter Benjamin on the enigmatic fourth part, the satyr play (the lost Proteus). In Benjamin's opinion, this last part weighs as heavy as the three tragedies together, giving the laughter of comedy the possibility of liberating the restricting weight of thoughts. Castellucci affirms that 'the tragedy goes on to disintegrate into a neurotic form through laughter. Comedy is its only catharsis'. For him, 'it was like reading the inverted view of the original order, the matriarchal order, as it gives way and surrenders. In short, (his) sympathy lies with Clytemnestra'. Therefore, at the end, Castellucci likes to return to the very start of the trilogy, interpreting it as 'an organic comedy', and reading it as an homage to 'the greatness of Clytemnestra' (1997b: 197–9). Deleuze and Guattari (1980) would stress the absence of both centre and totalizing structure and consider it as occasion, after the explosion of emotions, to start the process all over again. Along these anti-essentialist lines, they ask our attention for the multiple ('rhizomatic') character of the tragic experience, rather than for its mythic longing to return to one origin and centre. This can be understood as an exercise in 'deterritorialization' constantly followed by another one in 'reterritorializing', they would say, continuously incorporating other questions and struggles, discovering that meaning is in a constant flux (see Simon Goldhill's remarks on the notion of *dike* in *Oresteia*, 'this 'unworkable' notion that shifts all the time, ranging from legal justice to requital, 1992: 32).

On the other hand, there is also Castellucci's 'refusal to take for granted the cultural conclusion of the *Oresteia*: the establishment of the Areopagus, the absolution of Orestes and the definitive institution of a patriarchal and spiritual system to overcome the *ius naturale*, because if it is true that the *Eumenides* achieves this spiritual overcoming it is also true that the entire *Oresteia* is made up of those elements to be overcome. Therefore, he fancied 'reading the inverted view of the original order, the matriarchal order, as it gives way and surrenders'. Apparently, in both kind of approaches, what he liked was the possibility of returning, of imagining and dissolving worlds and playing with different ones. 'From the ending with the "Eumenides" I return back to beyond the beginning of the trilogy', he mentions, a radical plea not to restrict our imagination to one mythological and ontological worldview (1997: 197).

The production of his *Orestea* keeps the stage covered up with a number of gauzes which trouble and postpone any direct confrontation with the things shown. Reality as such does not have a chance to be detected, everything happens in worlds in transition. What is presented on the scene disturbs any easy categorizing: a (nearly empty) landscape, a Joseph Beuys- or a Heiner Müller-like atelier of history, images from a distant ritual past stumbling upon references to a more recent history (Picasso's *Guernica*), all of them left unfinished and scattered over the place, the scene literally covered by (the) dust (of history). This is a place where animals (donkeys, apes) and animal-like actors (the leader of the rabbit chorus, in *Agamemnon*) mingle with human ones, or better with human bodies and 'antibodies' (excessive, anorexic, amputated bodies) and where technology continually distorts sounds and voices. This is an environment where the text does not rule as text, but as a huge organic body that necessarily first 'fall[s] and disappear[s] in order to reemerge, one bit at a time, like a great cetacean inhaling', Castellucci's says, since 'the text works on the principle of latency, like Moby Dick for Ahab' (1997: 195). Text, bodies and stage are 'organic', as the title of this production says, to be apprehended in their physicality and materiality, and situated in an aesthetic climate where everything provokes intensive perceptions. Much verbal material comes from Lewis Carroll's famous storybooks for children *Alice's Adventures in Wonderland* (1865) and *Through the Looking-Glass* (1872), filled up with and recycled through Antonin Artaud's comments on them, a triple transition 'from Aeschylus to Carroll, from Carroll to Artaud and from Artaud to silence', as Castellucci observed. The general atmosphere of this tragedy simply was too atrocious and scary, the director said, to stage it in a direct way, therefore this detour over the fairy tale and the adventures of Alice (who suffered a fate comparable to Iphigeneia's one) (1997: 193).

Now and then, words that apparently belong to Aeschylus'text may be heard, relicts from an archaic period, taken out of an Italian translation that he considered 'outdated', because he mainly was interested 'in the dead state of the work, its dream-like dust'. The world of matriarchy, often enough acoustically evoked through whale sounds, and visually present in the full-breasted primordial bodies of women (Klytaimnestra, Elektra, Kassandra) challenge the patriarchal one that one hardly feels resurrected. Witnesses are the dead carcass of a billy-goat representing Agamemnon which, in *Choephori*, constantly needs to be reanimated through a bellows-like mechanic device and also the aimless wanderings of Orestes, the anti-hero, who must be reminded by Pylades (dressed as a clown) what part he is supposed to play. A mechanic arm that, in constant contractions, makes pumping and smacking noises, must help anorectic Orestes to hold the dagger that is bound to kill the mother (see figures 21.1 and 21.2).

On the one hand, this production surely is 'anti-affirmative' in the way that Anton Bierl proposed to call some productions of Oresteia 'negative, critical and pessimist', like Luca Ronconi's (1972) and Franco Parenti's (1985) productions (Bierl 1996: 77–106; 2004: 111–49). Indeed, on a political and cultural level, this trilogy does not lead to a new compromise (birth of democracy, progress, installation of a human court) nor to Hegelian synthesis, but, on the other hand, it cannot be completely discussed in a paradigm that only tries to recuperate and defend western unitary thinking. Asking ourselves whether the future can be considered a better place to live in, able to avoid the blood-shedding of the past, fits in the first paradigm. However, questions like the following ones, challenge it. The processes on the stage, do they continue to build upon the traditional 'humanist' interpretation of 'classics' (a world heritage in a never ending process of human emancipation, progress and expanding democracy, a world under 'construction') or do they radically question their organizing principles and ideological underpinnings (a world in 'deconstruction')? What kind of physical bodies have been included and excluded in the formation of this culture? (Butler, 1993) What hierarchies have we been using ever since our foundational stories have been preparing them for us? (Leonard 2005) And is there a 'beyond' in our traditional (mythical) ways of conceiving ourselves as western subjects (Pollock 2006; Leonard 2006)?

This *Orestea* is a world in constant metamorphosis and flux through the use of many intertexts and references, both from literary and visual sources: Hermann Melville's *Moby-Dick or The Whale* (1851), Jakob Bachofen's *Das Mutterrecht* (1861), Lewis

Figure 21.1   Beginning of the second act of *Choephoroi*. From left to right: Pylades,
(wearing a steeple-crowned clown's hat), Clytemnestra (lying on a bed), Orestes (trying out
the mechanical arm that will help him to kill Clytemnestra and Aegisthus) and a resurrected
billy-goat (referring to Agamemnon). Photograph courtesy of Sociètas Raffaello Sanzio ©
Sociètas Raffaello Sanzio

Carroll's *Alice's Adventures in Wonderland* (1865), Antonin Artaud's *Le théâtre et
son double* (1938), Michel Foucault's *Surveiller et Punir* (1975), Hermann Nitsch's
'splatter painting' and his depiction of Dionysian ceremonies and, of course, Pablo
Picasso's *Guernica* (1937). On top of that, one experiences an alienating and dis-
orienting manipulation of stage, sound and time, a frightening exploitation and mixing of human and animal bodies, and finally a staging of the death of traditional
language and representation (Artaud's disturbing use of heterogeneous kinds of languages, his '*glossolalia*'; Carroll's *Jabberwocky*). Ultimately, the unseen combination
of all these devices try to stimulate and start up a renewed interaction between the
spheres of reason and non-reason and prepare for a new western sensitivity. Its nomadic
design shows a plurality of possible worlds and the price it costs of remaining included
in one and the same. Yet, the overall atmosphere of amazement and mystery that
reigns throughout the whole production does not get resolved at the end. The skel-
eton of the trilogy is clearly recognizable, its three parts are staged, though in different degrees of expansion and reduction, but at the same time, something totally
new has arisen.

Figure 21.2 *Choephoroi*. Second act. Pylades (standing) and Orestes (sitting), in trying out the mechanical arm/device that will help Orestes to perform the killing of Aegisthus and Clytemnestra. Photograph courtesy of Socìetas Raffaello Sanzio © Socìetas Raffaello Sanzio

Giulio Cesare *(1997)*

Julius Caesar staged as a victim, rather than a winner, this is the underlying idea in this production where the real winners were: language, rhetoric and the unrepresentable. In this 'reworking' of Shakespeare's tragedy (and a number of Latin historians), in fact a drastic reduction of them, the Socìetas focuses on the question of political power and the danger of using it, of being misused by it, and hence on the constitutive ambiguity of rhetorical persuasion and its perennial appeal throughout history. No doubt a tragic topic, just as well as the warning that sons never can kill fathers without being caught into the same nightmare and lust for power. Caesar, captured and seduced by the uncontrollable and prodigious machinery of power, becomes an icon for all those who are equally trapped in the labyrinthine paths of language that end up in producing power. These rhetorical skills, the external political dress where all words are bound to get lost in, always rely upon a sophisticated technology, and for the Castelluccis the next (postdramatic) step was to question both the physical origins of language and the materiality of the staged bodies with the aid of sophisticated (medical) technology. Part I staged the public arena, the rhetorical empire where the characters are supposed to play their part; part II revealed the dark side of repressed emotions and a generalized feeling of uncertainty. But probably these topics were not what really was at stake, not the reason why this production will always be remembered as a shocking experience, as a part of theatre history. What fascinated and terrified the audience was the physical state and the choice of the actors, not professional ones, as always. Marcus Antonius, who was supposed to deliver the most famous of all monologues, was played by an actor who was recently tracheotomized, Cicero by an extremely obese individual ('he weighs 240 kilo', the dramaturgical notes mention), Caesar by a age-old little man, 'an authentic albino', Cassius and Brutus by two anorectic actors (who were relieved in the second act by two anorectic girls). Both Brutus and Cicero served an additional purpose, their bodies being used for a scrupulous analysis of the organic source of words. In the notes which served as a programme 'Cacophony for a staging: *Giulio Cesare*', Castellucci (1997a) explained that the actor playing Brutus introduced an endoscopy inside one of his nostrils, a device that

> allows to see the backward journey of the voice until reaching the threshold of the vocal chords. A central projection will allow to see the throat from which the voice comes out: as if, in the theatre, the proscenium would become a mouth, hence allowing us to see, on its bottom, the vocal chords of the same theatre, so that we are enabled to reach a literality which becomes vertigo. As a matter of fact, the image seen by the spectator leads to the total coincidence between the word and its vision (the vision of its carnal origin) and produces bewilderment because one doesn't really know which is the prevailing part: the word spoken or the sight of the letter.

At the same time, Brutus manipulated his voice 'breathing helium to increase high voice frequencies to the maximum'. And as in so many other of his productions, attempts were made here to bridge the differences between inside/outside and being/becoming, to reject the idea of a stable and fixed Self and to explore prelinguistic experience versus conceptualizing efforts. Rhetoric was studied in its literally inhabitation and colonizing of the body, from the moment that endoscopic devices visualized the vocal chords to the time that rhetorical effects really were produced on audiences. This was also a sophisticated way to go back, once again, to the origin of things and an invitation to the spectator to reconsider the story of his personal and collective genesis, although not in a positivistic sense. Indeed, the bodily metamorphosis through which Cicero goes (extreme corporeal excess, a birdlike mask, white gloves and leather horseshoes) and the extreme anorexia of Brutus and Cassius which reduce them to walking skeletons cannot be explained and situated in any naturalistic or positivistic perspective. What you see on the stage transcends and defies all your expectations and has been studied as examples of the threatening 'sublime': when, at the end of the second act, time slows down drastically, and Cassius stumbles around in an apocalyptic landscape, reduced to an already vanishing body, waiting to throw himself in his sword, moments of hesitation impose themselves on the spectator. This nightmare, by no means to be retraced in the world we know, signals the terror of the unknown and the threat of the unimaginable. The sublime that Kant with much persuasion wanted to divest of its terrifying dimensions in order to restore the forces of reason, was fully accepted as a temporary blackout by Lyotard, who called it 'the unrepresentable within representation itself' (Lyotard 1984: 81). As Luk Van den Dries mentions in his article on 'The sublime body':

> Unlike Kant, Lyotard situates the encounter with the sublime within artistic avant-garde practices. This encounter is geared towards putting the viewer in touch with 'le différend'. The sublime is thus ultimately threatening, frightening and irritating because it deprives us of certainty, it dismantles our consciousness, and opens up the shock of the new.
>
> (Van den Dries 2002: 86)

Giulio Cesare, a production based upon the fluidity of bodily presences, a series of tableaux questioning and confronting the western 'unimaginable', ends by putting the western condition into a crisis, but reintroduces, at the same time, some scary dimensions (human vulnerability and desire to dominate) which started up the oldest Greek tragedies.

Tragedia Endogonidia *(2002–2004)*

However, Raeffaello Sanzio's major project is their *Tragedia Endogonidia*, a series of eleven tragedies staged all over Europe in a three-year period, from Cesena 2002 (each episode is named after the initial letter of the city in which it is presented, hence C.#01) to Cesena 2004 (C.#11), over Avignon, Berlin, Brussels, Bergen, Paris, Roma, Strasbourg, London and Marseille, a nomadic enterprise in the most literal sense of the word. The notion 'Endogonidia' itself belongs to the world of microbiology and refers to the most basic forms of life which have the possibility of internal procreation without sex and this coexistence allows them to reproduce at infinitum, i.e. without a life of suffering and desire, mainly through a division of itself by itself. An excellent oxymoron and name for a theatrical project, since *Tragedia Endogonidia* contains the sharpest possible opposition between the finiteness of human life and infinity without an ending. A perfect illustration too of the tragic struggle of the hero who is bound to die after a life of desire and blindness and till the bitter end fights his biological condition, thinking that it is immortal. From the very start of this project, Castellucci wanted to examine the problematic nature of tragedy today, without staging any particular myth or allowing a chorus to participate. Is contemporary tragedy possible in a world without social and religious cohesion, without heroes who stand up and translate the opinions of a political community? The contemporary postmodern and late capitalistic world that thrives upon extreme forms of fragmentation and specialization is hardly compatible with the Greek community that shared and discussed a set of common values, a necessary condition to become a member of it. Yet, since this tragic feeling has influenced so deeply the western consciousness, in Castellucci's opinion, it became part of our psyche and can easily be translated in other aesthetic forms. Ever since, the gods of the Greek tragedy have been replaced by more anonymous powers: they are staged as an autonomous arrow-machine in Cesena and Bergen, a mechanical tree in London raping an actor, a car falling down from the ceiling in Paris, a massive military vehicle bursting into the theatre and threatening the audience in Strasbourg, powerful and easily recognizable images that free us from the dominance of all words and signs that are asked to become invisible again. In order to create a universal language that aims at restoring fundamental emotional answers, Castellucci restricts himself to a number of basic and recurring characters and themes that illustrate a limited number of tragic parameters. They constitute an open system that does not cease to transform during three years of production and therefore was presented at every occasion in different stages of its evolution. Mostly they questioned notions like time, space, tradition, death, destiny and dealt with the consequences of the 'scandal of being born'. A nearly geometric drawing of a man and a woman, present in every programme book, an image that was part of a golden disc that has been sent into space on board of a Voyager, carries the same undertone: this is us, this is how we look, we are embarked for a trip of which we do not know the purpose and the end. This is theatre about displaced humanity, about humans who constantly are teased by processes of time and duration, and especially by the enigmas of beginning and ending, birth and death, initiating language and being swallowed by it. It stages very archaic bits and pieces of the Western imagination and brings them along in cosmopolitan cities that do not have any longer an essence nor identity.

This nomadic theatre, in the absence of mythical stories, heavily relies upon the physical body, both of actors and public, generating all the time elliptic tracks between stage and audience, circuits and contact-zones between heterogeneous participants, obliging each member of the audience to consider that he/she is bound to become the hero of his/her own tragedy. Often enough, critics noticed that these kind of exchanges ended in a sphere of collective intimacy and vulnerability, people not knowing what happened to them, but always aware that something unseen and unexperienced did happen. Or, as Lyn Gardner mentioned in *Guardian* (15 May 2004): Castellucci is 'a director whose unsettling, astonishing, enraging theatre is often as difficult to watch as a train crash, but cannot be easily ignored'. Definitely no reassuring theatre, rather a trip into the completely unknown, a wet mop slapped into your face, a possibility to awake and rediscover yourself.

FURTHER READING

For a general introduction into the postmodern/postdramatic climate: Auslander 1997; Fuchs 1996; Malkin 1999; Pavis 1992; Watt 1998.

Some interesting studies on the body and physicality: Bleeker 2002; Fischer-Lichte et al. 2001; Gallop 1998; Schneider; 1997.

Concerning the importance of Artaud and the abject: Graver 1995.

CHAPTER TWENTY-TWO

Aristophanes between Israelis and Palestinians

Nurit Yaari

In September 2002 the Khan Theatre of Jerusalem performed *The War Over Home*, a satirical comedy written by Ilan Hatzor 'in the footsteps of Aristophanes'. The comedy's events take place in Jerusalem in the year 2012. After years of fighting, the country is struck by unemployment, poverty and hunger. In the first scene, a cabinet meeting, the prime minister's assistant presents his report:

> Two suicide bombers set themselves off near Netanya, bullets were shot across the Tel-Aviv Haifa highway, mortars fell on the road to Jerusalem, road mines exploded in Wadi Ara, on the way to the lake of Galilee, Katyusha missiles landed in Beer-Sheva, and rockets were fired at Haifa and Tzfat. In Ramat-Gan, The Safari's fence was hit; hungry lions and tigers devoured three residents of the neighbourhood.
>
> (scene 1)

Within the framework of this apocalyptic vision, *The War Over Home* reviews different reactions to this catastrophic situation: On the political national and international level, the reactions are of a 'more of the same' variety: The Israeli prime minister activates the army, his ministers seek the perfect salesman to be elected prime minister and choose a successful fishmonger from Jerusalem's market, while the Swedish mediator skips unsuccessfully between Ramallah and Jerusalem, vainly trying to persuade the respective leaders to sign an accord. On the social level, a popular protest is led by the energetic Dr. Lizy Strata, who decides to follow her ancient role model and put an end to the war by declaring a sex strike. On the private/personal level, Malkitzedek, an Israeli citizen of Jerusalem, decides to sign a 'personal peace treaty' with the Palestinians. Malkitzedek resides with his wife and child in a street proximate to the border between Israeli and Palestinian neighbourhoods; he and his family have been living flat on the floor for the past several years, making sure that their heads do not stick above the window frame for fear of snipers.

From this colourful amalgam we can differentiate the plots of three Aristophanic comedies – *The Acharnians, Knights* and *Lysistrata*. In all of these comedies, Aristophanes attacks the Athenian civil and military leadership (Kleon and his circle) for their deceitfulness and their imperialist gluttony, the Athenian citizens for their naïve belief in the empty promises of demagogues and the peace ambassadors for the decadence of their lifestyles and neglect of their public functions. By means of his legendary characters, Dicaeopolis, Demos and Lysistrata, Aristophanes is urging Athenians to protest against the corruption of the politicians who gain from war and to transform their wish for peace into action at all cost.

Following Aristophanes' political comedy, the events represented in *The War Over Home* reflect real events that transpired in Jerusalem in 2002. With the *Second (Al-Aqsa) Intifada* (*shaking off*, an Arabic term for uprising) in the background, suicide bombers exploded in buses and shopping centres, cars blew up in streets and passer-by were stabbed on a daily basis throughout Israeli cities. This horror was the everyday reality of Jews and Arabs, Israelis and Palestinians. By locating the events in 2012 and constructing the plot in a reiterative mode of 'eternal return', created by repeating the first and last scenes, *The War Over Home* emphasized the fact that nothing had been done in the last ten years to alter the stalemate that characterized 2002. Furthermore, its plot intoned that the daily agonies of un-employment, poverty and despair would not change in the next ten years, or the next hundred years unless a clear change took place, the responsibility for which the play assigned to its Israeli spectators.

Aristophanes had a very clear anti-war agenda and his political comedies declared it with a mélange of fantasy, vulgarity, blunt satire and acute criticism (Foley 1988: 33–47; Goldhill 1991: 167–222; Slater 2002: 5–8). In *The War Over Home*, the Khan Theatre group follows suit by mixing critical analysis of the Israeli–Palestinian conflict with grotesque representations of the lived reality, by ridiculing Israel's sacred cows – the Holocaust, the Army, the Family – and by suggesting a dream-like escape, the possibility of a better world, a peaceful, friendly, euphoric co-habitation of the civic space. Twentieth-century Israeli actors thus sing in the middle of the perform-ance an ironic song of apology in the form of Aristophanes' parabasis (in my trans-lation from the modern Hebrew text):

> We use this opportunity to notify the audience
> that they watch the performance at their own risk.
> We are just actors working in this theatre,
> working to earn a living.
> All the characters are fictional,
> any resemblance to living people
> or to real events is accidental.
> We, the actors, and all the creative members of the cast and crew,
> are firmly opposed to this play
> and hereby condemn the aberrant allusions to the present reality.
> We are sure that the performance does not reflect
> the people, the army and the Israeli reality.
> But this is what happens when you rely on plays
> written by a non-Jew, a Goy, Aristophanes.

In this chapter I am analyzing *The War Over Home* as an adaptation and production that follows Aristophanes' dramatic strategy – combining fantastic intrigue with contemporary analysis of society and politics – in reaction to the 2002 situation of the Israeli–Palestinian conflict. As appropriate to any discussion of current treatments of Aristophanes' comedies, this chapter combines theatre with politics. In order to help non-Israeli, non-Palestinian readers understand the choices that guided the dramaturgical strategy of the performance, I need to describe the socio-political context motivating *The War Over Home*. This involves a summary of the Israeli–Palestinian conflict and a description of the political/educational role played by the Israeli theatre since the 1967 war. The latter role, I believe, helped pave the way not only to productions such as *The War Over Home* but also to the transformation of Israeli public opinion, a change that eventually brought about the disengagement in Gaza and the emergence of a moderate political party at the centre of Israel's political map.

Aristophanes on the Israeli Stage

This was not the first time that Aristophanes was 'recruited' for the Israeli stage within the framework of political protest. Since 1948, Israelis and Arabs have lived in a persistent 'state of war'; it is no surprise, then, that Greek comedies were performed in Israel as part of a cultural discourse focusing on hopes for peace.

The first Aristophanic comedy to be performed in Israel was *Lysistrata*, at the Habima Theatre in Tel Aviv in 1958. The play was directed by the Greek director Minos Volonakis, with stage design and costumes by Nikolas Georgiadis. According to the Israeli press, Volonakis was invited to the Habima Theatre after a successful *Lysistrata* he directed in London and Oxford. The Israeli theatre critics wrote extensively on the excellent Hebrew translation (from the English adaptation Volonakis had used in London) done by Nissim Aloni, a promising young playwright and translator. They lauded the magnificent stage design, the joyful Greek songs and dances, the funny jokes, the vulgar movements and the theatricality of the two choruses but ignored the political issues dealt with in the play. For them this ancient comedy, a memento from a far away culture, offered the contemporary Israeli spectator a possible identification with longings for peace. Only David Ben Gurion, Israel's first Prime Minister, emphasized the important connection between past and present, Athens and Jerusalem when, after the premiere, he wrote the following in the Habima guest book: 'Although Lysistrata is Greek, she carries in her the dream of the prophets of Israel. This is the connection between Jerusalem and Athens. The dream will become a reality.'

The second staging of *Lysistrata*, was directed in 1968 by Oded Kotler, a young Israeli actor and director, at the Cameri Theatre in Tel Aviv. The performance took place at a very important political moment: after the victory of the Israeli army over the armies of Egypt, Jordan and Syria in the 1967 war, and the beginning of the peace talks with Egypt. The production emphasized both themes: the war between the sexes and the protest against war. But most of all it reflected the security felt by most Israelis at the war's conclusion and a victory that appeared to erase all threats to the survival of the State of Israel. The play's huge success was due to the combination of an excellent Hebrew translation (Nissim Aloni's translation was used again) fantastic costumes, witty movements and clever dances by the two choruses and the hilarious eroticism of Lysistrata's followers. *Lysistrata*'s 1968 stage image represented a gender-based longing for peace rather than a political satire ridiculing the figures and movements that prevent negotiation and mutual understanding. Aristophanes' *Peace*, directed that same year by Arye Saks at the Bimot Theatre in Tel Aviv, followed the same path: A joyful comedy offering a dreamlike vision of a peaceful future.

By 2000, with *Lysistrata 2000* performed at the Cameri Theatre of Tel Aviv, it had become clear that *Lysistrata* had replaced her political muscle and military temper with a celebration of women's emancipation. This ancient political comedy was now a sort of new comedy, a vehicle delivering mild bourgeois criticism. Set in the glamorous world of TV and the media, the adaptation written by Anat Gov and directed by Edna Mazya brought the play to contemporary Tel Aviv with vivid Hebrew and high society costuming. The jokes centred on women's liberation and the meta-theatrical opportunities offered by a hi-tech society. In one of the more creative meta-theatrical moments of the performance, the ringing of a cellular phone belonging to the actress playing Lysistrata broke into the fictional world – her baby-sitter was asking her to leave the stage and come home as her sick child was calling for her. After a moment of deliberation, the actress called her husband, an actor who played the role of the Spartan general, and persuaded him to go home to care for their son. As the actor left the stage, the actress resumed her role of Lysistrata and the performance continued. From the interviews given by the director and the adaptator as well as from the theatre critics and the spectators' reception of the performance, it was clear that *Lysistrata 2000* had no political issues to address, no social injustices to decry. The women and men on stage, representatives of healthy, well-dressed, well-fed Tel Aviv bourgeoisie, could be walking in today's Athens, Paris or New York; any hint of a socio-political context had been removed from the stage.

In 2002, when negotiations between Israelis and Palestinians had come to a standstill and the welcomed retreat from Lebanon had not realized its hopes for peace along the northern border, when the second *Intifada* again brought the conflict directly into the heart of Israel and the TV cameras focused on decimated civilians and Israeli tanks plying Palestinian roads, despair replaced disillusion. It was clear that Aristophanes was needed once more but that *Lysistrata* alone was inadequate for the task. A more complex plot had to be created that would capture the complexity of the current socio-political reality. In my role as the artistic consultant and dramaturg of the Khan Theatre in Jerusalem, I proposed to the theatre's artistic director and its principal director, Michael Gurevitch, to weave together several of Aristophanes' plots into a multilayered plot that will reflect the complexity of the situation. The Khan thus embarked on a peace project – *The War Over Home*. Gurevitch assembled a creative group of artists whose members were the playwright Ilan Hatzor, the poet-journalist Eli Mohar and the composer Yoni Rechter. As they started to work on the adaptation, Gurevitch began working with the Khan's actors according to his own theatrical method, a 'collective writing' of the performance through active participation of the actors and the creative team assembled for the production. It was clear that *The War Over Home* would incorporate the adaptation of scenes of three plots – *The Acharnians* (1–357; 729–835), *Knights* (1–615) and *Lysistrata* (1–253) – that exhibited different aspects of the protest against war. Other events were subsequently woven into the basic thematic/narrative material. The decision to intertwine three Aristophanic comedies was born of the wish to learn how to ease the audience into understanding that a change of mentality precedes the success of any negotiations meant to bring peace.

Multilayered Plot as Metaphor

The dramatic principle of creating a multilayered plot, employed in the building of *The War Over Home*, emerged from the need to reflect the complexity of the socio-political and cultural context of its representation. This multilayered dramatic plot-structure mirrored the kaleidoscopic, multicolour nature of the life in Jerusalem: the accumulation of historical, religious, architectural, social, political layers had turned into the overall metaphor of the production. In the short space of this chapter, I would like to demonstrate how this multilayered structure was used in the Khan Theatre's peace project to reflect the complexity that characterized the Israeli–Palestinian conflict as it did Israel's contemporary environment.

A short visit to the building housing the Khan Theatre, amidst its surroundings, can demonstrate the symbolic contribution of the Khan Theatre's architecture to the idea of a multilayered performance and illuminate the spectators' experience when entering the theatre, sitting in the auditorium and watching the play. The Khan Theatre is situated on a hill opposite the south-western wall surrounding the Old City of Jerusalem. It is situated in Abu Tor, a neighbourhood located on the road leading to Jerusalem's southern quarters. The Khan Theatre resides in a nineteenth-century Ottoman structure that served as an inn (literally, a *khan* is the Arabic term for inn) for travellers, especially at night when the Old City's gates were closed (see figure 22.1). The building itself was built over the ruins of a Crusader hostelry dating from the eleventh century. The Khan was renovated after 1968, as part of the development programme, initiated by Teddy Kolek (Jerusalem's almost legendary Mayor 1965–93), which pushed through a vision of ancient buildings taking on new cultural contents. The Khan's gala opening took place on 28 October 1967, and the director Philip Diskin was invited with his student's theatre group, 'The Circle', to perform on the renovated stage (see figure 22.2). In 1973 the well-known British director, Michael Alfreds, was appointed artistic director of the Khan Theatre and brought with him a group of dynamic young actors. Since then, the Khan Theatre has established itself as one of the most important creative theatres in Israel.

A view of the building shows that, despite its renovation, the Khan has clearly retained the architectural characteristics of an Ottoman inn, with its large arches and heavy columns. These characteristics mark the performative possibilities of the auditorium and stage, requiring special attention by theatre directors, stage designers, choreographers, actors and spectators alike.

Figure 22.1 An outside view of the Khan Theatre, Jerusalem, before reconstruction.
Photograph: Khan Theatre

No spectator visiting the Khan in Jerusalem can ignore its architecture, a style that appears to reflect the multicultural composition of the theatre's audience. Nor can any spectator ignore the composite of cultures and identities that the audience brings to the Israeli theatre every night. Because Israel is an immigrant-absorbing nation, the audience is generally composed of the native-born and new immigrants from as far as Russia or Ethiopia, religious residents of Mea Shearim (an ultra-Orthodox Jewish neighbourhood in Jerusalem) or secular couples from the newly developed western parts of the city. Settling down in their seats are spectators coming from the surrounding villages and small towns, settlers from the occupied territories, students from the Hebrew University and Palestinians from Jerusalem and nearby towns and villages (although their number declined during the first and second *Intifada*). So, we can see that every performance can be experienced as a multicultural event, a fact that the directors working in the Khan Theatre must take into account when planning their productions.

When we leave the theatre to walk around the Abu Tor neighbourhood, either gazing at its houses or extending our view to the whole of Jerusalem, we can see the same diversity everywhere – multiple layers of buildings in architectural styles belonging to different periods, objects and pieces of art reminiscent of cultures that left indelible marks on the country's culture and consciousness, with costumes, sounds

THE JERUSALEM KHAN THEATRE

GALA PREMIERE

OCTOBER 28, 1967

Figure 22.2 Design of the reconstructed stage of the Khan Theatre, Jerusalem. From the programme for the Gala Premiere. Photograph: Khan Theatre

and smells intermingling. The Khan Theatre is, in many ways, a juncture of the past and present, the holy and profane, contrast and complementarity.

A Multifaceted Conflict

For the historical layers of the Israeli–Palestinian conflict we have to start digging until we reach the Balfour Declaration (2 November 1917). In this document, the British promised the establishment of a 'national homeland' for Jews in Palestine, then under British rule (the period of the British Mandate). Space does not permit a thorough description of the events leading up to September 2002, when *The War Over Home* premiered, but I will nevertheless indicate several crucial milestones of the conflict in order to map the socio-political context.

On 29 November 1947 the United Nations decided on the division of the western part of the land between the Jordan River and the Mediterranean sea into two states – a Jewish State and an Arab state (leaving aside Jerusalem and Bethlehem to be ruled by the United Nations). The leaders of the Arab countries in the area objected to the decision and tried to get a hold of the whole area. Fierce attacks started on 30 November 1947, but grew more violent after the departure of the British army (14 May 1948) and the establishment of the state of Israel. By 15 May 1948, the armies of five Arab surrounding countries – Egypt, Jordan, Syria, Iraq and Lebanon – launched an attack on the Israeli state. The war lasted until 10 March 1949 and ended by ceasefire agreements (and not by peace treaties). The conclusion of this war which the Israelis named 'the War of Independence' and the Palestinians – the *Nakba*, or calamity, initiated two events in its wake: the establishment of the independent State of Israel, a Jewish state and home to the world's Jewry on the one hand and the creation of the Palestinian refugee problem on the other. Those refugees had either fled their homes during the war's combats, or were driven out of their villages by the conquering Israeli army. In consequence, individuals and extended families were gathered into refugee camps located in the neighbouring Arab countries; from the camps' squalid hovels as well as urban minarets, their leaders promising to take vengeance and hasten the return home.

Between 1948 and 1967, the Arab leadership in the countries surrounding Israel – Lebanon, Syria, Jordan and Egypt – added the Palestinian problem to their anti-Israel agenda. The 1967 ('Six Day') war changed the logistics of these campaigns when Israel captured territories from the attacking armies: from Syria (the Golan Heights), Jordan (Judea and Samaria) and Egypt (Sinai and Gaza). As a result, several Palestinian refugee camps were incorporated into the new borders of greater Israel. Israel soon faced two fronts: neighbouring Arab countries from the outside and the Palestinian refugees from the inside.

The Yom Kippur war (1973) and the Lebanon war (1982) together with the political stalemate that followed the euphoria of an illusory peace, sparked two Palestinian civilian revolts – the two *Intifadas* – against the Israeli occupation: The first *Intifada*, also known as *the war of stones*, took place between 1987 and 1993. It constituted an ongoing string of violent confrontations between Palestinians and Israelis, cut short only by the Oslo Accords, signed in 1995, which established the Palestinian National Authority. The second *Intifada*, entitled the *Intifada al-Aqsa*, began in 2000. It was triggered by Ariel Sharon's highly provocative visit to the esplanade of the Mosques during the hours of Muslim prayer. The second *Intifada* gave voice to Palestinians disillusion with the Oslo Accords and the negotiations between the Israelis and Palestinians, stalled over Israeli's denial of the refugees' 'right of return' to their original homes within pre-1948 Israel. The *Intifada* was characterized by escalated violence, with stones replaced by machine-guns and, eventually, mortars fired on Israeli settlements from Palestinian territory. Yet, the most devastating aspect of the second *Intifada* was the use of suicide bombers as a standard tactic in the Palestinian's strategy against Israel.

In September 2002, *The War Over Home* was performed with the second *Intifada* raging in the background. Yet, the *Intifada* was only the obvious layer of a monumental iceberg, constructed by tragedy upon tragedy: Two peoples living on the same land, which both called 'home,' sharing fractions of everyday existence yet diverging in religion, history and interpretation of the events. The perception of this being a zero-sum game, where one people's gain was the other's loss, inflamed the hostility. A historical paradox had arisen: Israel's creation as the home of the Jewish refugees, suffering a history of violent discrimination and persecution, had transformed Palestinians into homeless refugees. By returning to their home land, the Jews had driven out much of the Palestinian people from their own homes. While the wandering Jew had finally established roots, he had uprooted Palestinians from their farms, urban residences and businesses. Victims for the last two thousand years, Jews had become persecutors. This problematic state of affaires, known to each and every member of the theatre audience and interpreted according to his/her politics, underlies the satirical aspects and the comic situations so explicit in the performance of *The War Over Home*.

Israeli Theatre in Its Socio-political Context

Israeli theatre exhibits very tight linkage to its socio-political context. The first canonized Israeli play, *He Walked through the Fields*, performed in the Cameri Theatre in Tel Aviv in May 1948, presented the emerging Israeli society as a blend of 'old' Jews (those who came from Europe) and 'new' Jews (Israeli-born farmers and soldiers) against the background of the Independence war (Shamir 1959). On stage, Uri, the young hero, wearing his uniform to go to battle and leaving his new immigrant sweetheart, dies in a just war for national independence and statehood. The young hero on stage reflected the young spectators who came to the auditorium still in uniform, home on their short leaves from the front. Following the waves of immigration that deluged the state during the following two decades, theatre became an important instrument for inculcating the values, structure and ideology of emerging Israeli society (Ben-Zvi 1996; Abramson 1998).

It was precisely against this hegemonic ideology that Hanoch Levin, Israel's most prominent and prolific playwright to date, aimed his fierce political satires. *You, Me and the Next War* 1968; *Ketchup* 1969; *The Queen of the Bathtub* 1970 were written in the aftermath of the 1967 victory (Brown 1996). In these three cabarets, Levin questioned the notions of 'a just war' and 'a war for survival' by attacking all the sacred values that the Israeli state had extolled since its inception. Placed on the stage were generals who profited from war, ministers who built their careers on corpses, rituals sanctifying needless self-sacrifice and self-righteous Jews humiliating Arab labourers who were slaving away at menial trades. In a series of short sketches and songs, with a backdrop constructed of violent theatrical images, Levin projected a shameless society, drunk with arrogance, a mockery of the moral society meant to realize the Zionist dream.

Levin did not stop at political satire. Until his untimely death in 1999, he wrote fifty-eight plays in different styles and genres – comedies, tragicomedies, burlesques, mythical plays and tragedies (Levin 2003). He continued throughout to criticize Israel's hegemonic ideology(ies) while attempting to preach the importance of tolerance, acceptance of the other and co-existence (Levy and Yaari 1999).

During the 1970s and 1980s, another branch of socio-political theatre emerged at the Haifa Municipal Theatre under the artistic direction of Oded Kotler. Its directors, actors and playwrights gathered around Nola Chilton, an American director and acting teacher who had immigrated to Israel in 1964 and joined Kotler's troupe (Ben Zvi 2006). Haifa's Municipal Theatre became the centre for young playwrights having a critical bent, such as Yehoshua Sobol's *The Night of the 20th* (1974) *Weininger's Night* (1982), *The Palestinian Girl* (1985), *Jerusalem's Syndrome* (1987), Hillel Mittlepunkt's *The Moncky* (1975), *The Roof* (1975), *Deep Water* (1976), *Bouba* (1982), Yaakov Shabtai's *The Spotted Tiger* (1974), *The Chosen* (1976), *Eating* (1979). One characteristic element of their dramaturgy was the use of events in Jewish history to analyze issues high on the current Israeli agenda: national identity, religion, the other within and others outside, and the Jewish communal structure in the past and present (Taube 1993; Kaynar 1996; Rokem 2000). The watershed spurring this altered perspective was the 1973 war, which provoked Israel's theatre to turn its gaze inwards, an act that helped acknowledge the legitimacy of the 'other', of Palestinians and their national goals. Performances appeared to be gaining voices for the left.

In the early 1980s, with the outbreak of the Lebanon war, another important dramaturgical direction emerged – the use of classical plays to raise political issues and express protest against the war which broke out on 5 June 1982. In the wake of the Sabra and Shatilla massacres, instigated by the Lebanese militia with Israel's tacit consent, a massive rally, known as the '400,000 Demonstration', was held in the plaza before the Tel Aviv Municipality building on 26 September 1982. The rally signalled broad-based protest against the war and Israel's right-wing government, which continued in numerous street demonstrations as well as on the Israeli stage. Following a long international tradition of reinterpreting and restaging Euripides' *The Trojan Women* to reflect contemporary strife, three major Israeli repertoire theatres mounted plays related to the Trojan war. On 19 February 1983, Habima, the National Theatre, opened a production of *The Trojan Women* based on Jean-Paul Sartre's adaptation of Euripides' play. Tel Aviv's Cameri Theatre followed on 16 February 1984, with its production of Hanoch Levin's *The Lost Women of Troy*, an adaptation conjoining Euripides' *the Trojan Women* and *Hecuba*. On 1 October 1984, the Haifa Municipal Theatre mounted yet a third interpretation, based on Jean Giraudoux's *La Guerre de Troie n'aura pas lieu (Tiger at the Gates)*. All three shared one target: the waging of a covert, intriguing assault on Israel's penchant for war as a solution to political problems (Levy and Yaari 1998).

In the same vein, other important performances were staged; *Waiting for Godot*, directed by Ilan Ronen at the Haifa Municipal Theatre in 1984, became a landmark in this dramaturgical direction. The key to the performance of *Waiting for Godot* resides in its setting, casting and site. In the Haifa performance, the tree was transformed into a piece of iron-reinforced concrete, basic material in Israel's construction industry, which was characterized by an Arab labour force, either Palestinians from the occupied territories or Israeli–Arabs; Gogo and Didi were conceived as Arab construction workers, with their roles played by the Arab–Israeli actors Makram Khuri and Youssuf Abu Warda; Lucky, adopting the dress and movement of an old Druze (a non-Muslim Arab ethnic group living in northern Israel) was played by Doron Tavori, a Jewish–Israeli actor; while Pozo was played by Ilan Toren, another Jewish–Israeli actor, who portrayed him as a colonial landlord. The production's site was a renovated Arab building in Wadi Salib, in the heart of Haifa's old Arab neighbourhood. The performance, played in both Hebrew and Arabic before Jewish and Arab audiences, was enormously successful.

In 1987, a production of Strindberg's *Miss Julie* provided the Haifa Municipal Theatre with another occasion for transferring a play about conflict from one venue to another. Gedalia Besser, the director, cast Arab–Israeli actors – Youssuf Abu Warda and Salwa Nakara – as the servants and an Jewish–Israeli actress, Leora Rivlin, as Miss Julie. This ethno-national element added to the conflicts between the sexes and between masters and servants that inform the original classic. Youssuf Abu Warda, the actor who played the role of Jean, spoke about the director's decision: 'As Jean, I am not just a servant who seduces a woman from the upper class – I am an Arab who touches a Jewish woman. The director chose me to play the part because among other things, he thought it is good for an Arab actor to play the servant of a Jewish woman. It allows the director to spoon feed the spectators with his interpretation of the play as an example of the relationship between Jews and Arabs, because in our society, Arabs are generally the servants and Jews are the masters' (Livne 1987).

It is important to note here that for actors, the Haifa Municipal Theatre, located in the centre of Haifa, a city characterized by excellent terms of coexistence between Muslims, Christians, Bahaïs and Jews, functions as a meeting place where negotiation and integration can take place. Since the late 1970s, Arab–Israeli actors such as Makram Churi, Youssuf Abu-Warda, Salwa Nakara and Mouhamad Bakri have found a place in the theatre's troupe, playing leading roles in classical and contemporary plays. Another theatre located in Haifa is El Meidan, an Arab speaking theatre performing classical and modern Arab plays. In the city of Jaffa, where the Arab–Jewish coexistence is also good, an Arab–Hebrew theatre was founded in 1998 bringing together Arab and Jewish actors to mount cabarets, performances and theatrical events in which they can share each other's life experiences and create an understanding between the two communities.

The War Over Home

The summary of the socio-political and cultural context helps to explain the dramaturgical strategies employed in *The War Over Home*. Although Aristophanes' comedy was a natural choice when it comes to a political satire against war, another important decision made was to interweave three of Aristophanes' plots with other local plots into a multilayered, multicoloured satirical comedy. This strategy was used in order to project an image of a multilayered socio-political context and a multifaceted political-religious-cultural conflict. In contrast to the complexity of the plots, very clean-cut, clear-line/distinctions divided the characters who took part in the dramatic events. Three groups cut across the eleven scenes: the first, those advocating peace – the Jewish family (Malkizedek, Ziona and Yarden, see figure 22.3), the Palestinian family (Zahi, Nadia and Nidal), Dr Lizy Strata and her women followers (see figure 22.4); the second, those profiting from the war – Israel's Prime Minister, his advisors and ministers, generals, settlers, the Knesset's porter, the fishmonger

Figure 22.3 Ziona and Yarden in their house on the borderline (scene 1 *The War Over Home*) Photographer: Gadi Dagon. Copyright: Khan Theatre

who, like so many poor in their ignorance, follow right-wing parties with their capitalist ideology, and Moshe, Ziona's brother, a small war profiteer; the third group is comprised of mediators who use negotiations intended to resolve tragedies for their personal gain – in this case, the Swedish and Palestinian mediators.

The names of the characters are also significant, being symbolic of their positions regarding war and peace: Malkitzedek, a biblical name (Genesis 14.18–20 and Psalms 110.4) is constructed of two words in the manner following Aristophanes' Dicaeopolis: 'Melech' (in Hebrew: king) and Tzedek (in Hebrew: justice = *dike*); his wife's name, Ziona, brings to mind the ancient name for Israel – 'Zion' and 'Zionism' and their son Yarden (in Hebrew: the Jordan river). Zahi (in Arabic: to flourish, thrive, to succeed) is a peace-loving Palestinian, who before the *Intifada*, worked with Malkitzedek. Zahi joins Malkitzedk with his wife Nadia (in Arabic: she who assembles the people) and their son Nidal (in Arabic: a combat with weapons).

The comic movement of the sub-plots stresses the different choices taken in the transformation from war to peace and the victory of the new order: On the national and international political level, the situation only deteriorates. The fishmonger who was elected prime minister does not function differently than his predecessor; he, too, activates the army as a solution for every conflict. On the social level, the popular anti-war sex protest fails because of another woman's stratagem: Facing Lizy

Figure 22.4   Lizy Strata and her followers demonstrating outside the Israeli parliament in *The War Over Home*. Photographer: Gadi Dagon. Copyright: Khan Theatre

Strata's sex strike, the right-wing, female minister of education declares that in order to maintain the fighting strength of the army's heroes, she is initiating an alternative movement – to provide men with free sex at any time and place! Thus only the private peace treaty promises a better future for Malkitzedek, Zahi and their families. Soon their garden flourishes with fruits and vegetables; when joined by the soldiers and the Swedish and Palestinian mediators, it blooms. Finally, as the plot develops during the nine months of Ziona's pregnancy, it ends with a universal symbol of happiness, love, and hope – the birth of a new baby, a baby of peace.

The overall impression made by the performance was that of a carnival. Using scenic practices common to the humble vagabond tradition, ten actors played twenty multinational, cross-gender roles, including the three choruses: the generals, the women and the Settlers. The stage space changed rapidly from the public to the private sphere: the prime minister's kitchenette, Malkizedek's household, the gate of the knesset (Israel's parliament) and its cafeteria, a west bank settlement, and the garden surrounding Malkitzedek's house. In the closing scene, which takes place in Malkitzedek's garden – the stage flourishes with green grass and roses (an idyllic space for the ideal peace) – Malkitsedk, Zahi and their families promise their spectators a better, more wonderful future.

Using Aristophanes' dramatic strategies, the Khan's peace project defined its socio-political goal as stimulating a change in the Israeli mentality. This strategy was meant to open audiences to a deeper reading of the political situation and to greater comprehension of the leadership's political impotence. It was likewise aimed at preparing spectators to accept negotiations and the eventual necessary concessions. Thus, *The War Over Home* criticized the Israeli public for its blindness regarding the regime's manipulation of the Jewish history of persecutions and the Holocaust, the government's corruption, the militarism expressed in national glorification of the Israel defence forces, and its indifference to the everyday sufferings of the Palestinians. But it did more: With the aid of Aristophanes' plots, comedy was used to focus on a fundamental aspect of Israeli individual identity – survival at all costs – and demonstrate that it is an essential human instinct, the right of every human being, superior to any nationalistic/chauvinistic ideology: Peace, in the sense of the absence of war, is of little value to someone who is dying of hunger or cold. It will not remove the pain of torture inflicted on a prisoner of conscience. It does not comfort those who have lost their loved ones in floods caused by senseless deforestation in a neighbouring country. Peace can only last where human rights are respected, where the people are fed, and where individuals and nations are free (Dalai Lama 1989).

FURTHER READING

Arab–Israeli conflict

Baily 1990; Brickerton and Klausner 1998; Goldschelder 2002; Grossman 2003; Lukacs 1992.

Israeli theatre

Ben Zvi 1996. Ezraty and Solomon 2001; Levin 2003; Levy and Yaari 1998; Taube 2004; Urian 1997; 1995; Yaari 2006.

Arab–Palestinian theatre

Akad 2004; Hamdan 2006; Ibrahim 2006; Mast 2000; Masarwi 2006; Nasser 2006; Snir 1995. Kotzamani 2006; *PAJ* 28/2: 19–41 for a number of short articles on Arabic performance; Siam 1995.

Jerusalem (history and architecture)

Kroyanker 1994; Safdie 1989.

PART VI

Film

CHAPTER TWENTY-THREE

Working with Film: Theories and Methodologies

Joanna Paul

It is now a number of years since the publication of Maria Wyke's *Projecting the Past: Ancient Rome, Cinema and History* (1997), a work of considerable importance not only to the study of the relationship between the ancient world and the cinema, but also to the field of classical reception as a whole. Though forays into this aspect of reception had previously been made with some success (Solomon 1978; Winkler 1991), Wyke's fascinating and informative account of how and why modern popular culture turns to antiquity presented new possibilities for understanding the cultural exchanges between ancient and modern. The study of 'Classics and film' thus became a prominent strand of our discipline as it evolved into the twenty-first century, in both teaching and research (vindicating a reviewer's observation that 'it is not the least merit of this [Wyke's] stimulating book that it gives a strong impulse to future research', Catrein 1999: 246).

Ten years on, the time is ripe to reflect upon what working with film has meant; what it has contributed to Classics and Ancient History, classical reception studies, and the wider humanities; and what it may achieve in the future. As such, this chapter will not provide detailed investigations of specific cinematic receptions of antiquity beyond the examples necessary to furnish my arguments, but neither will it be simply a literature review of publications. Rather, what follows will try to identify and objectively examine some features of the critical terrain, asking whether work on Classics and film to date has fulfilled expectations of what can and might be done; for, despite its apparent centrality, it is still not certain that we are doing enough to exploit the scholarly and interpretative potentialities of working with film. It has been remarked that 'film is a comparatively new area in reception research and the development of critical approaches and methods rigorously tailored to the medium are as yet embryonic' (Hardwick 2003a: 71). This discussion, then, will assess the contribution of this strand of reception studies to our wider understanding of both Classics and reception, in both a theoretical and a practical sense, offering suggestions for which approaches might be pursued more vigorously, and which may be of limited usefulness.

Using Film in Teaching and Learning

Any consideration of how and why classicists work with film must acknowledge the role it plays in a pedagogical context. The discussion here will be brief, deferring to Marianne McDonald's contribution to this section for a useful insight into film as a 'teaching tool' (see also Winkler 2001: 3–9; Wyke 2003: 432–3). But still, it is important to begin my own discussion by noting that film's popularity as reception material often seems to be driven by the frequency of its use in teaching (particularly in higher education). Its role here follows, broadly, two different methodologies. Films may be used as objects of study in their own right, in a course which asks students to consider cinematic antiquities *as receptions*, possibly following some of the research approaches to be discussed in the next section; or they may be incorporated into other courses as *illustrative* tools – a unit on Roman spectacle may turn to *Ben-Hur* (1959) as a way of suggesting what a Roman chariot race would have been like. The pitfalls of this latter approach hardly need spelling out: even an amateur student of reception recognizes that the modern work appropriates and refigures the ancient source or text for particular ends, and should never be taken at face value as an unmediated representation of, say, the chariot race, even when that reception can be praised for the degree of attention it apparently pays to the ancient evidence (as was the case with *Ben-Hur*, for example).

Still, this kind of practice is indicative of film's particular appeal – an appeal which makes it both attractive and problematic as an object of academic study. The cinematic medium, by nature vivid and often exciting, is able to engage the spectator in a way that texts, or static images, may not. It is tried and tested as a way of enlivening jaded students, but even the most careful scholar can also be seduced by film's pretence at providing a window onto the ancient world. For some, this superficial allure, this reliance on what may be dismissed as brash spectacle, is reason enough to lament the presence of film in our discipline. Behind such an objection often lurks one of the most fascinating and contentious issues that accompanies working with film – that of the perceived gulf between elite and popular culture (Wyke 1997: 3–8). Though we would now resist defining Classics and Ancient History as inherently an elite discipline, it is undeniable that it has been perceived as such for much of its history, and the traces of this attitude are not easily erased. Conversely, film is seen as the archetypal mass medium, and when we observe the renewal of popular interest in the ancient world in recent years, it is clear that film and television are the main conduits for this. So, it is suggested, teaching with film is no more than a kind of cynical marketing ploy: capitalizing on the popularity of films such as *Gladiator* (2000), we turn to cinema simply to lure students into our lecture theatres, distastefully diluting a once lofty subject. In his introduction to a recent collection which explores reception's uses in Classics, Charles Martindale finds it 'worrying' that Classics students may spend more time studying *Gladiator* than Dante (2006: 11). Though he is quick to insist that this is 'certainly not to criticize the study of film or even of popular culture', it is hard not to be struck by the traces of an exclusive, if not elitist, notion of the humanities in evidence here (and Christopher

Rowe's response to Martindale's position, at a Classical Association meeting, made precisely that point: Rowe 2005).

There are a number of ways of responding to this debate. First, we can question the relative values attributed to 'high' and 'low' culture, and ask why studying popular culture is in itself undesirable – especially since Classics has long incorporated the study of ancient 'popular culture', such as arena games. Second, we should examine our assumptions about different kinds of film. Some may criticize mainstream Hollywood productions such as *Gladiator*, whilst finding it acceptable to work with European arthouse films such as Jean-Luc Godard's *Le Mépris* (1963), or the adaptations of Greek tragedy by Pier Paolo Pasolini (*Edipo Re* (1967); *Medea* (1970)). Since defensible aesthetic judgements no doubt motivate such distinctions, in some cases, then they cannot be dismissed out of hand; but it is also likely that some objections to researching and teaching with certain films could be revealed as simple intellectual snobbery, and so themselves devalued. Finally, film's popularity must also make us question the dangerous assumption that the scholarly community enjoys a kind of 'ownership' of the ancient world and classical learning (Hardwick 2003a: 85). In each of these areas, the debate provokes strong reaction, but it is not the purpose of this discussion to offer a polemic in support of working with film. Rather, I suggest that we welcome these conflicts as opportunities to continually question and reassess our work. It is no bad thing if the study of cinematic receptions still has to justify its existence, for it is by rigorously demonstrating the value of such work that we can ensure its success. This is not to say that Classics and film work must implicitly or explicitly seek to appease the doubters, but a good dose of self-reflection is a useful shield against the dazzle of the silver screen.

Whilst we address these important questions about the value of cinematic material in our discipline, film's pedagogical role ensures that it maintains a prominent position in the wider study of classical reception, since it is in the classroom that the *demand* for film seems most acute. This has particular commercial implications: the question of publishing trends will recur shortly, but we can note here that one of the most recent Classics and film publications, *Big Screen Rome* (Cyrino 2005), is more a teaching aid or textbook than an academic monograph, coming complete with questions for discussion at the end of each systematic survey of a film. A clearly useful book, it confirms the popularity of courses which teach cinematic receptions of antiquity. The question remains, then, does teaching set the agenda for Classics and film? If so, does it in some way inhibit our ambitions? Or can we do more – do we *need* to do more? – with film in the research arena (if this can be distinguished from teaching, which it surely cannot wholly be) in order to drive classical reception study forward to new, perhaps unexpected, conclusions?

The Dynamics of Reception in Classics and Film

We must begin by assessing what has happened so far in the field of Classics and film studies overall. There has been, it seems, a kind of evolution which roughly corresponds to the increasingly ambitious and rigorous development of classical

reception study more generally. The earliest studies of cinematic receptions of antiquity were largely 'catalogue'-style projects, in line with the 'positivistic tendency at
the end of the twentieth century, tedious but probably necessary at that point, to
equate the classical tradition with cataloguing connections and listing influences'
(Kallendorf 2004: 294). Early works such as *The Ancient World in the Cinema*
(Solomon 1978, 2001) or *The Epic Film: Myth and History* (Elley 1984) are primarily concerned with providing a comprehensive record of all films which fit their
chosen parameters of discussion, demonstrated by the numerous titles appended in
the filmographies. (Smith 2003 and Hirsch 1978 take a similar approach.) There is
much to be valued in this method, not least because these studies provide incon-
trovertible evidence of the wealth of material that exists for the scholar of cinematic
receptions of antiquity. Useful information on areas such as a film's production
history or its critical reception is collected and made easily accessible, with care
also taken to present some observations on how the film relates to ancient source
material – but in general, the level of analysis is fairly superficial. Solomon discusses
the question of historical authenticity at some length (2001: 27–35), and Elley begins
with some valuable thoughts on the nature of the epic tradition in a cinematic context (1984: 9–16), but this does not set the tone for the work as a whole. Of course,
it would be quite wrong to criticize these works for not providing exhaustive explorations of the theoretical nature of cinematic receptions of antiquity, since this was
never their intention. And since they admirably succeeded in fulfilling what *was*
presumably their intention – there is no need to replace *The Ancient World in the
Cinema* (only, we might hope, to update it in the future) – we might simply acknowledge this as something of a reception study cul-de-sac, without denigrating the achievements of Solomon et al. It is, then, slightly worrying when certain elements of Classics
and film study seem content to continue with the cataloguing approach. Allen M.
Ward's contribution to the recent volume *Gladiator: Film and History* (Winkler 2004)
is a dry catalogue of all the historical 'errors' found in Ridley Scott's film – down
to the breed of Maximus' dog, which was anachronistically played by a German
Shepherd – with little analysis of why we might compile a list of these inaccuracies,
or why they might be there in the first place. Axel Sütterlin's 1996 comparison
of the *Satyricon* in Petronius and Fellini is also basically a methodical structural
analysis of the two works, with little insight offered as to why Fellini might have
changed aspects of the original text (Catrein 1999: 244–6).

Other examples of this kind of approach are, though, few in number, and the shift
towards a more critical, analytical methodology (asking ' "how?" and "why?" as well
as "who?", "what?" and "where?" ': Kallendorf 2004: 294) is amply demonstrated by
other contributors to the *Gladiator* volume. Martin Winkler and Kathleen Coleman
each provided carefully thought-out accounts of *why* historical authenticity should
matter (Coleman 2004) – or, indeed, why it may *not* matter to filmmakers or audiences (Winkler 2004). These kinds of studies are therefore indicative of the methodology which has arguably come to dominate Classics and film studies since the
publication of Wyke's *Projecting the Past*: that is, accounts of a particular example
(or a group of examples) of cinematic reception, often constructed as a focused case
study, and endeavouring to provide not only accessible narratives of the circumstances
of the film's production and its relationship to ancient material, but also to analyze

and explain in some depth the implications of the act of reception itself. So, for example, Maria Wyke (Wyke 1997) argues that the Hollywood epics of the mid-twentieth century were powerfully shaped by contemporary politics – the anxieties of the post-war period, or the Cold War – projected back into ancient narratives. Similar claims can be made for many of the articles in the edited volumes of the past few years (especially Joshel, Malamud and McGuire 2001; Winkler 2004).

The basic methodology of this strand of cinematic reception studies is generally to identify a film (or films) which have an appreciable link with the ancient world – usually through an ancient setting and/or the adaptation of an ancient text – and then to explore the film's relationship with that ancient material, not simply with the aim of listing similarities and differences between ancient and modern, but with the intention of understanding what the reception – the film – can tell us about the receiving culture's view of antiquity *and of itself.* In short, to what *uses* is antiquity being put in a modern context? In turn, we might ask what use this kind of inquiry has. The discipline of Classics and Ancient History itself, I would argue, has much to gain from this kind of scholarship. By exploring the relationship between a film such as *Gladiator* and the historical record, we are offered new ways of confronting an eternal problem in the historiography of the ancient world – the gaps in the evidence, and the negotiations between concepts of 'fact' and 'fiction' that are required to fill them. For example, Robin Lane Fox, the academic consultant for *Alexander* (2004), welcomed the fact that the film encouraged him to think differently about aspects of Alexander's life that he had previously taken for granted (in comments made on the DVD commentary). In more general terms, this kind of reception study provides Classics with plenty of rich – and often strikingly immediate and relevant – evidence of how the modern world relates to the ancient, a topic which is of the utmost importance not only for understanding the relevance of our academic pursuits to the world in which we live, but also for allowing us to reflect more deeply on how (and why) those pursuits are themselves shaped by our historical and cultural situation. How much is our view of Roman arena spectacle, say, shaped by its prominence in ancient world films? If we have watched *Troy* (2004), regardless of our judgement on the film, to what extent does it act upon our next reading of the *Iliad*?

This is where some of the weightier theoretical aspects of reception come into play, for the reception theorist would argue that our viewing of *Troy* inevitably will affect our next reading of the *Iliad*. The two-way dynamics of the act of reception – the capacity of a reception to not only be influenced by the 'earlier' text but also to reach back in time and in a sense reconfigure that text – is an accepted concept in reception theory (see Martindale 1993), but, I would argue, it ought to be given more credence by scholars of Classics and film than has hitherto been the case. This is not to say that all film reception work is governed by an outdated notion of reception as simple, unidirectional influence or inheritance: interestingly, some of the earliest work which linked Classics and film discussed ancient texts and other sources using the language of cinema (Malissard 1970; Mench 1969). Though they are patently anachronistic on one level, we can also view such accounts as a logical consequence of recognizing the two-way flow of reception. If we allow that cinematic receptions of antiquity can reach back and 'affect' antiquity too, then it is possible that we can find some mileage in describing, say, Homer as 'cinematic' (a concept by no means limited to these brief academic articles, as the poems of Christopher Logue demonstrate: that adjective is used especially frequently to describe his translations/ adaptations of Homer). But still, particularly when working with cinematic receptions of literature, there is a need to think more carefully about the directional dynamics of reception. With *Troy*, for example, though there has been little time for considered responses to filter down into the scholarship (Martin Winkler's 2006b collection arrived too late for this article to take account of it), immediate reactions to the film by Classics scholars seemed to judge it (generally negatively) for what it took or discarded from Homer (Green 2004, for example, uses words such as loss, destruction, reduction, diminishment, discarding, and compression to characterize the adaptation), rather than fully working out its place in the reception history of the *Iliad*, in which all new receptions enter into a *dialogue* with the source – and each other. Overly evaluative, even emotive, responses may lead us to forget that cinematic adaptation can, and should, be understood as an interpretation of the source, rather than condemned as a desecration of it. The following observation from Lorna Hardwick is particularly relevant here:

> It used sometimes to be said that reception studies only yield insights into the receiving society. Of course they do this, but they also focus critical attention back towards the ancient source and sometimes frame new questions or retrieve aspects of the source which have been marginalized or forgotten.
>
> (Hardwick 2003a: 4)

Here, I think, is one area in which Classics and film studies could work harder, particularly when dealing with literature. As a kind of cultural monolith, cinema can monopolize our attention (the dazzle of the silver screen again). When we do hold it up against the ancient text, we are often more concerned with passing judgement on the film, frequently negatively, instead of asking how the modern reception might be made productive for the ancient source too. For example, a number of reviewers complained about the unsubtle appeals to heroic immortality that littered *Troy*, without sufficiently exploring why *kleos*, the epic glory sought by the Homeric heroes, might have been such an attractive theme for the filmmakers, and what impact the film's treatment of it has when we reread Homer (Green 2004: 179; Mendelsohn 2004: 47–8 is more thoughtful). Why not ask, then, whether the *poem*'s concern with epic commemoration might be viewed differently if we see film itself as a possible vehicle for that fame? Greater willingness to frame such questions, in line with this brief example, would be a welcome addition to studies of cinematic receptions of antiquity.

Locating Reception in Classics and Film Studies

There are other aspects of Classics and film work which prompt further questions and concerns regarding the theoretical underpinnings of cinema's relationship with antiquity. Again, cinema's engagement with literature is pivotal, one provocative (contentious even) area of scholarly inquiry being that which Maria Wyke labels 'Parallelism, allusion and quotation' (Wyke 2003: 441–3). Some investigations of Classics and film (particularly in evidence in Winkler's 2001 collection *Classical Myth and Culture in the Cinema*) adopt a comparative approach in order to identify 'formal or thematic parallelism' (Wyke 2003: 441) between an ancient text and film which generally does *not* seem to be linked to the ancient world (through setting, or through obvious claims to being an adaptation): for example, Hanna Roisman's comparison of narrative strategy in the *Odyssey* and *The Usual Suspects* (Roisman 2001), or an exploration of the *katabasis* theme in a variety of films (Holtsmark 2001). Roisman's pairing of the *Odyssey* together with *The Usual Suspects* is not, put crudely, about what cinema does with and to the ancient world, but is rather intended as, primarily, a vehicle for commenting on narratology. It is, as Roisman herself argues, thus primarily of pedagogic value in presenting complex texts and concepts to students in innovative (and relevant) ways (and see McDonald, this volume, ch. 25, for similar comments). The aims, then, are uncontroversial, but the chosen methodology raises important questions. One set of questions is about how and why such comparisons are chosen and whether they are necessary or successful is shedding light on the formal and thematic aspects of the ancient and modern texts. A second set of questions centres on the relationship between text and film.

Some kind of relationship between text and film is being posited here, but how are we to understand it? If a film has no clear link with classical antiquity (and how do we discern and evaluate this 'clarity' anyway?), in what sense might we be able to understand it as a reception of antiquity? The methodology exemplified by Roisman (2001) in examining correspondences in narrative approach then provides an excellent springboard for the consideration of some key issues relating to how we understand reception theory as a whole, which will in turn, I hope, encourage us to apply a more nuanced understanding of that theory to film work. (See, also, Roisman, this volume, ch. 24, for a productive application of the conclusions drawn in her 2001 article to two cinematic versions of the *Odyssey*.)

The theoretical point on which this issue seems to turn is, in fact, the location – the 'point' – of the very process of reception. (My observations here draw significantly on Batstone 2006, and other contributions to Martindale and Thomas 2006.) Do we understand 'the point of reception' to be located in *the film*'s reading of the classical past, or to be pushed back a stage into the *reader (viewer) of the film*? Or is it simultaneously in both? Christopher McQuarrie (*The Usual Suspects*' scriptwriter) may not have thought of his film as a reception of Homer, but if Roisman reads Homer into it, does it then constitute a classical reception? This is a live issue for reception study in general, but it is particularly pertinent for a number of films which, by seeming to flaunt some kind of relationship to antiquity, lure the classicists in, only for them to find themselves tangled in a movie whose relationship to the ancient past is characterized by a complex mix of ambiguity, authenticity, and evasion. The 'usual suspects' here (based on the attention they have received from classical scholars) might be the *Star Wars* series (1977–2005: see McDonald, this volume, ch. 25 and Winkler 2001b); and *O Brother, Where Art Thou?* (released 2000:

see Flensted-Jensen 2002 and Goldhill 2007). A brief focus on *O Brother* will serve to demonstrate how such a film might provide exciting and theoretically challenging material for the reception scholar, particularly regarding the question of where and how to locate cinematic reception. The film defines itself as an adaptation – itself a hard-to-define term – of Homer's *Odyssey* (a title card reads 'Based on Homer's *Odyssey*'), then proceeds with a 1930s-set narrative in which the main character, Everett Ulysses McGill, is on the run from a chain-gang, trying to return home to his wife Penny. The engagements with Homer operate on different levels, from the broad structural parallel of the obstacle-filled journey home, to the characterization which clearly links ancient and modern counterparts (Ulysses, Penny, a one-eyed 'Cyclops' figure, and so on). But this appeal to the ancient world is not a constitutive feature of the film as it is in, say, *Troy*, and, moreover, the film's directors, the Coen brothers, proclaimed in interviews that they had never read the *Odyssey* (*Time Out*, 30 August 2000). Where, then, is the reception in all of this?

To be sure, the proclamation that they had never read Homer was likely to be a conscious and provocative expression of 'authorial unreliability', in keeping with the Coens' postmodern style. It does not matter whether they were telling the 'truth' or not. What does matter is that this repression, even denial, of the act of reception *inherent to the film itself* exemplifies the uncertainty that exists if we try and pin down the location of the process. Is the reception of the *Odyssey* enacted by the Coen brothers, or by us when we watch the film? This example helps shed light on a possible bifurcation in the concept of reception. Reception theory has it that meaning is realized at the point of reception, which suggests that *O Brother*'s spectators have the autonomy to understand and configure the film's relationship with Homeric epic. Certainly, if we observe the relatively limited use of reception theory within the discipline of film studies, we see that it definitely focuses on the capacity of the *audience* to make meaning (Staiger 2000, 2005). But we also want to identify the process of reception that is enacted within the film itself – before it is ever 'read' by a movie-going audience. In this way we can assign the film's *creator* some autonomy in reading the ancient past – despite the difficulty in identifying a sole 'creator' in many films (so auteurs such as Godard or Fellini) and, no small matter, the theoretical discomfort in trying to ascertain authorial intention. The act of 'authorial reading' is surely no easier for us, the 'next' reader, to discern.

Evidently, this is not bifurcation of the point of reception so much as it is a blurring, or an instance of the chain-, even web-like nature of receptions in all media. In *Gladiator*, for example, Ridley Scott et al. created a film shaped by their readings of imperial Rome, resulting in a work which in turn has to be read by us – reminding us that we cannot study cinematic receptions of antiquity without acknowledging (or at least trying to) our own input as readers of those films too. (For a brief but incisive account of the complexities of this point, see Duncan Kennedy (2006: 290–1). There should be no real problem in understanding reception as occurring at *each* of these points, but the study of Classics and film is still often concerned with what Martindale calls 'fairly positivistic forms of historical inquiry' (Martindale 2006: 2): essentially historicizing approaches which examine *Gladiator* in order to figure out what Scott 'really thinks' about Commodus, at the expense of adequately incorporating what *we* think about Commodus (or Scott, or Commodus as portrayed by Scott, and so on). I would not call this approach mistaken, as Martindale does, but I would suggest that in order to fully exploit reception theory within Classics and film, it ought to be accompanied by interest in – or at least more rigorous questioning of – the full extent of the process of reception. Only then can we gain a more rounded picture of how cinematic engagements with antiquity might work. For example, given the Coen brothers' reluctance to discuss Homer in detail, and even their denial of 'receiving' him, could we distinguish between conscious and unconscious reception of classical material? What distinctions might we draw between scholarly and popular receptions of the film? What happens if a scholarly critic reads a multitude of Homeric parallels into *O Brother* and a member of the public reads none – is one a 'better' or a more 'correct' reading than the other? These questions inevitably recall the theme of elite versus mass culture that was raised earlier in the discussion. They perhaps also outline one way in which filmmakers and even the practitioners of Classics and film studies remain anxious about the 'inferiority' of their subject material, since reading ancient parallels into film is surely one way of augmenting film's cultural standing.

Film as Meta-reception

The preceding discussion has, I hope, demonstrated important ways in which film's role within classical reception studies can be made to work harder, and in so doing, contribute more effectively to the debates that still need to take place regarding what happens at the interface between ancient and modern. This is not a call for abstract theorization in place of studying actual cinematic material, but, rather, for productive combinations of the two. In terms of dissemination, it may also be the case that a different kind of scholarly work in this field is needed: having been dominated by the publication of edited collections of individual articles, which by their nature have limited scope for sufficiently grappling with these complex issues, we should perhaps hope to see more in the way of lengthier monographs, which can take the time to address such issues whilst still providing careful considerations of the material.

Furthermore, my aim here has been not to advocate using film simply as a convenient tool to help us address the complexities of reception theory from the perspective of Classics, but rather to assert film's unique contribution to our understanding of classical reception studies in general. As a 'reader' of antiquity, film's ability to construct and convey new and fascinating readings of an ancient text, or an aspect of ancient culture, should not be forgotten, and it is the particular nature of the medium that provides an important element of the appeal and utility of these readings. The obvious blend of word (and other aural dimensions) and visual image that makes up a film is clearly important and can have a distinct impact on the kind of reading of antiquity offered by the film. For example, as Maria Wyke demonstrated in *Projecting the Past*, a dominant feature of the mid-century ancient world epic was the potential contradiction between the film's narrative, which extolled the moral superiority of, say, persecuted Christians against the evil Romans, and the visual dimension of the film, which through its seductive spectacularization of imperial Rome encouraged audiences 'to position themselves not only as pure Christians but also as Romans luxuriating in a surrender to the splendours of film spectacle itself' (Wyke 1997: 31–2). Thus the film's reception of antiquity can incorporate two seemingly incompatible positions simultaneously.

Related to the use of sound and image is film's technological capability, which, on a fundamental level, also shapes its receptions in interesting ways. As a definitively modern medium, every time it engages with the ancient world, it forces us to confront the chasm between then and now, whilst frequently aiming to close that gap. Virtually every other kind of reception of antiquity (with the exception perhaps of computer games) occurs in a medium which existed in at least a broadly similar way in antiquity too, whereas cinema is a product only of the last century or so. When studying cinematic receptions, then, the fact that a very modern form of media is engaging with such ancient material is surely part of the fascination, and ought to provide more food for thought in terms of the implications of reception across different media, as well as across time. At the same time, though, the *raison d'être* of some ancient world films seems to be to try and make us forget the gulf between ancient and modern, using all the cinematic weaponry of realism and naturalism to give the impression that the cinema screen provides a window on the ancient world. This is especially true of the Hollywood epic, which aims – particularly in its physical recreation of the ancient world – at verisimilitude, and at exploiting the audience's willingness to trust filmed images as authoritative and *real*. 'Movies . . . plunge us into a vivid past – or bring that past directly into the present – seemingly without mediation' (Lowenthal 1985: 367). Herein lies one of the most important strategies of a cinematic reception, with clear implications for the wider understanding of classical reception in general: the nature of the film encourages us to forget that it is a reception of antiquity (or, returning to our discussion about where the 'point of reception' is, directs the audience to respond to the film as an unmediated encounter with antiquity, thus confining the 'point' of reception to the film viewer); whilst in fact – as much Classics and film scholarship has already shown – it is anything but. The gap between then and now is such that even as some films try and open a window onto the ancient world, they will inevitably not only *be* receptions but will also *utilize earlier receptions* in order to fill gaps in the historical knowledge *and* to shape their own particular vision of Rome. So, for example, *Gladiator*, a particularly vivid recreation of imperial Rome which trumpeted its 'accuracy' through its meticulous recreation of the Colosseum, also happily acknowledged the use of both Fascist appropriations of Roman iconography (Pomeroy 2004) and Victorian classical painting (Landau 2000: 64) in its production design.

Just as some Hollywood epics might function as models of disingenuously compressed and elided reception, other films can be seen as conscious dramatizations of that same process. Kenneth Mackinnon viewed certain cinematic adaptations of Greek tragedy as 'metatragedies': the works of Pier Paolo Pasolini in particular were, he argued, not merely adaptations of the ancient texts, but commentaries on their relationship to modern culture, thereby reflecting on, in a sense, their status as receptions (Mackinnon 1986: 126–64). We might add Federico Fellini's *Satyricon*

(1969) and *Roma* (1972) to this argument, as films which explicitly concern themselves with exploring the relationship between antiquity and modernity. *Satyricon* works as a particularly effective illustration of the dangers of relying on film to present a historicizing, trustworthy recreation of the classical past, using a wide variety of visual, aural, and narrative devices to convey the fragmentation and unintelligibility of that past. *Roma* uses a similar fragmentary strategy, showing how Fellini's notion of the city of Rome is compiled of many different aspects of its history and culture; antiquity itself cannot be uncovered as a pristine, intelligible entity, but can only be apprehended through the layers of reception that stretch between us and them. Film, particularly through its capacity to blend images and words into suggestive or mysterious montages, is thus just as well equipped to embody the process of reception as it is to insist on its irrelevance.

It is not only the European arthouse tradition which tackles such questions – even a recent Hollywood epic like *Alexander* was committed to incorporating the process of reception as an important theme, through a framing device which saw Ptolemy, in his old age, begin to dictate a written history of his younger days spent as one of Alexander's generals, thus motivating the film's flashback structure. As he muses, he makes quite clear that even at this short remove, the mythologization perpetuated by and around Alexander makes historicizing impossible. 'Did such a man as Alexander exist?', he asks. 'Of course not. We idolize him, make him better than he was.' At this point, the audience ought to be reminded of the inescapable power of chains of receptions to shape our view of the past, and the impossibility of getting back to the 'real' Alexander, through film or any other medium – even historiography. *Alexander* thus made a useful, even important, contribution to the debates over classical reception and its importance – but do the viewing public, still less academic commentators, acknowledge this? Probably not. The film was, relatively speaking, a critical and commercial failure, derided by audiences of all types for its unwieldy narrative structure, unsubtle characterization, and so on – and so serves, perhaps, as a useful endpoint for this discussion, returning full circle to some of the problems outlined at the beginning. For, given the ease with which some dismiss film as an object worthy of study anyway, a film which is perceived as 'bad' is even more likely to be rejected, even if it is aiming to convey some valuable observations – and to convey them outside the confines of the academy, which is surely to be commended. Films which tackle the complexities of the ancient world may often provoke dissatisfaction, but we should, I argue, be more ready to recognize not only their value as receptions, but also their willingness, often overlooked, to comment upon that very process themselves. Cinema provides a wealth of useful material with which to conduct more probing accounts of classical receptions, and so must be taken seriously if we are to give the field every opportunity to develop in new and interesting ways.

FURTHER READING

Readers who wish to gain additional perspectives of the general shape of Classics and film scholarship should consult two excellent articles by Wyke, 1998, 2003. *Der Neue Pauly* provides a fairly detailed entry on *Film* (vol. 13, cols 1133–41; currently only in German) with a useful bibliography, including many English works. The most important works that show Classics and film scholarship in practice are already mentioned in the main text of the article: to recap, they are Wyke 1997; Solomon 2001; Winkler 2001a; Joshel, Malamud and McGuire 2001; Winkler 2004, 2006a, 2006b. Recommended studies of classical reception which broadly reflect this article's standpoint are Martindale 1997 and Hardwick 2003a.

Other more specific examples of cinematic receptions of antiquity have necessarily been treated very briefly, but there is a good deal of scholarship for the interested reader to pursue. On Fellini and his depiction of antiquity, J.P. Sullivan's article in Winkler 2001a: 258–71, is recommended, as are Bondanella's discussions (1987, 1992). Fellini's own preface to the film is an invaluable source, and is reprinted in Bondanella 1978: 16–19, alongside additional useful articles. Cinematic adaptations of ancient literature are also an important aspect of this kind of classical reception. On Greek tragedy, besides Mackinnon 1986, two articles by Michelakis (2001, 2004a) are examples of some of the best work being carried out in this area. On adaptation more generally, Stam and Raengo 2005, Stam 2005 and Naremore 2000, are excellent.

CHAPTER TWENTY-FOUR

The *Odyssey* from Homer to NBC: The Cyclops and the Gods

Hanna M. Roisman

This chapter deals with the treatment of the Cyclops episode in two films based on Homer's *Odyssey*: the 1955 feature film *Ulysses*, directed by Mario Camerini and starring Kirk Douglas, screenplay by Franco Brusati, Mario Camerini, Ennio de Concini, Hugh Gray, Ben Hecht, Ivo Perilli and Irwin Shaw, and the 1997 NBC television mini-series production directed by Andrei Konchalovsky, starring Armand Assante, and scripted by Andrei Konchalovsky and Christopher Solimine. For all its grotesqueness and horror, the Cyclops story is a central and very rich episode in Homer's epic. In terms of the plot, it explains why Poseidon kept Odysseus away from home for ten years. In terms of theme, it touches on one of the more problematic aspects of the relationship between humans and gods that is explored in Homer's epic.

The first part of the chapter will focus on the rendition of the episode itself, with special attention to framing and characterization. The second part will deal with the treatment of Poseidon and, more broadly, with the relationship between man and god. Before starting, I'd like to state that this chapter will not deal with the differences in the format, technology, and original audiences (movie house versus home) of the two films. This is a subject unto itself and deserves attention. It does not, however, have bearing on matters that concern me in this chapter. These are, above all, how the filmmakers handled Homer's material and their differences in sensibility both from Homer's epic and from one another.

Rendition of the Cyclops Episode

For both films, the *Odyssey* served essentially as a source of material, from which the scriptwriters mined a hero with a classical name and a treasure trove of adventures. Both films are adventure stories, which dutifully run their hero through the chief adventures of his Homeric predecessor, while trying to make those adventures accessible to an audience unfamiliar with Homer. To these ends, both directors radically pare down the adventures, add material, and remodel Odysseus' character to suit contemporary tastes. In both films, the Cyclops episode is the one with the fewest departures from the original. However, abridgement of this episode occurs both in the action and at the structural level. In both films, the story includes the Greeks' entry into the cave, their entrapment by Polyphemus, their getting him drunk and blinding him; Polyphemus' display of consternation and confusion after his blinding, and Odysseus' taunting Polyphemus from the safety of his ship. Both films omit Odysseus' trick using the sheep, however. They show the men leaving the cave *with* the sheep, but not Odysseus binding three sheep together so that each threesome can carry out a man without the blind Polyphemus being able to feel them exit. Nor does Odysseus leave the cave clinging to the underbelly of Polyphemus' favourite ram. Originally, I thought that this omission was to save precious film time. But, since both films add other material to the episode, I soon realized the purpose was to simplify: to remove a complicated action with questionable appeal to modern urban audiences. The attention that Homer pays to Cyclops' husbandry is similarly removed.

The additions are similarly aimed at making the episode more accessible to audiences. In the 1955 film, most of the episode is taken up with a lengthy display of Ulysses and his men trampling on grapes to make more wine for the thirsty monster. This rather bizarre insertion serves as yet another of the many illustrations of Ulysses' cleverness, continually outsmarting the stupid monster. Advancing neither characterization nor plot, it endows the episode with a spurious sense of familiarity by exploiting the stereotype of Greek peasants trampling on grapes. Whether the 1950s audience realized that wine requires time to ferment and that Polyphemus was shown falling into a drunken torpor on grape juice, we cannot know. This addition does not appear in the NBC version, produced half a century later. Maybe the assumption was that modern audiences are familiar with the manufacture of alcoholic beverages.

At the structural level, it is noteworthy that both films remove the framing and ritual repetitions of the episode in Homer's *Odyssey*. There the Cyclops incident is one of a number of fantastic stories that Odysseus tells to entertain and impress his Phaeacian hosts. Neither film includes this conscious frame. In the 1955 film, the episode is shown as a flashback, the first of the incidents that Ulysses recalls as he stands on the Phaeacian shore. In the 1997 film, Odysseus narrates the episode directly to the outer audience as part of his chronological account of his leaving and return to his home in Ithaca. The removal of the framing may seem rather technical. But it has tremendous ramifications.

Homer's framing device served a number of functions. One was to direct the audience to consider Odysseus' recital not as absolute truth, but in the context of his visit with the Phaeacians. Judging from the sketchy information that Odysseus receives about his hosts from various sources – from Nausicaa, from the girl who leads him to Alcinous' palace (Athena), from the words of Alcinous in his addresses to the Phaeacians, and from his own observations (6.199–210, 262–72, 300–15; 7.30–132, 186–206, 317–28; 8.557–69) – Odysseus has some sense of his hosts and what they believe about themselves and the world. They see themselves as close to the gods, as possessing magic ships, as on a par with the Cyclops and the Giants, to whom they are cousins. They see (or at least portray) themselves as a quasi-mythical people who still enjoy intimate discourse and a close relationship with gods. Such people will be obliged to accept stories set in the dimension they claim themselves, and Odysseus tries to make his adventure with the Cyclops acceptable and satisfying to the audience he is addressing (Ahl and Roisman 1996: 92–121). In this narrative, Odysseus locates himself in a world that the Phaeacians are familiar with and tailors his story to their perceptions (Roisman 2001).

Odysseus uses the story to intimate to his audience how resourceful and dangerous he is even to sons of gods, and thus indirectly to assure his safe departure from their island. He tells how he overcame the Cyclops, from whom the Phaeacians had fled. He elaborates on his capacity for dissembling, letting his hosts know that he lied to Polyphemus by telling him that his ship had been destroyed when it had not, and thus warns the Phaeacians that if they think they have him at their mercy, he is as capable of concealing a ship from them as well. In case they want to keep him, he lets them know that he is able to break out of places. His story straddles the worlds of 'fiction' and 'history', in a way that makes them impossible to tell apart (Ahl and Roisman 1996: 109–15).

The frame also furthers the thematization of the episode. The audience may notice Odysseus' assertion that when he landed on the Cyclops' island, he was interested in finding out whether its inhabitants were violent and savage and not just, or hospitable and with a godly mind (9.175–6). This assertion echoes the narrator's description of Odysseus' thoughts in book six (120–1), when he landed on the Phaeacians' island. Similarly, when Odysseus addresses Polyphemus as a suppliant and begs him to show hospitality and respect for the gods by treating him and his men well and giving them gifts (9.259–71), the audience may recall the warm reception and many gifts that Odysseus had received from the Phaeacians in books seven and eight. These repetitions raise the contrast between civilization and barbarity that appears in the Cyclops episode to the level of a theme and make hospitality and gift-giving the criteria of civilized conduct.

This thematization is much weaker in the films. First, since the framing is removed, the rhetorical astuteness of the hero is also absent, and whatever fictional quality the story may have is lost. Thus ironically, what is presented in the epic as fiction turns into a 'reality' in the two films – as if one-eyed giants existed, and Odysseus indeed met one of them (cf. Lucian, *True History* 1.3). Second, instead of a more implicit notion of the importance of hospitality, both films draw a stark contrast between the ugly and barbaric Cyclops and the good-looking Greeks, and in both the hero preaches the related values of piety and hospitality to Polyphemus. Without the contextualization and recurrence permitted by framing, the contrast remains largely visual, the speeches remain largely behaviours, and the ideas behind them do not resound as they do in Homer.

Homer's framing also makes the Cyclops episode, like the others that Odysseus tells the Phaeacians, a poetic activity and Odysseus a storyteller-poet. The conception of hero as artist was possible because speech and action, counsel and fighting, were complementary functions of equal importance in the world of Homer's epics (Roisman 2005b). Neither film could conceive of Odysseus as a poet. The 1955 film presents him mainly as a macho warrior and inveterate adventurer, the 1997 film as a wise doer. Both characterizations reflect the dichotomization of art and action in the modern world and a view of artists as weak. Making Odysseus a storyteller allows him to relate both literal and figurative truth. It thus makes verisimilitude unnecessary. Indeed, Odysseus' tale has a stylized, ritualistic quality about it. Polyphemus enacts his cannibalism over three consecutive occasions, eating two men on the Greeks' first night in the cave (9.232–306, esp. 287–90), two more the next morning (9.307–17), and another two that evening (9.336–44). With this ritualization, the Cyclops' one-eyed monstrosity becomes emblematic of his cruel inhumanity, and the episode becomes a parable in which good vanquishes evil, and culture, brains and civilization, represented by Odysseus, overcome the primitive brute strength represented by the Cyclops.

This does not happen in the films. Both films are literalistic and strive to convey an impression of realism, despite the obviously fantastic quality of the episode. Both films thus remove the ritualistic, fairy-tale element of Homer's original, compacting the episode into a few hours in the cave, with a single occurrence of cannibalism. This saves film time and keeps the action moving, but it also leaches out Homer's parabolic meanings. Instead, both films try to rationalize the action by ascribing to Cyclops and Greeks alike rather concrete motives that are not present in Homer's original. Both films send the Greeks to the Cyclops' cave in search of food, while Homer had directed them there to satisfy Odysseus' curiosity about the nature of the island's inhabitants. This material motive, one might guess, would be more convincing to modern audiences, and an easier one to convey than elaborating on Odysseus' character to include so many intense and contradictory passions. In addition, both films provide explanations for Odysseus' misfortune in landing at the Cyclops' island and for the Cyclops' cruelties. Both films follow Homer's lead in relating that Odysseus offended Poseidon (or Neptune), and both films suggest that the Cyclops shares his father's resentment and anger. In the Homeric text, however, the offence occurs when Odysseus blinds the Cyclops; the text does not provide a reason for the Cyclops' behaviour (1.68–75; 9.517–35; 11.100–3). The films' motivation for the action replaces the awesome mystery of evil and the painful reality of uncaused suffering and misfortune found in the Homeric text with a settled and comprehensible world order.

With respect to characterization, both film heroes share with Homer's Odysseus his reputed good looks (if we disregard, of course, Polyphemus' words in 9.513–16), his curiosity, his fearlessness, his bravado and, above all, his ability to think on his feet, together with an unflinching readiness to use violence where necessary – all features that are essential either to the unfolding of the Cyclops episode or to the hero's audience appeal. Beyond this, however, each film finds ways to remodel Homer's hero to suit contemporary tastes.

In *Ulysses*, the hero comes across as more brawn than brains. As has been already noted, he and his men are drawn to the cave by material motives, in search of food, not by the intellectual curiosity of Homer's hero. Once in the cave, they are shown interested mainly in their stomachs: guzzling, roasting a kid or a lamb, and filching as much of the Cyclops' cheese as they can. When Eurylochus urges Ulysses to leave the cave before its owner returns, he reminds him to think more about his stomach and not to leave any food behind. When Eurylochus tells the men to hurry and carry the goods out of the cave to the ship, Odysseus remarks mockingly: 'Eurylochus, I know you are in a hurry, but please do not drop anything so precious as wine.' With his men, Ulysses pulls rank and uses force. Until the Cyclops shows his cannibalism, he repeatedly scorns and minimizes their fears. He constantly yells at them and roughly shoves them around. He orders them to sharpen the spike to put out Polyphemus' eye, but refuses to explain why. To be sure, he also offers himself as a sacrifice to Polyphemus, asking the giant whether he prefers to eat him boiled, grilled or roasted. But the offer sounds more like mockery of the Cyclops than a way of helping his men.

The 1997 Odysseus, created within the conventional demands of our own era, is portrayed as a 'nice guy' and psychologically adult leader. He is shown eating and revelling with his men in the Cyclops' cave, but the scene is not over-elaborated. He does not shout or shove his men around or call the blinded Cyclops 'stupid' as does his counterpart in the 1955 version. Rather, he shows himself to be fair and diplomatic. When the Cyclops finds Odysseus and his men eating his food, the hero tries to placate the angry monster, apologizing and offering him wine in compensation. After the Cyclops eats one of his men, he appears more sincerely ready to sacrifice himself to save the others, suggesting to the Cyclops that he eat him next. He makes sure, however, that the Cyclops will not want to do this by threatening that in killing him, the Cyclops will lose all the magic in his head and kill all the secrets of the world. The warning looks clever and does not detract from his good-guy credentials. This offer, however, runs counter to the emphasis the Homeric text places on Odysseus' determination to defeat his enemies by any means and on the value it accords his great ability for survival. After all, he is the only leader in the Homeric epics who lost all his troops, and not on the battlefield at Troy, but on the trip back home. The warning, however, helps to make the subsequent blinding, so hard to take in our squeamish age, acceptable to the audience: if such a nice guy was forced to this choice, it surely had to be done.

In each film, the character of the hero reflects the ideal masculinity of the age: rough-hewn in mid-century, more sensitive at the century's close. In both, the major trade-off for that currency is the main quality of the Homeric prototype: his tremendous resourcefulness. The resourcefulness of the two film heroes is limited to their ability to think on their feet and to devise ways out of knotty situations. It does not include the purposefulness, planning, anticipation and deliberation of Homer's Odysseus. As part of their plots, both film heroes come up with the idea of plying the Cyclops with wine and with the plan to put out his eye. In neither film, however, does the hero intentionally bring along the wine on his foray inland in anticipation that he might run into trouble and need it (9.196–215). In neither film is he shown deliberating on how to deal with the Cyclops (9.299–306). Homer's Odysseus first decides to kill the Cyclops and then changes his mind to blinding him when he realizes that he needs him alive to remove the heavy boulder blocking the cave's entrance. *Ulysses* skips over the first stage entirely. The 1997 Odysseus explains to one of his men why blinding the Cyclops is preferable to killing him. But neither is shown in the vital act of thinking through the implications of his moves and deciding between alternatives.

Now, of course, there is nothing wrong with adapting episodes and remodelling characters from the Classics. On the contrary, reinterpretation is vital to keeping the ancient text alive and relevant. The audience for these films, unfamiliar with Homer's epic and distant in time and culture from the values that inform it, gets a fast-moving adventure story featuring a hero whose motives they can appreciate and whose character they can admire. For one steeped in Homer, though, a sense of loss is perhaps unavoidable. By way of contrast, one can take the example of Euripides' satyr play, *The Cyclops*. Euripides introduced even greater changes than the film-makers; he omitted the frame and the ritualism of the episode; and he also reduced the stature of the Homeric hero, making him a complacent, self-righteous windbag, who was neither clever nor brave, and whose blinding of the Cyclops comes across as both stupid and cruel (Roisman 2005a: 71–3). But he made these changes in a dialogue with Homer: as a way of saying 'we don't have heroes today and perhaps never really did, but only flawed and bumbling human beings'. He could do this because his audience could refer back to the original and thus appreciate his dialogue. The modern filmmaker cannot be expected to engage in this way.

Poseidon

Among the functions of the Cyclops episode in Homer's poem, one is to elaborate on how Odysseus incurred Poseidon's wrath. Already in the opening pages we hear Zeus, speaking at a congress of the Olympians, explain that Poseidon was angry at Odysseus because Odysseus had blinded his son Polyphemus (1.68–75). Odysseus repeats the point at the end of his account of the Cyclops episode. Telling of his departure from the Cyclops' island, he quotes Polyphemus' moving prayer to his father to avenge the blinding by preventing Odysseus' return to Ithaca or, failing that, making sure that he comes home late, without his companions, and to troubles in his household (9.526–35).

Both films follow the lead of Homer's epic in attributing Odysseus' protracted homecoming to the anger of the sea god. As in Homer's epic, in both films it is this anger, manifested in violent sea storms, that keeps Odysseus from reaching home and drives him from one hair-raising encounter to the next. In both films, as in Homer's epic, too, the sea god is a recurrent presence, introduced at the beginning of the tale and referred to at key points thereafter. The films differ greatly from Homer, however, in their treatment of the sea god and the hero's relation to him. As we have seen, both films detach the anger of the sea god from the Cyclops episode. More fundamentally, they remove the entire matter from its historic and philosophic context in the Homeric world and anchor it in the Judeo-Christian worldview. To illustrate this transformation, I will first discuss Homer's treatment of Odysseus' offence and Poseidon's anger, with an eye to the assumptions it reflects about the nature of the godhead and the relationship between the human and divine, and then show how the films treat these motifs from the Judeo-Christian perspective.

In Homer's epic, Odysseus' offence is depicted as unintentional and inadvertent, and Poseidon's anger as highly personal. Given the Cyclops' great strength and cannibalism, it is clear that Odysseus had no option but to blind him if he wanted to exit his cave alive with those of his men whom the giant had not yet eaten. Although Odysseus boasts of his cleverness and gloats over Polyphemus' consternation, the blinding is in no way an intentional challenge to the deity. As noted above, we may suspect Odysseus' rendition of the incident to be self-serving. Nevertheless, there is nothing in the epic that in any way suggests that Odysseus violated any religious principle or injunction, as, for example, he might have done by failing to make due sacrificial offerings to a god or by boasting of his self-sufficiency, autonomy or superiority, as Ajax, the son of Oileus, is said to have done (4.499–511). Poseidon's anger at Odysseus is presented as a personal vendetta: Zeus tells the gods at the opening congress that Poseidon 'nurses a grudge' (1.68–9) against Odysseus; and when Poseidon learns that the other gods have decided to allow Odysseus to return home, the narrator tells us that he consoles himself with the thought that 'I can still give him his fill of trouble' (5.290). This depiction reflects the Homeric view of the gods as possessing human qualities and driven by human passions. Poseidon's anger is fuelled by much the same parental identification and protectiveness that might lead any human parent to seek vengeance under similar circumstances.

Homer's depiction also reflects the notion that the gods' superiority to human beings is anchored more in their power, derived from their identification with basic principles or forces of nature, than in any moral pre-eminence. Without exception, every shipwreck, drowning, and storm at sea in the epic is attributed to Poseidon's rage (e.g. 5.282–96, 339–41, 365–7, 445–6; 7.270–4; 9.283–5; 11.399–407; 23.234–8; 24.109–10), which becomes both the metaphor for and the explanation of the sea's unabated destructive energy (Otto 1954: 156–60; Burkert 1985: 136–9). Indeed, Poseidon's vendetta against Odysseus is shown as but one instance of the sea's power, made vivid in the lengthy description of several sea storms (5.282–450), and demonstrated, too, in Ajax' (son of Oileus) shipwreck (4.499–511), in the dispersal of the Greek fleet on their way home from Troy (3.130–83), and, above all, in the permanent end put to the Phaeacians' ability to give seafarers safe passage (13.172–87). For Homer's audience, who lived on islands and whose commerce and everyday lives were intimately bound up with the sea, Poseidon's deeds reflect the power of the sea to wreak havoc in their lives.

Homer's poem treats Odysseus' offence and ensuing sufferings in connection with the broader issue of the responsibility that persons bear for the ills that befall them. This issue is at the center of the disagreement between Zeus and Athena at the congress of the gods that opens the epic. Contemplating Aegisthus' murder by Orestes, Zeus decries the fact that men blame the gods for the evils they suffer, when, in fact, 'through their own folly they have sorrow beyond what is ordained' (1.33–4). Athena questions the generalizability of this observation. Acknowledging that Aegisthus deserved being killed, she intimates that Odysseus' sufferings are excessive and that Zeus has been overly harsh towards him (1.45–62). The issue is never quite resolved. Zeus's statement that men's recklessness causes them to suffer 'beyond what is ordained' suggests that human beings suffer no matter what they do, and the only difference is one of degree. His decision to bring Odysseus home after Athena objects to the harshness of Odysseus' punishment implies that he accepts Athena's criticism (1.64–79). The presentation of Odysseus' offence as inadvertent and essential to his survival and the rescue of his men exculpates Odysseus of wrongdoing. At the same time, one cannot say that Odysseus was not somewhat reckless in going into the Cyclops' cave in the first place; had he been more cautious, the entire incident would not have occurred. Indeed, his survival on his return to Ithaca may be mainly attributed to his circumspection after he lands there.

Essentially, what the Cyclops episode and Odysseus' sufferings at Poseidon's hands show is how easy it is for humans to fall foul of the gods, even without intent or ill will, and how important it is to retain the gods' favour. The epic reinforces the latter point by emphasizing the gods' role in bringing Odysseus back to Ithaca. At the end of the Olympian congress, Zeus calls upon the gods to join in working out Odysseus' homecoming (1.76–9). Hermes is dispatched to tell Calypso to release Odysseus from her clutches; Athena goes to Ithaca to stir up Telemachus. The goddess Ino/Leucothea comes to Odysseus' rescue as he is tossed about on his raft after leaving Calypso's island (5.336). What remains for the human hero who has lost the god's favour is to propitiate him. Thus, at their meeting in the underworld, the prophet Teiresias instructs Odysseus to make a sacrifice to Poseidon when he returns home (11.127–34; 23.274–81).

Homer's treatment of Poseidon and Odysseus' embroilment with him poses major problems for the filmmakers of the two movies. The most obvious difficulty is how to render the sea god – and the rest of the Greek pantheon – on screen. The problem, of course, stems from the Judeo-Christian concept of the deity as a single, distant and invisible god, who does not mingle with human beings, as the classical gods do, and cannot be apprehended by the senses.

The 1955 *Ulysses* represents Neptune by a statue, thereby removing him from the hero's world as a living presence, much as it does most of the gods. The only deity to appear on screen is Circe, and she is more a witch than an Olympian god. This solution is consistent with the generally anti-religious tenor of the film, but, at the same time, enables the filmmaker to show the ancients as idol worshippers and to distance himself from their religious beliefs. The NBC production, in contrast, brings Poseidon and the rest of the gods into the story and onto the screen. It depicts Poseidon as a face in the waves and a deep bass voice, while fully embodying Athena, Hermes, Aeolus and other gods. The anthropomorphic depiction of the gods goes beyond Homer, where the gods rarely appear to humans in their own form, but rather as people or birds, or through their voice alone. (For the few exceptions see *Il.* 1.198–200; 5.127–28, 330–33; 10.512; 11.195–99; 15.247–61; 17.333–4; 20.130–31; 24.223). It is, however, more in the spirit of Homer than the 1955 film and reflects the NBC filmmakers' ease, not found in *Ulysses*, with presenting a world infused by spirit and in which deities play an active role.

The question of how to handle the ancient pantheon presents a challenge for all cinematic adaptations of the Homeric texts. Beyond this, however, Homer's entire conception of the Poseidon theme is problematic from the Judeo-Christian perspective. In this perspective, the godhead is conceived of as morally superior to an erring or sinful humankind. Divine actions are viewed as expression not of personal passions, but of justice (and sometimes mercy). This perspective is implicit in the film's treatment of the hero's offence and the divine reaction. Where Homer's epic presents the personal vendetta of a vindictive god angered by an unintentional offence, the films present a conflict between the hero and the godhead, stemming from the hero's intentional violation of the hierarchical order between the human and divine. In both films, the offence that provokes the godhead is a deliberate act of defiance. In *Ulysses*, the offence is the rather crude act of destroying Neptune's temple and smashing his statue. The motive for the act is relayed at the start of the film: in the reference to Neptune in the blurb that precedes the action as the 'protector God of the conquered people' and in the narrator's reference to him as 'the Trojan god, the mighty Neptune'. Although the latter attribution is not quite accurate, as the gods of the Greeks and the Trojans are the same in the Homeric epics (though they took different sides), the implication is that Ulysses attacked the god of his defeated enemy. In the NBC production, the defiance is verbal rather than physical. It is embodied in the scene in which, following the victory at Troy, Odysseus stands facing the sea, raises his hands, and boasts: 'Do you see, you gods of sea and sky?! I conquered Troy! Me, Odysseus, a mortal man of flesh and blood, and bone and mind. I do not need you now. I can do anything.' His offence is his explicit challenge to the gods and his overweening belief in his self-sufficiency. The motive for this, too, is presented as the sea god's support for the Trojans. Odysseus, angry that Poseidon had 'played' with the Greeks for ten years and 'let blood spill', refuses to accept Poseidon's claim that he had been instrumental in getting the Greeks' wooden horse into Troy. Both films frame the defiance as an act of pride. In *Ulysses*, the narrator briefly states that Ulysses committed the deed 'in his pride'. In the NBC production, the entire scene described above shows Odysseus as prideful and arrogant. The scene ends with Odysseus steadfast in his defiance after Poseidon pronounces his punishment: 'You cannot stop me. . . . No one, no one, will stop me from seeing Ithaca', he declares.

My guess is that the makers of the films viewed pride as a prototypical vice of the hero in the ancient Greek canon. This assumption probably stems from the treatment of hybris, commonly identified as pride in Greek literature, where it is frequently criticized and depicted as bringing about the fall of those who are motivated by it (see further Fisher 1992). Pride is a convenient attribute to assign to the film heroes because it is also a major vice in the Christian tradition, so viewers could be expected to accept and understand how the heroes came to be punished for it. The paradigm of the defiant hero in conflict with the deity, however, better reflects the Judeo-Christian worldview than the Homeric one. Each film, in its own way, reflects the primal biblical narrative of Adam and Eve's defiance of god's commandment and their punishment for it. In both films, the sea god is envisioned as a moral authority and the hero as suffering the consequences for his offence against the moral order.

To be sure, the two films relate differently to the hero's offence, just as they do to the god who punishes it. In the 1955 film, Ulysses' defiance is the mark of his greatness. The written text that precedes the action admiringly bills Ulysses as a man 'who dared defy the god and continued his journey to Ithaca'. The film then shows Ulysses in repeated acts of defiance. In the storm that comes up after he leaves Troy, Ulysses rejects the suggestion of one of the shipmen that they should have sacrificed to Neptune, with the dismissive statement: 'There is no Neptune out there. There is nothing but wind, water, and death.' As he leaves the Cyclops' island, he vaunts his victory over Neptune: 'Who's master now, Neptune or Ulysses? The god with his trident or the man with his grapes?' In turning down the gift of immortality that Circe offers him, he tells her that he 'is there to battle with a god and has not yet been defeated'. On the island of the Phaeacians, he boasts to Alcinous: '. . . the anger of the gods pursued me, many disasters slowed me . . . but I am here, undestroyed!' Nowhere in the film is Ulysses taken to task for his defiance or for the pride behind it. On the contrary. The admiring tone of the opening blurb nullifies any criticism that the narrator's brief attribution of the act to Ulysses' pride may have implied.

The NBC production, in contrast, treats Odysseus' pride as a failing that must be overcome and charts his painful acquisition of humility. The Cyclops episode shows Odysseus brash and overconfident, as he boasts to the blinded giant: 'Blame your father, Poseidon. It is he who made me blind you. . . . Do you hear Poseidon? I am alive, Odysseus is alive.' After a series of misadventures culminating with the shattering of his ship, the drowning of his men, and his own furious attempt to keep afloat in a raging sea, we see him in a humbler mood. Once again addressing Poseidon's face in the waves, Odysseus now cries in anguish: 'Poseidon! Poseidon! What do you want? Poseidon, what do you want from me?' He tells the god that he has nothing left and asks what the god wants him to 'understand'. Having acknowledged his powerlessness, he is ready to hear Poseidon's teaching that 'without gods, man is nothing'. Before landing in Ithaca on the Phaeacians' ship, Odysseus indicates that he had learned his lesson: 'The Phaeacians carried me towards Ithaca, but it was Poseidon who allowed me to continue my journey, to consider his words. I understood that I was only one man in the world, nothing more, and nothing less.'

For all their differences, both films treat the hero's deliberate defiance as a defining element of his character. Both show a conflict with the godhead, where Homer had presented a one-sided vendetta. Moreover, where Homer had credited the gods for Odysseus' safe homecoming, both films give credit to the hero himself. In the 1955 film, Ulysses returns to Ithaca an unvanquished rebel who survives Neptune's wrath without having yielded to him. In an out-of-character statement, he tells his son that the gods had instructed him to disguise himself as a beggar. But he never gives thanks to the gods for his homecoming, although Penelope does. The NBC Odysseus is closer to Homer's in his essential piety. For example, he thanks the gods for giving him a son, and is on easy but respectful terms with Athena and recognizes her as his protectress. Moreover, as noted above, the conflict with the deity is brought to an end by Odysseus' understanding of his human limitations and of the power of the god. The filmmakers, however, have Alcinous state that 'I know only one long-lost hero, who being cursed by the gods could survive. It's cunning Odysseus'.

As with the characterization of the hero, the difference in the films' treatment of the Poseidon theme stems from and reflects differences in the times in which the films were produced. The 1955 film, produced in the Eisenhower years, challenges the conformities of the 1950s in the US, while reflecting the religious scepticism of post-war European intellectuals. It gives us an ultimately impotent god and a hero who gets away with literally throwing him off his pedestal and overboard. The image is not only of a hero who challenges the deity, but of a hero who challenges all established authority. With his repeatedly voiced contempt of the gods, the 1955 Ulysses is drawn as a rebel much in the spirit of James Dean, whose performances in *East of Eden* (1955) and *Rebel Without a Cause* (1955) looked forward to the anti-establishment mood of the 1960s. Yet it is also a safe film. In a way, it combines the Horatio Alger fantasy of making good by overcoming all odds, which was popular in mid-century America, with the Romantic fantasy of wrestling with the gods. While creating a hero whose defiance of authority appeals to youthful audiences, it allows older or more conservative viewers to see Ulysses' acts of destruction as smashing idols and his conduct as disbelief in a false religion. After all, the statue Ulysses smashes is of a heathen god, not of Christ or the Madonna.

The 1997 film, where the gods are given human form and the hero taught to respect them, reflects the more religious temper of the latter years of the twentieth century. To be sure, the anthropomorphic depictions of the Greek deities would be rejected by all three monotheistic religions. However, the sense of the gods' presence that the film conveys, Odysseus' easy intercourse with Athena and the other gods, and even his personal anger at Poseidon reflect the diffuse, non-doctrinaire New Age spirituality that drew the rebels and seekers at the end of the century. The 1997 film's message is also closer to the spirit of Homer's world than that of the 1955 film. In Homer's world, defiance of the gods, whether through acts of destruction or through boasting one's superiority or self-sufficiency, would have been regarded as sheer madness and much worse. No Homeric hero wilfully pitted himself against the gods, as both film heroes do. There was no question but that the gods were to be respected, feared, and placated, as they are in the NBC *Odyssey*.

FURTHER READING

Solomon (2001: 108–11) gives an informative account of the two movies. He points out the scarcity of cinematic treatments of the Homeric epics (107). To date, each of the epics has received five film treatments (including *Troy*, 2004). Solomon gives high marks to Lux-Ponti-DeLaurentiis's co-production of *Ulysses* (1955) asserting that although it is 'a bit shallow on the surface and crude in realization, it captures the spirit of the earliest fantasy novel of Western civilization' (111). He is more critical of the NBC production for abandoning the original structure's dive *in medias res* for a more chronological approach, as well as of the quality of the special effects (111). A short review by Roisman (2002) gives a brief account of the movie *Ulysses* episode by episode, and claims that although the movie modifies the original epic in many places, when it is faithful to the original it rings wonderfully of the ancient line. Kinzer (18 May 1997) in his review of *The Odyssey* cites Robert Halmi Sr., one of the four executive producers, as saying that Odysseus was a liar: 'He's not always right, but you always want to look at him. If I have an interpretation of the character, it is the first mythological Greek hero who stood in defiance of the gods. . . . He's very much in the face of the gods. He's trying to take charge of his own fate'. O'Connor (16 May 1997) thinks that the movie 'doesn't quite realize its grandiose ambitions'.

CHAPTER TWENTY-FIVE

A New Hope: Film as a Teaching Tool for the Classics

Marianne McDonald

After our youngest son had seen *Star Wars* for the twelfth or thirteenth time, I said, 'Why do you go so often?' He said, 'For the same reason you have been reading the Old Testament all your life'. He was in a new world of myth.

Bill Moyers, US broadcast journalist

Introduction: Myth and Film

By using the tools of myth and film, Classics can become a vital part of modern curricula. One can reach students by pointing out connections between what they know and what you want to teach. What is to be taught? First of all, acquaintance with the original myth in its historical and philosophical contexts. Then we move on to the modern relevance and how myth functions in a way that facilitates dealing with problems that everyone faces today. Thirdly, in this way one tries to stimulate interest in the study of the Classics, in both lower schools and universities, and build up enrolments. Films are useful vehicles for enticing students into familiarity with the Classics: the film can comment on the classic and the classic can give insight into the film. Films use a variety of devices to convey their messages, and stimulate viewers. In this, both films and Classics resemble and reassemble myth.

Myths take various shapes: they are not just stories that express humanity's concerns about life and death, they also address social and ideological constructs such as nationalism and individual identity. They can be founding myths to show the justification for a people's claim to a specific land (both Athens and Thebes had their variations of these myths). Or they can be myths that provide alternative explanations for the observable phenomena in nature. There are also myths that provide explanations for human behaviour – those are the main ones that will be featured in this chapter – and they come from Greek tragedy. A film resembles a myth in that it can access the subconscious, like a dream. The audience sits in a darkened room and many enter a state from which they seem to recover slowly; when the lights go up, they need to come floating back to the surface as if returning from a deep dive. Films also give rise to their own myths, such as the Old Wild West, or Outer Space. Films refer to other films, through visual quotations, just as quotations in novels and poems make references to previous novels and poems. The Classics themselves quarry the same mine that films do. Both relay myths arising from deep within the human psyche and both create and explore a collective memory of inherited knowledge and lore, some of it transmitted genetically as modern linguists like Noam Chomsky and media masters like Marshall McLuhan describe (Chomsky 1968; McLuhan 1966). So much of what constitutes the greatness of language becomes visual in film, but that translation permeates the audience's heart and mind in a new and effective way. Homer's *Iliad* (*c.*750 BC) once shaped ancient Greek minds and continues to be a major influence on western culture; film is its heir, albeit hardly as literate a form.

Many films try to follow the Classics closely, if not literally, others simply use them as inspiration (McDonald 1983, 1992). I will focus here on George Lucas's *Star Wars* (1977–2005) and Neil Jordan's *The Crying Game* (1992; see figure 25.1), and refer briefly to what can be called its sequel, *Breakfast on Pluto* (2005; see figure 25.2), making connections between these films and the classical myths that resonate within them. The main heroes in these films (Anakin/Darth Vader, Luke, Fergus and Kitten) follow the mythical trajectory of *hamartia* (fall), *anagnorisis* (recognition and insight) and redemption. The film critic Roger Ebert claims that 'George Lucas's *Star Wars* movies are among the most influential, both technically and commercially, ever made' (*Chicago Sun-Times*, 19 May 2005). They achieve their enormous popularity by using some of the myths most fundamental to man – particularly those that deal with the use and abuse of power, and others that address man's own ethical salvation – employing modern technology to elevate the stories' characters to godlike (should we say epic?) proportions. The human elements in *Star Wars* resonate with Sophocles' story of Oedipus, and access many other myths, beginning with a title card/crawl that says 'A long time ago in a galaxy far, far away' to establish the antiquity of these stories. The Greek gods become the 'force', which can be harnessed for both good and evil ends. Obi-Wan Kenobi in *A New Hope* says: 'The Force is what gives a Jedi his power. It's an energy field created by all living things. It surrounds us and penetrates us. It binds the galaxy together.' Jordan's *The Crying Game* has themes comparable to those found in Euripides' *Bacchae*, showing the passionate inner nature of man that breaks out of and at the same time defines its boundaries. Both also investigate the fluidity of gender and question gender roles. *Breakfast on Pluto* enters even more deeply into the subconscious and conjures an artistic conversion of reality into mythical themes as the story is told in a series of vignettes based on glowing recollections of events shaped by the optimistic imagination of the hero/heroine. It is an epic reconstruction of events that many people would regard as tragedy.

Reception theory has become more sophisticated since the 1980s. It is a way of analyzing the relationship between ancient and modern conditions, how politics have changed, how the cultural context is different and how performances are managed

Figure 25.1 Jaye Davidson (as Dil) and Stephen Rea (as Fergus) in *The Crying Game* (1992), directed by Neil Jordan. Photograph courtesy Miramax/Photofest © Miramax

Figure 25.2 Cillian Murphy (as Patrick 'Kitten' Brady) in *Breakfast on Pluto* (2005), directed by Neil Jordan. Photograph courtesy Sony Pictures Classics/Photofest © Sony Pictures Classics. Photographer Patrick Murphy

if the study involves something like Greek tragedy that necessarily factored in audience reaction and ways in which the individual fashions his or her own response.
There are other areas too: for example, the modern work can allude to the ancient
one in ways that are not literal. A film can show what the original myth described
in a surviving text (e.g. from the fifth century BC, thirty-two ancient Greek tragedies
and one Satyr play). There are structural correspondences and structural differences.
What might be acts in the ancient play, could become entire films in the modern
version that uses some of the ideas of the original (e.g. *The Phantom Menace* (1999)
and the final revelations at the end of *Oedipus Tyrannus* describe the childhood of
Anakin/Darth Vader, Laius as a young man, whereas the Oedipal drama per se takes
place only in the final two films (final in the sense of *Star Wars* time, not when the
films were made, which is the reverse), *The Empire Strikes Back* (1980) and *Return
of the Jedi* (1983). Myth has always been a means of confronting man's deepest fears
obliquely, facilitating recognition and understanding without causing lasting trauma.
The ancient Greek tragedians recognized the power of myth, and reworked some
of the same stories again and again. They returned to the same royal families and
made use of the same fundamental themes: confronting death; coming to terms with
identity; the shaping of society and the shaping of the individual by society. Many
of the most powerful films incorporate and question myths that are rooted in this
deep past, the psychological drives that shape not only history, but also an individual person's life. Bill Moyers in discussion with George Lucas said that psychiatrists
had told him that they used *Star Wars* in their treatment of children, and by
far their favourite character was not Anakin or Luke Skywalker but Darth Vader
(Lucas/Moyers, 1999). Lucas pointed out this was the father figure that loomed so
prominently in all children's lives, as Freud had indicated in his Oedipus Complex
(Berkowitz/Brunner 1970: 69–73).

Star Wars: An Oedipal Fantasy

George Lucas was born in 1944 in Modesto, California. He is a visionary filmmaker
and his *Star Wars* (1977–2005) is financially the most successful film series of
all time. He revolutionized the technology involved in film production and spear-
headed digital computerized effects. He was the first to be able to construct
characters and entire landscapes simply through computer technology. *Star Wars* is
composed of three prequels, *The Phantom Menace* (1999), *The Attack of the Clones*
(2002), *The Revenge of the Sith* (2005), and the final definitive three, *A New Hope*
(1977), *The Empire Strikes Back* (1980), and *The Return of the Jedi* (1983). The
first trilogy establishes the main themes: a Republic that needs to be defended, its
transformation into an empire dominated by an evil emperor, and a 'chosen one'
who goes bad. The second trilogy shows how the Republic is saved with freedom
and justice restored.

Anakin Skywalker, alias Darth Vader, was raised by a mother who did not know
the father (or, as she said, something that sounds suspiciously like a virgin birth):
'There was no father. I carried him, I gave birth, I raised him. I can't explain what

happened.' (For this and following quotes from the films see http://www.imbd. com/quotes.) This inspires a Wildean retort, 'Rather careless of you, wouldn't you say?' But the absent father is common in Greek mythology, particularly if the father is a god, as was the case with Heracles and Perseus. In some cases the situation is further complicated by the father being unknown, as when a child is exposed (Oedipus, Ion), and the child is raised by people other than his parents. Oedipus shared ignorance of his own father with Anakin, and Anakin's son, Luke Skywalker, also didn't know who his father was until in both his case and Oedipus' the father was dramatically identified. Anakin Skywalker, who was a slave, is bought by the Jedi master Qui-Gon Jinn, and leaves his mother to become a Jedi himself. Both Anakin and Luke were trained by teachers who were unrelated to them, rather like Jason (of Argonaut and Medea fame) being trained by Chiron, the centaur don of antiquity. The 'absent father' was the usual way that a child was raised in fifth-century BC Athens, given that men rather than women were the ones who assumed public roles (Slater 1968).

Children can be 'chosen' (cf. Buffy, the Vampire-Slayer). Achilles was one such child, described in a prophecy that had dire consequences for Achilles and Prometheus, and would have had for Zeus if he had mated with Thetis, Achilles's mother. Virgil's fourth *Eclogue* (ll. 8–45) speaks of a child who is 'blessed' and going to restore the Golden Age, an era of peace and plenty. In *The Phantom Menace*, Qui-Gon Jinn is a master trained by Yoda; both are Jedi Knights, a group recruited by genetic testing and educated rather like the Guardians in Plato's *Republic* (375^d–412^b). Qui-Gon asks his apprentice Obi-Wan Kenobi to look after Anakin Skywalker: 'He is the chosen one. He will bring balance. Train him.' He showed himself precocious as chosen children do (just as Heracles, while still in his crib, strangled two snakes sent by Hera to kill him, so Anakin wins a race beating all the adults who compete against him, and disables the deadly starship at the end of *The Attack of the Clones*). In *Star Wars*, a Jedi is needed to restore peace, freedom and prosperity. This 'chosen one' at first is intended to resolve the conflicts of the Trade Federation with the republic, and ultimately restore the republic after the empire takes over. The republic is continually identified with democracy, a form of government represented by the Greeks in Aeschylus' *Persians*, in contrast to the Persian empire, which was characterized by hubris, an insatiable drive for power, and a government where all are slaves but one (Euripides, *Hel.* 276). When the Persian queen Atossa asks who rules the Greeks, she is told they are slaves to no one and answer to no single man (*Pers.* 242). Both these plays (Aeschylus' *Persians*, and Euripides' *Helen*) contrast 'oriental' despotism to Greek democracy.

The transition from republic to empire is something now being investigated in the television series, *Rome* (HBO, 2005: http://www.hbo.com/rome). As Queen Jamillia says in *The Attack of the Clones*: 'We have to keep faith in the republic. The day we stop believing democracy can work is the day we lose it.' In *The Revenge of the Sith* (the top-grossing film of 2005), Padme Amidala (a member of the federation senate, married to Anakin/Darth Vader, mother of Luke Skywalker and Princess Leia) says of this transition: 'So this is how liberty dies – with applause.' Rhetorical justification soon follows victory, as Tacitus knew well when he spoke of the Roman Empire: 'They made it a desert and called it peace' (*Agricola*, 30.5). Earlier Thucydides observed that words lost their usual meanings as events changed, with, for instance, aggression being defined as courage (*Peloponnesian War*, 3.82). Anakin/Vader tells the emperor: 'The Separatists have been taken care of, my master' and the emperor answers: 'It is finished then. You have restored peace and justice to the galaxy'. Anakin Skywalker justifies himself to Obi-Wan: 'I have peace, freedom, and justice in my new Empire.' *The Attack of the Clones* features a gladiatorial fight worthy of what Rome had to offer, with its spectators and a Count Dooku (Dracula, anyone?), the ruler of Geonosian, acting for the phantom emperor (Darth Sidious) who will seize power from the republic and declare himself emperor at the end of the third episode. The liberation of Naboo comes from the combination of technological and spiritual skills, ingenuity and courage, evinced by the young Anakin, the chosen one proving himself as he disables the robot clones who are demolishing the defenders.

What is established in the first three films is a thesis that lies at the core of Greek tragedy, the gods teach wisdom through suffering.

Zeus ordained that man must learn by suffering:

> While they sleep,
> He drips in their hearts,
> The pain of remembered sorrow,
> And no matter how they resist,
> They learn wisdom,
> A grace the gods instil violently
> While seated on lofty thrones
> As they guide the universe.
> (Aesch. *Ag.* 176–83; all translations are my own)

Wisdom is what the Jedi learn, coupled with knowledge of 'the force'. This 'force' is rather like the Tao, or 'what is' for the Buddhist, knowledge that is achieved through meditation and practice, and that eventually leads to enlightenment. For the Greeks it would probably most resemble what Plato had regarded as the truth behind illusion: the forms that underlie the reality that one accesses by leaving the dark cave of ignorance (*Rep.* 10.617e). Not having access to this wisdom leads to the disasters described in Greek tragedy. Oedipus, for instance, is infected by a spiritual blindness that only suffering eventually cures. Blind anger, pride, excessive love of honour, and ignorance lead to his downfall. His cure comes from an endurance that time has taught him, and his own innate nature (*OC* 7–8). Anakin and Luke (and in Jordan's film, Fergus) have the same innate nature that Euripides says Dionysus has: most destructive or most beneficial, most violent or most gentle (*Ba.* 861).

Excess is dangerous (as the Greeks knew well, given the maxim inscribed on their temple at Delphi, 'Nothing in Excess'. Yoda in *The Phantom Menace* traces the path: 'Fear is the path to the dark side. Fear leads to anger. Anger leads to hate. Hate leads to suffering.' We are warned how people, republics, and empires fall. Anakin's path to the dark side begins when his mother dies and he kills not only those who killed her (Tusken Raiders, Sand People), but those who were innocent: 'I killed them. I killed them all . . . And not just the men, but the women and the children too. They're like animals, and I slaughtered them like animals'. In *Revenge of the Sith* he does the same thing to Count Dooku who at that point is his unarmed prisoner. He kills Master Mace Windu (another Jedi) to protect the Chancellor who will become the newly proclaimed emperor and later order him also to kill the young innocent Jedi as a pre-emptive measure: each violation leads him further down the dark path. Precedents for this go back to Achilles' blind slaughter of the Trojans, and human sacrifice of prisoners to avenge the loss of his beloved Patroclus in the *Iliad*. Oedipus did the same when he killed his father, a man who attacked him, and then proceeded to kill everyone who accompanied him (except for the clever escapee who later identified him). Blind anger is a prime cause of *hubris*, the arrogant violation of the norm to satisfy personal desires (*koros*), which is usually followed by *ate* (blind folly that leads to destruction). The obsessive pursuit of power and overestimation of one's strength lead to the downfall of both countries and individuals. There are parallel paths to the dark side in both Greek tragedy and *Star Wars*.

In *Revenge of the Sith* the respective positions are debated and distinctions are made:

CHANCELLOR:　All who gain their power are afraid to lose it. Even the Jedi.
ANAKIN:　　　The Jedi use their power for good.
CHANCELLOR:　Good is a point of view . . .
ANAKIN:　　　The Sith rely on their passion for their strength. They think inward, only about themselves . . . The Jedi are selfless . . . they only care about others.

Like the Classics, *Star Wars* also has an ethical component. The Jedi represent the moral philosophy that Plato and Aristotle were beginning to articulate, which would lead to a basis for social theory. These philosophers made the distinction between *philia*, a concern for others coupled with duty, and the more egotistic pursuits of *eros* based on personal need (see Plato's *Symposium* 203[b–d]). Lucas knew how to harness his audience's subconscious memory of the myths that are common to many cultures, stories that he gleaned from his work with the U.S. mythologist Joseph Campbell (Campbell 1972).

At the end of *Revenge of the Sith*, after being defeated by the master who trained him, Obi Wan Kenobi, Anakin/Vader is burned while he clutches the edge of a volcanically active space entity. He is burned from head to toe, just as Heracles (see Sophocles' *Women of Trachis*, 749–806) was consumed by the cloak imbued with the poisonous blood of his enemy, which his jealous wife sent to him (thinking it would win his love back); likewise, Jason's new *inamorata* was consumed by the fire from Medea's gifts to her (Euripides' *Medea*, 1136–1213). In each case, the external burns represent incontrollable inner passions.

Anakin/Vader is consumed with anger, not only on account of the loss of his mother, but also because he was not promoted as he felt he should have been in accord with his rank: he was appointed to the Jedi council as the Chancellor's personal representative but not given the rank of master. He protested: 'This is outrageous, it's unfair. I'm more powerful than any of you. How can you be on the council and not be a master?' This is as much a slight to his sense of personal honour as was Ajax's not being awarded Achilles' arms after the death of that hero. Those arms went instead to Odysseus, whose fighting skills Ajax considered inferior to his own. Anakin gives way to the temptation of power and vengeance against those who slighted him in the same way that Ajax planned to attack his former allies, the Greeks, in Sophocles' play (*c*.442 BC). Anakin also attacked his former allies and received the promotion that the Jedi had refused him from Darth Sidious.

In *A New Hope*, the galactic empire is established and the remnants of an advisory council (the imperial senate) abolished; the emperor Darth Sidious and Lord Vader rule. Power over the vassals has devolved to regional governors. Governor Tarkin claims 'Fear will keep the local systems in line'. Fear has kept many a government in power, as Sophocles' Menelaus knew:

> It's a bad citizen
> who does not obey those in authority;
> laws never function well in a city without fear.
> An army cannot be run sensibly
> without being protected by fear and respect.
> (*Ajax* 1071–6)

In *The Empire Strikes Back* more myths are accessed. Luke Skywalker goes on a hero's *katabasis* (descent to an underworld to gain added knowledge) under the tutelage of Yoda. Luke descends into an underground cave on Dagobah to fight with his phantom father who, when his face mask falls off, is seen to be himself. By the end of the film Vader is revealed as Luke's father (note the resemblance of 'Vader' to the German word for father, *Vater*) and the Oedipal struggle begins. First Luke fights to kill him, but Vader fights to try to gain his allegiance, which in Luke's terms, would mean his spiritual death. Underworld descents by Odysseus in Homer's *Odyssey* (*c*.725 BC) and Aeneas in Virgil's *Aeneid* (*c*.19 BC) allowed the heroes to gain knowledge not only of their past but what was to come, and certainly Luke's confrontation with his father was not only something in his subconscious, but an event in the future.

The Return of the Jedi shows two Oedipal conflicts, which are also conflicts between good and evil. This touches on some of the tragic conflicts in Greek tragedy, particularly in the figure of Oedipus. Luke fights his father (cutting off his hand), but refuses to deliver the death blow at the urging of Darth Sidious. Darth Vader redeems himself by saving his son from Darth Sidious who is unleashing force lightning on Luke, debilitating him with every salvo. Darth Vader and Oedipus share not only the fact that both are disabled, but have a dubious attitude towards killing (Darth Vader kills repeatedly for 'the cause' and Oedipus curses his own sons, knowing they will die from his curse, in *Oedipus at Colonus*). Anakin/Darth Vader kills Darth Sidious (the emperor) who became his mentor and surrogate father (even master) after he left Obi Wan Kenobi, another surrogate father whom he also killed to avenge the humiliation he received from him at the end of *The Revenge of the Sith*. He killed both while subject to the same anger and in response to the same sort of threat that Oedipus faced when his father hit him, trying to pass him on the road.

After the emperor is killed, Darth Vader asks Luke to remove his face armour, so that they can look at each other as human beings (not a machine to a human being). Luke reminds Vader that he (Vader) will die if he removes his mask, but Vader insists on doing so, it seems as a type of atonement. It may be a reaction to the shame he finally feels in response to his gratuitous killing so many innocents, and to his realizing the hollowness of the new empire. In his final choice, he resembles Ajax, who fell on his own sword out of shame.

There is reconciliation between Luke and his father:

LUKE: I'll not leave you here. I've got to save you.
ANAKIN: You already have, Luke.

Salvation is not from a Death Star that is collapsing around them, but from the shame that came from following the Dark Side, and pursuing total control over what no one could ever completely control. Lucas himself claimed that he was writing about greed for power and friendship (Lucas/Moyers, 1999). Hence, the ending of *The Return of the Jedi* parallels the ending of Euripides' *Heracles*, with Theseus rehabilitating his friend Heracles after he is plunged in despair. That play ends with the line: 'That man is mad who would prefer power and resources to good friends.' The interrelationship of people and the necessity for an ethical standard is crucial to both *Star Wars* and Greek tragedy.

The journey described in *Star Wars* comes full circle, from the gradual erosion of freedom and the transformation of a democracy/republic into an empire, and back to a democracy where friend no longer betrays friend for the sake of personal gain. Creons must learn to reconcile themselves with Antigones: both a just rule and personal rights must be respected. There is also personal redemption, as Ajax, Heracles and Oedipus found in different ways. Redemption can be regarded as a Christian accretion, but the seeds of it were in ancient myth. For Achilles, what justified his life was his immortal fame, something shared by Ajax, Heracles and Oedipus; Achilles and Heracles were deified because of their divine ancestry, and Ajax and Oedipus became deified heroes to be invoked at times of need. Anakin/Darth Vader is by far the most interesting character in *Star Wars* and he has the same off-putting characteristics as many Sophoclean heroes. As in *Oedipus at Colonus*, even the gods recognize the transformation of Oedipus into a culture hero or *daimon*. In *Star Wars* one of the final shots shows the spirits of Obi Wan Kenobi, Yoda and Anakin cheering on the success of Luke Skywalker and the democracy of the erstwhile rebels. Comparably, Oedipus would protect Theseus and democratic Athens in its hour of need.

The Crying Game: Bacchic Revels

Neil Jordan was born in 1950 in Sligo, Ireland. He was a writer to begin with and has published three novels, besides a book of short stories (*Night in Tunisia*, 1976). He wrote and directed his first feature film *Angel* (1989). His *Crying Game* was nominated for six Academy Awards, and won an Oscar for Best Original Screenplay.

Neil Jordan has also used myths to make his *Crying Game* touch the hearts of viewers. His myths often touch psychological realities, and this makes them all the stronger for modern audiences. He uses several myths that are national in origin (Irish, Greek) or religious (biblical), and others that transcend such boundaries: the myths of sexual, national and individual identity. Some myths are based on inner truths; others constitute an outer mask. The fact that this film has something for everyone, and taps into the mythic subconscious, is probably why it earned so much in the United States: based on the ratio of cost to box-office receipts, from a budget of $5 million to a take of nearly $60 million, it was the most profitable film of the year (1993). Some of the myths in *The Crying Game* derive from Jordan's own memories and signify something unique for him. But when memories are well chosen, they can trigger a reaction in the audience's own memory and elicit a frisson of recognition. There are specific parallels between Euripides' *Bacchae* and Jordan's *The Crying Game*. Both deal with the constituents of theatricality and identity: when does the *persona* (the Latin name for mask) become the person? Dionysus/Bacchus is the god of the theatre, and the god of wine. He is called a god most fierce, and most gentle; his nature has both aspects. He is the god of transformation, leader of the dance, and croupier for *The Crying Game*.

The plot of both the play and the film centres on vengeance and the discovery of one's own nature. Jody, a black man serving in the English army, is taken hostage by the IRA. Jody has several guards, but chooses to befriend the most vulnerable and humane, a man who is called Fergus. He shows Fergus a picture of his 'special friend', the beautiful Dil, and asks him, if he is killed, to find her and tell her he was thinking of her and to see how she is doing. Fergus and Jody are similar: they are both victims of prejudice (Irish in one case, black in the other); both are doing their duty; both want love. Their homosocial behaviour borders on the homosexual, and the camera reinforces the camaraderie. Because he won't free Jody's hands, Fergus has to hold Jody's penis for him when he urinates. Jody says, 'Thanks. I know that wasn't easy for you.' Fergus answers casually, 'The pleasure was all mine.' He laughs without understanding why. He has given a polite British reply to 'Thanks', but it might just have more meaning than he thought. Jody saw something in him, and he orchestrates the future using what he saw as a way to seduce Fergus. Comparably, Dionysus harnesses Pentheus' own sexual drives to bring about his destruction.

Fergus is told to execute Jody, but as Jody tries to escape he runs into a British Saracen tank and is killed, the IRA hiding place is destroyed, and Fergus escapes to London. He gets involved with Dil, but is horrified to discover he/she is a man. Jude, a brutal IRA agent with whom Fergus had been sleeping, and who had seduced Jody so that he could be captured, finds Fergus and tries to involve him in another operation. Jude and Dil have a shoot-out, in which Jude is killed. Fergus goes to prison for Dil.

Just as Dionysus takes vengeance on the Thebans, so Jody takes a comparable vengeance on Fergus. Dionysus seduces their king, Pentheus, into dressing up like a woman, and leads him to the mountains to spy on the frolicking maenads where, after being unmasked as a man, he is dismembered by his mother and other bacchantes. Dil is an extension of Jody's Dionysus, and one recalls the lines from *The Bacchae* as Pentheus comments on how attractive Dionysus appears, so like a woman with long hair, falling down her cheek, arousing desire in the onlooker (*pothou pleôs*, 456). Dil casts his/her spell over Fergus when he lip-synchs the song, *The Crying Game*. Jody symbolically dismembers Fergus by forcing him to question his own identity as a white man, as a nationalist, as a heterosexual, and as a human being. By the end of the film nothing will be as Fergus thought it was at the beginning: all his ideological constructs are deconstructed. His myths are shattered. Parallels are drawn between various games. Jody plays the imperialist's game, cricket, and flashbacks often show him clothed in that uniform (see C.L.R. James in *Breaking a Boundary*, 1963, in which he shows how cricket was used in Trinidad as a tool for colonial resistance, and the film by Ashutosh Gowariker, *Lagaan: Once Upon a Time in India*, 2001, protesting the British occupation in India). Another game here is the 'patriot' game. Fergus wonders if by following the IRA he has chosen the correct course when their method of winning is so brutal.

The Crying Game itself is a game of love and loss. It can be played various ways – by heterosexuals, homosexuals and the in-between. Symbolically this fluid identity is conveyed by the three renderings of the theme song, Geoff Stephens' *The Crying Game*: at first Dil lip-synchs it when it is sung by a woman, Kate Robbins; then sung by Dave Berry; and finally by Boy George, going from woman to man, and then in-between. The reappearance of the song at crucial times not only adds commentary to the film, but thereby functions like a Greek chorus.

Jody tells Fergus a type of Aesop fable about a scorpion and a frog. A scorpion asks a frog for a ride to cross a river. The frog refuses, saying the scorpion will sting him. The scorpion says that would be silly since they would then both drown. The frog is convinced, takes the scorpion, is stung mid-river, and asks the scorpion as they are sinking why he did it. The scorpion answers, 'I can't help it, it's in my nature.' The story figures again at the end of the film, and like the song *Crying Game*, it also functions like a Greek chorus, relaying added information whenever it recurs. The tale is used by Jody to show the difference between those who take and those who give, those who are cruel by nature, and those who are kind, the difference between cruel (masculine?) Jude (the IRA's brutal seductress) and gentle (feminine?) Fergus. This film raises questions about what constitutes one's nature, besides gender and sexuality. If there is anything this film attempts to do, it is to show the complexity of these issues. The distinctions appear as a cinematic dissolve: one feels the emotional trace. The same story of the frog and the scorpion was used by Orson Welles in his film *Mr. Arkadin* (1955, also known as *Confidential Report*). Mr. Arkadin is a tycoon who finds his former partners and has them killed. He is the scorpion, and true to his nature. In Jordan's film, the scorpion seems to be identified with the IRA and the merciless members who continue to pursue Fergus and force him to continue a violent path of 'patriotism'. A comparable point is made about the IRA in *Breakfast on Pluto*. The militants cannot accept sexual ambiguity and 'Kitten' must leave the act in which he/she plays Pocahontas, in order to amuse an IRA audience. That same humourless lack of compromise characterized Pentheus, who nevertheless, came under the spell of Dionysus as revenge was exacted.

In *The Crying Game*, speech itself is a type of a game. Dil speaks about Fergus in the third person to Col the bartender as a way of communicating with Fergus: the third person is another disguise. This also makes Fergus into an object and empowers Dil. The ultimate game is visual storytelling through theatre and film. The opening scene at the funfair, the site of illusion and play, is the first round in this game of discovery. The illusion will provide insight into multivalent truth: theatre is the source of Aristotelian *anagnorisis*, 'recognition'.

The tokens that are used in the games are various. They contribute to the construction of identity. At the fair, the pink teddy bear Jude clutches adds to her girl/toy quality (an appearance soon to be refuted as so much else in this film), and intensifies the racial distinction of her cream colours against Jody's brown skin. The cricket bat becomes part of Jody in Fergus's visions, a weapon for winning a game, and, according to Freudian definition, a symbolic penis, the weapon in the game of love. Another symbolic penis is the gun. Early on Fergus holds a gun to Jody's head; later Dil holds a gun to Fergus' head. Neither fire them. Jude misses when she tries to shoot. Both Fergus and Jude fail at using guns when they should; the male/female Dil uses the gun most effectively when he/she shoots Jude. Dil wins this game. He/she is an extension of Jody, both stand-ins for Dionysus at moments in this film. Dil is at home in his/her body and identity, whereas Fergus doesn't know either his body or his identity. Fergus forces Dil to disguise herself, but disguising 'her' is hopeless, and he/she returns as soon as possible to his norm of assuming the feminine gender while comfortable with 'her' masculine sex.

Jody returns as a god, not the *deus ex machina*, but the ghost in the machine of Fergus's memory, returning at inopportune times, and forcing Fergus to make connections. Fergus lets Dil make love to him. As their sexual activity is in progress, Fergus looks at a picture of Jody. He sees Jody playing cricket: both breathe heavily. Then when Fergus discovers Dil is a man (*anagnorisis*), and is repulsed to the point of vomiting, he sees Jody running and smiling, again dressed in his cricket clothes. Jody has won this round of the game of vengeance. Dionysus likewise reappears as the smiling god at the end of *The Bacchae*, when he gloats over his victory. But here there is a reversal in the film. When Dil learns that Fergus was instrumental in Jody's death, he/she debates about killing him. She points the gun at him, but can't shoot. Dil says: 'He won't let me', and looks at Jody's picture. Just as Fergus was unable to shoot Jody, so this becomes a karmic repetition. Dil does kill the other IRA member responsible for Jody's death (Jude, the only one still alive besides Fergus at this point), but Fergus goes to prison for her and she asks why. He answers by telling the Aesopean fable about the scorpion being true to its nature. It's obvious that both Fergus and Dil forgive, and show themselves superior to Dionysus. Cadmus indicts Dionysus in *The Bacchae* for his unforgiving nature: 'Gods should not rival men in their grudges' (*Ba.* 1348).

At the beginning of *The Bacchae*, Pentheus is repelled by the idea of an effeminate creature like Dionysus, but he gradually 'becomes' Dionysus and shares his desires. At the end Pentheus is elevated above the other women, appearing in a tree as Dionysus will also be elevated at the end of the play. He is shown to be a doublet of Dionysus, and his erotic partner. In May, 1998, during the biennial festival of the Istituto

Nazionale del Dramma Antico under the leadership of Professor Umberto Albini, I saw a performance in Sicily in the ancient Greek theatre of Siracusa, in which Dionysus seduced Pentheus in a bed in front of the audience, before dressing him as a woman. In one performance of *The Bacchae* in German, directed by Theodoros Terzopoulos (Düsseldorf, 2001), the lower part of the bodies of Dionysus and of the chorus seemed to be in perpetual motion and sexual ecstasy. It is this same discovery of desire that Jody awakes in Fergus. He is as effectively seduced by Jody/Dil as Pentheus was by Dionysus. Fergus's 'dismemberment' is symbolic when he vomits after seeing that Dil is a man. Later he recovers, apologizes to Dil, and reclaims what he first rejected.

Like Fergus in Yeats's poem, 'Fergus and the Druid', he sees his 'life go drifting like a river from change to change' (Yeats 1956: 33). *The Crying Game* is no less *The Changing Game*. Many names cannot be identified as male or female: Jaye (Davidson, the actor who plays Dil), Jody, and Jude. Ambiguity is the name of this game. Nobody is who or what they seem to be. Dionysus is also the master of disguise. He not only assumes a disguise himself, he also directs *The Death of Pentheus* and costumes Pentheus accordingly to reveal his own inner desires. Jody uses the disguise of heterosexuality. Dionysus came to Thebes in the guise of Dionysus' own priest. As soon as Jordan proposes a myth, he defuses it through its own ambiguity. *Chacun à son goût.* Perhaps the last laugh is Dionysus' after all. This film is powerful, as is *The Bacchae* from the fifth century BC, because we interpret it in the light of our own myths. Just as history is created by both the historian and the reader, so is the film created by the director as well as the viewer. *The Crying Game* understands the game, and has many willing players.

Conclusion

In the prequels to *Star Wars*, the requirements for the hero are well established. Campbell advised Lucas on the making of *Star Wars*, and his work traces the journey of the mythical hero (Campbell 1968). The hero's quest involves leaving home, travelling far, training, meeting challenges, and then being reintegrated. Both Anakin/Darth Vader in *Star Wars* and Fergus in *The Crying Game* take this journey, even descending into darkness (Anakin goes to the dark side, but is redeemed at the end; Fergus is a member of the IRA, but discovers he cannot kill albeit he sympathizes with the cause). By the end of each of the films they are both reintegrated: Darth Vader becomes Anakin again, paying his debt to society by his death, and Fergus is in jail, paying his debt (for a murder he did not commit, but protecting Dil, someone he loved). Both gained knowledge about their own natures so their reintegration is both personal and public. They can be themselves, and are reintegrated into a society, by means of *anagnorisis* and *philia*: knowledge joined with compassion for one's fellow human being (a virtue prized in Euripides' plays). Both of these films, like myths about heroes, tell stories of alienation, redemption, and reintegration into society (both protagonists, Anakin/Darth Vader and Fergus, regain a conscience after it had been lost).

My main goal in my 'Theatre, Myth, and Cinema' classes is to make the Classics understandable to students by drawing analogies with modern films that are familiar to them (in a class of five hundred, at least four hundred fifty raise their hands to indicate that they have seen *Star Wars*). Joanna Paul, who discusses well reception theories, this volume, ch. 23, in remarking on the 'limited usefulness' of films that do not seem to be linked to an ancient text does not consider how fruitful this approach may be for teachers and students in classes that introduced the Classics by means of films. Who determines which links are close and which are not, and what is their methodology? My aim is to have all of them read, for instance, *The Iliad*, *The Odyssey*, *Ajax*, *Oedipus Tyrannus*, *Oedipus at Colonus* and *The Bacchae* with renewed interest because they can relate to the situations addressed in the modern parallels. (Hanna Roisman, this volume, ch. 24, puts the myth of Ulysses in both the ancient and modern settings (with specific examples), and provides an interesting analysis of changes between Homer's text and time, and the new productions.) I also hope that they will develop an appreciation for texts that are the cultural treasures of the human race. Technology and visual representations certainly appeal to the modern appetite, but humanity will starve if it does not include Classics in its continued development. These myths that are true to the human spirit, with their tales of a hero's quest, reclaim an innocence that seems to be lost in the modern world:

> We shall not cease from exploration
> And the end of all our exploring
> Will be to arrive where we started
> And know the place for the first time.
>
> Through the unknown, remembered gate
> When the last of earth left to discover
> Is that which was the beginning.

(T.S. Eliot, *Four Quartets*, 'Little Gidding', pt 5; Wain 2005: 638)

FURTHER READING

There is now an extensive bibliography of books about films based on the Classics, but the two earliest are: Solomon 1978, mainly about Roman and biblical epics, and McDonald 1983, on Greek themes. Others show the academic imagination at work: Mackinnon 1986; Winkler 1991 and Winkler 2001a; and a very interesting study that concentrates on the Roman world rather than the Greek, Wyke 1997. For a discussion of how myths are transformed in the various media, see 'The Dramatic Legacy of Myth: Oedipus in Opera, Television and Film' in McDonald and Walton 2007. Another source for films based on the Classics can be found in McDonald 2003. There are also films based on performances of plays and operas: consult McDonald 1992 and 2001.

For background interpretative tools see Monaco 2000. For general background on Joseph Campbell's influences in *Star Wars*, see the Lucas and Moyers (video) 1999 and Hanson and Kay 2001, which demonstrate that there are few 'new myths'. See also Roisman 1999.

For the Irish and their long relationship with the Classics see McDonald and Walton 2002. There is a good discussion of sources for Neil Jordan's work in Giles 1997. For mythical themes concerning the hero and Greek family see Slater 1968, although I think his judgment is clouded by a Freudian misogyny.

For a complete filmography of Lucas's and Jordan's work, visit the International Movie Database (IMDB) at www.imdb.com.

PART VII

Cultural Politics

CHAPTER TWENTY-SIX

Possessing Rome: The Politics of Ruins in *Roma capitale*

Catharine Edwards

'Rome is everybody's city. Its monuments and its great public spaces have been a staple of the Western experience, like the Bible and the plays of Shakespeare,' observed the architectural historian Spiro Kostof in the catalogue for an exhibition held in Berkeley in 1973 documenting *The Third Rome*, the city as capital of united Italy 1871 to 1945 (Kostof 1973: 8). Kostof articulates an assumption which underlies much of what has been written by visitors to Rome over the centuries; Rome 'belongs' to its visitors as much as (if not more than) to its inhabitants. One aim of my chapter will be to analyze some aspects of this rhetoric of ownership with a particular focus on literature of the later nineteenth century. This was a time when Rome, largely unchanged since the era of Sixtus V, embarked on a process of radical transformation to fit its new role as capital city of a recently united Italy (*Roma capitale*). All at once the non-Italian would-be 'owners' of this romantic backwater felt themselves rudely dispossessed. The English travel writer Augustus Hare, for instance, in the 1900 edition of *Walks in Rome* (first published in 1871), complains at length: 'Thirty years of Sardinian rule . . . have done more for the destruction of Rome than all the invasions of the Goths and Vandals . . . The old charm is gone forever, the whole aspect of the city is changed' (1900: I. 10). Hare and his contemporaries were responding to a drastic change in Rome's fortunes. Yet their complaints also belong to a long tradition articulated by those who are not Roman by birth (though Hare himself had been born in the city) yet feel their own education and scholarship, their own intimacy with the city makes them, in a sense, its proper heirs.

For Kostof, the city of Rome has a transcultural symbolic resonance parallel to that of the Bible and Shakespeare. The analogy between city and literary text is one often drawn (e.g. by Favro 1996). Radical and irreversible changes to a city's physical fabric make this analogy in some respects a difficult one to sustain – a new 'reading', constituted by the addition or demolition of a particular building, for instance, might be thought to obliterate an earlier one. This chapter will also explore

initiatives on the part of the Italian government post 1871 to capitalize on the material remains of the ancient city of Rome as part of the new regime's presentation of
itself as 'the third Rome', following the Rome of the emperors and the Rome of
the popes. These initiatives changed dramatically the appearance of some of the best
known monuments in the city. Yet if the analogy of 'reading' cannot always be
sustained, the notion of reception has a particular force in this context. The 'meaning' or rather 'meanings' of the city and its buildings are not to be found only in
the intention of those who originally created them but also in the relationship between
the city and those who encounter it. The succession of ways in which different groups
have made sense of the city becomes an intrinsic part of what the city means. Thus
the frames and contexts – the 'reading practices' – which later governments have
created for the monuments of Roman antiquity (alongside the uses made of the
city in literature and art) have an undeniable impact on subsequent responses to
those monuments. Only virtual reality could offer us a vision of the twenty-first
century Capitoline without the Victor Emmanuel monument, or the Viminal without the Via Nazionale (for virtual reconstructions of some parts of the city see
http://www.cvrlab.org).

Rome was the culmination of the Grand Tours made by countless foreign aristo-
crats and scholars, with Britons especially numerous after the conclusion of the Seven
Years' War in 1763 (the relationship between the Grand Tour and developing
ideologies of imperialism is touched on suggestively by Chard (1996) and by Elsner
and Rubiés (1999: 46–7) but deserves further exploration). Visitors from Protestant
Britain were intrigued, overcome and/or alienated by the buildings, ceremonies and
rituals of the Catholic church. But it was the remains of pagan Rome which were
supposed to be the principal focus of their attention. To be present in Rome, to see
the ruined monuments of the classical past, was to activate, bring to life, the classical
education with which – in theory – every gentleman was equipped (conversely, Rome
would naturally be incomprehensible to those without such preparation). Recollect-
ing the experience twenty-five years later, Edward Gibbon described his own
response to seeing Rome for the first time: 'Each memorable spot where Romulus
stood or Tully spoke, or Caesar fell was at once present to my eye' (1984: 134).
James Boswell, visiting Rome as the climax of his Grand Tour in 1765, gives an
account of his explorations of the ancient sites of the city in the company of the
antiquary James Morison. After a tour of the Palatine, they visit what was believed
to be the site of Cicero's house. 'Struck by these famous places, I was seized with
enthusiasm. I began to speak Latin. Mr Morison replied . . . We made a resolution
to speak Latin continually during this course of antiquities. We have persisted, and
every day we speak with greater facility, so that we have harangued on Roman antiquities in the language of the Romans themselves' (1955: 65). Through displaying
his mastery of Latin, the visitor actualizes his identity as a Roman.

A few decades later, J.C. Eustace, in the preface to what was to be for some time
the dominant travel guide for the aristocratic British visitor, commented:

> Our early studies, as Gibbon justly observes, allow us to sympathize in the feelings of
> a Roman; and one might almost say of every school boy not insensible to the sweets

of his first studies, that he becomes in feelings and sentiments, perhaps even in language, a Roman. It is not then wonderful, that when in a riper age he visits that country and beholds those very scenes which he has imagined to himself so long before, he should feel an uncommon glow of enthusiasm.

(1812: I. 57–8)

The rhetoric of identification here operates on two levels. The boy's immersion in Latin texts equips him with the intellectual – and emotional – outlook of an ancient Roman. At the same time the study of the classical past is intimately connected with his own personal past, 'the sweets of his first studies' (Eustace's Catholicism perhaps adds another dimension here). Thus the experience of visiting the classical sites of Italy allows the sensitive visitor to fuse nostalgia for the vanished world of the ancient Romans with nostalgia for the vanished world of his own childhood.

It was by no means only Britons who felt themselves so connected with Rome. Goethe visited Italy for the first time aged thirty-seven; composed much later on the basis of his journals, his *Italian Journey* gives an account of this transformative experience (Mahoney 2002). Knowledgeable about the classical past, Goethe is not especially concerned to revisit specific classical texts. Yet the sight of Rome does take him back to his own childhood: 'All the dreams of my youth have come to life; the first engravings I remember – my father hung views of Rome in the hall – I now see in reality' (1962: 129). At the same time, he feels himself to be reborn in Rome (1962: 150). Rome then is associated with his earliest memories but, more than this, his metaphorical rebirth in Rome has made him a Roman.

The relationship of possession could be figured rather differently. The American writer Nathaniel Hawthorne, in a novel set in Rome, *The Marble Faun* (1864), conveys the relationship between Rome and the educated visitor in more sinister terms, comparing the city to a decaying corpse. He goes on to list at length the repugnant features of Rome in the mid-nineteenth century, its dreadful roads, its squalid sanitary arrangements, its wretched food, its idle and ignorant inhabitants with their pretended religious devotion, yet concludes that on leaving Rome, 'our heart-strings have mysteriously attached themselves to the eternal city and are drawing us thitherward again, as if it were more familiar, more intimately our home, than even the spot where we were born' (1910: 274–5). The visitor is torn. He becomes connected to Rome in spite of himself; Rome's claim supersedes that of any actual birthplace. We cannot help our attachment to Rome.

The perception of entitlement can skew responses to the remains of antiquity in curious ways. One character from Hawthorne's novel, visiting the Colosseum with his friends, makes the following observation:

The Coliseum is far more delightful, as we enjoy it now, than when eighty thousand persons sat squeezed together, row above row, to see their fellow creatures torn limb from limb. What a strange thought that the Coliseum was really built for us, and has not come to its best uses till almost two thousand years after it was finished!

(Hawthorne 1910: 130)

The Colosseum is only able to realize its 'true' meaning when experienced as a ruin by Protestant visitors (on the complex symbolic resonances of the Colosseum in later periods see Hopkins and Beard 2005).

While the romantic poets generally tended to resist engaging with cities, preferring rather to explore the natural world, Rome nevertheless exercised a peculiar fascination for Shelley and Byron in particular. Their writings on Rome played a key role in forging the sensibilities of later visitors, not least through anthologizing works such as those of Augustus Hare (discussed below). As Tim Webb has emphasized, it was in part because Rome, with its vast areas of resonant ruin and unchecked vegetation, was so unlike any other city that it held such appeal. It was in Shelley's words 'at once the Paradise, / The grave, the city and the wilderness' (*Adonais* 1821; cf. Webb 1996; McGann 1984). Much of the space encompassed by the ancient walls was desolate, deserted (adjectives used by striking frequency by visitors to describe the site of the Forum Romanum). Malaria left the surrounding Campagna largely uninhabited, while many visitors themselves succumbed, meeting a premature end in the city, and were buried in the Protestant cemetery beneath the pyramid of Gaius Cestius. Shelley found this a particularly entrancing spot: 'one might if one were to die, desire the sleep they seem to sleep', he wrote in a letter to Thomas Love Peacock in 1818 (1965: 14). Rome was to be the grave not only for John Keats, to whom Shelley dedicated *Adonais*, but also for Shelley's son, while Shelley's own heart was also interred not long after in the same cemetery (on the association of Rome with disease and death, see also Wrigley 1996; Pick 2005, esp. ch. 8).

Yet Rome was a city associated above all with the ancient dead: 'Rome is a city, as it were, of the dead, or rather of those who cannot die, and who survive the puny generations which inhabit and pass over the spot', as Shelley wrote to Peacock (1965: 14). In a sense they continued to inhabit it, crowding out the living. In a prose fragment entitled 'The Colosseum' (1818), Shelley describes a blind old man and his daughter sitting alone in the ancient amphitheatre. They are visited by a personified spirit of antiquity: 'He avoided, in an extraordinary degree, all communication with the Italians, whose language he seemed scarcely to understand, but was occasionally seen to converse with some accomplished foreigner . . . He spoke Latin, and especially Greek, with fluency' (1988: 224). Visitors from northern Europe versed in the tongues of antiquity are the only ones worthy of the spirit's attention.

Insistently, foreign visitors deny modern Romans' right to see themselves as the heirs of Roman antiquity (in this respect, as in a number of others, there are strong parallels with visitors' responses to Greece). Their very presence renders some uncomfortable. In his letter to Peacock, Shelley explicitly comments, 'at least in the first enthusiasm of your recognitions of ancient time, you see nothing of the Italians' (1965: 14). The city's modern inhabitants were to many visitors either invisible, revolting or – at best – picturesque (see figure 26.1). Modern day Italians are attacked for being venal, superstitious and lazy, for knowing little and caring less about the ruins of antiquity alongside which they live. The sclerosis induced by papal control of the city is an object lesson in the superiority of Protestantism and parliamentary government. This insistence on the worthlessness of modern Italians shores up the inevitably insecure claims to Rome's inheritance articulated by visitors.

Figure 26.1   Goatherd at Trajan's Forum. Alinari Archive, Florence

Italy's Capital

At the same time some very different conceptions of possession in relation to Roman antiquity were coming to be articulated in the speeches and writing of many Italians involved in the processes which would eventually lead to the unification of Italy. Significant political change was afoot during the early and middle decades of the nineteenth century (see Riall 1994). A republic was briefly declared in Rome in 1848, but suppressed the following year when the pope summoned military assistance from the French government. While the rest of the country was unified by 1861, Rome remained under papal control. Three leading figures in the movement for Italian unification, the political thinker Giuseppe Mazzini, the politician Camillo Cavour, and the military leader Giuseppe Garibaldi disagreed on many issues. Yet for all of them, in the end, only Rome could be the capital of the new nation. 'Rome or death!' was Garibaldi's battle cry (on his complex emotional relationship with the city see Pick 2005). The choice of Rome was to some extent determined by what it lacked – none of the various interest groups working for unification had a peculiar vested interest in the city (Agnew 1998: 230). At the same time, the symbolic resonance of Rome's past could underwrite a powerful future for the new Italian nation. Mazzini in a speech of 1859 articulates the notion of the third Rome with particular fervour. He exhorts his listeners to imagine themselves pausing on the Via Cassia:

> Stop here and gaze as far as you can toward the south and toward the Mediterranean. In the midst of these vast spaces you will glimpse, like a beacon in the ocean, an isolated point, a sign of distant grandeur. Kneel then and worship; for there beats the heart of Italy: there lies ROME in its eternal solemnity. And that eminent point is the Campidoglio of the Christian World. And a few steps away is the Campidoglio of the Pagan World. And those two fallen worlds await a third World, even more vast and sublime, which is being fashioned in the midst of its mighty ruins. And this is the Trinity of History whose word is in Rome.
>
> (tr. Springer 1987: 156–7)

Mazzini's exhortation conveys the emotive force an appeal to Rome might deploy as a unifying goal. Whatever the disappointments the process of unification might bring (Mazzini bitterly regretted that the new regime was to be a monarchy rather than a republic and soon fell out of favour) it was, he insisted, Rome he would remember on his death-bed (Mazzini 1986: 382).

Once again the city of Rome was to become an imperial capital; its monuments were to offer a sense of power, pride and discipline to Romans and Italians. Rome's international profile could be harnessed to launch the new nation on the international stage. Yet the city's symbolic potency carried its own dangers. As Kostof comments, 'The third Rome was competing not only with its neighbours in Europe but with itself' (1973: 10). Francesco Crispi (later to be Prime Minister) declared in 1884:

> Whoever enters this great city finds the synthesis of two great epochs, the one more marvellous than the other. The monuments which celebrate these epochs are the pride of the world; they are for Italians a powerful reminder of their duty . . . It is necessary for us also to establish and heighten monuments of civilization in Rome, so that posterity can say we were great like our fathers.
>
> (Atkinson et al. 1999: 47)

Contemporaries in Britain and Germany in particular were quick to remind the new Italian government of what this entailed. The German historian Ferdinand Gregorovius, who spent much of his life writing about medieval Rome, commented in a letter of 1886: 'Never on earth did people acquire a more illustrious capital, and with it an equally heavy responsibility before the entire civilised world' (Kostof 1976: 7). This inheritance, the assumption of responsibility for the physical fabric of the ancient city, as well as its symbolic associations, could prove a heavy burden. Would the new regime rise to this challenge?

The frenzy of construction which seized Rome in the aftermath of the breach of Porta Pia (when the army of United Italy finally took Rome from the papacy) in 1871 saw vast tracts of the city transformed. Enormous, if architecturally undistinguished, new governmental buildings appeared, some, such as the Ministry of Finance, on a scale to dwarf the most colossal of ruins (Schroeter 1978). The Minister of Finance, Quintino Sella, envisaged a refocusing of the city, with new structures concentrated to the north east. But a financial crisis soon struck (the city was virtually bankrupt by 1888), inducing the new government to pursue more modest plans, reusing existing structures in the historic centre, buildings which were to be made more accessible through the widening of old roads and the construction of new ones (Kostof 1976). Vast fortunes were made (and lost) by private speculators who, anticipating a deluge of new inhabitants, put up at great speed housing whose poor design and low-quality materials were almost universally condemned (a vivid picture of these, many of which were abandoned unfinished, to form a whole new category of ruins, is painted by Emile Zola in his novel *Rome* (1896: 248–59)). One monument was completed whose primary function was to encapsulate Italian identity, to symbolize the relationship of the new Rome to its predecessors, the structure commemorating Victor Emmanuel II, first king of united Italy, eventually erected on the slope of the Capitoline hill, dominating the symbolic heart of pagan and communal Rome (see figure 26.2).

The vast, brilliant white construction, begun in 1885, was built in the international Beaux-arts style (a style already associated with the imperialist projects of other western governments). The heroic equestrian statue of the king echoes that of Marcus Aurelius, the centrepiece of Michelangelo's nearby Capitoline piazza. A complex iconographic programme projects the image of a unified, secular state. The prominent

Figure 26.2   Victor Emmanuel Monument. Alinari Archive, Florence

role given to the martial figure of Dea Roma suggested the new state's ambition to emulate its imperial forebear (the iconography is well analyzed by Atkinson et al. 1999; cf. Dickie 1994; Brice 1998). The year the monument was dedicated, 1911, also saw the acquisition of Italy's first imperial possession with the conquest of Libya. In some respects, at least, the Fascist regime would not constitute a radically new departure (cf. Agnew 1998).

The choice of location for the monument sent out a powerful message, but it was a choice with major implications for the historic centre. Many deplored this rupture in the city's fabric; the Sindaco (Mayor) protested in 1883 to the Royal Commission – but in vain (*Dagli scavi al Museo* 1984: 54). The distinguished archaeologist Rodolpho Lanciani commented in his 'Notes from Rome' published in the *Athenaeum*, 3 March 1883: 'I cannot find the proper words to stigmatize the decision taken by the authorities. The raising of the monument . . . is a national calamity . . . it means the destruction of the famous hill, with its incomparable historical associations, with its particular features and looks and outlines, familiar to millions of men and dear to every one' (1988: 126–7). A vast quantity of archaeological material was recovered, though inadequately published (figure 26.3 documents some of the finds which came

Figure 26.3   Objects found during construction, 1874. Photo John Henry Parker.
© American Academy in Rome, Parker Collection

to light during construction). Only in the late twentieth century were attempts made to catalogue and publish in detail the finds from the Capitoline, as well as from the sites destroyed in the construction of other gargantuan public works, such as the Ministry of Finance, which covered the ancient Porta Collina (*Dagli scavi al museo* 1984).

This bold transformation of the Capitoline was only one aspect of the new government's attempts to appropriate the powerful resonances of the ruins of, above all, imperial Rome. Archaeology was to have a key role in the resurgent national consciousness. While for British romantic writers the ruins of Rome spoke of a past which could never be recovered, for many Italians they symbolized rather a living tradition (cf. Springer 1987). Already in 1843, the conservative nationalist Vincenzo Gioberti had asserted: 'Since the resurrection of a nation's monuments restores the very idea of its identity, it joins a nation's past with its future and serves . . . to unite resurgent peoples, awakening and keeping their hopes alive' (Springer 1987: 142). For centuries the papacy had had prime responsibility for the remains of ancient Rome, both pagan and Christian. Some popes, such as Pius VII (1800–23), had taken particular pains to present themselves as the rightful heirs of the Roman empire (a delicate ideological balancing act, as Springer emphasizes, 1987: 64–97). Though under Pius IX (1846–78) interest and resources had primarily been focused on the catacombs, Rome's Christian heritage, nevertheless the institutional structures in relation to ancient remains generally commanded a degree of international scholarly respect (Zevi in Lanciani 1989: 3–4). Under the new government, responsibility for antiquities was given to the Ministry of Public Instruction, as part of the general direction of art education and fine arts (by implication the primary function of antiquities was to be a source of models for modern artists – a conception which seemed outdated even by the standards of archaeology under the papacy). Key museums remained under the control of the Vatican, while others were variously the responsibility of the state and the city government (leading to tensions which, until very recently, continued to dog the care of antiquities in Rome, Zevi in Lanciani 1989: 5).

Some argued for the establishment of a vast archaeological park in Rome, centred on the Forum Romanum and Colosseum but also encompassing areas such as the Piazza Bocca della Verità (the ancient Forum Boarium). In the end the constrained resources of the city government (whose appeals for funds to the state were generally in vain (Kostof 1976: 8)) coupled with the emphasis generally given to road building, meant that archaeology was prioritized in only a small area of the city, focused on the Forum Romanum (Insolera and Perego 1983: 3–14). Significant excavations had been carried out earlier in the century as part of the Napoleonic regime's attempt to stake its claim as the heir to imperial Rome, with some continuation under the restored papal government (cf. Ridley 1992). Soon after September 1871, work was renewed on this most symbolically loaded of spaces. Lanciani was in charge of the project between 1882 and 1885. Giacomo Boni (like Lanciani an engineer rather than a philologist by training) directed excavations from 1898 to 1922. His stratigraphic approach was to revolutionize Italian archaeology (*Dagli scavi al museo* 1984: 76–83; *L'archeologia in Roma capitale tra sterro e scavo* 1983: 13–29).

The approach here (and in the handful of other sites in the city where conservation was given the upper hand, such as the Pantheon and those parts of the Baths of Diocletian not sacrificed to the Ministry of Finance and new roads) was to isolate the remains of ancient Roman monuments, removing the accretion of later structures (a policy pursued with much greater vigour in later decades under Mussolini) (Insolera and Perego 1983: 5–9). Vegetation, whose luxuriance had been a hallmark of Rome's ruins, was systematically removed, to prevent the further erosion caused particularly by root growth. Many individuals were enthused by the opportunities the new Rome offered the archaeologist. Corrado Ricci put forward a plan to excavate the imperial fora (whose remains were largely covered by later buildings, mostly in private ownership). Ricci's vastly ambitious projects would only be brought to fruition years later and even then only insofar as they were compatible with Fascist road-building (Insolera and Perego 1983: esp. 26–30; Barroero et al. 1983).

The ruined monuments of ancient Rome occupied an uneasy place in the forging of a new Italian nation in the middle and later decades of the nineteenth century (cf. Springer 1987). 'Juxtaposition . . . is a two-edged sword. While it draws attention to the connection between past and present (as in the Roman Forum next to the Vittoriano), it also opens up the possibility for invidious comparison between the achievements of the past and the present,' as Agnew comments (1998: 239). Many foreign commentators were quick to pass judgement. Articles in *The Times* (for instance of 10 January 1888) lamented that the opportunity to create a capital city of unparalleled beauty had been squandered by the Italian government.

Many Italians were keenly aware of this international scrutiny. The prolific Lanciani published much of his work in English, eager to communicate the almost overwhelming tide of new archaeological material to an international audience. His preface to *Ancient Rome in the Light of Recent Discoveries* (1888) overflows with enthusiasm: 'If in 1870 anyone had spoken to us of the probability of an imminent and complete excavation of the Forum, from end to end, we should have denied the possibility of such an enterprise being completed in a single generation. But now the golden dream has become a reality' (1888: xxii). This was intended as a riposte to the criticisms of the new state voiced in the international press. The monuments were undisturbed, he asserted, indeed they were better taken care of. Yet he too conceded there were losses, deploring the shabby new quarters which now encircled the old city: 'the blame must be cast especially on the Roman aristocracy, on our noble land-owners unworthy of the great names which to our misfortune they have inherited' (1888: xxv). Certainly most of the finds Lanciani enumerates disappeared in later years (Packer 1989: 139). It is notable that when he died Lanciani chose to leave his vast collection of papers to the Vatican Library – perhaps a belated acknowledgement that the papacy had not after all been such a poor curator of Rome's monumental past (Zevi in Lanciani 1989: 3).

To mark the fiftieth anniversary of Italian unification in 1911 a series of exhibitions was held throughout Italy, including several in Rome. Among these an exhibition of the Roman empire was organized by Lanciani in the restored remains of the Baths of Diocletian (*Dalla mostra al museo* 1983). Each province of the erstwhile empire was to contribute plaster casts of important Roman remains. The catalogue makes explicit the role of the exhibition as a reminder to other nations of their debt to a Rome which is to be identified with the modern Italian nation: 'it will be clear how all the countries which were once provinces are still governed by Roman laws and how their inhabitants still walk on roads *we* built' (1911: 9, my tr. and ital.). Lanciani's inaugural speech was reported to an audience of international scholars in the first volume of the *Journal of Roman Studies* by the British archaeologist Eugenie Strong. Lanciani concluded expressing the hope that 'the exhibition might remain as the basis of a future museum of the Roman empire, "where Italian youth may seek inspiration for all those virtues which rendered Rome, morally as well as materially, the mistress of the world"' (Strong 1911: 49). Strong adds her own comment: 'We can only re-echo this wish, praying that it be made to include not young Italy alone but the youth of other countries also.' Italians were not to have an exclusive right to the inspirational remains of the Roman empire. The conquest of Libya in 1911 made Italy the latest European nation to lay claim to its own empire, but Rome's imperial heritage was particularly contested at a time when other governments too sought to legitimize their imperial ambitions. In 1912, for instance, was published C.P. Lucas's *Greater Rome and Greater Britain*, exploring at great length parallels between the Roman empire and British rule in India (Majeed 1999).

Scholars might complain at the losses consequent on the construction of a new capital, the ancient sites tantalizingly revealed only to disappear again beneath a new road or office building. For aesthetes, the new archaeology was itself a source of pain. Many visitors deplored (and some continue to deplore) the decision to remove all vegetation from ancient monuments. Gregorovius' journal entry for 18 June 1871 lamented: 'Rome has become a white-washed sepulchre . . . Rosa has shaved even the Colosseum' (1911: 402). Henry James, in Rome in 1873, commented, 'beauty of detail has pretty well vanished, especially since the high growing wild flowers have been plucked away by the new government' (1994: 135). For Christopher Woodward, writing recently on the inspirational power of ruins, the Colosseum is now extinct: 'Today, it is the most monumental bathos in Europe: a bald, dead and bare circle of stones' (Woodward 2001: 31). In Rome, above all, archaeology and aesthetics were incompatible.

Hare's Rome

Augustus Hare was one of the most vociferous nineteenth-century critics of developments in the city. His guidebook *Walks in Rome*, which went through twenty-two editions, was the companion of innumerable anglophone visitors. Writing about the Roman Forum, Hare deplores the apathy of the earlier papal government. But he is also most unhappy at the handling of the newly extended excavations:

> While gaining in historic interest, the Forum has greatly lost in beauty since the recent discoveries. Artists will lament the beautiful trees which mingled with the temples, the

groups of *bovi* and *contadini* reposing in their shadow and above all the lovely vegetation which imparted light and colour to the top of the ruins. As almost every vestige
of verdure is carefully cleaned away when it springs up, the appearance is that of a
number of ruined sheds in a ploughed field with some fine columns interspersed. As
Forsyth truly observes, 'deep learning is generally the grave of taste'.

(Hare 1900: I. 114)

For Hare (an accomplished amateur artist), Rome's Italian inhabitants should be
picturesque figures in a landscape whose indolence is perfectly calibrated to preserve
undisturbed the crumbling charms of their setting.

Earlier generations of travel writers, anxious to preserve the exclusivity of the Grand
Tourists' Rome, deplored the influx of their fellow-countrymen, particularly those
of inferior social status (Buzard 1993: esp. ch. 1). Now the principal agent of change
in the city was the Italians themselves, awakened from their picturesque, if morally
inferior, lethargy to take possession of the city. In the 1900 edition of *Walks in Rome*,
the Italian government is consistently referred to as 'the Sardinians' – they constitute an alien invasion, parallel to the Goths and Vandals and equally destructive.
By implication these barbarians have no right to occupy the city. Rome's true heirs
are rather those such as Hare and other erudite visitors who truly appreciate the city's
melancholy beauty. Some changes in the centre of the city are for the better, he
concedes, but, 'There is not a single point in the entirely modern Rome which calls
for anything but contempt' (1900: II. 24).

Yet this is never just a matter of conflict between a national idea of Rome and a
cosmopolitan international idea of the city – nor indeed of a conflict between scholarship and aesthetics. As with so many others who have written about Rome, there
is a personal dimension to Hare's claim to the city. Earlier generations of tourists
infused Rome with nostalgia for the absent ancient past – but also for their own
childhood. Hare himself had been born in Rome in 1834; his profligate, fashionable, expatriate parents lived then as tenants of the Villa Strozzi (Barnes 1986). Shortly
before his birth, his uncle Augustus William Hare died while visiting Rome; the child
was named after him. Adopted by Augustus William Hare's widow, Hare left for
England at the age of seventeen months. His childhood was lonely and austere,
his relationship with his adoptive mother Maria Hare particularly intense. Years later
in 1857, travelling with Maria, he returned to Rome (where his natural mother and
sister still lived). Augustus and Maria enjoyed a number of lengthy stays in the
city over the next few years, despite the devotedly evangelical Maria's concerns that
her son might succumb to the attractions of the Catholic church. Hare recollected
these as the happiest times they spent together, though he does comment reveal-
ingly, 'I often found myself in difficulties between my two mothers' (Hare 1896:
II. 57). Years later, as Maria lingered on her death-bed, Augustus (who was already
an experienced writer of guide books for the publisher John Murray III) set to work
composing *Walks in Rome*.

When the book was first published in 1871 Rome itself was on the brink of
radical transformation. Subsequent editions chart the changes and Hare's responses
to them. Hare is especially critical of the destruction of the Villa Negroni, 'one of

the most flagrant instances of injustice under the Sardinian government' (1900: II. 25. On the history of the Villa Negroni see Wiseman 1992a). Right beside this villa had been Hare's own birthplace, the Villa Strozzi (also now absorbed into the expanding capital, 1900: II. 27). It is striking that the rhetoric of possession becomes more noticeable in later editions of *Walks in Rome*. The introduction to the 1900 edition quotes some lines from John Addington Symonds:

> Then, from the very soil of silent Rome,
> You shall grow wise, and walking, live again
> The lives of buried peoples, and become
> A child by right of that eternal home,
> Cradle and grave of empires, on whose walls
> The sun himself subdued to reverence falls.
>
> (1900: I. 15)

Here again we find a Rome unpeopled by inconvenient modern Italians. Instead the foreigner, whose learning and sympathies have earned him the right to be Rome's child, walks alone amid the ruins.

Chapter XVIII of *Walks in Rome* describes the Tomb of Gaius Cestius and, 'at the foot of the pyramid . . . the Old Protestant Cemetery'. Hare refers to the graves of Keats and Shelley, to that of Symonds (who died in Rome in 1893) – and also to that of his own uncle and namesake, Augustus William. Hare goes on to quote a passage from Samuel Rogers commenting on the power of this place to engage the foreign visitor's sympathy:

> You are yourself in a foreign land and they are for the most part your countrymen. They call upon you in your mother tongue – in English – in words unknown to a native, known only to yourself; and the tomb of Cestius, that old majestic pile, has this also in common with them. It is itself a stranger among strangers. It has stood there till the language spoken around it has changed; and the shepherd, born at the foot, can read the inscription no longer.
>
> (1900: II. 282–3)

English slips into Latin and once again the English visitor claims an affinity to the ancients closer than that an ignorant modern Italian could attain. At the same time, in the 1900 edition the account of the cemetery concludes with an attack on the new road whose construction has done much to ruin the tranquillity of this beguilingly melancholy spot (this unhappy juxtaposition is evident in Mackey's photograph, figure 26.4, taken in the 1890s).

Hare was of course not alone in criticizing the alterations made to Rome. But his nostalgia was especially complex and multilayered. He expresses intense longing for the now vanished Rome he had come to know as a young man, in the company of his adoptive mother, herself now dead. At the same time, we might speculate that for him Symonds' figure of the foreigner as a child again in and through Rome was especially poignant; Hare had been born in Rome but, adopted by his aunt, had left the city before he could remember anything of it. The nostalgia he felt was not so

Figure 26.4   Aurelian walls in Viale di Campo Boario with the Pyramid of Cestius.
Father Peter Paul Mackey, British School at Rome Archive (Mackey 1164)

much for his actual childhood, whose deprivations he catalogued comprehensively in *The Story of My Life* (6 vols, 1896–1900), but rather for the idyllic childhood he might so easily have had in the city of his birth, roaming free with his siblings amid the ilex trees, cypresses and fountains of the villas of the old Roman aristocracy. Hare, above all, could feel himself a Roman dispossessed.

Hare's *Walks in Rome* has accompanied many thousands of visitors to the city; his personal relationship to Rome has thus fed into the experiences of countless others. Each visitor makes his or her own Rome, drawing on books and images (themselves drawing on other books and images) and uniquely coloured by personal experience, desire, loss, ambition, disappointment. For foreigners, Rome has had a special place in the formation of imperial ambitions, in the articulation of class identity but also – in part because of the central role occupied by the study of antiquity in elite education – in many people's self-construction. Rome, always already familiar, carries a particular emotional potency. Yet even a first visit to this city is accompanied by nostalgia for an idea of Rome, something irretrievably lost and longed for.

The ancient world is 'a country of the imagination' (Goldhill 2002: 96). But what happens when we try to visit that country as a physical place? How do we deal with the claims others may make to be its rightful owners? To what extent can the Rome in which people live and work coexist with the Rome of the archaeologist, the Rome of the aesthete? The dramatic changes to the fabric of Rome in the late nineteenth and early twentieth century reflected an often incoherent and always contested view of the relationship between ancient Rome and modern Italy on the part of Italy's new government – and on the part of archaeologists eager to investigate the past. The conflicts between different views of the proper relationship between the city's past and its present continue unresolved in twenty-first century Rome. At the same time, the transformation of the eternal city in the years after 1871, which no visitor could ignore, profoundly destabilized foreign visitors' always uneasy sense of themselves as Rome's true heirs. Different readings of antiquity cannot always coexist comfortably. In Rome more than anywhere else perhaps we are brought face to face with the fact that an unmediated encounter with antiquity can never be realized. The Rome we want can never be ours.

NOTE

Particular thanks to Daniel Pick for acute comments on an earlier draft.

FURTHER READING

Moatti 1993 provides a brief but wide-ranging introduction to the complexities of subsequent engagements with the ancient city. Hibbert 1985 offers a readable and well informed narrative of the city's history, while Bondanella 1987, ch. 6, Romanticism and Risorgimento, offers a brief introduction to responses to the city in the context of Roman images in the modern world more generally. Edwards 1996 examines the role played by ancient texts in the formation of responses to the city on the part of more recent visitors. The essays in Liversidge and Edwards 1996 explore visual responses to Rome on the part of British visitors. Springer 1987 offers a fascinating comparison of British Romantic and Italian nationalist attitudes to the Roman past. Atkinson, Cosgrove and Notaro's 1999 essay analyzes the Victor Emmanuel monument in the context of the construction of imperial cities more generally, while Agnew 1998 offers a provocative comparison of *Roma Capitale* and Rome under Fascism. For a suggestive exploration of the resonance and reception of one particular monument in a variety of contexts, see Hopkins and Beard 2005.

CHAPTER TWENTY-SEVEN

'You unleash the tempest of tragedy': The 1903 Athenian Production of Aeschylus' *Oresteia*

Gonda Van Steen

Introduction

With the statement 'You unleash the tempest of tragedy', the allegorical character Tragedy addressed the classical playwright Aeschylus in an 'Ode to Tragedy' delivered on Athens' premier stage of 1903. The actress Marika Kotopoule, a mere seventeen years young, could hardly have made a more prophetic statement: within two weeks of her delivery of the controversial ode, the streets outside of the Greek Royal Theatre resembled a battlefield on which students and police clashed in the name of Aeschylus. What exactly led to such an 'excess' of reception? How could aesthetics and politics become such closely joined sides of one coin? And how had Aeschylus, who, for decades, had remained in the shadow of Sophocles and Euripides, so rapidly become *the* symbolic currency for which the Greeks were willing to shed blood?

Let me first introduce the *dramatis personae* and locale of the most controversial modern Greek production of Aeschylean tragedy, which delivered more drama offstage than onstage. In early November of 1903, the prestigious Greek Royal Theatre (*Vasilikon Theatron*) was about to appear with perhaps the most famous production in the modern Greek reception history of the revival of tragedy. The stirring 'Ode to Tragedy', which Kotopoule delivered and which set the stage for the infamous episode, had been composed by the champion of Demotic Greek, Kostes Palamas, especially for the opening night (1 November 1903) of a production of Aeschylus' *Oresteia*. Kotopoule stood in front of a statue of Aeschylus, which she crowned during her recitation, and asked the playwright's ghost to inspire 'glorious' revival tragedy with an innovative spirit (Eliades 1996: 70–3; Palamas 1903: 751). She then went on to play the role of Pallas Athena – a difficult part, but not beyond the skill and talent of this rising star of the Greek theatre world (Sideres 1976: 191, 192, 195).

All of Athens had its eyes on the stage whose opening two years earlier had been long awaited: the fancy playhouse of the Royal Theatre located in central Athens, which was sponsored by the Greek royal court. Carrying the burden of a national theatre of its time, the Royal Theatre was expected to inaugurate its classical revival repertoire with the production of an ancient tragedy of authority and grandeur. Aeschylus' trilogy would fit the bill three-fold, after the National Theatre's Shakespeare and other modern productions had failed to impress (Spathes 2005: 249–57). With pressures and expectations raised so high, however, the staging of the *Oresteia* became a political as well as a cultural challenge at a crucial moment in Greece's history of slow but steady nation-building: the country nominally reborn in 1821 aspired to leave the decades-long foreign interference and the most recent political, military, economic and financial setbacks behind, and to enter a new century confidently exploiting especially its 'cultural capital' (Bourdieu and Passeron 1973) – much in the way the 1896 Olympics, the first modern Olympics held in Athens, had inspired a new national consciousness and pride under international scrutiny. It is, therefore, not an exaggeration to posit that, in the 1903 *Oresteia* production of the Royal Theatre, considerations of Greek national identity played as substantial a role as issues of performance, performativity, translation practice, linguistic controversy and the endeavour to establish an impressive venue and repertoire for Greek revival tragedy under the eyes of Western Europe of the 1900s.

In a forthcoming book, the Greek language expert Peter Mackridge defines the Greek Language Question (*Glossiko Zetema*, see also Beaton 1994: 296–368; Horrocks 1997), or the decades-long struggle to define a national language, as perhaps the most poignant expression of the uncertainty about Greek identity (personal communication; cf. Mackridge forthcoming). In the largely uncharted domain of state-subsidized revival tragedy, this question boiled down to the director's – or the institution's – choice between delivering the text in the original ancient Greek or using a translation in the 'purist', classicizing Katharevousa language, the official idiom of the state, the bureaucracy, and formal education. The nineteenth-century Greek intelligentsia favoured and effectively advanced the artificially reconstructed register of the Katharevousa over the vernacular or *Demotike* (even though there were many shades to the *Demotike*, including literary and other written forms), in order to address the ideological needs of the nation-building project, with its many stakes vested in historical continuity and lineage. Both choices, however, were far from presenting viable theatrical options. The riotous reception of the 1903 *Oresteia* production, the clashes between conservative students and the police out to protect enthusiastic spectators, have gone down in history as a narrowly national issue, as nationalist rows symptomatic of the linguistic fanaticism which fuelled the Greek Language Question. A shift to broader issues of national identity, of which performance, translation and language remain constitutive elements, is long overdue.

The Players Offstage and the Greek
Language Turned Protagonist

Many prominent Greek personalities had stakes vested in bringing the unique premiere of Aeschylus' trilogy to the Royal Theatre. Thomas Oikonomou (1864–1927), its director, had gained acting experience with the famous and influential German court theatre founded by Georg II, Duke of Saxe-Meiningen (Georgousopoulos 2005: 223; Spathes 2005: 244, 262). Oikonomou chose to present Aeschylus' *Oresteia* in a prose adaptation in the formal Katharevousa language but, following the translation provided by the classical archaeologist Georgios Soteriades, he allowed for many Demotic touches and the occasional trite expression (Nirvanas 1968: 217–18). Kotopoule described the production's language as a simple, 'moderate Katharevousa' (Eliades 1996: 67), and so do modern scholars (e.g. Stauride-Patrikiou 2005: 22). Its idiom was, however, still too formalist and too far removed from even a high register of the vernacular for Ioannes Psychares (Psychares 1903: 1–2). The linguist Psychares, Palamas' well-known fellow-advocate for the Greek *Demotike*, strove to re-create modern Greek culture based on the language of the rural folk and its traditional culture. Psychares was thus the most fervent and often the most dogmatic spokesperson for the all-encompassing progressive cultural, educational, and political ideology encapsulated in the turn-of-the-century movement known as Demoticism. Soteriades was not a Demoticist himself and he even criticized the dogmatism of an extreme Demoticism, but his translation of Aeschylus' *Oresteia* was, nonetheless, attacked for being too Demotic (Mackridge 2005: 6–7; Patrikiou 2005: 156; Stauride-Patrikiou 2005: 22). With hindsight, many scholars have noted that Soteriades' translation was unnecessarily vilified for bringing spoken features of the Demotic language to his written translation and thus to the formal stage. Some retraced their steps to claim that Soteriades' Katharevousa was 'impeccable' (Andreades 1933: 25 n.2; Petras 1960: 29; see also Chasape-Christodoulou 2002: 1:517–19, referring to Palamas 1903, Xenopoulos 1903, and articles in the periodical *Noumas*, the contemporary Greek journal which served the spirit of militant Demoticism; but cf. Paulos Nirvanas 1968, who stressed Soteriades' act of mixing linguistic elements at the expense of a cohesive language). In sum, because the production's language was still noticeably different from the conventional Greek translations of classical tragedy in archaizing and therefore artificial Katharevousa or from some contemporary productions staged in – even more exclusionary – ancient Greek, Soteriades' translation became instantly controversial – or was made to be controversial, as I will argue (for one of the sustained debates on the translation's language, see the Greek periodical *Kritike* 1/19 of 1903).

Stagings of classical Greek tragedy at the height of the Greek Language Question were typically conducted either in the formalist Katharevousa or in the original ancient Greek. Conservatives of the time saw both choices as serving the nationalist purposes of official Hellenism. But the broad populace of non-elite Athenians embraced productions which were professionally staged in an accessible idiom, and thus received this *Oresteia* production enthusiastically. Aeschylus' trilogy was indeed a success with the Athenian public and played to full houses every night for about two weeks. Unlike many other stagings of classical tragedy, Oikonomou's production showed every sign of being theatrically viable (Eliades 1996: 76; Grammatas 2002: 2:19–20). But the director's 'all too liberal' choice and his success enraged a reactionary professor from the University of Athens, Georgios Mistriotes, who defended his own linguistic views most vociferously. Mistriotes was the firebrand standard-bearer of a line of mostly conservative philologists (some of whom turned amateur theatre directors). His Society for Staging Ancient Greek Drama was active from 1896 until 1906 and marked a decade of protectionist revival tragedy which laid exclusive claims to presenting 'patriotic' drama in the name of inherited Hellenic civilization (Chatzepantazes 2002: 1:1:139–40; De Herdt 2003: 1:89–93; Van Steen 2000: 94, 102, 113, 115–18, 119). Against the tide of the changing times, Mistriotes kept insisting on non-adapted tragedy stiffly delivered in 'correct' prosodic ancient Greek. In the absence of sufficient knowledge of authentic staging conditions, the student-amateurs of his society re-created and, in their opinion, perfected the positivistic style of philological 'faithfulness' and historical and archaeological 'accuracy', which had informed several earlier tragic revivals. Along with minimal action and movement, this antiquarian style featured monotonous, overly solemn, or hypertragic speech. Even amidst the fiercest criticism of his production theory and practice, Mistriotes saw himself as a well-positioned guardian of Greek patrimony and employed classical tragedy as a vehicle to deliver lessons in Greek patriotism, national unity, and conservative morality. In fact, he was one of the last and most tenacious defenders of the linguistic ideal which rejected modern Greek translations – in whichever register – of ancient Greek texts, and he sported an absolutist sense of the cultural and didactic duties of such a language policy. Non-translation of classical plays, however, meant limited dissemination and narrowed the potential for viable stage production. Circles of (mainly) students influenced by Mistriotes grew increasingly frustrated with the rise of tragic revival productions in the 'unworthy' idiom of the Demotic language or of an 'imperfect' Katharevousa. The sharpening divisions between modernists and classicists or classicizers came to a climax in the bloody riots known as the 1903 *Oresteiaka*.

Critics have traditionally painted the actions of Mistriotes and his acolytes in the black colours of anachronistic and incendiary archaeolatry based on linguistic differences. The incident of the *Oresteiaka* has repeatedly been singled out as *the* clash in which the language struggle over the ancient authors came to a head, with Mistriotes leading the supporters of non-translation against the advocates of translations which ranged from rigid Katharevousa to Demotic or vernacular Greek. While the scuffles of 1903 did attest to the high passions provoked by the language debate, they also voiced the larger public's continued preference for revival drama in a more accessible idiom, and pointed up the precarious status of foreign adaptations of classical tragedies in the 'homeland' of ancient drama.

The Unbearable Foreign Identity of an *Oresteia*

There was more to the student rioting than the Greeks' polarization along linguistic lines. Mistriotes and his ardent followers were perturbed also because Soteriades' adaptation was several steps removed from the ancient Greek prototype and had been fashioned after then-trendy German notions of Romanticized drama production. Soteriades' translation was not based on the original but rendered the text second-hand, if not third-hand (Sideres 1976: 195). Giannes Sideres, the early Greek theatre historian, created the long-standing record stating that Soteriades had derived his translation from Hans Oberländer's drastically-abridged German version in seven acts of the scholarly (but accessible) translation of Aeschylus' *Oresteia* made by Ulrich von Wilamowitz-Moellendorff; Oberländer's *Oresteia* had first opened in Berlin in early November of 1900 and to great acclaim (Sideres 1976: 169–70, 186–99, for the most cited record of the foreign and subsequent Greek productions; also Sideres 1973a and 1973b; cited by Symvoulidou 1998: 49, 50–51, among many others). Recent scholarship, however, has traced Kotopoule's own and admittedly later Greek stage version (1949) of the *Oresteia* back to a different adaptation in German produced by translator Paul Schlenther for a December 1900 staging of the trilogy at the Burgtheater in Vienna (Andrianou 2005: 132, 138; Siouzoule 2005: 142–4, 149–51; on the German-language productions and their influence on the Greek staging, see Flashar 1991: 113–23, 140, 395).

Wilamowitz characterized the German *Oresteia's* success as 'the fresh effect of an unknown great work of art [which] produced in performers and spectators a positively reverential feeling' (1930: 307). He continued in the vein of nationalist pride at a German premiere of the Greek trilogy: 'I am proud of having introduced [Aeschylus] to very many of my nation' (1930: 307). Later, however, Wilamowitz voiced reservations about presenting the *Eumenides* on stage: '[The *Oresteia* production in Vienna in 1900] confirmed my judgement that the *Eumenides* is not capable of being performed, notwithstanding its very effective opening. The trial scene and the solution of the conflict are not satisfying to our feelings: the stylization, by which the poet deliberately altered the tone, must have a chilling effect' (1930: 307). The tendencies towards nationalizing and stylizing classical tragedy, which coloured or subtracted from the historicism and antiquarianism intended by the philologist and translator, are important points of reference also in our discussion of the Greek, 'derivative' production of 1903 (Xenopoulos 1903: 88).

In 1903 Greece did not have many economic, financial or military resources. But it saw itself as the proud 'owner' of ancient drama and, after 1896, of the revival of the Olympic Games – two powerful sources of cultural and symbolic capital which often acted in tandem. Greek national pride explains why the Royal Theatre was able to spend large amounts of money on the *Oresteia* production. Gregorios Xenopoulos called the 1903 trilogy perhaps the most lavishly-done production that Athens had seen up until then (Xenopoulos 1903: 89; also Sideres 1976: 188, 194). Yet the expensive sets of the *Oresteia* production had a distinctly foreign flavour: the displays of reconstructions of Mycenaean architectural elements, as well as the many fancy props such as Agamemnon's weapons and chariot, and the more than one hundred eye-catching period costumes for the impressively large chorus, had been commissioned from artists and craftsmen based in Berlin or Vienna (Eliades 1996: 68; Flashar 1991: 140; Krumbacher 1909: 49–50; Sideres 1976: 188, 189, 191). The Greek production of the *Oresteia* featured a musical score (by Charles V. Stanford) which was foreign-imported as well (Petras 1960: 30; Sideres 1976: 191). The 1903 *Oresteia*, therefore, appeared to publicly forgo national autonomy and unified Greek 'essence'. If this Greek staging was in any way an authenticating revival, it tried, para-doxically, to replicate its European models in a faithful or at least a highly mediated manner (Patrikiou 2005: 163). The production's foreign form and ornate *opsis* trans-formed it into something of a 'Wagnerian melodrama', complete with choral parts reduced to Romanticist musical interludes (Georgousopoulos 1982–84: 1:232, 2:200; also Sideres 1976: 169–70, 197–9; but cf. Michelakis 2005: 16). This revival tragedy declined to boast, as it were, Hellenic-nationalist pride or 'patriotic' ideo-logy, even when – or precisely because – it was staged at the Royal Theatre and spon-sored by the (foreign-born) Greek court. The Royal Theatre was, after all, the venue expected to assume a representative, if not a ceremonial status for Greek national culture. Because the *Oresteia* trilogy was, moreover, the theatre's inaugural classical revival production, it should have served also as a *celebration* of national culture (Sideres 1976: 188). According to many contemporaries, the Royal Theatre should, at the very least, have upheld a stricter and more conservative linguistic if not aesthetic norm (Xenopoulos 1903: 88).

Even critics much more open than Mistriotes stated that they missed not only the Aeschylean text and the elevated modern Greek language to match it but also the 'hereditary' Greek style of the production. But, in complaints which usually go unmen-tioned, the professor again took the lead in voicing resentment at the decades-long Greek preference for western European imports over unifying 'national', or 'morally responsible', 'didactically profound', and 'authentically Greek' stagings. Romanticist and melodramatic adaptations had, since approximately the mid-nineteenth century, reimported Greek drama into Greece to affect, that is, to 'corrupt' and 'diminish' the Greeks. Mistriotes contended that these widespread practices 'betrayed' Greece along with the Greek language and failed to properly educate and enlighten the Greek public. The particularly strong commitment to antiquity that French Enlightenment and German Romanticism and *Bildung* had shown for decades was ultimately not good enough for Mistriotes to guarantee Greek national superiority. For him and his followers, foreign and Greek Romanticist conceptions and the dramaturgical fashions then in sway constantly threatened to upstage 'native' Greek nationalist priorities and patriotic responsibilities. According to Mistriotes, 'patriotic' produc-tions – not rich productions, but those which returned to ancient Greek and, as much as possible, to ancient Greece – were needed more than ever in those turn-of-the-century years of humiliating public setbacks at the hands of foreign as well as domes-tic forces. Productions which highlighted Greece's dependence on western theatre fashions could only be seen as 'unpatriotic'. But Mistriotes' vision of revival tragedy was doomed to fail, because he perpetuated the narrow philological treatments of classical drama when changing times called for innovative performative approaches and for new definitions of patriotism – for one, a patriotism which would feel less intimidated by foreign cultural and theatrical influences. The general Greek audi-ence clamoured for lighter genres, novel and accessible, and engaging performance styles, such as those of the *epitheorese*, or 'revue', and related Parisian vaudeville spec-tacles. Stagings of classical tragedy in Demotic became more common throughout the first half of the twentieth century, but only after incidents such as the *Oresteiaka* had rendered the Language Question notorious.

The Greek, the Bad and the Ugly

Karl Krumbacher cited some of Mistriotes' common charges against the translators and modernizers of ancient drama: he branded them as 'traitors of Greece,' who 'worked to enslave the nation' (Krumbacher 1909: 52–3). Soteriades' translation was, in Mistriotes' verdict, intent on 'destroying the unity of the Greek race'; it was ethnically divisive, 'anti-national', or 'non-Greek' (Polites, quoting from Mistriotes' public speech, 1950: 394). For about two weeks, Mistriotes fired up his students with his inflammatory rhetoric, directed as if against an organized political conspiracy which was unquestionably subversive. The students started to issue threats against the involved directors, managers, and actors, those 'murderers' of Aeschylus who had 'demoticized' him on the stage of Greece's theatre establishment – *and* had eulogized him as a Demotic champion by way of Palamas' introductory 'Ode to Tragedy' (Eliades 1996: 67, 79–80; Petras 1960: 29). The worst outburst, however, erupted on the evening of 16 November 1903, when Mistriotes' students marched on the Royal Theatre, interrupted the evening performance, demanded that the production's run be cut, and went on to clash with the police in street scuffles which left a handful dead, more than a dozen injured, and many more arrested (Eliades 1996: 78, 80; Petras 1960: 31; Sideres 1976: 198).

For Mistriotes, the issue revolved around whether the translated and adapted *Oresteia* could still stand as a 'patriotic' monument. He did not shy away from claiming a monopoly on a patriotism which, according to him, was in full synergy with classical antiquity and its ancient language. He railed against his opponents and defenders of the modernizing *Oresteia* in his – presumptuously titled – 'Philippic against the Vulgarizers', a fiery speech in search of classical rhetorical models (Demosthenes against Philippus II of Macedon) and published in the Athenian journal *Chronos* of 20 December 1903:

> Stand up, vile enemies, and show respect for the three millennia which look down angrily upon you from the Parthenon and the Propylaea. [C]ast your axe to the ground, with which you seek to sever the head of the Fatherland (*Patridos*), you mother-killers (*metraloiai*).
>
> (quoted also by Sideres 1973b: 96)

In the context of such a reactionary but militant 'patriotism', the frequent slurs of 'traitors', 'anti-Greeks', 'matricides' or even 'pan-Slavists' hurled at the Demoticists grew in number and acerbity (see the quotations from various relevant sources in Sideres 1973b: 90–99; also Sideres 1973a: 55). For Mistriotes, the practice of strict classicizing was to make productions of ancient tragedy legible and morally uplifting for the modern Greeks; therefore, any perceived lack of classicizing threatened to render the productions not only illegible to the Greeks but even nefarious.

Twentieth-century Greek linguistic and political debates recast the charge of a dearth of morally 'sound' patriotism in many of the old terms of insult and abuse. In this respect, too, the *Oresteiaka* left a bitter legacy. The label of 'matricide' remained part of the allegations issued by the linguistically and politically conservative right against the Demoticists, who, over time, became more clearly defined as the political left (Georgousopoulos 1982–84: 1:233). The crime of matricide is, of course, reified on stage as one of the central acts of Aeschylus' *Oresteia*, but it is also formally forgiven by the end of the trilogy. Mistriotes could not but perceive the 'Demotic' *Oresteia* as all the more offensive for condoning the matricide of the ancient Greek language. For him, not modern but ancient Greek was to be defined as the Greek 'mother-tongue'; ancient Greek fitted the metaphor of the '*metrike glossa*' – with another unabashed claim to linguistic continuity, autochthony, and integrity. He saw the slur of 'anti-Greek mother-killer' as a just attack on anyone violating the genealogical as well as linguistic unity of the Greek language, or on the one whose translating practice cut the Greeks off from their ancestral and (motherly) nurturing ancient Greek culture. The much-touted monolithic unity of the Greek language would help its speakers to ward off foreign intrusions as well as internal discord. Western cultural imperialist influences posed a real hazard, as did the aggressive inroads from the North which the Greeks feared that their Bulgarian neighbours would make. Bulgaria's expansionist ambitions and claims to Macedonia were financially supported by the conspiring Russians, at least in the opinion of Greek nationalists who believed that Macedonia was and should be Greek (Mackridge forthcoming).

In a related, extreme twist of nationalist paranoia, the charges against translator Soteriades included that he was a Russian errand-boy, who had been paid off in rubles to undermine the Greek state and its ancestral language (Eliades 1996: 69; Kalogiannes 1984: 65, 113 n.23; Krumbacher 1909: 58–9; Mackridge 2005: 5, 7; Nirvanas 1968: 214). The accusation of 'pan-Slavism' infused the debate on the *Oresteia* translation and production with inflammatory references to the earlier Gospel Riots, or the *Euangeli(a)ka*, the violent protests staged in 1901 against the Demotic translation of the New Testament published by Alexandros Palles. These *Euangelika* provided a blueprint or script, as it were, for conservative protesters to attack the linguistic advances and agendas of a progressive elite (not necessarily of the Greek people). What is most striking, however, is that the two main objects of progressive translation and reactionary obscurantism, the Christian scriptures and pagan classical tragedy, were conjoined as – at first sight unlikely – victims beleaguered by the common enemy of pedantic linguistic contestation. But this sweeping incorporation and alliance, too, was a feature of the nation-building construct of the much-heralded Helleno-Christian civilization (Mackridge 2005: 7), a construct created in the latter half of the nineteenth century only to fall to rampant and indiscriminate abuse during the middle decades of the twentieth century.

A brief description of the 'warm-up' to the actual Gospel Riots will help to explain the staying power of the charge of 'pan-Slavism'. The Russian-born queen of Greece, Queen Olga, had commissioned a new translation of the New Testament in the 'popular language' from Ioulia Karolou, her private secretary. Not unexpectedly, the Holy Synod of the Church of Greece blocked publication of the translation on the ground that its 'vulgar language' profaned the Gospels (Mackridge 2005: 4). In February of 1901, however, Queen Olga managed to proceed with a trial-run publication of one thousand copies – enough to provoke a public outcry and the strident allegation that the queen's Russian rubles paid for a translation that threatened to split the Greek language into dialects and, with it, the Greek nation. Such a manifest lack of Greek unity would leave especially Macedonia vulnerable to Bulgarian inroads, in the eyes of the Greek nationalists (Mackridge 2005: 5). In September of 1901, then, the Athenian newspaper *Akropolis* began running a serial of instalments of the Demoticist Palles' translation of the Gospels. The register of Palles' language and his choice of the profane medium of a newspaper enraged linguistic conservatives, university professors, students and even trade union leaders. During the protest rallies of several days, which demanded a broader ban on translations of the New Testament, casualties were incurred in scuffles between demonstrators and the police aided by the military. The Greek government itself fell (Mackridge 2005: 5–6). Slurs of 'pan-Slavism' were back in full force and were re-applied to the 'perpetrators' of the translation and production of Aeschylus' *Oresteia* two years later. Paulos Nirvanas sensibly regretted that all the burning political issues of the early twentieth century were, inevitably, tied to the language crises and their fallout: from the Great Idea to the Bulgarian and Slavic menace (at the expense of Macedonia), to the future of Hellenism itself (Nirvanas 1968: 214).

Essential to Mistriotes' strategy was the endeavour to place linguistic transgression on a par with religious transgression. This was not a big or even unexpected step for Greek conservatives to take, given that the Greek language had long been perceived not only as a solemnly ancient but also as a sacred language, which could only be 'corrupted' by Demotic Greek. The act of translating, however, which had long been contested with respect to the Gospels and to classical Greek tragedy, was more likely to be endorsed in the latter case, as long as the translator adhered to a strict Katharevousa. In the conservative perspective, ancient tragedy of the Greeks as 'the chosen people' functioned as an equivalent to the Old Testament. Telling is Andreades' quotation of an unidentified source apparently speaking for the Mistriotes camp: '[A]fter the attempt to vulgarize the New Testament, we now find ourselves faced with an attempt to vulgarize ancient tragedy, the Old Testament, so to speak, of the Greek people' (Andreades 1933: 25; also Petras 1960: 29; and, after him, Eliades 1996: 67). As the Greeks' Holy Bible, classical theatre demanded worshipful dependence from the modern Greeks, who tolerated tragedy's graphic descriptions of (offstage) violence and loss given their familiarity with such narrative components especially in the Old Testament. Aeschylus' *Persians*, for instance, had its counterpart in the biblical tale of David and Goliath; many nineteenth-century Greeks found the themes of retaliation against aggression and of glee after deserved victory appropriately represented in the playwright's oldest tragedy (Van Steen 2007). Mistriotes concluded his 'Philippic against the Vulgarizers' (in the journal *Chronos*, 20 December 1903) with words of praise for the 'martyrs of the language', who guarded with their blood both Greece's language and its religion. Such linguistic and religious attitudes imposed a matrix of immobility and stagnation on the reception of classical drama: any bold refiguration could be denounced as an act of sacrilege, as a profanation of everything sacred and holy that defined the Greek nation and race (Grammatas 2002: 2:20; Mackridge 2005: 7).

A German *Antigone*

The rows of the *Oresteiaka* point up fault lines in the complex dependencies between Greek revival tragedy, linguistic and translation practice, and the pressure to build a theatre and repertoire of manifest cultural capital. The immediate relevance of these relationships and their general importance as building blocks of Greek political and cultural identity are confirmed by Greek efforts to revive Sophocles' *Antigone* in Athens . . . belatedly. The play's Greek reception, too, re-veals a rather uncritical but widespread nineteenth- through early twentieth-century fascination with foreign-imported models of the kind that elicited Mistriotes' reaction. It was the compelling combination of a German adaptation and a Romanticist musical score that steered the earlier western European reception history of Sophocles' *Antigone*. The choral music composed by Felix Mendelssohn-Bartholdy had launched the *Antigone* of director Ludwig Tieck as *the* 'classical' production ever since its grand opening performance in Potsdam in 1841. The translation was by Johann Jakob Christian Donner and the production enjoyed the patronage of Friedrich Wilhelm IV of Prussia (Flashar 2001: 36–44, and 1991: 60–81, 85, 90–91, 110; Macintosh 1997: 286–9; Steiner 1984: 8–9). Most of the *Antigone* productions which sprang up all across western Europe were well-intentioned attempts to smooth over the 'intractable' aesthetics and conventions of Greek tragic theatre by means of the aural and visual delights of Romantic drama, to which the mid-nineteenth-century upper classes of theatre-goers had grown accustomed. The tremendously influential 'Mendelssohn *Antigone*', as the production became known, provoked a sense of belatedness in the Greek theatre world, because the Greeks had failed to revive the *Antigone* before the German adaptation stole the show and also because they had not embraced the successful modern version as quickly as other countries had done. By wasting such valuable opportunities, the Greeks, some thought, had failed to prove the authenticity of their own descent from the ancients. The search for historical continuity and classical ancestry indeed inspired many of the first modern Greek revival productions of ancient tragedy. Few saw the bold liberties which neo-classical and Romanticist adaptations took as encroaching upon the broad claim to continuity. Mistriotes, nonetheless, insisted on affirming the purity and unity of Greek origins through his own ancient-language revivals of Sophocles' tragedies, in particular.

Before Mistriotes staged his own *Antigone* in 1896 – a terrible flop – the play's Greek history had brought the issue of patriotic nationalism to the fore, and served as a lead to Greek revival drama's deliberate show of western 'progress' and modern sensibility. Especially the Romanticist Greek staging of Sophocles' *Antigone* of 1867 (in a Katharevousa translation by Alexandros Rizos Rankaves, see Rankaves 1895: 2: 164–5; Sideres 1976: 42–5) was modelled closely on the 1841 German version and amounted to a cosmopolitan and aristocratic-patriotic tribute to the king and the upper crust of Greek society (Chatzepantazes 2002: 1:1:138–40, 273–4 n.41, 1:2:633). With this first full-blown *Antigone* production of 1867, the semi-professional Greek actors and director intended to celebrate the royal wedding of King George I and the teenage Russian princess Olga (the later queen at the centre of the controversy of the *Euangelika*). The 'patriotic' (Sideres 1976: 43) tragedy was staged at the Herodes Atticus Theatre, which was newly excavated and fitted out, though not yet restored. An archaeology professor from the University of Athens, Athanasios Rousopoulos, was in charge of the direction. This academic basis – a common feature of mid-nineteenth- through early twentieth-century revival productions – demonstrates how willing and eager Greek intellectuals were to participate in the disciplined training in foreign-imported aesthetics and, in particular, western choral or orchestral music. The producers of the courtly *Antigone* of 1867 had no qualms about adopting full European-style sets, complete with a curtain and curtain frame, which they had erected in the orchestra to cover the back wall of the ancient Roman theatre (Sideres 1976: 43–4; Tsoutsoura 1993: 34). The Athenian production proudly showed off Mendelssohn's celebrated music; a full fifteen-member chorus of students sang the choral passages in Rankaves' translation (Chatzepantazes 2002: 1:2:634; Glytzoures 2001: 45; Sideres 1976: 43, 44).

The theatre historian Giannes Sideres characterized the rage for the Mendelssohn *Antigone* as the phenomenon of '*Antigonismos*', with a pun on the modern Greek word for 'antagonism' or 'rivalry' (*antagonismos*) (Sideres 1976: 82, with reference to a newspaper report in *Ephemeris* of 22 October 1888). In the competitive struggle to bring the first revival of Sophocles' *Antigone* to Greek soil, be it in its 'authentic' form or in adaptation, the German version held pride of place. For several decades to come, the *Antigone*-mania marked the tragedy and its author as vehicles of foreign-imported Romanticism through the siren call of music. The increasing interest which Greek translators took in Sophocles and in the *Antigone* did not achieve much to reappropriate the tragedy for Greece or to remedy the anemic condition of the Greek theatre world at large. The boost in translations was, if anything, the *result* of the mid through late nineteenth-century craving for the Mendelssohn *Antigone*: modern Greek translators merely hoped to get a piece of the action (cf. De Herdt 2003: 2:105–6). Some critics and scholars, however, continued to argue that any choral music should be adjusted and subordinated to the text and not vice versa and that, in Greece, revival tragedy should be owned by Greeks. When Mistriotes continued to loudly question the key position of Romanticist revival tragedy in Greek repertory and court-serving theatres, albeit with his keen, personal focus on the language of the performances, the nineteenth-century Greek tradition came to a rude awakening in the incident of the *Oresteiaka*.

Conclusion

The *Oresteiaka* episode provides a telling example of how Greek theatre history has tended to be fiercely nationalist. Its analysis gives us cause to question the nationalist paradigm; it also affirms our reasons to contextualize the reception of classical tragedy in its broader socio-political framework and to link this reception to the growth of Greek cultural identity. The *Oresteiaka* symbolized the struggle for the repatriation and domestic consolidation of ancient drama, in place and time, language, style, and aesthetic conception. The western annexation of classical theatre was as much anathema to Mistriotes and his students as the *Oresteia* production's linguistic transgression was deemed to 'betray' immediate territorial interests or to flaunt 'sacrilege'. The academic and conservative dream of high-cultural, 'patriotic' productions of ancient tragedy underscored Greece's rekindled irredentist ambitions: the irredentist dream of the 'Great Idea' to expand frontiers and to 'repatriate' the 'unredeemed' (formerly Byzantine) lands where large ethnic Greek populations still lived under Ottoman rule. Nationalist irredentism operated on a metaphorical level in Mistriotes' dramatic theory and practice. His philology of undaunted nostalgia – or reactionary and militant traditionalism, in the eyes of his detractors – wrenched the classical playwrights from Western cultural imperialism and aggression from the North, his 'unredeemed compatriots' enmeshed in foreign adaptations or conspiracies, as well as the ethnic ancient language – to be delivered not with the Erasmian but with the modern Greek pronunciation. Seeking a modern rebirth of the tragedians' 'timeless' language and ethos, the self-styled director Mistriotes treated classical drama more as the bearer of Hellenic ideology and Greek lineage than as a theatrical event of true performance. His showcasing of the canonical, 'immortal' plays reflected an academic but no less political vision of ancient tragedy: revival tragedy as an idealized moment of nationalist legitimation and as a means to continue to forge the neo-Hellenic links between language 'propriety' and 'unity' and official, 'patriotic' nation-building.

The 1903 Athenian production of Aeschylus' trilogy touched all the sensitive nerves of cultural reception, of politics, nationalism, language, morality and education. The outcry generated by the production marked one of the most significant acts of the cultural politics of reception in Greece, and it was far from the proverbial tempest in the teapot – as it has often been dismissed by recent students of modern Greek theatre history. For anyone eager to learn more about reception studies and its varied practices, the interest of the production of Aeschylus' *Oresteia*, now a century old, lies in its extraordinarily close engagement with the turn-of-the-century broader socio-cultural politics and their transformation into particular aesthetics and political realities. Critics have often overemphasized the linguistic debacle and have overlooked or toned down the foreign factor at the nub of the issue, which has been the focus of my attention. The *Oresteiaka* may well remain notorious as a language row and may continue to mark a low point in the modern Greek quarrel over the ancients. Its precise nature, however, must be analyzed in terms which probe beyond the linguistic or which, at the very least, make the translation and the ensuing linguistic divisions appropriately subservient to the production's broadly defined cultural translatability, or the nuanced resonances of the ancient text transferred to a complex society on the brink of modernity. The *Oresteiaka* episode may shed light also on how rocky the relationship can be between translation practice and the establishment of Greek revival tragedy – or just how many bumps there are in the road of the transition from ancients to modern ancients to moderns.

FURTHER READING

Hall 2004: 51–89. An excellent and concerted effort to theorize diverse receptive strands and an up-to-date discussion on the status of reception studies.

Euangelika 1901 – Oresteiaka 1903: Modernizing Pressures and Society's Acts of Resistance [in Greek], Athens, 2005. A very recent in-depth look at the two most notorious incidents which marked and marred the history of the modern Greek language. The volume is a collection of essays which were presented at a 2003 symposium held in Athens.

Macintosh, Michelakis, Hall, and Taplin 2005. A thorough recent study of the figure of Agamemnon and his circle in Aeschylus' tragedy and other sources and in ancient and modern reception histories.

Mackridge forthcoming, *Language and National Identity in Greece*, Oxford. Once published, Mackridge's book will prove to be one of the most useful English-language studies and in-depth analyses of the Greek Language Question within the context of the ideological debate about modern Greek identity. His book will focus on the long-running controversy (*c*.1776–1976) over which variety of Greek should be used as the official national written language. It will situate the language controversy against the background of various other languages which were spoken in the Southern Balkans and will address ways in which the Greeks have distinguished themselves from other nations by referring to their language. I thank Peter Mackridge for sharing his thoughts with me in advance of this much-anticipated publication and for offering generous comments on an earlier version of this chapter.

Steiner 1984. An impressive study of the reception of Sophocles' *Antigone* and the various philosophical, literary, artistic, and broadly cultural inquiries to which *Antigone* productions have given rise since the nineteenth century.

Van Steen 2000. A study of the reception history of Aristophanes' comedies in Greece of the late eighteenth through twentieth centuries.

CHAPTER TWENTY-EIGHT

Multicultural Reception: Greek Drama in South Africa in the Late Twentieth and Early Twenty-first Centuries

Betine van Zyl Smit

Introduction

The performance of Greek drama has flourished in South Africa in the last decades of the twentieth and at the start of the twenty-first centuries. Staging and adaptation have reflected the rich diversity of the country's cultures. Classical themes have been used to engage the new political dispensation as well as addressing global issues afresh. The abolition of racial segregation changed the themes, casts and audiences of plays (Van Zyl Smit 2003b: 16–17).

In South Africa art and politics often intersect. This is as true of the theatre and performance art as it is of literature and the figurative arts. Classical drama was part of the western elite culture imported by the colonial power. It encompassed performances by theatre companies from abroad, mainly from about 1850 to the 1920s, as well as local productions by amateur, academic and professional companies. Although many plays were staged in English, local translations, particularly into Afrikaans, were prominent from the 1920s onwards; while there were occasional performances in an indigenous language, none of the scripts were published. Initially, most of the Greek dramas, tragedy or comedy, were staged in what was then generally regarded as the 'classical' style. The actors wore loose garments, masks were not used, the members of the chorus were identically dressed, movement and speech were stylized and language formal and elevated.

Although at one level these performances were a celebration of the classical drama of ancient Greece, at another level the productions of Afrikaans translations in particular were also a celebration of the independence of Afrikaans language and culture. One way in which the fledgeling Afrikaans language enhanced its status and asserted its independence of the dominant hegemony of English was by aggressively developing its range and the variety of spheres in which it was viable. By choosing, for example, to stage an Afrikaans translation (by Theo Wassenaar) of Sophocles' *Oedipus Tyrannos* in Pretoria in 1938 to celebrate the centenary of the Great Trek when the ancestors of the Afrikaners left the Cape Colony, then under British rule, the Afrikaans community was using the prestige of Greek culture to enhance the validity of its own language and culture. The Afrikaners were staking a claim as equal inheritors of the great tradition of Greek drama. They wanted to prove that their language was on a par with English as a vehicle for the 'European' heritage. It can be argued that this claim was made, reiterated and enhanced by every Greek play that was performed in Afrikaans. It is notable that a considerable number of Greek dramas were not only translated into Afrikaans, but also published: of some more than one different translation (three of each of the *Oedipus* and *Antigone*, two versions of *Troades* and a further nine Greek plays) (Van Zyl Smit 2003b: 6–9).

Hybridity and Language

From the 1960s onward, however, an indigenous, alternative reception, predominantly Anglophone, developed. Productions became more experimental and local elements were often introduced. In the 1970s the alternative theatre became more radical and increasingly sought to confront the political realities of South African society. Attempts were made to reach all sectors of the community. At this time clear references to the plight of the oppressed in the country were introduced into the staging of Greek drama. Thus South African culture was fused with Greek culture in some of the plays of the theatre of protest. *Antigone in '71* was developed by the Theatre Council of Natal, a group strongly influenced by the Black Consciousness Movement that strove to affirm the dignity and pride of black South Africans and to confront the injustice and inhumanity of the apartheid system. The production included simulated hanging, newsreel footage of slum housing and a chorus of black women. The play was performed in township halls throughout the rural areas of Natal and brought its message to people previously unacquainted with theatre (Van Zyl Smit 2006: 291). The chord that Antigone's defiance struck with the opponents of apartheid was most memorably captured in the play-within-the-play in *The Island*, devised by Fugard, Kani and Ntshona, when Winston, a political prisoner, identifies the struggle of the woman of Greek legend with his own defiance of the injustice of the system. This powerful message was carried wherever *The Island* was performed, in South Africa and abroad. As regards performance style, these political interpretations of Greek drama, for the first time made use of contemporary idiom and local, everyday vocabulary and accent. This acculturation of Greek drama paved the way for a new indigenous mode of interpreting the texts in South Africa.

Many stage productions since the late twentieth century have been in a style that has been categorized as 'indigenous South African hybrid' (Hauptfleisch 1997: 67–81) and as 'syncretic theatre' (Balme 1999: 13–15). This style is thoroughly cross-cultural, as it makes use of elements from the formal, classical western traditions, from township musicals, performance poetry and traditional storytelling, and is often multilingual. Several recent versions of Greek tragedies and comedies have been staged in this mode. The energetic multiculturalism of such productions corresponds to the ideals of the post-apartheid society by manifesting a consciousness of the role the new South Africa may have, as an example of forging a peaceful transition to an equitable juxtaposition of languages and cultures in the globalized world.

A further feature of this hybrid style is the freedom with which different languages and registers of language are used. The polyglot mode reflects the modern urban environment where many of the eleven 'official' languages, plus urban dialects that combine elements from more than one language, are spoken daily. The linguistic treasures available to playwrights are thus immense. The multilingual nature of the theatre is part of its multiculturalism. In practice the language of communication in theatre is mostly English, as it is most widely understood, but one of the innovative features of SA theatre today is that the multilingualism in society is not just mirrored on the stage but strategically implemented to include or exclude parts of the audience and to comment on linguistic aspects of the power dynamics in the country.

The development of a multilingual text is often facilitated by the collective production process. Because the actors are ethnically diverse their languages reflect the linguistic and cultural diversity of everyday life in South Africa. One example of such a polyglot text is the Jazzart Theatre Company's 1994 workshopped version of *Medea*, which, although the dialogue was predominantly in English, also contained Xhosa and Afrikaans, while the actor who played Aetes spoke his native Tamil, which marked him very clearly as the foreign other. The Breughel theatre group's 1996 *Medeia-Ballade* started with the Kolchians speaking Xhosa to distinguish them from the Argonauts whose Afrikaans assimilated these representatives of the 'great Hellenic empire' to the 'civilized' brown and white inhabitants of South Africa. However, the Afrikaans dialogue of the Jazzart *Medea* was not the elevated register usual on the stage, but the dialect of the ordinary 'Coloured' people of the Western Cape. This enhanced the authenticity of the multilingualism of the performance.

Since the end of the apartheid regime, bonds between Dutch and Afrikaans writers have been renewed. One such collaboration in 2002 resulted in an Afrikaans version of the Belgian, Tom Lanoye's, *Mamma Medea* by the poet, Antjie Krog. Lanoye's Colchians speak Flemish in neat iambic pentameters, while the Greeks make use of colloquial Dutch prose. The translator, Krog, refined Lanoye's linguistic division to offer a remarkable range of current Afrikaans usage. The primitive Colchians pronounce their iambics in pure Afrikaans customary in formal high culture, while the powerful and technologically advanced Greeks deploy several mongrel variants of the language. Among the Colchians Medea, Chalkiope and their aunt Kirke maintain an elevated and even poetic form of discourse, while Aietes lards his language with expletives of a rather dated kind.

Of the Greeks, Jason varies his language according to circumstances and uses 'pure' language to impress or mislead, but his natural form of expression is 'dirty', studded with colloquial expletives. Jason's Argonaut companions, Telamon and Idas, each has his own idiolect: Idas shares Jason's preference for unsavoury language while Telamon prefers to mix his Afrikaans with English words and phrases. This is a strong trend in contemporary spoken Afrikaans, sometimes called 'Eng-Afrikaans', and is characteristic also of Kreousa, who makes her appearance to try to reconcile Medea to the new dispensation. Kreousa's ideas derive from pop psychology, to which her trendy discourse is well suited. Kreousa's language and speech are diametrically opposed to Medea's elevated poetic utterance which is one of the factors that isolate her among the Corinthians. Later Medea resorts to coarse language as if her association with Jason has started to corrupt her. In the final scene Medea slips into prose a few times and Jason into verse. These exchanges represent moments when they come close to understanding each other. The nuances of *Mamma Medea* are thus articulated not only by the surface meaning of the words, but emphasized by the style of utterance. Comic relief is provided by the Domestic Worker. The Colchian Nurse is replaced by a Corinthian domestic worker, played by a male actor in drag. This burlesque feature was enhanced by the character's exaggerated Cape 'Coloured' dialect.

Lanoye's bleak ending, with Medea and Jason each killing one of their children, is a savage comment on the acceptance of violence in the modern world. The joint culpability of Jason and Medea in *Mamma Medea* abolishes the distinction between barbarian and civilized, husband and wife, man and woman. *Mamma Medea* is a ferocious satire on modern society where moral judgements are often based on external appearance. Medea changes from an innocent, shy and sincere girl in Kolchis to a bitter woman without any illusions because of her contact with the ordered and 'civilized' Greeks. This condemns the seductive values of the 'first' world.

Krog's Afrikaans translation of *Mamma Medea* displays the rich variety of vocabulary, dialect and accent available to modern users of the language. Amid the lively polemics in the South African media about the future of Afrikaans, this play confidently asserts its viability and its range that can accommodate the needs of everyday conversation as well as elevated literary discourse.

Syncretism and Reconciliation

The confidence of artists in post-colonial South Africa that their own creation and culture have equal validity with the great cultures of the past is evident in multicultural syncretism where indigenous playwrights integrate their own material with classical drama, creating intercultural or cross-cultural performance.

One of the themes in Greek drama that has been highly relevant to the South African stage in the recent past is the resolution of violent conflict by means of reconciliation rather than further bloodshed. It is not surprising, therefore, that Aeschylus' *Oresteia* trilogy, which depicts the chain of murder and revenge within the ruling house of Argos and poses questions about the relationship of justice to vengeance and the struggle for reconciliation, has evoked responses in different generations of South African productions. Some of the playwrights also drew on the mythic material in Sophocles' *Electra*, Euripides' *Orestes* and his *Electra*.

The contrast in the conception of the productions and their reception highlights the profound changes in the political and social order as well as the theatre between South Africa in 1971, at the height of the repressive old regime, and in 2003, after nearly a decade of the new, inclusive and democratic order. Athol Fugard explored this material in his *Orestes* performed in 1971. *Orestes* was an improvisation with three actors. It was experimental in form and content. Mime and visual images with minimal spoken dialogue carried the performance, which Fugard created by super-imposing a contemporary incident, the bombing in 1964 of the Johannesburg station as a protest against apartheid, upon the mytho-dramatic source of Aeschylus' *Oresteia* (McMurtry 1998: 105). The contemporary characters suggested by the three actors are the bomber, John Harris, an elderly woman who was killed by the explo-sion, and a young girl, her grandchild, who was injured but survived. In the bare performance space, these three actors (two women and a man) transformed themselves into mother, daughter, son and then into Clytemnestra, Electra and Orestes. They thus embodied in turn contemporary South Africans, archetypes and the mythical family of Agamemnon. Agamemnon did not appear but his murder by Clytemnestra was acted out, unleashing the cycle of guilt and retribution. The actors read out three texts that established their threefold identities: a statement by Harris at his trial evoked contemporary South Africa; a passage on Electra, the Greek myth; and a text on the possibilities of interpersonal communication and performance, archetype and role.

Fugard had 'a sense that Harris stood in relation to his society as Orestes did to Clytemnestra. An intolerable burden of guilt for the crimes committed – the act of violence an attempt to escape the burden'. In apartheid South Africa, the citizen's membership of the body politic was restricted by law, the state did not protect individual rights, and freedom of speech was severely curtailed. Existence and identity were meaningless to the majority of the Family of South Africa. With no Eumenides to safeguard rights and maintain justice by crushing the offenders to dust, individuals assumed their function, were compelled to act violently (McMurtry 1998: 113).

Fugard's *Orestes* thus focused on the problem of violence, justice and retribution in South Africa, but by expanding this demonstration by means of the Greek myth and the archetypal forces behind the problem, it gained universal validity. The lack of a resolution in this play which has no ending corresponding to the Greek divine reconciliation, held a warning that violence would lead to further violence. This bleak ending was not unexpected at the height of the apartheid rule in 1971.

A production of the *Oresteia* that did not spell out the relevance of the tragic cycle for contemporary South Africa so unambiguously was a prestige production in 1981 of the state-funded Cape Performing Arts Board. It featured a German, Dieter Reible, directing an Afrikaans translation of a German adaptation, by Walter Jens, of the Greek trilogy. The cultural importance of this production was emphasized by the translator, Merwe Scholtz, and others writing background features in the local Afrikaans press before the opening (Conradie 1999: 20–2). Two notable features about the reaction of the public summarized by Conradie are, first, dismay at the 'unclassical' nature of the staging, which included neon lights, flaming, smoking firebrands, and blood flowing from the mangled corpses of Agamemnon, Kassandra and Aigisthos brought onto the stage; and, second, an insistence that the themes of the drama were not only universally relevant but particularly applicable in contemporary South Africa. However, the detail of the application was not spelled out. The play did not engage with local issues in any immediate way. The dialogue, spoken in Afrikaans, was the literary product of an academic translator. Indignant letters to the newspapers showed that theatre-egoers were unfamiliar with Reible's more adventurous and interpretive approach to Greek drama common in the northern hemisphere. This production still carried the hallmarks of the more sophisticated first world showing the colonized third world how a great classic could be staged in a modern way.

After the peaceful transition to majority rule, a number of playwrights and directors brought new interpretations of the cycle of violence and revenge in the royal house of Argos to bear on the new dispensation in South Africa. Mark Fleishman in 1998 workshopped material on this theme from the three Greek tragedians with a cast of drama students (Mezzabotta 2000: 10–14; Steinmeyer 2007). The resulting play, ironically called *In the City of Paradise*, boldly explored the possibility of achieving reconciliation by granting amnesty in the case of politically inspired acts of violence. This theme was particularly relevant at the time when the Truth and Reconciliation Committee (TRC) was nearing the end of its work during which many applications by perpetrators of violence under the apartheid regime had been heard, as well as victims' accounts of their experiences. In the play Orestes and Electra are tried for matricide, found guilty and sentenced to death by stoning. This due legal process is emphasized as the right course in contrast to taking the law into one's own hands, as Orestes had done. The danger of vigilantes acting without recourse to the constituted authorities is highlighted. However, when the sentence is about to be carried out, the herald intervenes and appeals to the historic juncture that calls for understanding not vengeance, forgiveness not retaliation. Because they have made a full disclosure, Orestes and Electra are to be granted amnesty. Thus the theme of reconciliation is underlined. Because Tyndareus in the play refuses to accept this outcome, the potential for future violence is also suggested. *In the City of Paradise* made clear that unless all South Africans accepted the principle of amnesty for past political crimes, a peaceful future would come under threat.

An amalgamation of extracts from the TRC hearings and translations of Greek tragedy to focus on the themes of vengeance and forgiveness in South Africa shaped Mervyn McMurtry's adaptation in 2000 of Sophocles' *Electra*. Additional material from the related plays by Aeschylus and Euripides was also integrated into the text. The prologue and choral odes were reworked and incorporated video excerpts of actual testimony before the TRC. Merging recent South African events with the famous mythical drama underlined the universality of the problem of terminating a cycle of retribution and resolving conflict by means of appeasement and amnesty rather than further bloodshed. This enhanced the unique achievement of the TRC, but did not minimize the harrowing process of achieving reconciliation.

Another reworking of the *Oresteia* in 2003 by an independent young South African director, Yael Farber, transferred the *Oresteia's* themes to South Africa in the immediate aftermath of the transition while the hearings of the TRC were being conducted. Farber chose the title *Molora* (Ashes) for her combination of the ancient account of the cycle of retribution with recent South African history. The TRC hearings revealed detailed accounts by perpetrators of atrocities of their deeds. In *Molora* Clytemnestra faces Electra who, as a child, witnessed the slaying of her father by her mother. Electra has been plotting revenge with her brother whose whereabouts are not known to the authorities. Clytemnestra uses some of the most notorious methods of torture of the South African police, such as the 'wet bag', to extract information from her daughter. The ancient Greek tragedy becomes a metaphor for revisiting the suffering of the black majority under apartheid. However, because of South Africa's avoidance of retaliation and vengeance and because of the peaceful achievement of a process of reconciliation, Farber alters the Greek story to show how the chain of violence can be broken. In her director's notes she elaborates on the example that the country's peaceful switch to majority rule held: 'Coming from South Africa, the question of revenge begs enormous consideration . . . I have long wanted to create a work that explores the cycle of violence and the dilemma of survivors who must have faced the choice between the impulse to avenge themselves and the choice to forgive.'

The fabric of the play reflects elements of the new syncretic style: The choral odes are sung in Xhosa by the Nqoko cultural singers of the Transkei. All the actors are black, save Clytemnestra. That makes a very obvious point. The chorus also represent the public at the TRC hearings and they persuade Electra to hand over the axe with which she plans to kill her mother.

This production was staged not only at the Grahamstown festival in South Africa but also in Germany and Japan. Farber emphasizes the importance of the message *Molora* has for the post 9/11 world (http://www.3sat.de/theater/programm/69773/index.html – accessed 30 May 2006 and http://www.litnet.co.za/teater/dsover.asp – accessed 1 June 2006).

Comedy as Critique and Celebration

Other Greek plays show a similar progression: from being staged to assert South Africa's claim as part of elite Western culture, to being radically transformed into new works claiming an indigenous interpretation of the traditional material (Van Zyl Smit 2003, 2005, 2006 passim). This applies to the staging of comedy as well as tragedy. Although ancient comedy has not been as popular in South Africa as tragedy, Aristophanes' plays have long been an established part of the training at drama schools. In addition to student productions, there have been a number of performances and adaptations where social and political criticism shows a strong engagement with issues of the day. One such version was André P. Brink's Afrikaans interpretation of *Birds*, produced in 1971. He renamed it *Die hand vol vere* (*A Handful of Feathers*), highlighting the playful approach befitting the comic genre.

Brink followed the structure of Aristophanes' comedy closely but transformed the characters into contemporary South Africans. The play became a vehicle for satirizing not only the narrowness and hypocrisy of politicians and other public figures, notably the ministers of the cabinet and of religion, but Brink also successfully introduced propaganda for the banned African National Congress; the flag chosen for the new country of the birds shows the organization's colours: yellow, green and black. None of the reviewers of the play picked this up. To those who recognized the colours and what they stood for, the chorus's cry of 'Viva Viva Viva Kammabokmakierieland!' must have had an added dimension, especially if they knew that the bokmakierie was a green and yellow bird with a black band under the throat. They would then also have added a second meaning to Pistorius' (the Pisthetairos figure) remark: 'There it is. Our flag of freedom.' Such overt support for a prohibited organization was dangerous, but none of the many readers and civic leaders who led a public outcry against Brink's adaptation seemed to understand it. Instead they attacked the play for promoting loose morals, smutty language and suggestive behaviour. They accused Brink of spreading sacrilege and contempt for patriotism. This reaction shows the seriousness with which the pillars of the Afrikaans community regarded the theatre. It also shows that for them the purpose of a play should be not only entertainment but moral upliftment.

By transforming Aristophanes' satire of Athenian life into a send-up of contemporary South Africa, Brink challenged the hitherto uncontested assumption amongst Afrikaners of the respect due to a 'classic'. In his use of earthy, everyday Afrikaans Brink domesticated the Greek writer and brought him to the notice of many whose views were rigidly conditioned by the tenets of Afrikaner and Christian nationalism.

During the 1970s the focus of stage performance had shifted to the theatre of protest and to indigenous South African productions that were often multiracial and multicultural. Adaptations of *Lysistrata* were prominent at the two theatres at the forefront of this movement. In 1974 The Company, the group that was to become the resident company of the Market Theatre in Johannesburg, staged as its first play *Lysistrata*, reworked for South Africa by the director Barney Simon. The Company was dedicated to non-racial theatre and some of its members had given up the security of employment at subsidized theatre companies. This bold and provocative first venture was widely reviewed. In 1977 The Space in Cape Town called its production, adapted by Dermod Judge, *Lysistrata S.A.* It was also played by a multiracial cast. These ventures outside state subsidized theatre defused some of the racial tension caused by the repressive regime as 'fears were dragged out into the open and poked fun at' (Astbury 1979).

The inauguration of the new regime in the country in 1994 inspired students to renew Aristophanic comedy even more drastically. Within two years two productions of *Frogs* gave Aristophanes a voice in the idiom of the new South Africa. The first was an adaptation by University of Cape Town drama students. It had been reworked from David Barrett's translation and included plenty of innovative local touches:

> Whereas the references to Aristophanes' contemporaries were retained in the dialogue scenes, some clever updating for South African spectators had been introduced into the separate choral sections, particularly in the *parabasis*. The names of Cleisthenes,

Archedemus, Phrynichus and Cleigenes were replaced (not always by wholly appropriate analogues, but ten out of ten for effort and ingenuity) by those of Terre'blanche (leader of the Afrikaner Weerstandsbeweging, a group of White right-wing extremists), Rajbansi (slippery Indian politician), Verwoerd (promulgator of apartheid, assassinated in 1966), and Mangope (Black puppet leader of the former 'homeland' of Bophuthatswana, who refused to participate in the recent elections). The resonance of these references helped to transmit something of the political flavour of Aristophanic comedy. Certainly, the chorus leader's impassioned appeal for constructive engagement by all Athenians recalled President Nelson Mandela's stirring inauguration speech, delivered only three days before the production opened, urging reconciliation and nation-building.

(Mezzabotta 1994)

This version of *Frogs* thus engaged with the political change in South Africa by amalgamating the Greek play with contemporary local material.

Another student production, *Paradox* (a pun on the pronunciation of the Afrikaans word for 'frogs', 'paddas'), at the University of Stellenbosch in 1996 investigated recent social and political changes. Democracy, achieved by the successful transition from the apartheid regime, had come even to the theatre! The audience were invited to exercise their democratic rights. They had to choose the best, not of Euripides or Aeschylus, but amongst local writers, to bring inspiration to the living. This Afrikaans version by Chris Vorster preserved the outline of the Greek comedy in that a godlike figure, and a slave, both women, undertake a journey to the Underworld to bring back a poet. A Master of Ceremonies, a female student in a tuxedo, served as a narrator and link between the audience and the actors. The large cast was overwhelmingly female, a woman taking the role even of Heracles. The traditional practice of male actors playing all roles, even those of women, was thus neatly reversed. Pluto became a 'Bitch Goddess' who presided over a rave club. Many aspects of the new dispensation, such as affirmative action, even the abolition of the death penalty, were satirized. Afrikaans had become 'the forbidden language' but was used in a lively and irreverent way in the show.

The climax was the democratic selection of the most inspirational poetic utterance. Vorster's radical innovation was to introduce the audience as judge. To facilitate selection five 'poetic' declarations had been printed on the programmes which thus became mock ballot papers, although the vote was by a show of hands. This cheeky updating appropriated Aristophanes' comedy as part of the new South African culture. The further implication of this romp was that it is no longer Dionysus who presides in the theatre. In the modern world, the theatre is ruled by its public. The underlying theme of the play was the importance of keeping the theatre culture alive.

Contemporary Trends

A fresh style in the performance of Greek drama in South Africa was unveiled in November 2002 when Roy Sargeant directed the *Bacchae* of Euripides at the newly instituted Dionysos festival at Kirstenbosch, the National Botanic Garden, in Cape Town. The play was performed by an all-male cast in an open-air stone amphitheatre. In keeping with the director's goal to stay as true as possible to the original Greek style of production, early morning (7 a.m.) performances were introduced. Sargeant aimed 'to tell the truth about the past'. The audience could draw their own conclusions about the themes of the drama: East and West, order and freedom, male and female, life and death. The chorus who remained on stage from the parodos played a central part. Their foreignness was suggested not only by their costumes, masks and musical instruments, but also by the fact that they were males representing women. The six young men moved as one, were dressed identically and wore identical half masks. Passages of heightened emotion were sung, while weightier pronouncements were spoken. The music was all performed on stage by castanets, drums and tambourines.

This production was well supported by theatre-goers and, accompanied as it was by a series of lectures on Greek drama, the god Dionysos, wine and wine-tasting of South African wines, made some impact on the public. *Oedipus the Tyrant* was produced at the same venue in 2003, and in 2004/5 Aristophanes' *Birds*. All these performances strove to maintain the ancient conventions as far as possible and have been very successful as examples of Greek culture still able to fascinate audiences of the modern world.

In addition to this 'traditional' presentation, a few daring adaptations of Greek tragedies in Cape Town revealed the complexity of the response of post-colonial theatre to the Classics. In 2001 Sabata Sesiu added music (African drumming, African jazz, choral singing and solo clarinet accompaniment to dialogue scenes), a half chorus, inspired partly by Greece, partly by Africa, dancing, mime, African storytelling (a choryphee or narrator dressed in African mask and buskins) and scenes of dialogue to a blend of Sophocles' *Antigone* and an African legend. This version, called *Giants*, likened the Creon character, Makhanda, to an African dictator and warned against the dangers of totalitarian rule, and, by implication, commended the new South African constitution with its guarantee of freedom and equality for all citizens.

Cape Town saw another 'new version' of Sophocles' *Antigone* in 2004. Sean Mathias and Myer Taub worked from a literal translation of the Greek. They envisaged an 'African' interpretation, with John Kani playing Creon. This performance had a deep resonance with previous South African *Antigones* because Kani in the 1960s, as a member of the Serpent Players, directed by Athol Fugard, took the part of Haemon, as the original actor had been arrested and imprisoned. His portrayal of the Creon role in *The Island*, first performed in 1973 and often revived, is legendary.

Mathias set out his intention 'to do a production that will contain all the elements of a third millennium life in a third world country. Therefore modern technology and modern music will sit alongside African poverty and the debris of an African war. I want the setting to describe the horror of a war-torn country and will not shy away from using violent images at times to plunge the audience into a different kind of reality.' This bleak background was very evident. The stage set represented the aftermath of war. There were corpses on the ground and a sentry patrolled the high wall built up from sandbags forming the backdrop. A big screen on stage brought news from TNN (Thebes News Network) about the outcome of the civil war. The simultaneous projection of events on stage on the screen suggested contemporary life with its blurring of reality and virtual reality, people's dependence on TV networks for legitimating reality, and the construction of history.

Creon, as the conception demanded, was very much the modern African ruler with his insistence on pomp and ceremony. A public service announcement on TNN showed a young man singing Creon's praises. This clear indication that Creon had usurped all the powers of the state was one of the many instances where a traditional African practice, here that of the 'imbongi' or praise-singer who celebrates the greatness of a leader, was blended with modern western technology. The use of English as the dominant language, with recourse to Xhosa at certain points, reflected contemporary reality. This *Antigone* was firmly grounded in the Greek original. The introduction of modern technology and modern costume strove to make clearer the application of the themes of the tragedy to the modern world. This was not always equally successful but it was a thought-provoking rendering of the great tragedy. Its setting evoked not only Africa, but also the images of Iraq which were being seen on screen throughout the world as this production was performed.

Another drama revisiting the vicissitudes of the royal house of ancient Thebes, *Jocasta Rising*, by Carol Michèle Kaplan also played in Cape Town in 2004. Sophocles' *Oedipus Tyrannos* was refashioned by focusing more on Jocasta and her fate. The action was set not only in ancient Thebes, but also in Cape Town in order to stress the universal validity of the theme of the suppression of the female. Technology, again a big screen, as well as prophecies transmitted by text messages, and colloquial Afrikaans interspersed in the English dialogue rooted the play in the contemporary world of the audience. Jocasta grows strong enough to accept the horror of the incest by refusing the role of suicide Sophocles gave her. As the play ends she is looking to the future that will give women their rightful place at the centre of power. This implies that there will be less death and destruction because, as is shown throughout the play, wars are primarily caused by male powermongers. Unfortunately the expectations generated by the theme were not fulfilled owing to the weak structure of the play, but it did offer a challenge to the orthodox rendering seen in Sargeant's production a few months earlier.

In 2005 Brett Bailey with his young company of black actors, Third World Bunfight, brought a revolutionary presentation of the *Medea* to the western Cape. Bailey relocated the Dutch company Dood Paard's 1998 *Medeia*, by Oscar van Woensel, in a post-colonial African wasteland. Bailey eschewed the proscenium theatre and set the play as well as the action in a shantytown. The audience had to walk to a squatter camp constructed in the veldt, and watch the play by moving after the actors as different scenes took place in different houses and spaces in the camp. A shack formed the backdrop to the first scene. In the centre of a sandy yard the chorus of African women danced and sang around a solitary tree. Musical accompaniment was provided by percussion instruments, such as rattles and sticks beaten together. All the women wore white except the young Medeia, who was clad in gold. The older Medeia's face was grey, covered in ash to symbolize her sorrow and suffering. The young Medeia led the dance while the older Medeia waited, silent and still, at the side.

This device of showing Medeia at the two most important times in her life was in line with the achronological presentation of the action. The young Medeia in her beauty, in love and happy, would become the mature woman, harrowed by her experience of love and betrayal. At the same time when the older Medeia was the focus of attention, the presence of the younger was a constant reminder of her former state. The scene, represented Colchis, a primitive community, but part of the world where the quest for money and power leads to war. The wall of the shack fell away and behind the shack a scene of fire, rape and pillage was revealed. Jason and the Argonauts had arrived. In this setting they became another of the marauding bands of fighters causing death and misery in many parts of the African continent. In their quest for the Golden Fleece they looted and rampaged. Medeia fell in love with Jason, and grasped the opportunity to escape with him from her confined life. Props and settings for this production were matched. Light was provided by candles in plastic bottles, or by a pickup truck parked at the side. These modes of lighting are often used in areas without electric power. The audience participated in the life of the shantytown by sharing their food, soup and 'vetkoek', a staple dish of the poor.

The suspense about the ultimate nature of the relationship between Jason and Medeia, the fate of their children and the nature of Medeia's revenge that usually forms the core of the structure of plays that deal with the Medea myth, was deliberately downplayed by the device of juggling the chronology of the events. This threw into relief many themes common in the modern world: the expectation of finding 'perfect love' as portrayed in mass culture, and the powerlessness of women. The corruption of some third world leaders was strikingly conveyed by the audience's glimpse, as they made their way to yet another scene, in an open-sided shack of an actor clad in 'African dictator's costume': a military uniform, cap and sunglasses. His Excellency for Life, King Pelias, lounged on top of a washing machine in a room filled with other home appliances such as TV sets and music centres so that it resembled a furniture store. The Corinthians' treatment of Medeia evoked the problem of xenophobia in South Africa and elsewhere.

Bailey's *Medeia* was a bold undertaking. It took the audience into the desolate circumstances in which many people live. They smelled the dust, saw the rudimentary structures that served as shelters and sat on the bare benches or on the ground like the inhabitants of squatter camps. The production was an ensemble effort with the dialogue reduced and much of the narrative coming from the Chorus, either sung or spoken, in English or Xhosa, in unison or by individuals. Bailey's manipulation of the chronological sequence of events underlined the harsh differences between the times of love and happiness and the times of betrayal, hatred and revenge. Medeia's shocking murder of her children (dolls in the play) was portrayed quite brutally but was an indictment not of Medeia only, but of the treatment she had received from Jason and from society. The Medeia of this play is a survivor, but she survives at the cost of losing all illusions about life and love.

As this overview indicates, the performance reception of Classical Greek drama in South Africa contains a blending of the ancient, colonial and local traditions, in different measures, at different times. Because local traditions are complex and varied in respect of language, attitude to the Western tradition, style of presentation and aim of performance the resulting products range from attempts at reviving the authentic Greek style of performance through different degrees of adaptation to acculturation and appropriation. South Africa's productive engagement with Greek drama seems set to continue as an important part of theatre performance.

FURTHER READING

Very little about the reception of Classical drama appears in general studies of South African theatre history and performance. However, as general background the works of Hauptfleisch (1997), Kruger (1999) and Orkin (1994) are invaluable. Articles dealing specifically with Classical drama, its translation, adaptation, performance and reception in different periods, may be found in *Akroterion* and the *South African Theatre Journal*. There are a number of reviews of productions of classical plays and adaptations in Denard's *Didaskalia* and Hardwick's (1996–ongoing) *Reception of Classical Texts project*. Wetmore (2002) contains useful analyses of a number of South African adaptations. There are a number of chapters of interest in Hardwick and Gillespie (2007), especially those by Steinmeyer and Rehm (on *The Island*).

CHAPTER TWENTY-NINE

Putting the Class into Classical Reception

Edith Hall

The hero of Thomas Hardy's tragic novel *Jude the Obscure*, a poor stonemason living in a Victorian village, is desperate to study Latin and Greek at university. He propels himself into the torment that results from harbouring such unrealistic aspirations at the moment when he gazes, from the top of a ladder leaning against a rural barn, on the spires of the University of Christminster (a fictional substitute for Oxford) (Richardson 2007). The spires, vanes and domes 'gleamed like the topaz' in the distance (Hardy 1974 [1895]: 41). The lustrous topaz shares its golden colour with the stone used to build Oxbridge colleges, but is one of the hardest minerals in nature. Jude's fragile psyche and health inevitably collapse when he discovers just how unbreakable are the social barriers that exclude him from elite culture and perpetuate his class position, however lovely the buildings that concretely represent them seem, shimmering on the horizon.

Hardy was writing from personal experience. As the son of a stonemason himself, and apprenticed to an architect's firm, he had been denied a public school and university education; like Jude Fawley, he had struggled to learn enough Greek to read the *Iliad* as a teenager (Seymour-Smith 1994: 39–40). Unlike Jude, Hardy rose through the social ranks to become a prosperous member of the literary establishment. But he never resolved his internal conflict between admiration for Greek and Latin authors and resentment of the supercilious attitude adopted by some members of the upper classes who had been formally trained in them. A similar conflict today remains unresolved within the study of Classics and its reception; many scholars suffer from a Hardyesque discomfort with the history of the discipline itself. Education in the ancient Latin and Greek languages has always been an exclusive practice, used to define membership in an elite, despite variations in the social and demographic arenas where the boundaries of exclusion have been drawn; the best documented case remains that fictively experienced by Jude – Classics in nineteenth-century England (Stray 1998; Larson 1999–2000). Yet the study of Greek and Roman antiquity has undergone an upheaval since World War Two, and more particularly since the 1960s. As a result it is now arguably less elitist than at any time in its history. Another result has been an upsurge of interest (historically connected with the Civil Rights movement) in the institution of ancient slavery, and a grudging new respect for Marxist and allied theories, primarily as applied by Geoffrey de Ste Croix (1981) and (to a lesser extent) George Thomson (1973, 1941), both of whom tackled class hierarchies head-on in relation to ancient history.

The first issue that needs to be addressed by anybody who wants to think about the relationship between social class and classical reception is this: (1) *why do the terms class and Classics sound so similar?* Both terms, in fact, originated in the ancient Mediterranean world. When the Romans heard their Latin noun *classis*, it contained a resonance that we do not hear when we say *class*: deriving from the same root as the verb *clamare* ('call out'), a *classis* consisted of a group of people 'called out' or 'summoned' together. It could be the men in a meeting, or in an army, or the ships in a fleet. The word has always been associated with Servius Tullius, the sixth of the legendary kings of early Rome, who was thought to have held the first census in order to find out, for the purposes of military planning, what assets his people possessed. It is this procedure that explains the ancient association of the term *class* with an audible call to arms. Yet in the middle of the eighteenth century the term was adopted in order to distinguish different strata within English society. The working poor of England began to be called members of 'the lower classes' rather than just 'the poor' or members of 'the lower orders'. The term *the poor* was too imprecise, and the notion of hierarchical 'orders' too inflexible and too infused with medieval and feudal notions of birth-rank to accommodate the new, unprecedented levels of social mobility. The term *class*, which (like its ancient prototype) implied a status with an economic basis rather than an inherited rank, was a result of the incipient erosion, during the industrial revolution, of the transparent and relatively stable hierarchical rank order which had earlier governed the English social structure. The French and German languages soon imitated the English one, replacing the terms *état* and *Stand* with *classe* and *Klasse*; by 1815 the now-familiar terms 'middle' and 'working classes' had become accepted parlance.

The plural Classics, meanwhile, had been used in English by 1711 to designate the corpus of Greek and Latin literature. But it is to the legendary first census that there must also be traced the origins of the terms *Classics*. In Servius' scheme, the men in the top of his six classes – the men with the most money and property – were called the *classici*. The top men were 'Classics', and this is why, by the time of the late second-century AD Roman miscellanist Aulus Gellius, by metaphorical extension the top authors could be called 'Classic Authors', *scriptores classici*, to distinguish them from inferior or metaphorically 'proletarian' authors, *scriptores proletarii* (*Noctes Attici* 19.8.15: (cf. Schein, this volume, ch. 6). Every tradition of writing, art and music – English Literature, Dutch painting, Jazz – now claims to have its own 'Classics'. But the most venerated Classics amongst all others have usually been the authors of Greece and Rome – the *primi inter pares* or 'first amongst equals' when compared with all the cultural *Classici* produced in world history. The addition of the definite article *the* to the term *Classics* enacts a final sub-division by which the *most* elite texts of all can be identified by the few refined individuals supposedly able to appreciate them. The unit at Harvard University which studies these Greek and Roman cultural 'Hyper-Classics' still styles itself *The Department of the Classics.* The involvement, historically, of the study of Greece and Rome with the maintenance of socio-economic hierarchies is thus so obvious in the very title *Classics* that since the late 1980s some scholars have considered abandoning it altogether, and replacing it with a label such as 'Study of the ancient Mediterranean' or 'Study of Greek and Roman antiquity'. But there is another possible response to the controversial and loaded nomenclature that the subject has inherited than simply to discard it. A better strategy, perhaps, is to use the problematic title to think with, in order to develop a sensitivity to the class issues raised by the study of 'Classical texts'.

The second and most important question that applying the concept 'class' to classical reception raises is this: (2) *to what class did the people under scrutiny, who were doing the 'receiving' of Greece and Rome, themselves in fact belong?* This question can be asked as much in relation to the fictional Jude Fawley (especially since he exists within a self-consciously 'realist' novel) as to the real-life author Thomas Hardy. But it is often a difficult question to answer. One reason is that no two analysts can ever agree on what exact sub-divisions within socio-economic classes pertained within any particular period of history: since the industrial revolution especially, there has been so much social confusion and mobility that precise sub-categories of class (for example, 'upper proletariat', 'under-class', 'service sector' or 'lower middle/white collar') can become difficult to apply consistently. Paul Fussell's 1983 'classic' of class analysis, *Class: A Guide Through the American Status System*, proposes a nine-tier stratification of contemporary American society, ranging from the super-rich (who have amassed such large fortunes that their descendants need never work) through to no fewer than five discrete categories of low-class persons: in descending order, these are skilled blue-collar workers, workers in factories and the service industry, manual labourers, the destitute unemployed and homeless, and the 'out-of-sight' members of the population incarcerated in prisons and institutions. Similar detailed sub-divisions can be identified in most historical societies. Another problem is the argument between Marxists, who stress the economic basis of class, and theorists influenced by the sociologist Max Weber, who stress the importance of *status* in terms of prestige derived from education and rank in determining true 'life chances'. Furthermore, working-class identity as it is commonly understood is often based on neither economic position nor prestige, but on more subjective criteria such as clothing, dialect, accent, place of origin, and recreational activities. This complexity has provided unwarranted ammunition to those who wish to deny altogether the blindingly obvious truth that in most of the societies manifested in world history, and certainly over the last five centuries, wealth and power have *always* been concentrated in the hands of a disproportionately small percentage of the population, who have lived off the labour of others; moreover, access to education and the means by which information, culture and therefore ideology are disseminated have *always* overlapped heavily with the possession of economic power. Any research into intellectual life in such societies, including research into classical reception, will therefore be distorted if what this chapter henceforward for the most part simply calls the 'lower' classes, who formed the majority of the population, are erased from the picture.

Yet hardly anybody has been interested in lower-class access to Classics. This becomes clear in comparison with the history of women's access, which has at last begun to be written (see e.g. Thomas 1994: 19–67; Beard 2000; Hardwick 2000a: ch. 2); a few important steps are being taken in investigating the study of Classics by colonized peoples in India (Vasunia 2007b), and by African Americans (Ronnick 2005). But scant attention has been paid to the implication of Classics in social exclusion that is class-based, or to the types of access to the cultures of ancient Greece and Rome which the lower classes have managed to gain. When such access has been achieved, it has always been in spite of educational deprivation. But another obstacle has often been the prejudice held by some members of the lower classes against cultural property understandably perceived as emblematic of their exploiters: as the miner in Tony Harrison's feature film *Prometheus* says to his small son, who has been given Greek tragedy to read as homework (Harrison 1998: 9): 'God knows why they feed yer all that crap'.

One reason for the neglect of class-conscious research is that many critics, especially in the USA, deny that class is a legitimate category of analysis. They feel that both class-conscious art and class-oriented criticism are reductive and partisan (see Konstan 1994: 47). Other critics reject the category of class because they fear it might narrow down the field of study and its potentialities. But the argument from the dangers of restriction can be used the other way: class-blindness has resulted in damaging controls exerted on the parameters of the discipline, and unnecessary limits on the ways in which Greek and Roman culture and their influence can be approached. Classical reception can be defined more interestingly if a wider social spectrum and more diverse media and genres are included in the picture. The third question that class-conscious researchers into classical reception need to ask is surely this: (3) *how much Latin and Greek education had the 'receivers' experienced, and how did they feel about it?* Blanket refusal to think about social class in the context of Classics was an attitude inherited from people like the Earl of Chesterfield, who in 1748 wrote to his son, 'Classical knowledge, that is, Greek and Latin, is absolutely necessary for everybody . . . the word *illiterate*, in its common acceptance, means a man who is ignorant of these two languages' (Stanhope 1932: 3. 1155). In a series of breath-taking acts of rhetorical exclusion, classical knowledge is here limited to linguistic knowledge, education to males, and literacy to reading competence in Greek and Latin.

Lord Chesterfield's distinctions explain why, until recently, so few classical schol-ars have ever evinced much enthusiasm in response to the history of modern-language translation, at least beyond the treatment of canonical ancient poets by equally can-onical post-Renaissance authors (e.g. Pope's translations of Homer). The length of time for which the classical languages constituted the near-exclusive property of an educated *elite* is itself remarkable. In his autobiographical poem *Autumn Journal*, Louis MacNeice (a Church of Ireland bishop's son, educated at public school) iron-ically pondered the relationship between the ancient languages and social privilege nearly two hundred years after Lord Chesterfield (MacNeice (1979 [1938]: 125):

> Which things being so, as we said when we studied
> The classics, I ought to be glad
> That I studied the classics at Marlborough and Merton,
> Not everyone here having had
> The privilege of learning a language
> That is incontrovertibly dead,
> And of carting a toy-box of hall-marked marmoreal phrases
> Around in his head.

Most prestige was attached not just to the ability to read Latin and Greek fluently, but to compose in these tongues in both poetry and prose (usually translated from British historians, essayists or parliamentarians). The Suffolk poet Robert Bloomfield, a former cobbler, was so astonished when he heard his popular classic *The Farmer's Boy* translated into Latin that he wrote another poem, darkly to warn his protagonist against despising his humble origins (Bloomfield 1827: vol. ii p. 128):

> Hey, Giles! in what new garb art dress'd?
> For Lads like you methinks a bold one;
> I'm glad to see thee so caress'd;
> But, hark ye! – don't despise your old one.
> Thou'rt not the first by many a Boy
> Who've found abroad good friends to own 'em;
> Then, in such Coats have shown their joy,
> E'en their own Fathers have not known 'em.

Tony Harrison, another poet born into a working-class family, studied Classics after winning a place at Leeds Grammar School. His poem *Classics Society (Leeds Grammar School 1552–1952)* expresses the class tensions crystallized in the pedagogical exercise of Latin Prose Composition (Harrison 1984: 120):

> We boys can take old Hansards and translate
> the British Empire into SPQR
> but nothing demotic or up-to-date,
> and *not* the English that I speak at home.

Yet during the centuries when elite 'education' continued to mean primarily education in Latin and Greek, far more people than ever acquired knowledge of these tongues were reading the Greeks and Romans in their own modern languages (see Hall forthcoming). In his path-breaking study of the intellectual movements that prepared the way for the seventeenth-century English revolution, Christopher Hill stressed that the first English translators of the Classics were a homogeneous group of non-University protestants and Puritans, and that one of their main goals, as ardent patriots, was to make ancient learning available to all Englishmen who could read. They 'regarded the creation of an enlightened lay public opinion as a bulwark of true religion and national independence' (Hill 1965: 28; see also Conley 1927). More recently, Jonathan Rose, in his brilliant historical account of the reading habits of the British working class (2001), has drawn attention to the excitement that many individual autodidacts experienced when they began to read certain of the Greek and Latin Classics (often Homer) in translation – the thrill of life-changing imaginative discovery. A real-life equivalent of Hardy's obscure Jude, an autodidactic stonemason called Hugh Miller (born in 1802), recalled the pleasure he had found as a boy in reading Pope's *Iliad* and *Odyssey*: 'I saw, even at this immature period, that no other writer could cast a javelin with half the force of Homer. The missiles went whizzing athwart his pages' (Miller 1843: 28–9). The fourth question that the class-conscious study of class reception entails is therefore this: (4) *through what kinds of books did the individual(s) discover and get access to the ancient world, and what kinds of modern-language translation would they have been likely to be able to use?*

Fortunately, research into the *history* of the role played by modern-language translations in the study of the ancient world has been facilitated by the more systematic study of reading culture which has developed amongst social historians over the last three decades. The contribution of such influential organizations as (in Britain) the Society for the Diffusion of Useful Knowledge has begun to be appreciated (Webb 1971: 66–7; Vincent 1989: 85, 110–11, 192). So has the wide range of books read by nineteenth-century African–American literary societies, which included Homer, Sappho, Pindar, Demosthenes and Virgil as well as Dante and Shakespeare (McHenry 2002: 56, 172–3). The impact of canonical works dependent on (rather than translated from) ancient authors is understood above all in France, where many people's reading knowledge of the Classics was for centuries derived mainly from François Fénelon's *Odyssey*-inspired novel *Les Aventures de Télémaque* (1699) and the seventeenth-century plays of Corneille and Racine, who dramatized the myths of Medea, Phaedra, and Iphigenia; works by all three authors featured amongst the thirty most cited titles in a French Ministry of Education questionnaire on rural reading filled in by prefects in 1866 (Lyons 2001: 164–5). Other scholars have noted the role played by *illustrated* texts in interesting illiterate people in the Classics (Richter 1987: 20–2). An early eighteenth-century French farm-boy from Lorraine, by the name of Valentin Jamerey-Duval, was illiterate until he came across an illustrated edition of *Aesop's Fables*. So drawn was he to the visual images that he asked some of his fellow-shepherds to explain the stories, and subsequently to teach him to read the book. As a result he developed an insatiable appetite for reading, and became a librarian to the Duke of Lorraine (Lyons 2001: 49). Aesop first rolled in English off William Caxton's printing press as early as 1484, and like Homer, Ovid and the ancient narratives telling the stories of Heracles and of the Argonauts, he has been a staple of illustrated children's books which have achieved deep social penetration, and the role played by these influential versions of classical authors in cultural history has yet to be the subject of serious scholarly attention.

More attention has focused on books designed to offer instructive 'digests' of ancient Classics, such as the excerpts from Aristotle, Polybius and Cicero included in *The Political Experience of the Ancient: In Its Bearing upon Modern Times*, published by the educationalist Seymour Tremenheere in 1852 (Webb 1971: 97). The cultural importance at all levels of society of *Aesop's Fables*, historically one of the most widely read texts after the bible, has begun to be acknowledged (Vincent 1989: 89). In eighteenth- and nineteenth-century Ulster, the bags of books touted round even the humblest of cottages by 'chapmen', or itinerant booksellers, certainly included Aesop's *Fables* but also – more surprisingly – a version of Ovid's *Ars Amatoria*. Other reading enjoyed by the 'common man' in Northern Ireland included a version of Musaeus' poem *Hero and Leander*, a history of Troy descended from the *Recuyell of the histories of Troye* printed by Caxton, and (for reasons of theology as much as a desire for classical learning) Josephus' *History of the Jewish War* (Adams 1987: 50, 58–9, 85, 103, 183, 185). In what is now Eire, classical literature was taught surreptitiously by the itinerant teachers of the hedge schools (McManus 2002; O'Higgins forthcoming).

The recent advent of freely available online modern-language translations of Greek and Roman ancient authors, through the work of initiatives such as Project Gutenberg, is undoubtedly set to improve non-specialist access to antiquity. This is the case even if the third-millennial phenomenon of the 'digital divide' separating those who have and do not have easy access to the internet is already creating a new type of social division that is different from that of socio-economic class, even if it usually overlaps with it. Once an author has been translated into a modern language, moreover, it may be that he *initially* begins to achieve widespread circulation not directly through a modern-language translation, but through some other popular medium. The fifth question that class-conscious research into classical reception could usefully ask would therefore be this: (5) *to which cultural media containing information about the Greeks and Romans would the people under investigation be most likely to have experienced systematic exposure?* These days the ancient Greeks and Romans are most likely to be encountered in the media of popular culture – novels, movies, television dramas and documentaries, cartoons, computer games, and comics (see e.g. Bridges 2007). Between the sixteenth and nineteenth centuries, far more people consumed texts, histories and myths from the ancient world by attending pageants, carnival festivities, the live theatre and the opera house than through the medium of the printed word (see especially Burke 1981). It was from Shakespeare's history plays that Renaissance groundlings learned their Roman history. It was through Italian opera and subsequently ballet that the myths immortalized in Ovid's *Metamorphoses* reached their widest eighteenth-century audiences. It was in the form of Ernest Legouvé's *Médée* that large numbers of mid-nineteenth century people without a word of Latin or Greek felt the theatrical impact of the death of Medea's children, whether in French, or in Italian, or English-language versions and imitations. One version, by John Heraud, in 1859 reached tens of thousands of lower-class spectators, seated in east London's enormous Standard Theatre. Even more learned their classical myths, and some spectacular episodes from ancient history (e.g. the Fall of Pompeii), in the form of the Victorian burlesque theatre – light-hearted musical adaptations of glamorous legends and classical drama (Hall and Macintosh 2005: 350–88, 401–27).

Working-class access to classical myth and history included the entertainments offered by travelling showmen. The famous Billy Purvis took his booth theatre around the circuit of northern race tracks, in which he displayed phantasmagorias illustrating scenes such as Neptune in his car, attended by Amphitrite and Tritons; Purvis's troupe of actors also performed paraphrases of plays on classical themes, including *The Death of Alexander the Great*, a revision of Nathaniel Lee's *The Rival Queen*s of 1677. The most famous of all early circus performers, Andrew Ducrow, specialized in 'hippodramatic' enactments of Hercules' labours, of Alexander the Great taming Bucephalus, of the rape of the Sabine women, and Roman gladiators in combat. Most of these were performed at Astley's Theatre in London, the clientele of which was heterogeneous, including both working-class and middle-class elements. Public houses in Victorian London sometimes hired entertainers who took up acrobatic poses based on classical statuary, such as 'Hercules wrestling with the Nemean Lion'. Similar forms of entertainment were sold by Victorian pornographers. From the 1840s onwards well-developed female models in skin-tight 'fleshings' could be seen in the popular *poses plastiques*, in which they imitated naked classical statues for the delectation of audiences which contemporary critics regarded as including the 'worst sort' of person. *Tableaux vivants* such as 'Diana Preparing for the Chase', at Liverpool's proletarian Parthenon Rooms in 1850, legitimized sexual voyeurism by the use of classical mythology (Hall and Macintosh 2005: 388–90).

Yet it is not enough to identify the class *position* of people reacting to the ancient Greek and Roman world in subsequent epochs: class *agenda* is even more important. When the educationalist Seymour Tremenheere compiled excerpts from ancient political theorists in order to enlighten the masses (see above), his intention was actually to *discourage* socialist agitation, and he therefore omitted Plato and his thought-provoking communistic Republic altogether. An arguably even more important question to ask is the sixth one to be suggested here: (6) *how has the reception of individual ancient texts and authors been affected by the class agenda of the new, post-antique readership or spectatorship?* There have always been plenty of working-class reactionaries, and many radicals and revolutionaries from higher up the social scale. Some ancient authors have been associated in certain periods with certain types of political view, espoused across the class spectrum, and research identifying this type of pattern remains largely undone. Here it is interesting to compare the different experiences undergone in England, and what in 1707 became Britain, by the Greek tragedians and Aristophanes respectively. Both genres of theatre were produced in and by the fifth-century Athenian democracy, and their contents were inextricably bound up with its ideals. But, until the twentieth century, only tragedy was used to support liberal causes and democratic reforms. Greek tragedy was associated with the 'Glorious Revolution', Whig ideology and, by the 1830s, with the extension of the franchise. Adaptations of Greek tragedy for performance on the professional stage of England, supportive of such political tendencies, can be identified from John Dennis's *Iphigenia* in 1700 to Thomas Talfourd's *Ion* in 1836 (Hall and Macintosh 2005). Aristophanes, on the other hand, was from before the Civil War identified with the Stuart monarchy and the dramatists who gathered round Charles I's French wife Henrietta Maria. After the Restoration in 1660, and more particularly after the French revolution, the writers attracted to Aristophanes were all different varieties of conservative, ranging from moralist Oxford academics in Holy Orders to wealthy patricians and counter-revolutionary agitators (Hall forthcoming). The most disreputable example of Aristophanic imitation is the novel *Simiocracy* (1884) by the Conservative MP Arthur Brookfield. It tells how the Liberal Party enfranchises orang-utans, and imports millions from Africa in order to retain power.

It is certain that researching the political agendas of the individuals who have responded to different ancient authors and artefacts has the potential to yield results that are not only intrinsically fascinating, but can illuminate the reputations and scholarly views that have attached themselves to these ancient authors. Indeed, since scholarship has usually provided the first line of interpretation of any particular author, in the form of editions and commentaries, it is *especially* important to pose the seventh question here suggested: (7) *how did the scholars responsible for the primary work on any particular ancient text personally see the world, and the place of classical literature within it?* For many of these scholars, class analysis would have been anathema. The effect of the *absence* of class-consciousness in the analysis of ancient literature during much of the twentieth century has been lucidly documented by Peter Rose (1992: 1–42). An exceptionally interesting example from slightly earlier is Basil Lanneau Gildersleeve, a brilliant classical scholar who in 1880 founded the prestigious *American Journal of Philology*, and is usually regarded as the founder of serious academic study of the classics in North America. His impact on the study of Pindar has been immeasurable: there is not a late nineteenth- or twentieth-century commentary or scholarly article on the epinician genre which is not still informed by Gildersleeve's dazzling commentary on the Olympian and Pythian odes (1885). Yet Gildersleeve's comments on Pindar are inseparable from his political outlook: he was intensely loyal to a nostalgic vision of the Old South, a vision forged before and during his service in the Confederate cavalry during the American Civil War, an experience which marked him indelibly (Hopkins 1986; DuBois 2003: 13–18). He had at some level identified the society he defended with the aristocratic, traditional, elegant world conjured up in Pindar's victory odes. That idealized picture had erased all the pain entailed by its underlying modes of production (peasant farming and slavery).

It is equally impossible to separate the politics espoused by the Philadelphia journalist I.F. Stone (a lifelong campaigner for African Americans and the poor, and opponent of American economic imperialism) from his study *The Trial of Socrates* (1989), in which he iconoclastically argued that Socrates deserved to be condemned because his actions had indeed been damaging to the Athenian democracy. Yet some of the most fascinating pages in that book concern not Socrates but Thersites, the low-class soldier who complains to the generals in the *Iliad* about the treatment of the ordinary troops. Stone points out how scholars from the Byzantine commentator Eustathius to the twentieth century have conspired with Homer in class snobbery and criticism of the first spokesman for low-class rights in the western literary tradition. The German reference work *Der Kleine Pauly*, which is still much used, goes so far as to describe Thersites as a *Meuterer, Laesterer und Prahlhans* – 'mutineer, slanderer and braggart'. For British scholars, authors, translators and artists, a quick look at the online *Oxford Dictionary of National Biography* can often provide speedy illumination not only of the class origins but of the political trajectory underlying any particular individual's publications. Simply to look up the name of the brilliant and influential translator of Aristophanes, John Hookham Frere, for example, is to reveal a bitter, disappointed plutocrat, the son of gentry, educated at Eton, fulminating from self-imposed exile in Malta against the democratic reforms he felt were eroding all the privileges previously enjoyed by his class. This has incalculable implications for his identification with Aristophanes, and his presentation, through translation, of the leaders of the Athenian *dēmos* (Hall forthcoming).

The case of Aristophanes underlines the importance of putting a further, eighth question in class-conscious classical reception: (8) *which ancient texts and passages within them have proved most susceptible to subsequent class-conscious readings?* The paramount example here is the *Odyssey*. One of the many reasons why this epic has proved so popular is that its cast of characters is not confined to an almost exclusively elite, aristocrat group: besides the several significant slave characters (Eumaeus, Eurycleia, Melantho), the poem includes a beggar, a mill woman, merchants and pirates, and a great deal of backbreaking labour (see Rose 1992: 92–140; Thalmann 1998). This overall effect is heightened by the setting on rugged Ithaca, where it is hard to secure a living from the land. But the most important factor in the focus of so many subsequent readings of the poem on class issues is the strategy by which Odysseus himself is disguised as the poorest type of free individual. For nearly ten books a king's perspective is fused with that of an indigent, ragged vagrant.

Yet the earliest responses to the *Odyssey* during the Renaissance did not emphasize its portrayal of class relationships. Odysseus was a prince in the high aristocratic tradition, a role certainly maintained in Giambattista della Porta's tragicomedy *Penelope* (1591), William Gager's Latin drama *Ulysses Redux* (1592), and Giacomo Badoaro's libretto for Monteverdi's opera *Il Ritorno d'Ulisse in Patria* (1640). Perhaps the earliest translocation of the *Odyssey* to a lower-class household occurred in the cheeky medium of ballad opera. *Penelope*, by John Mottley and Thomas Cooke (1728), sets the story of the *Odyssey* in a London tavern, the Royal Oak Ale-House; the publican is Penelope, wife of Ulysses, a sergeant in the grenadiers who has been absent fighting for nineteen years. There have subsequently been several other *Odyssey* plays and novels set in needy or proletarian communities (see Hall 2008). But the most widely disseminated responses to the *Odyssey* that relocate its action to low-class contexts have been in fairly recent cinema. *Sommersby* (1993, directed by Jon Amiel) concerns a confederate soldier who turns up at a homestead in the American south after the civil war, claiming to be its pig-farming householder Jack Sommersby, husband of Laurel and father of her son. Poverty, agricultural problems, and the wandering population of newly liberated slaves provide the background to a story that fuses the second half of the *Odyssey* with the true story of a returning soldier dramatized in the movie *La Retour du Martin Guerre* (1982). Created by the same men who went on to collaborate on the screenplay for *Sommersby*, Daniel Vigne and Jean-Claude Carrière, this had also been subtly influenced by the *Odyssey* and was a powerful evocation of the physical reality of life in pre-industrial sixteenth-century France. In Mike Leigh's *Naked* (1993), the Odysseus-figure Johnny is a Mancunian working-class drifter, and class conflict explodes in his disastrous confrontation with the 'suitor', represented by his girlfriend's rapacious upper-class landlord.

There have also been several films released over the last decade that explicitly use the *Odyssey* but translocate it to the working culture of the southern states of the USA. Victor Nunez's *Ulee's Gold* (1997) features a poor beekeeper in the Panhandle marshes of Florida, a former Vietnam combatant, who defends his home and womenfolk against lowlife criminals. The Coen Brothers' *O Brother, Where Art Thou?* (2000) identifies as its Odysseus-like hero one Ulysses Everett McGill, a loser and escaped convict from the 'white trash' of the deep south, in 1930s Mississippi, at the height of the great Depression (see Roisman, this volume, ch. 24). The story of unremitting agricultural labour told in Anthony Minghella's *Cold Mountain* (2003, based on a novel by Charles Frazier), almost sidelines its returning carpenter-soldier hero in favour of the relationship between the middle-class 'Penelope' Ada Monroe and the lowest-class person in the area (Ruby Thewes). Finally, Wim Wenders' *Don't Come Knocking* (2005) features Howard Spence, a sixty-year-old alcoholic movie actor, who on returning to his hometown in Elko, Nevada, rediscovers an old love interest and offspring; the travelogue consists of desperate escapades in a crummy casino, a drying-out cell in the local police station, and other demotic locations.

The *Odyssey* serves well to introduce the last question to be considered in this brief overview of methodologies for the investigation of class tensions within classical reception: (9) *the relationship between class and canon*. As society and its attitudes to social class have changed, so the periods of ancient history and the authors on the curriculum have been transformed. The *Iliad*, with its focus higher up the social scale than the *Odyssey*, was for centuries the more read and admired of the two poems, but in the early 1900s, the period of proletarian revolutions, it was relegated – so far permanently – to second place. Of course, the original emergence of the classical canon was a product of the ancient world's own judgements on what was deemed worthy of repeated reading, copying and transmission around its cultural centres, and these judgements usually had a class element within them. The elevated genres of epic and tragedy, with their aristocratic heroes, survived far better than mime, pantomime, satyr drama, and the Greek burlesque novel, with their irreverent attitudes, quotidian settings, obscenity, and perceived demotic appeal (see Hall 1995b). This point is brought out with incomparable clarity in Tony Harrison's (1990) play *The Trackers of Oxyrhynchus*, where the near-total loss and disparagement of the ancient genre of satyr drama is connected with both ancient aesthetic snobbery and twentieth-century class conflict.

Yet even within the corpus of transmitted texts, the 'canon' looks different from discrete vantage points in subsequent global history. The historians and biographers of Rome (Livy, Plutarch, Suetonius), who reverberated so loudly in the Renaissance and Early Modern periods, began to be rivalled by an interest in Greek history during the Enlightenment; democratic Athens only emerged as a model for mainstream admiration in the late eighteenth century, at the moment when her tragedies were essentially rediscovered in mainstream discourse. Radicals and autodidacts everywhere have always been attracted to ancient authors who had once been slaves, such as Aesop and Epictetus. In the former Soviet Union, the study of 'decadent' and 'bourgeois' individualist poets such as the Roman elegists was often discouraged, while Hesiod's *Works and Days*, Oppian's *Halieutica*, and other texts focused on agriculture and food provision were examined in detail. Soviet tastes can be demonstrated by a quick look through the useful English-language summaries of the articles included in the journal *Vestnik Drevnei Istorii* (*Messenger of Ancient History*, founded in 1937; see also Takho-Godi 1970).

This exercise would also reveal the significance of certain figures to a society as institutionally class-conscious as the Soviet Union, as they have also been to more anti-establishment working-class movements and their supporters. Spartacus, the Roman gladiator who led a slave revolt, is the best known in the west through Stanley Kubrick's film adaptation of the committed communist Howard Fast's 1951 novel. But the story had been used in the cause of reform from at least as early as the 1760 French tragedy *Spartacus* by Bernard-Joseph Saurin, who drew his noble image of the rebel slave from Plutarch's *Life of Crassus*. The other ancient patron of working-class movements has, since a similar date, been the Titan philanthropist Prometheus, who rebelled against Zeus's autocratic rule to give humankind fire, making possible all technological advances. His arrest and epoch-long confinement have always seemed symbolic of the industrial working classes' oppression and exploitation. Indeed, the man who coined the term *communism* to describe his egalitarian, feminist and utopian political aims was a nineteenth-century Christian socialist called John Goodwyn Barmby, who published a monthly magazine entitled *The Promethean: or Communist Apostle*. There is no topic in classical reception that would not benefit from the application of the nine-step inquiry into its class ramifications outlined in this chapter. But thinking about the vivid cultural presence across time of Spartacus' conflict with Crassus (see e.g. Wyke 1997: ch. 3; Urbainczyk 2004: 106–40; Hunnings 2007), and Prometheus' revolt against Zeus' autocracy (Harrison 1998: vii–xxix; Hardwick 2000a: 127–39; Hall 2004), would certainly prove a rousing way to begin putting the class into classical reception.

FURTHER READING

Fussell 1983; Hall 2004: 169–97; Hall 2008; Hall and Macintosh 2005: ch. 13; Hall Forthcoming, ch. 10; Konstan 1994; McHenry 2002; Ronnick 2004; P. Rose 1992; J. Rose 2001; Stray 1998; Thalmann 1998.

PART VIII

Changing Contexts

CHAPTER THIRTY

Reframing the Homeric: Images of the *Odyssey* in the Art of Derek Walcott and Romare Bearden

Gregson Davis

Prodigal, what were your wanderings about?
The smoke of homecoming, the smoke of departure.
From Derek Walcott: The Prodigal

The sea speaks the same language around the world's shores.
From Derek Walcott: The Odyssey: A Stage Version

The primary focus of this exploration of the postcolonial reception of Homer's *Odyssey* is on the poetry and poetic drama of the Caribbean Nobel laureate, Derek Walcott. Since his creative oeuvre encompasses both verbal and visual media, and his poetic diction is manifestly 'pictorial' in texture, the scope of the exploration will include a brief comparison between the modalities of reception discernible in his poetic corpus and those of the visual artist with whom he has expressed a deep aesthetic affinity – the great African–American painter, Romare Bearden (Walcott 1997: 222–35). An important point of convergence between the artistic principles professed by both artists is their interest in Homeric archetypes, and our discussion will therefore conclude with a glance at a few, specifically Odyssean, narrative motifs that recur in their works.

Our point of departure is Walcott's long-standing and fecund obsession with the Homeric heritage. In delineating the ramifications of this obsession it is worth clarifying at the outset the extent of his knowledge of the Homeric texts. Since his linguistic repertoire does not include ancient Greek, his acquaintance with the Homeric original is therefore indirect, though far from superficial. In addition to his familiarity with these canonical works through English translations, he is thoroughly conversant with the later European epic tradition that derives its inspiration from Homer. The secondary school educational curriculum that he absorbed as a precocious student in the classrooms of the former British island colony of St Lucia in the Caribbean archipelago equipped him with a basic proficiency in Latin, which enabled him to read Vergil's *Aeneid* in the original (cp. Greenwood 2005). As a voracious reader with unusually cosmopolitan tastes, he eventually went well beyond the standard school curriculum to familiarize himself with other major epic poems, such as Dante's *Divine Comedy*, which function, in part, as intermediaries in the transmission of the archetypal Homeric material. His creative assimilation of the epic tradition in both oblique and direct forms is exquisitely encapsulated in the short inaugural segment, labelled 'Archipelagoes', from the poem, 'Map of the New World' which appeared in the collection, 'The Fortunate Traveller' (Walcott 1980):

> [I] ARCHIPELAGOES
> At the end of this sentence, rain will begin.
> At the rain's edge, a sail.
>
> Slowly the sail will lose sight of islands;
> into a mist will go the belief in harbors
> of an entire race.
>
> The ten-years war is finished.
> Helen's hair, a gray cloud
> Troy, a white ashpit
> by the drizzling sea.
>
> The drizzle tightens like the strings of a harp.
> A man with clouded eyes picks up the rain
> and plucks the first line of the *Odyssey*.

Like the enlightened Keats of the ode, 'On First Looking into Chapman's Homer' (1817), Walcott's 'fortunate traveller' here undergoes an epiphanic experience in his encounter with the Homeric text that engenders new poetic horizons. The harp picked up by the modern bard in the final line announces an idiosyncratic incorporation and, at the same time, reframing of the *Odyssey* narrative.

Given the pervasiveness of the Homeric influence throughout his work as a whole, our analytic lens will be restricted to scrutinizing a few selected passages that may be regarded as representative of key aspects of his assimilative strategy. Thus his crowning masterpiece, the 'pseudo-epic' poem, *Omeros* (1990), will constitute a major point of reference for the discussion that follows. Some attention will also be devoted to kindred ideas conveyed in the dialogue of the play, *The Odyssey: A Stage Version* (1993a), as well as to a few passages in shorter lyric poems that allude explicitly to Homeric prototypes, such as 'Menelaus' and 'Homecoming: Anse La Raye'.

In an important talk inspired by a Romare Bearden exhibit, Walcott has elucidated his views on the most profound approach to imitating Homer (Walcott 1997). He holds up Joyce's *Ulysses* as the supreme embodiment of a non-trivial imitative strategy, because it ingeniously transposes central narrative episodes of the *Odyssey* into a contemporary cultural setting. In the Joycean reframing, psychological insight into character trumps adherence to generic norms and to the elevated style of the archaic heroic narrative. Walcott's own parallel strategy in *Omeros* is to endow humble fishermen on the island of St Lucia with attributes of character that recall the heroes of Homeric saga. Thus fishermen bearing French Creole names such as 'Achille' and 'Hector' become protagonists of a creative re-enactment of key motifs in the *Iliad* and *Odyssey*.

For Walcott's poetic muse, then, the Homeric model is seminal in so far as it furnishes an archive of character types and patterns of human relationships that transcend time and place, culture and geography. In articulating this point of view he has referred to such transcultural figures as 'iconic emblems' and, by way of illustration, adduces the Homeric Odysseus in whom he sees the paradigm of the Wanderer. As a visual emblem of this figure he fastens on 'the moving sail' – an image that is prominent in a Romare Bearden canvass on the Odysseus theme:

> What we have because of Homer, *permanently*
> because of Homer [. . .] are two emblems, at least.
> One is the Most Beautiful Woman in the World:
> Helen. That's indestructible, iconic, permanent
> for all cultures that share this part of history. The
> other emblem, of course, is the moving sail, alone
> on the ocean, not a ship but something small on
> a large expanse of water, trying to get somewhere –
> the image of the wanderer (call him Odysseus)
> made emblematic by the great poet.

The Wanderer, in this important formulation, is a complex figure that is worth unpacking in part, since it reappears in many guises throughout Walcott's poetic corpus. A notable recurrence in the lyric volume, *The Prodigal*, has provided one of the two epigraphs affixed to this essay (Walcott 2004):

> Prodigal, what were your wanderings about?
> The smoke of homecoming, the smoke of departure.

As the repetition of the word 'smoke' suggests (smoke is a key recurrent image in Walcott's poetry) the Wanderer often manifests a clouded vision of the experience of homecoming, which conceals a latent ambivalence. Among its other connotations, the wanderer figure signifies the cosmopolitan poet, ever on the move, who is haunted by a lingering sense of having betrayed his ancestral culture. Of the many poems devoted to the theme of 'Homecoming' that we find in Walcott's work, 'The Light of the World' is perhaps the most translucent vector of the returning poet's transient sentiment of having abandoned his people, or at least that unsung segment of the people embodied in the black population descended from slave ancestors. As the poet is being conveyed back to his hotel in a local bus while 'Marley was rocking on the transport's stereo', he is moved almost to tears at the sight of an old woman at the roadside (Walcott 1987: 49–50):

> An old woman with a straw hat over her headkerchief
> hobbled towards us with a basket; somewhere,
> some distance off, was a heavier basket

that she couldn't carry. She was in a panic.
She said to the driver: 'Pas quittez moi à terre',
which is, in her patois: 'Don't leave me stranded',
which is, in her history and that of her people:
'Don't leave me on earth' [. . .]

As the bus fills up with more passengers, the poet muses on the idea of abandonment, which he then personalizes:

Abandonment was something they had grown used to.

And I had abandoned them, I knew that there
sitting in the transport, in the sea-quiet dusk,
with men hunched in canoes, and the orange lights
from the Vigie headland, black boats on the water [. . .]

The idea of abandonment is interlinked with the implicit notion of a neglected poetic
theme, and it is plausible to read the later poem, *Omeros*, as making amends, in
the fullest measure, for that earlier neglect. Along with the speaker's sentiment of
betrayal, which can be read as a latent subtext of the Homeric paradigm, there is,
in Walcott's lyric narratives on the homecoming theme, an accompanying feeling
of apprehension about his poetic reception in his native island.

The poem that, in my view, best exemplifies this particular anxiety on the part of
the morally self-conscious wanderer/artist is 'Homecoming; Anse La Raye', which
recounts a return marred by the pain of rejection (Walcott 1984). In this iteration
of the homecoming motif the speaker observes wryly:

there are no rites
for those who have returned,
only, when her looms fade,
drilled in our skulls, the doom-
surge-haunted nights,
only this well-known passage [. . .]

The twin metaphorical coordinates of Penelope's loom and the dangerous ocean surge
here re-inscribe the Odyssean model in the mind of the returning poet and serve to
prepare the reader for the disheartening encounter to come later in the poem, in
which children playing on a St Lucian beach fail to recognize him as a native:

only this fish-gut-reeking beach
whose frigates tack like buzzards overhead,
whose spindly, sugar-covered children race
pelting up from the shallows
because your clothes,
your posture

seem a tourist's.
They swarm like flies
round your heart's sore.

The internal ambivalence of the wanderer/poet towards the bitter-sweet experience of homecoming comes to the surface, as we have seen, in the imagery of 'smoke', and is also expressed, metonymically, in the alternating rhythm of arrival and departure from the insular destination ('the smoke of arrival, the smoke of departure'). Whereas the ambivalence is virtually occluded in the original Homeric version of the warrior's protracted return, the image of an Odysseus whose deep urge to wander does not come to a close with his return to Ithaca becomes a powerful strand in later elaborations and permutations of the Odysseus myth. For instance, in Dante's famous transformation of the Ulysses figure in Canto 26 of the *Inferno*, the hero is represented as the type of the obsessive wanderer who is driven by a fatal hubristic craving for total knowledge of good and evil. In this medieval refashioning of the figure, the ineluctable impulse to depart finally takes precedence over the homing instinct in the mind of the ageing sailor/adventurer; in Walcott's remodelling, however, the two poles of arrival and departure that define the wanderer/poet's existence (what W.B. Stanford famously refers to as 'centrifugal' and 'centripetal' tendencies) remain equipotent in their magnetic attraction (Stanford 1954: 89). What is 'permanent', for Walcott, is the underlying emotional ambivalence, revealed in each iteration of the arrival/departure syndrome, that yields painfully acquired insight into the experiential paradox which beclouds all 'homecomings' – the perception that the very notion of 'homecoming' may be, at bottom, an oxymoron. As the disillusioned speaker of 'Homecoming: Anse La Raye' comes to understand, 'there are homecomings without home'. Given the transforming mirror of time, 'home' cannot be recuperated, and despite nostalgic desire for a pristine wholeness, it remains an unstable, if not destabilizing, concept that is constantly challenged by the shadow of memory.

In Walcott's lyric universe, then, the figure of the Wanderer retains a core, metapoetic dimension – a dimension that is omnipresent in the pages of *Omeros*, where 'Homer' is signifier for the universal bard and is continually re-incarnated as such in a variety of personae (e.g. Seven Seas). In the play, *The Odyssey: A Stage Version*, the figure of Blind Billy Blue performs a homologous role, as do the other singers that appear on the stage who bear the original Homeric names of Phemius and Demodokos. One important rhetorical function of these variants is, at the metapoetic level, to validate the Joycean (and by extension, Walcottian) move of jettisoning the high epic scaffolding employed by Homer. Nowhere is this function more transparent than in the dialogue between the sandalled bard of Chios and the composer of *Omeros*, in which the latter is told to ignore the divine apparatus: 'Forget the gods', Omeros growled, 'and read the rest' (Walcott 1990: 283). In terms of an implied reading of the Homeric epics, the injunction to the interlocutor to discard the Olympian scaffolding confirms the very aesthetic path being taken by the St Lucian bard in the course of the poem.

In the ensemble of emblematic figures that ultimately derive from the matrix of Homeric verse, a special place of honour is reserved for the trope of the bird. As in the case of the Wanderer, the bird acts as the vector of multiple significations that are mutually reinforcing. In both the *Odyssey* play and *Omeros* the bird, represented either on the wing or simply emitting a song, is a recurrent discursive image. As a preliminary approximation to outlining the polysemous range of the bird emblem, it will be useful to examine some of its occurrences in the verse drama.

The form that the emblem consistently assumes in the play is the swallow, as we learn immediately from the Prologue as pronounced by the choral bard, Billy Blue:

> When you hear this chord
> [*Chord*]
>   Look for a swallow's wings,
> A swallow arrowing seaward like a messenger
>
> Passing smoke-blue islands, happy that kings
> of Troy are going home and its ten years' siege is over.
>
> So my blues drifts like smoke from the fire of that war,
> Cause once Achilles was ashes, things sure fell apart.
>
> Slow-striding Achilles, who put the hex on Hector.
> A swallow twitters in Troy. That's where we start.

The swallow of this prologue appears in at least two of its prominent rhetorical aspects. On the wing it is 'like a messenger;' in other words, it delivers the news that constitutes the story or *mythos* as it enfolds in time. In addition to this primary narratological function of enunciating stages in the enactment of the plot, the swallow has the dramaturgical role of providing cues to the action and accompanying dialogue with its 'twitter'. The two functions – the 'seaward' direction of the narrative and the prompting twitter – are closely allied in the inaugural song of Billy Blue.

How does the swallow trope relate to Homeric paradigmatic motifs? In the first instance, the bird's association with bardic utterance links up with a common formulaic Homeric expression that describes the flow of epic dialogue, 'winged words'. Words on the wing, within the performative frame of Homeric verse carry the story along with their rhythmic pulse. With a swiftness that is endemic to Homer's dactylic hexameters the twitter serves to set the play's dialogue in motion. Walcott multiplies the role of the twittering swallow at many junctures in the rapid course of the play. Without attempting to account for each and every instance of the polysemous emblem, I shall concentrate on a few of the more salient manifestations.

Like Athena's theriomorph, the owl, Walcott's officious swallow performs the role of divine protector and premonitory counsellor of the wandering hero as well as of his maturing son, Telemachus. Thus in an exchange with Odysseus' loyal nurse, Eurycleia (act I, scene II) Telemachus receives privileged communication from a swallow:

TELEMACHUS: A swallow spoke to me from the wrist of that chair.
EURYCLEIA: You send for wine? what happened to your sea captain?
TELEMACHUS: The elect can take natural shapes, Eurycleia.
EURYCLEIA: Lord, bird t'ief this boy's wits.
TELEMACHUS: It twittered, 'He'll return'.

Whereas Eurycleia downplays the significance of Telemachus' epiphanic experience, the young man interprets the swallow's telltale whirr as a celestial prognostication of the revenge to be meted out by his father on the suitors: 'The whirr of one swallow starts destruction's engine'. Athena's impersonation of a bird in the Homeric narrative is here transposed and elaborated into the intermittent signalling swallow that is audible to the ear of the privileged protagonist. Walcott's Nestor in a later scene from the drama (act I, scene III) makes even more explicit the analogy between the emblematic bird of the Greek Athena and the ubiquitous swallow in the stage version when he remarks to Mentes, in a notable inversion of the impersonation, 'Athena was that swallow's inhabitant'. The Odysseus figure himself expounds his intimate relationship with the swallow to the circumspect Penelope, who has just told him about her famous trick of stitching and unstitching the shroud for Laertes (act II, scene IV):

PENELOPE: I'd unstitch it like a swallow's beak picking straw.
ODYSSEUS: Swallows are my friends.
PENELOPE: There's a nest in this house.

In these pregnant exchanges the swallow's twitter re-enacts a talismanic role that supports the more strictly dramaturgic one of marking stages in the forward progress of the story.

In Walcott's fluid theatrical adaptation, the bird may occasionally be emblematic not only of the advancing storyline, but of its connection with the broader *mythos* residing in the memory of the heroes, and thereby works as a metaphor for the bardic transmission of the tales from one audience to the next. This intermediate function of disclosing the interconnection between past and present episodes in the Trojan macro-saga is succinctly illustrated in the following brief exchange between Nestor and an attendant at his court at Pylos. As the visiting Telemachus tries to elicit clues as to his father's fate from the aged warrior who, as in the Homeric prototype, is the custodian of epic memory, the latter is made to recall the earlier momentous twitter of a swallow as he conjures up the past destiny of the doomed city (act I, scene III):

FIRST ATTENDANT: All of Troy's sorrow is borne in a swallow's flight
NESTOR: Ten years! And my heart is stabbed by a bird's twitter.

The foregoing adumbration of the semantic range traversed by Walcott's bird-sign would not be adequate without reference to its major significance as omen – a significance it conspicuously held in many ancient Mediterranean societies, including Egyptian, Hellenic, Etruscan and Roman. In the form of augury – the ritual praxis of predicting the future from the examination of the flight of birds – attention to winged creatures as celestial agents of communication was a prominent feature of Greco-roman lore and mythographic traditions. In the Homeric poems, no less than in Classical Greek drama, dream visions interpreted as prophecies of future events often contain bird allegories. In a highly condensed variant of the motif of the bird-portent, the sound of a swallow's whirring wings is taken as a premonitory sign of the bloody denouement of the epic saga. It is with the reassurance conveyed by this ominous sound that Odysseus warns the suitors, in a less oblique mode than heretofore, of their dire fate (act II, scene VI):

ODYSSEUS: What I endure will be suffered again.
                 [*A swallow passes*]
EURYMACHUS: What was that noise?
POLYBUS: Nothing. A swallow.
ODYSSEUS: Say your prayers.

The long poem, *Omeros*, which preceded the stage version of the *Odyssey* by approximately three years, is similarly replete with a bird imagery that is semantically dense in ways that are paralleled in the account we have given of the swallow's plural, interlocking roles. In the poetic narrative, however, Walcott employs a species of bird that is native to the New World, the sea-swift. As an equally complex emblem, the swift permeates the sea-scape of the quasi-epic narrative poem, *Omeros*. By virtue of its frequent recurrence, the bird and its watery habitat share a primary metonymic signification, in view of the central symbolic role of the sea in the life of the Odysseus figure. In explicating some of the swallow's figurative transmigrations I shall intersperse my analysis with frequent textual citations because, in the case of a poetic diction that is metaphorically dense, such as Walcott's, it is impossible to due justice to a nuanced order of 'intertextuality' (in the non-trivial sense) without recourse to concrete scrutiny of select loci.

A thorough exegesis of the overlapping meanings attributable to the sea-swift in Walcott's verse would take us too far away from our main theme. Suffice it to note, in passing, that the poet indulges in programmatic wordplay that foregrounds the centrality of the vocable, 'mer' ('sea'), in the syllabic breakdown of the poem's title (O-<u>mer</u>-os), and that the sea is often the figurative locus of past human experience (Walcott 1990: 14). The repeated appearances of the swift in its oceanic haunt are associated, at one level, with the rapid progress of the poem itself; but the germane interpretive levels are, as I have indicated, multiple. All the roles we have illustrated above in relation to the swallow emblem are fully documentable in the 'chapters' into which the poem is segmented, e.g. metteur-en-scène, bearer of tradition, protector of the wandering hero, intermediary narrator/messenger linking past and present, divine epiphany, augur. Rather than engaging in a point for point comparison of the interchangeable roles of swallow and swift in both texts, let us focus instead on a few passages from *Omeros* that complement and further refine observations made above in respect to the play.

As prelude to this complementary analysis, it is important to note that the poet provides the reader of the poem with a gloss that affirms the notional link, even symbolic identity, between swallow and swift. The gloss is made apropos of the description, or ecphrasis, of the embroidered work being stitched by Maud, a character in *Omeros* who is the wife of the expatriate Briton, Major Plunkett. In creating her 'immense quilt' Maud portrays a veritable ornithological guide which, in the poet's catalogue of its contents, comes to a climax with mention of the sea-swift (88):

terns, royal and bridled, wild ducks, migrating teal,
pipers (their fledgling beaks), wild waterfowl, widgeon.
Cypseloides Niger, l'hirondelle des Antilles

(their name for the sea-swift).

The parenthetical gloss explaining the nomenclature seals the purely symbolic identification of the 'swallow of the Antilles' with the 'swallow' of the Mediterranean.
An ancillary effect of the interconnected names is to underline the Homeric subtext that weaves together the two narratives embodied in the genres of poetic drama
and poem. At a very early stage of *Omeros* (chapter I.ii) the protagonist, Achille, has
an inaugural sighting of the sea-swift soon after he and his fellow-fishermen have
uprooted the laurel tree that they will use as material for building their canoe:

Achille looked up at the hole the laurel had left.
He saw the hole silently healing with the foam
of a cloud like a breaker. Then he saw the swift

crossing the cloud-surf, a small thing, far from its home [. . .]

The swift is thus assimilated, at a programmatic juncture of the poem, to the image
of the wanderer 'far from its home' and, in this particular incarnation, operates momentarily as a kind of surrogate for the Odysseus figure. Elsewhere in his poetry Walcott
avails himself of a visual pun that is crucial to understanding the symbolic complex
of bird, sails, and sailor. The V shape formed by the wings of a bird in flight is made
to fuse, diagrammatically, with the spread sails of a ship and, by a simple metonymic
extension, the sailor-wanderer who is 'far from home' and 'alone in a large expanse
of ocean' becomes essential to the equation.

In *Omeros* the chief Homeric prototype among the cast of characters is not – at
least on the surface of the plot – a contemporary version of Odysseus, but the hero
of the *Iliad*, the redoubtable Achilles. Such an ostensible distinction, however, obscures
the fact that Walcott's transformative muse deliberately conflates the two figures. The
conflation was, of course, already a structural feature of the Vergilian imitation of
Homer, which scholars of the Roman poet have long since noted (the *Aeneid* displays a clearly hybrid structure: the first half of the epic is dominated by 'Odyssean'
wanderings at sea in the quest for a home, while the latter half narrates conflicts on
land that call upon the Trojan hero's military prowess – his 'Achillean' side). Thus
in so far as 'Achille', the local counterpart of the Greek warrior, is a humble fisherman by vocation, he is also *ipso facto* a sailor whose existence is compassed by, and
derives meaning from, close, habitual interaction with sea. In view of the divergent
fates of Achilles and Odysseus in the tradition of the Trojan cycle epics, however,
the premonitory role of the Antillean *hirondelle* acquires a darker shade in the poem
than in the refashioned *Odyssey* play. In both Walcott texts, as we have seen, the
birds' appearances, in many instances, foreshadow pivotal episodes in the narrative;
but as far as the St Lucian Achille is concerned, the sad fate to which he is beck-
oned by the swift is a foregone conclusion that is irreversible.

It comes as no surprise, therefore, that Walcott's heroic fisherman who is in love with the beautiful maid, 'Helen', and who is doomed to a premature death, has a less than felicitous relationship with the sacred bird that punctuates the stages of his life. For him, the swift presages loss and, ultimately, death. Thus when he has an intuition that Helen is about to abandon him for his erotic rival, Hector, the reader is made to follow his ruminations (125):

> From his heart's depth he knew she was never coming
> back, as he followed the skipping of a sea-swift
> over the waves' changing hills, as if the humming
>
> horizon-bow had made Africa the target
> of its tiny arrow. When he saw the swift flail
> and vanish in a trough he knew he'd lost Helen.

A few lines later, in the closing sub-chapter of the verse, Achille arrives at the unsettling insight that not all swallows are benign (125):

> Steadily she kept her distance. He said the name
> that he knew her by – *l'hirondelle des Antilles*,
> the tag on Maud's quilt. The mate jigged the bamboo rods
>
> from which the baits trawled. Then it frightened Achille
> that this was no swallow but the bait of the gods,
> that she had seen the god's body torn from its hill.

The reference to the violence done to the body of the god reinvokes the uprooting of the *laurier-canelles* in the construction of the canoe – the inaugural episode of *Omeros* that is cast as an offence to the tree divinity. The cursed fisherman figure baited by the gods is emblematic, among other things, of the subaltern postcolonial black inhabitants of the Caribbean island, and in the course of the poem Achille makes a dream-like submarine journey back to his ancestral home in West Africa. The inner journey is a variant on the motif of *katabasis* (the descent of the hero to the nether world that is such a common feature of Ancient Mediterranean epics) (Davis 2007; Hardwick 2002: 236–56). In Walcott's reading of the old sagas, the underworld passage motif has a psychic correlate in the quest for self-knowledge ('he asked himself who he was': p.130). In this quest the accompanying swift attains to the stature of divine psychopomp ('leader of souls') who guides the hero towards the shores of his dead father – a sea journey that maps onto the mythological lore of many New World black diaspora peoples for whom 'Africa' is the name for the final resting-place to which the souls of the dead eventually return, travelling in a reverse direction from the catastrophic Middle Passage.

As a concluding observation on the nuanced treatment of the sea-swift in the imagery of *Omeros*, we may cite a passage that occurs in the final pages of the text, which retrospectively ascribes to the swift the all-encompassing function of guide to the narrative as a whole (319):

> I followed a sea-swift to both sides of this text;
> her hyphen stitched its seam, like the interlocking
> basins of a globe in which one half fits the next
>
> into an equator, both shores neatly clicking
> into a globe; except that its meridian
> was not North and South but East and West [. . .]
>
> Her wing-beat carries these islands to Africa,
> she sewed the Atlantic rift with a needle's line,
> the rift in the soul.

In this envoi the Caribbean 'rhapsode' (etymologically, 'stitcher of songs') rounds out his project of reinventing a common substratum for old and new versions of the epic tradition that finds its original matrix in the Homeric poems. What is claimed for the artistic 'swift' in this recapitulation is nothing less than the ambitious aim of the poem itself – a redemptive reintegration of Old and New Worlds that imaginatively bridges the 'rift' in the cultural soul of the postcolonial populace.

In what remains I hope to illuminate further the poet's transcultural compass by reconsidering a few of these major themes in relation to the visual art of Romare Bearden (1911–1988). My principal frame of reference for the juxtaposition will be Bearden's acclaimed cycle of collages depicting episodes from the *Odyssey* that he created in 1977. (Fine 2003: 88–91).

The transcultural dimension of his visualizations of these episodes is most starkly epitomized in the skin pigment that he uniformly imparts to the legendary actors. The mythic universe that he projects in his brightly coloured collages is populated by black-skinned males and females. Crucial to his reconstruction of a cultural seascape that is beyond history is the circumstance that dark pigmentation is not confined to mortals: even the powerful god of the sea, Poseidon, who is the inveterate enemy of Odysseus, is portrayed as black, as is his emblem, the formidable trident, that he wields with such vehemence against the returning Greek heroes. What is the ulterior significance of this blackness for the artist's idiosyncratic rendition and assimilation of the *Odyssey* story?

First and foremost, it exposes the fundamental irrelevance of racial identities (of which skin pigment is but one of the full panoply of superficial elements) for a deeper understanding of what it means to be a human being. That racial categorization leads to the invention of what Erik Erikson has accurately termed 'pseudo-species' is an insight that is now being amply validated by the new science of genomics. There is, however, an additional layer of literary-historical rationale to the portrayal of black bodies in a Homeric context. Bearden was no philologist, of course, but he appears to manifest an awareness of the Homeric type-scene that features the visit of the Olympian gods to the land of the Ethiopians. In Homer's worldview, as is well known to readers of the epics, the distant 'Ethiopians' (the word is derived from the Greek for 'people of burnt face') are conceived as leading a paradisiacal lifestyle and, what is even more remarkable from the perspective of modern racialist culturally engendered stereotypes, they enjoy a footing of social equality with the blessed gods who are their grateful guests at fabulous feasts. As Bearden is reputed to have observed to an interviewer who questioned him about the black pigment he bestowed on his figures, Poseidon 'always has to come up from Africa, where he wants to be with his friends there. And it is universal' (Fine 2003: 261, n.178; see frontispiece: figure 0.1). Clearly the artist is attempting to recover a rudimentary order of human experience that transcends time, race and culture. His concept of a 'universal' substrate inherent in Poseidon's desire to be with his black friends is, at bottom, very closely akin to Walcott's views, discussed above, on the subject of the timeless, transcendent iconic emblem.

The depiction of protagonists of an immemorial *mythos* as black is also a salient feature of Walcott's poetics, as we have seen in the context of the characters that are woven into the embroidery of *Omeros*. The stage version of the *Odyssey* contains analogous references to the black pigment of some of its dramatis personae. In a poetic drama that reconstructs a legendary cosmos the explicit references to skin colour are made in a deliberately casual way. The enchantress Circe, for example, proudly draws attention to her lustrous epidermis during her seduction of Odysseus: 'Rest your head on the length of this ebony arm'. Long ebony arms are certainly very prominent in the female lovers in Bearden's *Odyssey* series, with which Walcott was intimately familiar. Among the black characters who appear in the Walcott play are the fickle maidservant, Melantho (the root of whose Greek name registers her blackness) and the loyal nurse, Eurycleia, as we learn somewhat brusquely from Melantho's bitter outburst in response to an unwelcome order from her aged supervisor (act II, scene IV):

EURYCLEIA: Melantho, get back inside and clear the table.
MELANTHO: No, you crooked black bitch! I'm engaged to a prince.

In coming to terms with the ideational basis for the deployment of dark-skinned figures on the part of both visual artist and poet, it is essential to grasp that neither is primarily concerned with a revisionist pseudo-historical agenda (e.g. 'Eurydice and Circe were really black'), but rather with promulgating an image of an ancient Mediterranean world that existed 'before color prejudice' (Snowden 1983). Even more important to their common universalist perspective is the underlying paradox that the pigment of the figures is not, at bottom, germane to the story. The root idea of the interchangeability (and hence triviality) of skin pigmentation is graphically evident in Walcott's two contrasting representations in verse of the iconic emblem that he labels 'The Most Beautiful Woman in the World'. 'Helen' in this generic sense may be a black or white avatar, and it is no contradiction of this ahistorical conceptualization for Walcott to portray her as a stunning black maid in the pages of *Omeros*, on the one hand, and as a promiscuous white lover in a short lyric elegy, on the other. The latter incarnation occurs in the poem, 'Menelaus', (from the collection, *The Arkansas Testament*) where the voice of first person speaker is overheard ruefully reflecting on the past as he is wading in the sea (Walcott 1987: 101):

> Wood smoke smudges the sea.
> A bonfire lowers its gaze.

> Soon the sand is circled with ugly
> ash. Well, there were days
> when, through her smoke-grey
> eyes, I saw the white trash that was
> Helen [. . .]

As a final illustration of the lines of convergence between Walcott's and Bearden's remodellings of Homeric paradigms, we may adduce their similar depictions of the type of the female magician/witchdoctor. The type is, of course, abundantly represented in the folk traditions of many cultures, ancient and modern. As portrayed in the works of Bearden the avatar of the female magician often takes the form of the contemporary 'conjure-woman' of African diasporic subcultures, corresponding to the 'obeah-woman' in the Anglophone Caribbean (Powell et al. 2006). The intersection between these potent New World sorcerers and characters in the Homeric portrait gallery resides in the portrayal of the figure of Circe, and, to a lesser extent, that of Calypso – the nymphs who detain the wandering hero and retard his return to Ithaca. The ancillary motif of erotic desire is deeply interwoven into the fabric of the story as it is developed by both artists, whereas in Homer, Eros and witchcraft are unevenly distributed between the Circe and Calypso episodes.

In the iconography of Bearden's famous collages in the Odysseus series, the contrapuntal relationship between male Wanderer and female Enchantress is a paramount structural feature. For instance in his work, 'Odysseus leaves Circe' (frontispiece, figure 0.2), what Walcott has labelled the iconic emblem of 'the moving sail' is partly visible through an open window in Circe's bedroom, while the nude body of the black-skinned magician lies outstretched on the couch (Fine et al. 2003: 8a). Bearden's choice of focusing on the moment of the hero's triumphant departure is a window into his interpretation of the story, for it foregrounds the failure of the enchantress to keep her lover forever under her spell. In Greek and Roman mythography powerful female magicians, like Medea and Circe, conspicuously fail to prevail by magical means in their efforts to control the sexual loyalty of favoured male heroes, and uncontrollable Eros proves to be the *cas-limite* of the efficacy of love potions (Prince 2003).

The paradox of the powerful female magician who experiences the frustration of unreciprocated love is also a feature of Walcott's dramatization of the Circe and Calypso episodes. In this respect he adheres to the Homeric plot; but like Bearden, he transposes the witchcraft practices of the Greek magicians into Afro-Caribbean equivalents. Even the goddess Athena resorts to Afro-Haitian Vodun instruments, such as the scattering of flour in Vévé patterns, in executing her timely and supremely effective counter-magic in order to neutralize Circe's wiles:

CIRCE:	Someone was here.
	[*She rises, paces, distracted*]
ODYSSEUS:	The sheets are all soaked with your sweat.
CIRCE:	I heard: 'You're a monstrous bitch. You'll pay in the end.'
ODYSSEUS:	Who?

CIRCE:	A green-eyed goddess. You're her favorite.
ODYSSEUS:	Who was she?
CIRCE:	She sprinkled it round this bed. White sand.
ODYSSEUS [*Tasting it*]:	It's not sand, it's flour.

In Walcott's transcultural universe the interchangeability of swallow and owl, like that of Afro-Caribbean Shango and Greek chthonic ritual, attests to the equation, at a deeper level, of all forms of witchcraft and augury:

CIRCE:	Let me trace your palm's rivers. Sit; open to me.
ODYSSEUS:	I don't believe in that hoodoo, or in this card.
	[*He shows his palm. Circe reads it*]
CIRCE:	A cock to Shango or sombre Persephone.

As these theatrical excerpts make crystal clear, the parallel modalities by which Walcott and Bearden assimilate and reframe the heritage of 'iconic emblems' derivative of the Homeric tradition are rooted in their shared assumptions about the ability of the artist, verbal or visual, to penetrate to a universal substrate of human experience. As Walcott phrases it in the second of our two epigraphs:

The sea speaks the same language around the world's shores.

FURTHER READING

A very useful and well-informed introduction to Walcott's intellectual and artistic formation is the comprehensively annotated edition, by Baugh and Nepaulsingh (2004), of his long auto-biographical poem, *Another Life*. For a broader and more copious survey of his life and poetic career, consult the detailed biography by King (2000).

On Walcott's views on Homer as literary model and its artistic implications, his talk, Walcott (1997), is a succinct but precious source of insights into his aesthetics, and attests to his high regard for the influential re-workings of the Ulysses themes by Dante and James Joyce. The special edition of the journal, *South Atlantic Quarterly*, in which the talk was published, also contains useful short studies by an ensemble of international scholars on various aspects of his craft (Davis 1997b). There is a thoughtful discussion of his techniques of imitation in Terada 1992. The collection of articles by classical scholars that appeared in a special issue of *Classical World* (1999: 93.1. 71–81) focuses mainly on Walcott's remodelling of canonic literary texts from the Greco-Roman tradition.

Romare Bearden's artistic output is well illustrated and discussed in the substantial catalogue to a major retrospective exhibition of his work at the National Gallery in Washington (Fine et al. 2003). The catalogue includes excellent essays by Ruth Fine, Darah Kennel, Abdul Elleh and Jacqueline Francis on the cultural roots of his major themes and his place in the evolution of twentieth-century art. The Fine essay in that volume includes a well-illustrated section on the splendid series of collages that Bearden devoted to episodes from the *Odyssey*.

CHAPTER THIRTY-ONE

'Plato's Stepchildren': SF and the Classics

Sarah Annes Brown

Science fiction is an elastic term which may be applied to whimsical neo-medieval fantasies and to projections of far-future technology alike, to action-packed adventures in outer space and to more surreal and metaphysical explorations of inner space. Like any other genre it can be done well or badly, though (in a somewhat unfair *Catch 22* situation) the best SF tends to be assimilated to literary fiction, its generic alignment occluded or brushed aside. Although SF might seem a quintessentially modern genre, classical themes have permeated a great many SF productions – including the controversial 1968 *Star Trek* episode from which my chapter's title is derived – and some commentators have traced its origins back to the classical period.

The chief candidate for this originary role is Lucian of Samosata, a second-century CE satirist who was born in eastern Turkey but wrote in Greek. His fantastical *True History* certainly anticipates favourite science fictional devices, with its detailed description of wars in space and imaginative accounts of various alien species. One of these, a moon-dwelling race, is entirely male, although its members marry each other and bear children which grow in the calves of their legs (Lucian 1968: 1.22). Another species spends part of its lifecycle as a man, part as a tree. We can compare these speculative variations on humanity with similar visions of intriguing alterity in recent SF – the androgynous society depicted by Ursula K. Le Guin in *Left Hand of Darkness* (1969) and the alien 'pequeninos' who are reborn as trees after death in Orson Scott Card's *Speaker for the Dead* (1986) spring to mind. But Lucian's playful picaresque whimsy lacks SF's hallmark verisimilitude and his explorations of extraterrestrial life remain undeveloped. Ursula K. Le Guin and Orson Scott Card think through the problems faced by humankind when it interacts with non humans. Lucian, on the other hand, presents us with an entertaining romp, a kind of xenological raree show.

But even if Lucian's status as the inventor of science fiction remains open to question, classical literature has undoubtedly been fused together with SF by countless later writers – recent hybrids include the cult TV series *Xena, Warrior Princess*

(1995–2001), a cheerfully inauthentic historical fantasy set in 'ancient Greece', and Neil Gaiman's *Sandman* series of graphic novels (1988–2003), with its ambitious and inventive updating of Greek myths such as Orpheus. What follows is an attempt to explore and explain the unexpected affinities between classical culture and SF. Although most of the writers discussed below seem to have derived their knowledge of the 'classics' from intermediate sources, or simply by cultural osmosis as it were, their lack of direct scholarly engagement with the Latin and Greek originals in no way detracts from their vitality as distinctive vectors of the classical tradition. In fact their characteristic lack of anxiety or pedantry (comparable to the patterns of appropriation we may see in medieval texts or indeed within the classical tradition itself) invigorates their intervention in the field. Although there is an obvious ostensible mismatch between the 'classics' (high status, elite, ancient) and SF (low status, popular, modern) when we explore the interface between the two we are invited to interrogate the distinction between ancient and modern and cultivate a more relativist perspective on both cultural value and history.

As we shall see, SF works both to defamiliarize and to refamiliarize the classical tradition. In other words, it can make the classics seem stranger and more alien or uncomfortably close to home. In particular, SF's preoccupation with various kinds of time disruption, whether literal time travel or an alertness to the cyclical, gives a special edge to its engagement with the classics. The distinctions between past, present and future are compromised or collapse completely. This tendency is particularly conspicuous in texts which respond or allude to the fall of the Roman empire which emerges as a kind of apocalyptic Ur-narrative.

The Fall of Rome

The most famous science fictional work modelled on Rome's fall is undoubtedly Asimov's *Foundation* trilogy (1951–3) whose strongest influence was, as its author acknowledged, Gibbon's, *Decline and Fall of the Roman Empire* (1776–89). The (invented) discipline of 'psychohistory', allows Asimov's protagonist, Hari Seldon, to foretell the future, and the eventual decline of the powerful Galactic empire. In fact this empire's fall is simply an extrapolation from the past, a mirror image of Rome's decline. But the relationship between Rome and SF can be pushed back much further than Asimov's twentieth-century novels. For the modern reader, some of the very earliest responses to Rome's fall can produce a science-fictional frisson, reminding us of the many recent works which offer a bleak vision of our own civilization's future decay. Such works become, as it were, retrospectively and at the point of reception science fictional, and alert us to some of the historical and cultural pressures which make the literature of catastrophe so resonant. Reading them through the lens of modern SF may subtly reinflect their meaning. (For although influence can only work one way, the *effect* of influence is less bound by the laws of physics.) One such text is the Anglo-Saxon poem *The Ruin*. Roughly 1,300 years ago its anonymous author described his feelings when he beheld the buildings of a long vanished superior civilization.

The city buildings fell apart, the works
Of giants crumble. Tumbled are the towers
Ruined the roofs, and broken the barred gate,
Frost in the plaster, all the ceilings gape,
. . . the dead departed master-builders,
Until a hundred generations now
Of people have passed by . . .

Stone buildings stood, and the hot stream cast forth
Wide sprays of water, which a wall enclosed
In its bright compass, where convenient
Stood hot baths ready for them at the centre.
Hot streams poured forth over the clear grey stone,
To the round pool and down into the baths.

(Hamer 1970: 27–9)

The poet articulates his awe when contemplating the scale of the ancient ruins (probably those of Roman Bath) and his wonder at the luxuries enjoyed by the Romans. Although the poem's detail suggests an eye-witness report there are hints at a more universal and metaphorical application, and commentators have identified possible echoes of Biblical catastrophes such as the Tower of Babel or the ruined empires foretold in the Book of Revelation. The poem's possible association between past and future, between the fall of Rome and the end of civilization as a whole, prefigures many similar effects of montage in later literature. Indeed the fate of the poem's only surviving manuscript (in the Exeter Book, a tenth-century CE codex which contains the largest surviving collection of Old English literature) contributes to this sense of history's cycles being endlessly repeated – the poem's lament for the fragmented ruins is itself ruined and fragmented by fire damage. There is something compelling about such apocalyptic works – as Michael Alexander observes in his *Old English Literature*: 'everyone who reads a translation of *The Ruin* seems to respond to it' (p. 125).

It would surely be misleading to describe *The Ruin* as SF even though, in retrospect, it may create a 'science fiction effect'. But the model of the Roman empire's decline can be traced both directly and indirectly in a number of less equivocally science fictional works. In the early nineteenth century there was a craze for depictions (both visual and literary) of a decaying world. Notable examples are Gandy's painting *The Bank of England in Ruins* (1830) and Mary Shelley's novel of plague and extinction, *The Last Man* (1826). Although both are set in the future, both hark back, explicitly and self-consciously, to the classical past. The Gandy painting at first glance seems to be a depiction of a classical ruin but is in fact a projection of a future England in which the modern neo-classical architecture of the painter's own day will be in a state of picturesque but ominous decay. Shelley's novel is particularly interesting in its (almost gratuitous) importation of the classical world into an ostensibly futuristic text. The novel charts the eventual extinction of humankind from a cholera-like illness and is presented as an ancient manuscript, a sibylline prophecy foretelling events destined to happen in the twenty-first century, discovered by chance during a visit to Naples:

What appeared to us more astonishing, was that these writings were expressed in
various languages: some unknown to my companion, ancient Chaldee, and Egyptian
hieroglyphics, old as the Pyramids. Stranger still, some were in modern dialects, English
and Italian.

(Shelley 1994: 7)

As well as adding an uncanny illusion of verisimilitude this device associates humanity's decline with the earlier fall of Rome, and it is in Rome that the eponymous
hero composes his account of the plague. Yet again we can detect a dynamic of circularity and repetition at work in the literature of apocalypse.

Although works on related themes continued to be published – H.G. Wells's *The
Time Machine* (1895) is an important example – there was a marked surge of interest in the post-apocalyptic genre in the late twentieth century, largely fuelled by the
fear of nuclear war, although within the genre this anxiety is sometimes apparently
displaced onto other catalysts for decline such as alien invasion. This is the scenario
presented in John Christopher's *Tripods* trilogy (1967–8). Here the young hero, Will,
is a rebel in a future society which is ruled by the Tripods, alien invaders who have
subjugated the earth by enforcing a system of 'capping'. Once they are fourteen years
old, children have a metallic membrane attached to their skull which makes them
compliant and unquestioning. But Will is saved from this fate by the encouragement
of an old man, one of the few who have managed to avoid being capped. Will asks
the old man:

'Do you know how long it has been?'
    'That the Tripods have ruled? More than a hundred years. But to the Capped, it is
the same as ten thousand.'

(p. 37)

The same exaggerated sense of the passing of time since civilization's collapse is revealed
by the author of *The Ruin* who claims that a hundred generations have lived since
the Roman buildings first crumbled. And Will's awed incomprehension at the ruined
'great-cities' of the ancients recalls the Anglo-Saxon's poet's wonder at the Roman
baths. This is not necessarily an effect which has been consciously created by John
Christopher, but rather a function of the tendency for powerful narratives of human
decline, real or projected, to become entangled in the reader's mind.

It is perhaps not surprising that the patterns and effects of these two unconnected
texts of ruin and decay, *The Ruin* and the *Tripods* trilogy, should resemble one
another. More particularly striking is the way in which modern science fictional dystopias
don't just repeat a generic pattern of decay but seem (illogically) to give their vision
of future ruin a Dark Age-specific veneer. For example in *The Tripods* the nearest
city to Will is Winchester, a city strongly associated with the pre-industrial past as
the capital of Wessex. A particular effect is created by Christopher's choice of Winchester
– the resonance of Swindon or Basingstoke would have been quite different. What
characterizes this neo-medievalism is its illogic. Thus rather than just presenting a
return to the use of horses and tallow candles in the absence of cars and electric

lights – a natural, indeed inevitable, regression – the text depicts the recuperation of medieval motifs or language for no good reason. We can see another example of this trope in the far future section of David Mitchell's *Cloud Atlas* (2004), another novel which encourages the reader to see patterns and repetitions at work in the successive 'falls', minor and major, of humankind. Here the young narrator, living in a tribal community in post-apocalyptic Hawaii, uses the obsolete word 'coney' as though his society's (logical) regression to primitivism had been accompanied by an (illogical) regression to an archaic lexis: 'O, hot tears o' shame'n'sorryin' brimmed out. Head o' Bailey's dwellin' I was s'posed to be, but I'd got no stronger say-so'n a frighty lambkin an' no springier wit'n a coney in a trap' (p. 276). If we identify this neo-medievalism not as simple regression but as a re-enactment of a historical and archetypal fall from civilization to barbarism we can detect the ruins of Rome haunting Mitchell's modern post-apocalyptic text.

Further, more extended, examples of such obtrusive neo-medievalism include Walter M. Miller's *A Canticle for Leibowitz* (1960), a novel which, like Asimov's *Foundation* trilogy, is fully in control of its classical resonances and their effects. In the post-apocalyptic America depicted by Miller the paradigm of Rome's fall is obtrusively present. Most improbably the Christian church, in particular the monasteries, have emerged as America's sole culture bearers, hoarding relics of lost learning. Latin is once again the lingua franca. The 'vulgar dialects of the people had neither alphabet nor orthography' (p. 11). This future world is described as 'that darkest of ages' and the patterns of its society, with disparate largely heathen tribes living uneasily alongside the more cultured clerics, are strikingly similar to the perceived realities of the original Dark Ages. The following comment on literacy is typical:

> It was true that petty barons sometimes employed a scribe or two, but such cases were rare enough to be negligible, and were as often filled by monks as by monastery-schooled laymen.
>
> (p. 66)

Here the reference to 'barons' is nicely double edged as it recalls a feudal past but also reminds the reader of modern-day America with its oil and cattle barons. This sense of history as a palimpsest rather than a purely linear process, of a nuclear exchange triggering an inevitable replay of history from Rome's fall to the present, is confirmed at the end of the novel. By this point civilization is sufficiently 'advanced' to be on the brink of a second apocalypse, reinforcing the many previous reminders of history's cyclical nature.

In L. Sprague de Camp's 1941 novel, *Lest Darkness Fall*, the feared potential trigger of civilization's second decline is fascism rather than nuclear war. The hero, Padway, is visiting Mussolini's Rome, the site of a self-conscious attempt to re-enact the military, civic and architectural glories of the classical past. This sense of repetition is embedded in the novel's central conceit – that at certain moments of great instability there is a danger of 'timeslip', an involuntary and inexplicable return to the distant past. Padway's colleague portentously reflects that 'Now, Rome may soon again be the intersection point of great events. That means the web is weakening again here' (p. 6). Rather improbably this prophecy is almost immediately fulfilled when, on entering the Forum, Padway is suddenly transported back to the sixth century. Although the novel is in many ways a light-hearted fantasy there are hints that de Camp wants us to see in Rome's fall a warning for his own contemporaries. At one point Padway falls under the spell of a beautiful but psychopathic Gothic princess. She dismisses his anxieties about the future of Rome:

> Really? That's a strange thing to say. Of course, my own people, and barbarians like the Franks, have occupied most of the Western Empire. But they're not a danger to civilisation. They protect it from the real wild men like the Bulgarian Huns and the Slavs. I can't think of a time when our western culture was more secure.
>
> (p. 150)

Her assurances that Roman civilization will be safe as long her own people are strong enough to act as a buffer, a protection from the east, rings hollow in the context of de Camp's own time and the perception that a powerful Germany might usefully keep the Soviet Union at bay. Of course the apparent dynamic here – a past reality anticipates and echoes the present – is misleading. This is a work of fiction, and de Camp's 'past' is a reflex of his present, not its cause or precursor. For SF, and the fears for the future which it so often projects, can exert pressure on our reception of the classical past. Here for example we can see how de Camp shares the common western sense of being Rome's heirs when in fact our own 'civilization' is at least as indebted to the Gothic outsider.

Clearly the idea of Rome's decline and replacement by a far less refined if still vibrant culture persists as a model which permeates our own fears for the future. This implicit identification between the modern west and Rome is apparent in depictions of Rome itself as well as in science fictional works. For example, in Robert Harris's novel, *Pompeii*, two quintessentially modern genres, the political thriller and the disaster movie, are mapped on to a narrative of the distant past. One of the novel's epigraphs is a quotation from Tom Wolfe's *Hooking Up*:

> American superiority in all matters of science, economics, industry, politics, business, medicine, engineering, social life, social justice, and of course, the military was total and indisputable. Even Europeans suffering the pangs of wounded chauvinism looked on with awe at the brilliant example the United States had set for the world as the third millennium began.

The nightmare vision of fire, dust and panic conjured up at the novel's climax is thus particularly likely to remind readers of another wakeup call to a supposedly complacent superpower, the events of 9/11. And in Tom Holland's popular account of the fall of the Roman Republic, *Rubicon* (2003), we are similarly encouraged to discover and identify links between the position of Rome and that of the modern-day United States.

> Nor is it only the broad contours of geopolitics, of globalisation and the *pax Americana*, that can be glimpsed, albeit faint and distorted, in the glass. Our fads and

obsessions too, from koi carp to mockney to celebrity chefs, cannot help but inspire, in the historian of the Roman Republic, a certain sense of déjà vu.

(p. xx)

Although neither *Pompeii* nor *Rubicon* is SF their authors have the same kind of alertness to this frisson of déjà vu within the historical process as writers such as Asimov or Miller, and enjoy sending the reader on a verbal, virtual version of the 'timeslip' experienced by de Camp's Padway. (This science fictional sensibility may be linked to the fact that Holland is a prolific fantasy writer as well as an ancient historian while Harris's most famous book, *Fatherland*, is set in an alternate universe in which Hitler won the war.)

Another example of the Rome/present interface is explored in Stephen Baxter's novel *Coalescent*. Although a work of SF, one of the novel's two strands is set in fifth-century Roman Britain and its central character, Regina, charts a depressing decline from refined urban living to primitive survival. She is dispirited by her daughter's ignorance about the very recent Roman past, and by her superstitious fear of the ruins, anticipating the still greater gulf between past glory and present decay evoked in *The Ruin*: 'She knew Brica felt uncomfortable in such places as these ruins, as if she believed they were ghost-haunted relics built by giants of the past, as the children's tittle-tattle had it (p. 80). Regina eventually flees to Rome and creates a refuge in the catacombs where she founds a strange community of women which retains its Roman heritage in the face of barbarian invasion. This is the Roman equivalent of a nuclear bunker, and in the novel's other strand, set in our own time, a character muses on the period: 'It was an apocalypse, like living through a nuclear war' (422). It is tempting to speculate whether Baxter, a British writer born in 1957, was influenced by the memorably chilling 1984 nuclear war film *Threads*, with its parallel focus on a young woman who lived through a meltdown of civilization and brought up a daughter ignorant of pre-war times, although surrounded by ironic reminders of former marvels. Perhaps this paradigm of nuclear winter distorts Baxter's take on Roman Britain, making a gradual process of deromanization into a more shocking crisis.

Yet another conflation of Rome's fall and nuclear apocalypse is hinted at in *Titus* (2000), Julie Taymor's imaginative film version of *Titus Andronicus*. The film opens with young Lucius playing with toy Roman soldiers, modern soldiers and robots, spurting them all with ketchup, before a massive blast of light at the window throws him in terror to the ground. Although what follows suggests that only conventional weapons have been used, the rather heavy handed irony of the situation is characteristic of 1980s nuclear war narratives, as is the mismatch between an everyday setting in the prosperous west and its immediate total destruction. The film goes on to juxtapose elements from different periods of history with surreal illogic, retaining a good deal of Roman paraphernalia, but combining it with images and music from the 1930s and the present day. The martial scenes in particular, where motorbikes incongruously appear beside primitive weapons and armour, combine the different elements in order to create a post-apocalyptic atmosphere rather reminiscent of the cult Australian film *Mad Max* (1979), set in a near future world where order has broken down following global disaster. Thus *Titus* is able to highlight the play's portrait of a society in decay and of a Rome which can only cling on to its identity and deter the savages at the gate by becoming equally bloodthirsty, eventually joining forces with the barbaric outsiders.

Myths of Greece

The montage effect achieved in both *Coalescent* and *Titus*, whereby past and present are superimposed, is taken a step further in Fred Hoyle's *October 1st Is Too Late* (1966), an SF novel predicated on a strange temporal upheaval which causes different parts of the earth to move either backwards or forwards in time. Thus parts of America remain in 1966 whereas Mexico moves forwards many millennia and Greece goes back to the fifth century BC. Hoyle, like Walter M. Miller in *A Canticle for Leibowitz* (discussed above), takes a cyclical view of history. The novel's far future humans show the central characters a depressing film in which they see humanity destroy and rebuild itself countless times before deciding that stability can only be ensured by a vast reduction in numbers and an avoidance of competition. (At this point the central characters realize that the eastern United States, which they had assumed had returned to the eighteenth century because they could spot tiny settlements and campfires from the sky, is in fact located in a post-apocalyptic future.) The resulting society is, though peaceful, sterile and bland.

But despite Hoyle's interest in the rise and fall of civilizations he is more concerned with ancient Greece than with Rome, and the central section of the novel depicts the interaction between the modern protagonists and the inhabitants of fifth-century Athens. Although these are never made explicit there are ironic parallels between the earliest civilization depicted in the novel and the last. Both Athens and future Mexico are inhabited by comparatively tiny numbers of people and both allow their citizens enormous opportunities for leisure (the Greeks because of slavery, the future world because of technology). And a particular bond is developed between the future world and that of Ancient Greece when the unusually tall post-humans take over the temples and function as gods, commanding them to make peace with Sparta via an oracle. In offering a rational (if science fictional) explanation for Greek myths of the gods Hoyle typifies a trend within SF's reception of the classics. Future worlds offer the opportunity to transform the mysterious givens of mythology into the realities of future scientific or evolutionary developments.

Evolution, rather than science, is the key to Sherri Tepper's *The Gate to Women's Country* (1988), a novel in some ways comparable to *A Canticle for Leibowitz*. Both present post-apocalyptic worlds with improbably specific affinities with the distant past. Tepper's future world has embraced the mythology of ancient Greece. The women and men lead largely separate lives – most men spend their adult lives in a segregated garrison. (The regime in some ways reflects that of Sparta, a society so alien that accounts of its customs are themselves reminiscent of dystopian science fiction.) The men are obsessed with the father–son relationship of Odysseus and Telemachus while the women are equally preoccupied with the narrative of the Trojan war, in particular its female victims such as Iphigenia and Polyxena. Tepper's focus on Greece and Troy rather than on Rome seems at first to go against my suggestion that there is a special connection between *Rome* and post-apocalyptic fiction. But Tepper's novel is more fantastic than *Tripods* or *Leibowitz*, less concerned to project the future with verisimilitude than use the threat of nuclear war as the starting point for a fable. This characteristic of the novel comes into focus when we slowly realize that some of the men – those who choose to return to the women's city and a life of peace – are endowed with clairvoyant and telepathic skills, apparently the result of mutation. Prophecy, once a mysterious gift of the gods, is now a function of equally mysterious evolutionary forces. There is an ironic aptness to this gift being limited to men. Although the women's point of view is presented sympathetically by Tepper it can be argued that the paradigm of the ancient world has been reversed in this dichotomized society, and that young men, rather than young women such as Iphigenia and Polyxena, are the real sacrificial victims of a matriarchal system which is deliberately seeking to breed out 'male' violence by encouraging destructive wars in which many men are killed. By contrast with Sparta, this women's world weeds out aggression rather than weakness and, by contrast with Cassandra's role in Troy, prophecy is the preserve of men.

Tepper is not alone in forging a link between post-human 'superpowers' and the supernatural abilities possessed by gods (and some humans) in Greek mythology. In David Brin's *The Postman* (1985) we are presented with a post-apocalyptic world whose destruction occurred some time in our future, following successful research into recombinant DNA and other enhancements. The 'postman' is a wandering survivor from Oregon called Gordon who finds a tattered postman's uniform on a corpse, puts it on, and assumes the role of emissary from a 'Restored United States of America'. The location of this mythical entity is vaguely but portentously described as somewhere in the East, perhaps echoing the role of Byzantium which became the capital of the Roman world after Rome's decline. As well as symbolizing a vanished world in which order and stability were taken for granted, the 'postman' role punningly adumbrates post-human identity.

Mythological echoes permeate the novel. The defeat of a brave community by a band of aggressive survivalists is compared to the fall of Troy. We learn of 'supercomputers' who could communicate with men, and appear to witness a surviving example, the 'Cyclops'. It has nothing in common with Polyphemus, instead handing out benevolent and sophisticated advice which is susceptible of various interpretations:

[Kalo] laboriously read aloud from the computer printout.
    '. . . incipient seepage from plate tectonic boundaries . . . ground water retention variance . . .
    'We think we've got a line on what Cyclops meant,' Kalo offered. 'We'll start digging at the best two sites come dry season. Of course if we didn't interpret his advice right, it'll be our fault. We'll try agin' in some other spots he hinted at . . .
    The Mayor's voice had trailed off, for the Inspector was standing very still, staring at empty space.
    '*Delphi*,' Gordon had breathed, hardly above a whisper.

(p. 157)

Despite its oracular pronouncements this 'computer' turns out to be a fake, a box of tricks controlled by a few remaining scientists who manipulate light and sound, *Wizard of Oz* style, to maintain control. Thus the environment (like that of mythical ancient Greece) is in almost every way more primitive than our own but in just a few mysterious instances seems more advanced. At one point the leaders of two of the emergent 'tribes', a group of brutal survivalists and a community of liberal pacifists, engage in single combat. Both men, it is revealed, are rare surviving examples of post-humans, enhanced before the holocaust with unusual physical powers. The exaggeratedly muscular survivalist is compared to 'the legendary minotaur' while his morally superior and ultimately victorious opponent is described as 'sole relic of an age of near-gods' (306). Gordon looks on with awe, comparing their fight to that between the superhuman heroes of ancient myth, and feeling 'kinship with those ancient peoples who believed in giants – in manlike gods – whose battles boiled seas and pushed up mountain ranges.' This is not Brin's only engagement with the mythology of Greece. The survivalists are finally conquered when they are infiltrated by women from the most progressive and technologically sophisticated group who turn on their 'husbands' and kill them at a prearranged time. Like Tepper's heroines, this band of women is reliving the past in a self-conscious and highly literary way. We first encounter the group debating the methods of Lysistrata (one of the novel's dedicatees) and the Danaides. In the end the covert guerrilla tactics of the Danaides, Greek sisters who all agreed to kill their husbands on their wedding night, are adopted in preference to Lysistrata's peaceful sex strike. It is perhaps not surprising that a novel which explores the mythmaking ability of the future – the processes which can turn its very ordinary hero into a beacon of order and civilization in a chaotic world – should also be influenced by the legends of the distant past. Like Hoyle and Tepper, Brin reveals an urge to create a world in which the fictions of ancient myth can be reborn as future realities.

A more extended and programmatic fusion of Greek myth and SF is depicted in Dan Simmons' *Ilium* (2003) and its sequel *Olympos* (2005). Whereas most of the writers discussed here co-opt classical material in a comparatively casual and opportunistic way, Simmons' take on the classics is more scholarly. *Ilium*'s complex scenario is predicated on a re-enactment of the Trojan War in which events are controlled, as in Homer, by Greek gods. However, 'Mount Olympus' is located on a far future terraformed Mars and the gods are really mysterious post-humans whose 'divine' abilities are enabled by quantum technology. Simmons defamiliarizes the gods by describing them in a science fictional idiom:

> If you've never seen a god or goddess, all I can do is tell you that they are larger than life – literally, since Athena must be seven feet tall – and more beautiful and more striking than any mortal. I presume their nanotechnology and recombinant DNA labs made them that way.
>
> (p. 16)

The status of the Greeks and Trojans is rather different. They are neither post-humans nor humans from our earth's past. Rather, they are the creations of a process which, the novel suggests, takes place whenever a truly memorable work of fiction is written. New universes have come into being to give physical embodiment to the imaginations of Shakespeare and Homer, and the events of Simmons' novel take place following a permeation of the boundaries which normally separate these 'fictional' worlds from the 'real' earth:

> 'And you're saying that consciousness itself created these other universes? . . .
> 'Not just consciousness,' said Orphu. 'Exceptional types of consciousness that are like naked singularities in that they can bend space-time, affect the organisation of space-time, and collapse probability waves into discrete alternatives. I'm talking Shakespeare here. Proust. *Homer.*'
>
> (*Ilium*: 420)

One of the novel's central characters, a revived twenty-first-century classics scholar called Hockenberry, is tasked by the 'gods' with charting the progression of the Trojan war and noting any discrepancies from Homer. But as the novel continues Hockenberry himself begins to intervene in events, ensuring major deviations from Homer. It is Helen who persuades him that he must find the *Iliad*'s fulcrum if he wants to change its ending, leading Hockenberry to 'morph' into Athena and abduct Patroclus, thus inciting Achilles to wage war against the gods rather than Troy. It is typical of Simmons' sly metafictional play that he associates Hockenberry's interventions with established textual cruces in the *Iliad*. At one point Hockenberry morphs into Phoenix, Achilles' old tutor, in order to witness the embassy to Achilles. Hockenberry explains that there is something anomalous in the Homeric text at this point:

> The problem here is that Phoenix is an odd choice – he hasn't appeared in the story before, he's more of a Myrmidon tutor and retainer to Achilles than a commander, and it makes little sense that he would be sent to persuade his master. To top that off, when the ambassadors are walking along the oceans' edge – 'where the battle line of the breakers crash and drag' – on their way to Achilles' tent, the verb form that Homer uses is a dual form – a Greek verb set between singular and plural always relating to *two people* – in this case Ajax and Odysseus . . . It's as if the blind poet himself had been confused about whether there were two or three emissaries to Achilles and what, exactly, Phoenix's role was in the conversation that would decide all the players' fates.
>
> (341)

Teasingly a textual anomaly segues into a SF anomaly when Hockenberry realizes that he is *not* (as Phoenix) being invited to participate in the embassy to Achilles. This is the first deviation from the text of any substance the scholar has noticed. In order to maintain the story of the *Iliad* (and eventually change it) he must improvise, running after Ajax and Odysseus and telling them that Agamemnon ordered him to join the embassy at the last minute. Thus a circular effect is created, almost an uncanny charge, as it is hinted that Homer's own confusion about Phoenix's role in the embassy is somehow caused by *Hockenberry*, that Phoenix was not meant to join the party and that the fissures in the Homeric text represent a struggle at some level in the poet's mind between what was supposed to happen and Hockenberry's desperate intervention. A clearer example of this reverse dynamic comes when Odysseus is impressed by the cyborg Mahnmut's claim that he is 'no man' and declares 'I'll remember that' (p. 577). (Odysseus famously says he is called 'no man' when he is confronted by the Cyclops, leading to confusion whcn the Cyclops claims that 'no man' has harmed him.) Simmons' central conceit – that alternate universes are brought into being by the creative genius of individual writers – is problematized by these contradictory impulses within the novel which suggest that Homer's narrative was itself influenced by Simmons' own events and characters. Like many of the SF writers considered at the beginning of this piece Simmons complicates issues of time and causation, projecting a universe – or docuverse – with a cyclical rather than a teleological chronology.

Alternative History

Through their play with ideas of authority and authenticity Simmons's novels, in a sense, belong to an important subset of science fiction, the alternative history subgenre in which, for example, Hitler conquered Europe or Rome never fell – recent novels engaging with the latter scenario include Robert Silverberg's *Roma Eterna* (2003), Sophia McDougall's *Romanitas* (2005), and Neil Gaiman's 'August' (1991), an episode from the *Sandman* series of graphic novels. The dynamic of modern alternative history has a self-consciously ludic tendency, delighting in bathos, incongruity and metafictional play. (It is almost *de rigueur* for alternative history novels to contain further alternative history novels in which our own world, or something very like it, is presented as a fantasy.) Well known figures are inserted into the alternative narrative in bizarrely inappropriate roles – in one such novel by Michael Moorcock, *Warlord of the Air* (1971), we encounter a serious young policeman called Michael Jagger and a dashing airship captain, Theodor Korzeniowski. (Korzeniowski is better known to most of us in this reality as Joseph Conrad.) The same dynamic, whereby the narrative deviates from the original or real version and foregrounds this process, can be seen in the film *Troy* (2004). This is very much an 'alternative history' of Troy, in that it seems to slyly draw attention to its deviations from the principal sources rather than simply provide a more palatable conclusion. Hector articulates his dread that his baby son Astyanax may be hurled from the battlements with apparent prescience but at the end of the film both Andromache and Astyanax escape their usual fates and join Aeneas in flight. (If we look back at the encounter between Hector and Andromache in Book 6 of the *Iliad* we can see how the film has reversed the ironic disjuncture between Hector's words and his actions, for in Homer Hector prays for his son's glory.) When Agamemnon corners the priestess Briseis at the end of the film he taunts her with threats of slavery: 'You'll be my slave in Mycenae A Trojan priestess scrubbing my floors. And at night–' Although Briseis effectively deletes the whole *Oresteia* by stabbing Agamemnon to death at this point, the king's words seem to reference the 'real' story in which Agamemnon takes back another priestess from Troy, Cassandra, to be his slave and concubine.

But just as Lucian can be shown to have invented space opera, so it could be argued that alternative history has its origins in the classics. Stesichorus' *Palinode*, for example, is a (rather science fictional) alternative history of the Trojan war in which Helen was never removed to Troy but remained in hiding on an island, her place at Paris's side taken by a replica so perfect no one spotted the difference. The Greek tragedians would offer competing accounts of narratives such as the Electra story – in Euripides' *Electra* the disparities with the earlier representation of the myth offered by Aeschylus suggest a parodic undercutting of the earlier dramatist. Seneca's *Medea*, like Simmons' Ulysses, seems influenced by her previous literary avatars. Even the still more niche subgenre of alternative history predicated on Rome's survival has a classical precedent, but one located in history rather than reality. As a recent exhibition at the Courtauld, 'The Road to Byzantium' (2006), demonstrated, long after Rome's 'fall' its culture lived on in the east, producing exquisite and quintessentially classical domestic artefacts at the same time as the anonymous Anglo-Saxon author of *The Ruin* thought such wonders a thing of the distant past. The worlds of the classics and of science fiction can be seen as comparable fantasy environments which encourage inventive creativity in the works of both writers and film makers. The mythical past and the unknown future are equally resistant to being fixed or pinned down with canonical certainty.

NOTE

I am grateful to Tony Keen for many helpful comments and suggestions.

FURTHER READING

Although interest in the interface between the classical tradition and popular culture is growing, the relationship between SF and the Classics is still relatively uncharted territory. For a comparative early overview see Fredericks (1980). For a discussion of Lucian's place within the SF tradition see Roberts (2006: 21–31). Rome's relationship with SF is discussed by Bondanella (1987: 229–30).

CHAPTER THIRTY-TWO

Aristotle's *Ethics*, Old and New

Rosalind Hursthouse

Introduction

Nowadays, it is a platitude that there is no such thing as getting back to *the* right, objective, interpretation of texts so separated from us in time and culture as those of the ancient Greeks. But, taking that as given, there are still two distinctly different approaches that contemporary philosophers can take to the texts of the Great Dead Philosophers. They differ both in methodology and in upshot. (Compare the difference in methodology and upshot in productions of Shakespeare, when one is, for example, deliberately feminist, or Marxist or Japanese, and the other aims for authenticity.)

We can scrutinize our text through the lens of some aspect of modern philosophy, looking for similarities however anachronistic – and the upshot is that certain things in the ancient text come very strongly into focus and others fade into the background. Alternatively, we can take the most scholarly interpretation of the text available and scrutinize modern philosophy through *its* lens, and here the upshot is that certain things in the modern texts come strongly into focus and others fade into the background.

The methodology of the second approach resembles that of the traditional classicist in aiming for the most authentic interpretation of the text one can achieve; we read the author's other texts and the contemporary literature, and commentators closer to the author in time than us. The crucial difference is that, in the philosopher's approach, we take it, as a working hypothesis, that what the author says is *true*. This feature obviously makes it an inappropriate approach to take to, for example, Aristotle's *Physics*. The hypothesis that Aristotle got physics right and that we, post Newton and Einstein, have got it wrong is hardly plausible, and no one is interested in scrutinizing modern philosophy of physics through the lens of Aristotle's work. But moral philosophy does not date the way physics (that is, 'natural' philosophy) does. It is not implausible to hypothesize that what Aristotle says in the

Nicomachean and *Eudemian Ethics* is true and hence not inappropriate to take the second approach to these texts and look at modern moral philosophy through this lens.

When philosophers started doing so, about thirty years ago, what, hitherto unnoticed, began to come into focus was that the moderns were neglecting a number of topics of central importance to ethics that Aristotle had discussed. And out of the perception of these yawning gaps, modern virtue ethics was born. To show this, I must first give a necessarily brief and broad-brush picture of 'modern' moral philosophy, which we may think of as starting about fifty years ago.

By the 1950s and 1960s, Anglo-American moral philosophy had become entirely dominated by two theories derived from two somewhat earlier thinkers, Immanuel Kant (1724–1804), and John Stuart Mill (1806–73). The two theories acquired a vigorous new life in the 1950s and 1960s when, for the first time for many decades, it become not only permissible, but fashionable again, for philosophers to write about issues of right and wrong. (Moral philosophy went through a very dull period prior to that when all we did was analyze the language in which we talked about things being right and wrong, so we never talked about the issues at all.) Why this change occurred need not concern us here; suffice it to say that it did, and the proponents of the two different theories found themselves with something very exciting to do, namely write about lying, breaking promises, abortion, euthanasia, capital punishment and so on, in terms of their favoured theory. Simultaneously, they found another exciting thing to do (well, exciting for philosophers), which was to argue with each other about which was the better theory of the two.

And that was more or less the state of play. There was one discourse in which the two theories' proponents debated the rightness or wrongness of certain (types of) actions, such as abortion. Proponents of 'deontology' (the theory derived from Kant) argued that a certain type of action was right or wrong according to whether it accorded with, or violated, moral rules or principles such as 'Respect rights' or 'Do not kill'. Proponents of the other theory (utilitarianism or 'consequentialism') discussed the same issues, and very often came to different conclusions because, according to their theory – this was a crude, early version of consequentialism – actions were right or wrong solely according to their consequences for human happiness or misery. Then there was a second discourse, at the theoretical level, in which they argued with each other about the strengths of their theory and the weaknesses of the other's. And that was roughly the sum total of what the literature in moral philosophy was about.

In 1958, Elizabeth Anscombe, a classically trained philosopher, wrote a famous paper called 'Modern Moral Philosophy' (Anscombe [1958] 1997). It was a scathing attack on both the deontological and consequentialist approaches and in its penultimate paragraph, almost casually, she drew her readers' attention to 'how Plato and Aristotle talk' when they are doing moral philosophy, presenting this as manifestly both more insightful and realistic than the way the philosophers she was attacking talked. She also noted 'a huge gap, at present unfillable as far as we are concerned' between the ancient Greek philosophers' way of talking and the current one, which needed to be filled by accounts of certain concepts, including those of a *virtue* and of human 'flourishing'. She thus drew attention to two topics ignored by the prevailing literature, and the philosophers she inspired subsequently found more. Viewed through the lens of Aristotle's (and to a lesser extent, Plato's) ethical texts, the differences between deontology and consequentialism became insignificant; what struck the eye were their shared omissions.

Eight Topics in Aristotle with Which Moral Philosophy Should Be Concerned

Aristotle pays careful attention to the different reasons or motives people may have for doing the same thing. But the prevailing philosophical discourse about right and wrong actions usually ignored the agent's reasons for whatever action was done. The hypothesis that Aristotle was right to be concerned about the agent's reasons seems extremely plausible. Surely there is more to the moral assessment of an action as right or wrong than simply whether or not it accords with a correct moral rule, or what its consequences might be. Surely there is a problem about doing 'the right thing for the wrong reason'? Can it be right to do something you believe is wrong? Are not there very different motives that people have for doing things in the category of lying, or abortion or killing, and surely those motives very often enter into moral judgements or assessments of the action? And surely moral philosophers should be discussing such issues? But they were not.

Second, there was no discussion of the role of emotions in morality. But again, it seems obvious that how the agent feels about what she is doing sometimes makes a difference to the moral assessment of the action. (Of course this and the previous topic are related. If my reason for giving you an expensive present is that it is the only way I can think of getting into your good books, I will not feel about it the same way as I do if I give it to you simply because you are my friend and I want you to have it.) Moreover, Aristotle also assesses emotions, felt in particular circumstances, for certain reasons, as right and wrong and it is clear that we do too – we do not just limit our moral judgements to actions. We say that people should not get angry just because they are not getting their own way, that people should be delighted, rather than envious and distressed, when good things come to other people rather than them. But there was nothing about those moral judgements in the modern philosophical literature.

Third, we may be struck by the fact that, when we think about the different sorts of reasons that people have for doing what they do, we notice that sometimes people act for certain sorts of reasons quite characteristically and systematically. So, for instance, there are some people who only ever break a serious promise when they really can see no way to avoid breaking the promise without doing something worse. And there are other people who break promises – serious or trivial – almost whenever it suits them, because they do not give a damn. Now those two people are of very different sorts of moral character. We make moral judgements about people's character, as well as about their actions and their emotions, assessing them as kind, honest, trustworthy, generous, courageous, just, moderate in their pursuit of pleasure, or, alternatively, as cruel, dishonest, untrustworthy, cowardly, unjust, greedy or licentious. Character was so important to Aristotle that it provided the title for his (as we now say) ethical treatises – *ta ethika*. But where was the discussion of character in the modern philosophical literature? Nowhere.

Fourth, when we think about the moral assessment of character, we can think not only about our assessment of other people's but also about our assessment of our own. And we can have the thought, 'Here's a question that should concern me and which should surely be one concern in moral philosophy, namely "What sort of person should I be?" I should be aspiring to being better than I am, but in what way could I be better? But how, in what terms, should I think about that?' Surely this is a question that moral philosophy should have been addressing? Aristotle addresses it, but there was nothing in the modern philosophical literature.

Fifth, while we are thinking about character, it might strike us again that our moral characters are not something we are born with: they have to be inculcated. And we might not only hope that we can become better than we are, but think and hope that we can bring up our children perhaps to be better than we are, or at least to have a good start in turning out better than we have. And so we are led naturally to the topic of moral education. Is moral education not a topic that should be of interest to moral philosophers? It is to Aristotle, who stresses the importance of our being trained from childhood to take pleasure in and find abhorrent, the right things, and to habitually do what is just and courageous. This also was not in the literature.

Sixth, when we think about the moral education of our children, we thereby start thinking about our children, or, if we do not have them, at least about the up and coming generation. But while we are thinking about our own, or those that our friends have, we start thinking about the central importance of family relationships and, indeed, friendship, in our lives. Such relationships are surely not only of psychological importance. Surely the relationships between parent and child, siblings, long-term committed partners, and friends, are morally important? Should they not be part of what moral philosophy deals with? Aristotle devotes two whole books of the *Nicomachean Ethics* to *philia* a Greek term that covers all of those relationships in which there is mutual liking or love and goodwill. But none of them were discussed in the literature, which regularly stressed the importance of complete impartiality.

I think it is uncontentious to claim that all the above topics are ordinary and familiar matters of moral concern. And matters of moral concern are what moral philosophy is supposed to deal with. But I now want to mention two more that cannot, perhaps be described as 'ordinary and familiar' because they are a bit more abstract.

One is the notion of wisdom – practical or moral wisdom, as opposed to theoretical or academic knowledge. Practical wisdom is something that one does not think of as, in any way, the prerogative of people who have been fortunate enough to go through tertiary education. It is the kind of thing that can be found in people with little or no formal education at least as often as it is found amongst intellectuals, and we say it has to do with knowing about what is important in life and what is not, and what human beings are like, and how human life works. It is, as most adults know, what adolescents notably lack, however nice and well intentioned they are. Aristotle devotes a whole book of the *Nicomachean Ethics* to what we translate as 'practical wisdom' (*phronesis*), showing how essential it is to our acting well, and how it comes from experience and cannot be acquired 'theoretically' by attending lectures or reading books. And if you agree that this is also a concept that we have, here again is a topic of central importance to moral philosophy. But when we looked at the contemporary literature, there was not a suggestion that the idea had ever been contemplated. If anything, the suggestion was that a clever adolescent could acquire instant moral wisdom by reading the available philosophical literature!

So that is my seventh. My eighth is what one might describe as a moralized conception of happiness, that is, the ancient Greek concept of *eudaimonia*. *Eudaimonia* was what Anscombe meant by 'human "flourishing"', 'flourishing' now being, along with 'happiness', the English word that is used to translate it. *Eudaimonia* is the key concept in both of Aristotle's ethical treatises and was yet another topic ignored by the modern literature.

Happiness was indeed discussed by philosophers in the 1950s and 1960s, because the early modern utilitarians took it as their basic notion. But the concept of happiness that they discussed was supposed to be a non-moralized concept. It was supposed to be something that, more or less, you could get to either by introspection on whether or not you were having nice mental states, or by some story about its being the satisfaction of rational preferences, where that notion of *rationality* was supposed to be, once again, something that was quite non-moral. (This meant that psychopaths or sadists, if sufficiently logical in their reasoning, would count as being no less rational than good people; the fact that their preferences included getting their own way regardless of the cost to others was no reflection on their rationality.)

Although we no doubt all have a concept of happiness as subjective experience, I take it that most of us also have a different concept of it, which is indeed a moralized concept. It is one for which, in English, we do not have a very good word, because the modern use of 'happiness' has more or less taken over. But we can get to it by thinking, perhaps, in terms of our uses of the phrases '*true* happiness', or '*real* happiness', or 'the kind of happiness that's worth having'. We can also get to it by thinking of what good parents wish for their children. Good parents, who have their children's interests at heart, hope that their children will do well, and they hope that they will be happy. But if one thinks of what ordinary parents – ordinarily nice, responsible, people – hope for their children *when they hope that they will be happy*, I think we all know that they are not thinking in terms of their children growing up to lie around all the time in a drug-induced haze of contentment. That was not the kind of happiness they had in mind. It may indeed be that they hope, in our materialistic age, that their children will become fairly rich and successful, and think that that will be happiness, but even there, I do not suppose for a moment that they are anticipating being perfectly pleased with what, as it were, the good fairies had done at the christening, if their child became a rich and successful criminal, say a successful Mafioso drug baron. When they say 'I hope they will be rich and successful,' the background thought is, well, in the *right* sort of way. And the ones who have less materialistic hopes, and just hope that their child will be happy perhaps without being rich and successful, they, I think, usually hope that their child will grow up to do *worthwhile* things and have *worthwhile* relationships, and get enjoyment from those. As the italicized 'right' and 'worthwhile' indicate, these are both avowedly moralized concepts of happiness, as Aristotle's *eudaimonia* is, and discussion of that, as I say, was the other topic that was entirely lacking in the literature.

So there are *eight* – eight really big, important topics – all there in Aristotle. And when you hold him up as a lens to the moral philosophy of the 1950s and 1960s, what leaps out at you is: none of them. Well!

Modern Virtue Ethics: the Action Guidance Problem

To anyone familiar with Aristotle's ethics, it will seem odd that I have not yet mentioned the most obvious topic in him, namely that of virtue itself. I have not yet done so because, when philosophers began looking at modern moral philosophy through the lens of Aristotle, and noticed the absence of the other eight topics, we did not (despite Anscombe's advice) immediately notice that *virtue* was missing. (No doubt this was because it is hardly a word that occurs in ordinary conversation nowadays.) The initial moves we made criticized the prevailing two theories for their failure to take account of, say, one or two of the more familiar topics I cited above, that we had something to say about. What took a little longer was the realization that what holds all of those eight topics together in Aristotle is his treatment of virtue. And out of *that* thought, that is, the idea that if we make virtue our central guiding concept in moral philosophy, it brings in all of these others as part and parcel of it, the kind of modern virtue ethics that I do – which is the neo-Aristotelian sort – was born.

Modern virtue ethics – the ethical theory that takes *virtue* as its focal concept rather than rules (deontology) or consequences (utilitarianism/consequentialism) – now stands as a rival to those other two sorts of theory. But it took some time to get established as such a rival because, in its early days, it seemed to be faced with an insuperable lack of its own.

Recall that proponents of the other two theories had been concentrating exclusively on the question 'Is such-and-such an action right or wrong?' They had paid no attention to questions such as 'Are such and such emotions rightly felt or not?' or 'Is such and such a good moral character or not?' considering only 'Is this sort of action right or wrong?' In response to our criticisms, they did not abandon their theories, but began considering those other questions too, and finding ways in which their favoured theory could address them. Moreover (philosophers being what they are), they looked for ways to criticize the new theory of virtue ethics and found something that initially seemed fatal. Although, as they admitted, we had a lot to say about all of the questions that they had hitherto been missing out on, we had nothing to say about questions such as 'Is abortion right or wrong?' And, they said, the *most* important task for moral philosophy was to answer such questions – to come up with a theory that provided action guidance by giving an account of right action. Deontologists had such an account – actions are right if (and only if) they are in accordance with a correct moral rule. Consequentialists had such an account. Well, actually, they had several, but in one way or another they amount to 'Actions are right if (and only if) they have certain desirable consequences.' Virtue ethicists had no such account.

That was, at the time, true, and unfortunately, harking back to Aristotle or other ancient philosophers did not seem to help. Neither Aristotle, nor Plato, nor the Stoics have lengthy discussions of the rights and wrongs of particular sorts of action the way the prevailing moral philosophy did. And that left us with very little help. We could not, so to speak, go to the texts and say 'Well here's what Aristotle says about abortion, or euthanasia or breaking promises or lying . . . so let's try to reconfigure that a bit. What would it look like in a contemporary setting?' That probably would have been very hard anyhow, but he does not say anything about such topics at *all*.

The one idea that we did seem to get from him is that the way to think about an action's being right or wrong is to think about whether doing that very particular action, in the very particular circumstances that it would be done in, was what a virtuous agent would do if he (of course it is always 'he' in Aristotle) were in exactly those circumstances. There are many passages in which Aristotle says the virtuous man sets the standard, the virtuous man is the one who always knows what the right thing to do is on any particular occasion, the virtuous man succeeds in 'hitting the target' of right action. (See, for example, *Nicomachean Ethics*, book 2, passim) So we had that much to go on. But our saying 'An action is right if (and only if) it is what a virtuous agent would do in the circumstances' was met, unsurprisingly, with scorn and contempt. It is, after all, no more than a truism with which everyone can agree, but it clearly gave no action guidance. For action guidance, I need to know what the virtuous agent *would* do.

At one rather desperate stage, some of us thought we could get beyond the truism to something more concrete by appealing to a moral exemplar. So what virtue ethics tells you to do, when you are trying to work out what you ought to do, is *not* to think in terms of moral rules and *not* to think in terms of the possible consequences. Instead you should imagine, concretely, what you think a particular moral exemplar, say Socrates, or Jesus Christ would do in your circumstances. Now for *some* actions, given that we know quite a lot about what Socrates and Christ actually did and also what they praised and condemned, that would actually provide rather good action guidance. But it did have at least one obvious flaw, namely that for some others, it was no use at all and simply absurd. Was the raped fourteen-year-old girl supposed to get any guidance by asking herself 'If Socrates or Jesus were in my position, would he have an abortion?'

So, for something like fifteen years, the fact that virtue ethics could not provide practical action guidance was the most common objection to it as a rival to the other theories. Proponents of the two prevailing theories took it – not unjustifiably – to show that virtue ethics was not a normative ethical theory at all, but just a bunch of interesting ideas that the proponents of the real theories could incorporate – suitably amended, of course.

But we virtue ethicists were not very impressed by the amendments the others had made to Aristotle's ideas as they forced them into the moulds of their modern theories. We were, moreover, not inclined to accept the view that he had produced only a bunch of interesting ideas in moral philosophy which stood in need of the theoretical systemization of modern theory.

So we went back to the truism and thought about it again. Suppose someone wants to do what is right; the truism tells her that the action that is right in the circumstances she is in is what a virtuous agent would do in those circumstances. What do we know about any virtuous agent that could take us beyond this? Well, as a further truism, we know that a virtuous agent will (when acting in character) do what is virtuous and not do what is vicious. So suppose we assume that we have a list of the virtues and vices. (This apparently question-begging assumption will be considered below.) The virtues are, for example, honesty, courage, compassion, justice, generosity, loyalty . . . and a whole string of others. The vices are, for example, dishonesty, cowardice, callousness, injustice, meanness, disloyalty etc. So what we have is a large vocabulary of virtue and vice terms, and because we know that a virtuous agent does what is virtuous, not what is vicious, every single one of them generates an action-guiding rule – do what is honest, do not do what is dishonest, do what is generous, do not do what is mean, do what is courageous, do not do what is cowardly, do what is just, do not do what is unjust. And so on – and with a whole lot of further 'do nots', because we have a particularly rich vocabulary of vice terms.

And so – just like that – we managed to find what the other theories had been demanding that we come up with, namely, a set of action-guiding rules. (They are called the 'v-rules' which stands for 'virtue and vice rules'.)

Before considering the starting assumption ('Here is the list of the virtues and vices') we should consider the nature of the v-rules and the reaction to them when they were first introduced into the contemporary literature. One of the objections to them was that they were vague and/or tendentious. To this, the virtue ethicists responded that, far from being vague or unspecific, the v-rules, by the very fact that they use common, everyday language, of which we have an extremely nuanced understanding, are a great deal *more* specific than most of the rules that the deontologists (and 'rule-utilitarians') come up with.

Consider, for example, rules covering rights and wrongs with regard to telling the truth. An obvious starter as a non v-rule is 'Do not lie.' But, it is usually assumed, this calls for some qualification; few people want the prohibition against lying to be absolute. (Should one not lie to the Nazis at one's door about the Jews one has hidden in one's attic?) As it stands, the rule is too general, not specific enough about when one must not lie and when one may. It needs to be supplemented by some exception clauses. But these tend to get rather complicated – and tendentious. Furthermore, it is only a starter – we want a lot more from each other with regard to telling the truth than that we simply refrain from lying to each other. After all, we know how seriously we can mislead each other simply by remaining silent. Or by, not lying, but stating the true – but in the context extremely misleading – thing. And that kind of behaviour we often indeed do describe with no difficulty using our everyday language: we describe that as dishonest. So it is ruled out by the v-rule which says 'Do not do what is dishonest.' But the rule 'Do not lie' will not rule out as much as the v-rule does – it does not specify anything about such cases.

'We admit,' the other philosophers might say, 'that it is not only refraining from lying that is important, truth-telling and not deliberately misleading are important too. So we'll add the rule "Tell the whole truth".' But they should not should they? Aside from guaranteeing that people will be very boring, politeness and consideration will be ruled out. Think how much one dreads those people who say, 'I hope you will not mind my saying this *but . . .*' And then they tell you the truth. One could have done without it. One did not want a lie; one just could have done with the silence, or a true remark about something quite different. Now note that when the rule is 'Do what is honest' rather than 'Tell the whole truth', we do not expect someone following the v-rule to ram every unpleasant truth about us down our throats regardless of whether we want them to or not. Would you refuse to count anybody as honest unless they were the kind of person who did that? No, we do not single those people out as being particularly *honest*. Armed with our nuanced everyday language, we can describe them, perhaps, as being candid, or brutally frank, but that's not the same as giving them the accolade of saying that they have the virtue of honesty. Brutal frankness is not on anyone's list of virtues. So that is just one brief illustration of the way in which we defend the v-rules as being subtly nuanced and as capturing an enormous amount of the things that we want to rule in, and the things that we want to rule out.

Modern Virtue Ethics: the Justification Problem

Another objection to the v-rules was the very fact that they were couched in the virtue and vice terms. This made them morally laden and thereby, it was claimed, laid virtue ethics open to the spectre of the moral sceptic ('Why should anyone else agree with your list? It's just a matter of personal opinion') or cultural relativism. So I now return, as promised, to scrutinize the assumption that we can just give a list of the virtues and vices. The natural objection of the proponents of the other theories was – and is, no doubt, the objection that immediately occurred to my readers – 'How can you simply assume that? How do you know which character traits are the virtues and which character traits are the vices? Surely any list is open to much dispute – different individuals, and different cultures will put different character traits on the list and who is to say that yours/ours is the right one?'

Now this is indeed a problem – but, I want to stress, it is not one that is *peculiar* to virtue ethics. It is a perfectly general problem in moral philosophy, one that pertains to any ethical theory, because what it amounts to is the problem of justifying one's moral beliefs – hence 'the justification problem' in my sub-heading.

How does one justify one's belief that, say, abortion is always wrong, or always permissible or wrong in such and such cases but permissible in such and such cases? Well, as we all know, every argument has to start from somewhere, and when you do *applied* ethics, and argue about the rights and wrongs of abortion, you need some premises which you do not, while discussing the issue of abortion, argue for. When they discussed the issue, the deontologists assumed that certain rules or principles were the *correct* ones and the consequentialists assumed that consequences for human happiness or misery are the only things that really count (not the intrinsic nature of the acts for instance.) Similarly, the virtue ethicists assume that certain character traits are the virtues, and others the vices – *everyone* has to have some such assumptions as premises before they can apply their theory and start talking about real life issues.

Such discussions provide *some* justification for – some grounds for accepting – whatever conclusion about abortion is reached. But, of course, each theory's assumptions are open to dispute. Different individuals, different cultures, will say that different rules are the correct ones, will not agree that consequences are the only thing that matters morally and will have different views about what happiness consists in. So in each of the three cases, the justification for whatever conclusion about abortion has been reached is incomplete.

Modern philosophers do not ignore this problem. We regard it as an interesting and particularly difficult one in 'meta-ethics', about the rational status of moral beliefs. (Meta-ethics stands to ethics as philosophy of law stands to law. In meta-ethics, philosophers theorize about, for example, the foundations of ethics, and what, if anything, makes moral judgements true (convention? moral facts? our feelings?) Against a background that has made science the prevailing paradigm for objectivity, how are we to justify our moral beliefs as anything other than, on the one hand, a matter of personal opinion, or, if that seems obviously silly, as something other than the mere product of our culture? Under the name of 'the moral realism/anti-realism debate', it is currently one of hottest topics in Anglo-American philosophy quite generally, involving metaphysics, epistemology, philosophy of language, philosophy of mind and several other branches. Given all these ramifications, it has become highly specialized and abstract and, one might suppose, thereby quite cut off from any influence from Aristotle. But even here, some modern philosophers have found him instructive.

Looking at the modern debate through the lens of his ethical works, we may be struck by the role played by science. As a paradigm of objectivity, it sets the standard which beliefs must meet to be knowledge, and, since scientific knowledge is theoretical, it thereby requires that all knowledge must be theoretical. Now, despite knowing very little science, Aristotle had a perfectly good concept of theoretical knowledge and indeed regarded the virtue or excellence of the rational part of the soul that enabled one to attain it (*sophia*) as the most excellent excellence. But he also has the concept of *phronesis* which he is at pains to distinguish from *sophia*. It, too, is a form of knowledge; it too attains truth – real objective truth. But it is knowledge of truth of a different sort – 'practical truth', or truth pertaining to action. So on the working hypothesis that what Aristotle says is true, much of the modern debate may be seen as locked in a false dilemma. Our choice does not lie between 'moral beliefs are like scientific beliefs' and 'moral beliefs are subjective opinions or merely the products of our culture' (or something similarly subjective). We can entertain the possibility that moral beliefs can be objectively true without being anything like scientific truths. And some philosophers, inspired by Aristotle, are currently working on (the extremely difficult) problem of how to articulate that possibility.

I want to conclude by mentioning a less abstract and difficult aspect of this modern debate because it concerns an area in which virtue ethics fares much better than deontology and utilitarianism. The debate is fuelled by the empirical assumption that there really is widespread cultural variation in moral beliefs. But in moral beliefs about what? one might ask. There is a notable amount of cultural disagreement about particular deontological rules, and on what counts as happiness, a central concept for utilitarians. But, in the case of the virtues, though there may be quite a wide variety amongst cultures about how the virtue terms should be applied, the extent to which there is common cultural agreement about which character traits *are* the virtues is, I think, remarkable and worth noting.

There is an educational programme called The Virtues Project™ which was founded by three Canadians in 1991, recognized by the UN as a model global programme for all (NB) cultures in 1993, and which is now used in over 85 different countries. The founders say they went through 'the world's sacred texts' looking for what were named as virtues in all of them. They found over three hundred, but cut the list down to fifty-two, one for each week of the year, for pedagogical purposes. Not only were these all fifty two virtues that all the cultures represented in the texts had in common, but the list has now been successfully translated into just about every single living language. Of course, occasionally there is a language that does not have a word for one of them, though the speakers of the language recognize the virtue as soon as it is described. Similarly, neither we, nor the ancient Greeks, really have a word for the virtue of being rightly oriented with respect to anger. Aristotle says (*Nicomachean Ethics*, book IV, ch. 5) that his word, (*praotes*) 'leans towards the deficiency', and so do our translations, 'mildness' or 'patience', but we all recognize it as a much needed virtue when we remember the phenomenon of road-rage and the sad spiritlessness of people who submit unresentfully to flagrant injustice or abuse. But, by and large, the whole fifty-two are translatable into all of these other languages *as virtue terms*. And if the existence of moral cultural relativism is not mere dogma, ('It must exist!') but up for empirical falsification, it seems to me it has thereby been decisively disproved as far as the virtues are concerned.

One gathers that the founders of the Virtues Project™ expected to find agreement amongst the sacred texts because they assumed that our common human nature would surely – all over the world, regardless of the circumstances of culture – have led people to the same conclusions about which character traits we need in order to live fully human lives together. One also gathers that they made this assumption because of their religious beliefs, thinking of all human beings as spiritual beings to whom only spiritual growth, the development of their potential for the virtues, could bring 'genuine happiness'.

In secular terms, and substituting 'psychic' for 'spiritual', this is pure Aristotle. He claims that human beings 'have the virtues neither by nor contrary to nature, but are fitted by nature or receive them' (*Nicomachean Ethics*, book II, ch. 1) He claims that acquiring and exercising them is the only way to achieve *eudaimonia*. (*Nicomachean Ethics*, book I, chs 7–13.) Long sidelined as peculiarly classical ideas, these views are now being taken on board, unconsciously in the case of the Virtues Project™, quite consciously by some educational psychologists and authors of 'self-improvement' books. And very consciously – and enthusiastically – by modern virtue ethics.

FURTHER READING

Annas, J. (1993). Massive (almost 500 pages) and scholarly as it is, this book is so well written that it is accessible to non-specialists. The only comprehensive treatment of ancient ethical theory, it begins with Aristotle and also discusses Epicurus, the Sceptics, the Cyrenians and the Stoics, shedding much light *en route* on modern moral philosophy.

For a full exposition and defence of Hursthouse's neo-Aristotelian version of virtue ethics, written in an style accessible to non specialists, see Hursthouse 1999 and 2003.

For a useful introduction for students with a comprehensive bibliography see Kraut 2005.

CHAPTER THIRTY-THREE

Classicizing Bodies in the Male Photographic Tradition

Bryan E. Burns

The notion of a classical tradition is so closely tied to artistic representation of the male body that it pervades even the most modern of art forms. Recent artists such as Robert Mapplethorpe have photographed neo-classical marbles as well as living nudes in similar compositions (Tsuzuki and Celant 2005), and Andy Warhol specifically posed male nudes in the familiar poses of ancient statues (Barthes 1978; Warhol and Goldhill 2005). These references to antiquity, however, are mediated by photography's own heritage. Greek and Roman culture is now less often evoked as apology, but rather in celebration of an eroticism that was long concealed or denied (Davis 1991; Waugh 1996).

Allusions to antiquity, common in the academic nudes of drawing and painting, were even more important to nineteenth-century photography, when the medium's own artistic status was in doubt. Photographic technology was a dubious craft, suspect because of its ability to create misleading images, but nonetheless valued for its ability to document exact likenesses. The notion that photographs were directly representations suggested a new relationship between the viewer, whether behind the camera's lens or holding the printed image, and the viewed. This new gaze caused particular anxiety in relation to the male nude, whose erotic potential was now available in a more direct manner to both female and male consumers (Callen 2003). Seeking a legitimate place in modern markets, distinct from the burgeoning business of pornography, the male nude found a familiar cloak of artistic respectability in antiquity. Correspondences with ancient Greek art, both generally and with famous sculptures in particular, became a standard theme in the dialogue surrounding the potentially troubling male form in photography. But the ancient world was also open to many views, and connections ranged from public society's broad sense of shared heritage to the intimate relationship some individuals constructed with the classical past in the development and justification of homosexual identities.

This chapter explores the associations between ancient art and two figural types of the male nude: the London strongman and the Mediterranean youth. Image makers set these bodies in aesthetic contexts that brought appropriate classical models into play with each physical type. The sculpted body was a widely admired legacy from classical art, and visual parallels with ancient statues tempered reactions to the brazen presentation of strongmen's bare bodies. An instructional and inspirational prose developed in physical culture publications, relating an appreciation for Greek and Roman marbles with an admiration of heavily muscled flesh. A separate, self-consciously elevated discourse surrounded the images of more lightly muscled bodies, which circulated among artists and sophisticates, who debated their merit in terms of classicizing aesthetics. In letters and publications associated with the photographs of exotic youths, invocations of poets such as Homer and Anacreon, or the artists Pheidias and Praxitiles, elucidated the symbolic values of ancient art by which the images extended Greek traditions.

Classicizing nudes operated within a system of mass-produced photographic images, through which Victorian society developed shared, lasting attitudes to categories of people both at home and abroad. Through the allegedly objective lens of science, ethnographers and sociologists labelled undressed bodies as distinguished by ethnic traits and characteristics alleged to indicate primitivism and deviancy (Willis and Williams 2002; Seitler 2004). Eroticized views of non-western societies put particular emphasis on same-sex practices, broadly grouped as pederastic (Bleys 1996). Mediterranean countries were certainly implicated as southern lands of sexual license, while photographs of ruined temples and early excavations reinforced a respect for the classical heritage of Greece and Italy (Lyons et al. 2005). Though most frequently mentioned as vice or taboo, the promise of sexual liberation, veiled by the cultural tradition of the Grand Tour, drew many wealthy artists and aesthetes (Aldrich 1993).

One cultural figure who had a particularly significant voice in the association of photographic nudes, exotic landscapes and ancient art was the poet, biographer, art historian and essayist John Addington Symonds (1840–1893). Today, Symonds is best remembered for his ground-breaking studies of attitudes towards homosexuality, *A Problem in Greek Ethics* and *A Problem in Modern Ethics*, which were published privately in 1883 and 1891. The circulation of these writings was limited, extremely so at first, but Symonds long considered broader release and many of his less polemical works betray aspects of his private passion. Both his public and his private writings intersect with an extended network of image makers and consumers, who connected modern male nudes with the classical tradition. An enthusiastic admirer of both the strongman and the *ephebe*, Symonds serves as an excellent guide to the rhetoric surrounding the photographic nude. And in his treatment of the male nude in the classical tradition and the contemporary arts, Symonds reveals himself as a scholar, with his own political and personal passions (Blanshard 2000).

Heroes of a New Art

The importance of sculpture as a subject of photography is found from the very beginning of the development of photographic technology in the mid-nineteenth century.

Early pioneers focused their lenses on still-life objects, appropriate for long exposure and changing techniques. Classicist William Henry Fox Talbot (1800–1877) experimented with artworks found in his collection of plaster casts, initiating the photographic tradition of classicizing bodies – of plaster, stone, and flesh.

In 1839 Talbot invented one of the earliest techniques of photography, contemporary with Jaque Louis Mandé Daguerre, whose daguerreotype became the ubiquitous form of photography. Among Talbot's early subjects was a bust 'of Patroclus,' a plaster cast that he kept in his home study. He shot this statue repeatedly through the 1840s, experimenting with light and angle, eventually producing dozens of images of a remarkable variety (Taylor 1986–8). In his text accompanying two views of the bust, Talbot praised the merits of the sculpted subject – its whiteness reflecting light, its deep carving creating shadows, and of course its immobility during long exposures. The plaster cast was made from a marble bust in the Townley collection, now in the British Museum, where it went without a specific identification, just an anonymous 'Head of a Homeric Hero.' For Talbot, however, it was always 'Patroclus,' the faithful companion and helper of Achilles, who spent the nineteenth century patiently assisting the photographer (Schaaf 2000: 148).

As photographic technology progressed, the new medium gained status as a mechanical craft, as opposed to an artistic endeavour, valued most consistently for its veracity (Green-Lewis 1996: 37–64). When it came to photographing the full heroic body, athleticism and nationalism provided the context for a documentary, even if appreciative gaze, of the male body, which facilitated comparisons of ancient and modern physiques (Leoussi 2001). The unclothed male body served as the evidence of a sporting figure's celebrity status, just as uniforms, formal attire, and costumes distinguished photographic portraits of government officials, social elites, and theatrical performers. Athletic nudes were easily distinguished from pornographic nudes not by an artistic status, but by the celebrity of the model.

Eugen Sandow (1867–1925), for example, was a Prussian body-builder who became famous as a strong-man in London stage shows, more for the form of his body than for actual feats of strength and lifting (Chapman 1994). His fame spread through a series of cabinet card portraits by Henry Van der Weyde (1838–1924), who similarly photographed famous statesmen, authors, and actors. Sandow's image stood apart, however, because of the full presentation of his famous, nearly nude body (figure 33.1). The cabinet card portraits present Sandow as a living statue, erected on an inscribed podium and fitted with a fig leaf. Van der Weyde was an innovator in the use of electric lighting for studio portraits, a technique that allowed him to emphasize the sculpted definition of Sandow's physique. The hard, hairless body was further enhanced with cosmetics and powder, a practice which Sandow developed for stage performance, to create an even, polished appearance (Chapman 1994, 77). When captured by the camera, and reproduced as a marketable commodity, the sculptural aesthetic verified the superhuman status of the accomplished body builder and formed a crucial, visual element of the promotional campaign organized by Sandow himself.

Before the his fame spread to the general public, however, the classicizing aesthetics of Sandow's images captured the attention of discriminating viewers. When

Figure 33.1 *Eugen Sandow*, by Henry Van der Weyde, 1889. National Portrait Gallery, London

sent one of Van der Weyde's photographs by his friend Edmond Gosse in 1889, John Addington Symonds responded with a letter that foreshadowed the showman's success ('Sandow could make a colossal fortune') and also revealed the homoerotic desire that fueled some part of his success. As the object of an artistic gaze, the athlete's body was open to an aesthetic and appreciative evaluation, which Symonds articulated in direct comparison with classical sculpture:

> I hardly venture to write what I feel about the beauty of this photograph. It not only awakens the imaginative sense. But beats every work of art except for a few bits of the Pheidian period. And no sculpture has the immediate appeal to human sympathy which this superb piece of breathing manhood makes.
>
> (Younger 1999: 2)

The letter expressed not only his admiration for Sandow's form, but also his frustrated desire to possess 'copies of all the nude studies which have been taken of this hero'. He also expressed his worry that a direct request to the photographer went unanswered because of the ambiguity of English law concerning such 'pictures wh[ich] cannot fail to be *verführerisch* [seductive]'. Despite an evidently personal interest in the images of Sandow, Symonds also recognized their instructive appeal to a wider audience – the very quality that would make such imagery a crucial part of the physical culture industry. Anticipating the institutionalization of strong-man celebrity, Symonds intended to display the Sandow images in the public gymnasium he sponsored.

Sandow's heroic posturing took more dramatic levels, as he explored various media to recreate his image as a classical figure (Chapman 1994; Budd 1998). He took to wearing leopard-skin shorts or singlet, and was accordingly painted as a gladiator by E. Aubrey Hunt, wearing a 'real' leopard-skin stretched from one shoulder to hip. Heroic status was captured most literally in a photographic series by Napoleon Sarony, in which his pose mimicked the Farnese Hercules, leaning against a club wrapped in the lion-skin. The parallel was reinforced by another weary Hercules statue that stood at the entrance to Sandow's Institute of Physical Culture, opened in 1897 in London. Sandow was even captured in three-dimensional form, with a plaster cast of his body intended to document the perfection of 'European man.' The classification of his strength and beauty as distinctly European echoes the era's concerns to distinguish the ancient Greeks from Semitic peoples. And the notion of Sandow as an embodiment of western aesthetics and achievements is found throughout the chief device of his personal industry.

Sandow Magazine was a physical culture periodical whose publication commenced in 1898, enabling the entrepreneurial athlete to convince a broader audience of his place among the canonical heroes of the western tradition. His life story, as told in the magazine, turned on an introduction to Greek and Roman statues that inspired him to strive beyond the weakness of his sickly youth (Budd 1998, 44). It is no wonder, then, that the images which made him famous not only display a physical form similar to heroic sculptures, but that the composition of his photographs was modelled on those very marbles as well. *Sandow Magazine* detailed the laborious effort to immortalize his sculpted physique in plaster as another physical test for the hero, and celebrated the display of the completed work in the British Museum. Yet the plaster Sandow was soon removed from exhibition. Photography, through its subtly malleable form and mass distribution proved to be the most enduring medium of Sandow's icon and identity. And those documents of visual affinities between modern athlete and ancient god, initiated a lasting discourse that canonized heroic sculpture as the attainable ideal.

The trope of body builder as marble statue became well entrenched, as models were often set on a pedestal or given Hercules' club. The direct emulation of classical models became a staple of physical culture's visual language, with marbles repeatedly set forth as an archetype of masculinity (Dutton 1995; Wyke 1997). The French body-building magazine *La Culture Physique* made regular use of ancient sculpture as the ideal model and photography as the contemporary evidence of the ideal attained through the precise weight-training system developed by Edmond Desbonnet (1867–1953). Desbonnet himself appeared frequently in the magazine's illustrations; a cartoon advertisement in the premiere issue of February 1904 featured a marble sculpture of Desbonnet, inspiring a gentleman's transformation from slender elegance to bulky dominance. This same scenario played out in a later cartoon, which featured an uninitiated sophisticate shamed by the Farnese Hercules (Garb 1998).

Alongside Myron's *Discobolus*, the weary Hercules is perhaps the most familiar image of ancient figures recurring in physique publications. The Hercules also appeared photographed in *La Culture Physique* and was among the plaster casts of antiquities in Desbonnet's 'measuring studio.' It became a standard for those who sought, or promoted, symmetry alongside bulk, eventually appearing as an illustration of the forty-four muscles developed by free-weight exercises (Iyer 1940: viii–ix). A leaner form, the *Discobolus*, has inspired dozens, if not hundreds, of posed men in the continuing tradition of physique photography. Trainers regularly advocated the position, from Saldo Monte (1914) to Charles Atlas (1924: 61), who pronounced his development 'altogether more graceful and muscular' than the 'original' in Rome. Nonetheless, it was a woman, Diana Watts (Mrs Roger Watts) who first published an exercise programme literally modelled on the *Discobolus* and other classical poses (1914). Though Watts was tastefully draped in a short Grecian tunic, or dressed in a modest exercise costume, the men wore nothing more than a posing strap or fig leaf.

Photographs of each season's latest model striking the iconic pose were important to the rhetoric of physical culture, for the renewed image demonstrated that ordinary men could also attain the classic ideal. Desbonnet himself photographed disciples in his fitness centre, posed after the Apollo Belvedere, the Dying Gladiator, and other iconic sculptures. Very literal comparisons were also published in the pages of *La Culture Physique*, which included side-by-side photographs of the Borghese Mars and a Desbonnet instructor, Rudolphe in January 1905 (Garb 1998: 70–1). Lighting, angle, and pose were carefully arranged to highlight the similarities in developed form, but the human body was depilated and further polished with oil and makeup. The photograph itself was also retouched to add a fig leaf, matching the statue, as well as additional shading to delineate the human Rudolphe's iliac crest. The manipulated image of the human model underscores the importance of the visual statement to prove the sculpted form was an achievable goal for all men. Yet Desbonnet's heroic nudes clearly provoked responses beyond the intended inspiration. Also in 1905, *La Culture Physique* included an article defending its images as 'artistic,' suggesting that they were in fact open to a wider range of potential readings (Garb 1998: 73). Perhaps William Henry Fox Talbot was correct: sculptures are easier to photograph than flesh.

Poetic Visions

Symonds applied the notion of living statues to a more literary context in his essay 'The Genius of Greek Art,' in volume II of his *Studies of the Greek Poets*, originally published in 1875. In the opening passage Symonds conjures the image of the genius as 'a young man newly come from the wrestling-ground, anointed, chapleted, and very calm' (1893: vol. II, 362). Though we might glimpse this figure through fragments of text and stone, Symonds emphasized the distance between ourselves and the Greeks we admire in the Aeginetan marbles or a banquet scene on a vase, when reading Homer or Plato or Theocritus. Yet the genius also resided in nature, among the waves of the Aegean or on the slopes of Mount Hymettus, and Symonds recommended the lands of the Mediterranean to serve as 'our guides in the endeavour to restore the past of Hellas' (364). His examples of the 'southern landscape,' however, were more Italian than Greek, reflecting Symonds' travels to Sicily and his enchantment with the Bay of Naples, and its young inhabitants:

> Beneath the olive-trees, among the flowers and ferns, move stately maidens and bare-chested youths. Their eyes are starry-softened or flash fire, and their lips are parted to drink in the breath of life . . . These late descendants of Greek colonists are still beautiful – like moving statues in the sunlight and the shadow of the boughs . . . And where, if not here, shall we meet with Hylas and Hyacinth, with Ganymede and Hymenaeus, in the flesh?

> (366)

Symonds' vision was essentially renewed in photographic form (figure 33.2) by one of the many photographs of Neapolitan youths by Wilhelm von Gloeden (1856–1931). After settling himself in the town of Taormina on the rocky coast of Sicily, this German baron produced hundreds of classicizing images in the 1890s and early 1900s of young males. Although von Gloeden's photographs were initially sold as studies of the human form to artists and anatomists, they were of a stylistically different character than the drawings and earlier studio photographs known as *academies*. Whereas the traditional image for artists posed its single model as a statue or statuesquely, von Gloeden's evoked antiquity through the setting, costume, or props. And his models were seldom the mature men of professional modelling, but younger boys and teens, who were just as likely be posed in a subtly erotic pair or group as alone.

A clear distinction is present between the body type favored by von Gloeden and those of the physical culture industry, a difference characterized by American photographer Fred Holland Day (1864–1933) in the mythological yet practical terms that 'a Hercules can never be "made to do" for a Vulcan or a Ganymede' (Holland Day et al. 1996: 45). The boyish figure, essentially doubled front and back in figure 33.2, is nonetheless statuesque in build and especially pose. The model is seen in the sculptures associated with Praxiteles, like the Hermes from Olympia, with its softer musculature and fluid curve carrying through the torso to uneven hips. Accentuating the Hellenic, and also erotic, connotations of von Gloeden's image is the natural setting, recognized by the experienced viewer as the forested hills of the Mediterranean.

Von Gloeden's own description of his work, his inspiration and his goal, is strikingly similar to Symonds' description of figures in the landscape:

> Readings from Homer and Theocritus' Sicilian poetry stimulated my fantasy. Rocks and the sea, hills and forests recalled Arcadian shepherds and Polyphemus. Greek shapes excited me, just like the bronze colour of the descendants of the ancient Hellenes, and I tried to resurrect the ancient Greek life in these images.

> (quoted by Aldrich 1993: 150)

Figure 33.2   Untitled, by Wilhelm von Gloeden, no date. Erich Lessing/Art Resource, NY

The similarity may stem from the general spirit of the era, among those interested in classical revivals of one form or another and the particular connotations developed around 'Greek love' (Dowling 1994). It is tempting, however, to imagine von Gloeden not simply inspired by ancient poetry and the eternal landscape, but by Symonds' own vision as well. If von Gloeden had read *Studies of the Greek Poets* or other essays by Symonds, it would nicely balance the fact that the writer was among those who acquired von Gloeden's photographs.

We can't know the full range of works collected by Symonds, but the possibilities are well represented by a photo album belonging to the painter Paul Guerrier in the later twentieth century. Republished as *Et in Arcadia Ego*, the collection is presented as a 'chance find' preserved by a line of anonymous guardians who 'safeguarded the album' over the century that 'it has often been in danger' (Natter and Weiermair 2000: 5). Compiled at the turn of the century, this arrangement of 82 photographs by von Gloeden and contemporary photographers Guglielmo Plüschow, who was also his cousin, and Vincezo Galdi, is intact in its original order. The collection begins with a view of the empty Theatre at Epidaurus, literally setting the stage in Greece, with a series of broad architectural scenes. The sequence then follows the classical tradition to Italian settings, beginning with wide shots of villa courts on Capri that increasingly include male figures – both statues and living youths. As the photographs shift to the historical gardens of Rome and the interiors of ancient houses of Pompeii, the focus tightens on boys clad in toga and sandals posing alongside fountains and ruined walls. At mid-point, however, the monuments are left behind and the male body, with or without the toga, is set against natural landscapes, a plain plaster wall, or a simply draped backdrop.

These are the type of images that Symonds also collected, by the hundreds. Most were acquired from Plüschow, whom Symonds recommended friends to patronize with recommendations of particularly good models by name (Schueller and Peters 1969: vol. III, 645, 677). He also shared pictures with a small range of friends, alongside learned discussion of literature, arts, and society. In an 1890 letter to Edmond Gosse, Symonds wrote frankly about the appeal of Plüschow's work, despite the monotony, explaining that the photos were of interest in relation to his writing on the nude in art (Younger 1999: 4).

Symonds had already written an essay 'The Model' (1887), about the nature of the distance between photography and art, as represented by drawing and painting, with specific reference to the male nude. He made an extended comparison between the painted body of J. Hippolyte Flandrin's *A Young Man Sitting Naked beside the Sea: A Study* and a photograph of a model in the same pose – a photograph 'issued in Vienna for the use of art-students' (1887: 858). A young man is at the centre of each image, his body drawn in upon itself with arms wrapped around his legs and head resting upon his knees. Symonds admitted the superior ability of the photograph to capture 'nature . . . reality . . . truth,' but he claimed that it did so at the expense of something he called the 'intervention of the artist's mind . . . [the] feeling subjectivity which makes Flandrin's study of the young man alone upon the rock a painted poem' (1887: 859–60).

The comparison makes clear Symonds' disappointment with the particular photograph of a young man trapped in the photographer's studio. By comparison, his own reading of 'the painted poem' makes much of the surrounding ocean that contributes to a sense of 'resignation, the mystery of fate, the calm of acquiescence.' A greater appreciation of the painting's meaning to Symonds, however, is revealed by an 1876 letter to Horatio Forbes Brown, in which he described the painting as an expression of the modern spirit, 'bowed in silence and in sorrow' (Schueller and Peters 1969: vol. II, 421). In considering the photographic version, Symonds expressed a desire to see the bowed figure taken out of the studio, and set against the eternal Mediterranean. He proposed, 'we might transfer the model to a real rock, with the same scene of sea and coast painted behind him for a background; or better, we might place him in position on some spur of Capri's promontories with the Sorrentine headland for background' (1887: 860).

In his reverie, Symonds anticipated a photograph by von Gloeden of just such a model posed on a rocky outcrop, entitled *Caino* (figure 33.3). A series of distant mountain ridges replaces Flandrin's rocky coast, but the model is strikingly similar

Figure 33.3 *Caino*, by Wilhelm von Gloeden, 1905. Erich Lessing/Art Resource, NY

in appearance and pose, from the soft curls of his hair to the particular arrangement of one hand grasping the other wrist. Symonds was certainly not the first writer to consider the interplay between photographic representations of the body and those of other artistic media; nor would von Gloeden be the last to pose a model after Flandrin's study (Berman 1994: 358; Tsuzuki and Celant 2005: 16). But Symonds' writing and von Gloeden's photograph demonstrate the persuasive power of a seductive image, in that each one of them engaged the new model more fully than Flandrin's original.

Symonds went further, by encouraging movement and interaction with the photographed model, once set upon a Sorrentine rock: 'we should dwell upon the vigour of adolescent manhood, we should be curious perhaps to see the youth spring up, we should wonder how his lifted eyes might gaze on us, and what his silent lips might utter' (1887: 860). His imagined photograph captures the real likeness of a young body, perhaps something akin to the 'immediate appeal . . . of breathing manhood' he saw in the image of Eugen Sandow (Younger 1999: 2). But the new version of Flandrin's body is more akin to the ancient spirit once described by Symonds as 'erect, prayerful, praiseful, gazing out upon the world' (Schueller and Peters 1969: vol. II, 421). Set among the other sensual youths of the Italian landscape, the young man is now urged to take life, and to interact with the viewer, as a more classical figure.

Similarly, von Gloeden was not content to merely replicate Flandrin's image, though a faithful reproduction was clearly one goal. With that accomplished, the photographer seems to have followed Symonds' directive and on two later occasions produced images of another young man posed on a rock, lifting his head up from the knees, up from resignation and the sorrow of modernity. Yet for all the pleasure Symonds might have taken in these photographs, and despite the apparent willingness of von Gloeden to realize a true photographic vision of the painting, a tension remains between the writer and the photographer.

Symonds imagined his hypothetical photograph to be more provocative, but less artistic: 'the emotion stirred in us might be more pungent, and our interest more vivid; yet something, that indeed which makes the poem, would have disappeared' (1887: 860). The image was no longer affected by the artist's mood, Symonds explained; the camera's verisimilitude sharpened natural details, but lowered a symbolic threshold. Von Gloeden, it would seem, disagreed, and asserted his authorship on the original *Caino* image, with an inscription appropriate to classical art: W. von Gloeden Taormina fecit / W. von Gloeden made [this] in Taormina.

Both the creators and consumers of male nude photographs of this early era engaged with classical models. They envisioned idealized heroes and poetic embodiments through a medium that could elide differences between surviving sculptures of antiquity and statuesque figures of the modern day. Thus the moment captured by photographic technology could be perceived both as a remote past and a recurring present, enabling the illusion of looking into antiquity and the fantasy of statues come to life.

The two distinct types of bodies – strongmen and ephebes – were presented within specific visual formats that engaged artistic traditions. Aesthetic strategies that emphasized the similarity of modern body builders to sculpted heroes were meant to prove the achievement of physical goals, and were marketed in campaigns to convince ordinary people of the actual and potential realness of heroic bodies. To this end, the perceived ability of photography to document true likenesses was manipulated, and sculptures were brought to life in the viewer's contemporary world. Photographs of ephebic youths, however, were composed in styles meant to evoke a sense of distance, both temporal and geographic. The photographs of these models created a continuum with those of other eras and other artistic media, reinforcing the lived reality of the body posed before artists and viewers.

The homoeroticism pulsing within these treatments of a male artistic object was put into words by such viewers as John Addington Symonds. He responded to the male form as an artistic creation, a visual poem, a breathing sculpture. Symonds' reception of photographic images, whether it be mature body builder or youthful figure, demonstrates the crucial role of classical models both to his aesthetic readings of photography and to his articulation of male desire. Thus the classical dimension of Eugen Sandow's portraits and Wilhelm von Gloeden's figural studies could extend beyond their commercial intention or practical purpose in their formation of the male photographic tradition.

FURTHER READING

For a general overview of male photography, Waugh 1996 provides a coherent history of artistic developments and cultural contexts. Green-Lewis 1996 chronicles the early technologies of photography and surveys their reception in Victorian society. Individual essays convey the potentially erotic role of the classical figure in photography (Budd 1998), physical culture (Wyke 1997), and nationalist agendas (Leoussi 2001). Aldrich 1993: 136–61 puts Wilhelm von Gloeden, Fed Holland Day, and others in a broader context of writers and artists who visited Italy in their exploration of classical past and liberated present. For readers interested in the aesthetic and personal perspective of John Addington Symonds, the essays collected in Pemble 2000 provide a provocative overview of his life and writings.

CHAPTER THIRTY-FOUR

Homer in British World War One Poetry

Elizabeth Vandiver

Until recently, the influence of Homer on the British poets of World War One received scant attention. With the growth of reception studies in recent years, scholars have begun to recognize that the World War One poets' reception of Homer is an important topic for literary, social and cultural history (see Hardwick 2000a: 48–50; Hardwick 2003a: 93–96; Vandiver 1999; Vandiver 2007). Despite the obvious differences between Homeric warfare and the actual experiences of soldiers in World War One, Homeric epic provided a set of images, characters and tropes, in effect a whole shared vocabulary, for soldier-poets struggling to articulate and to understand their own war. On both the eastern and the western fronts, and from the beginning of the war to its end and after, poets refigured Homeric epic both to glorify and to protest the war, both to heroize and to humanize its victims. (For the terms 'refiguration' and 'appropriation', see Hardwick 2003a: 9–10.)

Introduction

In the early twentieth century, the British public-school curriculum laid a heavy emphasis upon classics, and many grammar schools, too, had robust classics programmes (Stray 1998: passim). But Homer was also a crucial source for middle-class and working-class poets, such as Wilfred Owen or Isaac Rosenberg; the Homeric paradigm of war was the image most readily available to poets of all classes who set out to write about war (see further, Vandiver 2007).

Homer's presence in poems written by men from across the educational spectrum is one indication of how deeply classics was interwoven into British popular culture; another such indication is that poets used Homeric tropes, images and settings to express widely differing views of the war. Lorna Hardwick has written that 'As the war became more and more horrifying, Homeric images increasingly became emblems of the poetics of dilemma and compassion' (2000: 50). This is certainly true for some poets, but by no means for all; the position of Homer in poetry about the war was more complex than this formulation implies. While writers of 'protest poetry', such as Wilfred Owen, are most familiar to modern readers, no less significant for our understanding of Homeric reception during World War One (though perhaps less congenial to modern tastes) are poets who used the Homeric paradigm of battle to exalt and affirm their own experiences of war, and indeed war itself. As Bergonzi has pointed out, critics have shown a marked tendency to privilege the poetry of protest over other poetic responses to the war: 'popular mythology assumes that the good war poets are poets of protest, and, in a somewhat circular argument, that their protest remains valuable because it is good poetry' (Bergonzi 1996: 15). This circular reading has pushed to one side those poets whose works glorified the war; with the obvious exception of Rupert Brooke, few such poets are now remembered, and it is not unusual for readers to 'excuse' Brooke's celebration of the war by noting that he died before he had a chance to experience war's full horrors. The implication is that, had Brooke only lived to fight at Gallipoli instead of dying on his journey there, he too would have turned from passionate support of the war to no less passionate protest.

Yet apart from Sassoon and Owen, even many 'canonical' poets such as Aldington, Blunden, or Rosenberg did not write obvious 'protest' poetry, however clearly they noted the war's horrors (Bergonzi 1996: 15). If we consider only the 'protest poets', we distort our understanding of poetic reaction to the war by simplifying that reaction into a single-minded and unilateral poetic voice. The actual range of reactions to the war, in poetry as in British culture in general, was complex and multi-sided, and the multivalent refiguration of Homer in war poetry is one indication of this complexity.

The appropriation of Homer for both praise and protest of the war continues until the Armistice and after; this casts doubt upon the long-held critical idea that the period up to July 1916 was one of relative naiveté and optimism and that a new disillusionment and cynicism appeared after the Battle of the Somme, and that war poetry in general moved from jingoistic patriotism through disillusionment to compassion (see e.g. Silkin 1972: 29–36). This idea has been increasingly questioned in recent years; as Bergonzi comments, 'The movement from illusion to disillusion is certainly there, in a number of well-known poets, but one must beware of seeing it as representative of all literary responses to the war' (1996: 215–16; cf. Hibberd 1986b: 108–9; Hibberd and Onions 1986: 3–7, 14–16, 27–8; and Watson 2004: passim).

Contemporary poetry's complex reaction to the war reflects the complexity of soldiers' views of the war in general – a complexity that historians have recently begun to treat with the seriousness it deserves. What Hynes and Todman have called the 'myth' of the war has been extremely powerful for many decades:

A generation of eager young Britons joined up to fight a war they didn't understand. They marched off to France and Flanders, leaving behind an idyllic Edwardian age that would never be recaptured. Once there, they fell under the command of a group of incompetent commanders . . . Time and again they were thrown forward in ill-conceived assaults that achieved nothing. . . . The pitiful survivors who returned to Britain were silenced by the trauma of their experiences – only the words of a tiny band of warrior poets could communicate the truth of what they had been through.

(Todman 2005: xi–xii; cf. Hynes 1990: x)

This myth has been tenacious, but as Holmes points out, it depends largely on hindsight and had its genesis in the disillusionment that developed in the 1920s, when it became clear that the veterans' (and others') high hopes for the peace would not be realized (2005: xxiv; cf. Hynes, ch. 21, 'The War Becomes Myth', 1990: 423–63). With hindsight, we can see that the victory of 1918 did not result in a Europe safe from future wars, and poetic expressions of outrage at the war's futility are therefore compelling in part because of our knowledge of what happened next, in the 1920s, 1930s, and 1940s. During the war itself, however, while some soldiers were undoubtedly certain that they were being butchered in a futile exercise of blind stupidity, this was by no means the only current interpretation of experience among combatants (and indeed, a revisionist school of modern historiography now questions the whole 'lions led by donkeys' interpretation of British military strategy; Holmes 2005: xx–xxiv; cf. Bond 2002). Powerful though protest such as Wilfred Owen's may be, we must remember that this was not the only poetic voice available at the time; there was a multiplicity of possible poetic stances, and this is evident in poems that refigure Homer no less than in other types of poetry. Some poets, almost from the war's earliest days, found the traditional paradigms of war – including the Homeric – insufficient or misleading. Others, however, never expressed such disillusionment, but continued until the end of the war to cite those traditional paradigms unironically.

The persistence of the Homeric conception of war as the primary template onto which soldier-poets tried to map their own experiences is all the more noteworthy, since this template was badly inaccurate in many ways; the war that awaited these young Homerists was very unlike the *Iliad*. Perhaps most importantly, Homer offered no preparation at all for modern warfare's realities of dismemberment, disfigurement, and lingering death; in the *Iliad* wounds come in two types, the immediately (or almost immediately) fatal and the superficial (Shay 1994: 127–9). The *Iliad* simply does not mention wounds that result in a slow, agonizing *process* of dying. Modern mechanized combat, therefore, must have been a hideous shock for soldiers who looked to Homer to understand war.

No less crucially, Homeric warfare does not allow for random and anonymous death. Homeric warriors almost always fight and kill one another *face to face*, and often know one another's names and lineage. Nor did Homer provide a precedent for the constant presence of the unburied dead, in No Man's Land and even in the trenches themselves, which formed so significant a part of the horrific experience of World War One, or for the almost total destruction of the landscape around the trenches. Precisely those aspects of trench warfare which have become canonical in our image of World War One – the anonymity of random death, the hideous mutilations, the ever-present corpses, the foul destruction of landscape – were the elements of warfare for which Homer offered no analog; and yet Homeric imagery, the Homeric view of battle, and Homeric concepts of honor and glory continued to provide a crucial source for discourse about war.

The Eastern Front: Gallipoli and Troy

The war poets' Homeric appropriations range from open and overt, including direct quotation of Homeric tags, to 'submerged' references that are more a matter of a poem's overall *mise-en-scène* or assumed background than of specific quotations. Both types of Homeric references, direct and submerged, appear throughout the war and on both fronts; however, the eastern front almost demanded open and direct reference to Homer. The Gallipoli peninsula, site of the April 1915–January 1916 campaign that inflicted extremely high casualties on troops from Britain, Australia, and New Zealand, is just across the Hellespont from the traditional site of Homer's Troy. Many poets draw specifically on this coincidence of location to connect the experiences of the soldiers of 1915 to those of Homer's warriors.

Poets mused on the parallels between Troy and the Dardanelles campaign even before arriving at Gallipoli. Rupert Brooke, for instance, most famous for his sonnet sequence '1914', died of blood-poisoning on the journey to Gallipoli (Marsh 1918: 180–2). A notebook found in his possession after his death contained fragments showing that Homer was very present in his mind: 'They say Achilles in the darkness stirred'; 'Priam and his fifty sons / Wake all amazed' (Marsh 1918: 177). Nowell Oxland, a far less well-known poet than Brooke who sailed for Gallipoli on 30 June 1915 and was killed in action on 9 August 1915, also turned to Homer as a means for articulating his own emotions during the voyage in his poem 'Outward Bound'. This poem was printed anonymously in the *Times* on 27 August 1915; later anthologies have used the title 'Outward Bound' as printed in the *Times*, but in Oxland's posthumously printed *Poems and Stories* the poem is called 'Farewell', and its dominant mood is clearly one of resigned leave-taking (Oxland 1920: 27–9).

'Outward Bound' begins with a detailed description of the landscape of the poet's native Cumberland, but then turns to references to the gods and the Greek expedition to Troy. The poem ends with the hope that, though the modern soldiers' bodies will not come home again, their spirits somehow may:

> Though the high gods smite and slay us,
> > Though we come not whence we go,
> As the host of Menelaus
> > Came there many years ago;
> Yet the self-same wind shall bear us
> > From the same departing place
> Out across the Gulf of Saros
> > And the peaks of Samothrace; . . .
> One with Cumberland for ever
> > We shall not go forth again.
> > > (Oxland 1920: 29)

Soldiers actually stationed at Gallipoli as well as those making the journey there found the Homeric connection compelling; over and over, poets mention Troy in the same breath as Gallipoli as they try to set their own experience in a recognizable framework. The best-known and most impressive example of all such poems is Patrick Shaw-Stewart's untitled 'I Saw a Man This Morning' (see further, Vandiver 2007).

Patrick Shaw-Stewart was born in 1888 and educated at Eton and Balliol College, Oxford. After enlisting, he was posted to Gallipoli and sailed in the same ship as Rupert Brooke, whom he knew. When Brooke died on April 23, 1915, Shaw-Stewart took part in the burial service on the Greek island of Skyros and commanded the firing party at the graveside. Shaw-Stewart served at Gallipoli from April 1915 until the January 1916 evacuation; he was killed in action in France on 30 December 1917 (Knox 1920: passim; Marsh 1918: 180–4).

'I Saw a Man This Morning', Shaw-Stewart's only known poem, was written on a blank page in his copy of Housman's *A Shropshire Lad* and found after his death; since it is in Shaw-Stewart's handwriting, Knox comments that 'It seems clear . . . that he wrote it himself, although he does not allude to it anywhere' (1920: 159). The Troy–Gallipoli connection is absolutely crucial:

1 I saw a man this morning
   Who did not wish to die:
I ask, and cannot answer,
   If otherwise wish I.

5 Fair broke the day this morning
   Against the Dardanelles;
The breeze blew soft, the morn's cheeks
   Were cold as cold sea-shells.

But other shells are waiting
10   Across the Aegean Sea,
Shrapnel and high explosive,
   Shells and hells for me.

O hell of ships and cities,
   Hell of men like me,
15 Fatal second Helen,
   Why must I follow thee?

Achilles came to Troyland
   And I to Chersonese:
He turned from wrath to battle,
20   And I from three days' peace.

Was it so hard, Achilles,
   So very hard to die?
Thou knowest, and I know not –
   So much the happier I.

25 I will go back this morning
   From Imbros over the sea;
Stand in the trench, Achilles,
   Flame-capped, and shout for me.
        (Knox 1920: 159–60)

This poem probably dates to 14 or 15 July 1915, when Shaw-Stewart was recalled after three days from a leave which he had expected to last a full week. In a letter of 17 July 1915, Shaw-Stewart describes this leave and its unexpected end, 'when I was suddenly recalled, as we were going up to the trenches' (Knox 1920: 143; for a full discussion of this letter and the poem's probable date, see Vandiver 2007). Shaw-Stewart's regiment had not been in the trenches for some weeks beforehand; through its engagement with the *Iliad*, the poem reflects the shock of this abrupt return to battle.

Shaw-Stewart compares his own absence from, and motivations for returning to, battle with Achilles' withdrawal and return, and by so doing exposes the distance and difference of his entire experience of war from the Homeric archetype. Achilles has clear motivations for fighting while Shaw-Stewart does not; Achilles withdraws from battle by his own choice, while Shaw-Stewart is a powerless recipient of orders.

In the beginning of the *Iliad*, Achilles questions his reason for fighting and says that, unlike Agamemnon, he himself has no quarrel with the Trojans (*Iliad* 1 ll. 157–160). Achilles was willing to fight so long as he received his due measure of honor and glory; but once these rewards are denied Achilles, he chooses to withdraw from battle, to return only when another even more compelling motivation, revenge for his comrade Patroklos, replaces the discarded motivation of glory. But for Shaw-Stewart, both the withdrawal from and the return to battle lack any such clear motivations; as the anguished and unanswered question, 'Fatal second Helen, why must I follow thee?' shows, Shaw-Stewart has no quarrel with the Turks and yet can find no sufficient substitute motive, either in the hope of glory *or* in the desire for personal vengeance, to justify his presence in battle. Shaw-Stewart references Achilles' wrath almost wistfully, as though wishing that he could, on his own part, feel so strong or so compelling an emotion. But unlike Achilles, Shaw-Stewart has not chosen to withdraw from battle; he was allowed to go on leave, but the choice was not his and now he must go back to battle, again through no personal choice but simply because he must. The poem's crucial question, 'Why must I follow thee', remains not only unanswered but unanswerable, as Shaw-Stewart offers no reason, not even the obvious answer 'duty'.

The final stanza reflects Shaw-Stewart's unrealizable longing to regain the Homeric warrior's power and highlights the uncloseable distance between Ilion and Gallipoli. Ogilvie comments that 'to a reader who has wept over the incident after the death of Patroklos when Achilles appears at the Greek trench and confounds the Trojans with three shouts (*Iliad* 18), Shaw-Stewart's lines enshrine a world of tragedy' (1964: 154), but other critics have not always fully understood or appreciated the exact point of this stanza's reference to Achilles. For instance, Hibberd and Onions gloss the last line's 'flame-capped' by saying 'Achilles's helmet was made by Hephaestus, god of fire' (1986: 193, n.18). While this is true, it misses Shaw-Stewart's precise reference to the scene when Athena crowns the unarmed Achilles with flame, *before* he receives the armor made by Hephaistos:

> Athene . . . about his head circled
> a golden cloud, and kindled from it a flame far-shining. . . .

> so from the head of Achilleus the blaze shot into the bright air.
> He went from the wall and stood by the ditch . . .
> There he stood, and shouted, and from her place Pallas Athene
> gave cry, and drove an endless terror upon the Trojans. . . .
> Three times across the ditch brilliant Achilleus gave his great cry,
> and three times the Trojans and their renowned companions were routed.
>   (*Iliad* 18 ll. 203–30, tr. Lattimore 1951)

The super-human, flame-capped Achilles, whose shout panics the Trojans, is asked to shout 'for' the all-too-human soldier in the 1915 trenches, presumably as the soldier goes 'over the top' towards his own death. For Shaw-Stewart, Achilles stands *in* the trench, not above it; the reference point here is very likely not only the *Iliad* itself, but also Tennyson's 'Achilles Over the Trench', a translation of *Iliad* 18 l. 202ff. Unlike Homer's and Tennyson's Achilles, who stands in full public view over the trench defending his comrades and routing the enemy, Shaw-Stewart's Achilles provides only private encouragement to one soldier entering battle, but himself stays behind in the trench. And in reality, such private encouragement is no help at all; Shaw-Stewart's Achilles is disengaged from the modern combat and ultimately powerless, a memory rather than a present help, and functions as a symbol of all that the soldier is leaving and losing. Along with Achilles in the trench, Shaw-Stewart leaves behind the *Iliad*'s assumption that war could confer honor, glory, or even the satisfaction of personal vengeance.

The Western Front: Julian Grenfell's 'Into Battle'

Poets writing on the western front also appropriated Homer; however, they often did so less overtly than eastern-front poets and scholars have missed the Homeric background of some major poems. For instance, Julian Grenfell's famous 'Into Battle' normally has been read without any recognition of its debt to Homer. This omission deprives the poem of its full impact, since the paradigm of war on which Grenfell draws is deeply and essentially Homeric.

Like his friend Patrick Shaw-Stewart, Julian Grenfell was born in 1888 and educated at Eton and at Balliol. After university, he enlisted in the army as a career officer. He wrote 'Into Battle' on 29 April 1915; it was published in the *Times* on 27 May, the day after Grenfell's death from a head wound suffered on 13 May (Grenfell 1916: 541; Mosley 1976: 257).

From its opening line 'The naked earth is warm with spring' (Hibberd and Onions 1986: 100) to the end of its sixth stanza, 'Into Battle' focuses on Nature as a beneficent force that comforts, strengthens, and encourages the warrior. The poem contains no mention of an enemy; supported by Nature, the warrior fights, but against whom is never specified. Also absent is any cause for which the warrior fights; for Grenfell, the warrior's prowess is its own justification. Grenfell was well acquainted with Homer and the Homeric presentation of battle; for Eton's annual Speech day on 4 June 1906, he chose to recite in Greek the *Iliad*'s description of Hektor's death (22 ll. 330–63), a scene which highlights Achilles' battle-prowess and the implacability of his desire for vengeance (Mosley 1976: 94; P. Hatfield, Eton College archivist, private communication, 8 September 2003). But in Grenfell's own poem, the goals of honour, glory, and personal vengeance are absent and pure 'joy of battle' exists by itself, as its own cause. Such battle-joy needs no political or moral justification: it simply *is*.

'Into Battle's' refiguration of Homer begins in the seventh stanza and continues through the end of the poem:

> In dreary, doubtful, waiting hours,
>   Before the brazen frenzy starts,
> The horses show him nobler powers;
>   O patient eyes, courageous hearts!
>
> And when the burning moment breaks,
>   And all things else are out of mind,
> And only joy of battle takes
>   Him by the throat, and makes him blind,
>
> Through joy and blindness he shall know,
>   Not caring much to know, that still
> Nor lead nor steel shall reach him, so
>   That it be not the Destined Will.
>
> The thundering line of battle stands,
>   And in the air death moans and sings;
> But Day shall clasp him with strong hands,
>   And Night shall fold him in soft wings.
>   (Hibberd and Onions 1986: 100–1)

The image of men and horses waiting for battle to begin, with the horses' calm providing a pattern for the men to follow, clearly recalls the end of *Iliad* 8:

> A thousand fires were burning there in the plain, and beside each
> one sat fifty men in the flare of the blazing firelight.
> And standing each beside his chariot, champing white barley
> and oats, the horses waited for the dawn to mount to her high place.
>   (*Iliad* 8 ll. 562–5, tr. Lattimore 1951)

It is at this point that we can begin to see how overlooking the subtle Homeric references hampers critics' readings of this poem. For instance, Silkin (1972) reads the horses as part of Grenfell's overall use of nature as an 'asserted corroboration of his [Grenfell's] activity', and so finds these lines unsuccessful: 'The last line shows again the inadequacy of the poetic equipment. "Patient" and "courageous" are not various, precise, or unanthropomorphic enough to establish the qualities of the animals themselves, so that he loses the strength of an independent corroborating agent' (74). But this objection disappears when we recognize the lines' Iliadic resonance. At the end of *Iliad* 8, Homer's horses, like Grenfell's, await the dawn patiently; for Homer as for Grenfell, the horses' quiet and calm acceptance of their lot provides a contrast to the implicit fears, anxieties, and hopes of the men who experience the wait for battle as 'dreary and doubtful'.

The horses' patient waiting signals the Homeric setting of these final stanzas, but the horses are by no means the only Homeric appropriation here. In this same stanza, the word 'brazen', too, recalls Homer. *Chalkeos* (bronze) and its compounds and cognates are very frequent terms in the *Iliad* in both literal and metaphoric uses (these terms describe, among other things, warriors' hearts, the sky, sleep, the war god Ares). 'Brazen frenzy' is an unsatisfactory metaphor for shells and machine-gun fire on the western front in 1915, but is completely appropriate as a description of Homeric heroes' clashing weapons.

The eighth stanza describes what is clearly an Homeric *aristeia* (a scene which foregrounds an individual warrior's prowess) as 'joy of battle takes / him by the throat and makes him blind'. This description resembles the word 'brazen' in being utterly inappropriate to the kind of battle that took place on the western front; although there certainly was hand-to-hand fighting with bayonets, most 'battles' in 1914–15 consisted of men walking into bursting shells and machine-gun fire, and it is difficult to see how 'joy of battle', the berserker's killing rage and delight in that rage, could really apply to such an experience of depersonalized carnage. Again, by using Homeric concepts and even Homeric diction, Grenfell assimilates his own experience of war to the very different Homeric model.

The final two stanzas maintain the poem's Homeric setting by evoking two specific scenes from the *Iliad* with the reference to the 'Destined Will' and the personifications of Day and Night. In the ninth stanza, 'the Destined Will' recalls the *Dios boulê*, the Will of Zeus, as it is cited in the opening lines of the *Iliad* (1.5). And in the last two lines Day and Night, capitalized and personified, recall Sleep and Death, who lift the body of Zeus' son Sarpedon from the battlefield and carry it back to his native country in *Iliad* 16 l. 666 ff.; Rupert Brooke's fragment 'Death and Sleep / Bear many a young Sarpedon home' is a similar though more explicit evocation of this Iliadic original (Marsh 1918: 177).

In this final stanza, more than anywhere else in the poem, a failure to recognize the Homeric nature of Grenfell's vision distorts critics' reading. So, for instance, Bergonzi 1996 comments that 'The concluding stanza is undoubtedly vulnerable, with its personified abstractions portentously intruding' (44). But in fact these 'personified abstractions' are not 'portentously intruding' at all – unless, that is, we consider the Homeric *mise-en-scène* of the entire poem to be a portentous intrusion. Grenfell's 'fighting man', like Homer's Sarpedon, will be lifted from the battlefield and carried in safety by benevolent personifications of natural forces. Such personifications may indeed be inappropriate as descriptions of battle in 1915, but in the conception of Grenfell's poem, they are neither intrusions nor inept.

The Western Front: Wilfred Owen and Isaac Rosenberg

So far, I have discussed poets who were educated in public schools whose curricula stressed the reading of classical texts in the original languages. There can be no doubt about the depth of such poets' classical learning, and it is therefore not surprising to find that Homer and the Homeric conception of war provide a constant background to their writings. However, Homer was also an important touchstone for poets who did not attend public school, as the works of Wilfred Owen and Isaac Rosenberg show.

Owen's best known classical reference is not to Homer, but to Horace; the climactic final line and a half of one of his most famous poems, '*dulce et decorum est / pro patria mori*', is of course a direct quotation from Horace *Odes* III.2. However, Owen's educational background meant that while he studied some Latin at school, he was unable to learn Greek there (Vandiver 1999: 442, n.27); it is all the more noteworthy, therefore, that some of his finest poems are rich in Homeric allusions. The most important of these is 'Strange Meeting'; this poem is in effect a Homeric *katabasis*, which parallels and refers to Odysseus' descent to the Underworld (Vandiver 1999: 445–53; Hardwick 2000: 53; see also Vandiver 2007). However, the Homeric connections of 'Strange Meeting' are Iliadic as well as Odyssean; as I have argued elsewhere, the words of the 'strange friend', the dead enemy who speaks most of the poem, directly recall key scenes from the *Iliad* (Vandiver 1999: 450–3). In particular, Owen's lines 'Then, when much blood had clogged their chariot wheels, / I would go up and wash them from sweet wells' (Owen 1983: I, 148) represent a complex interplay of two different Homeric references.

The first of these two references occurs at the end of *Iliad* 20, where Achilles' chariot wheels are spattered with blood:

> Before great-hearted Achilleus the single-foot horses
> trampled alike dead men and shields, and the axle under
> the chariot was all splashed with blood and the rails which encircled
> the chariot, struck by the flying drops from the feet of the horses,
> from the running rims of the wheels.
> (*Iliad* 20 ll. 498–502, tr. Lattimore 1951)

Owen's blood-clogged chariot wheels evoke images of traditional, heroic warfare (Vandiver 1999: 452–3; Taplin 1995: 223–4, n.34); but he calls up these images only to discard them immediately by pleading for their destruction through washing with water from 'sweet wells'. In contrast to the bloody chariot wheels, the 'sweet wells' sum up the attributes of peace, and here too the image derives from Homer. The source is Homer's vignette of peacetime Troy, before the Greeks came, which is recalled as Achilles and Hektor run past the washing-wells of the Trojan women:

> They raced along by the watching point . . .
> and came to the two sweet-running well springs. . . .
> Beside these
> in this place, and close to them, are the washing-hollows
> of stone, and magnificent, where the wives of the Trojans and their lovely
> daughters washed the clothes to shining, in the old days
> when there was peace, before the coming of the sons of the Achaians.
> (*Iliad* 22 ll. 145–56, tr. Lattimore 1951)

'Strange Meeting' brings together the horrific image of Achilles' blood-spattered chariot and the poignant image of washing-wells, as the soldier rejects the values of war
and claims for himself instead the domestic imagery of washing. The speaker would
wash the blood-spattered war chariots in the same fashion as the women of Troy
once washed clothes; the public and private, the aggressive and the domestic, are
combined in one brilliantly complex image that, by juxtaposing these two Iliadic
moments, shatters the whole paradigm of war as a field of worthy achievement – at
the same time that it recognizes the impossibility that the already-dead speaker's wish
could come to pass in reality.

Owen's 'Strange Meeting' is strong evidence that Homeric refiguration was not
the sole province of those who had received an upper-class education. This is all the
more noteworthy in the poems of Isaac Rosenberg, a working-class poet from a poor
immigrant London family. Rosenberg left school at fourteen and was largely self-
taught in literature. His working-class background meant that, unlike most soldier-
poets, he served as a private, not as an officer; he enlisted because his family needed
the money he would get by doing so (Rosenberg 1979: xv, xxiv). Many of his poems,
from both before and during the war, include generalized mythological images and
specifically Homeric ones.

'Break of Day in the Trenches', which Fussell considers 'the greatest poem of
the war', beautifully illustrates Rosenberg's use of Homer. Fussell comments that
'Break of Day' is 'partly a great poem because it is a great traditional poem' (2000:
250). Among the poem's traditional elements, the poppy is perhaps most important. Rosenberg introduces the poppy in the poem's fifth line ('as I pull the para-
pet's poppy / To stick behind my ear'; 1979: 103). This poppy provides the final
image of the poem:

> Poppies whose roots are in man's veins
> Drop, and are ever dropping;
> But mine in my ear is safe –
> Just a little white with the dust.
>   (Rosenberg 1979: 103–4)

Fussell refers the poppy here to 'the traditions of pastoral and of general elegy' (2002:
253); but as Hardwick has noted (2000: 51), this poppy in fact looks back beyond
the origins of elegy to Homer, and reflects the Homeric simile of *Iliad* 8 ll. 306–8:

> He bent drooping his head to one side, as a garden poppy
> bends beneath the weight of its yield and the rains of springtime;
> so his head bent slack to one side beneath the helm's weight.
>   (Tr. Lattimore 1951)

The Homeric poppy droops from the weight of rain, but Rosenberg's poppies drop
because of the thickness of man's blood at the flowers' roots. The complex resonances of 'poppies whose roots are in man's veins' are connected with Rosenberg's
use of root-imagery throughout his poetry (Silkin 1972: 260–5, 280; Bergonzi 1996:

112–13); among their other attributes, Rosenberg's poppies, rooted in blood and therefore doomed to death-in-life, are a visible token of the transitoriness of human existence. As they 'drop and are ever dropping', they reflect not only Homer's poppy-simile, but also his description of human beings as a 'generation of leaves' (*Il*.6 ll. 146–50). But Rosenberg inverts normal expectations by claiming that his own poppy, 'a little white with the dust', is 'safe'. In reality, a plucked flower would wither and die more quickly than growing ones, however ephemeral (cf. Fussell 2002: 252–3), while Rosenberg's poppies drop, not because they are cut but precisely because they are still rooted – in human mortality, in 'man's veins'. For Rosenberg, the cut flower is 'safe', or as safe as anything in the trenches can be (which is to say not safe at all), while the still growing flowers 'drop and are always dropping' from the blood at their roots.

The drooping or broken poppy as an image of a dying man itself has a complex history of reception, as it moved from its beginnings in Homer, through Sappho, Catullus, and Virgil, to arrive finally in the fields of Flanders, where it would become a symbol of the whole 'lost generation', most famously of course in John McCrae's 'In Flanders Fields' (see Fussell 2000: 246–50). Here, in Rosenberg's hands – or behind Rosenberg's ear – the poppy delicately performs its task of looking back, through the layers of earlier literature, to the Homeric scene where it first appears, and even more delicately reverses the reader's expectations so that the living poppies are in essence already dead while the plucked, inevitably withering poppy is 'safe'. The growing flowers *enact* death, while the cut flower, already whitened by the dust that corpses become, holds the poem's illusion of safety.

Conclusion: Gallipoli Revisited

Rosenberg strips war of its glory by his implicit refutation of heroic imagery. But at and even after the war's end, Homer could still be invoked to bestow the same sort of heroic glory earlier espoused by Grenfell and Brooke. The 1919 anthology *These Were the Men: Poems of the War* included an anonymous poem, 'The Dardanelles', spoken by the dead of Gallipoli. The poem concludes:

> There are other graves by the Dardanelles.
> Men whom immortal Homer sang
> Come to our ghostly camp fires' glow.
> Greet us as brothers and tell us 'Lo,
> So to *our* deeds old Troy rang'.
> Thus will the ages beyond our ken
> Turn to our story, and having read
> Will say with proudly uncovered head
> And reverent breath, 'Oh, God, they were men'.
> (Jaquet 1919: 76, italic original)

Since this poem was published anonymously, we cannot know precisely when it was written. However, its inclusion in an anthology published in 1919 indicates that the

unironic, heroizing use of Homer was still acceptable and, presumably, even congenial to the anthology's editor and his assumed readership.

Two years later, in 1921, the Irish author G.C. Duggan published a book-length
poem called *The Watchers on Gallipoli*, written in memory of his two brothers, killed
at Gallipoli. This book abounds in Homeric appropriations; for instance:

> The Heroes stir
> In their lone beds by reedy Scamander,
> And Helen's beauty lives again to see
> These western strangers, and Andromache
> Dreams of her Hector and Astyanax.
>   (1921: 33)

'The heroes stir / in their lone beds' could have been written by Brooke in 1915;
indeed, it is possible that Duggan's line is a direct echo of Brooke's, since Brooke's
fragment 'They say Achilles in the darkness stirred' appears in Marsh's *Memoir* (Marsh
1918: 177). Six years after Brooke's death, Duggan could still appropriate Homer
with no hint of ironic distancing.

Later in the twentieth century, the interrogation of Homer would lead to works
such as Walcott's *Omeros* and Logue's *War Music*, which foregrounds the elements
of brutality and senselessness that Homer interweaves into the *Iliad*'s multivalent
presentation of war. During World War One, however, such interrogation was not
the only possible mode of Homeric reception, nor was it yet impossible to read the
Iliad's presentation of glory and honor in a straightforward and unironic way. 'Break
of Day in the Trenches' brilliantly represents the ironic distancing and the rejection
of heroic values of one form of Homeric reception; but side by side with Rosenberg
and Owen were other poets who turned to Homer for straightforward, traditional
validation of their own or their comrades' sacrifice. By mid-century, Homer would
no longer exercise so strong a hold over poetic discourse and ways of imagining war;
but for writers struggling to comprehend the war of 1914–1918, Homer was one
of the primary tools available 'to think with', as poets strove either to validate or to
reject their own war by looking to Troy.

NOTE

I would like to thank the editors of this volume and Miriam Leonard for their comments on
this piece and Stephen Harrison for the reference to Tennyson's 'Achilles Over the Trench'.

FURTHER READING

There is at present no full-length study of the World War One poets and Homer or classics
in general; my book in progress, *Stand in the Trench, Achilles: Classical Receptions in British
Poetry of the Great War*, is intended to fill that lacuna. At present, the student wishing to
know more about Homeric reception in the war poets will find illuminating short discussions

in Ogilvie 1964; Hardwick 2000; and Hardwick 2003a. Vandiver 1999 examines Homeric references in C.H. Sorley's 'When you see millions of the mouthless dead' and Wilfred Owen's 'Strange Meeting'. Vandiver 2007 discusses Patrick Shaw-Stewart, E.A. Mackintosh, and Owen's 'Spring Offensive'.

Currently, the best advice for a student interested in World War One poetry and classical reception would be to read as much of the poetry as possible. Collected works editions are widely available for many of the more famous poets (e.g. Rupert Brooke, Wilfred Owen, Isaac Rosenberg, Siegfried Sassoon); for a broader exposure to trench poetry in general and for the work of more obscure poets, there are many useful anthologies. Hibberd and Onions 1986 is excellent, as is Silkin 1996. Finally, D. Hibberd's critical and biographical works on Wilfred Owen are rich mines of information about that poet's social and educational background, literary culture in England at the time of the war, and the war in general; see especially Hibberd 1986b, 1992, 2002.

PART IX

Reflection and Critique

CHAPTER THIRTY-FIVE

Reception Studies: Future Prospects

James I. Porter

Classical reception studies are booming. They have been doing so quietly for some time at the margins of the disciplines of classical studies, even though reception is in a strong sense all there is (Martindale 2007). One of the greatest ironies of classical studies is that they are *themselves* a form of reception studies, though professing classicists have been the last to acknowledge this. What is more, classical studies have long been predicated on the reception of the Greek and Roman past outside of Classics for their very own survival.

The resistance to reception within Classics is slowly fading, and rightly so, but reception has yet to be fully taken on board. The risks of avoidance are incalculable. To oppose the obvious fact that the classical past (so called) simply cannot exist without its being received is to live in the protective vacuum of an illusion – the illusion that classical studies and their objects are timeless and eternal, invulnerable to the impingements of history and to contingency (all the while working to erase those impingements in an effort to uncover the unblemished truth of their object). But turn this ideology of unchanging permanence around and you will find that classical studies have an extraordinarily powerful instrument in their hands. Henceforth they can boast to be a marker and a maker of historical change, of ideologies built around some of the most persistent ideals ever known, indeed of some of the most profoundly constitutive ideologies of modernity. These phenomena simply cannot be decoded without an intimate familiarity with the disciplines of Classics. Imagine that – *Classics*, those untimeliest, as Nietzsche called them, of disciplines, as a guide to *modernity*? But they are this, and much more besides.

So why has the quiet advance of reception studies become a boom? The general drift towards interdisciplinarity in the academy will have played a role, though to be sure reception of antiquity is not of itself an interdisciplinary venture, nor is it clear that reception studies have maximized their interdisciplinary potentials (more on this below). The exhaustion of high theory and the re-emergence of history, likewise prominent recent trends in the academy, have been further significant factors (Goldhill

2002; Martindale and Thomas 2006). Common sense may be the trump card, for reception studies have shown immense promise as a way of deepening the dialogue between modernity and classical antiquity.

What follows will be an overview of some of the future prospects that a critical reception of Greek and Roman antiquity can hold in store. These prospects, designed as talking-points and not as peremptory diktats, are formed around a biased and entirely provisional view of what reception studies are or can be.

The history of Greek and Roman studies as reception study

Reception is built into the bloodlines of classical studies, sometimes visibly, most often less than visibly. It was once a staple of Classics that it should discuss itself – its history, achievements, failings, directions and so on – in addition to going about its business. That is, the history of classical scholarship (with a strong bias towards philology in the narrow sense) was once a formal element of classical studies and recognized as such. Today, this has for the most part changed. Of course, the history of Classics continues, as ever, to be an implicit and ineliminable part of the disciplines that variously make it up: just to analyze a text (for example) is to conjure up the history of that text; a line of commentary can hardly be read without reading up on or about earlier commentaries; footnotes throw slivers of light upon predecessor generations; and in general arguments for novelty stand on the toes of giants, as well as on their shoulders. But the explicit history of classical studies no longer has an integral role to play in the classical disciplines, or in the formation and disciplining of future classicists. The history of classical scholarship was once a magisterial and occasionally Olympian industry – Boeckh's *Encyclopedia and Methodology of the Philological Sciences* is an example of the former, Wilamowitz's *History of Philology* of the latter. Then it became a minority interest, often carried on in spare research time (witness the new crop of studies on nineteenth-century scholarship that began appearing in the 1980s: e.g. Jenkyns 1980; Brink 1986). The reasons favouring the existence of the status of Classics in the past were plain (if disguised): winners get to write histories, and even to shape them. Nothing comparable exists today: there is no single vantage point from which the totality of classical studies can be viewed, let alone controlled. Moreover, the institutional support for this kind of synthetic vision is gone. (Try and imagine offering a course on the topic; now try and imagine anyone rushing to take it.) And so is the vision itself. Discussion of these difficulties and their embedded and genetic conditions is what is most needed today.

An in all, there are good reasons not to write histories of classical studies. To begin with, they invariably raise the spectre of contingency. Nothing can be more disconcerting than to realize how time-bound one's studies are and (will) have been. Surely there is no better way to date the study of the Classics than to pick up two older histories of them (let alone two specimens of Greek and Roman scholarship) and lay them side by side. Not only do no final truths emerge (though a good deal of time-honoured conventions do); it is also likely that no two histories will even remotely resemble one another. In place of the comforting illusion that even if times change antiquity no longer does, comparison of histories of scholarship or any series of studies around a single object reminds us of just the opposite illusion (or is it a fact?), namely that antiquity is changing all the time, from generation to generation and from scholar to scholar. Such vertigo is hard to bear for long. And yet one wants to believe that the more reflexivity that gets built into one's discipline, the greater the chances there will be of arriving at . . . what? A truer picture of antiquity? Or of the discipline itself? There is something uncontroversially valid-feeling about knowing how we know what we know. Knowledge might be forever imperfect without this self-knowledge. A unique act of courage needs to be summoned to take this leap into self-inquiry. But how can we get to the bottom of that? How do we know when we've arrived?

Probably one cannot. But it is salubrious to admit at least this, and to own up to the circumstances under which knowledge of something becomes possible at all, in the broadest sense: institutionally, socially, and culturally possible. That is partly what the history of disciplines is all about, much like reception studies more generally, which in some ways are the successor to the older disciplinary self-appraisals. This is one way in which knowledge can be truly self-productive – in the most unpredictable and beneficial of ways. And so it may happen that, in looking back upon scholarship from past centuries, one may see a bit of oneself in them. (Has our current modernity, for instance, ejected 'classicism' as traditionally conceived from the field of classical studies (Connolly 2001; Porter 2006b; Settis 2006)? What would it mean to do so?) Or one may investigate the myths of scholarship that currently frame its histories, or the micro-histories that attach to single institutions, such as those surrounding the Ritualist school at Cambridge (see Beard 2000). At any rate, the history of Greek and Roman studies, when it is not a history of personalities, remains in a fledgeling state today. (For an excellent start, see Stray 1998.)

In a world in which classicists are facing huge challenges of a very practical kind – as reflected in ever-dwindling enrollments, job prospects, funding, and symbolic resources (prestige and cultural capital) – it is incumbent on classicists to reassess themselves, their relevance, their place in the world, and their future. Exploring the history of their disciplines is the most natural point of entry to self-reflection and self-examination one could ask for. Such an approach is likely to reveal unexpected continuities with the past, seen now from a more modest vantage-point in the present.

Reception in Antiquity

It can be no accident that Greek and Roman studies have themselves been moving along a path that parallels reception studies. Only there the object has been something like the reception of antiquity within antiquity, without being so named. More and more scholars are turning to the ways in which antiquity conceived its own histories. And more and more it is becoming apparent that our sense of the past is shaped by *its* sense of its own past. Witness the recent explosion of studies on antiquarianism, nostalgia, pilgrimage and tourism, cults and their revivals. No longer unidimensional, linear, and progressive, ancient history appears like a cascade of Chinese boxes, each moment containing its own tightly packed historical pasts within itself. Greek and Roman studies and the history of those studies are increasingly becoming inseparable.

Concomitant with this trend, or set of trends, is the movement over the past two decades away from classicism, which is to say the revering of the traditional bastions of high classical culture of Greece and Rome – the canonical art and literature of the archaic and classical periods down to the early fourth century (essentially, down to Plato and Isocrates) and their Roman counterpart, the Augustan period of Vergil and Horace. Despite the efforts of Droysen, who put the age of Alexandria on the map with his three-volume masterpiece *Geschichte des Hellenismus* (1836–43), and a century on those of Wilamowitz, who championed the poetic achievements of the same age in his masterful two-volume *Hellenistische Dichtung* (1924), the Hellenistic age continued to be tarnished as a period of degeneracy and epigones, as a time when poets were scholars, librarians, and grammarians first, and only then poets, and so too they were crushed by the weight of the past and by a bookish approach to literature. The study of the Hellenistic period has only recently come back into fashion, along with its associated cultural developments: post-Socratic philosophy, the history of civic competitions and cult activities, and a bolder inquiry into the hybrid conditions of a Greek world in diaspora after Alexander spread Hellenism to the East and to Egypt – in other words, a fuller picture of a vital, flourishing and hardly degenerate Mediterranean world. In Roman scholarship, the post-classical imperial worlds of Seneca, Lucan, and Statius, and others, formerly shunned, are flourishing afresh. And the boundaries between earlier antiquity and late antiquity are slowly melting away. A new accent has been placed on the tense relations between Greeks and Romans under the empire from the first to third centuries CE. This is the age of the itinerant sophists and antiquarians, the travellers or pilgrims (or armchair travellers), the great lampoonists, and the final gasp of brilliant literary theory – the age of Dio of Prusa and Aulus Gellius, Pausanias and Arrian, Lucian and Longinus. All these are travellers who pass between cultures and through time zones: they inhabit the past and the present simultaneously; they speak and write in a language that is consciously modelled on the Attic Greek of the golden fifth century; they are strongly classicizing in their tastes: they look up to, and not only back to, the past; cities of the Greek mainland are treated as museums, but of the hands-on variety, and so on. All are receiving their pasts. Some are flaunting it.

In both the Hellenistic world and the later imperial world what is going on is an internal reception of antiquity. And once this fact emerges, it becomes evident (though it is really no secret) that antiquity never really ceased to be received in antiquity. The past as we know it was at no time clear-cut, but was always *only* layered, cluttered and palimpsestic. All the pillars of the Western classical tradition are made up of this same mosaic. Cults renewed their ties to the past at least from the Bronze Age onward (Snodgrass 1980); buildings incorporated and altered their predecessors, whether physically (Hurwit 2004) or by reference (Hölscher 2003, 2006); myths rewrote themselves, and really just are this rewriting; the ancient revisionings of Homer were as compelling, and as ineluctable, as the Homeric texts, which existed in no other way (see Lamberton and Keaney 1992; Nagy 1996;

Zeitlin 2001; Graziosi 2002), and which still exist this way for us, for there is no direct, unmediated access to the Homeric past.

The same holds for most of what we know about the Greek and Roman past. Indeed, countless texts come down to us thanks to the labors of epitomizers, anthologists, and commentators who permitted these texts to survive, albeit often only as fragments and quotations. But they do so as the remnants of an unbroken conversation that was carried on throughout antiquity, a conversation that is itself today slowly coming to be recognized as no less interesting and worthy of study than the gems of so-called primary texts that this ancient transmission has deposited on modern shores like a receding glacier. In philosophy, for example, work on the 'doxographical' tradition – representing the way antiquity talked about itself and its philosophers, from Theophrastus' *On the Senses,* a rich source of Presocratic thought, to Diogenes Laertius' *Lives of the Philosophers* to Aetius' *Placita* and works by other late authors – is proceeding apace (Laks 2002; Mansfeld 2004). Study of the ancient scholia and commentaries – hence, modern scholarship about ancient scholarship about ancient literature, language, and lore – is likewise gaining ground today (Meijering 1987; Most 1999; Nünlist forthcoming). This newfound interest in ancient secondary sources, reconceived as primary sources in their own right, is taking place within the framework of another set of studies that are just now coming to life. Here, the focus is on how knowledge was organized in the ancient world, and how it came to be transmitted – in education, in the sciences, in the pseudo-sciences, as allied with political projects and objectives, across cultural and language barriers, and so forth. Modern constructions of ancient categories are likewise beginning to flourish (Laks 1999, 2002). The implications for our own organizational categories and our own assumptions about this transmission are, needless to say, huge and yet to be explored. In fact, transmission and reception are not two faces of a single coin. Rather, they are two names for the selfsame activity. Classical studies are not merely the beneficiary of this activity. They are *subsumed* by it.

To assume that reception is a symptom of historical belatedness and only a late phenomenon in the ancient civilized world is to misgauge the phenomenon altogether. Above, I noted how the reception of Homer's texts was and is indistinguishable from those texts (see Budelmann and Haubold (ch. 1), and Graziosi (ch. 2), in this volume). Part of the reason is that reception is built directly into those texts. Poseidon's fear in *Iliad* 7 of being eclipsed by the ramshackle Achaean wall, indeed his bare mention of his worry, ironically ensures that at least half of his prediction that the memory of *their* wall will outlast that of *his* wall will come true, but it does not erase the worry. Obliteration (*aphanismos*), it turns out, is a gnawing question in the ancient tradition of Homer's reception, *not least because that reception is itself already a gnawing obsession in Homer.* Poseidon's anxiety about his Troy expresses a veiled meta-poetic worry already; *tis*-speeches ('someday someone will say . . .') predicting the future of a hero's fame (*kleos*) are another instance, as is the song of Demodocus or the fate of Aeneas' offspring ('. . . lest [his race] be without seed and obliterated (*aphantos*)' *Iliad* 20.300–6 (see Porter forthcoming). The examples can be multiplied *ad libitum.* Plainly, the theme of reception is rooted in the epic consciousness – as a most uncertain fate.

Reception Theory

So far I have been stressing the requirements of reception, which is to say the way in which reception necessarily structures access to antiquity. The problem with this formulation is that it suggests the wrong kind of picture, as though you could look through a viewfinder *into* a tube *at* an image, and only the final image mattered – that of a pure, uncontaminated antiquity – when in fact antiquity includes the viewfinder *and* the medium through which the looking is done. The past is mediated already in the past. The problem here, of course, is this: through what viewfinder do you look at the viewfinder and the medium?

Questions like this ought to fall under the purview of reception theory. Yet while so much of the new scholarship in reception is theoretically sophisticated, as the essays collected in Martindale and Thomas (2006) amply demonstrate, to date no theory tailored to the specific exigencies of Greek and Roman reception exists. The theory of reception as developed by the Konstanz School (Iser, Jauss, and others, following the earlier models of Gadamer and Ingarden), and its later American offspring, reader response theory, are frequently cited as precursors to classical reception study (see Martindale 1993; Hardwick 2003a; Martindale 2006: 1–13). Reception theory in this vein is hardly irrelevant, especially in its emphasis on the subject's constitutive role in the production of its interpretative objects. Still, recourse to a theory that was developed as a general model of textual interpretation is really a move *faute de mieux*, governed more by metonymy (a similarity of names) than by point of reference.

A number of topics in demand of immediate attention spring to mind: theories about subjectivity, cultural placement, knowledge as a form of attachment, problems of colonizing the past, the recuperation and the irrecuperability of antiquity, fragments and fragmentary wholes, anachronism and antiquarianism, classicism and anticlassicism, history and historicism, modern vs. postmodern reception, classical tradition vs. critical reception studies, disciplinary histories as cognitive mappings, and the effects of the ongoing remapping of the disciplines today on a new interdisciplinary reception studies. While no one global theory is likely to suffice to cover all of these areas, a few general parameters do need to be worked out. For example, because the past is actively produced as much as it is passively received, Greek and Roman reception theory must take into account the ever-changing nature of its objects. Traditions of reception are dynamic processes that flow in two directions at once, both forward and backward. We are still a long way off from a satisfactory theory that might describe, let alone explain, how this process works, though we know that it somehow does work, and that classicists and the Classics would not be here if it did not work.

Future Paths

The range taken by reception studies has tended to cluster around particular research areas, favouring certain periods (Enlightenment, Victorian, early modern periods) and themes (literary transpositions, including translations, gendered politics, icons of classicism), with literature and performance arts predominating (theatre, cinema, and, to a lesser degree, opera). A number of areas remain underexplored:

Histories of Greek and Roman Studies

As seen above, the history of Greek and Roman scholarship (with a strong bias towards philology in the narrow sense) was once a formal element of those studies and recognized as such. Today, this has for the most part changed. Such histories, when they occur, have an extra-disciplinary and somewhat gratuitous feel. Perhaps it is right that they should fall under the wing of reception studies, though again the problem of integration looms. At any rate, the history of Greek and Roman studies remains in a fledgling state today. The very idea of a history of the (so-called) classical disciplines needs to be rethought, especially if any headway is to be made in rethinking the disciplines themselves. At stake is nothing less than the very coherence of the profession of Greek and Roman studies in this contemporary, very postclassical world.

Techniques and tools of scholarship

While the zone above the *apparatus criticus* (to wit, the text) has been favoured in literary reception studies, only rarely does the *apparatus criticus* itself come in for scrutiny. Yet the critical apparatus is itself a text, and as such it is worthy of reception history. S. Gurd's recent study of the textual criticism of *Iphigenia at Aulis* (2005) is the first of its kind that dares to look below the line dividing the text from the *apparatus criticus* and to read successive uses of the *textus receptus* (an ever-changing object, as the *apparatus criticus* itself attests) and the textual scenarios it projects. Commentaries likewise contain rich histories of textual and other kinds of construction (Bollack and Judet de La Combe 1981; Bollack 1990; Most 1999). At stake in both of these areas and others like them (papyrology, source criticism, the archaeological field report, etc.) is the very conception of the objects of ancient Greek and Roman culture. Here, the very idea of what counts as 'secondary' is being revised (motto: *the secondary is primary*). Lessons can be learned from neighbouring fields, for example English textual criticism (e.g. McGann 1991, esp. 125). More work is needed here. (But in philology, see Most 1997, 2002; Burkert et al. 1998; in material culture, see Shanks 1996.)

Classical studies as reception studies

As the studies named in the foregoing paragraph all demonstrate, classical scholarship stands within the stream of reception, not outside of it. It ought to be possible to build this consciousness directly into the way scholarly problems come to be framed. Author-based courses can be structured around the ancient reception of these authors over time, and in different media – say, images of Homer (Most 2005), or of Socrates (Zanker 1988; Lapatin 2006). Textual traditions can be taught as mosaics of intertexts caught up in the dynamics of reception (Hinds 1998). Scholia can be better integrated into the same, not just as a source of validating readings but as a way of exemplifying antiquity's awareness of itself and as a precursor to scholarship today. The excitement of all such study is that it represents the most recent link in a multi-stranded chain. The delirium of historical contingency, past and present, could threaten to overwhelm, but that is a risk worth taking.

Intellectual history

Like it or not, reception has a native affinity to good old-fashioned intellectual history. German and Anglo-American perspectives have tended to predominate at the expense of other European and non-European perspectives. Here, too, a correction is needed. Italian studies beyond the Renaissance are scarce. What about reception of the Classics in Israel, or in South Africa, Latin and South America, or India? The collisions between Classics and colonialism/postcolonialism are just now getting the attention they deserve (Humphreys 2004; Hardwick 2004a; Goff 2005; Vasunia 2005b; Hardwick and Gillespie 2007). Comparisons between hegemonic Western classicism and non-Western classical traditions (Chinese, Islamic, Indian, and so on) are also worth exploring for the light they can shed on the mechanisms that produce and uphold classical ideals, not to mention any cross-fertilizations that might stand revealed.

Constructions of the classical ideal

The classical ideal is the myth of a golden era of a classically perfected era, lodged in fifth-century Athens, and familiar to readers of Winckelmann. The fragilities of this illusion are too many to name here. In place of a critique, consider the following from one of Nietzsche's early notebooks:

> One cannot understand our modern world unless one recognizes the immense influence that the purely fantastic has had on it. Reverence for classical antiquity, . . . that is, the only serious, unselfserving, self-sacrificing reverence that antiquity has received to date, is a monumental example of quixotism: and that is what philology is at its best. . . . One imitates something that is purely chimerical, and chases after a wonderland that never existed. The same impulse [to veneration] runs through classical antiquity: the way in which the Homeric heroes were copied, the entire traffic with myth has something of this [impulse]. Gradually, the whole of ancient Greece was made into an object worthy of Don Quixote.
>
> (Nietzsche 1988: 7: 7[1])

The odd temporalities of the classical ideal, involving not only the nomenclature of Greek and Roman studies but also their value, have a history and obey a logic that need to be unfolded and critically examined (Porter 2006a).

New themes

The range of themes addressed in reception studies is still in its infancy. One need is for longitudinal themes that presume a more or less continuous if historically variegated scope and that could border on independent studies in their own right. Take your pick, though a few less likely contenders would include philosophies of life and death; politics (including the politics of reception); the exportation of western models of classicism beyond western boundaries (e.g. in Malaysia; see Maier (1988)) and any rebound effects these might have on the originating models; or the history of materialism (as a counter to the idealizing histories of the past), one of whose expressions is the unlofty but chastening story of the (ongoing) commodification and commercialization of the past (cf. Vickers 1987). Foucault's *History of Sexuality* remains exemplary, if in need of reception study itself (see Leonard 2005 on the earlier Foucault; Porter in Martindale and Thomas 2006 for the late Foucault). Also neglected but worthy of recuperation are the unclassical elements within the presumed classical tradition within antiquity, viz., the minor, uncanonical strands, if not the very ousting of authors, works, and tendencies from the classical canon itself: (1) low, novelistic discourse (see Kurke 2006); (2) cynicism; aesthetic theory outside of the formalism and idealism of Plato and Aristotle and pitched against it (Porter forthcoming); (3) the modern invention of minority archipelagoes in antiquity and their associated styles (Greek and Roman archaic periods and the archaic mind; the Hellenistic age and Alexandrianism; Silver Latin; late antiquity); ancient forms of commentary (Sluiter 2000); ancient forms of dissent.

Material reception studies

Classical traditions are typically formed around and convey ideals, while the material supports of those ideals are typically rendered invisible. But classical traditions endure, as we saw, thanks to the material persistence of their traces. Archaeology and material culture have reception histories that deserve to be recovered, and which are being recovered above all in the area of modern Hellenism (Marchand 1996; Morris 2000), and not least around the formation of modern Greece (Hamilakis 2007). Studies of antiquity in this vein are implicitly part of reception studies (e.g. Alcock 2002), but so far have not been explicitly allied to this larger project. Finally, while there is much to be said in favour of emphasizing reception as a process, as 'recipience' (Whitmarsh 2006: 115), also needed is an emphasis on reception as a matter of sensuous rather than purely formal perception, what might be called *percipience*, as a way of eliciting the materiality and phenomenology of classical studies (Porter 2003). Winckelmann, Pater and Adrian Stokes are all excellent models for the sensuous perception and reception of ancient ideas and objects. Others in fields adjacent to Classics have been elaborating useful models of thick, phenomenally rich description.

Reception of reception

Is it too soon for the renewed field of reception studies to turn reflexively upon itself and to examine its own traditions from a critical and metatheoretical perspective? Only time will tell. Such a topic would bring the focus of reception studies up to the present or near-present – always an uncomfortable thing, but essential just the same. (See the Introduction to this volume.)

Reform in the Classroom:
Interdisciplinary Opportunities

Curricular reform is needed: why not make reception a field requirement for all matriculating classicists? A doctoral thesis on reception would not typically be considered a ticket to a job in the profession, at least in the States – if anything, quite the contrary. Nor do most Classics departments have designated positions for specialists in reception. With publishing outlets increasingly guaranteed, there should be no fears about tenurability and promotion. No doubt the greatest hesitation to date has been over the mission or 'core' of classical studies. Another is criterial. Standards of rigour in reception are far from established. And how do you test somebody's skill set in reception anyway? There are no datives or supines in reception studies, and the boundaries are potentially limitless, even of the critically conceived variety of reception studies. Supposing that reception studies has an obvious place in the academy, it is unclear where that place should be. In Classics departments? In modern languages? Comparative Literature? Or in History?

Criteria of 'relevance' aside, teaching reception has all the same benefits as reception studies have on their own: it demonstrates the situatedness and contingencies of Greek and Roman studies. An all too common assumption within Classics departments is that Classics has the prestige and responsibility, if not always the clout, to commandeer (to be synonymous with) liberal education and to draw students in for that reason: 'classical tradition' is a ticket to value, if not to a job. This is highly questionable. What really attracts students is their hunch that there is indeed some cachet to Classics, which they vaguely feel the pulls of, and also that they want proof of the claim, not the claim itself. Rather than resting on this assumption, why not explore alternatives? A critical, open-minded approach to problems of canonization, classicality and the ways in which Classics became 'Classics,' can be a powerful and seductive invitation to the study of how knowledge works in culture and society (Lianeri and Zajko 2008). Critical thinking and classical education in this way go hand in hand. One need not take the 'greatness' of the classical past for granted. One can instead ask how this claim to distinction came into existence and evolved, how it was sustained, transformed, questioned, perverted and so on. In this way, the concept of 'the classical' can receive some real substantive content: it can appear at the end of the curriculum as what was covered, however battered, bloodied, and wobbly it may be, not as the shining Thing one was after from the start. Recall that *homêrizein* (to Homerize) in Greek means 'to lie' – and other things less reputable ('to indulge one's natural lust' is found in a late novelist). It never hurts to start reception classes off with such disclosures.

A further pressing issue concerns the problem of training. While study of the reception of the Greek and Roman world is widespread and belongs to no one in particular, Greek and Roman reception studies are increasingly initiated by professing classicists, which raises the interesting question of what differences if any exist between reception studies carried out, as it were, from within the fold and those carried out by scholars who lack training let alone background in the postclassical target-fields of reception studies? Baldly put, the question is whether a non-classicist can competently conduct the history of Classics' reception. The flip-side of this is the question of what justifies a classicist's pretensions to knowledge about the reception of Greek and Roman material in other historical contexts and subject areas. Classicists who undertake reception studies are not only putting themselves out on a limb professionally. They are often obliged to reach well beyond their training – which is not inherently a bad thing, though it does make one want to ask once more why reception should fall outside of the professional training of classicists. A reverse argument might be that reception studies can be conducted without knowledge of Greek and Latin, let alone knowledge of the original Greek and Roman traditions in wearying detail, because reception begins (frequently) after those civilizations have collapsed. Why should someone studying the connections between Byron, Keats, or Goethe and Greco-Roman antiquity trouble herself with the philology of Aeschylus or Livy? Even if the premise behind the question is false or debatable, this does not meant that excellent work in reception should always require specialist philological expertise or detailed knowledge of the historical conditions and production of the source work, just as much reception has often been inspired by the Classics without being *stricto sensu* informed by them. Behind everything lies the problem of integration: how do all these bits of the puzzle fit together (assuming they should)?

Live Reception: Classical Studies and Public Intellectuals

My final topic will be a plea on behalf of the need for a new kind of classicist-academic: the engaged public intellectual who not only can create new public audiences for the field and the academy at large, but who also can enter into debates within the larger public sphere and can contribute in ways that only a perspective on the very origins of western culture and political life can afford. Indeed, the two missions, of self-survival and altruistic engagement, can be fruitfully aligned. Such a belief inspired a panel session at the annual meeting of the American Philological Association in 2005 co-organized by Joy Connolly and myself. The session, titled 'Can Public Intellectuals Think? Classics and the Public Sphere,' was conceived with a few different things in mind. First, it sprang from the conviction that, though the pressures of the present are urgent and real, Greek and Roman studies have more resources for ensuring their survival than classicists tend to think. One of these is the natural affinity of classical study to public intellectual life. The pursuit of the Classics has always been embedded in the production of public discourse. From its various moments of founding into late antiquity, the Renaissance, and beyond, the field has been every bit as much public and political as it has been a matter of the solitary scholar or grammarian poring over the relics of the past. If the public face of the classicist has not necessarily been validated by the profession, it has been and continues to be central to the function and construction of classical studies (understood as a collective totality), to its standing in society, and even to its prestige as a reservoir of (contested) tradition. Indeed, Classics has arguably held the prominent place in society it historically has enjoyed not because of its timeless value but precisely because Classics has been a publicly *contested* heritage, one of direct, if changing, value to each successive modernity.

The panel was conceived as a call to arms and an exhortation to acknowledge and develop the historical and contemporary links between Classics and public intellectual life – in classes and curricula, in scholarship, in its public appearances, and in its aspirations. Classics can and must rethink its historical and social functions in the light of its history as a peculiarly civic study, and the profession needs to examine the ways its daily practices of research and teaching enable – or disable – lines of communication with the public sphere. Not all classicists – and the same applies to humanist scholars generally – will or will want to be contacted by the media for quotation or to write books or blogs designed for non-professional readers. Yet in order to guarantee Classics a place at the table in the public sphere, classicists must begin by making their own historical role in building that table and by making themselves better understood by the public. To undertake this task is to participate in the 'living' reception of Greece and Rome (Harrison 2008).

The questions this panel sought to pose were the following: How can Classics capitalize on the intrinsic advantages granted to it by its disciplinary history? What are some of the ways in which classicists might learn to reach out and shape public discourse, appeal to existing public constituencies, enrich the understanding of Greek and Roman antiquity among the larger public, and indeed create new publics, without at the same time suffering from anxieties over the 'dilution' of professional standards? Can Classics departments tenure public intellectuals? What are some of the models available for public intellectuals in our field today? Can classicists imagine themselves as 'specific intellectuals' (Foucault), as 'organic intellectuals' (Gramsci), as 'figures of dissent' (Eagleton), as 'unacknowledged legislators' (Hitchens), or simply as public writers trained in the traditions of classical eloquence and civic virtue? What can Classics do in a world that has been characterized as drained and sapped of all intellectual force and responsibility? (So Furedi (2004), though one may wish to contest the characterization.)

Classics has plenty of resources at its immediate disposal for answering these and similar questions, whose relevance to reception history ought to be plain. Its subject matter is in good part filled with examples of public life, practice and virtue, from Socrates to Cicero. The history of the study of the Classics and indeed the entirety of its reception could be easily rewritten from the perspective of the role played by public intellectuals (Pico della Mirandola, Erasmus, W. von Humboldt, Gladstone, Nietzsche) – a perspective that, incidentally, is eminently teachable in the classroom. Unfortunately, studies of this dimension of Classics are under-represented, while histories of philology abound (see, however, Grafton 1997; Goldhill 2002; Winterer 2002; Leonard 2005). And there is the example of those contemporary scholars and poets working in the traditions of Greece and Rome who have risen to the ranks of public intellectuals (Mary Beard, Anne Carson, Paul Cartledge, Anthony Grafton, David Halperin, Victor Davis Hanson, Jonathan Lear, Daniel Mendelsohn, Martha Nussbaum, Josiah Ober and Gary Wills, to name just these). One should consider how Classics can intersect with wider publishing markets and various media outlets, bringing its research agendas and motivations into the public light. Last but not least, such a perspective can be used to begin to rethink Greek and Roman studies – what classicists do and what they teach – in terms of these same questions.

Needless to say, the broadest of these issues translate into other humanistic fields in the academy, and many classicists are already thinking up ways to translate the solipsism of specialized academic study into a more publicly accessible and meaningful activity. Classics has no intrinsic political perspective to offer, though it has shown itself capable of several, from hawkish right-wing illiberalism to left-wing liberal critiques to a softer, new critical humanism. A whole other dimension is lurking behind the technocratic veneer of the modern-day scholar – a dimension that reveals commitment, passion, a sense of urgency, and a desire to communicate meaningfully. But this interest remains largely untapped – in part, one suspects, because it is largely undirected: its primary outlets are in the classroom, or in the petty politics of the hallway and the departmental meeting. The problem here is not a lack of will, but a poverty on the level of structure. Why, for instance, is a *feuilleton* literature absent from the States or the UK but not on the continent? Why do Classics books not sell in vaster numbers? These questions point to the need to remould the ways in which scholars reach their publics. Scholastic journals and presses as they are currently conceived are decidedly not going to be the answer. (The more popularly pitched journal *Arion*, with its engaged humanism and pluralism, is a good antidote, but also one of a kind.) The occasional sound-bite in various media outlets helps give visibility to Classics but also threatens to tokenize its presence. Universities might well take up a leadership role, if they have the courage to do so – for the problem is endemic to the academy at large. In any event, in this utopic, revised world, Classics will want to join hands and make common cause with its neighbors. And *that* would be true interdisciplinarity in action, ensuring the reception of Classics in the largest and most vital sense of the word.

NOTE

Thanks to Miriam Leonard and the editors of this volume, above all Lorna Hardwick, for detailed comments on earlier drafts.

FURTHER READING

The classic statement of literary reception theory and history is Jauss 1970. Two recent studies of classicism and the classical ideal are Settis 2006, and the essays collected in Porter 2006b. See also Bassi and Euben 2003. An essay that nicely surveys many of the issues raised in the present chapter from the perspective of modern Greek studies is Jusdanis 2004, supplemented by Hamilakis 2004. See also the important study by Gourgouris 1996. On the politics of Classics and empire, see Vasunia 2003 and 2005b.

Bibliography

Abramson, G. 1998. *Drama and Ideology in Modern Israel*. Cambridge.

Achemenet. A resource site for the study of the Achaemenid Persian empire, www.achemenet. com, accessed 6 December 2006.

Achilleos, S. 2004. The *Anacreontea* and a tradition of refined male sociability. In Smyth 2004: 21–35.

Adams, G. 1729. *The Tragedies of Sophocles*. London.

Adams, J.R.R. 1987. *The Printed Word and the Common Man: Popular Culture in Ulster 1700–1900*. Belfast.

Adams, N. 1989. *Elektra* as opera and drama. Unpublished PhD dissertation, University of Pennsylvania.

Agnew, J. 1998. The impossible capital: monumental Rome under liberal and fascist regimes 1870–1943. *Geografiska Annaler*. Series B, *Human Geography* 80. Oxford: 229–40.

Ahl, F. and H.M. Roisman. 1996. *The Odyssey Reformed*. Ithaca, N.Y.

Akad, O. 2004. Le Théâtre Arabe. *Revue d'Histoire du Théâtre* 1/2: 33–40.

Al-Bayyati, Abd al-Wahhab. 1963. *The New Nisabour* [*Muhakama fi Nisabur*]. Cairo.

Albisetti, J. 1988. *Schooling Girls and Women: Secondary and Higher Education in the Nineteenth Century*. Princeton.

Alcock, S.E. 2002. *Archaeologies of the Greek Past: Landscape, Monuments, and Memories*. Cambridge.

Aldington, R. (tr.). 1930. *Euripides'* Alcestis. London.

Aldrich, R. 1993. *Seduction of the Mediterranean: Writing, Art, and Homosexual Fantasy*. London.

Alexander, M. 1983. *Old English Literature*. London.

Allan, W. 2001. Euripides in Megale Hellas: aspects of the early reception of tragedy. *Greece and Rome* 48: 67–86.

Allardyce Nicholl, B. 1925. *British Drama*, 4th edn. London, Toronto, Bombay, Sydney.

Allardyce Nicholl, B. 1952–9. *A History of English Drama 1660–1900*. Cambridge.

Allott, K. and M. Allott. 1979. *The Poems of Matthew Arnold*, 2nd edn. London.

Altena, H. 2005. The theater of innumerable faces. In Gregory 2005: 472–89.

Alter, R. (ed.). 2004. *Pleasure and Change: The Aesthetics of the Canon*. Oxford.

Amato, E. (ed.). 2006. *Approches de la troisième sophistique*. Brussels.

Amoroso, F. 1997. Ancient drama in modern Italian theatre. In Merkouris (ed.), 1997: 35–61.

Amory, Jr. C. 1929. *Persian Days.* Boston and New York.

Anderson, T.S. 1880. *My Wanderings in Persia.* London.

Andreades, A.M. 1933. *The Royal Theatre 1901–1908* [in Greek]. Athens.

Andrianou, E. 2005. The *lexis* of Georgios Soteriades in the *Oresteia* [in Greek]. In *Euangelika 1901*, 2005: 129–54.

Annas, J. 1993. *The Morality of Happiness.* Oxford.

Anon. 1943. *Aristophanes, Eleven Comedies.* Originally published by the Athenian Society, 1912. New York.

Anscombe, G.E.M. 1997 [1958, often repr.]. Modern moral philosophy. In Crisp and Slote (eds), 1997: 26–44.

Arendt, H. 1973 [1951]. *The Origins of Totalitarianism.* New York.

Armstrong, R.H. 1999. The archaeology of Freud's archaeology: recent work in the history of psychoanalysis. *International Review of Modernism* 3/1: 16–20.

Armstrong, R.H. 2005a. *A Compulsion for Antiquity: Freud and the Ancient World.* Ithaca.

Armstrong, R.H. 2005b. Contrapuntal affiliations: Edward Said and Freud's *Moses. American Imago* 62/2: 235–57.

Armstrong, R.H. 2005c. Translating ancient epic. In Foley (ed.), 2005: 174–95.

Armstrong, R.H. 2006. Theory and theatricality: classical drama and the early formation of psychoanalysis. *Classical and Modern Literature* 26/1: 79–109.

Armstrong, R.H. and C. Hackney-Dué (eds). 2007. *Homerizon.* Columbus, Ohio.

Arnold, A. 1877. *Through Persia by Caravan,* New York.

Arnold, M. 1972. *Selected Criticism.* Ed. C. Ricks. New York.

Arnold, M. 1857. *Poems,* 3rd edn. London.

Arrowsmith, W. 1961. The lively conventions of translations. In Arrowsmith and Shattuck (eds), 1961: 122–40.

Arrowsmith, W. 1963. Nietzsche on classics and classicists. *Arion* 2: 5–18.

Arrowsmith, W. and R. Shattuck (eds). 1961. *The Craft and Context of Translation: A Symposium.* Austin, Tex.

Assmann, J. 1997. *Moses the Egyptian: The Memory of Egypt in Western Monotheism.* Cambridge, Mass.

Astbury, B. 1979. *The Space/Die Ruimte/Indawo.* Cape Town.

Astrié, C. 2003. BR.#04. Societàs Raffaello Sanzio, Tragedia Endogonidia di Romeo Castellucci. *Idioma Clima Crono IV, Quaderni del Ciclo della Tragedia Endogonidia,* 14–15, Cesena.

Atkinson, D., D. Cosgrove and A. Notaro. 1999. Empire in modern Rome: shaping and remembering an imperial city, 1870–1911. In Driver and Gilbert (eds), 1999: 40–63.

Atlas, C. 1924. *Secrets of Muscular Power and Beauty.* New York.

Attardo, S. 1994. *Linguistic Theories of Humour.* Berlin.

Attardo, S. 2001. *Humorous Texts: A Semantic and Pragmatic Analysis.* Berlin.

Attardo, S. 2002. Translation and humour: an approach based on the General Theory of Verbal Humour (GTVH). *The Translator* 8/2: 173–94.

Attardo, S. and V. Raskin. 1991. Script theory revisited: joke similarity and joke representation model. *Humor* 4: 293–347.

Atwood, M. 2005. *The Penelopiad.* Edinburgh, New York and Melbourne.

Aunger, R. (ed.). 2001. *Darwinizing Culture: The Status of Memetics as a Science.* Oxford and New York.

Auslander, P. 1997. *From Acting to Performance: Essays in Modernism and Postmodernism.* London.

Austin, R.G. 1977. *P. Vergili Maronis Aeneidos Liber Sextus.* Oxford.

Avery, E.L., C.B. Hogan, A.H. Scouten, G.W. Stone and W. Van Lennep (eds). 1965–8. *The London Stage, 1660–1800: A Calendar of Plays and Afterpieces.* Carbondale, Ill.

Aycock, W. and T. Klein (eds). 1980. *Classical Mythology in Twentieth Century Thought and Literature.* Lubbock, Tex.

Azim, F. 2001. Post-colonial theory. In Knellwolf and Norris (eds), 2001: 237–47.

Bacon, H. 2001. Frost and the ancient muses. In Faggen (ed.), 2001: 75–100.

Baer, W. (ed.). 1996. *Conversations with Derek Walcott.* Kackson, Miss.

Bailey, C. (ed.). 1923. *The Legacy of Rome.* Oxford.

Bailey, S.D. 1990. *Four Arab–Israeli Wars and the Peace Process.* Basingstoke and London.

Bain, D. 1977. Euripides' *Electra* 518–44. *Bulletin of the Institute of Classical Studies* 24: 104–16.

Bain, K. and T. Hauptfleisch. 2001. Playing the changes: thoughts on the restructuring of the theatrical system and the arts industry in South Africa after apartheid. *South African Theatre Journal* 15: 8–24.

Baker, R.S. 1928–39. *Woodrow Wilson: Life and Letters.* 8 vols. London.

Baker, V. 1876. *Clouds in the East: Travels and Adventures on the Perso-Turkoman Frontier.* London.

Bakhtin, M. 1981. *The Dialogic Imagination: Four Essays.* Ed. M. Holquist, tr. C. Emerson and M. Holquist. Austin, Tex.

Balensiefen, L. 2005. Polyphem-Grotten und Skylla-Gewässer: Schauplätze der *Odyssee* in römischen Villen. In Luther (ed.), 2005: 9–31.

Balme, C.B. 1999. *Decolonizing the Stage: Theatrical Syncretism and Post-colonial Drama.* Oxford.

Barchiesi, A. 1984. *La traccia del modello: effetti omerici nella narrazione virgiliana.* Pisa.

Barchiesi, A. 2002. Review of J. Rüpke, *Von Göttern und Menschen erzählen. Formkonstanzen und Funktionswandel vormoderner Epik.* Stuttgart: 2001. *Bryn Mawr Classical Review* 26 June 2006.

Barchiesi, M. 1962. *Nevio epico: storia, interpretazione, edizione critica dei frammenti del primo epos latino.* Padua.

Barfoot, C.C. and van der Doel, R. (eds). 1995. *Ritual Remembering: History, Myth and Politics and Anglo-Irish Drama.* Amsterdam.

Barish, J. 1981. *The Antitheatrical Prejudice.* Berkeley.

Barker, A. and M. Warner (eds). 1992. *The Language of the Cave.* Edmonton, Alberta.

Barnes, M. 1986. *Augustus Hare.* London.

Barnes, T.D. 1996. Christians and the theater. In Slater (ed.), 1996: 161–80.

Barrault, J.-L. 1961. *The Theatre of Jean-Louis Barrault.* Tr. J. Chiari. London.

Barroero, L., A. Conti, A.M. Racheli and M. Serio. 1983. *Vai dei Fori Imperiali: la zona archeologica di Roma: urbanistica, beni artistici e politica culturale.* Rome.

Barsby, J. (ed.). 2002. *Greek and Roman Drama: Translation and Performance.* Tübingen.

Barthes, R. 1978. *Wilhelm von Gloeden interventi di Joseph Beuys, Michelangelo Pistoletto, Andy Warhol.* Naples.

Bassi, K. and P. Euben. 2003. Declassifying Hellenism. *Parallax* special issue 29/4.

Bassnett, S. 1991. *Translation Studies,* revd edn. London.

Bassnett, S. 2002. *Translation Studies,* 3rd edn. London and New York.

Bassnett, S. and A. Lefevere. (eds). 1990. *Translation, History and Culture.* London and New York.

Bassnett, S. and H. Trivedi (eds). 1999. *Post-colonial Translation: Theory and Practice.* London and New York.

Batstone, W.W. 2006. Provocation: the point of reception theory. In Martindale and Thomas (eds), 2006: 14–20.

Battezzato, L. (ed.). 2003. *Tradizione testuale e ricezione letteraria antica della tragedia greca.* Amsterdam.

Baugh, E. and C. Nepaulsingh. 2004. *Derek Walcott: Another Life.* Fully annotated, with a critical essay and comprehensive notes. London.

Bauman, T. and M.P. McClymons (eds). 1995. *Opera and the Enlightenment.* Cambridge.

Baumann, M. 1974. *Die Anakreonteen in englischen Übersetzungen: Ein Beitrag zur Rezeptionsgeschichte der anakreonteischen Sammlung.* Heidelberg.

Baxter, S. 2003. *Coalescent.* London.

Bayoumi, M. and A. Rubin. 2001. *The Edward Said Reader.* London.

Beacham, R., R. Bond and M. Ewans. 2002. Translation forum. In Barsby (ed.), 2002: 168–82.

Beard, M. 2000. *The Invention of Jane Harrison.* Cambridge, Mass.

Beard, M. 2004. Review of *Dionysus since 69: Greek Tragedy at the Dawn of the Third Millennium.* Oxford 2004. *Times Literary Supplement,* 15 October.

Beard, M. and J. Henderson. 1995. *Classics: A Very Short Introduction.* Oxford and New York.

Beaton, R. 1994. *An Introduction to Modern Greek Literature.* Oxford.

Bebbington, D.W. 1998. Gladstone and Grote. In Jagger (ed.), 1998: 157–76.

Bebbington, D.W. 2005. *The Mind of Gladstone: Religion, Homer, and Politics.* Oxford.

Bell, G. 1928 [1898]. *Persian Pictures.* Intro. E. Denison Ross. London. Originally published anonymously as *Safar Nameh: Persian Pictures – A Book of Travel,* 1898.

Belloc, H. 1931. *On Translation.* The Taylorian Lecture, 1931. Oxford.

Benamou, M. and C. Caramello (eds). 1977. *Performance in Postmodern Culture.* Milwaukee.

Benhabib, S.J. Butler, D. Cornell and N. Fraser (eds). 1995. *Feminist Contentions: A Philosophical Exchange.* London and New York.

Benjamin, S.G.W. 1887. *Persia and the Persians.* Boston.

Benjamin, W. 1969. *Illuminations.* Tr. H. Zohn. New York.

Benjamin, W. 1969. The work of art in the age of mechanical reproduction. In Benjamin (ed.), 1969: 217–51. Originally published in *Zeitschrift für Sozialforschung* 5/1: 40–68, 1936.

Benjamin, W. 1990. Ursprung des deutschen Trauerspiels (1928). In *Gesammelte Schriften* [*Collected Works*] 1: 1–238. Ed. by R. Tiedemann and H. Schweppenhaeuser. Frankfurt-am-Main.

Benveniste, É. 1973. *Indo-European Language and Society.* Tr. E. Palmer. London.

Ben-Zvi, L. (ed.). 1996. *Theater In Israel.* Ann Arbor.

Ben–Zvi, L. 2006. Staging the other Israel: the documentary theater of Nola Chilton. *The Drama Review* 50/3: 42–55.

Berenson, B. 1954. *Aesthetics and History.* New York.

Bergonzi, B. 1996. *Heroes' Twilight: A Study of the Literature of the Great War,* 3rd edn. Manchester.

Berkowitz, L. and T.F. Brunner (trs and eds). 1970. *Sophocles'* Oedipus Tyrannus: *a new translation, passages from ancient authors, religion and psychology: some studies. Criticism.* New York.

Berlinerblau, J. 1999. *Heresy in the University: The Black Athena Controversy and the Responsibilities of American Intellectuals.* New Brunswick.

Berman, G. 1994. F. Holland Day and his 'classical' models: summer camp. *History of Photography* 18: 348–67.

Bernal, M. 1987. On the transmission of the alphabet to the Aegean before 1400 B.C. *BASOR* [*Bulletin of the American Schools of Oriental Research*] 267: 1–19. Tr. into Arabic, rev. and intro. by A. Etman, 1997. Cairo.

Bernal, M. 1997. *Black Athena. The Afro-Asiatic Roots of Classical Civilization, I: The Fabrication of Ancient Greece 1785–1985.* Chapel Hill, N.C. Arabic tr. A. Etman 1997. Cairo.

Bernstein, R. 1998. *Freud and the Legacy of Moses.* Cambridge.

Bery, A. and P. Murray. 2000. *Comparing Postcolonial Literatures: Dislocations.* London and New York.

Besserman, L. (ed.). 1996. *The Challenge of Periodization: Old Paradigms and New Perspectives.* New York.

Bhabha, H. 1993. *The Location of Culture.* London.

Bieber, M. 1930. Maske. *Realencyclopadie der Altertumswissenschaft* 14/2: cols 2070–2120. Stuttgart.

Bierl, A. 1996. *Die Orestie des Aischylos auf der modernen Bühne: Theoretische Konzeptionen und ihre szenische Realisierung.* Stuttgart.

Bierl, A. 2004. *L'Orestea di Eschilo sulla scena moderna. Concezione teoriche e realizzazioni sceniche.* Rome.

Biet, C. 1994. *Oedipe en monarchie: tragédie et théorie juridique à l'âge classique.* Klincksieck.

Bigwood, J.M. 1978. Ctesias as historian of the Persian wars. *Phoenix* 32: 19–41.

Binge, L.W.B. 1969. *Ontwikkeling van die Afrikaanse Toneel 1832–1950.* Pretoria.

Blanshard, A. 2000. Hellenic fantasies: aesthetics and desire in John Addington Symonds' *A Problem in Greek Ethics. Dialogos* 7: 97–121.

Bleeker, M. 2002. *The Locus of Looking: Dissecting Visuality in the Theatre.* Amsterdam.

Bleeker, M., S. De Belder, A. Van Hoof and K. Vanhoutte. 2002. Interview with Romeo Castellucci. In Bleeker et al. (eds), 2002: 217–31.

Bleeker, M., S. De Belder, K. Debo, L. Van den Dries and K. Vanhoutte. 2002. *Bodycheck: Relocating the Body in Contemporary Performing Art.* Amsterdam and New York.

Bleys, R. 1996. *The Geography of Perversion: Male-to-Male Sexual Behaviour Outside the West and the Ethnographic Imagination, 1750–1918.* London.

Blondell, R. (tr.). 1999. *Euripides'* Alcestis. New York.

Blondell, R. 2002. *The Play of Character in Plato's Dialogues.* Cambridge.

Bloomer, W.M. 2005a. Marble Latin: encounters with the timeless language. In Bloomer (ed.), 2005b: 207–16.

Bloomer, W.M. (ed.). 2005b. *The Contest of Language.* Notre Dame, Ind.

Bloomfield, R. 1827. *The Poems.* 3 vols. London.

Boas, F.S. 1966 [1914]. *University Drama in the Tudor Age.* Oxford.

Boedeker, D. and K.A. Raaflaub (eds). 1998. *Democracy, Empire, and the Arts in Fifth-century Athens.* Cambridge, Mass.

Bollack, J. 1990. *L'Œdipe roi de Sophocle: Le texte et ses interprétations.* Villeneuve d'Ascq, France.

Bollack, J. and P. Judet de la Combe (eds). 1981. *L'Agamemnon d'Eschyle: Le texte et ses interprétations.* Lille and Paris.

Bond, B. 2002. *The Unquiet Western Front: Britain's Role in Literature and History.* Cambridge.

Bondanella, P. (ed.). 1978. *Federico Fellini: Essays in Criticism.* New York and Oxford.

Bondanella, P. 1987. *The Eternal City: Roman Images in the Modern World.* Chapel Hill, N.C.

Bondanella, P. 1992. *The Cinema of Federico Fellini.* Princeton.

Boon, R. and J. Plastow (eds). 1998. *Theatre Matters: Performance and Culture on the World Stage.* Cambridge.

Borges, J.L. 1964. Averroes' search. Tr. J.E. Irby. In *Labyrinths: Selected Stories and Other Writings.* Ed. D.A. Yates and J.E. Irby. New York: 148–55.

Borges, J.L. 1985. La Busca de Averroes. *Prosa Completa*. Vol. 2. *El-aleph*. Barcelona.

Borthwick, E.K. 1979. Aristophanes and Agathon: a contrast in hair styles. *Eranos* 77: 166–7.

Børtnes, J. and T. Hägg (eds). 2006. *Gregory of Nazianzus: Images and Reflections*. Copenhagen.

Bosman, F.C.L. 1980. *Drama en toneel in Suid-Afrika, II: 1856–1912*. Pretoria.

Boswell, J. 1955. *Boswell on the Grand Tour: Italy, Corsica and France, 1765–6*. Ed. F. Brady and F. Pottle. New York.

Bosworth, A.B. and E.J. Baynham (eds). 2000. *Alexander the Great in Fact and Fiction*. Oxford.

Bosworth, C.E. 1993. The Hon. George Nathaniel Curzon's travels in Russian central Asia and Persia. *Iran* 31: 127–36.

Bosworth, C.E. 1995. E.G. Browne and his *A Year amongst the Persians*. *Iran* 33: 115–22.

Bothmer, D. von (ed.). 1987. *Papers on the Amasis Painter and his World*. Malibu.

Bourdieu, P. 1977 [1972]. *Outline of a Theory of Practice*. Tr. R. Nice. Cambridge.

Bourdieu, P. and Passeron, J.-C. 1973. Cultural reproduction and social reproduction. In Brown (ed.), 1973: 71–112.

Bovon, A. 1963. La représentation des guerriers perses et la notion de barbare dans la 1ère moitié de Ve siècle. *Bulletin de Correspondence Hellénique* 87: 579–602.

Boyer, P. 1990. *Tradition as Truth and Communication: A Cognitive Description of Traditional Discourse*. Cambridge.

Boyle, A.J. (ed.). 1993. *Roman Epic*. London.

Braden, G. 1978. *The Classics and English Renaissance Poetry*. New Haven and London.

Bradley, E. (Cuthbert Bede). 1853. *The Adventures of Mr Verdant Green*. London.

Bradley-Birt, F.B. 1909. *Through Persia: From the Gulf to the Caspian*. London.

Bradshaw, M. 1996. Mary Shelley's *Last Man*: the end of the world as we know it. In Stockwell and Littlewood (eds), 1996: 163–75.

Braidotti, R. 2004. *Nomadic Subjects. Embodiment and Sexual Difference in Contemporary Feminist Theory*. New York.

Brathwaite, E.K. 1967. *Odale's Choice*. London and Ibadan.

Brathwaite, E.K. 1984. *History of the Voice: The Development of Nation Language in Anglophone Caribbean Poetry*. London.

Bréchet, C. 1999. Le *De Audiendis Poetis* de Plutarque et le procès platonicien de la poésie. *Revue de Philologie* 73: 209–44.

Bremer, J.M. 1981. Greek Hymns. In Versnel (ed.), 1981: 193–215.

Briant, P. 1989. Histoire et idéologie. Les Grecs et la décadence Perse. In Mactoux and Geny (eds), 1989: 33–47. Tr. as History as ideology: the Greeks and 'Persian' decadence. In Harrison (ed.), 2002: 193–210.

Briant, P. 2002 [1996]. *From Cyrus to Alexander. A History of the Persian Empire*. Tr. P.T. Daniels. Winona Lake, Ind. Originally published 1996 as *Histoire de l'Empire Perse de Cyrus à Alexandre*. Paris.

Brice, C. 1998. *Monumentalité publique et politique à Rome: Le Vittoriano*. Rome.

Brickerton, I.J. and C.L. Klausner. 1998. *A Concise History of the Arab–Israeli Conflict*, 3rd edn. New Jersey.

Bridges, E. 2007. The guts and the glory: Pressfield's *Spartans at the Gates of Fire*. In Bridges et al. (eds), 2007: 405–21.

Bridges, E., E. Hall and P.J. Rhodes (eds). 2007. *Cultural Responses to the Persian Wars: Antiquity to the Third Millennium*. Oxford.

Briggs, W.W. and H.W. Benario (eds). 1986. *Basil Lanneau Gildersleeve: An American Classicist*. Baltimore.

Bright, D. (ed.). 1998. *The Passionate Camera: Photography and Bodies of Desire*. London.

Brilliant, R. 1984. *Visual Narratives: Storytelling in Etruscan and Roman Art*. Ithaca, N.J.

Brin, D. 1997. *The Postman*. London.

Brink, A.P. 1971. Die Hand vol vere. Unpublished playscript.

Brink, C.O. 1986. *English Classical Scholarship: Historical Reflections on Bentley, Porson and Housman*. Cambridge.

Broadie, S. and C. Rowe. 2002. *Aristotle's* Nicomachean Ethics. Tr. C. Rowe. Oxford.

Brooks, A. 1997. *Postfeminisms: Feminism, Cultural Theory and Cultural Forms*. London and New York.

Brosius, M. 1991. Two views on Persian history in eighteenth century England. In Sancisi-Weerdenburg and Drijvers (eds), 1990: 79–89.

Brosius, M. 1996. *Women in Ancient Persia (559–331 BC)*. Oxford.

Brower, R. 1959. *Alexander Pope: The Poetry of Allusion*. Oxford.

Brown, E. 1996. Politics of desire: Brechtian 'epic theater' in Hanoch Levin's postmodern satire. In Ben-Zvi (ed.), 1996: 173–200.

Brown, M. 1999. Passion and love: anacreontic song and the roots of romantic lyric. *English Literature and History (ELH)* 66: 373–404.

Brown, P. 1971. *The World of Late Antiquity: From Marcus Aurelius to Muhammad*. London.

Brown, P. 1989. *The Body and Society: Men, Women and Sexual Renunciation in Early Christianity*. London.

Brown, P. 1992. *Power and Persuasion in Late Antiquity: Towards a Christian Empire*. Madison.

Brown, R.K. (ed.). 1973. *Knowledge, Education and Cultural Change*. London.

Browne, E.G. 1926 [1893]. *A Year amongst the Persians. Impressions as to the Life, Character and Thought of the People of Persia. Received during Twelve Months' Residence in that Country in the Years 1887–1888 by EGB. With a Memoir by Sir E. Denison Ross*. Cambridge.

Brunt, A. 1993. *Studies in Greek History and Thought*. Oxford.

Buckley, T. 1849. *The Tragedies of Sophocles*. London.

Budd, M.A. 1998. Every man a hero: sculpting the homoerotic in physical culture photography. In Bright (ed.), 1998: 41–57.

Budelmann, F. 2004. Greek tragedies in West African adaptations. *Proceedings of the Cambridge Philological Society* 50: 1–28. Repr. in Goff 2005: 118–46.

Budelmann, F. 2007. Trojan Women in Yorubaland: Femi Òsòfisan's *Women of Owu*. In Hardwick and Gillespie (eds), 2007.

Budelmann, F. and P. Michelakis (eds). 2001. *Homer, Tragedy and Beyond. Essays in Honour of P.E. Easterling*. London.

Buffière, F. 1956. *Les mythes d'Homère et la pensée grecque*. Paris.

Bulman, J.C. 1996. *Shakespeare, Theory and Performance*. London.

Burgess, J. 2001. *The Tradition of the Trojan War in Homer and the Epic Cycle*. Baltimore.

Burian, P. 1997. Translation yesterday and today. In Easterling (ed.), 1997: 271–4.

Burke, A. 2003. Interviews in classical performance research: 1 Journalistic interviews. In Hardwick (ed.), 1996–, www2.open.ac.uk/ClassicalStudies/GreekPlays/essays/burkeinterview.htm

Burke, A. and P. Innes. 2004. Interviews as a methodology for performance research: (2) academic interviews – an invitation for discussion. *The Reception of the Texts and Images of Ancient Greece in Late Twentieth-century Drama and Poetry in English*, www.2.open.ac.uk/ClassicalStudies/GreekPlays/essays/burkeacademic.htm, accessed 18 January 2007.

Burke, P. 1981. The classical tradition and popular culture in early modern Europe. In *Les intermédiaires culturels: actes du Colloque du Centre méridional d'histoire social, des mentalités et des cultures, 1978*: 237–44. Aix-en-Provence.

Burke, P. 2004. *What Is Cultural History?* Cambridge and Malden, Mass.

Burkert, W. 1985. *Greek Religion: Archaic and Classical.* Tr. J. Raffian. Oxford and Harvard.

Burkert, W. 1987. The making of Homer in the sixth century B.C.: rhapsodes versus Stesichoros. In von Bothmer (ed.), 1987: 43–62; repr. in Cairns (ed.), 2001: 117–26.

Burkert, W. 1992. *The Orientalizing Revolution: Near Eastern Influence on Greek Culture in the Early Archaic Age.* Tr. M.E. Pinder and W. Burkert, Cambridge, Mass.

Burkert, W., E. Matelli, L. Orelli and M.L.G. Marciano (eds). 1998. *Fragmentsammlungen philosophischer Texte der Antike = Le raccolte dei frammenti di filosofi antichi: Atti del seminario internazionale, Ascona, Centro Stefano Franscini 22–27 settembre 1996. Aporemata 3.* Göttingen.

Burkitt, K. 2007. Imperial reflections: the post-colonial verse-movel as post-epic. In Hardwick and Gillespie (eds), 2007.

Burnyeat, M. 1997. First words: a valedictory lecture. *Proceedings of the Cambridge Philological Society* 43: 1–19.

Burris, S. 1990. *The Poetry of Resistance: Seamus Heaney and the Pastoral Tradition.* Athens.

Burrow, C. 1993. *Epic Romance: Homer to Milton.* Oxford.

Burrow, C. 1997. Virgil in English translation. In Martindale (ed.), 1997: 21–37.

Bushnell, R. 2005. *A Companion to Tragedy.* Oxford.

Butler, G. 1990. *Demea.* Cape Town.

Butler, J. 1993. *Bodies That Matter: On the Discursive Limits of Sex.* London and New York.

Butler, J. 1995. Contingent foundations. In Benhabib et al. (eds), 1995: 35–58.

Buxton, R. 2004. *Robert Frost and Northern Irish Poetry.* Oxford.

Buzard, J. 1993. *The Beaten Track: European Tourism, Literature and the Ways to Culture, 1800–1918.* Oxford.

Cairns, D. (ed.). 2001. *Oxford Readings in Homer's* Iliad. Oxford.

Calame, C. 1986. Facing otherness: the tragic mask in ancient Greece. *History of Religions* 26: 125–42.

Calame, C. and R. Chartier (eds). 2004. *Identités d'auteur dans l'Antiquité et la tradition européenne.* Grenoble.

Calder, W.M. III and A. Demandt (eds). 1990. *Eduard Meyer: Leben und Leistung eines Universalhistorikers.* Leiden.

Callen, A. 2003. Doubles and desire: anatomies of masculinity in the later nineteenth century. *Art History* 26: 669–99.

Callow, S. 1985. *Being an Actor.* Harmondsworth.

Cameron, A. 1991. *Christianity and the Rhetoric of Empire: The Development of Christian Discourse.* Berkeley.

Campbell, D.A. 1988. *Greek lyric II.* Cambridge, Mass.

Campbell, J. 1968 [1948]. *The Hero with a Thousand Faces,* 2nd edn. Princeton.

Cannon, G. 1990. *The Life and Mind of Oriental Jones: Sir William Jones, the Father of Modern Linguistics.* Cambridge.

Cardini, R. and M. Regoliosi (eds). 1998. *Che cos'è il classicismo?* Rome.

Carlson, M. 2004. Oedipus, a history of rewritings: Egyptian Oedipuses – comedies or tragedies. In Decreus and Kolk (eds), 2004: 368–75.

Carlson, M. (ed.). 2005. *The Arab Oedipus: Four Plays.* New York.

Carne-Ross, D.S. 1968. A mistaken ambition of exactness. *Delos* 2: 171–97.

Carne-Ross, D.S. 1989. Jocasta's divine head: English with a foreign accent. *Arion,* 3rd series, 1: 106–41.

Carpenter, T. 1989. *The Musical Language of* Elektra, in *Richard Strauss*: Elektra. Ed. D. Puffett. Cambridge Opera Handbooks. Cambridge.

Cartledge, P.A. 1997. 'Deep plays': theatre as process in Greek civic life. In Easterling (ed.), 1997: 3–35.

Cartledge, P.A. 1999. Democratic politics ancient and modern: from Cleisthenes to Mary Robinson. *Hermathena* 166: 5–29.

Cartledge, P.A. 2006. Democracy, origins of: contribution to a debate. In Raaflaub and Wallace (eds), 2006: 155–69.

Caruth, C. 1991. Unclaimed experience: trauma and the possibility of history. *Yale French Studies* 79: 181–92.

Castellucci, C. and R. 1992. *Il teatro della Societas Raffaello Sanzio: Dal teatro iconoclasta alla super-icona*. Milan.

Castellucci, C. and R. 2001. *Les pélérins de la matière: Théorie et praxis du théâtre. Ecrits de la Socìetas Raffaello Sanzio*. Besançon.

Castellucci, R. 1997a. Cacophony for a staging: Giulio Cesare. *Programme Notes*: 2–12.

Castellucci, R. 1997b. The *Oresteia* through the looking-glass. *Theaterschrift* 11: 190–9.

Castellucci, R., C. Guidi and C. Castellucci. 2001. *Epopea della polvere. Il teatro della Socìetas Raffaello Sanzio 1992–1999. Amleto, Masoch, Orestea, Guilio Cesare, Genesi*. Milan.

Catrein, C. 1999. Review of Sütterlin 1996 and Wyke 1997. *Classical Review* 49/1: 244–6.

Césaire, A. 1955. *Discours sur le Colonialisme*. Paris. Tr. J Pinkham. Repr. 1972. New York.

Chapman, D.L. 1994. *Sandow the Magnificent: Eugen Sandow and the Beginnings of Bodybuilding*. Urbana, Ill.

Chapman, G. (ed.). 1967. *Chapman's Homer*, 2nd edn. 2 vols. Princeton.

Charalabopoulos, N. 2001. The stagecraft of Plato: the Platonic dialogue as a meta-theatrical prose drama. Unpublished PhD thesis, University of Cambridge.

Chard, C. 1996. Introduction. In Chard and Langdon (eds), 1996: 1–29.

Chard, C. and H. Langdon. 1996. *Transports: Travel, Pleasure and Imaginative Geography*. New Haven.

Chasapē Christodoulou, E. 2002. *Ancient Greek Myth in Modern Greek Drama. From the Era of the Cretan Theatre until the End of the Twentieth Century* [in Greek]. 2 vols. Thessaloniki.

Chatzepantazes, Th. 2002. *From the Nile to the Danube: The Chronicle of the Development of the Greek Professional Theatre, within the Broader Framework of the Eastern Mediterranean, from the Foundation of the Independent State to the Asia Minor Catastrophe* [in Greek]. Herakleio, Crete.

Chesterman, A. (ed.). 1989. *Readings in Translation Theory*. Helsinki.

Chomsky, N. 1968. *Language and Mind*. New York.

Christopher, J. 1984. *The Tripods Trilogy*. Harmondsworth.

Chuvin, P. 1990. *A Chronicle of the Last Pagans*. Cambridge Mass.

Citroni, M. 1998. Percezioni di classicità nella letteratura latina. In Cardini and Regoliosi (eds), 1998: 1–34.

Citroni, M. 2006. The concept of the classical and the canons of model authors in Roman literature. Tr. R.A. Packham. In Porter (ed.), 2006: 204–34.

Clarke, A. 2003. *Growing Up Stupid Under the Union Jack*. Kingston. Originally published Toronto 1980.

Clarke, M.J., B.G.F. Currie and R.O.A.M. Lyne (eds). 2006. *Epic Interactions: Perspectives on Homer, Virgil and the Epic Tradition*. Oxford.

Clarke, M.L. 1945. *Greek Studies in England 1700–1830*. Cambridge.

Clarke, W.G. and William A.W. (eds). 1952. *Hamlet, The Plays and Sonnets of William Shakespeare*, II, *Great Books of the Western World*, Chicago, London and Toronto.

Classe, O. (ed.). 2000. *Encyclopedia of Literary Translation into English*. London and Chicago.

Clayton, B. 2004. *A Penelopean Poetics: Reweaving the Feminine in Homer's* Odyssey, Lanham, Boulder, New York, Toronto and Oxford.

Cohen, B. (ed.). 2000. *Not the Classical Ideal: Athens and the Construction of the Other in Greek Art and Drama.* Leiden.

Coldiron, M. 2002. Masks in the ancient and modern theatre. *New Theatre Quarterly* 18: 393–4.

Coleman, K. 2004. The pedant goes to Hollywood: the role of the academic consultant. In Winkler (ed.), 2004: 45–52.

Collins, E.T. 1896. *In the Kingdom of the Shah: The Journey of a Medical Man through Persia.* London.

Collins, J.C. 1891. *Illustrations of Tennyson.* London.

Conley, C.H. 1927. *The First English Translators of the Classics.* New Haven, Conn.

Connolly, J. 2001. Problems of the past in imperial Greek education. In Too (ed.), 2001: 339–72.

Conradie, P.J. 1996. Debates surrounding an approach to African tragedy. *South African Theatre Journal* 10/1: 25–34.

Conradie, P.J. 1999. Die resepsie van enkele Afrikaanse opvoerings van Griekse tragedies. *Akroterion* 44: 14–23.

Constantinidis, S.E. 1987. Classical Greek drama in modern Greece: mission and money. *Journal of Modern Greek Studies* 5/1: 15–32.

Cooke, A.B. and Vincent, J.R. 1974. *The Governing Passion.* Brighton.

Corrigan, R. 1958–60. Character as destiny in Hofmannsthal's *Electra. Modern Drama* 1–2.

Corsi, M. 1939. *Il teatro all'aperto in Italia.* Milan.

Cribiore, R. 2001. *Gymnastics of the Mind: Greek Education in Hellenistic and Roman Egypt.* Princeton.

Cribiore, R. 2007. *The School of Libanius in Late Antique Antioch.* Princeton.

Crisp, R. 2002. *Aristotle,* Nicomachean Ethics. Cambridge.

Crisp, R. and M. Slote (eds). 1997. *Virtue Ethics: Oxford Readings in Philosophy.* Oxford.

Crombez, T. 2005. The stain and deficiency of tragedy. *Janus* 19: 93–100.

Cronin, M. 1996. *Translating Ireland: Translation. Languages. Cultures.* Cork.

Cronin, R., A. Chapman and A.H. Harrison (eds). 2002. *A Companion to Victorian Poetry.* Oxford.

Cropp, M., K. Lee and D. Sansone (eds). 1999/2000. *Euripides and Tragic Theatre in the Late Fifth Century. Illinois Classical Studies* 24–5.

Crow, B. with C. Banfield. 1996. *An Introduction to Post-colonial Theatre.* Cambridge.

Cudjoe, S. (ed.). 1993. *Eric E. Williams Speaks: Essays on Colonialism and Independence.* Wellesley.

Cudjoe, S. 1997. Eric Williams and the politics of language. *Callaloo* 20/4: 753–63.

Cumming, J.E. 1995. Gluck's *Iphigeneia* operas: sources and strategies. In Bauman and McClymons (eds), 1995: ch. 11.

Curzon, G. 1892. *Persia and the Persian Question.* London and New York.

Cyrino, M. 2005. *Big Screen Rome.* Malden and Oxford.

Dagli scavi al museo: come da ritrovamenti archeologici si construisce il museo. 1984. Venice.

Daif, S. 2003. *Studies in Contemporary Arab Poetry,* 10th edn. Dar El Maaref.

Dain, A. and P. Mazon. 1958. *Sophocle, 2.* Paris.

Dakin Quinn, R. 1997. An open letter to institutional mothers. In Looser and Kaplan (eds), 1997: 174–82.

Dalai Lama. 1989. Nobel Peace Prize lecture of the 14th Dalai Lama, 11 December 1989. Repr. in *Ocean of Wisdom. Guidelines for Living,* 1990. San Francisco.

Dalla mostra al museo: dalla mostra archeologica del 1911 al Museo della civiltà romana. 1983. Venice.

Dalzell, A., C. Fantazzi and R.J. Schoeck (eds). 1991. *Acta conventus neo-latini Torontonensis: Proceedings of the Seventh International Congress of Neo-Latin Studies.* Binghamton, N.Y.

Dash, J.M. 1998. *The Other America: Caribbean Literature in a New World Context.* Charlottesville and London.

Davidson, J., F. Muecke and P. Wilson (eds). 2006. *Greek Drama III.* London.

Davie, J. 1996. *Euripides'* Alcestis. London.

Davies, J.K. 2002. Greek history: a discipline in transformation. In Wiseman (ed.), 2002: 25–46.

Davis, G. 1997a. *Aimé Césaire.* Cambridge.

Davis, G. (ed.). 1997b. *The Poetics of Derek Walcott: Intertextual Perspectives. South Atlantic Quarterly* special issue 96/2. Durham, N.C.

Davis, G. 1997c. The disavowal of epic in Derek Walcott's *Omeros. South Atlantic Quarterly* 96/2: 321–53.

Davis, G. 2003. *Ut pictura poesis*: a testament. *Agenda* special issue on Derek Walcott, 39: 198–9.

Davis, G. 2007. 'Homecomings without Home': representations of postcolonial *nostos* (homecoming) in the lyric of Aimé Césaire and Derek Walcott. In Graziosi and Greenwood (eds), 2007.

Davis, M.D. 1991. *The Male Nude in Contemporary Photography.* Philadelphia.

Day, J. and J.L. Kingsley. 1829. Original papers in relation to a course of liberal education. *American Journal of Sciences and Arts* 15: 297–351.

De Camp, L.S. 1979. *Lest Darkness Fall.* London.

De Herdt, K. 2003. 'Je crains que vous ne me trouviez trop moderne pour un Grec'. Over Griekse vertalingen van Oudgriekse teksten, ca. 1860–1910. 2 vols. Unpublished Ph.D. dissertation, University of Gent, Belgium.

De Ste. Croix, G.E.M. 1981. *The Class Struggle in the Ancient Greek world: From the Archaic Age to the Arab Conquests.* London.

Deane, S. (ed.). 1991. *The Field Day Anthology of Irish Writing.* Derry.

Decreus, F. 2007. The same kind of smile? About the use and abuse of theory in defining the relations between Classics and post-colonialism. In Hardwick and Gillespie (eds), 2007.

Decreus, F. and M. Kolk (eds). 2004. Rereading Classics in east and west: post-colonial perspectives on the tragic. *Documenta* 22/4. Gent.

Del Guidice, L. and N. Van Deusen (eds). 2005. *Performing Ecstasies: Music, Dance, and Ritual in the Mediterranean.* Ottawa.

Deleuze, G. and F. Guattari. 1980. *Mille plateaux. Capitalisme et schizophrénie.* Paris.

Deleuze, G. and F. Guattari. 1983. *Anti-Oedipus: Capitalism and Schizophrenia.* Tr. R. Hurley, M. Seem and H.R. Lane. Minneapolis.

Delorme, C. 1970. Narcissisme et éducation dans l'œuvre romanesque d'André Gide. *Revue des lettres modernes*, nos 223–7 = *André Gide/Études gidiennes* 1: 13–121.

Denard, H. (ed.). Ongoing. *Didaskalia*, www.didaskalia.net.

Denham, Sir J. 1969. *Poetical Works.* Ed. T.H. Banks, 2nd edn. Hamden, Conn.

Depew, M. and D. Obbink (eds). 2000. *Matrices of Genre: Authors, Canons and Society.* Cambridge, Mass., and London.

Derrida, J. 1995. *Archive Fever: A Freudian Impression.* Tr. E. Prenowitz. Chicago.

Dickie, J. 1994. La Macchina da Scrivere: the Victor Emmanuel monument in Rome and Italian nationalism. *The Italianist* 14: 261–85.

Dickinson, P. 1970. *Aristophanes Plays: 1.* London and New York.

DNB. 1908–9. *Dictionary of National Biography*, 2nd edn, 22 vols. London.

Diggle, J. (ed.). 1981. *Euripides' Iphigeneia he en Taurois* in *Euripidis Fabulae* II, Oxford Classical Texts.

Dilks, D. 1977. Baldwin and Chamberlain. In Gash (ed.), 1977: 271–404.

Dillon, J. and S. Wilmer (eds). 2005. *Rebel Women*. Dublin.

Dindorf, W. (ed.). 1855 *Scholia Graeca in Homeri Odysseam*. Oxford.

Djisenu, J. 2007. Cross-cultural bonds between ancient Greece and Africa: implications for contemporary staging practices. In Hardwick and Gillespie (eds), 2007.

Doherty, L. 1995. *Siren Songs: Gender, Audiences and Narrative in the* Odyssey. Ann Arbor.

Doherty, L. 2001. *Gender and the Interpretation of Classical Myth*. London.

Dominik, W.J. 2007. Writing, power and politics in classically derived Afrikaans drama. In Hilton and Gosling (eds), 2007: 93–117.

Donadoni, S.F. 1986. Gli Egiziani e le lingue degli altri. In Donadoni, *Cultura dell' antico Egitto*: 193–206. Rome.

Donnell, A. and S.L. Welsh. (eds). 1996. *The Routledge Reader in Caribbean Literature*. London.

Dougherty, C. 2005. *Prometheus*. New York.

Dover, K.J. 1987. The speakable and the unspeakable. In Dover, *Greek and the Greeks: Collected Papers,* 1: 176–81. Oxford. Rpr. (with one revision) from *Essays in Criticism* 30 (1980).

Dowling, L. 1994. *Hellenism and Homosexuality in Victorian Oxford*. Ithaca and New York.

Drachmann, A.B. (ed.). 1903–27. *Scholia vetera in Pindari carmina*. Leipzig. Repr. Stuttgart 1997.

Driver, F. and D. Gilbert (eds). 1999. *Imperial Cities: Landscape, Display and Identity*. Manchester.

Droysen, J.G. 1836–43. *Geschichte des Hellenismus*. 2 vols. Hamburg.

Dryden, J. 1956–2000. *The Works of John Dryden*. Ed. H.T. Swedenberg et al. 20 vols. Berkeley, Los Angeles and London.

DuBois, P. 2003. *Slaves and Other Objects*. Chicago and London.

Duckworth, G.E. 1952. *The Nature of Roman Comedy: A Study in Popular Entertainment*. Princeton.

Duggan, G.C. 1921. *The Watchers on Gallipoli: A Poem*. Dublin.

Dutton, K.R. 1995. *The Perfectible Body: The Western Ideal of Male Physical Development*. New York.

Eagleton, T. 2003. *Figures of Dissent: Critical Essays on Fish, Spivak, Žižek and Others*. London: Verso.

Easterling, P.E. 1993. The end of an era? Tragedy in the early fourth century. In Sommerstein et al. (eds), 1993: 559–69.

Easterling, P.E. 1994. Euripides outside Athens: a speculative note. *Illinois Classical Studies* 19: 73–80.

Easterling, P.E. 1996. Canon. *The Oxford Classical Dictionary*, 3rd edn. Oxford and New York: 286.

Easterling, P.E. (ed.). 1997a. *The Cambridge Companion to Greek Tragedy*. Cambridge.

Easterling, P.E. 1997b. From repertoire to canon. In Easterling (ed.), 1997a: 211–27.

Easterling, P.E. 2002. A taste for the classics. In Wiseman (ed.), 2002: 21–37.

Easterling, P.E. 2005. *Agamemnon* for the Ancients. In Macintosh et al. (eds), 2005: 23–36.

Easterling, P.E. and E. Hall (eds). 2002. *Greek and Roman Actors: Aspects of an Ancient Profession*. Cambridge.

Eastwick, E. 1864. *Three Years' Residence in Persia*. London.

Edmunds, L. and R.W. Wallace (eds). 1997. *Poet, Public and Performance in Ancient Greece*. Baltimore and London.

Edwards, C. (ed.). 1999. *Roman Presences: Receptions of Rome in European Culture, 1789–1945.* Cambridge.

Edwards, C. 1996. *Textual Approaches to the City.* Cambridge.

Edwards, C. 1997. Unspeakable professions: public performance and prostitution in ancient Rome. In Hallett and Skinner (eds), 1997: 66–95.

El Kafoury, S.A. 2004. Egyptian literature in Classics: a bibliometric study (in Arabic). MA thesis, Cairo University. English abstract in *Annual of Egyptian Society of Greek and Roman Studies* (AESGRS) 2004, 5: 211–14.

Eliades, Ph. 1996. *Kotopoule: Biographical Corpus* [in Greek]. Athens.

Eliot, T.S. 1948. Introduction (1928). In Eliot (ed.), *Ezra Pound: Selected Poems.* London: 7–21.

Elley, D. 1984. *The Epic Film: Myth and History.* London.

Elsner, J. and J.-P. Rubiés (eds). 1999. *Voyages and Visions: Towards a Cultural History of Travel.* London.

Emigh, J. 1996. *Masked Performance: The Play of Self and Other in Ritual and Theatre.* Philadelphia.

Enciclopedia dello spettacolo. 1954–62. 9 vols. Rome. Supplemented 1982 by vol. 10, *Cinema, Teatro, Balleto.* Rome.

Erbse, H. (ed.). 1969–88. *Scholia Graeca in Homeri Iliadem.* Berlin.

Erskine, A. 2001. *Troy between Greece and Rome: Local Tradition and Imperial Power.* Oxford.

Etman, A. 1974. The problem of Heracles' apotheosis in the *Trachiniae* of Sophocles and in *Hercules Oetaeus* of Seneca: a comparative study of the tragic and Stoic meaning of the myth. PhD thesis (in Greek). Athens.

Etman, A. 1979. Oedipus between his mythical origins and his national anxiety on the Egyptian stage. *Al Bayan* (Kuwait) February–May: 155–8.

Etman, A. 1982. Abdel-Wahab el-Bayati and his poetic fiery muses. *Al-Kuwait* 16: 21–5.

Etman, A. 1983a. The stealer and poems inspired *El Dawlw Mawrhi* 27 46

Etman, A. 1983b. Reflections on Greek mythology in El Sayab's poems. *Fusul* 3/4: 37–46.

Etman, A. 1985. The classical sources of Arabic theatre. XIIe Congrés International d'Archéologie Classique, Athens, 4–10 September 1983, *Practica Tomos* 1: 126–9.

Etman, A. 1990. *Cleopatra and Antony: A Study in the Art of Plutarch, Shakespeare and Ahmed Shawqy,* 2nd edn. Cairo.

Etman, A. 1993. *Les Sources Classiques du Théâtre de Tewfik El-Hakim: Etude Comparée,* 2nd edn. Cairo.

Etman, A. (ed.). 1995. Pioneers and a hundred years of Classics. *Classical Papers* 4. University of Cairo.

Etman, A. 1997–8. Greek into Latin through Arabic. *Journal of Oriental and African Studies* 9: 29–38.

Etman, A. 1998. Taha Hussein and the future of classical culture in Egypt and the Arab world. *Memorial Volume for Taha Hussein,* 687–770. Cairo.

Etman, A. 2000. The tragedy *Maïe* and its classical sources. *Turath El Masrah.* National Centre of Theatre, Music and Popular Arts, July: 5–80.

Etman, A. 2001a. The patriotism of Cleopatra between Munirah El Mahdyah and Ahmed Shawqi Turath El Masrah. *National Centre of Theatre, Music and Popular Arts* 2: 56–71.

Etman, A. 2001b. Gli Studi Classici e il loro influsso sulla Letteratura Creativa in Egitto e nel Mondo Arabo. *ACME* 54: 3–10. Milan.

Etman, A. 2002. The reception of ancient Greek drama in Egypt and the Arab world Sixth International Symposium on Ancient Greek Drama, September 2000. *Leukosia* 223–6.

Etman, A. 2003. Cleopatra VII as a literary myth. *Mythe et Modernité. Actes du Colloque International, Thessalonique 31 octobre–2 novembre 2002.* Edition du Laboratoire de Litterature Comparée.

Etman, A. 2004a. The Greek concept of tragedy in the Arab culture: how to deal with an Islamic Oedipus? In Decreus and Kolk (eds), 2004: 281–99.

Etman, A. 2004b. *The* Iliad *of Homer.* Cairo.

Etman, A. (ed.). 2006. *The* Iliad *Through Ages. The Proceedings of the Seminar (29 May–1 June 2004) on the Centenary of Soliman El Bostany's Translation and the Publication of a New Translation from the Greek Text into Arabic.* Supreme Council of Culture. Cairo.

Euangelika 1901–Oresteiaka 1903: Modernizing Pressures and Society's Acts of Resistance [in Greek]. 2005. Athens.

Euben, P.J., J.R. Wallach and J. Ober (eds). 1994. *Athenian Political Thought and the Reconstruction of American Democracy.* Ithaca, N.Y., and London.

Eustace, J.C. 1812. *A Classical Tour through Italy.* 4 vols. London.

Evans, R. 2007. Perspectives on post-colonialism in South Africa: the Voortrekker monument's classical heritage. In Hardwick and Gillespie (eds), 2007.

Ewans, M. 1982. *Wagner and Aeschylus: the* Ring *and the* Oresteia. London.

Ewans, M. (ed.). 2000. *Sophocles: Three Dramas of Old Age.* London.

Ewans, M. 2007. *Opera from the Greek: Studies in the Poetry of Appropriation.* Aldershot.

Ewbank, I.-S. 2005. Striking too short at Greeks: the transmission of *Agamemnon* to the English Renaissance stage. In Macintosh et al. (eds), 2005: 37–52.

Ezraty, I. and A. Solomon. 2001. Staging reconciliation: the Arab–Hebrew theatre of Jaffa makes a model. *Theater* 31/2: 35–43.

Faggen, R. (ed.). 2001. *The Cambridge Companion to Robert Frost.* Cambridge.

Fantuzzi, M. and Hunter, R. 2005. *Tradition and Innovation in Hellenistic Poetry.* Cambridge.

Farrell, J. 2004. Roman Homer. In Fowler (ed.), 2004: 254–71.

Favro, D. 1996. *The Urban Image of Augustan Rome.* Cambridge.

Felson Rubin, N. 1994. *Regarding Penelope: From Character to Poetics.* Princeton.

Ferrari, G. 1989. Plato and poetry. In Kennedy (ed.), 1989: 92–148.

Field, G.C. 1930. *Plato and His Contemporaries.* London.

Fine, R. 2003. Romare Bearden: the spaces between. In Fine et al. (eds), 2003: 92.

Fine, R. et al. 2003. *The Art of Romare Bearden.* Exhibition Catalogue. National Museum of Art. Washington.

Fischer, H. (ed.). 1884. *Georg Rudolf Weckherlins Gedichte.* Tübingen.

Fischer-Lichte, E., C. Horn and M. Warstat. 2001. *Verkörperung.* Tübingen and Basel.

Fisher, N.R.G. 1992. *Hybris: A Study in the Values of Honour and Shame in Ancient Greece.* Warminster.

Fitch, E. 1924. Pindar and Homer. *Classical Philology* 19: 57–65.

Flashar, H. 1991. *Inszenierung der Antike: Das griechische Drama auf der Bühne der Neuzeit, 1585–1990.* Munich.

Flashar, H. 2001. *Felix Mendelssohn–Bartholdy und die griechische Tragödie: Bühnenmusik im Kontext von Politik, Kultur und Bildung.* Leipzig.

Flashar, H. and S. Vogt (eds). 1995. *Altertumswissenschaft in den 20er Jahren.* Stuttgart.

Fleishman, M. 1990. Workshop theatre as oppositional form. *South African Theatre Journal* 4/1: 88–118.

Fleishman, M. 1994. Medea. Unpublished playscript. Cape Town.

Fleishman, M. 1997. Physical images in the South African theatre. *South African Theatre Journal,* 11/1–2: 199–214.

Flensted–Jensen, P. 2002. Something old, something new, something borrowed: the *Odyssey* and *O Brother Where Art Thou?*. *Classica et Mediaevalia* 53: 13–30.

Flower, M. 2000. Alexander the Great and panhellenism. In Bosworth and Baynham (eds), 2000: 96–135.

Foley, F. 2000. The comic body in Greek art and drama. In Cohen (ed.), 2000: 275–311.

Foley, H. 1988. Tragedy and politics in Aristophanes' *Acharnians*. *Journal of Hellenic Studies* 108: 33–47.

Foley, H. 1999. Modern performance and adaptation of Greek tragedy. *Transactions and Proceedings of the American Philological Association* 129: 1–12.

Foley, J.M. 1999. *Homer's Traditional Art*. Pennsylvania.

Foley, J.M. 2002. *How to Read an Oral Poem*. Urbana, Ill., and Chicago.

Foley, J.M. (ed.). 2005. *A Companion to Ancient Epic*. Oxford.

Foot, M.R.D. and Matthew, H.C.G. (eds). 1968–94. *The Gladstone Diaries*. 14 vols. Oxford.

Fornara, C.W. 1992. Studies in Ammianus II: Ammianus' knowledge and use of Greek and Roman literature. *Historia* 411: 420–38.

Fortin, E.L. 1981. *Dissidence et philosophie au Moyen Age: Dante et ses antécédents*. Montreal.

Forsyth, K. 1989. Hofmannsthal's *Elektra*: from Sophocles to Strauss. In Puffett (ed.), 1989: ch. 2.

Fotopoulos, D. 1986. *Endymatologia sto Elleniko Theatro*. Athens.

Fotopoulos, D. 1990. *Paramythia Peran tis Opseos*. Athens.

Fowler, G. 1841. *Three Years in Persia; with Travelling Adventures in Koordistan*. London.

Fowler, R. 1987. *The Nature of Early Greek Lyric: Three Preliminary Studies*. Toronto.

Fowler, R. (ed.). 2004. *The Cambridge Companion to Homer*. Cambridge.

France, P. (ed.). 2000. *The Oxford Guide to Literature in English Translation*. Oxford.

Fredericks, S.C. 1980. Greek mythology in modern science fiction. In Aycock and Klein (eds), 1980: 89–106. Lubbock, Tex.

Freud, S. 1953–74. *The Standard Edition of the Complete Psychological Works of Sigmund Freud*. General editor and tr. James Strachey. London.

Friel, B. 1981. *Translation*. In *Selected Plays*. London.

Friis Johansen, K. 1967. *The* Iliad *in Early Greek Art*. Copenhagen.

Fuchs, E. 1996. *The Death of Character: Perspectives on Theater after Modernism*. Bloomington and Indianapolis.

Fugard, A. 1993. *Township Plays*. Oxford.

Fugard, A. 1995. *The Island*. In Fugard, *The Township Plays*. Oxford: 193–227.

Fugard, A. 2002. *Antigone* in Africa. In McDonald and Walton (eds), 2002: 128–47.

Fuhrmann, M. 1959. Friedrich August Wolf zur 200. Wiederkehr seines Geburtstages am 15 February 1959. *Deutsche Vierteljahrschrift für Literaturwissenschaft und Geistesgeschichte* 33: 187–236.

Fulbrook, M. 2002. *Historical Theory*. London.

Furedi, F. 2004. *Where Have All the Intellectuals Gone? Confronting 21st Century Philistinism*. London and New York.

Fussell, P. 1983. *Class: A Guide Through the American Status System*. New York.

Fussell, P. 2000. *The Great War and Modern Memory*, 25th anniversary edn. Oxford.

Galinsky, K. (ed.). 2005. *The Cambridge Companion to the Age of Augustus*. Cambridge.

Galinsky, K. 2007. Film. In Kallendorf (ed.), 2007: 393–407.

Gallop, J. 1998. *Thinking Through the Body*, New York.

Gamwell, L. and Wells, R. (eds). 1989. *Sigmund Freud and Art: His Personal Collection of Antiquities*. London.

Garb, T. 1998. *Bodies of Modernity: Figure and Flesh in Fin-de-Siècle France*. London.

Garber, M. 2001. *Academic Instincts.* Princeton and Oxford.

Garland, R. 2004. *Surviving Greek Tragedy.* London.

Garnsey, P. 1996. *Ideas of Slavery from Aristotle to Augustine.* Cambridge.

Gash, N. 1977. *The Conservatives.* Ed. R.A. Butler. London.

Gay, P. 1985. *Freud for Historians.* Oxford and New York.

Genova, P.A. 1994. A crossroads of modernity: André Gide's *Le Traité du Narcisse. South Central Review* 11/3: 1–24.

Georgousopoulos, K. 1982–84. *Keys and Codes of the Theatre* [in Greek]: 1 *Ancient Drama*; 2 [Modern] *Greek Theatre.* Athens.

Georgousopoulos, K. 1993. Interpreting ancient drama in twentieth-century Greece [in Greek]. In Merkouris (ed.), 1993: 103–25.

Georgousopoulos, K. 2002. The revival of ancient Greek drama in the twentieth century: theories and stage practice [in Greek]. In *The Uses of Antiquity in Modern Greek Culture* [in Greek]: 41–9. Athens.

Georgousopoulos, K. 2005. The reception of the *Oresteia* of Thomas Oikonomou [in Greek]. In *Euangelika 1901–Oresteiaka 1903: Modernizing Pressures and Society's Acts of Resistance* [in Greek]: 221–8, Athens.

Gera, D.L. 1993. *Xenophon's* Cyropaedia: *Style, Genre and Literary Technique.* Oxford.

Ghazoul, F. 1994. The Greek component in the poetry and poetics of Muhammad Afifi literature. *Journal of Arabic Literature* 25: 136–51.

Ghazoul, F. 2002. Tracking the Graeco-Roman trail in the poetry of Nazik al Malaika Muqaranat. *Comparisons* 1: 19–28.

Gibbon, E. 1984. *Memoirs of My Life.* Ed. G. Bonnard. Harmondsworth.

Gibbs, J. 2007. Antigone and her African sisters: West African versions of a Greek original. In Hardwick and Gillespie (eds), 2007.

Gide, A. 1924. *Incidences.* Paris.

Gide, A. 1935. *Œuvres complètes,* vol. 9. Paris.

Gide, A. 1958. *Romans, Récits, et Soties, Œuvres Lyriques.* Bibliothèque de la Pléiade. Paris.

Gikandi, S. 1996. *Maps of Englishness: Writing Identity in the Culture of Colonialism.* New York.

Gilbert, H. and Tompkins, J. 1996. *Post-colonial Drama: Theory, Practice, Politics.* London and New York.

Giles, J. 1997. *The Crying Game.* London.

Gill, C. 1998. Altruism or reciprocity in Greek ethical philosophy. In Gill et al. (eds), 1998: 303–28.

Gill, C. 1999. *Plato:* The Symposium. Tr. with an introduction and notes. London.

Gill, C., N. Postlethwaite and R. Seaford (eds). 1998. *Reciprocity in Ancient Greece,* Oxford.

Gillespie, S. and D. Hopkins (eds). 2005. *The Oxford History of Literary Translation in English, 3, 1660–1790.* Oxford.

Gilliam, B. 1991. *Richard Strauss's* Elektra. Oxford.

Gilroy, P. 1993. *The Black Atlantic.* London and New York.

Giraldi, L.G. 1696. *Opera Omnia.* 2 vols. Leiden.

Gladstone, W.E. 1879 [1865]. *Gleanings of Past Years, 1843–79.* 7 vols. London.

Gladstone, W.E. 1857. *Oxford Essays.* London.

Gladstone, W.E. 1858. *Studies on Homer and the Homeric Age.* 3 vols. Oxford and London.

Gladstone, W.E. 1869. *Juventus Mundi: The Gods and Men of the Heroic Age.* London.

Gladstone, W.E. 1874. The shield of Achilles. *Contemporary Review* 23: 329–44.

Gladstone, W.E. 1879. The Olympian system versus the solar theory. *Nineteenth Century* 32: 746–68.

Gladstone, W.E. 1887. Universitas hominum: or, the unity of history. *North American Review*, 145: 589–602.

Gladstone, W.E. 1890. *Landmarks of Homeric Study*. London.

Gladstone, W.E. 1894. *The Odes of Horace Translated into English*. London.

Gladstone, W.E. 1971. *Midlothian Speeches, 1879*. Intro. M.R.D. Foot. Leicester.

Glicksohn, J.-M. 1984. Les Lumières, la Musique et la Grèce. In *L'Avant-Scène Opera* 62: 70–80.

Gliksohn, J.-M. 1985. *Iphigénie: de la Grèce antique à l'europe des lumières*. Paris.

Gluck, C.W. 1960. *Iphigénie en Tauride*. Edition Eulenberg 917. London.

Glytzoures, A. 2001. *The Stage Director's Art in Greece: The Emergence and the Establishment of the Art of the Stage Director in Modern Greek Theatre* [in Greek]. 2 vols. Athens.

Goethe, J.W. von. 1962. *Italian Journey*. Tr. W.H. Auden and E. Mayer. Harmondsworth.

Goff, B. (ed.). 2005. *Classics and Colonialism*. London.

Goff, B. 2007. Antigone's Boat: the colonial and the postcolonial in *Tegonni: an African Antigone* by Femi Òsòfisan. In Hardwick and Gillespie (eds), 2007.

Goff, B. and M. Simpson. 2007. *Crossroads in the Black Aegean: Oedipus, Antigone and Dramas of the African Diaspora*. Oxford.

Goldhill, S. 1986. *Reading Greek Tragedy*. Cambridge.

Goldhill, S. 1991. *The Poet's Voice*. Cambridge.

Goldhill, S. 1992. *Aeschylus: The Oresteia*. Cambridge.

Goldhill, S. 1990. The great Dionysia and civic ideology. In Winkler and Zeitlin (eds), 1990: 97–129.

Goldhill, S. (ed.). 2001. *Being Greek under Rome: Cultural Identity, the Second Sophistic, and the Development of Empire*. Cambridge.

Goldhill, S. 2002. *Who Needs Greek?: Contests in the Cultural History of Hellenism*. Cambridge.

Goldhill, S. 2006. Imperfect Aeschylus. *Times Literary Supplement* 24 May.

Goldhill, S. 2007. *Naked* and *O Brother, Where Art Thou?*: the politics and poetics of epic cinema. In Graziosi and Greenwood (eds), 2007.

Goldhill, S. and R. Osborne (eds). 1999. *Performance Culture and Athenian Democracy*. Cambridge.

Goldhill, S. and S. von Reden. 1999. Plato and the performance of dialogue. In Goldhill and Osborne (eds), 1999: 257–89.

Goldscheider, C. 2002. *Cultures in Conflict: The Arab–Israeli Conflict*. Westpoint, Conn., and London.

Gorak, J. 1991. *The Making of the Modern Canon*. London.

Gorak, J. (ed.). 2001. *Canon vs. Culture: Reflections on the Current Debate*. London and New York.

Gould, J. 1992. Plato and performance. In Barker and Warner (eds), 1992: 13–25.

Goulet, A. 1985. *Fiction et vie sociale dans l'œuvre d'André Gide*. Paris.

Gourgouris, S. 1996. *Dream Nation: Enlightenment, Colonization, and the Institution of Modern Greece*. Stanford.

Gower, B.S. and M.C. Stokes (eds). 1992. *Socratic Questions: New Essays on the Philosophy of Socrates and its Significance*. London and New York.

Grafton, A. 1997. *Commerce with the Classics: Ancient Books and Renaissance Readers*. Ann Arbor.

Grafton, A. and L. Jardine. 1986. *From Humanism to the Humanities: Education and the Liberal Arts in Fifteenth- and Sixteenth-century Europe*. London.

Grafton, A., G. Most and S. Settis (eds). 2007. *The Classical Tradition*. Cambridge, Mass.

Grammatas, Th. 2002. *Greek Theatre in the Twentieth Century: Cultural Models and Originality* [in Greek]. 2 vols. Athens.

Gramsci, A. 1988. *An Antonio Gramsci Reader: Selected Writings 1916–1935*. Ed. D. Forgacs. New York.

Graver, D. 1995. *The Aesthetics of Disturbance: Anti-Art in Avant-Garde Drama*. Ann Arbor.

Graziosi, B. 2001. Competition in wisdom. In Budelmann and Michelakis (eds), 2001: 57–74.

Graziosi, B. 2002. *Inventing Homer: The Early Reception of Epic*. Cambridge.

Graziosi, B. and E. Greenwood (eds). 2007. *Homer in the Twentieth Century: Between World Literature and the Western Canon*. Oxford.

Graziosi, B. and J. Haubold. 2005. *Homer: The Resonance of Epic*. London.

Green, P. 2004. Heroic hype, new style: Hollywood pitted against Homer. *Arion* 12/1: 171–87.

Green, R. 2002. Towards a reconstruction of performance style. In Easterling and Hall (eds), 2002: 93–126.

Green-Lewis, J. 1996. *Framing the Victorians: Photography and the Culture of Realism*. Ithaca, N.Y.

Greenwood, E. 2004. Classics and the Atlantic triangle: Caribbean readings of Greece and Rome via Africa. *Forum of Modern Language Studies*. 40/4: 365–76.

Greenwood, E. 2005. 'We speak Latin in Trinidad': uses of Classics in Caribbean literature. In Goff (ed.), 2005: 65–91.

Greenwood, E. 2007. Arriving backwards: the return of *The Odyssey* in the English-speaking Caribbean. In Hardwick and Gillespie (eds), 2007.

Gregorovius, F. 1911. *Roman Journals 1852–74*. Tr. A. Hamilton. London.

Gregory, J. (ed.). 2005. *A Companion to Greek Tragedy*. Oxford.

Grenfell, E.A.P. (Lady Desborough) 1916. *Pages from a Family Journal*. Eton.

Griffith, M. 1977. *The Authenticity of* Prometheus Bound. Cambridge.

Griffith, M. 1983. Personality in Hesiod. *Classical Antiquity* 2: 37–65.

Grimm, M. 1829–31. *Correspondance Littéraire*. Paris.

Grossman, D. 2003. *Death as a Way of Life: Israel Ten Years after Oslo*. New York.

Grote, G. 1846–56. *A History of Greece*. London.

Gruen, E.S. 1992. *Culture and National Identity in Republican Rome*. Ithaca.

Grundy, G.B. 1901. *The Great Persian War and its Preliminaries. A Study of the Evidence, Literary and Topographical*. London.

Gugelberger, G.M. 1991. Decolonizing the canon: considerations of third world literature. *New Literary History* 22: 505–24.

Guillory, J. 1993. *Cultural Capital: The Problem of Literary Canon Formation*. Chicago.

Guillory, J. 1995. Canon. In Lentricchia and McLaughlin (eds), 1995: 233–49.

Gurd, S.A. 2005. *Iphigenias at Aulis: Textual Multiplicity, Radical Philology*. Ithaca.

Gutas, D. 1998. *Greek Thought, Arabic Culture*. London.

Guthrie, T. 1965. *In Various Directions: A View of Theatre*. London.

Guymond de la Touche, C. 1771. *Iphigénie en Tauride, Tragédie*. Lyon.

Hadas, M. and J.H. McLean (trs). 1936. *Euripides' Alcestis*. New York.

Hadzsits, G.D. and D.M. Robinson. 1922. Editor's preface. In Showerman (ed.), 1922: ix–x.

Hainaux, R. (ed.). 1957. *World Theatre* 6/4: 277.

Hainsworth, B. (ed.). 1993. *The Iliad: A Commentary, 3: Books 9–12*. Cambridge.

Hall, E. 1989. *Inventing the Barbarian. Greek Self-Definition through Tragedy*. Oxford.

Hall, E. 1995a. Lawcourt dramas: the power of performance in Greek forensic oratory. *Bulletin of the Institute of Classical Studies* 40: 39–58.

Hall, E. 1995b. The ass with double vision: politicising an ancient Greek novel. In Margolies and Joannou (eds), 1995: 47–59.

Hall, E. 2002. The singing actors of antiquity. In Hall and Easterling (eds), 2002: 3–38.

Hall, E. 2004. Towards a theory of performance reception. *Arion* 12/1: 51–89.

Hall, E. 2007. Aeschylus' *Persians* via the Ottoman empire to Saddam Hussein. In Bridges et al. (eds), 2007: 167–99.

Hall, E. 2007a. The English-speaking Aristophanes. In Hall and Wrigley (eds), 2007.

Hall, E. Forthcoming. *Beyond the Wine-Dark Sea: A Cultural History of the* Odyssey. London.

Hall, E. 2008. Navigating the realms of gold: translation as access route to the Classics. In Lianeri and Zajko (eds), forthcoming. Oxford.

Hall, E. and P.E. Easterling (eds). 2002. *Greek and Roman Actors: Aspects of an Ancient Profession.* Cambridge.

Hall, E. and F. Macintosh. 2005. *Greek Tragedy and the British Theatre 1660–1914.* Oxford.

Hall, E. and A. Wrigley (eds). 2007. *Aristophanes in Performance 412 BCE–2005 CE.* Oxford.

Hall, E., F. Macintosh and O. Taplin (eds). 2000. *Medea in Performance, 1500–2000.* Oxford.

Hall, E., F. Macintosh and A. Wrigley (eds). 2004. *Dionysus Since 69: Greek Tragedy at the Dawn of the Third Millennium.* Oxford.

Hall, P. 2000. *Exposed by the Mask: Form and Language in Drama.* London.

Hall, S. 1990. Cultural identity and diaspora. In Rutherford (ed.), 1990: 222–37.

Hallett, J.P. and M. Skinner (eds). 1997. *Roman Sexualities.* Princeton.

Halliwell, S. 1992. Plato and the psychology of drama. In Zimmermann (ed.), 1992: 55–73.

Halliwell, S. 1993. The function and aesthetics of the Greek tragic mask. In Slater and Zimmermann (eds), 1993: 195–210.

Halliwell, S. 1997. *Aristophanes: A New Verse Translation. Birds, Lysistrata, Assembly, Women, Wealth.* Oxford.

Halliwell, S. 1998. *Aristotle's* Poetics, 2nd edn. London.

Halliwell, S. 2000. Aristophanes. *Encyclopedia of Literary Translation into English.* Ed. O. Classe. London and Chicago.

Halliwell, S. 2002. *The Aesthetics of Mimesis: Ancient Texts and Modern Problems.* Princeton.

Hamburger, M. (ed.). 1954. *H. von Hofmannsthal. Selected Plays and Libretti.* New York.

Hamdan, M. 2000. L'expérience théatrale palestinienne en Israël de 1948–2005: quelques repères. *Théâtre/Public* 181: 106–12.

Hamdy, M.E. 1966. *Arab Writers and Myth.* Cairo.

Hamer, R. (ed.). 1970. *A Choice of Anglo-Saxon Verse.* London.

Hamilakis, Y. 2004. The fragments of modernity and the archaeologies of the future: a reply to Gregory Jusdanis. *Modernism/modernity* 11/1: 55–9.

Hamilakis, Y. 2007. *The Nation and Its Ruins: Antiquity, Archaeology, and National Imagination in Greece.* Oxford.

Hanson, M.J. and M.S. Kay. 2001. *Star Wars: The New Myth.* Philadelphia.

Hardwick, L. 1992. Convergence and Divergence in reading Homer. In Emlyn-Jones et al. (eds), *Homer: Readings and Images.* London: 227–48.

Hardwick, L. 1995. Classical distances. In Sewart (ed.), 1995: 1: 283–6.

Hardwick, L. 1996–Ongoing. *The Reception of Classical Text and Images of Ancient Greece in Late Twentieth-century Drama and Poetry in English.* Milton Keynes and at www2.open. ac.uk/ClassicalStudies/GreekPlays.

Hardwick, L. 1997. Reception as simile: the poetics of reversal in Homer and Derek Walcott. *International Journal of the Classical Tradition* 3: 326–38.

Hardwick, L. 1999. The theatrical review as a primary source for the modern reception of Greek drama: a preliminary evaluation. In Hardwick (ed.), 1996–ongoing, www2.open.ac. uk/ClassicalStudies/GreekPlays/essays/Reviews.html.

Hardwick, L. 2000. *Translating Words, Translating Cultures.* London.

Hardwick, L. 2001. Who owns the plays? Issues in the translation and performance of Greek drama on the modern stage. *Eirene* 37, Theatralia special edition: 23–39.

Hardwick, L. 2002. Classical texts in post-colonial literatures: consolation, redress and new beginnings in the work of Derek Walcott and Seamus Heaney. *International Journal of the Classical Tradition* 9/2: 236–56.

Hardwick, L. 2003a. *Reception Studies: New Surveys in the Classics* 33. *Greece and Rome.* Oxford.

Hardwick, L. 2003b. Classical theatre in modern Scotland: the democratic stage. In Hardwick and Gillespie (eds), 2003: 1–12.

Hardwick, L. 2004a. Greek drama and anti-colonialism: decolonizing Classics. In Hall et al. (eds), 2004: 219–42.

Hardwick, L. 2004b. 'Shards and suckers': contemporary receptions of Homer. In Fowler (ed.), 2004: 344–62.

Hardwick, L. 2004c. Sophocles' *Oedipus* and conflicts of identity in post-colonial contexts. In Decreus and Kolk (eds), 2004: 376–86.

Hardwick, L. 2005a. Refiguring classical texts: aspects of the post-colonial condition. In Goff (ed.), 2005: 107–17

Hardwick, L. 2005b. Staging *Agamemnon*: the languages of translation. In Macintosh et al. (eds), 2005: 207–21.

Hardwick, L. 2005c. The praxis of what is 'European' in modern performances of Greek drama: the multi-lingual turn. *Parodos* 6: 6–8.

Hardwick, L. 2006a. Remodelling reception: Greek drama as diasporic performance. In Martindale and Thomas (eds), 2006: 204–15.

Hardwick, L. 2006b. 'Murmurs in the cathedral': the impact of translations from Greek poetry and drama on modern work in English by Michael Longley and Seamus Heaney. *Yearbook of English Studies* 36/1: 204–15.

Hardwick, L. 2007a. Contests and continuities in classical traditions: African migrations in Greek drama. In Hilton and Gosling (eds), 2007: 43–72.

Hardwick, L. 2007b. Postcolonial studies. In Kallendorf (ed.), 2007: 312–27.

Hardwick, L. 2007c. Shades of multi-lingualism and multi-vocalism in modern performances of Greek tragedy in post-colonial contexts. In Hardwick and Gillespie (eds), 2007.

Hardwick, L. and C. Gillespie (eds). 2003. *The Role of Greek Drama and Poetry in Crossing and Redefining Cultural Boundaries.* Milton Keynes.

Hardwick, L. and C. Gillespie (eds). 2007. *Classics in Post-colonial Worlds.* Oxford.

Hardwick, L., P. Easterling, S. Ireland, N. Lowe and F. Macintosh (eds). 2000. *Theatre Ancient and Modern.* Milton Keynes.

Hardy, T. 1974 [1896]. *Jude the Obscure.* Intro. Terry Eagleton. London.

Hare, A. 1900 [1871]. *Walks in Rome.* London.

Hare, A. 1896–1900. *The Story of my Life.* 6 vols. London.

Harl, M. 1993. Église et enseignement dans l'Orient grec au cours des premiers siècles. In Harl, *Le déchiffrement du sens: études sur l'herméneutique chrétienne d'Origène à Grégoire de Nysse.* Paris: 417–31.

Harris, A. 2001. Not waving or drowning: young women, feminism, and the limits of the next wave debate. *Outskirts: Feminisms along the Edge* 8, www.chloe.uwa.edu.au/outskirts/archive/VOL8/article4.html.

Harris, R. 2003. *Pompeii.* London: Hutchinson.

Harrison, J. (tr.). 2004. *Euripides'* Hecuba. Cambridge.

Harrison, G.W.M. (ed.). 2005. *Satyr Drama, Tragedy at Play.* Swansea.

Harrison, N. 2003. *Postcolonial Criticism: History, Theory and the Work of Fiction.* Cambridge.

Harrison, S.J. (ed.). 1990. *Oxford Readings in Vergil's* Aeneid. Oxford.

Harrison, S.J. (ed.). 2008. *Living Classics: Greece and Rome in Contemporary Poetry in English.* Oxford.

Harrison, S.J. 2007. Some Victorian Versions of Greco–Roman Epic. In Stray (ed.), 2007c.

Harrison, T. (tr.). 2005. *Euripides'* Hecuba. London.

Harrison, T. (tr.). 1981. *The Oresteia.* London.

Harrison, T. 1984. *Selected Poems.* Harmondsworth.

Harrison, T. 1990. *The Trackers of Oxyrhynchus.* London and Boston.

Harrison, T. 1991. Facing up to the muses: presidential address to the Classical Association, 1988. *Proceedings of the Classical Association* 85: 7–32.

Harrison, T. 1998. *Prometheus.* London.

Harrison, T. (ed.). 2002. *Greeks and Barbarians.* Edinburgh.

Harrison, T. 2000. *The Emptiness of Asia. Aeschylus' Persians and the History of the Fifth Century.* London.

Harrison, T. (tr.). 2005. *Euripides'* Hecuba. London.

Hartmann, R. 1981. *Richard Strauss: The Staging of his Operas and Ballets.* New York.

Hartog, F. 1988. *The Mirror of Herodotus. The Representation of the Other in the Writing of History.* Tr. J. Lloyd. Berkeley.

Hartshorne, E.Y. 1937. *The German Universities and National Socialism.* Cambridge, Mass., and London.

Haskell, F. and N. Penny. 1981. *Taste and the Antique: The Lure of Classical Sculpture, 1500–1900.* New Haven.

Haubold, J. 2002. Greek epic: a near eastern genre? *Proceedings of the Cambridge Philological Society* 48: 1–19.

Haubold, J. 2007. Modes of resonance: tradition vs. reception. In Graziosi and Greenwood (eds), 2007.

Hauptfleisch, T. 1992. Post-colonial criticism, performance theory and the evolving forms of the South African theatre. *South African Theatre Journal* 6/2: 64–83.

Hauptfleisch, T. 1997. *Theatre and Society in South Africa. Some Reflections in a Fractured Mirror.* Pretoria.

Havelock, E.A. 1963. *Preface to Plato.* Oxford.

Hawthorne, N. 1910. *The Marble Faun.* London.

Haynes, K. 2003. *English Literature and Ancient Languages.* Oxford.

Hayward, T.A. 1983. The Latin epigraphs in *The Bothie of Tober-na-Vuolich. Victorian Poetry* 21: 145–55.

Heaney, S. 1975. *North.* London.

Heaney, S. 1987. *The Haw Lantern.* London.

Heaney, S. 1990. *The Cure at Troy: A Version of Sophocles'* Philoctetes. London.

Heaney, S. 1995. *The Redress of Poetry.* London.

Heaney, S. 1996. *The Spirit Level.* London.

Heaney, S. 1998. *Opened Ground: Poems 1966–1996.* London.

Heaney, S. 2001. *Electric Light.* London.

Heaney, S. 2003. Eclogues *in extremis*: on the staying power of pastoral. *Proceedings of the Royal Irish Academy,* 103C: 1–12.

Heaney, S. 2004. *Sophocles'* Antigone*: The Burial at Thebes.* London.

Heath, M. 1996. *Aristotle,* Poetics. Warminster.

Heath, M. 2004. *Menander: A Rhetor in Context.* Oxford.

Hein, H. and C. Korsmeyer (eds). 1993. *Aesthetics in Feminist Perspective.* Bloomington and Indianapolis.

Heitner, R. 1964. The *Iphigeneia in Tauris* theme in drama of the eighteenth century. *Comparative Literature* 16: 289–309.

Helmstadter, R.J. 1985. Conscience and politics: Gladstone's first book. In Kinzer (ed.): 3–42.

Henderson, J. 1991. *The Maculate Muse: Obscene Language in Attic Comedy*, 2nd edn. New Haven.

Henderson, J. 1996. *Three Plays by Aristophanes: Staging Women*. London and New York.

Henderson, J. 2000. *Aristophanes III: Birds, Lysistrata, Women at the Thesmophoria*. Cambridge, Mass., and London.

Hennessy, A. (ed.). 1992. *Intellectuals in the Twentieth-century Caribbean, 2: Unity in Variety – The Hispanic and Francophone Caribbean*. London and Basingstoke.

Henrichs, A. 1995. Philologie und Wissenschaftsgeschichte: Zur Krise eines Selbstverständnisses. In Flashar and Vogt (eds), 1995: 423–57.

Henry, A. 2004. *Not My Mother's Sister: Generational Conflict and Third-wave Feminism*. Bloomington and Indianapolis.

Hermans, T. 1999. *Translation in Systems*. Manchester.

Hesk, J. 2000. *Deception and Democracy in Classical Athens*. Cambridge.

Heslin, J. 2005. *The Transvestite Achilles: Gender and Genre in the Achilleid of Statius*. Cambridge.

Heubeck, A., S. West and J.B. Hainsworth (eds). 1988. *Homer's* Odyssey: *A Commentary*, 1. Oxford.

Hibberd, D. 1986a. Who were the war poets, anyway? In Roucoux (ed.), 1986: 108–20.

Hibberd, D. 1986b. *Owen the Poet*. Athens.

Hibberd, D. 1992. *Wilfred Owen: The Last Years, 1917–1918*. London.

Hibberd, D. 2002. *Wilfred Owen: A New Biography*. London.

Hibberd, D. and J. Onions (eds). 1986. *Poetry of the Great War: An Anthology*. New York.

Hibbert, C. 1985. *Rome: The Biography of a City*. Harmondsworth.

Highet, G. 1949. *The Classical Tradition: Greek and Roman Influences on Western Literature*. New York and London.

Hill, C. 1965. *Intellectual Origins of the English Revolution*. Oxford.

Hilton, J.L. and A. Gosling. 2007. *Alma Parens Originalis? The Receptions of Classical Literature and Thought in Africa, Europe, the United States, and Cuba*. Bern.

Hinds, S. 1998. *Allusion and Intertext: Dynamics of Appropriation in Roman Poetry*. Cambridge.

Hirsch, F. 1978. *The Hollywood Epic*. South Brunswick, N.J.

Hitchens, C. 2000. *Unacknowledged Legislation: Writers in the Public Sphere*. London.

Hobsbawm, E. and T. Ranger (eds). 1983. *The Invention of Tradition*. Cambridge.

Hofmannsthal, H. von. 1947–59. Szenische Vorschriften zu *Elektra*. In *Prosa II, Gesammelte Werke in Einzelausgaben*. Ed. H. Steiner. Frankfurt.

Hofmannsthal, H. von. 1959. *Aufzeichnungen*. Frankfurt.

Hofmannsthal, H. von. 1997. *Sämtliche Werke VII, Dramen 5*. Ed. K. Bohnenkamp and M. Mayer. Frankfurt.

Hofmannsthal, H. von and Strauss, R. 1951. *Correspondence between Strauss and Hofmannsthal*. London.

Holland, T. 2003. *Rubicon*. London.

Holland Day, F., V. Posever Curtis and J. Van Nimmen (eds). 1996. *F. Holland Day: Selected Texts and Bibliography*. World Photographers References Series 8. Oxford.

Hollows, J. and Moseley, R. (eds). 2006. *Feminism in Popular Culture*. Oxford and New York.

Holmes, R. 2005. *Tommy: The British Soldier on the Western Front, 1914–1918*. London.

Hölscher, T. 2003. *The Language of Images in Roman Art: Art as a Semantic System in the Roman World*. Tr. A. Snodgrass and A.-M. Künzl-Snodgrass. Cambridge.

Hölscher, T. 2006. Greek styles and Greek art in Augustan Rome: issues of the present versus records of the past. In Porter (ed.), 2006: 237–59.

Holtsmark, E.B. 2001. The *Katabasis* theme in modern cinema. In Winkler (ed.), 2001: 23–50.

Hopkins, D. 1986. The Charleston background. In Briggs and Benario (eds), 1986: 1–27.

Hopkins, D. 2000. Classical translation and imitation. In Womersley (ed.), 2000: 76–93.

Hopkins, D. 2005. Theories of translation: Dryden and his contemporaries. In Gillespie and Hopkins (eds), 2005: 55–66.

Hopkins, K. and M. Beard. 2005. *The Colosseum*. London.

Horden, P. (ed.). 1985. *Freud and the Humanities*. London.

Horrocks, G. 1997. *Greek: A History of the Language and Its Speakers*. London.

Howard, P. 1963. *Gluck and the Birth of Modern Opera*. London.

Howard, P. 1981. *C.W. von Gluck*. Cambridge.

Howe, S. 1998. *Afrocentrism: Mythical Pasts and Imagined Homes*. London.

Hughes, T. 1861. *Tom Brown at Oxford*. London.

Hughes, T. (tr.). 1999. *Aeschylus' The Oresteia*. London.

Humphreys, S.C. 2004. *The Strangeness of Gods: Historical Perspectives on the Interpretation of Athenian Religion*. Oxford.

Hunnings, L. 2007. Nineteenth-century Spartacus: proletariat, Pole and Christ. In Stray (ed.), 2007c.

Hunter, R. 2004. Homer and Greek literature. In Fowler (ed.), 2004: 235–53.

Hunter, R. and Fantuzzi, M. 2005. *Tradition and Innovation in Hellenistic Poetry*. Cambridge.

Hursthouse, R. 1999. *On Virtue Ethics*. Oxford.

Hursthouse, R. 2003. Virtue ethics. *Stanford Encyclopedia of Philosophy online*. http://plato.stanford.edu/entries/ethics–virtue.

Hurwit, J.M. 2004. *The Acropolis in the Age of Pericles*. New York.

Hussein, T. 1926. *Pre-Islamic Poetry*. Later, revised edn, *Pre-Islamic Literature*. Cairo.

Hussein, T. 1938. *The Future of Culture in Egypt* [*Mustaqbul al-thaqafa fi misr*]. Cairo.

Hynes, S. 1990. *A War Imagined: The First World War and English Culture*. London.

Ibrahim, G. 2006. Lysistrata. *PAJ: A Journal of Performance and Art* 28/2: 34–6.

Ige, J.O. 2007. The sacred cities of the mind: Roy Campbell and the Classics. In Hilton and Gosling (eds), 2007: 159–77.

Inglebert, H. 2004. Education et culture chez les chrétiens de l'Antiquité tardive. In Pailler and Payen (eds), 2004: 333–41

Insolera, I. and F. Perego. 1983. *Archeologia e città: storia moderna dei Fori di Roma*. Bari.

International Movie Database (IMDB). www.imdb.com, accessed 19 May 2006.

Irele, F.A. 2001. *The African Imagination: Literature in Africa and the Black Diaspora*. Oxford.

Irele, F.A. and S. Gikandi (eds). 2004. *The Cambridge History of African and Caribbean Literature*. Cambridge.

Irmscher, J. 1980. Klassische Altertumswissenschaft im 'Dritten Reich': Quellen und Forschungen. *Klio* 62: 219–24.

Iyer, K.V. 1940. *Physique and Figure*. Bangalore.

Jackson, A.V.W. 1906. *Persia Past and Present. A Book of Travel and Research*. New York.

Jaeger, W.W. 1931. *Das Problem des Klassischen und die Antike: Acht Vorträge gehalten auf der Fachtagung der klassischen Altertumswissenschaft zu Naumburg 1930*. Leipzig. Reprint, 1972. Darmstadt.

Jagger, P.J. 1998. *Gladstone*. London.

James, C.L.R. 1980. *Spheres of Existence. Selected Writings*. London.

James, C.L.R. 1993. A convention appraisal: Dr. Eric Williams, First Premier of Trinidad and Tobago, a biographical sketch. In Cudjoe (ed.), 1993: 327–51.

James, C.L.R. 1994. *Beyond a Boundary*. London.

James, C.L.R. 1996. Discovering literature in Trinidad: the nineteen-thirties. In Donnell and Welsh (eds), 1996: 163–5.

James, H. 1994. *Travelling in Italy with Henry James: Essays*. Ed. F. Kaplan. London.

Jameson, M.H. (ed.). 1985. *The Greek Historians. Papers Presented to A.E. Raubitschek*. Saratoga, Calif.

Janaway, C. 1995. *Images of Excellence: Plato's Critique of the Arts*. Oxford.

Janko, R. 1982. *Homer, Hesiod and the Hymns: Diachronic Development in Epic Diction*. Cambridge.

Jaquet, E.R. (ed.). 1919. *These Were the Men: Poems of the War, 1914–1918*. London, Edinburgh and New York.

Jauss, H.R. 1970. *Literaturgeschichte als Provokation*. Frankfurt am Main.

Jauss, H.R. 1982. *Toward an Aesthetic of Reception*. Tr. T. Bahti. Minneapolis.

Jauss, H.R. 2001. The identity of the poetic text in the changing horizon of understanding. In Machor and Goldstein (eds), 2001: 7–28.

Jebb, R.C. (tr.). 2004 [1898]. *Sophocles: Plays*. Philoctetes. Intro. F. Budelmann. London.

Jebb, R.C. (tr.). 2004 [1900]. *Sophocles: Plays*. Antigone. Intro. R. Blondell. London.

Jenkins, R. 1995. *Gladstone*. London.

Jenkyns, R. 1980. *The Victorians and Ancient Greece*. Oxford.

Jenkyns, R. 2002. The classical tradition. In Cronin et al. (eds), 2002: 229–45.

Jenkyns, R. 2006. The idea of the epic in the nineteenth century. In Clarke et al. (eds), 2006: 301–29.

Jensen, K. 1996. The Humanist reform of Latin and Latin teaching. In Kraye (ed.), 1996: 63–81.

Jeyifo, B. (ed.). 2001. *Conversations with Wole Soyinka*. Jackson.

Jeyifo, B. (ed.). 2002. *Modern African Drama*. New York and London.

Johnson, M. 1992. Reflections of inner life: masks and masked acting in ancient Greek tragedy and Japanese Noh drama. *Modern Drama* 35: 20–34.

Johnson, S. 1905. *Lives of the Poets*. Ed. G. Birkbeck Hill. 3 vols. Oxford.

Johnston, D. (ed.). 1996. *Stages of Translation: Essays and Interviews on Translating for the Stage*. Bath.

Jones, E. 'A Perpetual Torrent': Dryden's Lucretian style. In Patey and Keegan (eds), 1985: 47–63.

Jones, E. 1953. *Sigmund Freud: Life and Work*, 1: *The Young Freud 1856–1900*. London.

Jordan, N. (written and dir. by). 1992. *The Crying Game*. Film.

Jordan, N. (screenplay and dir. by). 2005. *Breakfast on Pluto*. Based on the novel of the same title by Pat McCabe, 1998, London.

Jory, E.J. 1996. The drama of the dance: prolegomena to an iconography of imperial pantomime. In Slater (ed.), 1996: 139–59.

Joseph, G. and H. Tucker. 1999. Passing on: death. In Tucker (ed.), 1999: 110–24.

Joshel, S., M. Malamud and D. McGuire, jr. (eds). 2001. *Imperial Projections: Ancient Rome in Modern Popular Culture*. Baltimore.

Jürs-Munby, K. 2006. Introduction. In Lehman (ed.), 2006.

Jusdanis, G. 2004. Farewell to the classical: excavations in modernism. *Modernism/modernity* 11/1: 37–53.

Kachtemkar, R. and S. Rappe (eds). 2006. *The Blackwell Companion to Socrates*. Oxford.

Kallendorf, C. 2000. Rezeptionsgeschichte Comes of Age: *Der Neue Pauly* and the Classical Tradition, 1. A review of *Der Neue Pauly. Enzyklopädie der Antike in 15 Bänden*, vols. 1–7, 13 Stuttgart, 1996–9. *International Journal of the Classical Tradition* 7/1: 58–66.

Kallendorf, C. 2004. Rezeptionsgeschichte comes of age: *Der Neue Pauly* and the classical tradition, II. A review of *Der Neue Pauly: Enzyklopädie der Antike*, vols. 8–12/2 (Altertum), 14–15/3 (Rezeptions-und Wissenschaftsgeschichte), and 16 (Register, Listen, Tabellen), Stuttgart and Weimar, 2000–3. *International Journal of the Classical Tradition* 11/2: 293–301.

Kallendorf, C. 2005. Virgil's post-classical legacy. In Foley (ed.), 2005: 574–88.

Kallendorf, C. (ed.). 2007. *A Companion to the Classical Tradition*. Oxford.

Kalogiannes, G.Ch. 1984. *The Noumas and Its Era 1903–1931: Linguistic and Ideological Struggles* [in Greek]. Athens.

Kannicht, R. 1982. Poetry and art: Homer and the monuments afresh. *Classical Antiquity* 1: 70–86.

Karantinos, S. 1951. H Skenothesia ton *Nephelon*. In the programme of the Agiou Konstantinou 1951 National Theatre production of *Clouds*.

Kaster, R.A. 1988. *Guardians of Language: The Grammarian and Society in Late Antiquity*. Berkeley.

Kaynar, G. 1996. 'Get out of the picture, kid in a cap': on the interaction of the Israeli drama and reality convention. In Ben-Zvi (ed.), 1996: 285–301.

Keating, K. (ed.). 1970. *Matthew Arnold: Selected Prose*. Harmondsworth.

Keen, A.G. 2005. Alternative histories of the Roman empire in Stephen Baxter and Robert Silverberg. Paper delivered at a work-in-progress research seminar, Open University, Milton Keynes.

Kelly, D. Forthcoming. *Lineages of Empire: The Historical Roots of British Imperial Thought* [special volume for the *Proceedings of the British Academy*]. London.

Kennedy, D.F. 1997. Modern receptions and their interpretative implications. In Martindale (eds), 1997: 38 55.

Kennedy, D.F. 2006. Afterword: the uses of 'reception'. In Martindale and Thomas (eds), 2006. 288–93.

Kennedy, G. (ed.). 1989. *The Cambridge History of Literary Criticism, 1*. Cambridge.

Kent, R.G. 1953. *Old Persian. Grammar, Texts, Lexicon*, 2nd edn. New Haven.

Kermode, F. 1983. *The Classic: Literary Images of Permanence and Change*, Cambridge, Mass.

Kermode, F. 1988. *History and Value*. Oxford.

Khedr, M. 2002. La Bibliothèque d'Alexandrie, symbole de dialogue dans *Les Noces de la Nymphe des bibliothèques* d'Ahmed Etman. *Actes du Colloque International: Dialogue et Controverse*. Faculté des Lettres, Departement de Français, Cairo: 309–29.

Kiberd, D. 1995. *Inventing Ireland*. London.

Kiberd, D. 1998. Romantic Ireland's dead and gone. *Times Literary Supplement* 12 June: 12–14.

Kierkegaard, S. 1987. *Either/Or*. Part 1 originally published in Danish in 1843, edited and translated by H.V. and E.H. Hong [Kierkegaard's Writings, 3]. Princeton.

King, B. 2000. *Derek Walcott: A Caribbean Life*. Oxford.

Kinneir, J.M. 1813. *A Geographical Memoir of the Persian Empire, Accompanied by a Map*. London.

Kinsella, T. (ed.). 1986. *The New Oxford Book of Irish Verse*. Oxford.

Kinzer, B.L. (ed.). 1985. *The Gladstonian Turn of Mind*. Toronto.

Kinzer, S. 1997. Adventures of a Man who Defied the Gods: A Tale Retold with a New Goal of 'Reality'. *New York Times*, May 18, p. D12.4.

Kleiner, D.M. 2005. Semblance and storytelling in Augustan Rome. In Galinsky (ed.), 2005: 197–233.

Kloss, G. 2001. *Erscheinungsformen komischen Sprechens bei Aristophanes*. Berlin and New York.

Knauer, G.N. 1964a. *Die Aeneis und Homer*. Göttingen.

Knauer, G.N. 1964b. Vergil's *Aeneid* and Homer. *Greek, Roman and Byzantine Studies* 5: 61–84. Repr. in S.J. Harrison (ed.), 1990: 390–412.

Knellwolf, C. and C. Norris. 2001. *The Cambridge History of Literary Criticism*, 9. *Twentieth-century Historical, Philosophical and Psychological Perspectives*. Cambridge.

Knight, D. 1951. *Pope and the Heroic Tradition: A Critical Study of his* Iliad. New Haven.

Knox, B. 1959. *Oedipus at Thebes. Sophocles' Tragic Hero and His Time*. New Haven.

Knox, R. 1920. *Patrick Shaw-Stewart*. London and Melbourne.

Koestler, A. 1964. *The Act of Creation*. London.

Konstan, D. 1994. The classics and class conflict. *Arethusa* 27: 47–70.

Koselleck, R. 2002. *The Practice of Conceptual History: Timing History, Spacing Concepts*. Stanford.

Kostof, S. 1973. *The Third Rome, 1870–1950: The Traffic and the Glory*. Berkeley.

Kostof, S. 1976. Drafting a master plan for 'Roma Capitale': an exordium. *Journal of the Society of Architectural Historians* 25: 4–20.

Kotsidu, H. 1991. *Die musischen Agone der Panathenäen in archaischer und klassischer Zeit: eine historisch-archäologische Untersuchung*. Munich.

Kotzamani, M. 2006. Lysistrata on the Arabic Stage. *PAJ: A Journal of Performance and Art* 28/2: 13–41.

Kougioumtzis, M. 1989. Maskes ston Choro Archaiou Dramatos, *Symposium Proceedings of the International Conference of Ancient Drama*. Athens: 139–42.

Koun, K. 1982. Eimaste Brosta se mia Poiese poli Megali, *Ta Nea* 28 July.

Koun, K. 1997. *Kanoume Theatro gia tin Psyche mas*, 4th edn. Athens.

Kovacs, D. (tr.). 1994. *Euripides'* Alcestis. Cambridge, Mass.

Kovacs, D. 2005. Text and transmission. In Gregory (ed.), 2005: 379–93.

Kraemer, J. 1956–57. Arabische Homerverse. *Zeitschrift der Deutchen Morgenländischen Gesellschaft* 106: 259–316, and *Zu den 'Arabischen Homerversen'* 107: 511–18. Wiesbaden

Krause, E., L. Huber and H. Fischer (eds). 1991. *Hochschulalltag im 'dritten Reich': Die Hamburger Universität 1933–1945*. Berlin and Hamburg.

Kraut, R. 2005. Aristotle's Ethics. *Stanford Encyclopedia of Philosophy online*, 1st pub. 1 May 2001; substantively rev. 3 June 2005, http://plato.stanford.edu/entries/aristotle-ethics/, accessed 20 December 2006.

Kraye, J. 1996. *The Cambridge Companion to Renaissance Humanism*. Cambridge.

Kritike [in Greek] 1903. Special issue [1: 19] on the *Oresteiaka*.

Krog, A. (tr.). 2002. *Tom Lanoye's* Mamma Medea. Cape Town.

Kroyanker, D. 1994. *Jerusalem Architecture*. New York.

Kruger, L. 1999. *The Drama of South Africa: Plays, Pageants and Publics since 1910*. London.

Kruger, L. 2003. History plays in Britain: dramas, nations and inventing the present. In Worthen and Holland (eds), 2003: 151–76.

Krumbacher, K. 1909. *Populäre Aufsätze*. Leipzig.

Kuhrt, A. 1983. The Cyrus cylinder and Achaemenid imperial policy. *Journal for the Study of the Old Testament* 25: 83–97.

Kuhrt, A. 1995. *The Ancient Near East c. 3000–300 BC*. 2 vols. London.

Kuhrt, A. and H. Sancisi-Weerdenburg. 1987. Introduction in H. Sancisi-Weerdenburg and A. Kuhrt (eds), 1987: ix–xiii.

Kurke, L. 2006. Plato, Aesop, and the beginnings of mimetic prose. *Representations*, 94: 6–52.

L'archeologia in Roman capitale tra sterro e scavo. 1983. Venice.

Labarbe, J. 1949. *L'Homère de Platon*. Liège.

Lacan, J. 1998. *Le séminaire, livre V: Les formations de l'inconscient*. Paris.

Lacroix, J. 1874. *Oeuvres de Théâtre*, 3. Paris.

Laks, A. 1999. Histoire critique et doxographie: pour une histoire de l'historiographie de la philosophie. *Études philosophiques* 4: 465–77.

Laks, A. 2002. 'Philosophes Présocratiques': Remarques sur la construction d'une catégorie de l'historiographie philosophique. In Laks and Louguet (eds), 2002: ch. 1.

Laks, A. and C. Louguet (eds). 2002. *Qu'est–ce que la philosophie présocratique? What is Presocratic Philosophy?* Cahiers de philologie. Série Apparat critique, 20. Villeneuve–d'Ascq.

Lamberton, R. 1986. *Homer the Theologian: Neoplatonist Allegorical Reading and the Growth of the Epic Tradition*. Berkeley.

Lamberton, R. and J.J. Keaney (eds). 1992. *Homer's Ancient Readers: The Hermeneutics of Greek Epic's Earliest Exegetes*. Princeton.

Lambton, A.K.S. 1995. Major-General Sir John Malcolm (1769–1833) and *The History of Persia*. *Iran* 33: 97–10.

Lamming, G. 1993. Trinidad and the revolution in political independence. In Cudjoe (ed.), 1993: 317–25.

Lan, D. (tr.). 1994. *Ion*. London.

Lanciani, R. 1888. *Ancient Rome in the Light of Recent Discoveries*. London.

Lanciani, R. 1988 [1883]. *Notes from Rome*. Ed. A. Cubberley. Rome. Originally published in *Athenaeum*, 3 March 1883.

Lanciani, R. 1901. *The Destruction of Ancient Rome: A Sketch of the History of the Monuments*. London.

Lanciani, R. 1911. *Catalogo della mostra archeologica nelle Terme di Diocleziano*. Bergamo.

Lanciani, R. 1989. *Storia degli scavi di Roma*. Intro. F. Zevi. Rome.

Landau, D. 2000. Gladiator*: The Making of the Ridley Scott Epic*. Basingstoke.

Lanoye, T. 2001. *Mamma Medea*. Amsterdam.

Lapatin, K. 2006. Picturing Socrates. In Kachtemkar and Rappe (eds), 2006: 110–58.

Larkin Galiñanes, C. 2005. Funny fiction; or, jokes and their relation to the humorous novel. *Poetics Today* 26/1: 79–111.

Larson, V.T. 1999–2000. Classics and the acquisition and validation of power in Britain's 'imperial century' 1815–1914. *International Journal of the Classical Tradition* 6: 185–225.

Lattimore, R. (tr.). 1951. *The Iliad of Homer*. Chicago and London.

Lattimore, R. (tr) 1953. *Aeschylus'* Agamemnon. Chicago.

Lattimore, R. (tr.) 1955. *Euripides'* Alcestis. Chicago.

Lazarus, N. 1999. *Nationalism and Cultural Practice in the Postcolonial World*. Cambridge.

Lear, J. 1992. Inside and outside the *Republic*. *Phronesis* 37: 84–215.

Lecoq, J. 2000. *The Moving Body*. Tr. D. Bradby. London.

Lee, H.D.P. 1987. *Plato*, The Republic. Tr. and revd with an introduction. Harmondsworth.

Leezenberg, M. 2007. From the Peloponnesian war to the Iraq war: a post-liberal reading of Greek tragedy. In Hardwick and Gillespie (eds), 2007.

Lefevere, A. and Bassnett, S. 1990. Introduction: Proust's grandmother and the thousand and one nights – the 'cultural turn' in translation studies. In Bassnett and Lefevere (eds), 1990: 1–13.

Lefkowitz, M.R. and G.M. Rogers (eds). 1996. Black Athena *Revisited*. Chapel Hill and London.

Lehmann, H.-T. 2006. *Postdramatic Theatre*. London and New York. First pub. *Postdramatisches Theater* 1999. Frankfurt.

Leiter, S.L. 1991. *From Stanislavski to Barrault: Representative Directors of the European Stage*. London.

Lennard, H.B. (tr.). 1889. *Ion*. London.

Lennox, C. (tr.). 1759. Brumoy's Theatre of the Greeks in *Le Théâtre des Grecs*. London.

Lentricchia, F. and T. McLaughlin (eds). 1995. *Critical Terms for Literary Study*. Chicago.

Lenz, M. 1910. *Geschichte der königlichen Friedrich–Wilhelms–Universität zu Berlin. Bd. 1: Gründung und Ausbau*. Halle.

Leo, F. 1913. *Geschichte der römischen Literatur*. Berlin.

Leonard, M. 2003. Antigone, the political and the ethics of psychoanalysis. *Proceedings of the Cambridge Philological Society* 49: 130–54.

Leonard, M. 2005. *Athens in Paris: Ancient Greece and the Political in Post-war French Thought*. Oxford.

Leonard, M. 2006. Lacan, Irigaray, and Beyond: Antigones and the politics of psychoanalysis. In Zajko and Leonard (eds), 2006: 121–39.

Leontis, A. 1995. *Topographies of Hellenism*. Ithaca, N.Y.

Leoussi, A.S. 2001. Myths of Ancestry. *Nations and Nationalism* 7: 467–86.

Leppin, H. 1992. *Histrionen: Untersuchungen zur sozialen Stellung von Bühnenkünstlern im Westen des Römischen Reiches zur Zeit der Republik und des Principat*. Bonn.

Levin, H. 2003. *The Labor of Life, Selected Plays*. Tr. B. Harshav. Stanford.

Levine, L.W. 1996. *The Opening of the American Mind: Canons, Culture, and History*. Boston.

Levy, S. and N. Yaari. 1998. Three Trojan Israeli women: theatrical modes of political opposition. *Journal of Drama and Theatre* 4: 99–123.

Levy, S. and N. Yaari. 1999. The onstage atrocities of Hanoch Levin: Israeli metamorphoses of Greek tragedies. In Patsalidis and Sakellaridou (eds), 1999: 133–44.

Lewis, D.M. 1977. *Sparta and Persia*. Leiden.

Lewis, D.M. 1985. Persians in Herodotus. In Jameson (ed.), 1985: 89–105. Repr. in Lewis 1997: 345–61.

Lewis, D.M. 1997. *Selected Papers in Greek and Near Eastern History*. Ed. P.J. Rhodes. Cambridge.

Lianeri, A. The Homeric moment? Translation, historicity, and the meaning of the classics. In Martindale and Thomas (eds), 2006: 141–52.

Lianeri, A. and V. Zajko (eds). 2008. *Translation and the Classics*. Oxford.

Lim, R. 2003. Converting the unchristianizable: the baptism of stage performers in late antiquity. In Mills and Grafton (eds), 2003: 84–126.

Liveley, G. 2006. Surfing the third wave? Postfeminism and the hermeneutics of reception. In Martindale and Thomas (eds), 2006: 55–66.

Liversidge, M. and C. Edwards (eds). 1996. *Imagining Rome: British Artists and Rome in the Nineteenth Century*. London.

Livingstone, R.W. (ed.). 1923 [1921]. *The Legacy of Greece*. Oxford.

Livne, N.Y. 1987. Abu-Warda searches for a solution. [In Hebrew]. *Koteret Rashit*. 1 July 1987.

Lloyd-Jones, H. 1975. Gladstone on Homer. *Times Literary Supplement*, 3 January 1975: 15–17. Repr. in Lloyd-Jones 1982: 114–15.

Lloyd-Jones, H. 1982. *Blood for the Ghosts: Classical Influences in the Nineteenth and Twentieth Centuries*. London.

Lloyd–Jones, H. 1994. Sophocles *Antigone*. Cambridge Mass.

Logan, B. 2003. Whose play is it anyway? *Guardian*, 12 March: 16–17.

Lohse, G. 1991. Klassische Philologie und Zeitgeschehen. Zur Geschichte eines Seminars an der Hamburger Universität in der Zeit des Nationalsozialismus. In Krause et al. (eds), 1991. Berlin/Hamburg: 775–826.

Lokke, K.E. 2004. *Tracing Women's Romanticism: Gender, History, and Transcendence*. London and New York.

Loomba, A., S. Kaul, M. Bunzl, A. Burton and J. Esty (eds). 2005. *Postcolonial Studies and Beyond*. Durham and London.

Looser, D. and A. Kaplan (eds). 1997. *Generations: Academic Feminist in Dialogue*. Minneapolis.

Loppert, M. 1992. Gluck, Christoph Willibald; section 6, 'The Italian Reform Operas' and section 7, 'The Paris Operas'. *The New Grove Dictionary of Opera*. London: 2.456–9.

Loraux, N. 1986. *The Invention of Athens: The Funeral Oration in the Classical City*. Tr. A. Sheridan. Cambridge, Mass.

Lord, A. 2000. *The Singer of Tales*, 2nd edn. Cambridge, Mass.

Losemann, V. 1977. *Nationalsozialismus und Antike: Studien zur Entwicklung des Faches Alte Geschichte 1933–45*. Hamburg.

Loulidi, Y. 1998. *Greek Mythology in Contemporary Arab Theatre* (in Arabic). Morocco.

Loulidi, Y. 2004. Greek mythology in the Arab tragedy: a return of the myth or to the myth. In Decreus and Kolk (eds), 2004: 399–405.

Lowell, R. 1978. *Aeschylus* Agamemnon. New York.

Lowenthal, D. 1985. *The Past is a Foreign Country*. Cambridge.

Lubin, D.M. 2003. *Shooting Kennedy: JFK and the Culture of Images*. Berkeley.

Lucas, G. (story, screenplay and dir. by). 1977. *Star Wars: A New Hope*. AKA: *Adventures of the Starkiller: The Star Wars* (original script title); and *Star Wars IV: A New Hope* (video box title).

Lucas, G. (writer). 1980. *Star Wars: The Empire Strikes Back*. Screenplay by Leigh Brackett. Directed by Irvin Kershner. AKA *Star Wars V: The Empire Strikes Back* (video box title).

Lucas, G. (writer). 1983. *The Return of the Jedi*. Screenplay by L. Kasdan. Directed by R. Marquand. AKA *Star Wars VI: Return of the Jedi* (USA) (video box title).

Lucas, G. (written and dir. by). 1999. *Star Wars*: Episode I, *The Phantom Menace*.

Lucas, G. (story, screenplay and dir. by). 2002. *Star Wars*: Episode II, *The Attack of the Clones*.

Lucas, G. (story, screenplay and dir. by). 2005. *Star Wars*: Episode III, *The Revenge of the Sith*.

Lucas, G. and B. Moyers. 1999. *The Mythology of Star Wars*. Video. Films for the Humanities and Sciences. Lawrenceville, N.J.

Lucian, 1968. *Complete Works*. 8 vols. Cambridge, Mass.

Lucwich, A. 1884. *Aristarchs homerische Textkritik nach den Fragmenten des Didymos*, vol. 1. Leipzig.

Lukacs, Y. (ed.). 1992. *The Israeli–Palestinian Conflict: A Documentary Record 1967–1990*. Cambridge, New York and Melbourne.

Luraghi, N. (ed.). 2002. *Herodotus in Context*. Oxford.

Lurje, M. 2004. *Die Suche Nach der Schuld: Sophokles' Oedipus Rex, Aristotles' Poetik und das Tragödienverständnis der Neuzeit*. Munich and Leipzig.

Luther, A. (ed.). 2005. *Odyssee-Rezeptionen*. Frankfurt.

Lyons, C.L., J.K. Papadopoulos, L.S. Stewart and A. Szegedy-Maszak. 2005. *Antiquity and Photography: Early Views of Ancient Mediterranean Sites*. London and Los Angeles.

Lyons, M. 2001. *Readers and Society in Nineteenth-century France: Workers, Women, Peasants*. Basingstoke.

Lyotard, J.-F. 1977. The unconsciousness as mise-en-scène. In Benamou and Caramello (eds), 1977: 87–98.

Lyotard, J.-F. 1984. *The Postmodern Condition*. Manchester.

Lyttelton, Lord and Gladstone, W.E. 1861. *Translations*. London.

Macaulay, T.B. 1860. *The Lays of Ancient Rome*. London.

Macaulay, T.B. 1877. *Critical and Historical Essays*. London.

Machor, J.L. and P. Goldstein. 2001. *Reception Study: From Literary Theory to Cultural Studies*. New York and London.

Macintosh, F. 1994. *Dying Acts: Death in Ancient Greek and Modern Irish Tragic Drama*. Cork.

Macintosh, F. 1997. Tragedy in performance: nineteenth and twentieth-century productions. In Easterling (ed.), 1997: 284–323.

Macintosh, F. 2000. Introduction: the performer in performance. In Hall et al. (eds), 2000: 1–31.

Macintosh, F. 2001. Oedipus in Africa. *Omnibus* 42: 8–9.

Macintosh, F. 2005a. Greek tragedy and the cosmopolitan ideal. In Hall and Macintosh (eds), 2005: 521–554.

Macintosh, F. 2005b. Viewing *Agamemnon* in nineteenth-century Britain. In Macintosh et al. (eds), 2005: 139–62.

Macintosh, F. 2007. From the Court to the National: the Theatrical legacy of Murray's *Bacchae*. In Stray (ed.), 2007a.

Macintosh, F. Forthcoming. *Sophocles'* Oedipus Rex*: A Production History*. Cambridge.

Macintosh, F., P. Michelakis, E. Hall and O. Taplin (eds). 2005. *Agamemnon in Performance, 458BC–2004AD*. Oxford.

Mack, P. 1996. Renaissance rhetoric and dialectic. In Kraye (ed.), 1996: 82–99.

Mackinnon, K. 1986. *Greek Tragedy into Film*. London and Sydney.

Mackridge, P. 1998. Byzantium and the Greek Language Question in the nineteenth century. In Ricks and Magdalino (eds), 1998: 49–61. London.

Mackridge, P. 2005. Greek as a sacred language: modern Greek translations of the New Testament. Unpublished paper delivered at Princeton University, 29 March.

Mackridge, P. Forthcoming. *Language and National Identity in Greece*. Oxford.

MacNeice, L. 1979. *Collected Poems*, 2nd edn. London.

Mactoux, M.-M. and E. Geny (eds). 1989. *Mélanges P. Lévêque*. 7 vols. Bésançon.

Magnus, P. 1963. *Gladstone: A Biography*. London.

Mahoney, D.F. 2002. Autobiographical writings. In Sharpe (ed.), 2002: 147–59.

Maier, H.M.J. 1988. *In the Centre of Authority: The Malay Hikayat Merong Mahawangsa*. Studies on Southeast Asia. Ithaca.

Maingot, A.P. 1992. Politics and populist historiography in the Caribbean. In Hennessy (ed.), 1992: 145–74.

Majeed, J. 1999. Comparativism and references to Rome in British imperial attitudes to India. In Edwards (ed.), 1999: 88–109.

Malcolm, J. 1815. *A History of Persia*. 2 vols. London.

Malcolm, J. 1827. *Sketches of Persia*. 2 vols. London.

Malissard, A. 1970. Homère, Virgile et le langage cinématographique. *Caesarodunum* 5: 155–69.

Malkin, J.R. 1999. *Memory-theater and Postmodern Drama*. Ann Arbor.

Mandela, N. 1994. *Long Walk to Freedom*. London.

Mansfeld, J. 2004. *Doxography of Ancient Philosophy*. Stanford Encyclopedia of Philosophy. Stanford.

Marchand, S.L. 1996. *Down from Olympus: Archaeology and Philhellenism in Germany, 1750–1970*. Princeton.

Margadant, J.B. 1990. *Madame le professeur: Women Educators in the Third Republic*. Princeton.

Margolies, D. and M. Joannou (eds). 1995. *Heart of a Heartless World: Essays in Cultural Resistance in Honour of Margot Heinemann*. London.

Mariotti, S. 1986. *Livio Andronico e la traduzione artistica*. Urbino.

Maritz, J. 2007. Sculpture at Heroes' Acre, Harare, Zimbabwe: Classical Influences? In Hardwick and Gillespie (eds), 2007.

Markley, A.A. 2004. *Stateliest Measures: Tennyson and the Literature of Greece and Rome*. Toronto.

Marrou, H.-I. 1956. *A History of Education in Antiquity*. Madison.

Marsh, E. 1918. *Rupert Brooke: A Memoir*. New York.

Marshall, C.W. 1999. Some fifth-century masking conventions. *Greece and Rome* 46: 188–202.

Martindale, C. 1993. *Redeeming the Text: Latin Poetry and the Hermeneutics of Reception*. Cambridge.

Martindale, C. (ed.). 1997. *The Cambridge Companion to Virgil*. Cambridge.

Martindale, C. 2006. Introduction: thinking through reception. In Martindale and Thomas (eds), 2006: 1–13.

Martindale, C. 2007. Reception. In Kallendorf (ed.), 2007: 297–311.

Martindale, C. and A.B. Taylor (eds). 2004. *Shakespeare and the Classics*. Cambridge.

Martindale, C. and R.F. Thomas (eds). 2006. *Classics and the Uses of Reception*. Oxford.

Masarwi, R. 2006. Layla. *PAJ: A Journal of Performance and Art* 28/2: 36–8.

Mason, H.A. 1959. *Humanism and Poetry in the Early Tudor Period*. London:

Mason, H.A. 1963. Is Juvenal a classic? In Sullivan (ed.), 1963: 93–176.

Mason, H.A. 1969. Creative translation: Ezra Pound's *Women of Trachis*. *Cambridge Quarterly* 4: 244–72.

Mason, H.A. 1972. *To Homer Through Pope: An Introduction to Homer's* Iliad *and Pope's Translation*. London.

Mason, H.A. 1976. Horace's Ode to Pyrrha. *Cambridge Quarterly* 7: 27–62.

Mason, H.A. 1981. Living in the present: is Dryden's 'Horat. Ode 29 Book 3' an example of 'creative translation'? *Cambridge Quarterly* 10: 91–129.

Mason, T. 1990. Abraham Cowley and the wisdom of Anacreon. *Cambridge Quarterly* 19: 103–37.

Mast, E. 2000. Sahmatah: awakening history. *TDR: The Drama Review* 44/3: 113–30.

Matthew, H.C.G. 1997. *Gladstone, 1809–1898*. Oxford.

Mavromoustakos, P. 1999a. Ancient Greek drama on the modern Greek stage: from the *Persians* of 1571 to the approaches of the twentieth century. In Mavromoustakos (ed.), 1999b: 77–87 (in Greek).

Mavromoustakos, P. (ed.). 1999b. *Productions of Ancient Greek Drama in Europe during Modern Times*. Proceedings of a conference held in Corfu 1997. Papers in Greek, English and French with summaries in English. Athens.

Mayer, W. and P. Allen. 2000. *John Chrysostom*. London.

Mayeur, F. 1979. *L'Éducation des filles en France aux xixe siècle*. Paris.

Mazhar, A. 2003. Intertextual subversions and appropriations in Shakespeare's *Antony and Cleopatra*, Shawqi's *The Death of Cleopatra* and Etman's *Cleopatra Loves Peace*. *Journal of Oriental and African Studies* 12: 97–133.

Mazzini, G. 1986. *Note autobiografiche*. Ed. R. Pertici. Milan.

McCabe, P. 1998. *Breakfast on Pluto*. New York.

McDonald, M. 1983. *Euripides in Cinema: The Heart Made Visible*. Philadelphia.

McDonald, M. 1992. *Ancient Sun, Modern Light: Greek Drama on the Modern Stage*. New York and Oxford.

McDonald, M. 2000a. Black Dionysus: Greek tragedy from Africa. In Hardwick et al. (eds), 2000: 95–108.

McDonald, M. (tr.). 2000b. *Sophocles'* Antigone. London. Repr. in McDonald et al. (eds), 2005.

McDonald, M. 2001. *Sing Sorrow: Classics, History, and Heroines in Opera*. Westport, Conn.

McDonald, M. 2003. *The Living Art of Greek Tragedy*. Bloomington, Ind. Rpr. 2004. French translation, *L'arte vivente della tragedia greca*, tr. Francesca Albini, additions by Umberto

Albini, Firenze 2004; Greek translation, *I zosa techne tis archaias hellenikes tragodias,* tr. Helen Tserezole, Athens 2005.

McDonald, M. (tr.). 2005. *Euripides'* Hecuba. London.

McDonald, M. 2007. The dramatic legacy of myth: Oedipus in opera, television and film. In McDonald and Walton (eds), 2007: 608–53.

McDonald, M. and J.M. Walton (eds). 2002. *Amid Our Troubles: Irish Versions of Greek Tragedy.* London.

McDonald, M. and J.M. Walton (eds). 2007. *The Cambridge Companion to Greek and Roman Theatre.* Cambridge.

McDonald, M., K. McLeish and F. Raphael (trs). 2005. *Greek Tragedy.* London.

McGann, J.J. 1991. *The Textual Condition.* Princeton.

McGann, J.J. 1984. Rome and its romantic significance. In Patterson (ed.), 1984: 83–104.

McGuinness, F. (tr.). 2004. *Euripides'* Hecuba. London.

McHenry, E. 2002. *Forgotten Readers: Recovering the History of African American Literary Societies.* Durham, N.C., and London.

McLeish, K. (tr.). 1997. *Ion.* London.

McLuhan, M. 1966. *Understanding Media: The Extensions of Man.* New York.

McLynn, N. 2006. Among the Hellenists: Gregory and the Sophists. In Børtnes and Hägg (ed.), 2006: 213–38.

McManus, A. 2002. *The Irish Hedge School and its Books, 1695–1831.* Dublin.

McMullen, S. 1985. From the armchair to the stage: Hofmannsthal's *Elektra* in its theatrical context. *Modern Language Review* 80/3: 637–51.

McMurtry, M. 1998. 'Greeks bearing gifts': Athol Fugard's *Orestes* project and the politics of experience. *Modern Drama* 41/1: 105–18.

McMurtry, M. 2000. Electra. Unpublished playscript.

Meijering, R. 1987. *Literary and Rhetorical Theories in Greek Scholia.* Groningen.

Meineck, P. and I.C. Storey. 2000. *Aristophanes'* Clouds. Indianopolis and Cambridge.

Mench, F. 1969. Film sense in the *Aeneid. Arion* 8: 380–97. Repr. in Winkler (ed.), 2001: 219–32.

Mendelsohn, D. 2004. A little *Iliad. New York Review of Books* 51/11: 46–9.

Merkouris, S. (ed.). 1993. *Ancient Greek Theatre: Its Influence on Europe* [in Greek]. Athens.

Merkouris, S. (ed.). 1997. *A Stage for Dionysus: Theatrical Space and Ancient Drama.* Athens.

Merritt-Hawkes, O.A. 1935. *Persia. Romance and Reality.* London.

Mertens, W. and R. Haubl. 1996. *Der Psychoanalytiker als Archäologe: Eine Einführung in der Methode der Rekonstruktion.* Stuttgart.

Mezzabotta, M.R. 1994. Frolicking frogs rap in Cape Town. *Didaskalia* 1/3, www.didaskalia.net/issues/vol1no3/mezzabotta, accessed 12 January 2007.

Mezzabotta, M.R. 2000. Ancient Greek drama in the new South Africa. In Hardwick et al. (eds), 2000: 246–68.

Michelakis, P. 2001. The past as a foreign country? Greek tragedy, cinema and the politics of space. In Budelmann and Michelakis (eds), 2001: 241–57.

Michelakis, P. 2004a. Greek tragedy in cinema: theatre, politics, history. In Hall et al. (eds), 2004: 199–217.

Michelakis, P. 2004b. Early film adaptations of Greek tragedy: cinema, theatre, culture. Unpublished paper.

Michelakis, P. 2005. Introduction: Agamemnons in performance. In Macintosh et al. (eds), 2005: 1–20.

Michelakis, P. 2006a. *A Companion to Euripides'* Iphigenia at Aulis. London.

Michelakis, P. 2006b. Reception, performance, and the sacrifice of Iphigenia. In Martindale and Thomas (eds), 2006: 216–26.

Michelini, A.N. 1987. *Euripides and the Tragic Tradition*. Madison.

Millbank, A. 1998. *Dante and the Victorians*. Manchester.

Miller, H. 1843. *My Schools and Schoolmasters: or, the Story of my Education*. Edinburgh.

Miller, M.C. 1997. *Athens and Persia in the Fifth Century: A Study in Cultural Receptivity*. Cambridge.

Miller, W.M. 1990. *A Canticle for Leibowitz*. London.

Millon, H.A. and L. Nochlin (eds). 1978. *Art and Architecture in the Service of Politics*. Cambridge, Mass.

Mills, K. and A. Grafton (eds). 2003. *Conversion in Late Antiquity and the Early Middle Ages: Seeing and Believing*. Rochester, N.Y.

Millspaugh, A.C. 1925. *The American Task in Persia*. New York and London.

Minogue, S. (ed.). 1990. *Problems for Feminist Criticism*. London and New York.

Mitchell, D. 2004. *Cloud Atlas*. London.

Moatti, C. 1993. *The Search for Ancient Rome*. London.

Momigliano, A. 1945. Review of F. Altheim, *Die Soldatenkaiser*, Frankfurt and Main. *Journal of Roman Studies* 35/1–2: 129–31.

Momigliano, A. 1966. *Terzo contributo alla storia degli studie classici e del mondo antico*. 2 vols. Rome.

Momigliano, A.D. 1994. *Studies on Modern Scholarship*. Ed. G.W. Bowersock and T.J. Cornell. Tr. T.J. Cornell. Berkeley.

Monaco, J. 2000. *How to Read a Film: Movies, Media, Multimedia*, 3rd edn. New York and Oxford.

Monoson, S.S. 2000. *Plato's Democratic Entanglements: Athenian Politics and the Practice of Philosophy*. Princeton, N.J.

Montanari, F. 1979–95. *Studi di filologia omerica antica*. 2 vols. Pisa.

Monte, S. 1914. *How to Pose*. London.

Moore, B.B. 1915. *From Moscow to the Persian Gulf: Being the Journal of a Disenchanted Traveller in Turkestan and Persia*. New York.

Moore, D. (ed.). 2001. *Black Athena Writes Back: Martin Bernal Responds to his Critics*. Durham, N.C.

Morgan, T.J. 1998. *Literate Education in the Hellenistic and Roman Worlds*. Cambridge.

Morley, J. 1903. *The Life of William Ewart Gladstone*. 3 vols. London.

Morris, I. 2000. *Archaeology as Cultural History: Words and Things in Iron Age Greece*. Malden, Mass.

Morris, I. and B. Powell (eds). 1997. *A New Companion to Homer*. Leiden.

Morris, S. 1997. Homer and the Near East. In Morris and Powell (eds), 1997: 599–623.

Morton, R.S. 1940. *A Doctor's Holiday in Iran*. New York and London.

Mosley, N. 1976. *Julian Grenfell: His Life and the Times of His Death, 1888–1915*. New York.

Most, G.W. (ed.). 1997. *Collecting Fragments [Fragmente Sammeln]*. Aporemata 1. Göttingen.

Most, G.W. (ed.). 1998. *Editing Texts [Texte Edieren]*. Aporemata 2. Göttingen.

Most, G.W. (ed.). 1999. *Commentaries [Kommentare]*. Aporemata 4. Göttingen.

Most, G.W. 2000. Generating genres: the idea of the tragic. In Depew and Obbink (eds), 2000: 15–35.

Most, G.W. (ed.). 2001. *Historicization [Historisierung]*. Aporemata 5. Göttingen.

Most, G.W. (ed.). 2002. *Disciplining Classics [Altertumswissenschaft als Beruf]*. Aporemata 6. Göttingen.

Most, G.W. 2003. Violets in crucibles: translating, traducing, transmuting. *Transactions of the American Philological Association* 133/2: 381–90.

Most, G.W. 2005. How many Homers? In Santoni (ed.), 2005: 1–14.

Mueller, C. and A. Krajewska-Wieczorek. 2000. *Sophocles'* Antigone. Hanover, N.H.

Mueller, M. 1980. *Children of Oedipus and Other Essays on the Imitation of Greek Tragedy 1550–1800.* Toronto.

Müller, K.O. 1830. *The History and Antiquities of the Doric Race.* Tr. H. Tufnell and G.C. Lewis. 2 vols. London.

Mulrooney, D. 2002. *Orientalism, Orientation, and the Nomadic Work of Pina Bausch.* Frankfurt.

Munday, J. 2001. *Introducing Translation Studies: Theories and Applications.* London and New York.

Murnaghan, S. 1987. Penelope's Agnoia: knowledge, power, and gender in the *Odyssey.* In Skinner (ed.), 1987: 103–15.

Murray, G. (tr.). 1920. *Aeschylus'* Agamemnon. London.

Murray, G. 1927. *The Classical Tradition in Poetry: The Charles Eliot Norton Lectures.* Oxford.

Murray, O. 1987. Herodotus and oral history. In Sancisi-Weerdenburg and Kuhrt (eds), 1987: 93–115. Repr. Luraghi (ed.), 2002: 16–44.

Murray, O. (ed.). 1990. *Sympotica. A Symposium on the Symposion.* Oxford.

Murray, P. 1992. Inspiration and mimesis in Plato. In Barker and Warner (eds), 1992: 27–46.

Murray, P. (ed.). 1996. *Plato on Poetry:* Ion, Republic *376e–398b; 595–608b.* Cambridge Greek and Latin Classics series. Cambridge.

Mustard, W.P. 1904. *Classical Echoes in Tennyson.* New York. Repr. 1971.

Näf, B. 1986. *Von Perikles zu Hitler: Die Athenische Demokratie und die Deutsche Althistorie bis 1945.* Bern.

Näf, B. (ed.). 2001. *Antike und Altertumswissenschaft in der Zeit von Faschismus und Nationalsolialismus. Kolloquium Universität Zurich 14–17 Oktober 1998.* Mandelbachtal and Cambridge.

Nagy, G. 1990. *Pindar's Homer: The Lyric Possession of an Epic Past.* Baltimore.

Nagy, G. 1996. *Poetry as Performance: Homer and Beyond.* Cambridge.

Nagy, G. 1999. *The Best of the Achaeans: Concepts of the Hero in Archaic Greek Poetry,* 2nd edn. Baltimore.

Nagy, G. 2002. *Plato's Rhapsody and Homer's Music: The Poetics of the Panathenaic Festival in Classical Athens.* Cambridge, Mass.

Nagy, G. 2004. L'aède épique en auteur: la tradition des Vies d'Homère. In Calame and Chartier (eds), 2004: 41–68.

Nails, D. 1995. *Agora, Academy and the Conduct of Philosophy.* Dordrecht and Boston.

Naipaul, V.S. 2001. *The Middle Passage: Impressions of Five Colonial Societies.* London.

Naremore, J. (ed.). 2000. *Film Adaptation.* London.

Nasser, H.K. 2006. Stories from under occupation: performing the Palestinian experience. *Theatre Journal* 58/1: 15–37.

Natter, T.G. and P. Weiermair (eds). 2000. *Wilhelm von Gloeden-Wilhelm von Plüschow-Vincenzo Galdi: Et in Arcadia Ego: Turn-of-the-Century Photography.* Zurich.

Nelis, D.P. 2005. Apollonius of Rhodes. In Foley (ed.), 2005: 353–63.

Neville, A. 1563. *The Lamentable Tragedie of Oedipus the Sonne of Laius Kyng of Thebes out of Seneca.* London.

Newiger, H.-J. 1969. Hofmannsthals *Elektra* und die griechische Tragödie, *Arcadia* 4: 138–63.

Ngugi wa Thiong'o. 1986. *Decolonizing the Mind*. Oxford.

Nicholl, A.B. 1952–9. *A History of English Drama 1660–1900*. Cambridge.

Niethammer, F.I. 1808. *Der Streit des Philanthropinismus und Humanismus in der Theorie des Erziehungsunterrichts unserer Zeit*. Jena.

Nietzsche, F. 1956. *The Birth of Tragedy from the Spirit of Music and The Genealogy of Morals*. Tr. F. Golffing. New York.

Nietzsche, F. 1967. *The Birth of Tragedy and the Case of Wagner*. Tr. W. Kaufmann. New York.

Nietzsche, F. 1988. *Friedrich Nietzsche. Sämtliche Werke. Kritische Studienausgabe in 15 Einzelbänden*, 2nd edn. Ed. G. Colli and M. Montinari. 15 vols. Berlin.

Nietzsche, F. 1990 [1956]. *The Genealogy of Morals*. Tr. F. Golffing. New York.

Nightingale, A.W. 1995. *Genres in Dialogue: Plato and the Construct of Philosophy*. Cambridge.

Nirvanas, P. 1968. The *Oresteiaka* [in Greek]. In *Collected Works* [in Greek]. Ed. G. Valetas, 4: 214–20. Athens.

Nisbet, R.G.M. 1995. *Collected Papers on Latin Literature*. Oxford.

Nisetich, F.J. 1989. *Pindar and Homer. American Journal of Philology, Monographs* 4. Baltimore.

Nkrumah, K. 1965. *Neo-Colonialism: The Last Stage of Imperialism*. London.

Noiray, M. 1979. Gluck's methods of composition in his French operas. Unpublished M. Litt thesis. Oxford.

Nünlist, R. Forthcoming. *The Ancient Critic at Work: Terms and Concepts of Literary Criticism in Greek Scholia* (working title). Cambridge.

Nylander, C. 1970. *Ionians in Pasargadae*. Uppsala.

O'Connor, J.J. 1997. Perilous Journey Home Upon the Wine-Dark Sea. (Review) *New York Times*, May 16, p. D18.

O'Higgins, D. Forthcoming. Infelix Paupertas: scholarship of the eighteenth century Irish poor. *Arethusa*.

Ober, J. 1989. *Mass and Elite in Democratic Athens. Rhetoric, Ideology and the Power of the People*. Princeton.

Ober, J. 2005. *Athenian Legacies. Essays on the Politics of Going on Together*. Princeton and Oxford.

Ober, J. and C. Hedrick (eds). 1996. *Demokratia: A Conversation on Democracies, Ancient and Modern*. Princeton.

Ogilvie, R.M. 1964. *Latin and Greek: A History of the Influence of the Classics on English Life from 1600 to 1918*. London.

Okpewho, I. 1991. Soyinka. Euripides and the anxiety of empire. *Research in African Literatures* 30/4: 32–55.

Olmstead, A.T. 1948. *History of the Persian Empire*. Chicago.

ODNB. 2004. *Oxford Dictionary of National Biography*. 60 vols. Oxford.

Orkin, M. 1994. *Drama and the South African State*. Manchester.

Osborne, P. 1995. *The Politics of Time: Modernity and Avant-garde*. London.

Otto, W.F. 1954. *The Homeric Gods: The Spiritual Significance of Greek Religion*. Tr. M. Hadas. London. Repr. New York, 1979.

Ouseley, W. 1819–23. *Travels in Various Countries of the East; More Particularly Persia*. 3 vols. London.

Owen, W. 1983. *The Complete Poems and Fragments*. 2 vols. Ed. J. Stallworthy. New York.

Oxaal, I. 1968. *Black Intellectuals Come to Power. The Rise of Creole Nationalism in Trinidad and Tobago*. Cambridge, Mass.

Oxland, N. *c*.1920. *Poems and Stories*. Printed for private circulation. London.

Packer, J. 1989. Politics, urbanism and archaeology in 'Roma capitale'. *American Journal of Archaeology* 93: 137–41.

Page, D.L. (ed.). 1972. *Aeschyli Tragoediae*. Oxford.

Pailler, J.M. and P. Payen (eds). 2004. *Que reste-t-il de l'éducation classique: Relire «le Marrou» Histoire de l'éducation dans l'Antiquité*. Toulouse.

Palamas, K. 1903. The Tempest of the *Oresteia* [in Greek]. *Kritike* 1/19: 745–51. Reprinted in *Collected Works* [in Greek], vol. 6, 1972: 373–81. Athens.

Palmer-Sikelianos, E. 1993. *Upward Panic*. Ed. J. Anton. Chur and Philadelphia.

Panayotakis, C. 1997. Baptism and crucifixion on the mimic stage. *Mnemosyne* 50: 302–19.

Panofsky, E. 1955. *Meaning in the Visual Arts*. New York.

Parker, D. 1961. The Acharnians *by Aristophanes*. New York, Scarborough, Ont. and London.

Parker, D. 1992/3. WAA: an intruded gloss. *Arion* 3. 2/2–3: 251–6.

Parker, G.F. 2005. 'Talking scripture out of church': Parson Adams and the partiality of translation. *Translation and Literature*, 14: 179–95.

Parker, J. 2001. *Dialogic Education and the Problematics of Translation in Homer and Greek Tragedy*. Lewiston, Queenston and Lampeter.

Parker, R. 1996. *Athenian Religion: A History*. Oxford.

Parry, M. 1971. *The Making of Homeric Verse*. Oxford.

Pater, W. 1914 [1894]. *Greek Studies: A Series of Lectures*. London.

Patey, D.L. and T. Keegan (eds). 1985. *Augustan Studies: Essays in Honor of Irvin Ehrenpreis*. Newark, London and Toronto.

Patrikiou, H. (ed.). 1998. *The Translation of Ancient Greek Drama in All the Languages of the World* [in Greek]. Athens.

Patrikiou, H. 2005. The Language Question as pretext for the interpretive impasse: the example of the stage revival of tragedy [in Greek]. *Euangelika 1901*: 155–85.

Patsalidis, S. and Sakellaridou, E. (eds). 1999. *(Dis)Placing Classical Greek Theatre*. Thessaloniki.

Patterson, A. (ed.). 1984. *Roman Images*. Baltimore.

Paulin, T. 1985. *The Riot Act: A Version of Sophocles'* Antigone. London.

Pavis, P. 1992. *Theatre at the Crossroads of Culture*. London and New York.

Pemble, J. (ed.). 2000. *John Addington Symonds: Culture and the Demon Desire*. New York.

Petras, S. 1960. *The Royal Theatre and Greek Operetta* [in Greek]. Athens.

Pfeiffer, R. 1968. *History of Classical Scholarship from the Beginnings to the End of the Hellenistic Age*. Oxford.

Pfeiffer, R. 1976. *History of Classical Scholarship from 1300 to 1850*. Oxford.

Pick, D. 2005. *Rome or Death: The Obsessions of General Garibaldi*. London.

Pickard-Cambridge, A.W. 1988 [1968]. *The Dramatic Festivals of Athens*, 2nd edn. Revd J. Gould and D.M. Lewis, with supplement and corrections, repr. 1991. Oxford.

Pinter, H. 1960. *The Birthday Party*. London.

Planché, J.R. 1872. *Recollections and Reflections*, vol. 1. London.

Pluggé, D.E. 1938. *History of Greek Play Production in American Colleges and Universities from 1881 to 1936*. New York.

Polites, G.N. 1950. The theatre criticism of the *Noumas* [in Greek]. *Anglo–Hellenike Epitheorese* 4/10: 393–6.

Pollock, G. 2006. Beyond Oedipus: feminist thought, psychoanalysis, and mythical figurations of the feminine. In Zajko and Leonard (eds), 2006: 67–117.

Pomeroy, A.J. 2004. The vision of a fascist Rome in *Gladiator*. In Winkler (ed.), 2004: 111–23.

Pomeroy, S.B. (ed.). 1991. *Women's History and Ancient History*. Chapel Hill and London.

Pope, A. 1939–69. *The Twickenham Edition of the Poems of Alexander Pope.* General editor John Butt. 11 vols. London.

Popov, L.K. 1997. *The Family Virtues Guide.* New York.

Popov, L.K. 2000. *The Virtues Project™ Educator's Guide.* California.

Pormann, P.E. 2006. The Arab Cultural Awakening (Naha), 1870–1950, and the classical tradition. *International Journal of the Classical Tradition* 13: 3–20.

Porter, J.I. 2000. *Nietzsche and the Philology of the Future.* Stanford.

Porter, J.I. 2003. The materiality of classical studies. *Parallax* 29/4: 64–74.

Porter, J.I. 2006a. What is 'classical' about classical antiquity? In Porter 2006b: 1–65.

Porter, J.I. (ed.). 2006b. *Classical Pasts: The Classical Traditions of Greece and Rome.* Princeton.

Porter, J.I. 2007a. Hearing voices: the Herculaneum papyri and classical scholarship. In Seydl and Coates (eds), 2007: 95–113.

Porter, J.I. 2007b. Making and unmaking: the Achaean wall and the limits of fictionality in Homeric criticism. In Armstrong and Hackney-Dué (eds), 2007.

Porter, J.I. Forthcoming. *The Origins of Aesthetic Inquiry in Antiquity: Matter, Experience and the Sublime.* Cambridge.

Porter, J.R. 1999/2000. Euripides and Menander: *Epitrepontes,* Act IV. In Cropp et al. (eds), 1999/2000: 157–73.

Postlewait, T. and B.A. McConachie (eds). 1989. *Interpreting the Theatrical Past: Essays in the Historiography of Performance.* Iowa.

Potter, R. (tr.). 1777. *Aeschylus'* Agamemnon. Norwich.

Potter, R. (tr.). 1781. *Euripides'* Alcestis. London.

Potter, R. (tr.). 1781. *Ion.* London.

Potter, R. (tr.). 1788. *Sophocles'* Antigone. London.

Powell, B.B. 1991. *Homer and the Origin of the Greek Alphabet.* Cambridge.

Powell, R., M.E. De Guilio, A. Garcia, V. Trout and C. Wang. 2006. *Conjuring Bearden.* Catalogue of the Exhibition. Nasher Museum of Art at Duke University. Durham, N.C.

Prichard, J.C. 1831. *The Eastern Origin of the Celtic Nations Proved.* London.

Prince, C.K. 2007. A divided child, or Derek Walcott's post-colonial philology. In Hardwick and Gillespie (eds), 2007.

Prince, M. 2003. Medea and the inefficacy of love magic: Propertius 1.1 and Tibullus 1.2. *Classical Bulletin* 79/2: 205–18.

Psychares, I. 1903. The translation of the *Oresteia* [in Greek]. *Ho Noumas* 72. 30 November: 1–2.

Puffett, D. (ed.). 1989. *Richard Strauss:* Elektra. Cambridge.

Quayson, A. 2002. *Strategic Transformations in Nigerian Writing.* Oxford and Bloomington.

Raaflaub, K.A. and R. Wallace (eds). 2006. *Origins of Democracy in Ancient Greece: Interpretations and Controversies.* Princeton.

Rabinowitz, N.S. and A. Richlin. 1993. *Feminist Theory and the Classics.* New York and London,.

Radt, S. (ed.). 1985. *Tragicorum graecorum fragmenta* 3. Göttingen.

Ralles, A. 1903. Euripides' *Cyclops* [in Greek]. *Ho Noumas* 72. 30 November: 1.

Ramazani, J. 1997. The wound of history: Walcott's *Omeros* and the post-colonial poetics of affliction. *Proceedings of the Modern Literature Association* 112/3: 405–15.

Ramm, A. 1985. Gladstone's religion. *Historical Journal,* 28: 327–40.

Ramm, A. 1989–90. Gladstone as man of letters. *Nineteenth Century Prose* 17: 1–29.

Rankaves, A.R. 1895. *Memoirs* [in Greek], vol. 2. Athens.

Rankine, P.D. 2006. *Ulysses in Black: Ralph Ellison, Classicism and African American Literature.* Madison, Wis.

Rappe, S. 2001. The new math: how to add and to subtract pagan elements in Christian education. In Too (ed.), 2001: 405–32.

Raskin, V. 1985. *Semantic Mechanisms of Humor*. Dordrecht and Boston.

Rawlinson, G. 1885. *The Seven Great Monarchies of the Ancient Eastern World*. New York.

Ray, H.P. 2007. *Memory as History: The Legacy of Alexander in Asia*. New Delhi.

Redpath, T. 1981. Tennyson and the literature of Greece and Rome. In Tennyson 1981: 105–30.

Rees, R. 2008. *Ted Hughes and the Classics*. Oxford.

Rehm, R. 1992. *Greek Tragic Theatre*. London.

Rehm, R. 2002. *The Play of Space: Spatial Transformation in Greek Tragedy*. Princeton and Oxford.

Rehm, R. 2003. *Radical Greek Theatre: Greek Tragedy and the Modern World*. London.

Rehm, R. 2007. 'If you are a woman': theatrical womanizing in Sophocles' *Antigone* and Fugard, Kani, and Ntshona's *The Island*. In Hardwick and Gillespie (eds), 2007.

Reid, J.D. 1993. *Oxford Guide to Classical Mythology in the Arts*. 2 vols. New York and Oxford.

Reinelt, J.G. and J.R. Roach. 1992. *Critical Theory and Performance*. Ann Arbor.

Reinhardstoettner, K. von. 1886. *Plautus: spätere Bearbeitungen plautinischer Lustspiele; ein Beitrag zur vergleichenden Litteraturgeschichte*. Leipzig.

Reiss, K. 1989. Text types, translation types and translation assessment. In Chesterman (ed.), 1989: 105–15.

Revard, S.P. 1991. Cowley's *Anacreontiques* and the translation of the Greek *Anacreontea*. In Dalzell (ed.), 1991: 595–607.

Revermann, E. 1999/2000. Tragedy and Macedon: some conditions of reception. In Cropp et al. (eds), 1999–2000: 451–67.

Reynolds, M. 2003. *The Sappho History*. Chippenham and Eastbourne.

Riall, L. 1994. *The Italian Risorgimento: State, Society and National Unification*. London.

Rice, C.C. 1916. *Mary Bird in Persia*. Foreword by the Rt Rev. C.H. Stileman. London.

Rice, E. 1990. *Freud and Moses: The Long Journey Home*. New York.

Richards, D. 2000. Canvas of blood: Okigbo's African modernism. In Bery and Murray (eds), 2000: 229–39.

Richards, D. 2007. Another architecture. In Hardwick and Gillespie (eds), 2007.

Richards, S. 1995. In the border country: Greek tragedy and contemporary Irish Drama. In Barfoot and van der Doel (eds), 1995: 191–200.

Richardson, E. 2007. Jude the Obscure: Victorian classical outcasts. In Stray (ed.), 2007b: 28–45.

Richardson, N.J. 1975. Homeric professors in the age of the Sophists. *Proceedings of the Cambridge Philosophical Society* 21: 65–81.

Richter, N. 1987. *La Lecture et ses institutions: la lecture populaire, 1700–1918*. Le Mans.

Ricks, C. 1989. *Tennyson*. Basingstoke.

Ricks, D. and P. Magdalino (eds). 1998. *Byzantium and the Modern Greek Identity*. London.

Ridley, R. 1992. *The Eagle and the Spade: The Archaeology of Rome during the Napoleonic Era, 1809–1814*. Cambridge.

Ridout, N. 2005. Tragedy at home. Società Raffaello Sanzio at Laban. *PAJ: A Journal of Performance and Art* 81: 83–92.

Ringer, F.K. 1979. *Education and Society in Modern Europe*. Bloomington.

Rizzo, S. 1986. Il latino nell' Umanesimo. In *Letteratura Italiana, 5: Le questioni*, edited by A.A. Rosa. Turin: 379–408.

Robert, M. 1977. *From Oedipus to Moses: Freud's Jewish Identity*. London.

Robinson, M. 1982. The ancient and the modern: a comparison of Metastasio and Calzabigi. *Studies in Music from the University of Western Ontario* 7/2: 137–47.

Robson, J.E. 2006. *Humour, Obscenity and Aristophanesi*. Tübingen.

Roche, P. (tr.). 1974. *Euripides' Alcestis*. New York.

Rockett, E. and K. 2003. *Neil Jordan: Exploring Boundaries*. Dublin.

Rodenwaldt, G. 1916. Zur Bedeutung des Klassischen in der bildenden Kunst. *Zeitschrift für Ästhetik und allgemeine Kunstwissenschaft* 11: 113–31.

Rogerson, A.I. 2007. Conington's Roman Homer. In Stray (ed.), 2007b: 94–106.

Rohde, E. 1961 [1893]. *Psyche: The Cult of Souls and Belief in Immortalilty among the Greeks*. Darmstadt.

Rohlehr, G. 1997. The culture of Williams: context, performance, legacy. *Callaloo* 20/4: 849–88.

Roisman, H. 1999. Teiresias and Obi-Wan: outside the scope of the plot. *New England Classical Journal* 26/4: 23–35.

Roisman, H. 2001. Verbal Odysseus: narrative strategy in the *Odyssey* and in *The Usual Suspects*. In Winkler (ed.), 2001: 51–71.

Roisman, H. 2002. Ulysses (1954). *Amphora* 1: 10–11. Film reviews section.

Roisman, H. 2005a. The *Cyclops* and the *Alcestis*: tragic and the absurd. In Harrison (ed.), 2005: 67–82.

Roisman, H. 2005b. Nestor the good counsellor. *Classical Quarterly* 551: 17–38.

Rojo López, A.M. 2002. Frame semantics and the translation of humour. *Babel* 48/1: 34–77.

Rokem, F. 2000. *Performing History*. Iowa.

Ronnick, M.V. 2004. 12 Black Classicists. *Arion* 11: 85–102.

Ronnick, M.V. (ed.). 2005. *The Autobiography of William Sanders Scarborough: An American Journey from Slavery to Scholarship*. Foreword by Henry Louis Gates, Jr. Detroit, Mich.

Root, M.C. 1979. *The King and Kingship in Achaemenid Art: Essays in the Creation of an Iconography of Empire*. Leiden:

Root, M.C. 1985. The Parthenon frieze and the Apadana reliefs at Persepolis: reassessing a programmatic relationship. *American Journal of Archaeology* 89: 103–20.

Root, M.C. 1991. From the heart: powerful persianisms in the art of the western empire. In Sancisi-Weerdenburg and Kuhrt (eds), 1991: 1–29.

Rorabaugh, W.J. 2002. *Kennedy and the Promise of the Sixties*. Cambridge.

Rose, J. 2001. *The Intellectual Life of the British Working Classes*. New Haven, Conn.

Rose, P. 1992. *Sons of the Gods, Children of Earth : Ideology and Literary Form in Ancient Greece*. Ithaca, N.Y., and London.

Rose, P. 2006. Divorcing ideology from Marxism and Marxism from ideology: some problems. *Arethusa* 39: 101–36.

Rosenberg, I. 1979. *Collected Works*. Ed. I. Parsons. New York.

Rosenmeyer, P.A. 1992. *The Poetics of Imitation: Anacreon and the Anacreontic Tradition*. Cambridge.

Rosenthal, F. 1992. *The Classical Heritage in Islam*. London and New York.

Ross, E.D. 1931. *The Persians*. Oxford.

Rosslyn, F. (ed.). 2002. *Pope's* Iliad: *A Selection with Commentary*, 2nd edn. London.

Roth, M. 2000. 'Anacreon' and drink poetry: or, the art of feeling very very good. *Texas Studies in Literature and Language* 42: 14–45.

Rotimi, O. 1971. *The Gods are Not to Blame*. Oxford.

Roucoux, M. (ed.). 1986. *English Literature of the Great War Revisited*. Proceedings of the Symposium on the British Literature of the First World War. Amiens.

Rowe Karlyn, K. 2006. Feminism in the classroom: teaching towards the third wave. In Hollows and Moseley (eds), 2006: 57–75.

Rowe, C.J. (ed.). 1998. *Plato*, Symposium. With intro., tr. and com. Warminster.

Rowe, C.J. 2005. Reply to Charles Martindale: comments made in debate on 'Reception and the Classics of the Future', at the Annual Meeting of the Classical Association 2005. *Bulletin of the Council of University Classical Departments* 34, www.rhul.ac.uk/Classics/CUCD/ rowe05.html, accessed October 2006.

Rowell, C.H. 1996. An interview with Derek Walcott. In Baer (ed.), 1996: 122–34.

Ruch, W., A. Attardo and R. Raskin. 1993. Towards an empirical verification of the General Theory of Verbal Humor. *Humor* 6/2: 123–36.

Ruhnken, D. 1825. *Opuscula* I, 2nd edn. Leiden.

Ruíz Zafon, C. 2004. *The Shadow of the Wind*. London.

Rutherford, J. 1990. *Identity, Community, Culture, Difference*. London.

Rutherford, R.B. 1995. *The Art of Plato: Ten Essays in Platonic Interpretation*. London.

Ryle, G. 1966. *Plato's Progress*. Cambridge.

Sabata, S. 1999. Giants. Unpublished playscript.

Safdie, M. 1989. *Jerusalem the Future of the Past*. Boston.

Said, E. 1979 [1978]. *Orientalism*. New York.

Said, E. 1993. *Culture and Imperialism*. London.

Said, E. 2001. Yeats and decolonization. In Bayoumi and Rubin (eds), 2001: 291–313.

Said, E. 2003. *Freud and the Non-European*. London.

Saïd, S. 2002. Greeks and barbarians in Euripides' tragedies: the end of differences? In Harrison (ed.), 2002: 62–100. 1st pub. 1984 as Grecs et barbares dans les tragédies d'Euripide: le fin des différences, *Ktema* 9: 27–53.

Saïd, S. 2004. Permanence et Transformation des 'Classiques': Les conversions de la poésie de Plutarque à Basile le Grand. In Pailler and Payen (eds), 2004: 227–39.

Sancisi-Weerdenburg, H. (ed.). 1987. *Achaemenid History 1: Sources, structure and synthesis*. Leiden.

Sancisi-Weerdenburg, H. 1987a. Introduction. In Sancisi-Weerdenburg (ed.), 1987: xi–xiv. Leiden.

Sancisi-Weerdenburg, H. 1987b. The fifth oriental monarchy and hellenocentrism: Cyropaedia VIII and its influence. In Sancisi-Weerdenburg (ed.), 1987: 117–31.

Sancisi-Weerdenburg, H. 1987c. Decadence in the empire or decadence in the sources? From sources to synthesis: Ctesias. In Sancisi-Weerdenburg (ed.), 1987: 33–45.

Sancisi-Weerdenburg, H. 1991. Introduction in Sancisi-Weerdenburg and Drijvers (eds), 1991: 1–35.

Sancisi-Weerdenburg, H. and J.W. Drijvers (eds). 1990. *Achaemenid History 5: The Roots of the European Tradition*. Leiden.

Sancisi-Weerdenburg, H. and J.W. Drijvers (eds). 1991. *Achaemenid History 7: Through Travellers' Eyes*. Leiden.

Sancisi-Weerdenburg, H. and A. Kuhrt (eds). 1987. *Achaemenid History 2: The Greek Sources*. Leiden.

Sancisi-Weerdenburg, H. and A. Kuhrt (eds). 1991. *Achaemenid History 6: Asia Minor and Egypt. Old Cultures in a New Empire*. Leiden.

Sanesi, I. 1911. *La Commedia*. Milan.

Sansweet, S.J. 1998. *Star Wars Encyclopedia*. New York.

Santoni, A. (ed.). 2005. *L'Autore multiplo. Pisa, Scuola Normale Superiore, 18 Ottobre 2002*. Pisa.

Saunders, T.J. 2004. *Plato: Laws*. Preface by R.F. Stalley. Harmondsworth.

Saunders, T.J. (ed.). 2005 [1987]. *Early Socratic Dialogues*. Harmondsworth.

Savory, T. 1957. *The Art of Translation*. London.

Schaaf, L.J. 2000. *The Photographic Art of William Henry Fox Talbot*. Princeton.

Scharfenberger, E. 2002. Aristophanes' *Thesmophoriazousai* and the challenges of comic translation: the case of William Arrowsmith's *Euripides Agonistes*. *American Journal of Philology* 123: 429–63.

Schein, S.L. 2007. An American Homer for the twentieth century. In Graziosi and Greenwood (eds), 2007.

Scherer, J. 1987. *Dramaturgies d'Oedipe*. Paris.

Schneider, R. 1997. *The Explicit Body in Performance*. London and New York.

Schroeter, E. 1978. Rome's first national state architecture: the *Palazzo delle Finanze*. In Millon and Nochlin (eds), 1978: 128–49.

Schueller, H.M. and R.L. Peters (eds). 1967–9. *The Letters of John Addington Symonds*. Detroit.

Schwartz, P. 1988. *The Best of Company: The Story of Johannesburg's Market Theatre*. Craighall.

Scodel, R. 2002. *Listening to Homer: Tradition, Narrative and Audience*. Ann Arbor.

Scolnicov, H. and P. Holland (eds). 1989. *The Play Out of Context: Transferring Plays from Culture to Culture*. Cambridge.

Scott, J. 2005. *Electra after Freud: Myth and Culture*. Ithaca and London.

Segal, C. 2001. *Oedipus Tyrannus: Tragic Heroism and the Limits of Knowledge*, 2nd edn. Oxford.

Seitler, D. 2004. Queer physiognomies: or, how many ways can we do the history of sexuality? *Criticism* 46: 71–102.

Selaiha, N. 2002. Antigone in Palestine. *Al Ahram Weekly* 585: 9–15 May: 16.

Sellar, W.Y. 1897. *Virgil*. Oxford.

Settis, S. 2006 [2004]. *The Future of the 'Classical'*. Tr. A. Cameron. Cambridge and Malden, MA. First published 2004 as *Futuro del 'Classico'*. Torino.

Sewart, D. (ed.). 1995. *One World Many Voices*. 2 vols. Birmingham.

Seydl, J. and V. Coates (eds). 2007. *Antiquity Recovered: The Legacy of Pompeii and Herculaneum*. Malibu.

Seymour-Smith, M. 1991. *Hardy*. London.

Shamir, M. 1959. *He Walked Through the Fields*. Tr. A. Hodes. Jerusalem.

Shankman, S. 1983. *Pope's* Iliad: *Homer in the Age of Passion*. Princeton.

Shankman, S. (ed.). 1996. *The* Iliad *of Homer, Translated by Alexander Pope*. Harmondsworth.

Shanks, M. 1996. *Classical Archaeology of Greece: Experiences of the Discipline*. London and New York.

Shapiro, A. and P. Burian (trs). 2003. *Aeschylus* Agamemnon. Oxford.

Sharpe, L. (ed.). 2002. *The Cambridge Companion to Goethe*. Cambridge.

Shay, J. 1994. *Achilles in Vietnam: Combat Trauma and the Undoing of Character*. New York.

Shelley, B. 1965. *The Complete Works of B. Shelley*, 10, *Letters 1818–1822*. Ed. R. Ingpen and W.E. Peck. London.

Shelley, M. 1994. *The Last Man*. Oxford.

Sherlock, P. and R. Nettleford. 1990. *The University of the West Indies: A Caribbean Response to the Challenge of Change*. London and Basingstoke.

Showerman, G. 1922. *Horace and His Influence*. Boston.

Siam, D. 1995. Interview with Emil Habibi. *Contemporary Theatre Review* 3/2: 107–12.

Sider, L. 2003. (ed.). *Soundscape: Exploring the Art of Sound with the Moving Images*. London.

Sideris [Sideres], G. 1973a. The freedom-fighters of the *Noumas* translate tragedies into Demotic [in Greek]. *Theatro* 2nd series 6/31: 46–56.

Sideris [Sideres], G. 1973b. The *Oresteiaka*: troubles to prevent the [ancient] tragedies from being played in translation! [in Greek]. *Theatro* 2nd series 6/34–6: 88–99.

Sideris [Sideres], G. 1976. *The Ancient Theatre on the Modern Greek Stage, 1817–1932* [in Greek]. Athens.

Sierz, A. 2005. Sir Tom in the Doghouse. *Daily Telegraph*. 10 October: 25.

Silk, M.S. (ed.). 1996. *Tragedy and the Tragic: Greek Theatre and Beyond*. Oxford.

Silk, M.S. 2004. Shakespeare and Greek tragedy: strange relationship. In Martindale and Thomas (eds), 2004: 241–60.

Silkin, J. 1972. *Out of Battle: The Poetry of the Great War*. London.

Silkin, J. 1996. *Penguin Book of First World War Poetry*. London and New York.

Simmons, D. 2003. *Ilium*. London.

Simpson, M. 2007. The curse of the canon: Ola Rotimi's *The Gods Are Not To Blame*. In Hardwick and Gillespie (eds), 2007.

Simpson, St J. 2003. From Persepolis to Babylon and Nineveh: the rediscovery of the ancient Near East. In Sloan (ed.), 2003: 192–201.

Sinclair, R.K. 1998. *Democracy and Participation in Athens*. Cambridge.

Siouzoule, N. 2005. From Aeschylus to Soteriades [in Greek]. *Euangelika 1901*: 141–54.

Skinner, M. (ed.). 1987. Rescuing Creusa: new methodological approaches to women in antiquity. *Helios* 13/2: special issue.

Skutsch, O. (ed.). 1985 *The* Annals *of Quintus Ennius*. Oxford.

Slater, N.W. and B. Zimmermann (ed.). 1993. *Intertextualität in der griechisch-römischen Komödie*, Drama, 2. Stuttgart.

Slater, N.W. 2002. *Spectator Politics*. Philadelphia.

Slater, P. 1968. *The Glory of Hera: Greek Mythology and the Greek Family*. Princeton,

Slater, W.J. (ed.). 1996. *Roman Theater and Society*. Ann Arbor.

Sloan, K. (ed.). 2003. *Enlightenment. Discovering the World in the Eighteenth Century*. London.

Sluiter, I. 2000. The dialectics of genre: some aspects of secondary literature and genre in antiquity. In Depew and Obbink (eds), 2000: 183–203.

Smith, G.A. 2003 [1991]. *Epic Films: Casts, Credits and Commentary on Over 300 Historical Spectacle Movies*. Revd and expanded edn. Jefferson N.C.

Smyth, A. (ed.). 2004. *A Pleasing Sinne: Drink and Conviviality in Seventeenth-century England*. Cambridge.

Snir, R. 1995. Palestinian theatre: historical development and contemporary distinctive identity. *Contemporary Theatre Review* 3/2: 29–74.

Snodgrass, A.M. 1980. *Archaic Greece: The Age of Experiment*. Berkeley.

Snodgrass, A.M. 1998. *Homer and the Artists: Text and Picture in Early Greek Art*. Cambridge.

Snowden, F. 1983. *Before Color Prejudice: The Ancient View of Blacks*. Cambridge, Mass.

Societas Raffaello Sanzio. 2002–4. *Tragedia Endogonidia* in *Idioma, Clima, Crono*, I–VIII. Edizioni casa del bello estremo. Cesena. Published in English, with French and Italian translations.

Solberg, R. 1999. *Alternative Theatre in South Africa: Talks with Prime Movers since the 1970s*. Pietermaritzburg.

Solomon, J. 2001 [1978]. *The Ancient World in the Cinema*. South Brunswick. Revd and expanded edn. New Haven and London.

Solomos, A. 1974. *The Living Aristophanes*. Tr. A. Solomos and M. Felheim. Ann Arbor.

Sommerstein, A.H. 1973a. *Aristophanes:* Lysistrata, The Acharnians, The Clouds, revd edn 2002. Harmondsworth.

Sommerstein, A.H. 1973b. On translating Aristophanes: ends and means. *Greece and Rome*, 20: 140–54.

Sommerstein, A.H. 1981. *The Comedies of Aristophanes:* Knights. Warminster.

Sommerstein, A.H. 1982. *The Comedies of Aristophanes:* Clouds. Warminster.

Sommerstein, A.H. 1994. *Aristophanes'* Thesmophoriazousai. Warminster.

Sommerstein, A.H., S. Halliwell, J. Henderson and B. Zimmerman (eds). 1993. *Tragedy, Comedy and the Polis*. Bari.

Sourvinou-Inwood, C. 1991. *'Reading' Greek Culture*. Oxford.

Sowerby, R. 2004. The Decorum of Pope's *Iliad*. *Translation and Literature* 13: 49–79.

Soyinka, W. 1973. *The Bacchae of Euripides: A Communion Rite*. London.

Soyinka, W. 1976. *Myth. Literature and the African World*. Cambridge.

Soyinka, W. 1999. *The Burden of Memory: The Muse of Forgiveness*. Oxford.

Spathes [Spathis], D. 2005. The stage director and the production of the *Oresteia* at the Royal Theatre [in Greek]. *Euangelika 1901*: 229–66.

Spathis [Spathes], D. 1986. Sophocles' *Philoctetes* adapted by N. Pikkolos: the first appearance of ancient tragedy in modern Greek theatre [in Greek]. In Spathis (ed.), 1986: 145–98.

Spathis [Spathes], D. 1986. *Enlightenment and Modern Greek Theatre* [in Greek]. Thessaloniki.

Spence, D. 1987. *The Freudian Metaphor: Towards Paradigm Change in Psychoanalysis*. New York.

Springer, C. 1987. *The Marble Wilderness: Ruins and Representation in Italian Romanticism, 1775–1850*. Cambridge.

Staiger, J. 2000. *Perverse Spectators: The Practices of Film Reception*. New York.

Staiger, J. 2005. *Media Reception Studies*. New York.

Stam, R. 2005. *Literature through Film: Realism, Magic, and the Art of Adaptation*. Malden and Oxford.

Stam, R. and A. Raengo (eds). 2005. *Literature and Film: A Guide to the Theory and Practice of Film Adaptation*. Malden and Oxford.

Stam, R. and E. Shohat. 2005. Traveling multiculturalism: a trinational debate in translation. In A. Loomba et al. (eds), 2005: 293–316.

Stanford, W.B. 1954. *The Ulysses Theme*. Oxford.

Stanford, W.B. 1976. *Ireland and the Classical Tradition*. Dublin and New Jersey.

Stanhope, P.D., Fourth Earl of Chesterfield. 1932. *Letters*. Ed. B. Dobree. London.

Stanley, S. 2001. *New Grove Dictionary of Music and Musicians.*, 2nd edn, 29 vols. London [7th edn counting from the original *Dictionary*].

Stannard, D.E. 1980. *Shrinking History*. Oxford and New York.

Stauride-Patrikiou, R. 2005. Old ideas and new fears [in Greek]. *Euangelika 1901*: 13–24.

Steiner, G. 1975. *After Babel*. Oxford.

Steiner, G. 1984. *Antigones*. Oxford.

Steiner, G. 1998 [1975]. *After Babel: Aspects of Language and Translation*, 3rd edn. Oxford.

Steiner, H. (ed.). 1947–59. *Prosa II, Gesammelte Werke in Einzelausgaben*. Frankfurt.

Steinmeyer, E. 2007a. Elektra in the marvel universe. In Hilton and Gosling (eds), 2007: 317–40.

Steinmeyer, E. 2007b. Post-apartheid *Electra*: in the city of paradise. In Hardwick and Gillespie (eds), 2007.

Stephens, S. and P. Vasunia (eds). Forthcoming. *Greece, Rome and National Cultures*. Oxford.

Stewart, J. 1959. *Jane Ellen Harrison: A Portrait from Letters*. London.

Stockwell, P. and D. Littlewood (eds). 1996. *Impossibility Fiction: Alternativity – Extrapolation – Speculation*. Amsterdam.

Stokes, A.D. 1978. *The Stones of Rimini*. Ed. L. Gowing. *The Critical Writings of Adrian Stokes*. London.

Stokes, M.C. 1992. Socrates' mission. In Gower and Stokes (eds), 1992: 26–81.

Stone, I.F. 1988. *The Trial of Socrates*. London.

Stone, M. 1999. A flexible Rome: fascism and the cult of *romanità*. In Edwards (ed.), 1999: 205–20.

Strauss, R. 1953. *Recollections and Reflections*. Ed. W. Schuh, tr. L.J. Lawrence. London.

Stray, C.A. 1994. Paradigms regained: towards a historical sociology of textbooks. *Journal of Curriculum Studies* 26/1: 1–29.

Stray, C.A. 1998. *Classics Transformed: Schools, Universities, and Society in England, 1830–1960*. Oxford.

Stray, C.A. 2007. Education. In Kallendorf (ed.), 2007: 5–14.

Stray, C.A. (ed.). 2007a. *Gilbert Murray Reassessed: Hellenism, Theatre, and International Politics*. Oxford.

Stray, C.A. (ed.). 2007b. *Oxford Classics: Teaching and Learning 1800–2000*. London.

Stray, C.A. (ed.). 2007c. *Remaking the Classics: Literature, Genre and Media in England 1800–2000*. London.

Stray, C.A. Forthcoming. *Classical Books*. London.

Stromaier, G. 1980. Homer in Baghdad. *Byzantinoslavica: Revue Internationale des Etudes Byzantines* 41: 191–200.

Strong, S.A. [Eugenie]. 1911. The exhibition illustrative of the provinces of the Roman empire at the baths of Diocletian, Rome. *Journal of Roman Studies* 1: 1–49.

Strunk, O. (ed.). 1998 [1950]. *Source Readings in Music History*. 5 vols. Rev. edn. New York.

Sullivan, J.P. (ed.). 1963. *Critical Essays on Roman Literature: Satire*. London.

Sullivan, J.P. 2001. The Social Ambience of Petronius' *Satyricon* and Fellini's *Satyricon*. In Winkler (ed.), 2001: 258–71.

Sütterlin, A. 1996. *Petronius Arbiter und Federico Fellini: Ein strukturanalytischer Vergleich*. New York.

Swain, S. 1996. *Hellenism and Empire: Language, Classicism, and Power in the Greek World, AD50–250*. Oxford.

Swanwick, A. (tr.). 1865. *The Dramas of Aeschylus*. London.

Sweet, R. 1978–80. *Wilhelm von Humboldt: A Biography*. 2 vols. Columbus.

Sykes, P.M. 1902. *Ten Thousand Miles in Persia or Eight Years in Irán*. New York.

Sykes, P.M. 1915. *A History of Persia*, vol. 1. London.

Sykes, P.M. 1922. *Persia*. Oxford.

Symonds, J.A. 1887. The model. *Fortnightly Review* 42: 857–61.

Symonds, J.A. 1893. *Studies of the Greek Poets*, 3rd edn. London.

Symvoulidou, Ch. 1998. Translation and theatre criticism 1889–1990: a diachronic approach based on the modern Greek productions of the plays of Aeschylus [in Greek]. In Patrikiou (ed.), 1998: 47–63.

Tackels, B. 2005. *Les Castellucci. Ecrivains de plateau*. Besançon.

Takho-Godi, A. 1970. Classical studies in the Soviet Union. *Arethusa* 3: 123–7.

Talib, I.S. 2002. *The Languages of Postcolonial Literatures*. London.

Tanner, L.E. 1934. *Westminster School: A History*. London.

Taplin, O. 1977. *The Stagecraft of Aeschylus*. Oxford.

Taplin, O. 1978. *Greek Tragedy in Action*. London.

Taplin, O. 1995. *Homeric Soundings: The Shaping of the Iliad*. Oxford.

Taplin, O. 1997. The pictorial record. In Easterling (ed.), 1997: 69–90.

Taplin, O. 1999. Spreading the word through performance. In Goldhill and Osborne (eds), 1999: 33–57.

Taplin, O. 2001. Mask in Greek tragedy and in *Tantalus*. A paper delivered at a conference on *Tantalus* hosted by the Centre for Hellenic Studies in May 2001, www.apgrd.ox.ac.uk/people/imagesdocs/ottantalus.htm, accessed 10 February 2006.

Taplin, O. 2002. Contemporary poetry and Classics. In Wiseman (ed.), 2002: 1–19.

Taplin, O. 2007. *Pots and Plays: Interactions between Tragedy and Greek Vase-painting of the Fourth Century BC.* Los Angeles.

Tarrant, D. 1955. Plato as dramatist. *Journal of Hellenic Studies* 75: 82–9.

Tatarkiewicz, W. 1958. Les quatre significations du mot 'classique'. *Revue internationale de philosophie* 43: 5–11.

Taube, M. 1993. *Modern Israeli Drama in Translation.* Portsmouth, N.H.

Taube, M. 2004. *An Anthology of Israeli Drama for the New Millennium.* New York.

Taylor, D. 1986. *Sophocles'* Antigone. London.

Taylor, P. 1993. All present and erect, *Independent*, 17 May.

Taylor, S.L. 1986–8. Fox Talbot as an artist: the 'Patroclus' series. *Bulletin of the University of Michigan Museums of Art and Archaeology* 8: 38–55.

Tennyson, H. (ed.). 1981. *Studies in Tennyson.* Totowa, N.J.

Terada, R. 1992. *Derek Walcott's Poetry: American Mimicry.* Boston, Mass.

Thalmann, W.G. 1998. *The Swineherd and the Bow: Representations of Class in the Odyssey.* Ithaca, N.Y., and London.

Theocharidis, G. 1940. *Beiträge zur Geschichte des byzantinischen Profantheaters im IV und V Jahrhundert, hauptsächlich auf Grund der Predigten des Johannes Chrysostomus Patriarchen von Konstantinopel.* Thessaloniki.

Thiel, H. van. (ed.). 1991. *Homeri Odysseia.* Hildesheim.

Thiel, H. van. (ed.). 1996. *Homeri Ilias.* Hildesheim.

Thirlwall, C. 1835–44. *A History of Greece.* 8 vols. London.

Thomas, C.N. 1994. *Alexander Pope and his Eighteenth-century Women Readers.* Carbondale, Ill.

Thomas, R. 2001a. *Virgil and the Augustan Reception.* Cambridge.

Thomas, R. 2001b. The Georgics of resistance: from Virgil to Heaney. *Vergilius* 47: 117–47.

Thomson, C. 1782. *Remarks and Explanation of the Great Seal of the United States of America.* Philadelphia.

Thomson, G. 1973 [1941]. *Aeschylus and Athens*, 4th edn. London.

Tillotson, G. and K. 1965. *Mid-Victorian Studies.* London.

Todman, D. 2005. *The Great War: Myth and Memory.* London and New York.

Tomlinson, C. 2003. *Metamorphoses: Poetry and Translation.* Manchester.

Too, Y.L. (ed.). 2001. *Education in Greek and Roman Antiquity.* Leiden and Boston.

Toury, G. 1995. *Descriptive Translation Studies – And Beyond.* Amsterdam and Philadelphia.

Trivedi, H. 2007. Western Classics, Indian Classics: postcolonial contestations. In Hardwick and Gillespie (eds), 2007.

Trivedi, H. and M. Mukherjee (eds). 1996. *Interrogating Post-colonialism: Theory. Text and Context.* Shimla.

Tsoutsoura, M. 1993. A historical perspective on the problems and aesthetics of the revival of the Chorus at the Delphic Festivals [in Greek]. *Porphyras* 14/66: 31–45.

Tsuzuki, K. and G. Celant (eds). 2005. *Robert Mapplethorpe and the Classical Tradition: Photographs and Mannerist Prints.* Berlin.

Tucker, H. (ed.). 1999. *A Companion to Victorian Literature and Culture.* Oxford.

Tuplin, C.J. 1990. Persian decor in *Cyropaedia*. In Drijvers and Sancisi-Weerdenburg (eds), 1990: 17–29.

Tuplin, C.J. 2004. Doctoring the Persians: Ctesias of Cnidus, physician and historian. *Klio* 86, 305–47

Turner, F.M. 1981. *The Greek Heritage in Victorian Britain.* New Haven.

Turner, F.M. 1993. *Contesting Cultural Authority: Essays in Victorian Intellectual Life.* Cambridge.

Tuten, N.L. and Zubizarreta, J. 2001. *The Robert Frost Encyclopedia.* Westport, Conn.

Twiddy, I. 2006. Seamus Heaney's versions of pastoral. *Essays in Criticism* 56: 50–71.

Underwood, S. 1998. *English Translators of Homer: From George Chapman to Christopher Logue.* Plymouth.

Upton, C.-A. (ed.). 2000. *Moving Target: Theatre Translation and Cultural Relocation.* Manchester, UK, and Northampton, Mass.

Urbainczyk, T. 2004. *Spartacus.* Bristol.

Urian, D. (ed.). 1995. Palestinians and Israelis in the theatre. *Contemporary Theatre Review* 3: 2.

Urian, D. 1997. *The Arab in Israeli Drama and Theatre.* London.

Valakas, K. 2002. The use of the body by actors in tragedy and satyr play. In Easterling and Hall (eds), 2002: 69–91.

Valentini, V. and B. Marranca. 2004. The universal: the simplest place possible. *PAJ: A Journal of Performance and Art.* 26/2: 16–25.

Van den Dries, L. 2002. The sublime body. In Bleeker et al. (eds), 2002: 71–95.

Van Steen, G.A.H. 2000. *Venom in Verse: Aristophanes in Modern Greece.* Princeton.

Van Steen, G.A.H. 2001. Playing by the censor's rules? Classical drama revived under the Greek junta (1967–1974). *Journal of the Greek Diaspora* 27/1–2: 133–94.

Van Steen, G.A.H. 2005. Forgotten theater, theater of the forgotten: classical tragedy on modern Greek prison islands. *Journal of Modern Greek Studies* 23/2: 335–95.

Van Steen, G.A.H. 2007. Enacting history and patriotic myth: Aeschylus' *Persians* on the eve of the Greek War of Independence. In Bridges et al. (eds), 2007: 299–329.

Van Zyl Smit, B. 2003a. The reception of Greek tragedy in South Africa. *Eirene* 39: 234–53.

Van Zyl Smit, B. 2003b. The reception of Greek tragedy in the 'old' and the 'new' South Africa. *Akroterion* 48: 3–20.

Van Zyl Smit, B. 2005. Aristophanes in South Africa. *South African Theatre Journal* 19: 254–76.

Van Zyl Smit, B. 2006. *Antigone* in South Africa. In Davidson et al. (eds), 2006: 281–98.

Van Zyl Smit, B. 2007. *Medea* in Afrikaans. In Hilton and Gosling (eds), 2007: 73–92.

Vance, N. 1997. *The Victorians and Ancient Rome.* Oxford.

Vandiver, E. 1999. 'Millions of the mouthless dead': Charles Hamilton Sorley and Wilfred Owen in Homer's Hades. *International Journal of the Classical Tradition* 5: 432–55.

Vandiver, E. 2007. Classical echoes in British poetry of the First World War. In Stray (ed.), 2007c.

Varakis, A. 2003. The use of masks in the modern staging of Aristophanes in Greece. Unpublished PhD thesis, Royal Holloway, University of London.

Varakis, A. 2004. Research on the ancient mask. *Didaskalia* 6/1, www.didaskalia.net/issues/vol6no1/varakis.html, accessed 14 February 2006.

Vasunia, P. 2001. *The Gift of the Nile. Hellenizing Egypt from Aeschylus to Alexander.* Berkeley.

Vasunia, P. 2003. Hellenism and empire: reading Edward Said. *Parallax* 9/4: 88–97.

Vasunia, P. 2005a. Greater Rome and Greater Britain. In Goff (ed.), 2005: 38–64.

Vasunia, P. 2005b. Greek, Latin, and the Indian civil service. *Proceedings of the Cambridge Philological Society* 51: 35–71.

Vasunia, P. 2007. Alexander and Asia: Droysen and Grote. In Ray (ed.), 2007: 89–102.

Vasunia, P. 2007a. Dalpatram's *Lakshmi* and Aristophanes' *Wealth.* In Hall and Wrigley (eds), 2007.

Vasunia, P. 2007b. Persia. In Grafton et al. (eds), 2007.

Vasunia, P. Forthcoming a. Alexander Sikandar. In Stephens and Vasunia (eds), forthcoming. Oxford.

Vasunia, P. Forthcoming b. *Empire without End: Postcolonial Theory and the Ancient World*. London.

Vasunia, P. Forthcoming c. *Greece, Rome, and the British Empire*. Oxford.

Vellacott, P. (tr.). 1953. *Euripides'* Alcestis. Harmondsworth.

Vellacott, P. (tr.). 1954. *Euripides'* Ion. Harmondsworth.

Venuti, L. 1995. *The Translator's Invisibility: A History of Translation*. London.

Venuti, L. 2000. Neoclassicism and enlightenment. In France (ed.), 2000: 55–64.

Venuti, L. 2002. Translating humour: equivalence, compensation, discourse. *Performance Research* 7/2: 6–16.

Venuti, L. (ed.). 2004. *The Translation Studies Reader*, 2nd edn. New York and London.

Vernant, J.-P. 1988. Oedipus without the Complex. In Vernant and Vidal-Naquet (eds), 1988: 85–112.

Vernant, J.-P. and P. Vidal-Naquet. 1988. *Myth and Tragedy in Ancient Greece*. Tr. Janet Lloyd. New York.

Versnel, H.S. (ed.). 1981. *Faith, Hope and Worship: Aspects of Religious Mentality in the Ancient World*. Leiden.

Vervain, C. 2005. Performing ancient drama in mask: the case of Greek new comedy. *New Theatre Quarterly* 79: 245–64.

Vervain, C. and Wiles, D. 2001. The masks of Greek tragedy as point of departure for modern performance. *New Theatre Quarterly* 67: 254–72.

Vestin, M. and G. Sneltved (ed.). 2004. *The Face and the Mask of the Actor: Methodica 2003*. Stockholm.

Vickers, M.J. 1987. Value and simplicity: eighteenth-century taste and the study of Greek vases. *Past and Present* 116: 98–137.

Vidal-Naquet, P. 1988. Oedipus in Athens. In Vernant and Vidal-Naquet (eds), 1998: 301–28.

Vincent, D. 1989. *Literacy and Popular Culture: England 1750–1914*. Cambridge.

Vlastos, G. 1991. *Socrates: Ironist and Moral Philosopher*. Cambridge.

Voltaire F.-M.A. de. 1947. *Candide or Optimism*. Tr. J. Butt. London.

Vorster, C. 1996. *Paradox* with apology to Aristophanes. Unpublished playscript.

Vovolis, T. 2003. The voice and the mask in ancient Greek tragedy. In Sider (ed.), 2003: 73–82.

Vovolis, T. and G. Zamboulakis. 2004. The acoustical mask of Greek tragedy. In Vestin and Sneltved (eds), 2004: 107–31.

Wagner, R. 1892–9. *Richard Wagner's Prose Works*. Tr. W. Ashton Ellis. London.

Wain, J. 2005 [1990]. *The Oxford Anthology of English Poetry: Blake to Heaney*. Vol. 2.

Walcott, D. 1980. *The Fortunate Traveller*. New York.

Walcott, D. 1984. *Collected Poems: 1948–1984*. New York.

Walcott, D. 1987. *The Arkansas Testament*. New York.

Walcott, D. 1990. *Omeros*. London and New York.

Walcott, D. 1993a. *The Odyssey: A Stage Version*. London.

Walcott, D. 1993b. *The Antilles: Fragments of Epic Memory – The Nobel Lecture*. New York.

Walcott, D. 1997. Reflections on *Omeros*. *South Atlantic Quarterly*, special issue 96/2: 229–46.

Walcott, D. 1998. *What the Twilight Says*. London.

Walcott, D. 2004. *The Prodigal*. New York.

Walcott, D. and R. Bearden. 1983. *The Caribbean Poetry of Derek Walcott and the Art of Romare Bearden*. New York.

Walder, D. 1993. *Township Plays*. Oxford.

Wallace, R.W. 1997. Poet, public and 'theatocracy': audience performance in classical Athens. In Edmunds and Wallace (eds), 1997: 97–111.

Walton, J.M. 1980. *Greek Theatre Practice.* Westport, Conn.

Walton, J.M. 1987. *Living Greek Theatre: A Handbook of Classical Performance and Modern Production.* Westport, Conn.

Walton, J.M. 1996. *The Greek Sense of Theatre: Tragedy Reviewed,* 2nd edn. Amsterdam.

Walton, J.M. 1999. Essence or perception: Greek drama for a new century. In Patsalidis and Sakelaridou (eds), 1999: 325–39.

Walton, J.M. 2002. Hit or myth: the Greeks and Irish Drama. In McDonald and Walton. (eds), 2002: 3–36.

Walton, J.M. (tr.). 2002 [1997]. *Six Greek Comedies.* London.

Walton, J.M. 2003. *Tantalus. Didaskalia* 5/2, www.didaskalia.net/issues/vol5no2/walton.html, accessed 14 February 2006.

Walton, J.M. 2005. Translation or transubstantiation. In Macintosh et al. (ed.), 2005: 189–206.

Walton, J.M. 2006a. *Found in Translation: Greek Drama in English.* Cambridge.

Walton, J.M. 2006b. The line or the gag: translating classical comedy. *Centre for Translation and Intercultural Studies Occasional Papers* 3: 29–46. Ed. S. Fekry Hanna.

Walzer, R. 1962. *Greek into Arabic. Essays on Islamic Philosophy.* Columbia.

Warburg, A. 1999. *The Renewal of Pagan Antiquity: Contributions to the Cultural History of the European Renaissance.* Tr. D. Britt, intro. K.W. Forster. Los Angeles.

Warhol, A. and S. Goldhill. 2005. *Andy Warhol. Eros and Mortality: The Late Male Nudes.* New York.

Warr, G. (tr.). 1900. *The Oresteia of Aeschylus.* London.

Watson, J.S.K. 2004. *Fighting Different Wars: Experience, Memory, and the First World War in Britain.* Cambridge.

Watson-Williams, H. 1967. *André Gide and the Greek Myth: A Critical Study.* Oxford.

Watt, S. 1998. *Postmodern/Drama. Reading the Contemporary Stage.* Ann Arbor.

Watts, D. 1914. *Renaissance of the Greek Ideal.* New York.

Waugh, T. 1996. *Hard to Imagine: Gay Male Eroticism in Photography and Film from their Beginnings to Stonewall.* New York.

Way, A. (tr.). 1894. *The Plays of Euripides.* London.

Wearing, J.P. 1991. *The London Stage, 1930–1939: A Calendar of Plays and Players.* London.

Webb, R. 2005. The protean performer: mimesis and identity in late antique discussions of the theater. In Del Guidice and Van Deusen (eds), 2005: 3–11.

Webb, R. 2006. Logiques du mime dans l'Antiquité Tardive. *Pallas* 71: 127–36.

Webb, R.K. 1971. *The British Working-class Reader 1790–1848.* New York.

Webb, T. 1996. 'City of the soul': English romantic travellers in Rome. In Liversidge and Edwards (eds), 1996: 20–37.

Weber, S. 2005. *Targets of Opportunity: On the Militarization of Thinking.* London.

Webster, T.B.L. 1967. *Monuments Illustrating Tragedy and Satyr Play,* 2nd edn. *Bulletin of the Institute of Classical Studies* suppl. 20. London.

Webster, T.B.L. 1978. *Monuments Illustrating Old and Middle Comedy,* 3rd edn. rev. by J.R. Green. *Bulletin of the Institute of Classical Studies* suppl. 39. London.

Webster, T.B.L. 1995. *Monuments Illustrating New Comedy,* 3rd edn, rev. and enlarged by J.R. Green and A. Seeberg. *Bulletin of the Institute of Classical Studies* suppl. 50. London.

Wegeler, C. 1996. *– wir sagen ab der internationalen Gelehrtenrepublik: Altertumswissenschaft und Nationalsozialismus: das Göttinger Institut für Altertumskunde 1921–1962.* Vienna.

Welch, R. 1993. *Changing States: Transformations in Modern Irish Writing.* London.

Wellek, R. 1968. Classicism in literature. *Wiener* 1: 449–56.

Wellek, R. 1973. Romanticism in literature. *Wiener* 4: 187–98.

West, F. 1984. *Gilbert Murray: A Life.* London and Canberra.

West, M.L. 1997. *The East Face of Helicon: West Asiatic Elements in Greek Poetry and Myth.* Oxford.

West, M.L. (ed.). 1998. *Homeri Ilias* 1. Teubner.

West, M.L. 1999. The invention of Homer. *Classical Quarterly* 49: 364–82.

West, M.L. (ed. and tr.). 2003. *Homeric Hymns, Homeric Apocrypha, Lives of Homer.* Cambridge, Mass.

West, S. 1988. The transmission of the text. In Heubeck et al. (eds), 1998: 33–48.

Wetmore, K.J. 2002. *The Athenian Sun in an African Sky: Modern African Adaptations of Classical Greek Tragedy.* Jefferson and London.

Wetmore, K.J. Jr. 2003. *Black Dionysus: Greek Tragedy and African American Theatre.* Jefferson, N.C., and London.

Whitmarsh, T. 2006. True histories: Lucian, Bakhtin and the pragmatics of reception. In Martindale and Thomas (eds), 2006: 104–15.

Whittall, A. 1989. Dramatic structure and tonal organization. In Puffett (ed.), 1989: 55–73.

Wiener, P.P. (ed.). 1973. *Dictionary of the History of Ideas.* 4 vols. New York.

Wiesehöfer, J. 1978. *Der Aufstand Gaumatas und die Anfänge Dareios I.* Bonn.

Wiesehöfer, J. 1996. *Ancient Persia.* London.

Wilamowitz-Moellendorff, U. von. 1884. *Homerische Untersuchungen.*

Wilamowitz-Moellendorff, U. von (tr.). 1907. *Griechische Tragödien.* Vol. 2. Orestie, 5th edn. Berlin.

Wilamowitz-Moellendorff, U. von. 1924. *Hellenistische Dichtung in der Zeit des Kallimachos.* 2 vols. Berlin.

Wilamowitz-Moellendorff, U. von. 1930 [1928]. *My Recollections 1848–1914.* Tr. G.C. Richards. London. [*Erinnerungen 1848–1914,* Leipzig. 1928].

Wiles, D. 1991. *The Mask of Menander.* Cambridge.

Wiles, D. 1999. Working with masks. *Reception of Classical Texts Research Project,* www2.open.ac.uk/ClassicalStudies/GreekPlays/e_archive/1999/MarchSeminar.htm, accessed 10 March 2006.

Wiles, D. 2000. *Greek Theatre Performance: An Introduction.* Cambridge.

Wiles, D. 2003. *A Short History of Western Performance Space.* Cambridge.

Wiles, D. 2004a. The use of masks in modern performances of Greek drama. In Hall et al. (eds), 2004: 245–64.

Wiles, D. 2004b. The mask in Greek tragedy. *Dionyso* 3: 206–14.

Wiles, D. 2007. *Mask and Performance in Greek Tragedy. From Ancient Festival to Modern Experimentation.* Cambridge.

Willetts, R.F. (tr.). 1958. *Ion.* Chicago.

Williams, B. 1993. *Shame and Necessity.* Berkeley, Los Angeles and London.

Williams, E. 1944. *Capitalism and Slavery.* Chapel Hill.

Williams, E. 1964 [1962]. *History of the People of Trinidad and Tobago.* London. 1st pub. 1962, Trinidad.

Williams, E. 1969. *Inward Hunger: The Education of a Prime Minister.* London.

Williams, E. 1970. *From Columbus to Castro: The History of the Caribbean, 1492–1969.* London.

Williams, E. 1981. *Forged from the Love of Liberty: Selected Speeches of Dr. Eric Williams.* Ed. K. Sutton. Trinidad.

Williams, E. 1997. Massa day done: public lecture at Woodford Square, 22 March 1961. *Callaloo* 20/4: 724–30.

Williams, E.C. 1907. *Across Persia*. London.

Williams, R. 2004a. Digital resources for practice-based research: the new comedy masks project. *Literary and Linguistic Computing* 19/3: 415–26.

Williams, R. 2004b. The digital matrix in 3D. *Digicult Info* 9: 3–9.

Williams, R.H. 1983. *Keywords*. Rev. edn. New York.

Williams, T. 2001. Truth and representation: the confrontation of history and mythology in *Omeros*. *Callaloo* 24/1: 276–86.

Willis, I. 2007. The empire never ended. In Hardwick and Gillespie (eds), 2007.

Willis, D. and C. Williams. 2002. *The Black Female Body: A Photographic History*. Philadelphia.

Wilmer, S.E. 1999. Seamus Heaney and the tragedy of stasis. In Patsalidis and Sakellaridou (eds), 1999: 221–31.

Wilmer, S.E. 2003. Irish Medeas: revenge or redemption? An Irish solution to an international problem. *Eirene* 39: 254–63.

Wilmer, S.E. 2007. Finding a post-colonial voice for Antigone: Seamus Heaney's burial at Thebes. In Hardwick and Gillespie (eds), 2007.

Winckelmann, J.J. 1755. *Gedancken über die Nachahmung der griechischen Wercke in der Malerey und Bildhauer-Kunst*. Friedrichstadt.

Winckelmann, J.J. 2006 [1764]. *History of the Art of Antiquity*. Tr. H.F. Mallgrave. Los Angeles. First pub. 1764. *Geschichte der Kunst des Alterthums*. Dresden.

Winders, J. 1991. *Gender, Theory, and the Canon*. Madison, Wis.

Winkler, J.J. 1990. *The Constraints of Desire*. New York.

Winkler, M. (ed.). 1991. *Classics and Cinema*. London and Toronto.

Winkler M. (ed.). 2001a. *Classical Myth and Culture in the Cinema*. New York and Oxford.

Winkler, M. 2001b. *Star Wars* and the Roman Empire. In Winkler 2001: 272–90.

Winkler, M. 2002. The face of tragedy: from theatrical mask to cinematic close-up. *Mouseion* 3/2: 43–70.

Winkler, M. (ed.). 2004. Gladiator*: Film and History*. Malden and Oxford.

Winkler, M. (ed.). 2006a. Spartacus*: Film and History*. Malden and Oxford.

Winkler, M. (ed.). 2006b. Troy*: From Homer's* Iliad *to Hollywood Epic*. Malden and Oxford.

Winkler, J. and F. Zeitlin (eds). 1990. *Nothing to Do with Dionysus?* Princeton.

Winterer, C. 2002. *The Culture of Classicism: Ancient Greece and Rome in American Intellectual Life, 1780–1910*. Baltimore.

Wiseman, T.P. 1992a. *Talking to Virgil: A Miscellany*. Exeter.

Wiseman, T.P. 1992b. A Roman villa. In Winkler (ed.), 1992a: 71–110.

Wiseman, T.P. (ed.). 2002. *Classics in Progress; Essays on Ancient Greece and Rome*. Oxford.

Wohl, V. 2002. *Love among the Ruins: The Erotics of Democracy in Classical Athens*. Princeton.

Wolf, F.A. 1985. *Prolegomena ad Homerum*. Ed. and tr. A. Grafton, G. W. Most and J.E.G. Zetzel. Princeton.

Womersley, D. (ed.). 2000. *A Companion to Literature from Milton to Blake*. Oxford.

Woodruff, P. 2005. Justice in translation: rendering ancient Greek tragedy. In Gregory (ed.), 2005: 490–504.

Woodward, C. 2001. *In Ruins*. London.

Worbs, M. 1983. *Nervenkunst: Literatur und Psychoanalyse in Wien der Jahrhundertwende*. Frankfurt.

Worrall, N. 1989. *Modernism to Realism on the Soviet Stage*. Cambridge.

Worthen, W.B. and P. Holland (eds). 2003. *Theorizing Practice: Redefining Theatre History*. London.

Wright, D. 2001.*The English Amongst the Persians. Imperial Lives in Nineteenth-century Iran*. Rev. paperback edition. London.

Wrigley, R. 1996. Infectious enthusiasms: influence, contagion and the experience of Rome. In Chard and Langdon (eds), 1996: 75–116.

Wyke, M. 1997a. Herculean muscle! The classicizing rhetoric of bodybuilding. *Arion* 4/3: 51–79.

Wyke, M. 1997b. *Projecting the Past: Ancient Rome, Cinema and History.* London.

Wyke, M. 1998. Classics and contempt: redeeming cinema for the classical tradition. *Arion* 6/1: 124–36.

Wyke, M. (ed.). 1999. *Parchments of Gender: Deciphering the Body.* Oxford.

Wyke, M. 2003. Are you not entertained? Classicists and cinema. *International Journal of the Classical Tradition* 9/3: 430–45.

Wynn, A. 2003. *Persia in the Great Game. Sir Percy Sykes: Explorer, Consul, Soldier, Spy.* London.

Xenopoulos, G. 1903. A review of the Royal Theatre's *Oresteia* of Aeschylus as translated by Mr. G. Soteriades [in Greek]. *Panathenaia* 7. 15 November: 86–9.

Yaari, N. 1993. The mask in the ancient theatre. *Assaph C* 9: 51–62.

Yaari, N. 2006. Le Théâtre de Hanokh Levin. *Théâtre/Public* 181: 101–5.

Yamagata, N. 2005. Plato, memory and performance. *Oral Tradition* 20: 111–29.

Yeats, W.B. 1956. *Collected Poems.* New York.

Yerushalmi, Y.H. 1989. Freud on the 'historical novel': from the manuscript draft 1934 of *Moses and Monotheism. International Journal of Psycho-Analysis* 70: 375–95.

Yerushalmi, Y.H. 1991. *Freud's Moses: Judaism Terminable and Interminable.* New Haven and London.

Younger, J.G. 1999. Ten unpublished letters by John Addington Symonds at Duke University. *Victorian Newsletter* 95: 1–10.

Yunis, H. 1996. *Taming Democracy: Models of Political Rhetoric in Classical Athens.* Ithaca.

Yunis, H. 1998. The constraints of democracy and the rise of the art of rhetoric. In Boedeker and Raaflaub (eds), 1998: 223–40.

Zajko, V. 2006. Hector and Andromache: identification and appropriation. In Martindale and Thomas (eds), 2006: 80–91.

Zajko, V. and M. Leonard (eds). 2006. *Laughing with Medusa. Classical Myth and Feminist Thought.* Oxford.

Zanetto, G., D. Canavero, A. Capra and A. Sgobbi (eds). 2004. *Momenti della ricezione omerica: poesia lirica e teatro.* Milan.

Zanker, P. 1988. *The Power of Images in the Age of Augustus.* Tr. A. Shapiro. Ann Arbor.

Zarrilli, P.B., B.A. McConachie, G.J. Williams and C.F. Sorgenfrei (eds). 2006. *Theatre Histories: An Introduction.* London.

Zeitlin, F. 1996. *Playing the Other.* Chicago.

Zeitlin, F. 2001. Visions and revisions of Homer. In Goldhill (ed.), 2001: 195–266.

Zeitlin, F. 2004. Dionysus in 69. In Hall et al. (eds), 2004: 49–75.

Zeman, H. 1972. *Die deutsche anakreontische Dichtung: Ein Versuch zur Erfassung ihrer ästhetischen und literarhistorischen Erscheinungsformen im 18. Jahrhundert.* Stuttgart.

Zeman, H. 1999. Anakreontische Dichtung, Anakreontik. *Der Neue Pauly* 13: 130–3.

Zimmermann, B. (ed.). 1992. *Antike Dramatheorien und ihre Rezeption, Drama: Beitr. Zum antiken Drama und seiner Rezeption, Bd. 1.* Stuttgtart.

Ziolkowski, T. 1993. *Virgil and the Moderns.* Princeton.

Zola, E. 1896. *Rome.* Tr. E.Vizetelly. London.

Zuntz, G. 1965. *An Inquiry into the Transmission of the Plays of Euripides.* Cambridge.

Index